A HISTORY OF WESTERN SOCIETY

A HISTORY OF WESTERN SOCIETY

THIRD EDITION

VOLUME C: FROM THE REVOLUTIONARY ERA TO THE PRESENT

JOHN P. McKAY
BENNETT D. HILL
JOHN BUCKLER

University of Illinois at Urbana-Champaign

HOUGHTON MIFFLIN COMPANY BOSTON
Dallas Geneva, Illinois
Lawrenceville, New Jersey Palo Alto

Text Credits Lines from "The White Man's Burden" from *Rudyard Kipling: Definitive Edition.* Reprinted by permission of Doubleday & Company, Inc., The National Trust, and A. P. Watt Ltd. Portion of Y. Yevtushenko, "Stalin's Heirs" from M. Tatu, *Power in the Kremlin: From Khrushchev to Kosygin* (New York: Viking, 1968), p. 248. Reprinted by permission of the publisher.

Chapter opener credits appear on page 1045.

Cover: *Portrait of Jeanne Hebuterne,* 1918, by Amadeo Modigliani. The Norton Simon Art Foundation.

Printed in the U.S.A.

Library of Congress Catalog Card Number: 86–81470

ISBN: 0–395–42413–5

CDEFGHIJ–RM–8987

About the Authors

John P. McKay Born in St. Louis, Missouri, John P. McKay received his B.A. from Wesleyan University (1961), his M.A. from the Fletcher School of Law and Diplomacy (1962), and his Ph.D. from the University of California, Berkeley (1968). He began teaching history at the University of Illinois in 1966 and became a professor there in 1976. John won the Herbert Baxter Adams Prize for his book *Pioneers for Profit: Foreign Entrepreneurship and Russian Industrialization, 1885–1913* (1970). He has also written *Tramways and Trolleys: The Rise of Urban Mass Transport in Europe* (1976) and has translated Jules Michelet's *The People* (1973). His research has been supported by fellowships from the Ford Foundation, the Guggenheim Foundation, the National Endowment for the Humanities, and IREX. His articles and reviews have appeared in numerous journals, including *The American Historical Review, Business History Review, The Journal of Economic History,* and *Slavic Review.* He edits *Industrial Development and the Social Fabric: An International Series of Historical Monographs.*

Bennett D. Hill A native of Philadelphia, Bennett D. Hill earned an A.B. at Princeton (1956) and advanced degrees from Harvard (A.M., 1958) and Princeton (Ph.D., 1963). He taught history at the University of Illinois at Urbana, where he was department chairman from 1978 to 1981. He has published *English Cistercian Monasteries and Their Patrons in the Twelfth Century* (1968) and *Church and State in the Middle Ages* (1970); and articles in *Analecta Cisterciensia, The New Catholic Encyclopaedia, The American Benedictine Review,* and *The Dictionary of the Middle Ages.* His reviews have appeared in *The American Historical Review, Speculum, The Historian, The Catholic Historical Review,* and *Library Journal.* He has been a fellow of the American Council of Learned Societies and has served on committees for the National Endowment for the Humanities. Now a Benedictine monk at St. Anselm's Abbey, Washington, D.C., he is also a Lecturer at the University of Maryland at College Park.

John Buckler Born in Louisville, Ky., John Buckler received his B.A. from the University of Louisville in 1967. Harvard University awarded him the Ph.D. in 1973. From 1984 to 1986 he was the Alexander von Humboldt Fellow at Institut für Alte Geschichte, University of Munich. He is currently an associate professor at the University of Illinois, and is serving on the Subcommittee on Cartography of the American Philological Association. In 1980 Harvard University Press published his *The Theban Hegemony, 371–362 B.C.* His articles have appeared in journals both here and abroad, like the *American Journal of Ancient History, Classical Philology, Rheinisches Museum für Philologie, Classical Quarterly, Wiener Studien,* and *Symbolae Osloenses.*

CONTENTS

MAPS xi

PREFACE xiii

21

THE REVOLUTION IN POLITICS, 1775–1815 667

LIBERTY AND EQUALITY 668
The Roots of Liberalism / The Attraction of Liberalism

THE AMERICAN REVOLUTION, 1775–1789 670
The Origins of the Revolution / Independence / Framing the Constitution / The Revolution's Impact on Europe

THE FRENCH REVOLUTION, 1789–1791 675
The Breakdown of the Old Order / Legal Orders and Social Realities / The Formation of the National Assembly / The Revolt of the Poor and the Oppressed/ A Limited Monarchy

WORLD WAR AND REPUBLICAN FRANCE, 1791–1799 682
The Beginning of War / The Second Revolution / Total War and the Terror / The Thermidorian Reaction and the Directory, 1794–1799

THE NAPOLEONIC ERA, 1799–1815 688
Napoleon's Rule of France / Napoleon's Wars and Foreign Policy

Notes

Suggested Reading

22

THE REVOLUTION IN ENERGY AND INDUSTRY 699

THE INDUSTRIAL REVOLUTION IN ENGLAND 700
Eighteenth-Century Origins / The First Factories / The Problem of Energy / "Steam Is an Englishman"/ The Coming of the Railroads / Britain at Midcentury

THE SPREAD OF THE INDUSTRIAL REVOLUTION 710
The Challenge of Industrialization / Agents of Industrialization

CAPITAL AND LABOR 714
The New Class of Factory Owners / The New Factory Workers / Conditions of Work / A Mature Working Class

THE ALTERNATIVE TO INDUSTRIALIZATION 720
The Growth of Population / The Potato Famine in Ireland

Notes

Suggested Reading

23

IDEOLOGIES AND UPHEAVALS, 1815–1850 727

THE PEACE SETTLEMENT 728
The Congress of Vienna / Intervention and Repression / Metternich and Conservatism

RADICAL IDEAS AND EARLY SOCIALISM 735
Liberalism / Nationalism / French Utopian Socialism / The Birth of Marxian Socialism

THE ROMANTIC MOVEMENT 741
Romanticism / Literature / Art and Music

REFORMS AND REVOLUTIONS 746
National Liberation in Greece / Liberal Reform in Great Britain / The Revolution of 1830 in France

THE REVOLUTION OF 1848 751
A Democratic Republic in France / The Austrian Empire in 1848 / Prussia and the Frankfurt Assembly

Notes

Suggested Reading

24

LIFE IN URBAN SOCIETY 761

TAMING THE CITY 762
Industry and the Growth of Cities / The Public Health Movement / The Bacterial Revolution / Urban Planning and Public Transportation

RICH AND POOR AND IN BETWEEN 771
Social Structure / The Middle Classes / The Working Classes

THE FAMILY 780
Premarital Sex and Marriage / Prostitution / Kinship Ties / Women and Family Life / Child Raising

SCIENCE AND THOUGHT 787
The Triumph of Science / Social Science and Evolution / Realism in Literature

Notes

Suggested Reading

25

THE AGE OF NATIONALISM, 1850–1914 795

NAPOLEON III IN FRANCE 796
The Second Republic and Louis Napoleon / Napoleon III's Second Empire

NATION BUILDING IN ITALY AND GERMANY 799
Italy to 1850 / Cavour and Garibaldi / Germany Before Bismarck / Bismarck Takes Command / The Austro-Prussian War of 1866 / The Taming of Parliament / The Franco-Prussian War of 1870–1871

THE MODERNIZATION OF RUSSIA 808
The "Great Reforms" / The Industrialization of Russia / The Revolution of 1905

THE RESPONSIVE NATIONAL STATE, 1871–1914 813
The German Empire / Republican France / Great Britain and Ireland / The Austro-Hungarian Empire

MARXISM AND THE SOCIALIST MOVEMENT 821
The Socialist International / Unions and Revisionism

Notes

Suggested Reading

26

THE WEST AND THE WORLD 827

BUILDING A WORLD ECONOMY 828
Trade and Communications / Foreign Investment / The Opening of China and Japan / Western Penetration of Egypt

THE GREAT MIGRATION 835
The Pressure of Population / European Migrants / Asian Migrants

WESTERN IMPERIALISM 840
The Scramble for Africa / Imperialism in Asia / Causes of the New Imperialism / Critics of Imperialism

RESPONSES TO WESTERN IMPERIALISM 849
Empire in India / The Example of Japan / Toward Revolution in China

Notes

Suggested Reading

27
THE GREAT BREAK: WAR AND REVOLUTION 859

THE FIRST WORLD WAR 860
The Bismarckian System of Alliances / The Rival Blocs / The Outbreak of War / Reflections on the Origins of the War / The First Battle of the Marne / Stalemate and Slaughter / The Widening War

THE HOME FRONT 872
Mobilizing for Total War / The Social Impact / Growing Political Tensions

THE RUSSIAN REVOLUTION 878
The Fall of Imperial Russia / The Provisional Government / Lenin and the Bolshevik Revolution / Trotsky and the Seizure of Power / Dictatorship and Civil War

THE PEACE SETTLEMENT 885
The End of the War / Revolution in Germany / The Treaty of Versailles / American Rejection of the Versailles Treaty

Notes

Suggested Reading

28
THE AGE OF ANXIETY 895

UNCERTAINTY IN MODERN THOUGHT 896
The New Physics / Freudian Psychology / Philosophy: Logical Empiricism and Existentialism / The Revival of Christianity / Twentieth-Century Literature

MODERN ART AND MUSIC 903
Architecture and Design / Modern Painting / Modern Music

MOVIES AND RADIO 907

THE SEARCH FOR PEACE AND POLITICAL STABILITY 909
Germany and the Western Powers / The Occupation of the Ruhr / Hope in Foreign Affairs, 1924–1929 / Hope in Democratic Government

THE GREAT DEPRESSION, 1929–1939 916
The Economic Crisis / Mass Unemployment / The New Deal in the United States / The Scandinavian Response to Depression / Recovery and Reform in Britain and France

Notes

Suggested Reading

29
DICTATORSHIPS AND THE SECOND WORLD WAR 925

AUTHORITARIAN AND TOTALITARIAN STATES 926
Conservative Authoritarianism / Modern Totalitarianism / Totalitarianism of the Left and the Right

STALIN'S RUSSIA 929
From Lenin to Stalin / The Five-Year Plans / Life in Stalinist Society / Women in Soviet Russia

MUSSOLINI'S ITALY 936
The Seizure of Power / The Regime in Action

HITLER'S GERMANY 939
The Roots of Nazism / Hitler's Road to Power / The Nazi State and Society / Hitler's Popularity

NAZI EXPANSION AND THE SECOND WORLD WAR 947
Aggression and Appeasement, 1933–1939 / Hitler's Empire, 1939–1942

Notes

Suggested Reading

30
THE RECOVERY OF EUROPE AND THE AMERICAS 957

ALLIED VICTORY AND THE COLD WAR, 1942–1950 958
The Grand Alliance / The Tide of Battle / The Origins of the Cold War / West Versus East

THE WESTERN EUROPEAN RENAISSANCE 968
The Postwar Challenge / Economic "Miracles" / Toward European Unity / Decolonialization

SOVIET EASTERN EUROPE 978
Stalin's Last Years / Reform and De-Stalinization / The Fall of Khrushchev

THE WESTERN HEMISPHERE 982
Postwar Prosperity in the United States / The Civil Rights Revolution / Economic Nationalism in Latin America / The Cuban Revolution

Notes

Suggested Reading

31

LIFE IN THE POSTWAR ERA 991

SCIENCE AND TECHNOLOGY 992
The Stimulus of World War Two / The Rise of Big Science / The Life of Scientists and Technologists

TOWARD A NEW SOCIETY 1000
The Changing Class Structure / Social Security Reforms and Rising Affluence / Renewed Discontent and the Student Revolt

WOMEN AND THE FAMILY 1007
Marriage and Motherhood / Women at Work

Notes

Suggested Reading

32

THE RECENT PAST, 1968 TO THE PRESENT 1015

THE TROUBLED ECONOMY 1016
Money and Oil / Inflation, Debt, and Unemployment / Some Social Consequences

THE ATLANTIC ALLIANCE 1023
Germany and the European Settlement / Political Crisis in the United States / Recent Developments

THE SOVIET BLOC 1030
The Czechoslovak Experiment / The Soviet Union / The Solidarity Revolution

THE FUTURE IN PERSPECTIVE 1039

CHAPTER OPENER CREDITS 1045

NOTES ON THE ILLUSTRATIONS 1045

INDEX 1048

MAPS

21.1 Napoleonic Europe in 1810 692

22.1 Cottage Industry and Transportation in Eighteenth-Century England 701

22.2 The Industrial Revolution in England, ca 1850 709

22.3 Continental Industrialization, ca 1850 711

22.4 The Irish Potato Famine 723

23.1 Europe in 1815 729

23.2 Peoples of the Habsburg Monarchy, 1815 734

24.1 European Cities of 100,000 or More, 1800 and 1900 763

24.2 The Modernization of Paris, ca 1850–1870 769

25.1 The Unification of Italy, 1859–1870 800

25.2 The Unification of Germany, 1866–1871 806

26.1 European Investment to 1914 831

26.2 The Partition of Africa 843

26.3 Asia in 1914 846

27.1 The Balkans After the Congress of Berlin, 1878 865

27.2 The Balkans in 1914 865

27.3 The First World War in Europe 870

27.4 Shattered Empires and Territorial Changes After World War One 890

28.1 The Great Depression in the United States, Britain, and Europe 917

29.1 The Growth of Nazi Germany, 1933–1939 948

30.1 World War Two in Europe 960

30.2 World War Two in the Pacific 961

30.3 Territorial Changes After World War Two 969

30.4 European Alliance Systems 973

30.5 The New States in Africa and Asia 977

32.1 OPEC and the World Oil Trade 1018
32.2 The Use of Nuclear Power in the 1980s 1031
32.3 World Population Density 1040
32.4 Estimated World Per Capita Income in the Early 1980s 1041

PREFACE

A HISTORY OF WESTERN SOCIETY grew out of the authors' desire to infuse new life into the study of Western civilization. We knew full well that historians were using imaginative questions and innovative research to open up vast new areas of historical interest and knowledge. We also recognized that these advances had dramatically affected the subject of European economic, intellectual, and, especially, social history, while new research and fresh interpretations were also revitalizing the study of the traditional mainstream of political, diplomatic, and religious development. Despite history's vitality as a discipline, however, it seemed to us that both the broad public and the intelligentsia were generally losing interest in the past. The mathematical economist of our acquaintance who smugly quipped "What's new in history?"—confident that the answer was nothing and that historians were as dead as the events they examine—was not alone.

It was our conviction, based on considerable experience introducing large numbers of students to the broad sweep of Western civilization, that a book reflecting current trends could excite readers and inspire a renewed interest in history and our Western heritage. Our strategy was twofold. First, we made social history the core element of our work. Not only did we incorporate recent research by social historians, but also we sought to re-create the life of ordinary people in appealing human terms. At the same time we were determined to give great economic, political, intellectual, and cultural developments the attention they unquestionably deserve. We wanted to give individual readers and instructors a balanced, integrated perspective, so that they could pursue on their own or in the classroom those themes and questions that they found particularly exciting and significant. In an effort to realize fully the potential of our fresh yet balanced approach, we made many changes, large and small, in the second edition.

In preparing the third edition we have worked hard to keep our book up-to-date and to make it still more effective. First, every chapter has been carefully revised to incorporate recent scholarship. Many of our revisions relate to the ongoing explosion in social history, and once again important findings on such subjects as class relations, population, women, and the family have been integrated into the text. New scholarship also led to substantial revisions on many other questions, such as the Neolithic agricultural revolution, political and economic growth in ancient Greece, the rise and spread of Christianity, the Germanic nobility, medieval feudalism, the origins of the Renaissance, Louis XIV and the French nobility, eighteenth-century absolutism, the French Revolution and Napoleon, nationalism, life in the postwar era, and events of the recent past. We believe that the incorporation of newer interpretations of the main political developments in the medieval, early modern, and French revolutionary periods is a particularly noteworthy change in this edition. Better integration of political and social development contributes to this improvement.

Second, we have carefully examined each chapter for organization and clarity. Chapters 7, 8, 9, 11, 14, and 15 have been thoroughly reorganized, while Chapters 17, 18, 21, and 23 have been reordered to a lesser extent. The result of these changes is a more logical presentation of material and a clearer chronological sequence. Similarly, the reorganization of Chapters 30 and 31 and the addition of Chapter 32 have permitted a more complete discussion of changes since World War Two and an innovative interpretation of this complicated era. We have also taken special care to explain terms and concepts as soon as they are introduced.

Third, we have added or expanded material on previously neglected topics to help keep our work fresh and appealing. Coverage of religious developments, with special emphasis on their popular and social aspects, now extends from ancient to modern times and includes several new sections. The reader will also find new material on many other topics, notably the Minoans, Greek and Roman wars, medieval Germany, the Hanseatic League, the African slave trade, Hume and d'Holbach, the pre-revolutionary French elite, Mill, and events since the late 1960s.

Finally, the illustrative component of our work has been completely revised. There are many new illustrations, including a tripling of the color plates that let both great art and earlier times come alive. Twenty new maps containing social as well as political material have also been added, while maps from the second edition have been re-edited and placed in a more effective format. As in earlier editions, all illustrations have been carefully selected to complement the text, and all carry captions that enhance their value. Artwork remains an integral part of our book, for the past can speak in pictures as well as words.

Distinctive features from earlier editions remain in the third. To help guide the reader toward historical understanding we have posed specific historical questions at the beginning of each chapter. These questions are then answered in the course of the chapter, each of which concludes with a concise summary of the chapter's findings. The timelines added in the second edition have proved useful, and still more are found in this edition.

We have also tried to suggest how historians actually work and think. We have quoted extensively from a wide variety of primary sources and have demonstrated in our use of these quotations how historians sift and weigh evidence. We want the reader to realize that history is neither a list of cut-and-dried facts nor a senseless jumble of conflicting opinions. It is our further hope that the primary quotations, so carefully fitted into their historical context, will give the reader a sense that even in the earliest and most remote periods of human experience history has been shaped by individual men and women, some of them great aristocrats, others ordinary folk.

Each chapter concludes with carefully selected suggestions for further reading. These suggestions are briefly described in order to help readers know where to turn to continue thinking and learning about the Western world. The chapter bibliographies have been revised and expanded in order to keep them current with the vast and complex new work being done in many fields.

Western civilization courses differ widely in chronological structure from one campus to another. To accommodate the various divisions of historical time into intervals that fit a two-quarter, three-quarter, or two-semester period, *A History of Western Society* is being published in three versions, each set embracing the complete work:

One-volume hardcover edition, A HISTORY OF WESTERN SOCIETY; two-volume paperback, A HISTORY OF WESTERN SOCIETY *Volume I: From Antiquity to the Enlightenment* (Chapters 1–17), *Volume II: From Absolutism to the Present* (Chapters 16–32); three-volume paperback, A HISTORY OF WESTERN SOCIETY *Volume A: From Antiquity to the Reforma-*

tion (Chapters 1–13), *Volume B: From the Renaissance to 1815* (Chapters 12–21), *Volume C: From the Revolutionary Era to the Present* (Chapters 21–32).

Note that overlapping chapters in both the two- and the three-volume sets permit still wider flexibility in matching the appropriate volume with the opening and closing dates of a course term. Furthermore, for courses beginning with the Renaissance rather than antiquity or the medieval period, the reader can begin study with Volume B.

Learning and teaching ancillaries, including a *Study Guide, Computerized Study Guide, Instructor's Manual, Test Items, Computerized Test Items,* and *Map Transparencies,* also contribute to the usefulness of the text. The excellent *Study Guide* has been revised by Professor James Schmiechen of Central Michigan University. Professor Schmiechen has been a tower of strength ever since he critiqued our initial prospectus, and he has continued to give us many valuable suggestions and his warmly appreciated support. His *Study Guide* contains chapter summaries, chapter outlines, review questions, extensive multiple-choice exercises, self-check lists of important concepts and events, and a variety of study aids and suggestions. One innovation in the *Study Guide* that has proved useful to the student is the step-by-step Reading with Understanding exercises, which take the reader by ostensive example through reading and studying activities like underlining, summarizing, identifying main points, classifying information according to sequence, and making historical comparisons. To enable both students and instructors to use the *Study Guide* with the greatest possible flexibility, the guide is available in two volumes, with considerable overlapping of chapters. Instructors and students who use only Volumes A and B of the text have all the pertinent study materials in a single volume, *Study Guide, Volume 1* (Chapters 1–21); likewise, those who use only Volumes B and C of the text also have all the necessary materials in one volume, *Study Guide, Volume 2* (Chapters 12–32). The multiple-choice sections of the *Study Guide* are also available in a computerized version that provides the student with tutorial instruction.

The *Instructor's Manual,* prepared by Professor Philip Adler of East Carolina University, contains learning objectives, chapter synopses, suggestions for lectures and discussion, paper and class activity topics, and lists of audio-visual resources. The accompanying *Test Items,* also by Professor Adler, offers more than 1100 multiple-choice and essay questions and approximately 500 identification terms. The test items are available to adopters on computer tape and disk. In addition, a set of forty color map transparencies is available on adoption.

It is a pleasure to thank the many instructors who have read and critiqued the manuscript through its development: James W. Alexander, University of Georgia; Susan D. Amussen, Connecticut College; Jack M. Balcer, Ohio State University; Ronald M. Berger, State University College at Oneonta, New York; Charles R. Berry, Wright State University; Shirley J. Black, Texas A & M University; John W. Bohnstedt, California State University at Fresno; Paul Bookbinder, University of Massachusetts—Boston, Harbor Campus; Jerry H. Brookshire, Middle Tennessee State University; Thomas S. Burns, Emory University; Robert Clouse, Indiana State University; Norman H. Cooke, Rhode Island College; Charles E. Daniel, University of Rhode Island; Gary S. Cross, Pennsylvania State University; Lawrence G. Duggan, University of Delaware; J. Rufus Fears, Indiana University; John B. Freed, Illinois State University; James Friguglietti, Eastern Montana College; Charles L. Geddes, University of Denver; James Gump, University of San Diego; Charles D. Hamilton, San Diego State University; Barbara Hanawalt, Indiana University; Thomas J. Heston, West Chester State College; Edward J. Kealey, College of the Holy Cross; Isabel F. Knight, Pennsylvania State University; Charles A. Le Guin, Portland State University; Richard Lyman, Simmons College; Rhoda McFadden, Montgomery County Community College; Christian D. Nokkentved, University of Illinois at Chicago; John E. Roberts, Jr., Lincoln Land Community College; William J. Roosen, Northern Arizona University; Lawrence Silverman, University of Colorado; Armstrong Starkey, Adelphi University; Robert E. Stebbins, Eastern Kentucky University; Bailey S. Stone, University of Houston; C. Mary Taney, Glassboro State College; Allen M. Ward, University of Connecticut; and Donald Wilcox, University of New Hampshire.

Many of our colleagues at the University of Illinois kindly provided information and stimulation for our book, often without even knowing it. N. Frederick

Nash, Rare Book Librarian, gave freely of his time and made many helpful suggestions for illustrations. The World Heritage Museum at the University continued to allow us complete access to its sizable holdings. James Dengate kindly supplied information on objects from the museum's collection. Caroline Buckler took many excellent photographs of the museum's objects and generously helped us at crucial moments in production. Such wide-ranging expertise was a great asset for which we are very appreciative. Bennett Hill wishes to express his sincere appreciation to Ramón de la Fuente of Washington, D.C., for his support, encouragement, and research assistance in the preparation of this third edition. John Buckler extends his thanks to Elke Bernlocher.

Each of us has benefited from the generous criticism of his co-authors, although each of us assumes responsibility for what he has written. John Buckler has written the first six chapters; Bennett Hill has continued the narrative through Chapter 16; and John McKay has written Chapters 17 through 32. Finally, we continue to welcome from our readers comments and suggestions for improvements, for they have helped us greatly in this ongoing endeavor.

JOHN P. MCKAY
BENNETT D. HILL
JOHN BUCKLER

21

THE REVOLUTION IN POLITICS, 1775–1815

*T*HE LAST YEARS of the eighteenth century were a time of great upheaval. A series of revolutions and revolutionary wars challenged the old order of kings and aristocrats. The ideas of freedom and equality, ideas that have not stopped shaping the world since that era, flourished and spread. The revolution began in North America in 1775. Then in 1789 France, the most influential country in Europe, became the leading revolutionary nation. It established first a constitutional monarchy, then a radical republic, and finally a new empire under Napoleon. The armies of France also joined forces with patriots and radicals abroad in an effort to establish new governments based on new principles throughout much of Europe. The world of modern domestic and international politics was born.

What caused this era of revolution? What were the ideas and objectives of the men and women who rose up violently to undo the established system? What were the gains and losses for privileged groups and for ordinary people in a generation of war and upheaval? These are the questions on which this chapter's examination of the French and American revolutions will be based.

LIBERTY AND EQUALITY

Two ideas fueled the revolutionary period in both America and Europe: liberty and equality. What did eighteenth-century politicians and other people mean by liberty and equality, and why were those ideas so radical and revolutionary in their day?

The call for liberty was first of all a call for individual human rights. Even the most enlightened monarchs customarily claimed that it was their duty to regulate what people wrote and believed. Liberals of the revolutionary era protested such controls from on high. They demanded freedom to worship according to the dictates of their consciences instead of according to the politics of their prince. They demanded the end of censorship and the right to express their beliefs freely in print and at public meetings. They demanded freedom from arbitrary laws and from judges who simply obeyed orders from the government.

These demands for basic personal freedoms, which were incorporated into the American Bill of Rights and other liberal constitutions, were very far-reaching. Indeed, eighteenth-century revolutionaries demanded more freedom than most governments today believe it is desirable to grant. The Declaration of the Rights of Man, issued at the beginning of the French Revolution, proclaimed, "Liberty consists in being able to do anything that does not harm another person." A citizen's rights had, therefore, "no limits except those which assure to the other members of society the enjoyment of these same rights." Liberals called for the freedom of the individual to develop and to create to the fullest possible extent. In the context of the aristocratic and monarchial forms of government that then dominated Europe, this was a truly radical idea.

The call for liberty was also a call for a new kind of government. The revolutionary liberals believed that the people were sovereign—that is, that the people alone had the authority to make laws limiting the individual's freedom of action. In practice, this system of government meant choosing legislators who represented the people and who were accountable to them. Moreover, liberals of the revolutionary era believed that every people—every ethnic group—had this right of self-determination and thus the right to form a free nation.

By equality, eighteenth-century liberals meant that all citizens were to have identical rights and civil liberties. Above all, the nobility had no right to special privileges based on the accident of birth.

Liberals did not define equality as meaning that everyone should be equal economically. Quite the contrary. As Thomas Jefferson wrote in an early draft of the American Declaration of Independence, before changing "property" to the more noble-sounding "happiness," everyone was equal in "the pursuit of property." Jefferson and other liberals certainly did not expect equal success in that pursuit. Great differences in wealth and income between rich and poor were perfectly acceptable to liberals. The essential point was that everyone should legally have an equal chance. French liberals and revolutionaries said they wanted "careers opened to talent." They wanted employment in government, in business, and in the professions to be based on ability, not on family background or legal status.

Equality of opportunity was a very revolutionary idea in eighteenth-century Europe. Legal inequality between classes and groups was the rule, not the exception. Society was still legally divided into groups with special privileges, such as the nobility and the clergy, and groups with special burdens, like the peasantry. In many countries, various middle-class groups—professionals, businessmen, townspeople, and craftsmen—enjoyed privileges that allowed them to monopolize all sorts of economic activity. It was this kind of economic inequality, an inequality based on artificial legal distinctions, against which liberals protested.

The Roots of Liberalism

The ideas of liberty and equality—the central ideas of classical liberalism—have deep roots in Western history. The ancient Greeks and the Judeo-Christian tradition had affirmed for hundreds of years the sanctity and value of the individual human being. The Judeo-Christian tradition, reinforced by the Reformation, had long stressed personal responsibility on the part of both common folk and exalted rulers, thereby promoting the self-discipline without which liberty becomes anarchy. The hounded and persecuted Protestant radicals of the later sixteenth century had died for the revolutionary idea that individuals were entitled to their own religious beliefs.

Although the liberal creed had roots deep in the Western tradition, classical liberalism first crystallized at the end of the seventeenth century and during the Enlightenment of the eighteenth century.

Liberal ideas reflected the Enlightenment's stress on human dignity and human happiness on earth. Liberals shared the Enlightenment's general faith in science, rationality, and progress: the adoption of liberal principles meant better government and a better society for all. Almost all the writers of the Enlightenment were passionately committed to greater personal liberty. They preached religious toleration, freedom of press and speech, and fair and equal treatment before the law.

Certain English and French thinkers were mainly responsible for joining the Enlightenment's concern for personal freedom and legal equality to a theoretical justification of liberal self-government. The two most important were John Locke and the baron de Montesquieu, considered earlier. Locke (page 530) maintained that England's long political tradition rested on "the rights of Englishmen" and on representative government through Parliament. Locke admired especially the great Whig noblemen who had made the bloodless revolution of 1688, and he argued that a government that oversteps its proper functions —protecting the natural rights of life, liberty, and private property—becomes a tyranny. Montesquieu (page 585) was also inspired by English constitutional history. He, too, believed that powerful "intermediary groups"—such as the judicial nobility of which he was a proud member—offered the best defense of liberty against despotism.

The Marquis de Lafayette was the most famous great noble to embrace the liberal revolution. Shown here directing a battle in the American Revolution, he returned to champion liberty and equality in France. For admirers he was the "hero of two worlds." *(Anne S. K. Brown Military Collection, John Hay Library, Brown University)*

The Attraction of Liberalism

The belief that representative institutions could defend their liberty and interests appealed powerfully to ambitious and educated bourgeois. Yet it is important to realize that liberal ideas about individual rights and political freedom also appealed to much of the aristocracy, at least in western Europe and as formulated by Montesquieu. Representative government did not mean democracy, which liberal thinkers tended to equate with mob rule. Rather, they envisioned voting for representatives as being restricted to those who owned property, those with "a stake in society." England had shown the way. After 1688 it had combined a parliamentary system and considerable individual liberty with a restricted franchise and unquestionable aristocratic pre-eminence. In the course of the eighteenth century, many leading French nobles, led by a judicial nobility inspired by Montesquieu, as shown in Chapter 18, were increasingly eager to follow the English example.

Eighteenth-century liberalism, then, appealed not only to the middle class, but also to some aristocrats. It found broad support among the educated elite and the substantial classes in western Europe. What it lacked from the beginning was strong mass support. For comfortable liberals, the really important questions were theoretical and political. They had no need to worry about their stomachs and the price of bread. For the much more numerous laboring poor, the great questions were immediate and economic. Getting enough to eat was the crucial challenge. These differences in outlook and well-being were to lead to many misunderstandings and disappointments for both groups in the revolutionary era.

THE AMERICAN REVOLUTION, 1775–1789

The era of liberal revolution began in the New World. The thirteen mainland colonies of British North America revolted against their mother country and then succeeded in establishing a new unified government.

Americans have long debated the meaning of their revolution. Some have even questioned whether or not it was a real revolution, as opposed to a war for independence. According to some scholars, the Revolution was conservative and defensive in that its demands were for the traditional liberties of Englishmen; Americans were united against the British, but otherwise they were a satisfied people, not torn by internal conflict. Other scholars have argued that, on the contrary, the American Revolution was quite radical. It split families between patriots and Loyalists and divided the country. It achieved goals that were fully as advanced as those obtained by the French in their great revolution a few years later.

How does one reconcile these positions? Both contain large elements of truth. The American revolutionaries did believe they were demanding only the traditional rights of English men and women. But those traditional rights were liberal rights, and in the American context they had very strong democratic and popular overtones. Thus the American Revolution was fought in the name of established ideals that were still quite radical in the context of the times. And in founding a government firmly based on liberal principles, the Americans set an example that had a forceful impact on Europe and speeded up political development there.

The Origins of the Revolution

The American Revolution had its immediate origins in a squabble over increased taxes. The British government had fought and decisively won the Seven Years' War (page 625) on the strength of its professional army and navy. The American colonists had furnished little real aid. The high cost of the war to the British, however, had led to a doubling of the British national debt. Anticipating further expense defending its recently conquered western lands from Indian uprisings like that of Pontiac, the British government in London set about reorganizing the empire with a series of bold, largely unprecedented measures. Breaking with tradition, the British decided to maintain a large army in North America after peace was restored in 1763. Moreover, they sought to exercise strict control over their newly conquered western lands and to tax the colonies directly. In 1765 the government pushed through Parliament the Stamp Act, which levied taxes on a long list of commercial and legal documents, diplomas, pamphlets, newspapers, almanacs, dice, and playing cards. A stamp glued to each article indicated the tax had been paid.

The effort to increase taxes as part of tightening up the empire seemed perfectly reasonable to the British. Heavier stamp taxes had been collected in Great Britain for two generations, and Americans were being asked only to pay a share of their own defense.

The Boston Tea Party This contemporary illustration shows men disguised as Indians dumping East India Company tea into Boston's harbor. The enthusiastic crowd cheering from the wharf indicates widespread popular support. *(Library of Congress)*

Moreover, Americans had been paying only very low local taxes. The Stamp Act would have doubled taxes to about two shillings per person. No other people in the world (except the Poles) paid so little. The British, meanwhile, paid the world's highest taxes in about 1765—twenty-six shillings per person. It is not surprising that taxes per person in the newly independent American nation were much higher in 1785 than in 1765, when the British no longer subsidized American defense. The colonists protested the Stamp Act vigorously and violently, however, and after rioting and boycotts against British goods, Parliament reluctantly repealed the new tax.

As the fury of the Stamp Act controversy revealed, much more was involved than taxes. The key question was political. To what extent could the home government refashion the empire and reassert its power while limiting the authority of colonial legislatures and their elected representatives? Accordingly, who should represent the colonies, and who had the right to make laws for Americans? While a troubled majority of Americans searched hard for a compromise, some radicals began to proclaim that "taxation without representation is tyranny." The British government replied that Americans were represented in Parliament, albeit indirectly (like most Englishmen themselves), and that the absolute supremacy of Parliament throughout the empire could not be questioned. Many Americans felt otherwise. As John Adams put it, "A Parliament of Great Britain can have no more rights to tax the colonies than a Parliament of Paris." Thus imperial reorganization and Parliamentary supremacy came to appear as grave threats to Americans' existing liberties and time-honored institutions.

Americans had long exercised a great deal of independence and gone their own way. In British North America, unlike England and Europe, no powerful established church existed, and personal freedom in questions of religion was taken for granted. The colonial assemblies made the important laws, which were seldom overturned by the home government. The right to vote was much more widespread than in England. In many parts of colonial Massachusetts, for example, as many as 95 percent of the adult males could vote.

Moreover, greater political equality was matched by greater social and economic equality. Neither a hereditary nobility nor a hereditary serf population existed, although the slavery of the Americas consigned blacks to a legally oppressed caste. Independent farmers were the largest group in the country and set much of its tone. In short, the colonial experience had slowly formed a people who felt themselves separate and distinct from the home country. The controversies over taxation intensified those feelings of distinctiveness and separation and brought them to the fore.

In 1773 the dispute over taxes and representation flared up again. The British government had permitted the financially hard-pressed East India Company to ship its tea from China directly to its agents in the colonies, rather than through London middlemen, who then sold to independent merchants in the colonies. Thus the company secured a vital monopoly on the tea trade, and colonial merchants were suddenly excluded from a highly profitable business. The colonists were quick to protest.

In Boston, men disguised as Indians had a rowdy "tea party" and threw the company's tea into the harbor. This led to extreme measures. The so-called Coercive Acts closed the port of Boston, curtailed local elections and town meetings, and greatly expanded the royal governor's power. County conventions in Massachusetts protested vehemently and urged that the acts be "rejected as the attempts of a wicked administration to enslave America." Other colonial assemblies joined in the denunciations. In September 1774, the First Continental Congress met in Philadelphia, where the more radical members argued successfully against concessions to the crown. Compromise was also rejected by the British parliament, and in April 1775 fighting began at Lexington and Concord.

Independence

The fighting spread, and the colonists moved slowly but inevitably toward open rebellion and a declaration of independence. The uncompromising attitude of the British government and its use of German mercenaries went a long way toward dissolving long-standing loyalties to the home country and rivalries among the separate colonies. *Common Sense* (1775), a brilliant attack by the recently arrived English radical Thomas Paine (1737–1809), also mobilized public opinion in favor of independence. A runaway best seller with sales of 120,000 copies in a few months, Paine's tract ridiculed the idea of a small island ruling a great continent. In his call for freedom and republican government, Paine expressed Americans' growing sense of separateness and moral superiority.

On July 4, 1776, the Second Continental Congress adopted the Declaration of Independence. Written by Thomas Jefferson, the Declaration of Independence boldly listed the tyrannical acts committed by George III (1760–1820) and confidently proclaimed the natural rights of man and the sovereignty of the American states. Sometimes called the world's greatest political editorial, the Declaration of Independence in effect universalized the traditional rights of Englishmen and made them the rights of all mankind. It stated that "all men are created equal . . . they are endowed by their Creator with certain unalienable rights . . . among these are life, liberty, and the pursuit of happiness." No other American political document has ever caused such excitement, both at home and abroad.

Many American families remained loyal to Britain; many others divided bitterly. After the Declaration of Independence, the conflict often took the form of a civil war pitting patriot against Loyalist. The Loyalists tended to be wealthy and politically moderate. Many patriots, too, were wealthy—individuals such as John Hancock and George Washington—but willingly allied themselves with farmers and artisans in a broad coalition. This coalition harassed the Loyalists and confiscated their property to help pay for the American war effort. The broad social base of the revolutionaries tended to make the liberal revolution democratic. State governments extended the right to vote to many more people in the course of the war and re-established themselves as republics.

On the international scene, the French sympathized with the rebels from the beginning. They wanted revenge for the humiliating defeats of the Seven Years' War. Officially neutral until 1776, they supplied the great bulk of guns and gunpowder used by the American revolutionaries, very much as neutral great powers supply weapons for "wars of national liberation" today. By 1777 French volunteers were arriving in Virginia, and a dashing young nobleman, the marquis de Lafayette (1757–1834), quickly became one of Washington's most trusted generals. In 1778 the French government offered the Americans a formal alliance, and in 1779 and 1780 the Spanish and Dutch declared war on Britain. Catherine the

The Signing of the Declaration, July 4, 1776 John Trumbull's famous painting shows the dignity and determination of America's revolutionary leaders. An extraordinarily talented group, they succeeded in rallying popular support without losing power to more radical forces in the process. *(Yale University Art Gallery)*

Great of Russia helped organize a League of Armed Neutrality in order to protect neutral shipping rights, which Britain refused to recognize.

Thus, by 1780 Great Britain was engaged in an imperial war against most of Europe as well as the thirteen colonies. In these circumstances, and in the face of severe reverses in India, the West Indies, and at Yorktown in Virginia, a new British government decided to cut its losses. American negotiators in Paris were receptive. They feared that France wanted a treaty that would bottle up the new United States east of the Alleghenies and give British holdings west of the Alleghenies to France's ally, Spain. Thus the American negotiators ditched the French and accepted the extraordinarily favorable terms Britain offered.

By the Treaty of Paris of 1783, Britain recognized the independence of the thirteen colonies and ceded all its territory between the Appalachians and the Mississippi River to the Americans. Out of the bitter rivalries of the Old World, the Americans snatched dominion over half a continent.

Framing the Constitution

The liberal program of the American Revolution was consolidated by the federal Constitution, the Bill of Rights, and the creation of a national republic. Assembling in Philadelphia in the summer of 1787, the delegates to the Constitutional Convention were determined to end the period of economic depression, social uncertainty, and very weak central government that had followed independence. The delegates decided, therefore, to grant the federal, or central, government important powers: regulation of domestic and foreign trade, the right to levy taxes, and the means to enforce its laws.

Strong rule was placed squarely in the context of representative self-government. Senators and congressmen would be the lawmaking delegates of the voters, and the president of the republic would be an elected official. The central government was to operate in Montesquieu's framework of checks and balances. The executive, legislative, and judicial branches would systematically balance each other.

Benjamin Franklin in France Franklin served with distinction as American ambassador to France during the War for Independence. Shown signing the crucial Treaties of Commerce and Alliance in 1778, Franklin was lionized by the French as scientist and sage. *(Brown Brothers)*

The power of the federal government would in turn be checked by the powers of the individual states.

When the results of the secret deliberation of the Constitutional Convention were presented to the states for ratification, a great public debate began. The opponents of the proposed constitution—the Anti-Federalists—charged that the framers of the new document had taken too much power from the individual states and made the federal government too strong. Moreover, many Anti-Federalists feared for the personal liberties and individual freedoms for which they had just fought. In order to overcome these objections, the Federalists solemnly promised to spell out these basic freedoms as soon as the new constitution was adopted. The result was the first ten amendments to the Constitution, which the first Congress passed shortly after it met in New York in March 1789. These amendments formed an effective bill of rights to safeguard the individual. Most of them—trial by jury, due process of law, right to assemble, freedom from unreasonable search—had their origins in English law and the English Bill of Rights of 1689. Others—the freedoms of speech, the press, and religion—reflected natural-law theory and the American experience.

The American Constitution and the Bill of Rights exemplified the great strengths and the limits of what came to be called "classical liberalism." Liberty meant individual freedoms and political safeguards. Liberty also meant representative government but did not necessarily mean democracy with its principle of one man, one vote.

Equality—slaves excepted—meant equality before the law, not equality of political participation or economic well-being. Indeed, economic inequality was resolutely defended by the elite who framed the Constitution. The right to own property was guaranteed by the Fifth Amendment, and if the government took private property, the owner was to receive "just compensation." The radicalism of liberal revolution in America was primarily legal and political, not economic or social.

The Revolution's Impact on Europe

Hundreds of books, pamphlets, and articles analyzed and romanticized the American upheaval. Thoughtful Europeans noted, first of all, its enormous long-term implications for international politics. A secret report by the Venetian ambassador to Paris in 1783 stated what many felt: "If only the union of the Provinces is preserved, it is reasonable to expect that, with the favorable effects of time, and of European arts and sciences, it will become the most formidable power in the world."[1] More generally, American independence fired the imaginations of those few aristocrats who were uneasy with their privileges and of those commoners who yearned for greater equality. Many Europeans believed that the world was advancing now and that America was leading the way. As one French writer put it in 1789: "This vast continent which the seas surround will soon change Europe and the universe."

Europeans who dreamed of a new era were fascinated by the political lessons of the American Revolution. The Americans had begun with a revolutionary defense against tyrannical oppression, and they had been victorious. They had then shown how rational beings could assemble together to exercise sovereignty and write a permanent constitution—a new social contract. All this gave greater reality to the concepts of individual liberty and representative government. It reinforced one of the primary ideas of the Enlightenment, the idea that a better world was possible.

Louis XVI Idealized in this stunning portrait by Duplessis as a majestic, self-confident ruler and worthy heir of Louis XIV, Louis XVI was actually shy, indecisive, and somewhat stupid. *(Château de Versailles/Giraudon/Art Resource)*

THE FRENCH REVOLUTION, 1789–1791

No country felt the consequences of the American Revolution more directly than France. Hundreds of French officers served in America and were inspired by the experience. The most famous of these, the young and impressionable marquis de Lafayette left home as a great aristocrat determined only to fight France's traditional foe, England. He returned with a love of liberty and firm republican convictions. French intellectuals and publicists engaged in passionate analysis of the federal Constitution, as well as the constitutions of the various states of the new United States. The American Revolution undeniably hastened upheaval in France.

Yet the French Revolution did not mirror the American example. It was more violent and more complex, more influential and more controversial, more loved and more hated. For Europeans and most of the rest of the world, it was *the* great revolution of the eighteenth century, the revolution that opened the modern era in politics.

The Breakdown of the Old Order

Like the American Revolution, the French Revolution had its immediate origins in the financial difficulties of the government. As we noted in Chapter 18, the efforts of Louis XV's ministers to raise taxes had been thwarted by the Parlement of Paris, strengthened in its opposition by widespread popular support. When renewed efforts to reform the tax system met a similar fate in 1776, the government was forced to finance all of its enormous expenditures during the American war with borrowed money. The national debt and the annual budget deficit soared. By the 1780s fully half of France's annual budget went for ever-increasing interest payments on the ever-increasing debt. Another quarter went to maintain the military, while 6 percent was absorbed by the costly and extravagant king and his court at Versailles. Less than one-fifth of the entire national budget was available for the productive functions of the state, such as transportation and general administration. It was an impossible financial situation.

One way out would have been for the government to declare partial bankruptcy, forcing its creditors to accept greatly reduced payments on the debt. The powerful Spanish monarchy had regularly repudiated large portions of its debt in earlier times, and France had done likewise, after an attempt to establish a French national bank ended in financial disaster in 1720. Yet by the 1780s the French debt was held by an army of aristocratic and bourgeois creditors, and the French monarchy, though absolute in theory, had become far too weak for such a drastic and unpopular action.

Nor could the king and his ministers, unlike modern governments, print money and create inflation to cover their deficits. Unlike England and Holland, which had far larger national debts relative to their populations, France had no central bank, no paper currency, and no means of creating credit. French money was good gold coin. Therefore, when a depressed economy and a lack of public confidence made it increasingly difficult for the government to obtain new gold loans in 1786, it had no alternative but to try to increase taxes. And since France's tax system was unfair and out of date, increased revenues were possible only through fundamental reforms. Such reforms would affect all groups in France's complex and fragmented society and opened a Pandora's box of social and political demands.

Legal Orders and Social Realities

As in the Middle Ages, France's 25 million inhabitants were still legally divided into three orders or "estates"—the clergy, the nobility, and everyone else. As the nation's first estate, the clergy numbered about 100,000 and had important privileges. It owned about 10 percent of the land and paid only a "voluntary gift" to the government every five years. Moreoever, the church levied a tax (the tithe) on landowners, which averaged somewhat less than 10 percent. Much of the church's income was actually drained away from local parishes by political appointees and worldly aristocrats at the top of the church hierarchy, to the intense dissatisfaction of the poor parish priests.

The second legally defined estate consisted of some 400,000 noblemen and noblewomen—the descendants of "those who fought" in the Middle Ages. The nobles owned outright about 25 percent of the land in France, and they, too, were taxed very lightly. Moreoever, nobles continued to enjoy certain manorial rights, or privileges of lordship, that dated back to medieval times and allowed them to tax the peasantry for their own profit. This was done by means of exclusive rights to hunt and fish, village monopolies on baking bread and pressing grapes for wine, fees for justice, and a host of other "useful privileges." In addition, nobles had "honorific privileges," such as the right to precedence on public occasions and the right to wear a sword. These rights conspicuously proclaimed the nobility's legal superiority and exalted social position.

Everyone else was a commoner, a member of the third estate. A few commoners were rich merchants or highly successful doctors and lawyers. Many more were urban artisans and unskilled day laborers. The vast majority of the third estate consisted of the peasants and agricultural workers in the countryside. Thus the third estate was a conglomeration of vastly different social groups, united only by their shared legal status as distinct from the privileged nobility and clergy.

In discussing the long-term origins of the French Revolution, historians have long focused on growing tensions between the nobility and the comfortable members of the third estate, usually known as the bourgeoisie, or middle class. A dominant historical interpretation has held sway for at least two generations. According to this interpretation, the bourgeoisie was basically united by economic position and class interest. Aided by the general economic expansion discussed in Chapter 19, the middle class grew rapidly in the eighteenth century, tripling to about 2.3 million persons, or about 8 percent of France's population. Increasing in size, wealth, culture, and self-confidence, this rising bourgeoisie became progressively exasperated by archaic "feudal" laws restraining the economy and by the growing pretensions of a reactionary nobility, which was closing ranks against middle-class needs and aspirations. As a result, the French bourgeoisie eventually rose up to lead the entire third estate in a great social revolution, a revolution that destroyed feudal privileges and established a capitalist order based on individualism and a market economy.

In recent years, a flood of new research has challenged these accepted views, and once again the French Revolution is a subject of heated scholarly debate. Above all, revisionist historians have questioned the existence of a growing social conflict between a progressive capitalistic bourgeoisie and a reactionary feudal nobility in eighteenth-century France. Instead, these historians see both bourgeoisie and nobility as being riddled with internal rivalries and highly fragmented. The great nobility, for example, was profoundly separated from the lesser nobility by differences in wealth, education, and worldview. Differences within the bourgeoisie—between wealthy financiers and local lawyers, for example—were no less profound. Rather than standing as unified blocs against each other, nobility and bourgeoisie formed two parallel social ladders, increasingly linked together at the top by wealth, marriage, and Enlightenment culture.

Revolutionist historians stress in particular three developments in their reinterpretation. First, the nobility remained a fluid and relatively open order. Throughout the eighteenth century, substantial numbers of successful commoners continued to seek and obtain noble status through government service and purchase of expensive positions conferring nobility. Thus the nobility of the robe continued to attract the wealthiest members of the middle class and to permit social mobility. Second, key sections of the nobility were no less liberal than the middle class, which until revolution actually began, generally supported the judicial opposition led by the Parlement of Paris. Finally, the nobility and the bourgeoisie were not really at odds in the economic sphere. Both looked to investment in land and government service as their preferred activities, and the ideal of the merchant capitalist was to gain enough wealth to retire from trade, purchase estates, and live nobly as a large landowner. At the same time, wealthy nobles often acted as aggressive capitalists, investing especially in mining, metallurgy, and foreign trade.

The revisionists have clearly shaken the belief that the bourgeoisie and the nobility were inevitably locked in growing conflict before the revolution. But in stressing the similarities between the two groups, especially at the top, they have also reinforced the view, long maintained by historians, that the Old Regime had ceased to correspond with social reality by the 1780s. Legally, society was still based on rigid orders inherited from the Middle Ages. In reality, France had already moved far toward being a society based on wealth and economic achievement, where an emerging elite that included both aristocratic and bourgeois notables was frustrated by a bureaucratic monarchy that had long claimed the right to absolute power.

The Formation of the National Assembly

The Revolution was under way by 1787, though no one could have realized what was to follow. Spurred by a depressed economy and falling tax receipts, Louis XVI's minister of finance revived old proposals to impose a general tax on all landed property, as well as provincial assemblies to help administer the tax, and he convinced the king to call an Assembly of Notables to gain support for the idea. The assembled notables, who were mainly important noblemen and high-ranking clergy, were not in favor of it. In return for their support, they demanded that control over all government spending be given to the provincial assemblies, which they expected to control. When the government refused, the nobles responded that such sweeping tax changes required the approval of the Estates General, the representative body of all three estates, which had not met since 1614.

Facing imminent bankruptcy, the king tried to reassert his authority. He dismissed the nobles and established new taxes by decree. In stirring language, the Parlement of Paris promptly declared the royal initiative null and void. The Parlement went so far as to specify some of the "fundamental laws" against which no king could transgress, such as national consent to taxation and freedom from arbitrary arrest and imprisonment. When the king tried to exile the judges, a tremendous wave of protest swept the country. Frightened investors also refused to advance more loans to the state. Finally, in July 1788, a beaten Louis XVI called for a spring session of the Estates General. Absolute monarchy was collapsing.

What would replace it? Throughout the unprecedented election campaign of 1788 and 1789, that question excited France. All across the country, clergy, nobles, and commoners came together in their respective orders to draft petitions for change and to elect their respective delegates to the Estates General. The local assemblies of the clergy showed considerable dissatisfaction with the church hierarchy, and two-thirds of the delegates were chosen from the poorer parish priests, who were commoners by birth. The nobles, already badly split by wealth and education, remained politically divided. A conservative majority was drawn from the poorer and more numerous provincial nobility, but fully a third of the nobility's representatives were liberals committed to major changes.

As for the third estate, there was great popular participation in the elections. Almost all male commoners twenty-five years or older had the right to vote. However, voting required two stages, which meant that most of the representatives finally selected by the third estate were well-educated, prosperous members of the middle class. Most of them were not businessmen, but lawyers and government officials. Social status and prestige were matters of particular concern to this economic elite. There were no delegates from the great mass of laboring poor—the peasants and the artisans.

The petitions for change from the three estates showed a surprising degree of agreement on most issues, as recent research has clearly revealed. There was general agreement that royal absolutism should give way to constitutional monarchy, in which laws and taxes would require the consent of an Estates General meeting regularly. All agreed that, in the future, individual liberties must be guaranteed by law and that the position of the parish clergy had to be improved. It was generally acknowledged that economic development required reforms, such as the abolition of internal trade barriers. The striking similarities in the grievance petitions of the clergy, nobility, and third estate reflected the broad commitment of France's elite to liberalism.

Yet an increasingly bitter quarrel undermined this consensus during the intense election campaign: *how* would the Estates General vote, and precisely *who* would lead in the political reorganization that was generally desired? The Estates General of 1614 had sat as three separate houses. Any action had required the agreement of at least two branches, a requirement that had guaranteed control by the privileged orders—the nobility and the clergy. Immediately after its victory over the king, the aristocratic Parlement of Paris ruled that the Estates General should once again sit separately, mainly out of respect for tradition but partly to enhance the nobility's political position. The ruling was quickly denounced by certain middle-class intellectuals and some liberal nobles. They demanded instead a single assembly dominated by representatives of the third estate, to ensure fundamental reforms. Reflecting a growing hostility toward aristocratic aspirations, the abbé Sieyès argued in 1789 in his famous pamphlet, *What Is the Third Estate?*, that the nobility was a tiny, overprivileged minority and that the neglected third estate constituted the true strength of the French nation. When the government agreed that the third estate should have as many delegates as the clergy and the nobility combined, but then rendered its act meaningless by upholding voting by separate order, middle-class leaders saw fresh evidence of an aristocratic conspiracy.

In May 1789, the twelve hundred delegates of the three estates paraded in medieval pageantry through the streets of Versailles to an opening session resplendent with feudal magnificence. The estates were almost immediately deadlocked. Delegates of the third estate refused to transact any business until the king ordered the clergy and nobility to sit with them in a single body. Finally, after a six-week war of nerves, a few parish priests began to go over to the third estate, which on June 17 voted to call itself the National Assembly. On June 20, excluded from their hall because of "repairs," the delegates of the third estate moved to a large indoor tennis court. There they swore the famous Oath of the Tennis Court, pledging never to disband until they had written a new constitution.

The king's actions were then somewhat contradictory. On June 23, he made a conciliatory speech to a joint session, urging reforms, and then ordered the three estates to meet together. At the same time, he apparently followed the advice of relatives and court nobles, who urged the king to dissolve the Estates General by force. The king called an army of eighteen thousand troops toward Versailles, and on July 11 he dismissed his finance minister and his other more liberal ministers. Faced with growing opposition since 1787, Louis XVI had resigned himself to bankruptcy. Now he sought to reassert his divine and historic right to rule. The middle-class delegates had done their best, but they were resigned to being disbanded at bayonet point. One third-estate delegate reassured a worried colleague: "You won't hang—you'll only have to go back home."[2]

The Revolt of the Poor and the Oppressed

While the third estate pressed for symbolic equality with the nobility and clergy in a single legislative body at Versailles, economic hardship gripped the masses of France in a tightening vise. Grain was the basis of the diet of ordinary people, and in 1788 the harvest had been extremely poor. The price of bread, which had been rising gradually since 1785, began to soar. By July 1789, the price of bread in the provinces climbed as high as eight sous per pound. In Paris, where bread was subsidized by the government in an attempt to prevent popular unrest, the price rose to four sous. The poor could scarcely afford to pay two sous per pound, for even at that price a laborer with a wife and three children had to spend half of his wages to buy the family's bread.

Harvest failure and high bread prices unleashed a classic economic depression of the preindustrial age.

Storming the Bastille This contemporary drawing conveys the fury and determination of the revolutionary crowd on July 14, 1789. This successful popular action had enormous symbolic significance, and July 14 has long been France's most important national holiday. *(Photo: Flammarion)*

With food so expensive and with so much uncertainty, the demand for manufactured goods collapsed. Thousands of artisans and small traders were thrown out of work. By the end of 1789, almost half of the French people would be in need of relief. One person in eight was a pauper, living in extreme want. In Paris the situation was desperate in July 1789: perhaps 150,000 of the city's 600,000 people were without work.

Against this background of dire poverty and excited by the political crisis, the people of Paris entered decisively onto the revolutionary stage. They believed in a general, though ill-defined, way that the economic distress had human causes. They believed that they should have steady work and enough bread to survive. Specifically, they feared that the dismissal of the king's moderate finance minister would throw them at the mercy of aristocratic landowners and grain speculators. Stories like that quoting the wealthy financier Joseph François Foulon as saying that the poor "should eat grass, like my horses," and rumors that the king's troops would sack the city began to fill the air. Angry crowds formed and passionate voices urged action. On July 13, the people began to seize arms for the defense of the city, and on July 14, several hundred of the most determined people marched to the Bastille to search for gunpowder.

An old medieval fortress with walls ten feet thick and eight great towers each a hundred feet high, the Bastille had long been used as a prison. It was guarded by eighty retired soldiers and thirty Swiss guards. The governor of the fortress-prison refused to hand over the powder, panicked, and ordered his men to fire, killing ninety-eight people attempting to enter. Cannon were brought to batter the main gate, and fighting continued until the governor of the prison surrendered. While he was being taken under guard to city hall, a band of men broke through and hacked him to death. His head and that of the mayor of Paris, who had been slow to give the crowd arms, were stuck on pikes and paraded through the streets. The next day, a committee of citizens appointed the marquis de Lafayette commander of the city's armed forces. Paris was lost to the king, who was forced to recall the finance minister and to disperse his troops. The uprising had saved the National Assembly.

As the delegates resumed their long-winded and inconclusive debates at Versailles, the people in the countryside sent them a radical and unmistakable message. All across France, peasants began to rise in spontaneous, violent, and effective insurrection against their lords, ransacking manor houses and burning feudal documents that recorded the peasants' obligations. Neither middle-class landowners, who often owned manors and village monopolies, nor the larger, more prosperous farmers were spared. In some areas, the nobles and bourgeoisie combined forces and organized patrols to protect their property. Yet the peasant insurrection went on. Recent enclosures were undone, old common lands were reoccupied, and the forests were seized. Taxes went unpaid. Fear of vagabonds and outlaws—the so-called Great Fear—seized the countryside and fanned the flames of rebellion. The long-suffering peasants were doing their best to free themselves from aristocratic privilege and exploitation.

Faced with chaos, yet fearful of calling on the king to restore order, some liberal nobles and middle-class delegates at Versailles responded to peasant demands with a surprise maneuver on the night of August 4, 1789. The duke of Aiguillon, one of France's greatest noble landowners, declared that

> *in several provinces the whole people forms a kind of league for the destruction of the manor houses, the ravaging of the lands, and especially for the seizure of the archives where the title deeds to feudal properties are kept. It seeks to throw off at last a yoke that has for many centuries weighted it down.*[3]

He urged equality in taxation and the elimination of feudal dues. In the end, all the old exactions were abolished, generally without compensation: serfdom where it still existed, exclusive hunting rights for nobles, fees for justice, village monopolies, the right to make peasants work on the roads, and a host of other dues. Though a clarifying law passed a week later was less generous, the peasants ignored the "fine print." They never paid feudal dues again. Thus the French peasantry, which already owned about 30 percent of all the land, quickly achieved a great and unprecedented victory. Henceforth, the French peasants would seek mainly to consolidate their triumph. As the Great Fear subsided, they became a force for order and stability.

A Limited Monarchy

The National Assembly moved forward. On August 27, 1789, it issued the Declaration of the Rights of Man. This great liberal document had a very American flavor, and Lafayette even discussed his draft in detail with the American ambassador in Paris, Thomas Jefferson, the author of the American Declaration of Independence. According to the French declaration, "men are born and remain free and equal in rights." Mankind's natural rights are "liberty, property, security, and resistance to oppression." Also, "every man is presumed innocent until he is proven guilty." As for law, "it is an expression of the general will; all citizens have the right to concur personally or through their representatives in its formation. . . . Free expression of thoughts and opinions is one of the most precious rights of mankind: every citizen may therefore speak, write, and publish freely." In short, this clarion call of the liberal revolutionary ideal guaranteed equality before the law, representative government for a sovereign people, and individual freedom. This revolutionary credo, only two pages long, was propagandized throughout France and Europe and around the world.

Moving beyond general principles to draft a constitution proved difficult. The questions of how much power the king should retain and whether he could permanently veto legislation led to another deadlock. Once again the decisive answer came from the poor, in this instance the poor women of Paris.

To understand what happened, one must remember that the work and wages of women and children were essential in the family economy of the laboring poor. In Paris great numbers of women worked, particularly within the putting-out system in the garment industry—making lace, fancy dresses, embroidery, ribbons, bonnets, corsets, and so on. Many of these goods were beautiful luxury items, destined for an aristocratic and international clientele.[4] Immediately after the fall of the Bastille, many of France's great court nobles began to leave Versailles for foreign lands, so that a plummeting demand for luxuries intensified the general economic crisis. International markets also declined, and the church was no longer able to give its traditional grants of food and money to the poor. Unemployment and hunger increased further, and the result was another popular explosion.

On October 5, some seven thousand desperate women marched the twelve miles from Paris to Versailles to demand action. A middle-class deputy looking out from the assembly saw "multitudes arriving from Paris including fishwives and bullies from the market, and these people wanted nothing but bread." This great crowd invaded the assembly, "armed with scythes, sticks and pikes." One coarse, tough old woman directing a large group of younger women defiantly shouted into the debate: "Who's that talking down there? Make the chatterbox shut up. That's not the point: the point is that we want bread."[5] Hers was the genuine voice of the people, essential to any understanding of the French Revolution.

The women invaded the royal apartments, slaughtered some of the royal bodyguards, and furiously searched for the despised queen, Marie Antoinette. "We are going to cut off her head, tear out her heart, fry her liver, and that won't be the end of it," they shouted, surging through the palace in a frenzy. It seems likely that only the intervention of Lafayette and the National Guard saved the royal family. But the only way to calm the disorder was for the king to go and live in Paris, as the crowd demanded.

The next day, the king, the queen, and their son left for Paris in the midst of a strange procession. The heads of two aristocrats, stuck on pikes, led the way. They were followed by the remaining members of the royal bodyguard, unarmed and surrounded and mocked by fierce men holding sabers and pikes. A mixed and victorious multitude surrounded the king's carriage, hurling crude insults at the queen. There was drinking and eating among the women. "We are bringing the baker, the baker's wife, and the baker's boy," they joyfully sang. The National Assembly followed the king to Paris. Reflecting the more radical environment, it adopted a constitution that gave the virtually imprisoned "baker" only a temporary veto in the lawmaking process. And, for a time, he and the government made sure that the masses of Paris did not lack bread.

"To Versailles" This print is one of many commemorating the women's march on Versailles. Notice on the left that the fashionable lady from the well-to-do is a most reluctant revolutionary. *(Photo: Flammarion)*

The next two years until September 1791 saw the consolidation of the liberal Revolution. Under middle-class leadership, the National Assembly abolished the French nobility as a legal order and pushed forward with the creation of a constitutional monarchy, which Louis XVI reluctantly agreed to accept in July 1790. In the final constitution, the king remained the head of state, but all lawmaking power was placed in the hands of the National Assembly, elected by the economic upper half of French males. Eighty-three departments of approximately equal size replaced the complicated old patchwork of provinces with their many historic differences. The jumble of weights and measures that varied from province to province was reformed, leading to the introduction of the simple, rational metric system in 1793. The National Assembly promoted economic freedom. Monopolies, guilds, and workers' combinations were prohibited, and barriers to trade within France were abolished in the name of economic liberty. Thus the National Assembly applied the critical spirit of the Enlightenment to reform France's laws and institutions completely.

The assembly also threatened nobles who had emigrated from France with the loss of their lands. It nationalized the property of the church and abolished the monasteries as useless relics of a distant past. The government used all former church property as collateral to guarantee a new paper currency, the *assignats,* and then sold these properties in an attempt to put the state's finances on a solid footing. Although the church's land was sold in large blocks, a procedure that favored nimble speculators and the rich, peasants eventually purchased much of it as it was subdivided. These purchases strengthened their attachment to the revolutionary state.

The most unfortunate aspect of the reorganization of France was that it brought the new government into conflict with the Catholic church. Many middle-class delegates to the National Assembly, imbued with the rationalism and skepticism of the eighteenth-century philosophes, harbored a deep distrust of popular piety and "superstitious religion." They were interested in the church only to the extent that they could seize its land and use the church to strengthen the new state. Thus they established a national church, with priests chosen by voters. In the face of resistance, the National Assembly required the clergy to take a loyalty oath to the new government. The clergy became just so many more employees of the state. The pope formally condemned this attempt to subjugate the church. Against such a backdrop, it is not surprising that only half the priests of France took the oath of allegiance. The result was a deep division within both the country and the clergy itself on the religious question, and confusion and hostility among French Catholics were pervasive. The attempted reorganization of the Catholic church was the revolutionary government's first important failure.

WORLD WAR AND REPUBLICAN FRANCE, 1791–1799

When Louis XVI accepted the final version of the completed constitution in September 1791, a young and still obscure provincial lawyer and member of the National Assembly named Maximilien Robespierre (1758–1794) evaluated the work of two years and concluded, "The Revolution is over." Robespierre was both right and wrong. He was right in the sense that the most constructive and lasting reforms were in place. Nothing substantial in the way of liberty and equality would be gained in the next generation, though much would be lost. He was wrong in the sense that a much more radical stage lay ahead. New heroes and new ideologies were to emerge in revolutionary wars and international conflict.

The Beginning of War

The outbreak and progress of revolution in France produced great excitement and a sharp division of opinion in Europe and the United States. Liberals and radicals such as the English scientist Joseph Priestly (1733–1804) and the American patriot Thomas Paine saw a mighty triumph of liberty over despotism. Conservative spirits like Edmund Burke (1729–1797) were deeply troubled. In 1790 Burke published *Reflections on the Revolution in France,* one of the great intellectual defenses of European conservatism. He defended inherited privileges in general and those of the English monarchy and aristocracy in particular. He predicted that unlimited reform would lead only to chaos and renewed tyranny. By 1791 fear was growing outside France that the great hopes raised by the Revolution might be tragically dashed. The moderate German writer Friedrich von Gentz was apprehensive that, if moderate and intelligent revolution failed in France, all the old evils would be ten times worse: "It would be felt that men could be happy only as slaves, and every tyrant, great or small, would use this confession to seek revenge for the fright that the awakening of the French nation had given him."[6]

The kings and nobles of Europe, who had at first welcomed the revolution in France as weakening a competing power, began to feel threatened themselves. At their courts they listened to the diatribes of great court nobles who had fled France and were urging intervention in France's affairs. When Louis XVI and Marie Antoinette were arrested and returned to Paris after trying unsuccessfully to slip out of France in June 1791, the monarchs of Austria and Prussia issued the Declaration of Pillnitz. This carefully worded statement declared their willingness to intervene in France, but only with the unanimous agreement of all the Great Powers, which they did not expect to receive. Austria and Prussia expected their threat to have a sobering effect on revolutionary France without causing war.

The crowned heads of Europe misjudged the revolutionary spirit in France. When the National Assembly had disbanded, it had sought popular support by decreeing that none of its members would be eligible for election to the new Legislative Assembly. This meant that, when the new representative body was duly elected and convened in October 1791, it had a different character. The great majority were still prosperous, well-educated, and middle class, but they were younger and less cautious than their predecessors. Loosely allied as "Jacobins," so named after their political club, the new representatives to the Assembly were passionately committed to liberal revolution.

The Jacobins increasingly lumped "useless aristocrats" and "despotic monarchs" together, and they easily whipped themselves into a patriotic fury with bombastic oratory. So the courts of Europe were attempting to incite a war of kings against France; well then, "we will incite a war of people against kings. . . . Ten million Frenchmen, kindled by the fire of liberty, armed with the sword, with reason, with eloquence would be able to change the face of the world and make the tyrants tremble on their thrones."[7] Only Robespierre and a very few others argued that people do not welcome liberation at the point of a gun. Such warnings were brushed aside. France would "rise to the full height of her mission," as one deputy urged. In April 1792, France declared war on Francis II, archduke of Austria and king of Hungary and Bohemia.

France's crusade against tyranny went poorly at first. Prussia joined Austria in the Austrian Netherlands (present-day Belgium), and French forces broke and fled at their first encounter with armies of this First Coalition. The road to Paris lay open, and it is possible that only conflict between the eastern monarchs over the division of Poland saved France from defeat.

Military reversals and Austro-Prussian threats caused a wave of patriotic fervor to sweep France. The Legislative Assembly declared the country in danger. Volunteer armies from the provinces streamed through Paris, fraternizing with the people and singing patriotic songs like the stirring *Marseillaise,* later the French national anthem.

In this supercharged wartime atmosphere, rumors of treason by the king and queen spread in Paris. Once again, as in the storming of the Bastille, the common people of Paris acted decisively. On August 10, 1792, a revolutionary crowd attacked the royal palace at the Tuileries, capturing it after heavy fighting with the Swiss Guards. The king and his family fled for their lives to the nearby Legislative Assembly, which suspended the king from all his functions, imprisoned him, and called for a new National Convention to be elected by universal male suffrage. Monarchy in France was on its deathbed, mortally wounded by war and popular revolt.

The Second Revolution

The fall of the monarchy marked a rapid radicalization of the Revolution, which historians often call the "second revolution." Louis's imprisonment was followed by the September Massacres, which sullied the Revolution in the eyes of most of its remaining foreign supporters. Wild stories seized the city that imprisoned counter-revolutionary aristocrats and priests were plotting with the allied invaders. As a result, angry crowds invaded the prisons of Paris and summarily slaughtered half the men and women they found. In late September 1792, the new, popularly elected National Convention proclaimed France a republic. The republic adopted a new revolutionary calendar, and citizens were expected to address each other with the friendly "thou" of the people, rather than with the formal "you" of the rich and powerful.

All of the members of the National Convention were Jacobins and republicans, and the great majority continued to come from the well-educated middle class. But the convention was increasingly divided into two well-defined, bitterly competitive groups—the Girondists and the Mountain, so called because its members, led by Danton and Robespierre, sat on the uppermost left-hand benches of the assembly hall. Many indecisive members seated in the "Plain" below floated back and forth between the rival factions.

The division was clearly apparent after the National Convention overwhelmingly convicted Louis XVI of treason. By a single vote, 361 of the 720 members of the convention then unconditionally sentenced him to death in January 1793. Louis died with tranquil dignity on the newly invented guillotine. One of his last statements was, "I am innocent and shall die without fear. I would that my death might bring happiness to the French, and ward off the dangers which I foresee."[8]

Both the Girondists and the Mountain were determined to continue the "war against tyranny." The Prussians had been stopped at the indecisive battle of Valmy on September 20, 1792, one day before the republic was proclaimed. Republican armies then successfully invaded Savoy and captured Nice. A second army corps invaded the German Rhineland and took the city of Frankfurt. To the north, the revolutionary armies won their first major battle at Jemappes and occupied the entire Austrian Netherlands by November 1792. Everywhere they went, French armies of occupation chased the princes, "abolished feudalism," and found support among some peasants and middle-class people.

But the French armies also lived off the land, requisitioning food and supplies and plundering local treasures. The liberators looked increasingly like foreign invaders. International tensions mounted. In February 1793, the National Convention, at war with Austria and Prussia, declared war on Britain, Holland, and Spain as well. Republican France was now at war with almost all of Europe, a great war that would last almost without interruption until 1815.

As the forces of the First Coalition drove the French from the Austrian Netherlands, peasants in western France revolted against being drafted into the army. They were supported and encouraged in their resistance by devout Catholics, royalists, and foreign agents.

In Paris, the quarrelsome National Convention found itself locked in a life-and-death political struggle between the Girondists and the Mountain. The two groups were in general agreement on questions of policy. Sincere republicans, they hated privilege and wanted to temper economic liberalism with social concern. Yet personal hatreds ran deep. The Girondists feared a bloody dictatorship by the Mountain, and the Mountain was no less convinced that the more moderate Girondists would turn to conservatives and even royalists in order to retain power. With the middle-class delegates so bitterly divided, the laboring poor of Paris emerged as the decisive political factor.

The great mass of the Parisian laboring poor always constituted—along with the peasantry in the summer of 1789—the elemental force that drove the Revolution forward. It was the artisans, shopkeepers, and day laborers who had stormed the Bastille, marched on Versailles, driven the king from the Tuileries, and carried out the September Massacres. The petty traders and laboring poor were often known as the *sans-culottes,* "without breeches," because they wore trousers instead of the knee breeches of the aristocracy and the solid middle class. The immediate interests of the sans-culottes were mainly economic, and in the spring of 1793, the economic situation was as bad as the military situation. Rapid inflation, unemployment, and food shortages were again weighing heavily on the poor.

Moreover, by the spring of 1793, the sans-culottes were keenly interested in politics. Encouraged by the so-called angry men, such as the passionate young ex-priest and journalist Jacques Roux, the sans-culottes were demanding radical political action to guarantee them their daily bread. At first the Mountain joined the Girondists in violently rejecting these demands. But in the face of military defeat, peasant revolt, and hatred of the Girondists, the Mountain and especially Robespierre became more sympathetic. The Mountain joined with sans-culottes activists in the city government to engineer a popular uprising, which forced the convention to arrest thirty-one Girondist deputies for treason on June 2. All power passed to the Mountain.

Robespierre and others from the Mountain joined the recently formed Committee of Public Safety, to which the convention had given dictatorial power to

The Reign of Terror A man, woman, and child accused of political crimes are brought before a special revolutionary committee for trial. The Terror's iron dictatorship crushed individual rights as well as treason and opposition. *(Photo: Flammarion)*

deal with the national emergency. These developments in Paris triggered revolt in leading provincial cities, such as Lyons and Marseilles, where moderates denounced Paris and demanded a decentralized government. The peasant revolt spread and the republic's armies were driven back on all fronts. By July 1793, only the areas around Paris and on the eastern frontier were firmly controlled by the central government. Defeat appeared imminent.

Total War and the Terror

A year later, in July 1794, the Austrian Netherlands and the Rhineland were once again in the hands of conquering French armies, and the First Coalition was falling apart. This remarkable change of fortune was due to the revolutionary government's success in harnessing, for perhaps the first time in history, the explosive forces of a planned economy, revolutionary terror, and modern nationalism in a total war effort.

Robespierre and the Committee of Public Safety advanced with implacable resolution on several fronts in 1793 and 1794. In an effort to save revolutionary France, they collaborated with the fiercely patriotic and democratic sans-culottes. They established, as best they could, a planned economy with egalitarian social overtones. Rather than let supply and demand determine prices, the government decreed the maximum allowable prices, fixed in paper assignats, for a host of key products. Though the state was too weak to enforce all its price regulations, it did fix the price of bread in Paris at levels the poor could afford. Rationing and ration cards were introduced to make sure that the limited supplies of bread were shared fairly. Quality was also controlled. Bakers were permitted to make only the "bread of equality"—a brown bread made of a mixture of all available flours. White bread and pastries were outlawed as frivolous luxuries. The poor of Paris may not have eaten well, but they ate.

They also worked, mainly to produce arms and munitions for the war effort. Craftsmen and small manufacturers were told what to produce and when to deliver. The government nationalized many small

The French Revolution

May 5, 1789	Estates General convene at Versailles
June 17, 1789	Third Estate declares itself the National Assembly
June 20, 1789	Oath of the Tennis Court
July 14, 1789	Storming of the Bastille
July–August 1789	The Great Fear in the countryside
August 4, 1789	National Assembly abolishes feudal privileges
August 27, 1789	National Assembly issues Declaration of the Rights of Man
October 5, 1789	Parisian women march on Versailles and force royal family to return to Paris
November 1789	National Assembly confiscates church lands
July 1790	Civil Constitution of the Clergy establishes a national church
	Louis XVI reluctantly agrees to accept a constitutional monarchy
June 1791	Arrest of the royal family while attempting to flee France
August 1791	Declaration of Pillnitz by Austria and Prussia
April 1792	France declares war on Austria
August 1792	Parisian mob attacks palace and takes Louis XVI prisoner
September 1792	September Massacres
	National Convention declares France a republic and abolishes monarchy
January 1793	Execution of Louis XVI
February 1793	France declares war on Britain, Holland, and Spain
	Revolts in provincial cities
March 1793	Bitter struggle in the National Convention between Girondists and the Mountain
April–June 1793	Robespierre and the Mountain organize the Committee of Public Safety and arrest Girondist leaders
September 1793	Price controls to aid the sans-culottes and mobilize war effort
1793–1794	Reign of Terror in Paris and the provinces
Spring 1794	French armies victorious on all fronts
July 1794	Execution of Robespierre
	Thermidorean Reaction begins
1795–1799	The Directory
1795	End of economic controls and suppression of the sans-culottes
1797	Napolean defeats Austrian armies in Italy and returns triumphant to Paris
1798	Austria, Great Britain, and Russia form the Second Coalition against France
1799	Napoleon overthrows the Directory and seizes power

workshops and requisitioned raw materials and grain from the peasants. Sometimes planning and control did not go beyond orders to meet the latest emergency: "Ten thousand soldiers lack shoes. You will take the shoes of all the aristocrats in Strasbourg and deliver them ready for transport to headquarters at 10 A.M. tomorrow." Failures to control and coordinate were failures of means and not of desire: seldom if ever before had a government attempted to manage an economy so thoroughly. The second revolution and the ascendancy of the sans-culottes had produced an embryonic emergency socialism, which was to have great influence on the subsequent development of socialist ideology.

While radical economic measures supplied the poor with bread and the armies with weapons, a Reign of Terror (1793–1794) was solidifying the home front. Special revolutionary courts, responsible only to Robespierre's Committee of Public Safety, tried rebels and "enemies of the nation" for political crimes. Drawing on popular, sans-culottes support centered in the local Jacobin clubs, these local courts ignored normal legal procedures and judged severely. Some 40,000 French men and women were executed or died in prison. Another 300,000 suspects crowded the prisons and often brushed close to death in a revolutionary court.

Robespierre's Reign of Terror was one of the most controversial phases of the French Revolution. Most historians now believe that the Terror was not directed against any single class. Rather, it was a political weapon directed impartially against all who might oppose the revolutionary government. For many Europeans of the time, however, the Reign of Terror represented a terrifying perversion of the generous ideals of 1789. It strengthened the belief that France had foolishly replaced a weak king with a bloody dictatorship.

The third and perhaps most decisive element in the French republic's victory over the First Coalition was its ability to continue drawing on the explosive power of patriotic dedication to a national state and a national mission. This is the essence of modern nationalism. With a common language and a common tradition, newly reinforced by the ideas of popular sovereignty and democracy, the French people were stirred by a common loyalty. The shared danger of foreign foes and internal rebels unified all classes in a heroic defense of the nation.

In such circumstances, war was no longer the gentlemanly game of the eighteenth century, but a life-and-death struggle between good and evil. Everyone had to participate in the national effort. According to a famous decree of August 23, 1793:

The young men shall go to battle and the married men shall forge arms. The women shall make tents and clothes, and shall serve in the hospitals; children shall tear rags into lint. The old men will be guided to the public places of the cities to kindle the courage of the young warriors and to preach the unity of the Republic and the hatred of kings.

Like the wars of religion, war in 1793 was a crusade; this war, though, was fought for a secular rather than a religious ideology.

As all unmarried young men were subject to the draft, the French armed forces swelled to 1 million men in fourteen armies. A force of this size was unprecedented in the history of European warfare. The soldiers were led by young, impetuous generals, who had often risen rapidly from the ranks and personified the opportunities the Revolution seemed to offer gifted sons of the people. These generals used mass attacks at bayonet point by their highly motivated forces to overwhelm the enemy. By the spring of 1794, French armies were victorious on all fronts. The republic was saved.

The Thermidorian Reaction and the Directory, 1794–1799

The success of the French armies led Robespierre and the Committee of Public Safety to relax the emergency economic controls, but they extended the political Reign of Terror. Their lofty goal was increasingly an ideal democratic republic, where justice would reign and there would be neither rich nor poor. Their lowly means were unrestrained despotism and the guillotine, which struck down any who might seriously question the new order. In March 1794, to the horror of many sans-culottes, Robespierre's Terror wiped out many of the "angry men," led by the radical social democrat Jacques Hébert. Two weeks later, several of Robespierre's long-standing collaborators, led by the famous orator Danton, marched up the steps to the guillotine. Knowing that they might be next, a strange assortment of radicals and moderates in the convention organized a conspiracy. They howled down Robespierre when he tried to speak to the National Convention on 9 Thermidor (July 27, 1794). On the following day, it was Robespierre's turn to be shaved by the revolutionary razor.

As Robespierre's closest supporters followed their leader, France unexpectedly experienced a thorough reaction to the despotism of the Reign of Terror. In a general way, this "Thermidorian reaction" recalled the early days of the Revolution. The respectable middle-class lawyers and professionals who had led the liberal Revolution of 1789 reasserted their authority. Drawing support from their own class, the provincial cities, and the better-off peasants, the National Convention abolished many economic controls, printed more paper currency, and let prices rise sharply. It severely restricted the local political organizations where the sans-culottes had their strength. And all the while, the wealthy bankers and newly rich speculators celebrated the sudden end of the Terror with an orgy of self-indulgence and ostentatious luxury.

The collapse of economic controls, coupled with runaway inflation, hit the working poor very hard. The gaudy extravagance of the rich wounded their pride. The sans-culottes accepted private property, but they believed passionately in small business and the right of all to earn a decent living. Increasingly disorganized after Robespierre purged their radical spokesmen, the common people of Paris finally revolted against the emerging new order in early 1795. The Convention quickly used the army to suppress these insurrections. For the first time since the fall of the Bastille, bread riots and uprisings by Parisians living on the edge of starvation were effectively put down by a government that made no concessions to the poor.

In the face of all these catastrophes, the revolutionary fervor of the laboring poor finally subsided. As far as politics was concerned, their interest and influence would remain very limited until 1830. There arose, especially from the women, a great cry for peace and a turning toward religion. As the government looked the other way, the women brought back the Catholic church and the worship of God. In one French town, women fought with each other over which of their children should be baptized first. After six tumultuous years, the women of the poor concluded that the Revolution was a failure.

As for the middle-class members of the National Convention, they wrote yet another constitution, which they believed would guarantee their economic position and political supremacy. The mass of the population could vote only for electors, who would be men of means. Electors then elected the members of a reorganized legislative assembly, as well as key officials throughout France. The assembly also chose the five-man executive—the Directory.

The men of the Directory continued to support French military expansion abroad. War was no longer so much a crusade as a means to meet the ever-present, ever-unsolved economic problem. Large, victorious French armies reduced unemployment at home, and they were able to live off the territories they conquered and plundered.

The unprincipled action of the Directory reinforced widespread disgust with war and starvation. This general dissatisfaction revealed itself clearly in the national elections of 1797, which returned a large number of conservative and even monarchist deputies who favored peace at almost any price. Fearing for their skins, the members of the Directory used the army to nullify the elections and began to govern dictatorially. Two years later, Napoleon Bonaparte ended the Directory in a coup d'état and substituted a strong dictatorship for a weak one. Truly, the Revolution was over.

THE NAPOLEONIC ERA, 1799–1815

For almost fifteen years, from 1799 to 1814, France was in the hands of a keen-minded military dictator of exceptional ability. One of history's most fascinating leaders, Napoleon Bonaparte realized the need to put an end to civil strife in France, in order to create unity and consolidate his rule. And he did. But Napoleon saw himself as a man of destiny, and the glory of war and the dream of universal empire proved irresistible. For years he spiraled from victory to victory; but in the end he was destroyed by a mighty coalition united in fear of his restless ambition.

Napoleon's Rule of France

In 1799, when he seized power, young General Napoleon Bonaparte was a national hero. Born in Corsica into an impoverished noble family in 1769, Napoleon left home to become a lieutenant in the French artillery in 1785. After a brief and unsuccessful adventure fighting for Corsican independence in 1789, he returned to France as a French patriot and a dedicated revolutionary. Rising rapidly in the new army, Napoleon was placed in command of French forces in Italy and won brilliant victories there in 1796 and 1797. His next campaign, in Egypt, was a failure, but Napoleon made his way back to France before the fiasco was generally known. His reputation remained intact.

Napoleon soon learned that some prominent members of the legislative assembly were plotting against the Directory. The dissatisfaction of these plotters stemmed not so much from the fact that the Directory was a dictatorship, as from the fact that it was a weak dictatorship. Ten years of upheaval and uncertainty had made firm rule much more appealing than liberty and popular politics to these disillusioned revolutionaries. The abbé Sieyès personified this evolution in thinking. In 1789 he had written in his famous pamphlet, *What Is the Third Estate?,* that the nobility was grossly overprivileged and that the entire people should rule the French nation. Now Sieyès's motto was "confidence from below, authority from above."

Like the other members of his group, Sieyès wanted a strong military ruler. The flamboyant thirty-year-old Napoleon was ideal. Thus the conspirators and Napoleon organized a takeover. On November 9, 1799, they ousted the Directors, and the following day soldiers disbanded the assembly at bayonet point. Napoleon was named first consul of the republic, and a new constitution consolidating his position was overwhelmingly approved in a plebiscite in December 1799. Republican appearances were maintained, but Napoleon was already the real ruler of France.

Napoleon Crossing the Alps: David Bold and commanding, with flowing cape and surging stallion, the daring young Napoleon Bonaparte leads his army across the Alps from Italy to battle the Austrians in 1797. This painting by the great Jacques-Louis David (1748–1825) is a stirring glorification of Napoleon, a brilliant exercise in mythmaking. *(The Granger Collection)*

The essence of Napoleon's domestic policy was to use his great and highly personal powers to maintain order and put an end to civil strife. He did so by working out unwritten agreements with powerful groups in France, whereby these groups received favors in return for loyal service. Napoleon's bargain with the solid middle class was codified in the famous Civil Code of 1804, which reasserted two of the fundamental principles of the liberal and essentially moderate revolution of 1789: equality of all citizens before the law and absolute security of wealth and private property. Napoleon and the leading bankers of Paris established a privately owned Bank of France, which loyally served the interests of both the state and the financial oligarchy. Napoleon's defense of the economic status quo also appealed to the peasants, who had bought some of the lands confiscated from the church and nobility. Thus Napoleon reconfirmed the gains of the peasantry and reassured the middle class, which had already lost a large number of its revolutionary illusions in the face of social upheaval.

At the same time, Napoleon accepted and strengthened the position of the French bureaucracy. Building on the solid foundations that revolutionary governments had inherited from the Old Regime, he perfected a thoroughly centralized state. A network of prefects, subprefects, and centrally appointed mayors depended on Napoleon and served him well. Nor were members of the old nobility slighted. In 1800 and again in 1802 Napoleon granted amnesty to a hundred thousand émigrés on the condition that they return to France and take a loyalty oath. Members of this returning elite soon ably occupied many high posts in the expanding centralized state. Only a thousand diehard monarchists were exempted and remained abroad. Napoleon also created a new imperial nobility in order to reward his most talented generals and officials.

The Napoleonic Era

November 1799	Napoleon overthrows the Directory
December 1799	French voters overwhelmingly approve Napoleon's new constitution
1800	Napoleon founds the Bank of France
1801	France defeats Austria and acquires Italian and German territories in the Treaty of Lunéville
	Napoleon signs a concordat with the pope
1802	Treaty of Amiens with Britain
March 1804	Execution of the Duke of Engheim
December 1804	Napoleon crowns himself emperor
October 1805	Battle of Trafalgar: Britain defeats the French and Spanish fleets
December 1805	Battle of Austerlitz: Napoleon defeats Austria and Prussia
1807	Treaties of Tilsit: Napoleon redraws the map of Europe
1810	Height of the Grand Empire
June 1812	Napoleon invades Russia with 600,000 men
Winter 1812	Disastrous retreat from Russia
March 1814	Russia, Prussia, Austria, and Britain form the Quadruple Alliance to defeat France
April 1814	Napoleon abdicates and is exiled to Elba
February–June 1815	Napoleon escapes from Elba and rules France until suffering defeat at Battle of Waterloo

Napoleon's great skill in gaining support from important and potentially hostile groups is illustrated by his treatment of the Catholic church in France. In 1800 the French clergy was still divided into two groups: those who had taken an oath of allegiance to the revolutionary government and those in exile or hiding who had refused to do so. Personally uninterested in religion, Napoleon wanted to heal the religious division so that a united Catholic church in France could serve as a bulwark of order and social peace. After long and arduous negotiations, Napoleon and Pope Pius VII (1800–1823) signed the Concordat of 1801. The pope gained for French Catholics the precious right to practice their religion freely, but Napoleon gained the most politically. His government now nominated bishops, paid the clergy, and exerted great influence over the church in France.

The domestic reforms of Napoleon's early years were his greatest achievement. Much of his legal and administrative reorganization has survived in France to this day. More generally, Napoleon's domestic initiatives gave the great majority of French people a welcome sense of order and stability. And when Napoleon added the glory of military victory, he rekindled a spirit of national unity that would elude France throughout most of the nineteenth century.

Order and unity had their price: Napoleon's authoritarian rule. Free speech and freedom of the press—fundamental rights of the liberal revolution, enshrined in the Declaration of the Rights of Man—were continually violated. Napoleon constantly reduced the number of newspapers in Paris. By 1811 only four were left, and they were little more than organs of government propaganda. The occasional elections were a farce. Later laws prescribed harsh penalties for political offenses.

These changes in the law were part of the creation of a police state in France. Since Napoleon was usually busy making war, this task was largely left to Joseph Fouché, an unscrupulous opportunist who had earned a reputation for brutality during the Reign of Terror. As minister of police, Fouché organized a ruthlessly efficient spy system, which kept thousands of citizens under continuous police surveillance. People suspected of subversive activities were arbitrarily detained, placed under house arrest, or even consigned to insane asylums. After 1810 political suspects were held in state prisons, as they had been during the Terror. There were about 2,500 such political prisoners in 1814.

Napoleon on Campaign This picture of the bloody Battle of Bordino in Russia in 1812 captures important features of Napoleonic warfare. While cannon boomed, infantry fired, and cavalry charged, commanders watching from on high directed their forces like pieces on a chessboard. *(Brown Brothers)*

Napoleon's Wars and Foreign Policy

Napoleon was above all a military man, and a great one. After coming to power in 1799, he sent peace feelers to Austria and Great Britain, the two remaining members of the Second Coalition, which had been formed against France in 1798. When these overtures were rejected, French armies led by Napoleon decisively defeated the Austrians. In the Treaty of Lunéville (1801) Austria accepted the loss of its Italian possessions, and German territory on the west bank of the Rhine was incorporated into France. Once more, as in 1797, the British were alone, and war-weary, like the French.

Still seeking to consolidate his regime domestically, Napoleon concluded the Treaty of Amiens with Great Britain in 1802. Britain agreed to return Trinidad and the Caribbean islands, which it had seized from France in 1793. The treaty said very little about Europe, though. France remained in control of Holland, the Austrian Netherlands, the west bank of the Rhine, and most of the Italian peninsula. Napoleon was free to reshape the German states as he wished. To the dismay of British businessmen, the Treaty of Amiens did not provide for expansion of the commerce between Britain and the Continent. It was clearly a diplomatic triumph for Napoleon, and peace with honor and profit increased his popularity at home.

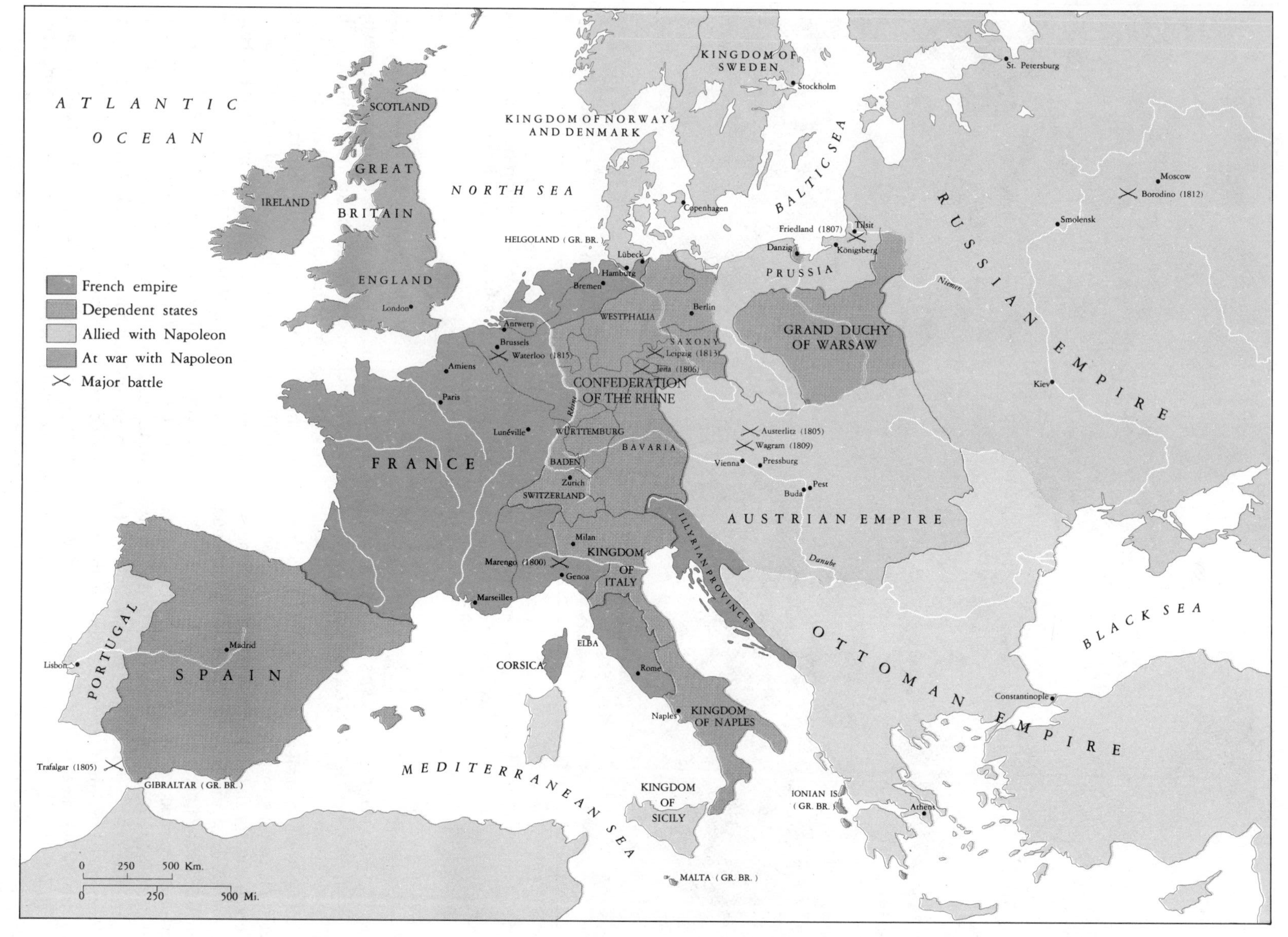

ATLANTIC OCEAN
French empire
Dependent states
Allied with Napoleon
At war with Napoleon
Major battle
SCOTLAND
GREAT BRITAIN
IRELAND
ENGLAND
London
NORTH SEA
KINGDOM OF NORWAY AND DENMARK
KINGDOM OF SWEDEN
Stockholm
Copenhagen
BALTIC SEA
St. Petersburg
HELGOLAND (GR. BR.)
Lübeck
Hamburg
Bremen
Friedland (1807)
Tilsit
Danzig
Königsberg
PRUSSIA
Niemen
RUSSIAN EMPIRE
Moscow
Borodino (1812)
Smolensk
Kiev
Berlin
WESTPHALIA
SAXONY
Leipzig (1813)
Jena (1806)
GRAND DUCHY OF WARSAW
Antwerp
Brussels
Waterloo (1815)
Amiens
Paris
CONFEDERATION OF THE RHINE
Rhine
Lunéville
WURTTEMBURG
BAVARIA
BADEN
Zurich
SWITZERLAND
FRANCE
Austerlitz (1805)
Wagram (1809)
Vienna
Pressburg
Buda
Pest
AUSTRIAN EMPIRE
Danube
Milan
KINGDOM OF ITALY
Marengo (1800)
Genoa
Marseilles
ILLYRIAN PROVINCES
PORTUGAL
Madrid
Lisbon
SPAIN
CORSICA
ELBA
Rome
KINGDOM OF NAPLES
Naples
OTTOMAN EMPIRE
BLACK SEA
Constantinople
Trafalgar (1805)
GIBRALTAR (GR. BR.)
MEDITERRANEAN SEA
KINGDOM OF SICILY
IONIAN IS. (GR. BR.)
Athens
MALTA (GR. BR.)
0 250 500 Km.
0 250 500 Mi.

In 1802 Napoleon was secure but unsatisfied. Ever a romantic gambler as well as a brilliant administrator, he could not contain his power drive. Aggressively redrawing the map of Germany so as to weaken Austria and attract the secondary states of southwestern Germany toward France, Napoleon was also mainly responsible for renewed war with Great Britain. Regarding war with Britain as inevitable, he threatened British interests in the eastern Mediterranean and tried to restrict British trade with all of Europe. Britain had technically violated the Treaty of Amiens by failing to evacuate the island of Malta, but it was Napoleon's decision to renew war in May 1803. He concentrated his armies in the French ports on the Channel in the fall of 1803 and began making preparations to invade England. Yet Great Britain remained mistress of the seas. When Napoleon tried to bring his Mediterranean fleet around Gibraltar to northern France, a combined French and Spanish fleet was, after a series of mishaps, virtually annihilated by Lord Nelson at the Battle of Trafalgar on 21 October 1805. Invasion of England was henceforth impossible. Renewed fighting had its advantages, however, for the first consul used the wartime atmosphere to have himself proclaimed emperor in late 1804.

Austria, Russia, and Sweden joined with Britain to form the Third Coalition against France shortly before the Battle of Trafalgar. Actions like Napoleon's assumption of the Italian crown had convinced both Alexander I of Russia and Francis II of Austria that Napoleon was a threat to their interests and to the European balance of power. Yet the Austrians and the Russians were no match for Napoleon, who scored a brilliant victory over them at the Battle of Austerlitz in December 1805. Alexander I decided to pull back, and Austria accepted large territorial losses in return for peace as the Third Coalition collapsed.

Victorious at Austerlitz, Napoleon proceeded to reorganize the German states to his liking. In 1806 he abolished many of the tiny German states, as well as the ancient Holy Roman Empire, whose emperor had traditionally been the ruler of Austria. Napoleon established by decree a German Confederation of the Rhine, a union of fifteen German states minus Austria, Prussia, and Saxony. Naming himself "protector" of the confederation, Napoleon firmly controlled western Germany.

Map 21.1 Napoleonic Europe in 1810

Napoleon's intervention in German affairs alarmed the Prussians, who had been at peace with France for more than a decade. Expecting help from his ally Russia, Frederick William III of Prussia mobilized his armies. Napoleon attacked and won two more brilliant victories in October 1806 at Jena and Auerstädt, where the Prussians were outnumbered two to one. The war with Prussia and Russia continued into the following spring, and after Napoleon's larger armies won another victory, Alexander decided to seek peace.

For several days in June 1807, the young tsar and the French emperor negotiated face to face on a raft anchored in the middle of the Niemen River. All the while, the helpless Frederick William rode back and forth on the shore, anxiously awaiting the results. As the German poet Heinrich Heine said later, Napoleon had but to whistle and Prussia would have ceased to exist. In the subsequent treaties of Tilsit, Prussia lost half of its population, while Russia accepted Napoleon's reorganization of western and central Europe. Alexander also promised to enforce Napoleon's recently decreed economic blockade against British goods and to declare war on Britain if Napoleon could not make peace on favorable terms with his island enemy.

After the victory of Austerlitz and even more after the treaties of Tilsit, Napoleon saw himself as the emperor of Europe and not just of France. The so-called Grand Empire he built had three parts. The core was an ever-expanding France, which by 1810 included Belgium, Holland, parts of northern Italy, and much German territory on the east bank of the Rhine. Beyond French borders Napoleon established a number of dependent satellite kingdoms, on the thrones of which he placed (and replaced) the members of his large family. Third, there were the independent but allied states of Austria, Prussia, and Russia. Both satellites and allies were expected after 1806 to support Napoleon's continental system and thus to cease all trade with Britain.

The impact of the Grand Empire on the peoples of Europe was considerable. In the areas incorporated into France and in the satellites (see Map 21.1), Napoleon introduced many French laws, abolishing feudal dues and serfdom where French revolutionary armies had not already done so. Some of the peasants and middle class benefited from these reforms. Yet while he extended progressive measures to his cosmopolitan empire, Napoleon had to put the prosperity and special interests of France first in order to safeguard his power base. Levying heavy taxes in money and men for his armies, Napoleon came to be regarded more as a conquering tyrant than as an enlightened liberator.

The first great revolt occurred in Spain. In 1808 a coalition of Catholics, monarchists, and patriots rebelled against Napoleon's attempts to make Spain a French satellite with a Bonaparte as its king. French armies occupied Madrid, but the foes of Napoleon fled to the hills and waged uncompromising guerrilla warfare. Spain was a clear warning. Resistance to French imperialism was growing.

Yet Napoleon pushed on, determined to hold his complex and far-flung empire together. In 1810, when the Grand Empire was at its height, Britain still remained at war with France, helping the guerrillas in Spain and Portugal (see Map 21.1). The continental system, organized to exclude British goods from the Continent and force that "nation of shopkeepers" to its knees, was a failure. Instead, it was France that suffered from Britain's counter-blockade, which created hard times for French artisans and the middle class. Perhaps looking for a scapegoat, Napoleon turned on Alexander I of Russia, who had been fully supporting Napoleon's war of prohibitions against British goods.

Napoleon's invasion of Russia began in June 1812 with a force that eventually numbered 600,000, probably the largest force yet assembled in a single army. Only one-third of this force was French, however; nationals of all the satellites and allies were drafted into the operation. Originally planning to winter in the Russian city of Smolensk if Alexander did not sue for peace, Napoleon reached Smolensk and recklessly pressed on. The great battle of Borodino that followed was a draw, and the Russians retreated in good order. Alexander ordered the evacuation of Moscow, which then burned, and refused to negotiate. Finally, after five weeks in the burned-out city, Napoleon ordered a retreat. That retreat was one of the great military disasters in history. The Russian army and the Russian winter cut Napoleon's army to pieces. Only 30,000 men returned to their homelands.

Leaving his troops to their fate, Napoleon raced to Paris to raise yet another army. Possibly he might still have saved his throne if he had been willing to accept a France reduced to its historical size—the proposal offered by Austria's foreign minister Metternich. But Napoleon refused. Austria and Prussia deserted Napoleon and joined Russia and Great Britain in the Fourth Coalition. All across Europe, patriots called for a "war of liberation" against Napoleon's oppression, and the well-disciplined regular armies of Napoleon's enemies closed in for the kill. This time the coalition held together, cemented by the Treaty of Chaumont, which created a Quadruple Alliance to last for twenty years. Less than a month later, on April 4, 1814, a defeated, abandoned Napoleon abdicated his throne. After this unconditional abdication, the victorious allies granted Napoleon the island of Elba off the coast of Italy as his own tiny state. Napoleon was even allowed to keep his imperial title, and France was required to pay him a large yearly income of 2 million francs.

The allies also agreed to the restoration of the Bourbon dynasty, in part because demonstrations led by a few dedicated French monarchists indicated some support among the French people for that course of action. The new monarch, Louis XVIII (1814–1824), tried to consolidate that support by issuing the Constitutional Charter, which accepted many of France's revolutionary changes and guaranteed civil liberties. Indeed, the Charter gave France a constitutional monarchy roughly similar to that established in 1791, although far fewer people had the right to vote for representatives to the resurrected Chamber of Deputies. Moreover, after Louis XVIII stated firmly that his government would not pay any war reparations, France was treated leniently by the allies, who agreed to meet in Vienna to work out a general peace settlement.

Yet Louis XVIII—old, ugly, and crippled by gout—totally lacked the glory and magic of Napoleon. Hearing of political unrest in France and diplomatic tensions in Vienna, Napoleon staged a daring escape from Elba in February 1815. Landing in France, he issued appeals for support and marched on Paris with a small band. French officers and soldiers who had fought so long for their emperor responded to the call. Louis XVIII fled, and once more Napoleon took command. But Napoleon's gamble was a desperate long shot, for the allies were united against him. At the end of a frantic period known as the Hundred

Days, they crushed his forces at Waterloo on June 18, 1815, and imprisoned him on the rocky island of St. Helena, far off the western coast of Africa. Old Louis XVIII returned again—this time "in the baggage of the allies," as his detractors scornfully put it—and recommenced his reign. The allies now dealt rather harshly with the apparently incorrigible French (see Chapter 23). And Napoleon, doomed to suffer crude insults at the hands of sadistic English jailers on distant St. Helena, could take revenge only by writing his memoirs, skillfully nurturing the myth that he had been Europe's revolutionary liberator, a romantic hero whose lofty work had been undone by oppressive reactionaries. An era had ended.

The revolution that began in America and spread to France was a liberal revolution. Inspired by English history and some of the teachings of the Enlightenment, revolutionaries on both sides of the Atlantic sought to establish civil liberties and equality before the law within the framework of representative government. Success in America was subsequently matched by success in France. There liberal nobles and an increasingly class-conscious middle class overwhelmed declining monarchial absolutism and feudal privilege, thanks to the common people—the sans-culottes and the peasants. The government and society established by the Declaration of the Rights of Man and the French constitution of 1791 were remarkably similar to those created in America by the federal Constitution and the Bill of Rights. Thus the new political system, based on electoral competition and civil equality, came into approximate harmony with France's evolving social structure, which had become increasingly based on wealth and achievement rather than on tradition and legal privileges.

Yet the Revolution in France did not end with the liberal victory of 1789 to 1791. As Robespierre led the determined country in a total war effort against foreign foes, French revolutionaries became more democratic, radical, and violent. Their effort succeeded, but at the price of dictatorship—first by Robespierre himself and then by the Directory and Napoleon. Some historians blame the excesses of the French revolutionaries for the emergence of dictatorship, while others hold the conservative monarchs of Europe responsible. In any case, historians have often concluded that the French Revolution ended in failure.

This conclusion is highly debatable, though. After the fall of Robespierre, the solid middle class, with its liberal philosophy and Enlightenment world-view, reasserted itself. Under the Directory, it salvaged a good portion of the social and political gains that it and the peasantry had made between 1789 and 1791. In so doing, the middle-class leaders repudiated the radical social and economic measures associated with Robespierre, but they never re-established the old pattern of separate legal orders and absolute monarchy. Napoleon built on the policies of the Directory. With considerable success he sought to add the support of the old nobility and the church to that of the middle class and the peasantry. And though Napoleon sharply curtailed thought and speech, he effectively promoted the reconciliation of old and new, of centralized government and careers open to talent, of noble and bourgeois in a restructured property-owning elite. Little wonder, then, that Louis XVIII had no choice but to accept a French society solidly based on wealth and achievement. In granting representative government and civil liberties to facilitate his restoration to the throne in 1814, Louis XVIII submitted to the rest of the liberal triumph of 1789 to 1791. The core of the French Revolution had survived a generation of war and dictatorship. Old Europe would never be the same.

NOTES

1. Quoted by R. R. Palmer, *The Age of the Democratic Revolution,* Princeton University Press, Princeton, N.J., 1959, 1.239.
2. G. Lefebvre, *The Coming of the French Revolution,* Vintage Books, New York, 1947, p. 81.
3. P. H. Beik, ed., *The French Revolution,* Walker, New York, 1970, p. 89.
4. O. Hufton, "Women in Revolution," *Past and Present* 53 (November 1971): 91–95.
5. G. Pernoud and S. Flaisser, eds., *The French Revolution,* Fawcett Publications, Greenwich, Conn., 1960, p. 61.
6. L. Gershoy, *The Era of the French Revolution, 1789–1799,* Van Nostrand, New York, 1957, p. 135.
7. Ibid., p. 150.
8. Pernoud and Flaisser, pp. 193–194.

SUGGESTED READING

In addition to the fascinating eyewitness reports on the French Revolution in P. Beik, *The French Revolution,* and G. Pernoud and S. Flaisser, eds., *The French Revolution* (1960), A. Young's *Travels in France During the Years 1787, 1788 and 1789* (1969) offers an engrossing contemporary description of France and Paris on the eve of revolution. Edmund Burke, *Reflections on the Revolution in France,* first published in 1790, is the classic conservative indictment. The intense passions the French Revolution has generated may be seen in the nineteenth-century French historians, notably the enthusiastic Jules Michelet, *History of the French Revolution;* the hostile Hippolyte Taine; and the judicious Alexis de Tocqueville, whose masterpiece, *The Old Regime and the French Revolution,* was first published in 1856. Important recent general studies on the entire period are R. R. Palmer, *The Age of the Democratic Revolution* (1959, 1964), which paints a comparative international picture; E. J. Hobsbawm, *The Age of Revolution, 1789–1848* (1962); C. Breunig, *The Age of Revolution and Reaction, 1789–1850* (1970); O. Connelly, *French Revolution—Napoleonic Era* (1979); and L. Dehio, *The Precarious Balance: Four Centuries of the European Power Struggle* (1962). C. Brinton's older but delightfully written *A Decade of Revolution, 1789–1799* (1934) complements his stimulating *Anatomy of Revolution* (1938, 1965), an ambitious comparative approach to revolution in England, America, France, and Russia. A Cobban, *The Social Interpretation of the French Revolution* (1964), and F. Furet, *Interpreting the French Revolution* (1981), are exciting reassessments of many well-worn ideas, to be compared with W. Doyle, *Origins of the French Revolution* (1981); G. Lefebvre, *The Coming of the French Revolution* (1947); and N. Hampson, *A Social History of the French Revolution* (1963). G. Rudé makes the men and women of the great days of upheaval come alive in his *The Crowd in the French Revolution* (1959). R. R. Palmer studies sympathetically the leaders of the Terror in *Twelve Who Ruled* (1941). Two other particularly interesting, detailed works are C. L. R. James, *The Black Jacobins* (1938, 1980), on black slave revolt in Haiti, and J. C. Herold, *Mistress to an Age* (1955), on the remarkable Madame de Staël. On revolution in America, E. Morgan, *The Birth of the Republic, 1763–89* (1956), and B. Bailyn, *The Ideological Origins of the American Revolution* (1967), are noteworthy. Three important recent studies on aspects of revolutionary France are D. Jordan's vivid *The King's Trial: Louis XVI vs. the French Revolution* (1979); W. Sewell, Jr.'s imaginative *Work and Revolution in France: The Language of Labor from the Old Regime to 1848* (1980); and P. Higonnet, *Class, Ideology and the Rights of Nobles During the French Revolution* (1981).

P. Geyl, *Napoleon, For and Against* (1949), is a delightful discussion of changing historical interpretations of Napoleon, which may be compared with a more recent treatment by R. Jones, *Napoleon: Man and Myth* (1977). Good biographies are J. M. Thompson, *Napoleon Bonaparte: His Rise and Fall* (1952); F. H. M. Markham, *Napoleon* (1964); and V. Cronin, *Napoleon Bonaparte* (1972). L. Bergeron, *France Under Napoleon* (1981), is an important synthesis. Wonderful novels inspired by this period include Raphael Sabatini's *Scaramouche,* a swashbuckler of revolutionary intrigue with accurate historical details; Charles Dickens's classic *Tale of Two Cities;* and Leo Tolstoy's monumental saga of Napoleon's invasion of Russia (and much more), *War and Peace.*

22

THE REVOLUTION IN ENERGY AND INDUSTRY

HILE THE REVOLUTION in France was opening a new political era, another revolution was transforming economic and social life. This was the Industrial Revolution, which began in England in the 1780s and spread after 1815 to continental Europe and then around the world. Because the Industrial Revolution was less dramatic than the French Revolution, some historians see industrial development as basically moderate and evolutionary. In the long perspective, however, it was rapid and brought about radical changes. Perhaps only the development of agriculture during Neolithic times had a similar impact and significance.

The Industrial Revolution profoundly modified much of human experience. It changed patterns of work, transformed the social class structure, and eventually even altered the international balance of political power. It may quite possibly have saved Europe from the poverty of severe overpopulation and even from famine. How did this happen? How and why did drastic changes occur in industry, and how did these changes affect people and society? These are the questions this chapter will seek to answer. Chapter 24 will examine in detail the emergence of accompanying changes in urban civilization.

THE INDUSTRIAL REVOLUTION IN ENGLAND

The Industrial Revolution began in England. It was something new in history, and it was quite unplanned. With no models to copy and no idea of what to expect, England had to pioneer not only in industrial technology but also in social relations and urban living. Between 1793 and 1815, these formidable tasks were complicated by almost constant war with France. As the trailblazer in economic development, as France was in political change, England must command special attention.

EIGHTEENTH-CENTURY ORIGINS

The Industrial Revolution grew out of the expanding Atlantic economy of the eighteenth century, which served mercantilist England remarkably well. England's colonial empire, augmented by a strong position in Latin America and in the African slave trade, provided a growing market for English manufactured goods. So did England itself. In an age when it was much cheaper to ship goods by water than by land, no part of England was more than twenty miles from navigable water. Beginning in the 1770s, a canal-building boom greatly enhanced this natural advantage (see Map 22.1). Nor were there any tariffs within the country to hinder trade, as there were in France before 1789 and in politically fragmented Germany.

Agriculture played a central role in bringing about the Industrial Revolution in England. English farmers were second only to the Dutch in productivity in 1700, and they were continuously adopting new methods of farming as the century went on. The result, especially before 1760, was a period of bountiful crops and low food prices. The ordinary English family did not have to spend almost everything it earned just to buy bread. It could spend more on other items, on manufactured goods—leather shoes or a razor for the man, a bonnet or a shawl for the woman, toy soldiers for the son, and a doll for the daughter. Thus demand for goods within the country complemented the demand from the colonies.

England had other assets that helped give rise to the Industrial Revolution. Unlike eighteenth-century France, England had an effective central bank and well-developed credit markets. The monarchy and the aristocratic oligarchy, which had jointly ruled the country since 1688. provided stable and predictable government. At the same time, the government let the domestic economy operate fairly freely and with few controls, encouraging personal initiative, technical change, and a free market. Finally, England had long had a large class of hired agricultural laborers, whose numbers were further increased by the enclosure movement of the late eighteenth century. These rural wage earners were relatively mobile—compared to village-bound peasants in France and western Germany, for example—and along with cottage workers they formed a potential industrial labor force for capitalist entrepreneurs.

All these factors combined to initiate the Industrial Revolution, which began in the 1780s—after the American war for independence and just before the French Revolution. Thus the great economic and political revolutions that have shaped the modern world occurred almost simultaneously, though they began in different countries. The Industrial Revolution was, however, a longer process. It was not complete in England until 1830 at the earliest, and it had no real impact on continental countries until after the Congress of Vienna ended the era of revolutionary wars in 1815.

The First Factories

The pressure to produce more goods for a growing market was directly related to the first decisive breakthrough of the Industrial Revolution—the creation of the world's first large factories in the English cotton textile industry. Technological innovations in the manufacture of cloth led to a whole new system of production and social relationships. Since no other industry experienced such a rapid or complete transformation before 1830, these trail-blazing developments deserve special consideration.

Although the putting-out system of merchant capitalism (page 621) was expanding all across Europe in the eighteenth century, this pattern of rural industry was most fully developed in England. Thus it was in England, under the pressure of growing demand, that the system's shortcomings first began to outweigh its advantages. This was especially true in the textile industry after about 1760.

The constant shortage of thread in the textile industry focused attention on ways of improving spinning. Many a tinkering worker knew that a better spinning wheel promised rich rewards. Spinning of the traditional raw materials—wool and flax—proved hard to change, but cotton was different. Cotton textiles had first been imported into England from India by the East India Company, and by 1760 there was a tiny domestic industry in northern England. After many experiments over a generation, a gifted carpenter and jack-of-all-trades, James Hargreaves, invented his cotton spinning jenny about 1765. At almost the same moment a barber-turned-manufacturer named Richard Arkwright invented (or possibly pirated) another kind of spinning machine, the water frame. These breakthroughs produced an explosion in the infant industry. By 1790 the new machines produced ten times as much cotton yarn as had been made in 1770. By 1800 the production of cotton thread was England's most important industry.

Hargreaves's jenny was simple and inexpensive. It was also hand operated. In early models, from six to twenty-four spindles were mounted on a sliding carriage, and each spindle spun a fine, slender thread. The woman moved the carriage back and forth with one hand and turned a wheel to supply power with the other. Now it was the weaver who could not keep up with his vastly more efficient wife.

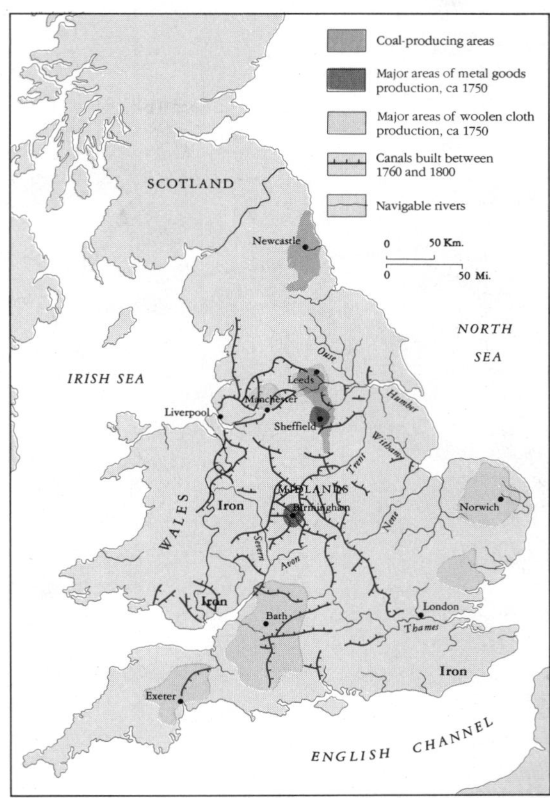

MAP 22.1 Cottage Industry and Transportation in Eighteenth-Century England England had an unusually good system of navigable waterways even before river-linking canals made it better.

Arkwright's water frame employed a different principle. It quickly acquired a capacity of several hundred spindles and demanded much more power —water power. The water frame thus required large specialized mills, factories that employed as many as a thousand workers from the very beginning. The water frame could spin only coarse, strong thread, which was then put out for respinning on hand-powered cottage jennies. Around 1790 Samuel Crompton's innovation, the "mule," began to require more power than the human arm could supply. (Crompton's invention was so named because it

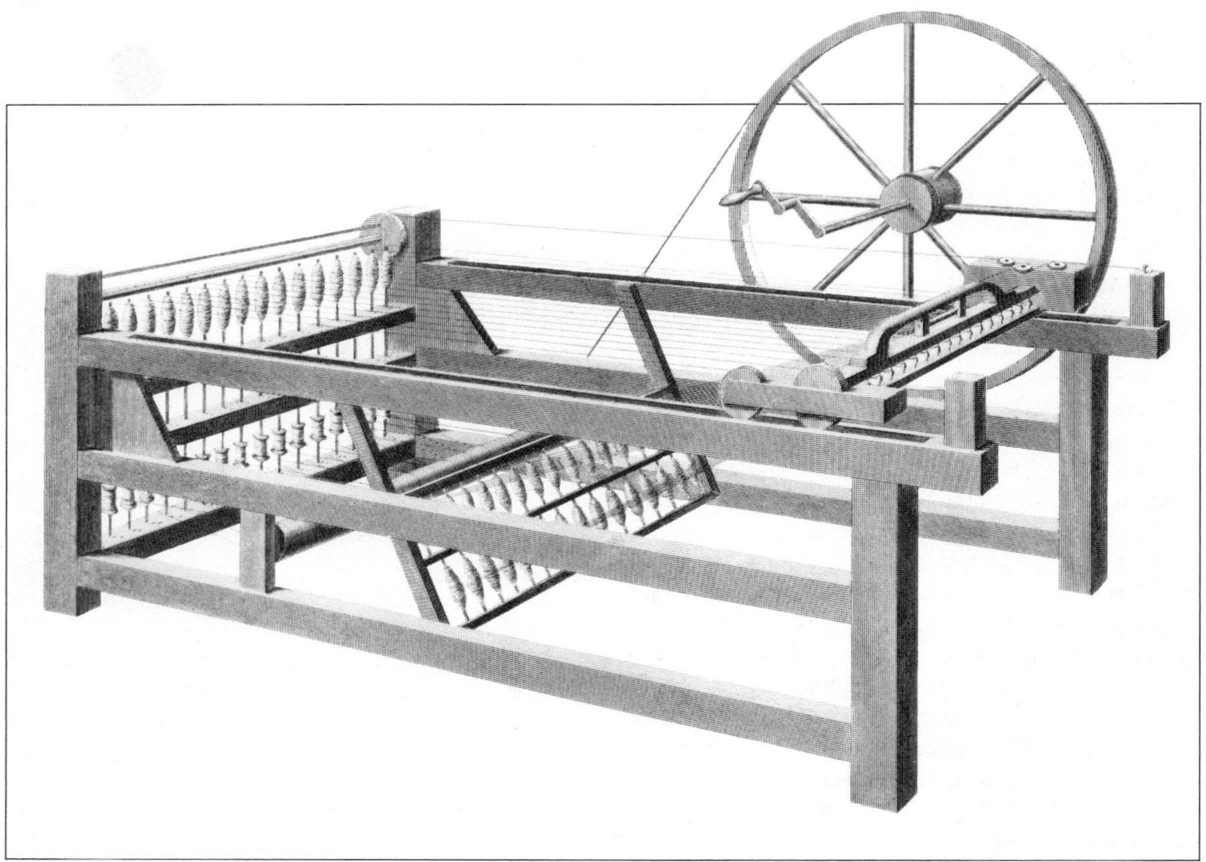

Hargreaves's Spinning Jenny The loose cotton strands on the slanted bobbins passed up to the sliding carriage and then on to the spindles in back for fine spinning. By 1783 one woman could spin by hand a hundred threads at a time on an improved model. *(University of Illinois, Champaign)*

united the best aspects of the jenny and the water frame, just as a mule combines the traits of its dam the horse and its sire the donkey.) After that time, all cotton spinning was gradually concentrated in factories.

The first consequences of these revolutionary developments were much more beneficial than is generally believed. Cotton goods became much cheaper, and they were bought and treasured by all classes. In the past, only the wealthy could afford the comfort and cleanliness of underwear, which was called "body linen" because it was made from expensive linen cloth. Now millions of poor people, who had earlier worn nothing underneath their coarse, filthy outergarments, could afford to wear cotton slips and underpants.

The family was freed from its constant search for adequate yarn from scattered, part-time spinners, since all the thread needed could be spun in the cottage on the jenny or obtained from a nearby factory. The wages of weavers, now hard pressed to keep up with the spinners, rose markedly until about 1792. Weavers were among the best-paid workers in England. They were known to walk proudly through the streets with £5 notes stuck in their hatbands, and they dressed like the middle class.

One result of this unprecedented prosperity was that large numbers of agricultural laborers became weavers. Meanwhile, however, mechanics and capitalists were seeking to invent a power loom to save on labor costs. This Edmund Cartwright achieved in 1785. But the power looms of the factories worked poorly at first, and handloom weavers continued to receive good wages until at least 1800.

Working conditions in the early factories were less satisfactory than those of cottage weavers and spinners. But until the late 1780s, most English factories were in rural areas, where they had access to water power. These factories employed a relatively small percentage of all cotton textile workers. People were reluctant to work in them, partly because they resembled the poorhouses where destitute inmates had to labor for very little pay. Therefore, factory owners turned to young children as a source of labor. More precisely, they turned to children who had been abandoned by their parents and put in the care of local parishes. The parish officers often "apprenticed" such unfortunate orphans to factory owners. The parish thus saved money and the factory owners gained workers over whom they exercised almost the authority of slaveowners. The hours were terrible, the conditions appalling. But only the nakedness of this exploitation was new. These children and the women who came to work beside them in the next generation were simply doing in the factory, under different conditions, the same kind of work they had long done in their cottages. It is some consolation that such exploitation of small children was at this point more nearly ending than beginning.

The creation of the world's first modern factories in the English cotton textile industry in the 1770s and 1780s, which grew out of the putting-out system of cottage production, was a momentous development. Both symbolically and in substance, the big new cotton mills marked the beginning of the Industrial Revolution in England.

The Problem of Energy

The growth of the cotton textile industry might have been stunted or cut short, however, if water from rivers and streams had remained the primary source of power for the new factories. But this did not occur. Instead, an epoch-making solution was found to the age-old problem of energy and power. It was this solution to the energy problem—a problem that has reappeared in recent times—that permitted continued rapid development in cotton textiles, the gradual generalization of the factory system, and the triumph of the Industrial Revolution.

Human beings, like all living organisms, require energy. Adult men and women need 2,000 to 4,000 calories (units of energy) daily, simply to fuel their bodies, work, and survive. Energy comes from a variety of sources; energy also takes different forms, and one form may be converted into another. Plants have been converting solar energy into caloric matter for eons. And human beings have used their toolmaking abilities to construct machines that convert one form of energy into another for their own benefit.

Prehistoric people relied on plants and plant-eating animals as their sources of energy. With the development of agriculture, early civilizations were able to increase the number of useful plants and thus the supply of energy. Some plants could be fed to domesticated animals, like the horse. Stronger than human beings, these animals converted the energy in the plants into work. In the medieval period, people began to develop water mills to grind their grain and windmills to pump water and drain swamps. More efficient use of water and wind in the sixteenth and seventeenth centuries enabled human beings to accomplish more; intercontinental sailing ships are a prime example. Nevertheless, even into the eighteenth century, society continued to rely for energy mainly on plants, and human beings and animals continued to perform most work. This dependence meant that Western civilization remained poor in energy and power.

Lack of power lay at the heart of the poverty that afflicted the large majority of people. The man behind the plow and the woman at the spinning wheel could employ only horsepower and human muscle in their labor. No matter how hard they worked, they could not produce very much. What people needed were new sources of energy and more power at their disposal. Then they would be able to work more efficiently, produce more, and live better.

Where was more energy to be found? Almost all energy came directly or indirectly from plants and therefore from the land: grain for people, hay for animals, and wood for heat. The land was also the principal source of raw materials needed for industrial production: wool and flax for clothing; leather for shoes; wood for housing, tools, and ironmaking. And though swamps could be drained and marshes reclaimed from the sea, it was difficult to expand greatly the amount of land available. True, its yield could be increased, such as by the elimination of fallow; nonetheless there were definite limits to such improvements.

The shortage of energy was becoming particularly severe in England by the eighteenth century. Because of the growth of population, most of the great forests of medieval England had long ago been replaced by fields of grain and hay. Wood was in ever shorter sup-

Making Charcoal After wood was carefully cut and stacked, iron masters slowly burned it to produce charcoal. Before the Industrial Revolution, a country's iron industry depended largely on the size of its forests. *(University of Illinois, Champaign)*

ply; yet it remained tremendously important. It was the primary source of heat for all homes and industries. It was also the key to transportation, since ships and wagons were made of wood. Moreover, wood was, along with iron ore, the basic raw material of the iron industry. Processed wood (charcoal) was the fuel mixed with iron ore in the blast furnace to produce pig iron. The iron industry's appetite for wood was enormous, and even very modest and constant levels of iron production had gone far toward laying bare the forests of England, as well as parts of Europe. By 1740 the English iron industry was stagnating. Vast forests enabled Russia in the eighteenth century to become the world's leading producer of iron, much of which was exported to England. But Russia's potential for growth was limited, too, and in a few decades Russia would reach the barrier of inadequate energy that was already holding England back.

"Steam Is an Englishman"

As this early energy crisis grew worse, England looked toward its abundant and widely scattered reserves of coal as an alternative to its vanishing wood. Coal was first used in England in the late Middle Ages as a source of heat. By 1640 most homes in London were heated with it, and it also provided heat for making beer, glass, soap, and other products. Coal was not used, however, to produce mechanical energy or to power machinery. It was there that coal's potential was enormous, as a simple example shows.

One pound of good bituminous coal contains about 3,500 calories of heat energy. A miner who eats 3,500 calories of food can dig out 500 pounds of coal a day, using hand tools. Even an extremely efficient converter, which transforms only 1 percent of the heat energy in coal into mechanical energy, will pro-

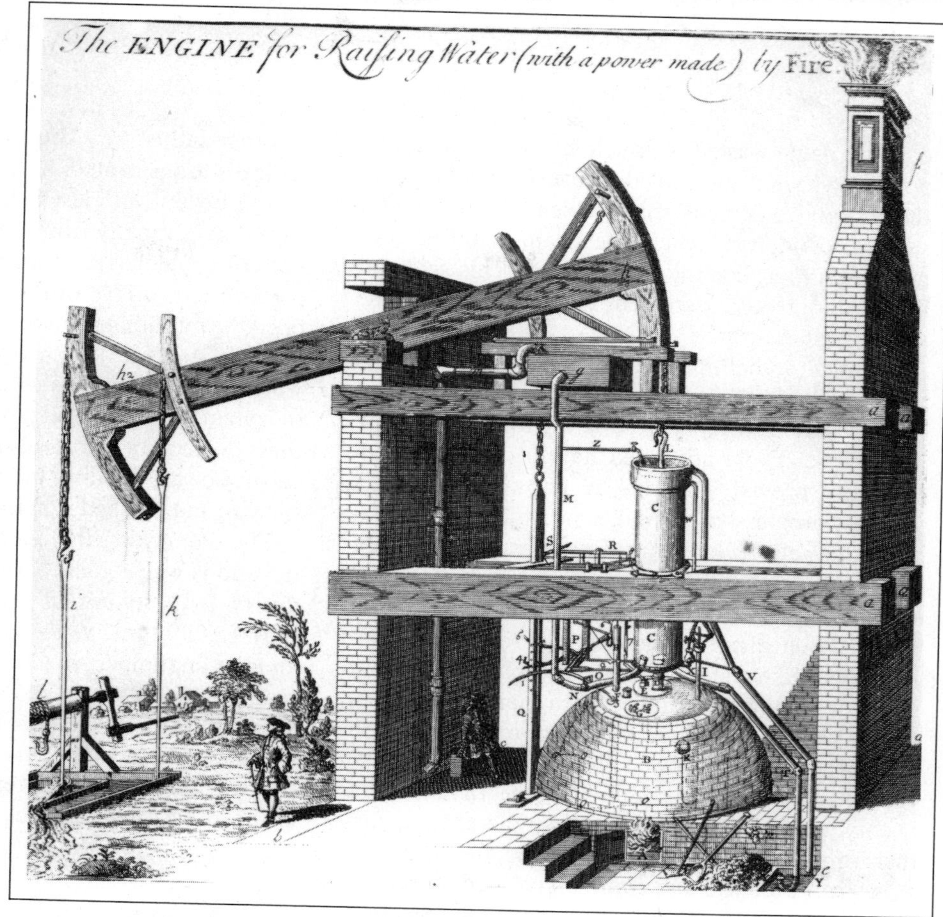

The Newcomen Engine The huge steam-filled cylinder (C) was cooled by injecting water from the tank above (G) through a pipe (M). Atmospheric pressure then pushed down the piston, raised the beam, and pumped water from the mine. *(Science Museum, London)*

duce 27 horsepower-hours of work from the 500 pounds of coal the miner cut out of the earth. (The miner, by contrast, produces only about 1 horsepower-hour in the course of a day.) Much more energy is consumed by the converter, but much more work can be done.

Early steam engines were just such inefficient converters. As more coal was produced, mines were dug deeper and deeper and were constantly filling with water. Mechanical pumps, usually powered by animals walking in circles at the surface, had to be installed. At one mine, fully five hundred horses were used in pumping. Such power was expensive and bothersome. In an attempt to overcome these disadvantages, Thomas Savery in 1698 and Thomas Newcomen in 1705 invented the first primitive steam engines.

Both engines were extremely inefficient. Both burned coal to produce steam, which was then injected into a cylinder or reservoir. In Newcomen's engine, the steam in the cylinder was cooled, creating a partial vacuum in the cylinder. This vacuum allowed the pressure of the earth's atmosphere to push the piston in the cylinder down and operate a pump. By the early 1770s, many of the Savery engines and hundreds of the Newcomen engines were operating successfully, though inefficiently, in English mines.

In the early 1760s, a gifted young Scot named James Watt (1736–1819) was drawn to a critical study of the steam engine. Watt was employed at the time by the University of Glasgow as a skilled craftsman making scientific instruments. The Scottish universities were pioneers in practical technical education, and in 1763 Watt was called on to repair a Newcomen engine being used in a physics course. After a series of observations, Watt saw why the Newcomen engine wasted so much energy: the cylinder was being heated and cooled for every single stroke of the piston. To remedy this problem, Watt added a separate condenser, where the steam could be condensed without cooling the cylinder. This splendid invention greatly increased the efficiency of the steam engine.

To invent something in a laboratory is one thing; to make it a practical success is quite another. Watt needed skilled workers, precision parts, and capital, and the relatively advanced nature of the English economy proved essential. A partnership with a wealthy, progressive toymaker provided risk capital and a manufacturing plant. In the craft tradition of locksmiths, tinsmiths, and millwrights, Watt found skilled mechanics who could install, regulate, and repair his sophisticated engines. From ingenious manufacturers like the cannonmaker John Wilkinson, who learned to bore cylinders with a fair degree of accuracy, Watt was gradually able to purchase precision parts. This support allowed him to create an effective vacuum and regulate a complex engine. In more than twenty years of constant effort, Watt made many further improvements. By the late 1780s, the steam engine was a practical and commercial success in England. As a nineteenth-century saying put it, "Steam is an Englishman."

The steam engine of Watt and his followers was the Industrial Revolution's most fundamental advance in technology. For the first time in history, humanity had, at least for a few generations, almost unlimited power at its disposal. For the first time, inventors and engineers could devise and implement all kinds of power equipment to aid people in their work. For the first time, abundance was at least a possibility for ordinary men and women.

The steam engine was quickly put to use in many industries in England. It made possible the production of ever more coal to feed steam engines elsewhere. The steam-power plant began to replace water power in the cotton-spinning mills during the 1780s, contributing greatly to that industry's phenomenal rise. Steam also took the place of water power in flour mills, in the malt mills used in breweries, in the flint mills supplying the china industry, and in the mills exported by England to the West Indies to crush sugar cane.

Steam power promoted important breakthroughs in other industries. The English iron industry was radically transformed. The use of powerful, steam-driven bellows in blast furnaces helped ironmakers switch over rapidly from limited charcoal to unlimited coke (which is made from coal) in the smelting of pig iron after 1770. In the 1780s Henry Cort developed the puddling furnace, which allowed pig iron to be refined in turn with coke. Strong, skilled ironworkers—the puddlers—"cooked" molten pig iron in a great vat, raking off globs of refined iron for further processing. Cort also developed heavy-duty steam-powered rolling mills, which were capable of spewing out finished iron in every shape and form.

The economic consequences of these technical innovations was a great boom in the English iron industry. In 1740 annual British iron production was only 17,000 tons. With the spread of coke smelting and the first impact of Cort's inventions, production reached 68,000 tons in 1788, 125,000 tons in 1796, and 260,000 tons in 1806. In 1844 Britain produced 3 million tons of iron. This was truly phenomenal expansion. Once scarce and expensive, iron became the cheap, basic building block of the economy.

The Coming of the Railroads

Sailing ships had improved noticeably since the Age of Discovery, and the second half of the eighteenth century saw extensive construction of hard and relatively smooth roads, particularly in France before the Revolution. Yet it was passenger traffic that benefited most from this construction. Overland shipment of freight, relying solely on horsepower, was still quite limited and frightfully expensive; shippers used rivers and canals for heavy freight whenever possible. It was logical therefore that inventors would try to use steam power to improve inland transportation.

As early as 1800, an American ran a "steamer on wheels" through city streets. Other experiments followed. In the 1820s, English engineers perfected steam cars capable of carrying fourteen passengers at ten miles an hour—as fast as the mail coach. But the noisy, heavy steam automobiles frightened passing horses and damaged themselves as well as the roads with their vibrations. For the rest of the century, horses continued to reign on highways and city streets.

Early Railroad Construction presented innumerable challenges, like the building of bridges to span broad rivers and deep gorges. Civil engineers responded with impressive feats and their profession bounded ahead. *(BBC Hulton/The Bettmann Archive)*

The coal industry had long been using plank roads and rails to move coal wagons within mines and at the surface. Rails reduced friction and allowed a horse or a human being to pull a heavier load. Thus, once a rail capable of supporting a heavy locomotive was developed in 1816, all sorts of experiments with steam engines on rails went forward. In 1825, after ten years of work, George Stephenson built an effective locomotive. In 1830 his *Rocket* sped down the track of the just-completed Liverpool and Manchester Railway at sixteen miles per hour. This was the world's first important railroad, fittingly steaming in the heart of industrial England.

The line from Liverpool to Manchester was a financial as well as a technical success, and many private companies were quickly organized to build more rail lines. These companies had to get permission for their projects from Parliament and pay for the rights of way they needed; otherwise, their freedom was great. Within twenty years, they had completed the main trunk lines of Great Britain. Other countries followed quickly with similar railway construction.

The significance of the railroad was tremendous. The railroad dramatically reduced the cost and uncertainty of shipping freight overland. This advance had many economic consequences. Previously, mar-

The Third-Class Carriage The French artist Honoré Daumier was fascinated by the railroad and its human significance. This great painting focuses on the peasant grandmother, absorbed in memories. The nursing mother represents love and creativity; the sleeping boy, innocence. *(The Metropolitan Museum of Art. Bequest of Mrs. H. O. Havemeyer, 1929. The H. O. Havemeyer Collection)*

kets had tended to be small and local; as the barrier of high transportation costs was lowered, they became larger and even nationwide. Larger markets encouraged larger factories with more sophisticated machinery. Such factories could make goods cheaper, enabling people to pay less for them. They also tended to drive most cottage workers, many urban artisans, and other manufacturers out of business.

In all countries, the construction of railroads contributed to the growth of a class of urban workers. Cottage workers, farm laborers, and small peasants did not generally leave their jobs and homes to go directly to work in factories. However, the building of railroads created a strong demand for labor, especially unskilled labor, throughout a country. Like farm work, hard work on construction gangs was done in the open air with animals and hand tools. Many farm laborers and poor peasants, long accustomed to leaving their villages for temporary employment, went to build railroads. By the time the work was finished, life back home in the village often seemed dull and unappealing, and many men drifted to towns in search of work—with the railroad companies, in construction, in factories. By the time they sent for their wives and sweethearts to join them, they had become urban workers.

The railroad changed the outlook and values of the entire society. The last and culminating invention of the Industrial Revolution, the railroad dramatically revealed the power and increased the speed of the new age. Racing down a track at sixteen miles per hour or, by 1850, at a phenomenal fifty miles per hour was a new and awesome experience. As a noted French economist put it after a ride on the Liverpool and Manchester in 1833, "There are certain impressions that one cannot put into words!"

Some great painters, notably J. M. W. Turner (1775–1851) and Claude Monet (1840–1926), succeeded in expressing this sense of power and awe. So did the massive new train stations, the cathedrals of the industrial age. Leading railway engineers like Isambard Kingdom Brunel and Thomas Brassey, whose tunnels pierced mountains and whose bridges spanned valleys, became public idols—the astronauts of their day. Everyday speech absorbed the images of railroading. After you got up a "full head of steam," you "highballed" along. And if you didn't "go off the track," you might "toot your own whistle." The railroad fired the imagination.

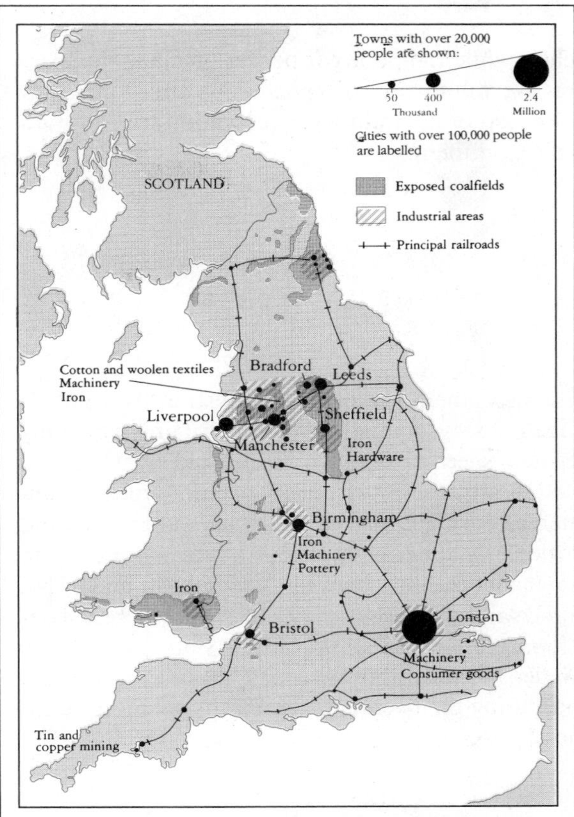

Map 22.2 The Industrial Revolution in England, ca 1850 Industry concentrated in the rapidly growing cities of the north and the midlands, where rich coal and iron deposits were in close proximity.

Britain at Midcentury

In 1851 London was the site of a famous industrial fair. This exposition was held in the newly built Crystal Palace, an architectural masterpiece made entirely of glass and iron, both of which were now cheap and abundant. For the hundreds of thousands who visited, one fact stood out. The little island of Britain—England, Wales, and Scotland—was the "workshop of the world." It alone produced two-thirds of the world's coal and more than half of its iron and cotton cloth. Britain was the first industrial nation (see Map 22.2).

Britain had unlocked and developed a new source of energy. With practically unlimited power, the British economy had significantly increased its production of manufactured goods. Between 1780 and 1800, Britain doubled its production of industrial goods. Between 1801 and 1851, the gross national product (GNP) rose three and a half times at constant prices. In other words, the British increased their wealth and their national income dramatically. At the same time, the population of Great Britain boomed, growing from about 9 million in 1780 to almost 21 million in 1851.

Since the economy grew much faster than the number of people, average real income per person increased markedly. (*Real income* is the actual monetary value of people's wages after adjusting for the effects of inflation or deflation.) In fact, average real income per person in Britain just about *doubled* between 1801 and 1851, from £13 per person to £24 per person. Put very simply, and all other things being equal, the woman or man of 1851 could buy twice as much as the woman or man of 1801. Considering the poverty of the eighteenth century, poverty that all the drama and excitement of the French Revolution did little or nothing to reduce, this would appear to be a monumental achievement.

But perhaps all other things were not equal. Perhaps workers, farmers, and ordinary people did not share in the new wealth. Perhaps only the rich got richer, while the poor got poorer or made no progress. We will turn to this great issue after looking at the spread of the Industrial Revolution from Britain to the Continent.

THE SPREAD OF THE INDUSTRIAL REVOLUTION

The new methods of the Industrial Revolution spread slowly at first. Whereas Britain's economy began to speed up about 1780 and had created an industrial urban society by 1850, the economies of continental Europe began to follow only after 1815 and particularly after about 1830. First Belgium took up the challenge; then between about 1840 and 1860, France and the various states of Germany began developing rapidly, as did the United States. After 1870, Sweden, Russia, and Japan started to industrialize, and during the twentieth century many more countries did so.

The Challenge of Industrialization

If poverty was so widespread in Europe and if industrial development created so much more wealth per person in Great Britain, why did continental countries wait years and even decades before they followed the British example? The eighteenth century was certainly an era of agricultural improvement, population increase, expanding foreign trade, and growing cottage industry. England led in these developments, but other countries participated in the general trend. Thus, when the pace of English industry began to accelerate in the 1780s, countries like France began to copy the new methods. English industry enjoyed clear superiority, but the Continent was not very far behind.

By 1815, however, the situation was quite different. In spite of wartime difficulties, English industry maintained the momentum of the 1780s and continued to grow and improve rapidly between 1789 and 1815. On the Continent, the unending political and economic upheavals that began with the French Revolution had another effect. They disrupted trade, created runaway inflation, and fostered social anxiety. War severed normal communications between England and the Continent, severely handicapping continental efforts to use new British machinery and technology. Moreover, the years from 1789 to 1815 were, even for the privileged French economy, a time of "national catastrophe"—in the graphic words of a recent French scholar.[1] Thus, whatever the French Revolution and the Napoleonic era meant politically, economically and industrially they meant that France and the rest of Europe were much further behind Britain in 1815 than in 1789.

This widening gap made it more difficult for other countries to follow the British example in energy and industry after 1815. British goods were being produced very economically, and they had come to dominate world markets completely while the continental states were absorbed in war between 1792 and 1815. In addition, British technology had become so advanced and complicated that very few engineers or skilled technicians outside England understood it. Moreover, the technology of steam power had grown much more expensive. It involved large investments in the iron and coal industries and, after 1830, required the existence of railroads, which were very costly. Continental businessmen had great difficulty finding the large sums of money the new methods demanded, and there was a shortage of laborers accustomed to working in factories. Landowners and government officials were often so suspicious of the new form of industry and the changes it brought that they did little at first to encourage it. All these disadvantages slowed the spread of modern industry (see Map 22.3).

After 1815, however, when continental countries began to industrialize seriously, they had at least two important advantages. First, they did not need to develop, ever so slowly and expensively, their own advanced technology. Instead, they could simply "borrow" the new methods developed in Great Britain, as well as engineers and some of the financial resources they lacked. European countries like France and Russia had a second asset that many non-Western areas lacked in the nineteenth century. They had strong independent governments, which did not fall under foreign political control. These governments could fashion economic policies to serve their own interests, as they proceeded to do. They would eventually use the power of the state to promote the growth of industry.

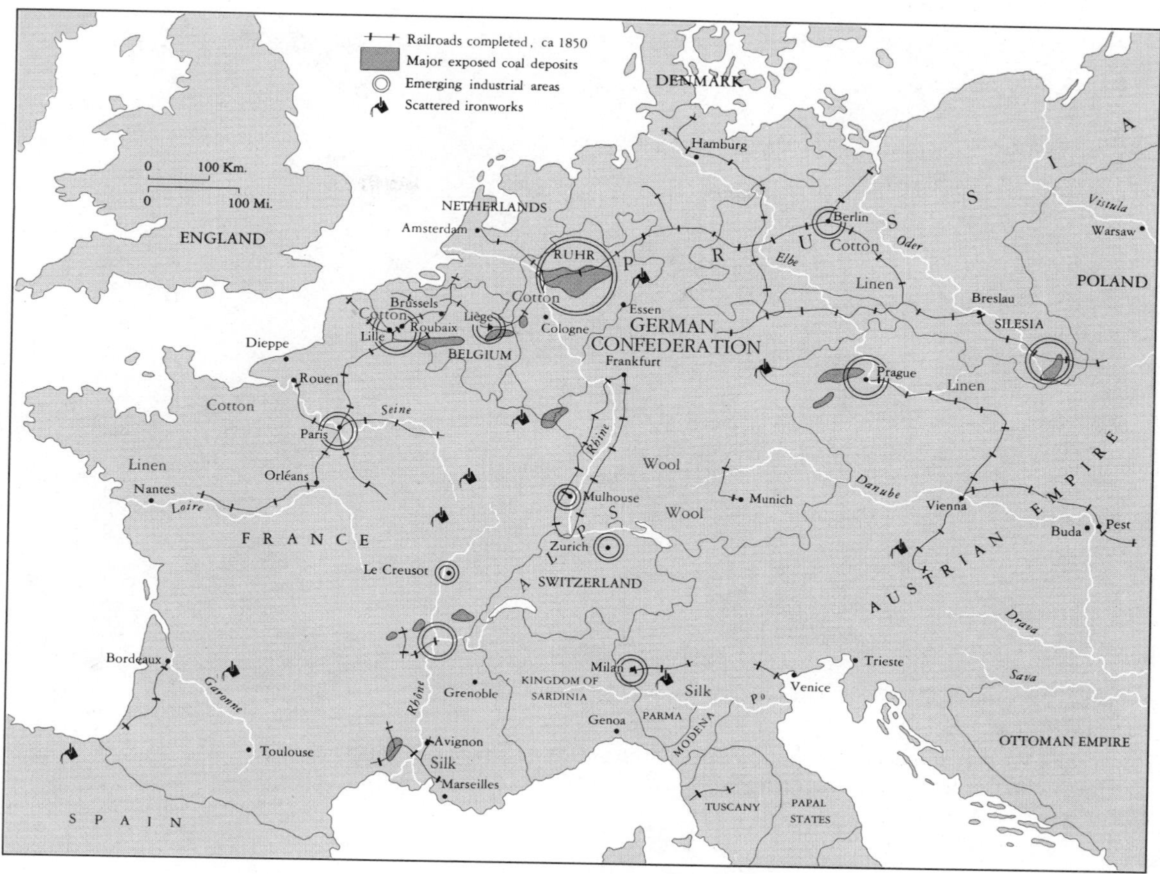

MAP 22.3 Continental Industrialization, ca 1850 Though continental countries were beginning to make progress by 1850, they still lagged far behind England. For example, continental railroad building was still in an early stage, whereas the English rail system was essentially complete.

AGENTS OF INDUSTRIALIZATION

To understand better the spread of modern industry, one should look at the fascinating careers of a few of the businessmen, workers, and apostles of industrialization who were involved. For economic life is as much the product of particular human efforts as of vast impersonal forces.

The British realized the great value of their technical discoveries and tried to keep their secrets to themselves. Until 1825 it was illegal for artisans and skilled mechanics to leave Britain; until 1843 the export of textile machinery and other equipment was forbidden. Many talented, ambitious workers, however, slipped out of the country illegally and introduced the new methods abroad.

One such man was William Cockerill, a Lancashire carpenter. He and his sons began building cotton-spinning equipment in French-occupied Belgium in 1799. In 1817 the most famous son, John Cockerill, purchased the old summer palace of the deposed bishops of Liège at Seraing, around five miles from Liège in southern Belgium. Cockerill converted the palace into a large industrial enterprise, which produced machinery, steam engines, and then railway locomotives. He also established modern ironworks and coal mines at Liège, as well as other operations throughout western Europe.

Cockerill's plants at Liège and Seraing became an industrial nerve center, continually gathering new information and transmitting it across Europe. Many skilled British workmen came, illegally, to work for

Cockerill's Works light up the night and display the awesome power of the new industrial technology in this lithograph of 1852. *(The British Museum)*

Cockerill, and some went on to found their own companies throughout Europe. Newcomers brought the latest plans and secrets, so that Cockerill could boast that, ten days after an industrial advance occurred in Britain, he knew all about it in Belgium. Thus, British technicians and skilled workers were a powerful force in the spread of early industrialization.

Another instructive career is that of Fritz Harkort, a pioneer in the German machinery industry. Harkort came from an old commercial family in Westphalia. He studied engineering developments in England while serving there as a Prussian army officer during the Napoleonic wars. Impressed and enchanted with what he saw, Harkort concluded that Germany had to match all these English achievements as quickly as possible. Setting up shop in an abandoned castle in the still-tranquil Ruhr valley, Harkort felt an almost religious calling to build steam engines and become the "Watt of Germany."

Harkort's basic idea was simple, but it was enormously difficult to carry out. Steam engines had been greatly improved in the course of thirty years, and the new models Harkort was trying to copy required much accuracy and know-how. Lacking skilled laborers to do the job, Harkort turned to England for experienced, though expensive, mechanics. He could not be choosy. As he later reminisced, "I had to cut several of my English workers down from the gallows, so to speak, if only in order to get some of them."[2] Harkort longed for the day he could afford to replace the haughty foreigners with his fellow countrymen.

Getting materials posed a great problem as well. German ironsmiths could not supply the thick iron boilers Harkort needed, and he had to import them from England at great cost and with frequent damage. There was a modest market for Harkort's engines, for the German coal industry was beginning to expand. But German roads were so bad—Harkort denounced them as deathtraps for man and beast—that steam engines had to be built at the works, completely dismantled and shipped piece by piece to the buyer, and then reassembled by Harkort's technicians. No wonder Harkort was a very early promoter

Heavy Industry required skilled workers and large capital investments. In this illustration English dignitaries visit a plant with a new technology for making steel wheels. *(BBC Hulton/The Bettmann Archive)*

of railroads, which, he predicted in 1829, "will bring countless revolutions to the world."

In spite of all these problems, Harkort built engines, sold them throughout Germany and the rest of Europe, and won fame and praise. His ambitious efforts also resulted in large financial losses for himself and his partners. These proved fatal, for Harkort's enterprise, like almost all the others of the day, was a private, capitalistic undertaking. It could not lose money indefinitely. In 1832, after sixteen years of activity and accomplishment, Harkort was forced out of his company by his financial backers, who cut back operations to reduce losses. In one sense, then, his career was a failure; yet Harkort was a pioneering visionary, the most creative German businessman of his era. His career illustrates both the great efforts of a few important business leaders to duplicate the British achievement and the extreme difficulty of the task.

Support from the government often helped businessmen in continental countries to overcome some of their difficulties. Tariff protection was one such support. For example, after Napoleon's wars ended in 1815, France was suddenly flooded with cheaper and better English goods. The French government responded by laying high tariffs on many English imports, in order to protect the French economy. After 1815 continental governments bore the cost of building roads and canals to improve transportation, and they also bore to a significant extent the cost of building railroads.

The career of the German journalist and thinker Friedrich List (1789–1846) reflects government's greater role in the Industrial Revolution on the Continent than in England. List considered the growth of modern industry of the utmost importance because manufacturing was a primary means of increasing people's well-being and relieving their poverty. Moreover, List was a dedicated nationalist. He wrote that the "wider the gap between the backward and advanced nations becomes, the more dangerous it is to remain behind." For an agricultural nation was not only poor but weak, increasingly unable to defend itself and maintain its political independence. To promote industry was to defend the nation.

The practical policy List focused on in articles and in his *National System of Political Economy* (1841) was the tariff. He supported the formation of a customs union, or *Zollverein,* among the separate German states. Such a tariff union came into being in 1834. It allowed goods to move between the German member states without tariffs, and a single uniform tariff was erected against all other nations. List wanted a high protective tariff, which would encourage infant industries, allowing them to develop and eventually to hold their own against their more advanced British counterparts. List denounced the English doctrine of free trade as little more than England's attempt "to make the rest of the world, like the Hindus, its serfs in all industrial and commercial relations." By the 1840s List's ideas were increasingly popular in Germany and elsewhere.

Banks, like governments, also played a larger and more creative role on the Continent than in England. Previously, almost all banks in Europe had been private, organized as secretive partnerships. Such banks were content to deal with a few rich clients and a few big merchants. They avoided industry. In the 1830s, two important Belgian banks pioneered in a new direction. They operated as big corporations with many stockholders, large and small. Thus their financial resources were large. The banks were able to use that money to develop industrial companies. They became, in short, industrial banks.

Similar banks became important in France and Germany in the 1850s. They established and developed many railroads and many companies working in heavy industry. The most famous such bank was the Crédit Mobilier of Paris, founded by Isaac and Emile Pereire, two young Jewish journalists from Bordeaux. The Crédit Mobilier advertised extensively. It used the savings of thousands of small investors, as well as the resources of big ones. The activities of the bank were far-reaching; it built railroads all over France and Europe. As Emile Pereire had said in 1835, "It is not enough to outline gigantic programs on paper. I must write my ideas on the earth."

Industrial banks like the Crédit Mobilier mobilized the savings of thousands of small investors and invested those savings in industry and transportation, particularly in the 1850s. In doing so, the directors of these banks helped their countries find the capital needed for industrialization. They also often made themselves very wealthy.

CAPITAL AND LABOR

Industrial development brought new social relations and problems between capital and labor. A new group of factory owners and industrial capitalists arose. These men strengthened the wealth and size of the middle class, which had previously been made up mainly of merchants and professional people. The nineteenth century became the golden age of the middle class. Modern industry also created a much larger group—the factory workers. For the first time, large numbers of men and women came together under one roof to work with complicated machinery for major capitalists and large companies. What was the nature of relations between these two new groups—capital and labor? Did the new industrial middle class ruthlessly exploit the workers, as Karl Marx and others have charged?

The New Class of Factory Owners

Early industrialists operated in a highly competitive economic system. As the careers of Watt and Harkort illustrate, there were countless production problems, and success and large profits were by no means certain. Manufacturers, therefore, waged a constant battle to cut their production costs and stay afloat. Most profit had to go back into the business for new and better machinery. "Dragged on by the frenzy of this terrible life," according to one of his dismayed critics, the struggling manufacturer had "no time for niceties. He must conquer or die, make a fortune or drown himself."[3]

The early industrialists came from a variety of backgrounds. Many, like Harkort, were from well-established merchant families, who provided capital and contacts. Others, like Watt and Cockerill, were of modest means, especially in the early days. Artisans and skilled workmen of exceptional ability had unparalleled opportunities. The ethnic and religious groups that had been discriminated against in the traditional occupations controlled by the landed aristocracy jumped at the new chances. Quakers and Scots were tremendously important in England; Protestants and Jews dominated banking in Catholic France. Many of the industrialists were newly rich, and, not surprisingly, they were very proud and self-satisfied.

Cotton Mill Workers Family members often worked side by side in industry. Here women and children are combing raw cotton and drawing it into loose strands called rovings, which will then be spun into fine thread. *(The Mansell Collection)*

As factories grew larger, opportunities declined, at least in well-developed industries. It became considerably harder for a gifted but poor young mechanic to end up as a wealthy manufacturer. Formal education became more important as a means of advancement, and formal education at the advanced level was expensive. In England by 1830 and in France and Germany by 1860, leading industrialists were more likely to have inherited their well-established enterprises, and they were financially much more secure than their fathers and grandfathers. They were also aware of a greater gap between themselves and their workers.

The New Factory Workers

The social consequences of the Industrial Revolution have long been hotly debated. Since any honest observer will see that some conditions got better and others got worse, vigorous debate is likely to continue. (Also, industry promoted rapid urbanization with its own great problems, as will be shown in Chapter 24.) Nevertheless, for workers and ordinary families, the Industrial Revolution brought a great transformation, which was, on balance, desirable. It marked a great step forward from the pattern of preindustrial life for the common people and the poor.

The condition of English workers in the Industrial Revolution has always generated the most controversy among historians, because England was the first country to industrialize and because the social consequences seem harshest there. Before 1850, other countries had not proceeded very far with industrialization, and almost everyone agrees that the economic conditions of European workers improved after 1850. The countries that followed England were able to benefit from English experience in social as well as technical matters. Thus the early English Industrial Revolution provides the strongest case for the harmful social consequences of modern industrial development, at least prior to 1914, and it is fitting to focus on it.

From the beginning, the Industrial Revolution in England had its critics. Among the first were the romantic poets. William Blake (1757–1827) called the early factories "satanic mills" and protested against the hard life of the London poor. William Wordsworth (1770–1850) lamented the destruction of the rural way of life and the pollution of the land and water. Doctors and reformers wrote eloquently of problems in the factories and new towns. Some handicraft workers—notably the Luddites, who attacked whole factories in northern England in 1812 and after—smashed the new machines, which they believed were putting them out of work.

Another early critic was Friedrich Engels (1820–1895), the future revolutionary and colleague of Karl Marx. After studying conditions in northern England, this young middle-class German published *The Condition of the Working Class in England* in 1844. Engels cast the problem of industrial life in class terms. "At the bar of world opinion," he wrote, "I charge the English middle classes with mass murder, wholesale robbery, and all the other crimes in the calendar."[4] Engels's charge of middle-class exploitation and increasing worker poverty was embellished by Marx and later socialists. It was extremely influential.

Meanwhile, other observers believed that conditions were improving for the working class. Andrew Ure wrote in 1835 in his study of the cotton industry that conditions in most factories were not harsh and were even quite good. Edwin Chadwick, a great and conscientious government official, well acquainted with the problems of the working class, concluded that the "whole mass of the laboring community" was increasingly able "to buy more of the necessities and minor luxuries of life."[5]

If all the contemporary indictments of observers like Engels and all the defenses of those like Ure were counted up, those who thought conditions were getting worse for working people would probably be the majority. Yet it is clear that opinions differed greatly. In an attempt to go deeper into the problem, historians must look at different kinds of sources.

Statistical evidence is one such source. It should help resolve the conflicting opinions of contemporary and often biased observers. If working people suffered a great decline, as Engels and later socialists asserted, then they must have bought less and less food, clothing, and other necessities as time went on. The purchasing power of the working person's wages must have declined drastically.

At the end of the nineteenth century, dispassionate British statisticians tried to pull together all the evidence on wages and prices and thereby measure what working-class people could or could not have bought. Such an approach was only partially successful. England was not in a prestatistical age during its Industrial Revolution, but there were many gaps and shortcomings in the available numbers. Nevertheless, this approach does offer important insights.

During the period from about 1750 to 1790, when cottage industry was still dominant, the purchasing power of the average British laborer's wages seems to have risen somewhat. The workers—primarily cottage workers, artisans, and farm hands—could buy more goods, like food and clothing, over the years. Wages in industry were substantially higher than in agriculture, and all kinds of wages rose faster in the industrializing areas of the north than in the purely agricultural counties of the south. The cautious conclusion must be that from 1750 to 1790 the growth of industry made for a more abundant life for working people, in terms of material goods.

The years from 1792 to 1815, a period of constant war against revolutionary and Napoleonic France, brought very different circumstances. Wages rose, but they did not keep up with inflation. Food prices rose most, as the price of wheat approximately doubled from 1790 to 1810. The condition of the working poor declined.

Between 1815 and 1850, the purchasing power of workers' wages increased again. Money wages remained steady or fell somewhat, but prices fell more. The fullest studies show that the real wages of the average worker—agricultural and industrial—increased 25 percent between 1800 and 1825 and another 40 percent between 1825 and 1850.[6] The trend was definitely upward, but the course was erratic. Between 1820 and 1840, real wages increased by only 5 to 10 percent. However, the wages of unskilled workers in British industry were again, as before 1790, about twice as high as those of unskilled workers in British agriculture. In short, throughout the Industrial Revolution, with the exception of the wartime period, there was apparently substantial economic improvement for British workers.

This important conclusion must be qualified, though. Increased purchasing power meant more goods, but it did not necessarily mean greater happiness. Also, these figures do not say anything about how the level of unemployment may have risen, for the simple reason that there are no good unemployment statistics from this period. Furthermore, the hours in the average workweek increased; to an unknown extent, workers earned more simply because they worked more. Finally, the wartime decline was of great importance. The war years were formative years for the new factory labor force. They were also some of the hardest yet experienced. They colored the early experience of modern industrial life in somber tones.

Another way to consider workers' standard of living is to look at the goods they purchased. Again the evidence is somewhat contradictory. Speaking generally, workers ate somewhat more food of higher nutritional quality as the Industrial Revolution progressed, except during wartime. Diets became more varied; people ate more potatoes, dairy products, fruits, and vegetables.

Clothing improved, but housing for working people did not. In short, per capita use of specific goods supports the position that the standard of living of the working classes rose, at least moderately, during the Industrial Revolution. The rich did get richer. So did the poor to some extent, especially if they worked in industry.

Conditions of Work

What about working conditions? Did workers earn more only at the cost of working longer and harder? Were workers exploited harshly by the new factory owners?

The first factories were cotton mills, which began functioning along rivers and streams in the 1770s. Cottage workers, accustomed to the putting-out system, were reluctant to work in factories even when they received relatively good wages, because factory work was different from what they were used to and unappealing. In the factory, workers had to keep up with the machine and follow its tempo. They had to show up every day and work long, monotonous hours. Factory workers had to adjust their daily lives to the shrill call of the factory whistle.

Cottage workers were not used to that kind of life and discipline. All members of the family worked hard and long, but in spurts, setting their own pace. They could interrupt their work when they wanted to. Women and children could break up their long hours of spinning with other tasks. On Saturday afternoon the head of the family delivered the week's work to the merchant-manufacturer and got paid. Saturday night was a time of relaxation and drinking, especially for the men. Recovering from his hangover on Tuesday, the weaver bent to his task on Wednesday and then worked frantically to meet his deadline on Saturday. Like some students today, he might "pull an all-nighter" on Thursday or Friday in order to get his work in.

Also, early factories resembled English poorhouses, where totally destitute people went to live on welfare. Some poorhouses were industrial prisons, where the inmates had to work in order to receive their food and lodging. The similarity between large brick factories and large stone poorhouses increased the cottage workers' fear of factories and their hatred of factory discipline.

It was cottage workers' reluctance to work in factories that prompted the early cottonmill owners to turn to abandoned and pauper children for their labor. As we have seen, they contracted with local officials to employ large numbers of these children, who had no say in the matter. Pauper children were often badly treated and terribly overworked in the mills, as they were when they were apprenticed as chimney sweeps, market girls, shoemakers, and so forth. In the eighteenth century, semiforced child labor seemed necessary and was socially accepted. From our modern point of view, it was cruel exploitation and a blot on the record of the new industrial system.

By 1790 the early pattern was rapidly changing. The use of pauper apprentices was in decline, and in 1802 it was forbidden by Parliament. Many more factories were being built, mainly in urban areas, where they could use steam rather than water power and attract a work force more easily than in the countryside. The need for workers was great. Indeed, people came from near and far to work in the cities, both as factory workers and as laborers, builders, and domestic servants. Yet, as they took these new jobs, working people did not simply give in to a system of labor that had formerly repelled them. Rather, they helped modify the system by carrying over old, familiar working traditions.

Cotton Mill near Manchester The simple rural scene in the foreground of this 1834 engraving contrasts vividly with the massive brick factory building dominating the landscape. *(BBC Hulton/The Bettmann Archive)*

For one thing, they came to the mills and the mines as family units. This was how they had worked on farms and in the putting-out system. The mill or mine owner bargained with the head of the family and paid him or her for the work of the whole family. In the cotton mills, children worked for their mothers or fathers, collecting wastes and "piecing" broken threads together. In the mines, children sorted coal and worked the ventilation equipment. Their mothers hauled coal in the narrow tunnels below the surface, while their fathers hewed with pick and shovel at the face of the seam.

The preservation of the family as an economic unit in the factories from the 1790s on made the new surroundings more tolerable, both in Great Britain and in other countries during the early stages of industrialization. Parents disciplined their children, making firm measures socially acceptable, and directed their upbringing. The presence of the whole family meant that children and adults worked the same long hours (twelve-hour shifts were normal in cotton mills in 1800). In the early years, some very young children were employed solely to keep the family together. Jedediah Strutt, for example, believed children should be at least ten years old to work in his mills, but he reluctantly employed seven-year-olds to satisfy their parents. Adult workers were not particularly interested in limiting the minimum working age or hours of their children, as long as they worked side by side. Only when technical changes threatened to place control and discipline in the hands of impersonal managers and foremen did they protest against inhuman conditions in the name of their children.

But some enlightened employers and social reformers in Parliament definitely felt otherwise. "In an age of rising standards of humanitarianism the few were determined to impose higher standards on the many; and were able to exploit developing means of mass communication to do it."[7] These reformers had important successes.

Girl Dragging Coal Tubs Published by reformers in Parliament in 1842, this picture shocked public opinion and contributed to the Mines Act of 1842. *(The British Library)*

Their first major accomplishment was the Factory Act of 1833. It limited the workday for children between nine and thirteen to eight hours and that of adolescents between fourteen to eighteen to twelve hours. The law also prohibited the employment of children under nine; they were to be enrolled in the elementary schools factory owners were required to establish. Since efficiency required standardized shifts for all workers, the Factory Act shattered the pattern of whole families working together in the factory. The employment of children declined rapidly. Similarly, the Mines Act of 1842 prohibited all women and boys under ten from working underground.

Ties of blood and kinship remained important in other ways in England in the formative years between about 1790 and 1840. Many manufacturers and builders hired workers not directly but through subcontractors. They paid the subcontractors on the basis of what the subcontractors and their crews produced—for smelting so many tons of pig iron or moving so much dirt or gravel for a canal or roadbed. Subcontractors in turn hired and fired their own workers, many of whom were friends and relations. The subcontractor might be as harsh as the greediest capitalist, but the relationship between subcontractor and work crew was close and personal. This kind of traditional relationship was more acceptable to workers than impersonal factory discipline. This system also provided people an easy way to find a job. Even today, a friend or relative who is a foreman is frequently worth a hundred formal application forms.

Ties of kinship were particularly important for newcomers, who often traveled considerable distances to find work. Many urban workers in Great Britain were from Ireland. Forced out of rural Ireland by population growth and deteriorating economic conditions from 1817 on, Irish in search of jobs could not be choosy; they took what they could get. As early as 1824, most of the workers in the Glasgow cotton mills were Irish; in 1851 one-sixth of the population of the great port of Liverpool was Irish. Even when Irish workers were not related directly by blood, they were held together by ethnic and religious ties. Like other immigrant groups elsewhere, they worked together, formed their own neighborhoods, and not only survived but thrived.

A Mature Working Class

By about 1850, the working people of urban Britain had, like British industry, gone a long way toward attaining maturity. Family employment in the factory had given way to the employment of adults, for whom the discipline of the clock and the regularity of the machine were familiar taskmasters. Gone were violent demonstrations against industrialization. In their place were increasing acceptance of the emerging industrial system and an ongoing effort to make that system serve workers better.

In Great Britain and in other countries later on, workers slowly created a labor movement to serve their needs. In 1799, partly in panicked reaction to the French Revolution, Parliament had passed the Combination Acts outlawing unions and strikes. These acts were widely disregarded by workers. Societies of skilled factory workers organized unions, as printers, papermakers, carpenters, and other such craftsmen had long since done. The unions sought to control the number of skilled workers, limit apprenticeship to members' own children, and bargain with owners over wages. They were not afraid to strike; there was, for example, a general strike of adult cotton spinners in Manchester in 1810. In the face of widespread union activity, Parliament repealed the Combination Acts in 1824, and unions were tolerated though not fully accepted after 1825.

The next stage in the development of the British trade-union movement was the attempt to create a single large national union. This effort was led not so much by working people as by social reformers like Robert Owen (1771–1858). Owen, a self-made cotton manufacturer, had pioneered in industrial relations by combining firm discipline with concern for the health, safety, and hours of his workers. After 1815 he experimented with cooperative and socialist communities, including one at New Harmony, Indiana. Then, in 1834, Owen organized one of the largest and most visionary of the early national unions, the Grand National Consolidated Trades Union. When this and other grandiose schemes collapsed, the British labor movement moved once again after 1851 in the direction of bread-and-butter craft unions. The most famous of these "new model" unions was the Amalgamated Society of Engineers. These craft unions won real benefits for their members by fairly conservative means and thus became an accepted part of the industrial scene.

The maturity of British workers was also expressed in direct political activity in defense of their own interests. After the collapse of Owen's national trade union, a great deal of the energy of working people went into the Chartist movement, whose goal was political democracy. The key Chartist demand—that all men be given the right to vote—became the great hope of millions of aroused people. Workers were also active in campaigns to limit the workday in the factories to ten hours and to permit duty-free importation of wheat into Great Britain to secure cheap bread. Thus working people played an active role in shaping the new industrial system. Clearly, they were neither helpless victims nor passive beneficiaries.

THE ALTERNATIVE TO INDUSTRIALIZATION

What was the alternative to the Industrial Revolution and the new urban society? What would have been the likely course of events—the likely alternative for Europe—if industrialization had not occurred? It is impossible to know exactly, yet a look at general developments and at the case of Ireland, which did not industrialize, may shed some light on this question.

The Growth of Population

The drama of industrialization must be viewed alongside the drama of rapid population growth. Europe's population began growing after 1720 (pages 618–620), leading to severe pressures on available resources and overpopulation in many areas. Large numbers of people had serious difficulty growing or buying the food they needed. There was widespread underemployment, acute poverty, and constant migration in search of work.

All these forces operated during and after the era of the French Revolution. Europe had roughly 140 million people in 1750, 188 million in 1800, and 266 million in 1850—an increase of almost 40 percent in each half-century. Overpopulation worsened between 1800 and 1850 on much of the Continent, most noticeably in Flanders, parts of Scandinavia, and southwestern Germany. One result was migration from the countryside to nearby cities and towns, where unskilled laborers were already irregularly em-

"Be United and Industrious" This handsome membership certificate of the "new model" Amalgamated Society of Engineers exalts the nobility of skilled labor and the labor movement. Union members are shown rejecting the call of Mars, the God of War, and accepting well-deserved honors from the Goddess of Peace. Other figures represent the strength of union solidarity, famous English inventors, and the trades of the members. *(Bridgeman Art Library)*

Evicting Irish Peasants, 1848 Unable to pay their rent, famine-stricken peasants are ordered from their home, which is already being torn down. Soldiers with fixed bayonets stand ready to quell any disturbance. *(Illustrated London News/Library of Congress)*

ployed and poorly paid. Another result was that growing numbers of peasants liquidated their small and inadequate landholdings and went abroad. Thus, in the early nineteenth century, particularly in the hungry 1840s, many German and Swedish settlers tried their luck and skill on prairie lands of the American Midwest.

The pressure of increasing numbers and rural poverty was most severe in Ireland. Although Ireland supplied many workers for factories in Britain, Ireland itself did not industrialize in the nineteenth century. Therefore, although Ireland was a particularly oppressed and exploited nation, its fate could have been that of much of Europe if not for the Industrial Revolution.

The Potato Famine in Ireland

Late eighteenth-century Ireland was a conquered country. The great mass of the population (outside the northern counties of Ulster, which were partly Presbyterian) were Irish Catholic peasants, who rented their land from a tiny minority of Church of England Protestants, many of whom lived in England (page 650). These Protestant landlords lacked the improving zeal of their English counterparts. They knew they were perched on top of a volcano that erupted periodically, but they were quite content to use their powers to grab as much as possible, as quickly as possible.

The result was that the condition of the Irish peasantry around 1800 was abominable. The typical peasant family lived in a wretched cottage made of mud and could afford neither shoes nor stockings. Hundreds of shocking accounts describe hopeless poverty. Sir Walter Scott wrote:

The poverty of the Irish peasantry is on the extreme verge of human misery; their cottages would scarce serve for pig styes even in Scotland; and their rags seem the very refuse of a sheep, and are spread over their bodies with such an ingenious variety of wretchedness that you would think nothing but some sort of perverted taste could have assembled so many shreds together.

For a French traveler, Ireland was "pure misery, naked and hungry. . . . I saw the American Indian in his forests and the black slave in his chains, and I believed that I was seeing in their pitiful condition the most extreme form of human misery; but that was before I knew the lot of poor Ireland."[8] Yet in spite of these terrible conditions, population growth sped onward. The 3 million of 1725 reached 4 million in 1780 and doubled to 8 million in 1840. Between 1780 and 1840, 1.75 million men and women left Ireland for Britain and America.

The population of Ireland grew so quickly for three reasons: extensive cultivation of the potato, early marriage, and ruthless exploitation of peasants by landlords. The potato, first introduced into Ireland in the late sixteenth century, was the principal food of the Irish peasantry by the last years of the eighteenth century. The reason for dependence on the potato was originally the pressure of numbers, which forced the peasants to wring as many calories as they could out of a given piece of land. But once peasants began to live almost exclusively on potatoes, many more people could exist. A single acre of land spaded and planted with potatoes could feed a family of six for a year, whereas it would take at least two and probably four acres of grain and pasture to feed the same number. Moreover, the potato was not choosy and could thrive on boggy wastelands.

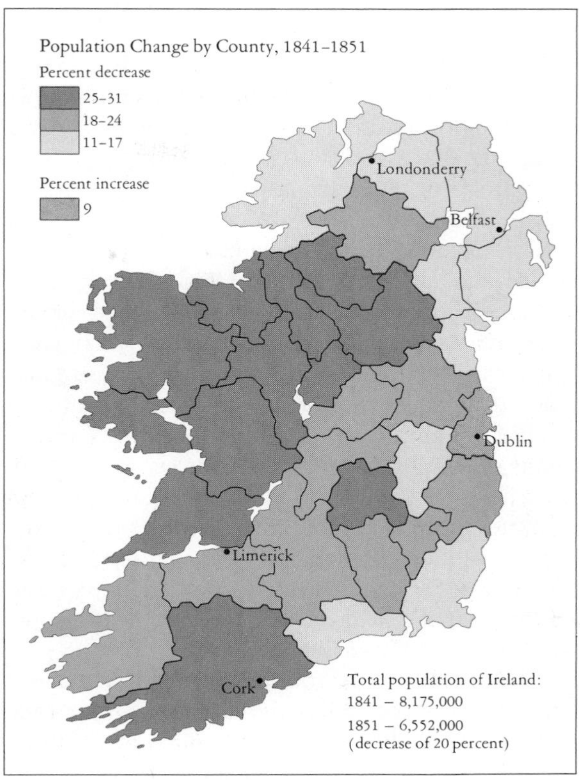

Map 22.4 The Irish Potato Famine Though all Ireland suffered, population losses were highest in the west where dependency on the potato was greatest.

Needing only a potato patch of an acre or two for survival, Irish boys and girls married much earlier than did their counterparts in rural England and France by the end of the eighteenth century. Setting up housekeeping was easy, for a cabin of mud and stone could be slapped together in a few days with the willing assistance of the young couple's neighbors and relatives. A mat for a bed, a chair or two, a table, and an iron pot to boil potatoes were easily acquired. To be sure, the young couple was accepting the life of extreme poverty that travelers and people of good conscience lamented. They would literally live on potatoes—ten pounds a day every day all year long for the average male—moistened with a cup of milk if they were lucky.

Nonetheless, the decision to marry early and have large families was quite reasonable, given Irish conditions. The landlords, not the peasants, owned and controlled the land. Because land was leased only for short periods on uncertain terms, peasants had no incentive to make permanent improvements. Any increase in profits went to the landlord, and anything beyond what preserved the peasants from absolute starvation was extorted from them. Poverty thus being inescapable in rural Ireland, it was better shared with a wife or husband. Children were a precious asset, as in many poor countries today, for there was no welfare or social security system, and an infirm or aged person's best hope of escaping starvation was a dutiful son or a loving daughter.

As the population continued to grow, conditions became increasingly precarious. The peasantry depended on a single crop, the size of which varied substantially from year to year. Potato failures cannot be detected in time to plant other crops, nor can potatoes be stored for more than a year. Furthermore, a potato economy is a subsistence economy. It lacks a well-developed network of roads and trade capable of distributing other foods in time of disaster. From

1820 on, deficiencies in the potato crop became increasingly serious. Disease in the potato crop was becoming more common, and the accompanying fever epidemics that struck the population were growing more frequent. Some great catastrophe in the near future was almost completely inevitable.

In 1845 and 1846 and again in 1848 and 1851, the potato crop failed in Ireland and throughout much of Europe. The general result was high food prices, widespread suffering, and social unrest. In Ireland, which was furthest down the road to rural overpopulation and dependence on a disease-prone plant, the result was unmitigated disaster—the Great Famine. Blight attacked the young plants, the leaves withered, and the tubers rotted. Widespread starvation and mass fever epidemics followed. Cannibalism occurred, although starving people generally lived on the carcasses of diseased cattle, dogs, and horses and on herbs of the field. In some places, dead people were found with grass in their mouths.

Total losses were staggering. The population of Ireland was roughly 8 million in 1845, and without the famine it would have reached 9 million in 1851 (see Map 22.4). But that year, Ireland's population was only 6.5 million. Fully 1 million emigrants fled the famine between 1845 and 1851 (2 million left between 1840 and 1855), going primarily to the United States and Great Britain. Thus at least 1.5 million people died or went unborn because of the disaster. The British government's efforts at famine relief were too little and too late. Moreover, the government continued to collect its taxes, and the landlords continued to demand their rents. Tenants who could not pay were evicted and their homes broken up or burned. Famine or no, Ireland was still the conquered jewel of foreign landowners.

The Great Famine shattered and reversed the pattern of Irish population growth. Alone among the nations of Europe, Ireland's numbers declined in the nineteenth century, to 4.4 million in 1911. Ireland remained a land of continuous out-migration. It also became a land of late marriage and widespread celibacy, as the landowning classes discouraged potato farming and converted much of the country into pasture for cattle and sheep. After great population decline and untold suffering, Ireland found a new demographic equilibrium within the framework of a poor pastoral economy.

The fate of Ireland has real relevance for an understanding of the Industrial Revolution. The rapid population growth without industrialization that occurred in Ireland between 1780 and 1845 occurred elsewhere, too—in central Russia, in western Germany, and in southern Italy, to name only three crucial regions. In these areas, there were indications of acute poverty and overpopulation, and the potato played a crucial role as it had done in Ireland. In Prussia, for example, annual potato production grew from 1 to 11 million tons from 1815 to 1860. By 1850 in some parts of Europe, bread was a luxury; workers and peasants were subsisting almost entirely on potatoes. In 1500 the average German had eaten about 200 pounds of meat a year; in 1850 his counterpart ate about 40 pounds.[9] The standard of living was declining. Other Irelands were in the making.

Population growth threatened to produce a morass of rural poverty, a demographic catastrophe, or both. In this connection, the historian T. S. Ashton once argued that the Industrial Revolution was the salvation rather than the curse of England and of the parts of Europe fortunate enough to follow England's lead. He may have overstated the case, but Ashton was surely closer to the truth than those who persist in arguing the contrary. The alternative to the revolution in energy and industry would probably have been, sooner or later, disaster.

NOTES

1. M. Lévy-Leboyer, *Les banques européennes et l'industrialisation dans la première moitié du XIXe siècle,* Presses Universitaires de France, Paris, 1964, p. 29.
2. Quoted by D. S. Landes, *The Unbound Prometheus: Technological Change and Industrial Development in Western Europe from 1750 to the Present,* Cambridge University Press, Cambridge, Eng., 1969, p. 150.
3. J. Michelet, *The People,* University of Illinois Press, Urbana, 1973 (originally published, 1846), p. 64.
4. F. Engels, *The Condition of the Working Class in England,* trans. and ed. W. O. Henderson and W. H. Chaloner, Stanford University Press, Stanford, Calif., 1968, p. xxiii.

5. Quoted in W. A. Hayek, ed., *Capitalism and the Historians,* University of Chicago Press, Chicago, 1954, p. 126.
6. P. Deane and W. A. Cole, *British Economic Growth, 1688–1959,* Cambridge University Press, Cambridge, Eng., 1964, p. 25.
7. P. Mathias, *The First Industrial Nation: An Economic History of Britain, 1700–1914,* Charles Scribner's Sons, New York, 1969, p. 205.
8. Quoted by G. O'Brien, *The Economic History of Ireland from the Union to the Famine,* Longmans, Green, London, 1921, pp. 21–24.
9. W. L. Langer, *Political and Social Upheaval, 1832–1852,* Harper & Row, New York, 1969, p. 188.

SUGGESTED READING

There is a vast and exciting literature on the Industrial Revolution. D. S. Landes's *The Unbound Prometheus* (1969), cited in the Notes, and S. Pollard, *Peaceful Conquest: The Industrialization of Europe* (1981), are the best general treatments of European industrial growth since 1750. P. Mathias, *The First Industrial Nation: An Economic History of Britain, 1700–1914* (1969); P. Deane, *The First Industrial Revolution* (1966); and P. Mantoux, *The Industrial Revolution in the Eighteenth Century* (1961), admirably discuss the various aspects of the English breakthrough and offer good bibliographies. (See also the Suggested Reading for Chapter 23.) W. Rostow, *The Stages of Economic Growth: A Non-Communist Manifesto* (1960), is a popular, provocative study. R. Cameron brilliantly traces the spread of railroads and industry across Europe in *France and the Economic Development of Europe, 1800–1914* (1961). The recent works of A. S. Milward and S. B. Saul, *The Economic Development of Continental Europe, (1780–1870* (1973) and *The Development of the Economies of Continental Europe, 1850–1914* (1977), may be compared with J. Clapham's old-fashioned classic, *Economic Development of France and Germany* (1963). C. Kindleberger, *Economic Growth in France and Britain, 1851–1950* (1964), is a stimulating study, especially for those with some background in economics. Other important works in recent years on industrial developments are C. Tilly and E. Shorter, *Strikes in France, 1830–1848* (1974); D. Ringrose, *Transportation and Economic Stagnation in Spain, 1750–1850* (1970); L. Schofer, *The Formation of a Modern Labor Force* (1975), which focuses on the Silesian part of Germany; and W. Blackwell, *The Industrialization of Russia,* 2nd ed. (1982).

The debate between "optimists" and "pessimists" about the consequences of industrialization in England goes on. P. Taylor, ed., *The Industrial Revolution: Triumph or Disaster?* (1970), is a useful introduction to different viewpoints, while W. A. Hayek, ed., *Capitalism and the Historians* (1954), is a good collection of essays stressing positive aspects. It is also fascinating to compare Friedrich Engels's classic condemnation, *The Condition of the Working Class in England,* with Andrew Ure's optimistic defense, *The Philosophy of Manufactures,* first published in 1835 and reprinted recently. E. P. Thompson continues and enriches the Engels tradition in *The Making of the English Working Class* (1963), an exciting book rich in detail and early working-class lore. An unorthodox but moving account of a doomed group is D. Bythell, *The Handloom Weavers* (1969). F. Klingender, *Art and the Industrial Revolution,* rev. ed. (1968), is justly famous, and M. Ignatieff, *A Just Measure of Pain* (1980), is an engrossing study of prisons during English industrialization. D. S. Landes, *Revolution in Time: Clocks and the Making of the Modern World* (1983), is a brilliant integration of industrial and cultural history.

Among general studies, many of which are cited in the Suggested Reading for Chapter 23, G. S. R. Kitson Clark, *The Making of Victorian England* (1967), is particularly imaginative. A. Briggs, *Victorian People* (1955), provides an engrossing series of brief biographies. H. Ausubel discusses a major reformer in his work, *John Bright* (1966), and B. Harrison skillfully illuminates the problem of heavy drinking in *Drink and the Victorians* (1971). On poverty and politics in Ireland, K. H. Connell, *The Population of Ireland, 1750–1850* (1950), and S. Cronin, *Irish Nationalism: A History of Its Roots and Ideology* (1981), are excellent points of departure, while C. Smith, *The Great Hunger* (1962), is a moving account of the famine. The most famous contemporary novel dealing with the new industrial society is Charles Dickens's *Hard Times,* an entertaining but exaggerated story. *Mary Barton* and *North and South* by Elizabeth Gaskill are more realistic portrayals, and both are highly recommended, as is Emile Zola's *Germinal,* a grim, powerful story of love and hate during a violent strike by French coal miners.

23

IDEOLOGIES AND UPHEAVALS, 1815–1850

THE MOMENTOUS economic and political transformation of modern times began in the late eighteenth century with the Industrial Revolution in England and then the French Revolution. Until about 1815, these economic and political revolutions were separate, involving different countries and activities and proceeding at very different paces. The Industrial Revolution created the factory system and new groups of capitalists and industrial workers in northern England, but almost continuous warfare with France checked its spread to continental Europe. Meanwhile, England's ruling aristocracy suppressed all forms of political radicalism at home and joined with crowned heads abroad to oppose and eventually defeat revolutionary and Napoleonic France. The economic and political revolutions worked at cross-purposes and even neutralized each other.

After peace returned in 1815, the situation changed. Economic and political changes tended to fuse, reinforcing each other and bringing about what the historian Eric Hobsbawm has incisively called the "dual revolution." For instance, the growth of the industrial middle class encouraged the drive for representative government, while the demands of the French sans-culottes in 1793 and 1794 inspired many socialist thinkers. Gathering strength and threatening almost every aspect of the existing political and social framework, the dual revolution rushed on to alter completely first Europe and then the world. Much of world history in the last two centuries can be seen as the progressive unfolding of the dual revolution.

Yet three qualifications must be kept firmly in mind. In Europe in the nineteenth century, as in Asia and Africa in more recent times, the dual revolution was not some inexorable mechanical monster grinding peoples and cultures into a homogenized mass. The economic and political transformation it wrought was built on complicated histories, strong traditions, and highly diverse cultures. Radical change was eventually a constant, but the particular results varied enormously.

Nor should the strength of the old forces be underestimated. In Europe especially, the traditional elites —the monarchs, noble landowners, and bureaucrats —long proved capable of defending their privileges and even of rerouting the dual revolution to serve their interests.

Finally, the dual revolution posed a tremendous intellectual challenge. The meanings of the economic, political, and social changes that were occurring, as well as the ways they could be shaped by human action, were anything but clear. These questions fascinated observers and stimulated new ideas and ideologies.

How, then, did the political revolution, derailed by class antagonisms in France and resisted by European monarchs, break out again in the era of early industrialization? And what ideas did thinkers develop to describe and shape the transformation going on before their eyes? These are the questions this chapter will explore.

THE PEACE SETTLEMENT

The eventual triumph of revolutionary economic and political forces was by no means certain in 1814. Quite the contrary. The conservative, aristocratic monarchies with their preindustrial armies and economies (Great Britain excepted) appeared firmly in control once again. France had been decisively defeated by the off-again, on-again alliance of Russia, Prussia, Austria, and Great Britain. That alliance had been strengthened and reaffirmed in March 1814, when the allies pledged not only to defeat France but to hold it in line for twenty years thereafter. The Quadruple Alliance had then forced Napoleon to abdicate in April 1814 and restored the Bourbon dynasty to the French throne (page 694). But there were many other international questions outstanding, and the allies agreed to meet in Vienna to fashion a general peace settlement. Interrupted by Napoleon's desperate gamble during the Hundred Days, the allies concluded their negotiations at the Congress of Vienna after Napoleon's defeat at Waterloo.

Most people felt profound longing for peace. The great challenge for statesmen in 1814 was to construct a peace settlement that would last and not sow the seeds of another war. Their efforts were largely successful and contributed to a century unmarred by destructive, generalized war (see Map 23.1).

MAP 23.1 Europe in 1815 Europe's leaders re-established a balance of political power after the defeat of Napoleon.

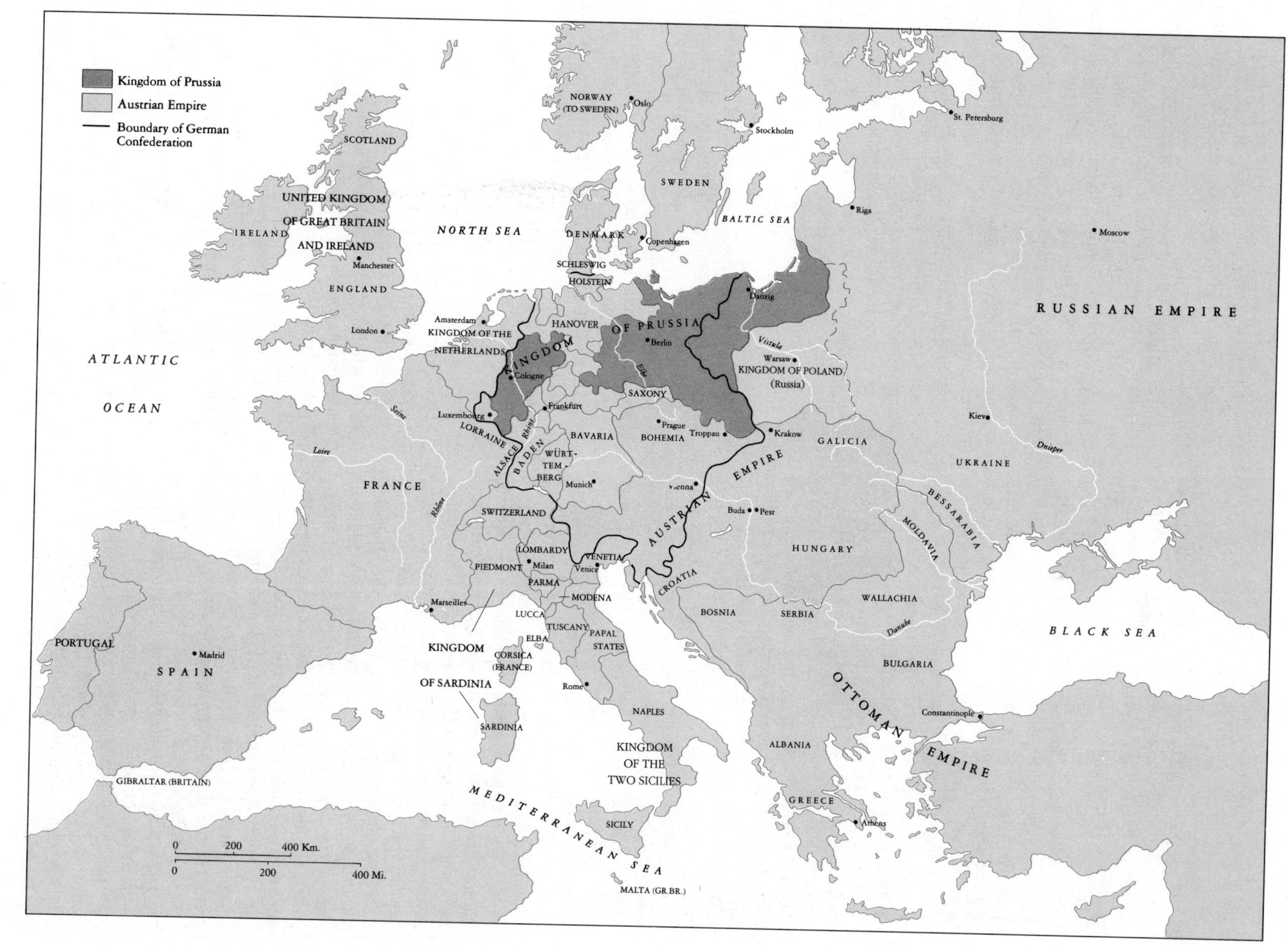
Kingdom of Prussia
Austrian Empire
Boundary of German Confederation
SCOTLAND
UNITED KINGDOM OF GREAT BRITAIN AND IRELAND
IRELAND
Manchester
ENGLAND
London
NORTH SEA
ATLANTIC OCEAN
NORWAY (TO SWEDEN)
Oslo
Stockholm
St. Petersburg
SWEDEN
BALTIC SEA
Riga
Moscow
DENMARK
Copenhagen
SCHLESWIG
HOLSTEIN
Danzig
RUSSIAN EMPIRE
Amsterdam
KINGDOM OF THE NETHERLANDS
HANOVER
KINGDOM OF PRUSSIA
Berlin
Vistula
Warsaw
KINGDOM OF POLAND (Russia)
Cologne
Elbe
SAXONY
Luxembourg
Frankfurt
Prague
BOHEMIA
Troppau
Krakow
GALICIA
Kiev
Dnieper
UKRAINE
Seine
Loire
LORRAINE
Rhine
ALSACE
BADEN
BAVARIA
WÜRT-TEM-BERG
Munich
Vienna
AUSTRIAN EMPIRE
FRANCE
Rhône
SWITZERLAND
Buda
Pest
BESSARABIA
MOLDAVIA
HUNGARY
LOMBARDY
VENETIA
PIEDMONT
Milan
Venice
PARMA
MODENA
CROATIA
Marseilles
WALLACHIA
BOSNIA
SERBIA
LUCCA
TUSCANY
Danube
BLACK SEA
PORTUGAL
Madrid
SPAIN
KINGDOM OF SARDINIA
ELBA
PAPAL STATES
CORSICA (FRANCE)
BULGARIA
Rome
OTTOMAN EMPIRE
Constantinople
NAPLES
SARDINIA
ALBANIA
KINGDOM OF THE TWO SICILIES
GIBRALTAR (BRITAIN)
MEDITERRANEAN SEA
GREECE
Athens
SICILY
0 200 400 Km.
0 200 400 Mi.
MALTA (GR.BR.)

The Congress of Vienna

The allied powers were concerned first and foremost with the defeated enemy, France. Agreeing to the restoration of the Bourbon dynasty, the allies signed the first Peace of Paris with Louis XVIII on May 30, 1814.

The allies were quite lenient toward France. France was given the boundaries it possessed in 1792, which were larger than those of 1789. France lost only the territories it had conquered in Italy, Germany, and the Low Countries, in addition to a few colonial possessions. Although there was some sentiment for levying a fine on France to pay for the war, the allies did not press the matter when Louis XVIII stated firmly that his government would not pay any reparations. France was even allowed to keep the art treasures Napoleon's agents had looted from the museums of Europe. Thus the victorious powers did not punish harshly, and they did not foment a spirit of injustice and revenge in the defeated country.

When the four allies met together at the Congress of Vienna, assisted in a minor way by a host of delegates from the smaller European states, they also agreed to raise a number of formidable barriers against renewed French aggression. The Low Countries—Belgium and Holland—were united under an enlarged Dutch monarchy capable of opposing France more effectively. Moreover, Prussia received considerably more territory on France's eastern border, so as to stand as the "sentinel on the Rhine" against France. In these ways the Quadruple Alliance combined leniency toward France with strong defensive measures. They held out a carrot with one hand and picked up a bigger stick with the other.

In their moderation toward France the allies were motivated by self-interest and traditional ideas about the balance of power. To Metternich and Castlereagh, the foreign ministers of Austria and Great Britain, as well as their French counterpart Talleyrand, the balance of power meant an international equilibrium of political and military forces, which would preserve the freedom and independence of each of the Great Powers. Such a balance would discourage aggression by any combination of states or, worse, the domination of Europe by any single state. As they saw it, the task of the powers was thus twofold. They had to make sure that France would not dominate Europe again, and they also had to arrange international relations so that none of the victors would be tempted to strive for domination in its turn. Such a balance involved many considerations and all of Europe.

The balance of power was the mechanism used by the Great Powers—Austria, Britain, Prussia, Russia, and France—to settle their own dangerous disputes at the Congress of Vienna. There was general agreement among the victors that each of them should receive compensation in the form of territory for their successful struggle against the French. Great Britain had already won colonies and strategic outposts during the long wars, and these it retained. Metternich's Austria gave up territories in Belgium and southern Germany but expanded greatly elsewhere, taking the rich provinces of Venetia and Lombardy in northern Italy as well as its former Polish possessions and new lands on the eastern coast of the Adriatic (see Map 23.1). There was also agreement that Prussia and Russia should be compensated. But where, and to what extent? That was the ticklish question that almost led to renewed war in January 1815.

The vaguely progressive, impetuous Alexander I of Russia had already taken Finland and Bessarabia on his northern and southern borders. Yet he burned with ambition to restore the ancient kingdom of Poland, on which he expected to bestow the benefits of his rule. The Prussians were willing to go along and give up their Polish territories, provided they could swallow up the large and wealthy kingdom of Saxony, their German neighbor to the south.

These demands were too much for Castlereagh and Metternich, who feared an unbalancing of forces in central Europe. In an astonishing about-face, they turned for diplomatic support to the wily Talleyrand and the defeated France he represented. On January 3, 1815, Great Britain, Austria, and France signed a secret alliance directed against Russia and Prussia. As Castlereagh concluded somberly, it appeared that the "peace we have so dearly purchased will be of short duration."

The outcome, however, was compromise rather than war. When rumors of the alliance were intentionally leaked, the threat of war caused the rulers of Russia and Prussia to moderate their demands. They accepted Metternich's proposal: Russia established a small Polish kingdom, and Prussia received two-fifths rather than all of Saxony (see Map 23.1). This compromise was very much within the framework of balance-of-power ideology and eighteenth-century diplomacy: Great Powers became greater, but not too

The Congress of Vienna While the Great Powers hammered out a peace settlement, a host of delegates from all over Europe celebrated with endless balls, receptions, and romantic intrigues. Here the "dancing congress" enjoys a glittering evening-dress ball given by the Austrian emperor and empress. *(The Bettmann Archive)*

much greater. In addition, France had been able to intervene and tip the scales in favor of the side seeking to prevent undue expansion of Russia and Prussia. In so doing France regained its Great Power status and was no longer isolated, as Talleyrand gleefully reported to Louis XVIII.

Unfortunately for France, as the final touches were being put on the peace settlement at Vienna, Napoleon suddenly reappeared on the scene. Escaping from his "comic kingdom" on the island of Elba in February 1815 and rallying his supporters for one last campaign during the Hundred Days, Napoleon was defeated at Waterloo and exiled to St. Helena. Yet the resulting peace—the second Peace of Paris—was still relatively moderate toward France. Fat old Louis XVIII was restored to his throne for a second time. France lost some territory, had to pay an indemnity of 700 million francs, and had to support a large army of occupation for five years.

The rest of the settlement already concluded at the Congress of Vienna was left intact. The members of the Quadruple Alliance did, however, agree to meet periodically to discuss their common interests and to consider appropriate measures for the maintenance of peace in Europe. This agreement marked the beginning of the European "congress system," which lasted long into the nineteenth century and settled international crises through diplomatic conferences.

Intervention and Repression

There was also a domestic political side to the re-establishment of peace. Within their own countries, the leaders of the victorious states were much less flexible. In 1815, under Metternich's leadership, Austria, Prussia, and Russia embarked on a crusade against the ideas and politics of the dual revolution. The crusade lasted until 1848.

The first step was the Holy Alliance, formed by Austria, Prussia, and Russia in September 1815. First proposed by Russia's Alexander I, the alliance proclaimed the intention of the three eastern monarchs to rule exclusively on the basis of Christian principles and to work together to maintain peace and justice on all occasions. Castlereagh refused to sign, characterizing the vague statement of principle as "a piece of sublime mysticism and nonsense." Yet it soon became a symbol of the repression of liberal and revolutionary movements all over Europe.

In 1820 revolutionaries succeeded in forcing the monarchs of Spain and the southern Italian kingdom of the Two Sicilies to grant liberal constitutions against their wills. Metternich was horrified: revolution was rising once again. Calling a conference at Troppau in Austria, under the provisions of the Quadruple Alliance, he and Alexander I proclaimed the principle of active intervention to maintain all autocratic regimes whenever they were threatened. Austrian forces then marched into Naples and restored Ferdinand I to the throne of the Two Sicilies. The French armies of Louis XVIII likewise restored the Spanish regime—after the Congress of Troppau had rejected Alexander's offer to send his Cossacks across Europe to teach the Spanish an unforgettable lesson.

Great Britain remained aloof, arguing that intervention in the domestic politics of foreign states was not an object of British diplomacy. In particular, Great Britain opposed any attempts by the restored Spanish monarchy to reconquer its former Latin American possessions, which had gained their independence during and after the Napoleonic wars. Encouraged by the British position, the young United States proclaimed its celebrated Monroe Doctrine in 1823. This bold document declared that European powers were to keep their hands off the New World and in no way attempt to re-establish their political system there. In the United States, constitutional liberalism, an ongoing challenge to the conservatism of continental Europe, retained its cutting edge.

In the years following the crushing of liberal revolution in southern Italy in 1821 and in Spain in 1823, Metternich continued to battle against liberal political change. Sometimes he could do little, as in the case of the new Latin American republics. Nor could he undo the dynastic changes of 1830 in western Europe. Nonetheless, until 1848 Metternich's system proved quite effective in central Europe, where his power was greatest.

Metternich's policies dominated not only Austria and the Italian peninsula but the entire German Confederation, which the peace settlement of Vienna had called into being. The confederation was composed of thirty-eight independent German states, including Prussia and Austria. (The Hungarian half of the Austrian Empire was not a member.) These states met in complicated assemblies dominated by Austria, with Prussia a willing junior partner in the planning and execution of repressive measures.

It was through the German Confederation that Metternich had the infamous Carlsbad Decrees issued in 1819. The decrees required the thirty-eight German member states to root out subversive ideas in their universities and newspapers. They also established a permanent committee with spies and informers to investigate and punish any liberal or radical organizations. Metternich's ruthless imposition of repressive internal policies on the governments of central Europe contrasted with the intelligent moderation he had displayed in the general peace settlement of 1815.

Metternich and Conservatism

Metternich's determined defense of the status quo made him a villain in the eyes of most progressive, optimistic historians of the nineteenth century. Yet rather than denounce the man, it is more useful to try to understand him and the general conservatism he represented.

Born into the middle ranks of the landed nobility of the Rhineland, Prince Klemens von Metternich (1773–1859) was an internationally oriented aristocrat. In 1795 his splendid marriage to Eleonora von Kaunitz, granddaughter of Austria's famous statesman and heiress to vast estates, opened the door to the highest court circles and a brilliant diplomatic career. Austrian ambassador to Napoleon's court in 1806 and Austrian foreign minister from 1809 to

1848, the cosmopolitan Metternich always remained loyal to his class and jealously defended its rights and privileges to the day he died. Like most other conservatives of his time, he did so with a clear conscience. The nobility was one of Europe's most ancient institutions, and conservatives regarded tradition as the basic source of human institutions. In their view, the proper state and society remained that of pre-1789 Europe, which rested on a judicious blend of monarchy, bureaucracy, and aristocracy.

Metternich's commitment to conservatism was coupled with a passionate hatred of liberalism. He firmly believed that liberalism, as embodied in revolutionary America and France, had been responsible for a generation of war with untold bloodshed and suffering. Liberal demands for representative government and civil liberties had unfortunately captured the imaginations of some middle-class lawyers, businessmen, and intellectuals. Metternich thought that these groups had been and still were engaged in a vast conspiracy to impose their beliefs on society and destroy the existing order. Like many conservatives then and since, Metternich blamed liberal revolutionaries for stirring up the lower classes, whom he believed to be indifferent or hostile to liberal ideas, desiring nothing more than peace and quiet.

The threat of liberalism appeared doubly dangerous to Metternich because it generally went with national aspirations. Liberals, especially liberals in central Europe, believed that each people, each national group, had a right to establish its own independent government and seek to fulfill its own destiny. The idea of national self-determination was repellent to Metternich. It not only threatened the existence of the aristocracy, it also threatened to destroy the Austrian Empire and revolutionize central Europe.

Metternich This portrait by Sir Thomas Lawrence reveals much of Metternich the man. Handsome, refined, and intelligent, Metternich was a great aristocrat passionately devoted to the defense of his class and its interests. *(The Bettmann Archive)*

The vast Austrian Empire of the Habsburgs was a great dynastic state. Formed over centuries by war, marriage, and luck, it was made up of many peoples speaking many languages (see Map 23.2). The Germans, long the dominant element, had supported and profited by the long-term territorial expansion of Austria; yet they accounted for only a quarter of the population. The Magyars (Hungarians), a substantially smaller group, dominated the kingdom of Hungary—which was part of the Austrian Empire—though they did not account for a majority of the population even there.

The Czechs, the third major group, were concentrated in Bohemia and Moravia. There were also large numbers of Italians, Poles, and Ukrainians, as well as smaller groups of Slovenes, Croats, Serbs, Ruthenians, and Rumanians. The various Slavic peoples, together with the Italians and the Rumanians, represented a widely scattered and completely divided majority in an empire dominated by Germans and Hungarians. Different ethnic groups often lived in the same provinces and even the same villages. Thus the different parts and provinces of the empire differed in languages, customs, and institutions. They were held together primarily by their ties to the Habsburg emperor.

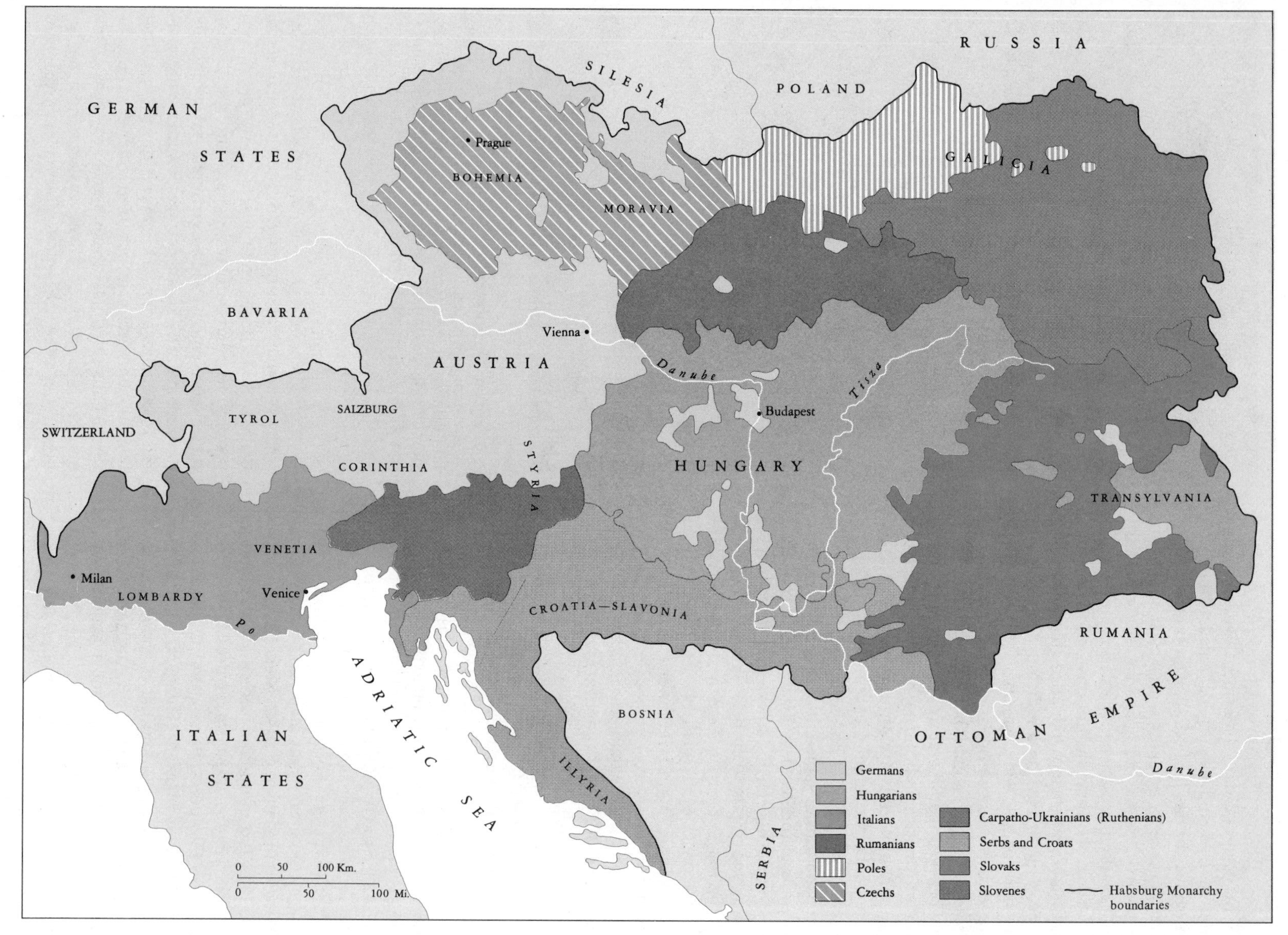

RUSSIA
GERMAN STATES
SILESIA
POLAND
Prague
BOHEMIA
MORAVIA
GALICIA
BAVARIA
Vienna
AUSTRIA
Danube
Budapest
Tisza
TYROL
SALZBURG
SWITZERLAND
STYRIA
HUNGARY
CORINTHIA
TRANSYLVANIA
VENETIA
Milan
LOMBARDY
Venice
Po
CROATIA–SLAVONIA
RUMANIA
ADRIATIC SEA
BOSNIA
ITALIAN STATES
OTTOMAN EMPIRE
ILLYRIA
Danube
SERBIA
Germans
Hungarians
Italians
Rumanians
Poles
Czechs
Carpatho-Ukrainians (Ruthenians)
Serbs and Croats
Slovaks
Slovenes
Habsburg Monarchy boundaries
0 50 100 Km.
0 50 100 Mi.

MAP 23.2 Peoples of the Habsburg Monarchy, 1815 The old dynastic state was a patchwork of nationalities. Note the widely scattered pockets of Germans and Hungarians.

The multinational state Metternich served was both strong and weak. It was strong because of its large population and vast territories; it was weak because of its many and potentially dissatisfied nationalities. In these circumstances, Metternich virtually had to oppose liberalism and nationalism, for Austria was simply unable to accommodate those ideologies of the dual revolution. Other conservatives supported Austria because they could imagine no better fate for the jumble of small nationalities wedged precariously between masses of Germans and hordes of Russians in east central Europe. Castlereagh even went so far as to say that Austria was the "great hinge upon which the fate of Europe must ultimately depend." Metternich's repressive conservatism may not hold appeal for many people today, but it had understandable roots in the dilemma of a multinational state in an age of rising nationalism.

RADICAL IDEAS AND EARLY SOCIALISM

The years following the peace settlement of 1815 were years of profound intellectual activity. Intellectuals and social observers were seeking to understand the revolutionary changes that had occurred and were still taking place. These efforts led to ideas that still motivate the world.

Almost all of these basic ideas were radical. In one way or another they opposed the old, deeply felt conservatism that Metternich exemplified so well. The revived conservatism, with its stress on tradition, a hereditary monarchy, a strong and privileged landowning aristocracy, and an official church, was rejected by radicals. Instead, radicals developed and refined alternative visions—alternative ideologies—and tried to convince society to act on them. With time, they were very successful.

LIBERALISM

The ideas of liberalism—liberty and equality—were by no means defeated in 1815. First realized successfully in the American Revolution and then achieved in part in the French Revolution, this political and social philosophy continued to pose a radical challenge to revived conservatism. Liberalism demanded representative government as opposed to autocratic monarchy, equality before the law as opposed to legally separate classes. Liberty also continued to mean specific individual freedoms: freedom of the press, freedom of speech, freedom of assembly, and freedom from arbitrary arrest. In Europe, only France with Louis XVIII's Constitutional Charter and Great Britain with its Parliament and historic rights of English men and women had realized much but by no means all of the liberal program in 1815. Elsewhere, liberal demands were still a call for revolutionary change.

Yet although "classical" liberalism still had its cutting edge, it was not as sharp a tool as it had been. This was especially true of liberal economic principles, which called for unrestricted private enterprise and no government interference in the economy. This philosophy was popularly known as the doctrine of *laissez faire.*

The idea of a free economy had first been persuasively formulated by a Scottish professor of philosophy, Adam Smith (1723–1790). Smith, whose *Inquiry into the Nature and Causes of the Wealth of Nations* (1776) founded modern economics, was highly critical of eighteenth-century mercantilism. Mercantilism, he said, meant stifling government regulations as well as unjust privileges for private monopolies and government favorites. Far preferable was free competition, which would give all citizens a fair and equal opportunity to do what they did best. Smith argued effectively that freely competitive private enterprise would result in greater income for everyone, not just the rich.

Unlike some of his contemporaries, Smith applauded the modest rise in real wages of British workers in the eighteenth century and went so far as to say, "No society can surely be flourishing and happy, of which the far greater part of the members are poor and miserable." Smith also believed that greater competition meant higher wages for workers, since manufacturers and "masters are always and everywhere in a sort of tacit, but constant and uniform, combination, not to raise the wages of laborers above their actual rate." In short, Adam Smith was a spokesman for general economic development, not narrow business interests.

In the early nineteenth century, the British economy was progressively liberalized, as old restrictions on trade and industry were relaxed or eliminated. This liberalization promoted continued rapid economic growth in the Industrial Revolution. At the same time, however, economic liberalism and laissez-faire economic thought were tending to become a doctrine serving business interests. Businessmen used the doctrine to defend their right to do exactly as they wished in their factories. Labor unions were outlawed because they supposedly restricted free competition and the individual's "right to work."

The teachings of a kindly parson, Thomas Malthus (1776–1834), helped make economic liberalism an ideology of business interests in many people's minds. In his "Essay on the Principle of Population" (1798), Malthus argued that population would always tend to grow faster than the supply of food. In Malthus's opinion, the only hope of warding off such "positive checks" to population growth as war, famine, and disease was "prudential restraint." That is , young men and women had to limit the growth of population by the old tried-and-true means of marrying late in life. But Malthus was not optimistic about this possibility. The powerful attraction of the sexes would cause most people to marry early and have many children.

The wealthy English stockbroker and economist David Ricardo (1772–1823) was even less optimistic. His depressing "iron law of wages" posited that, because of the pressure of population growth, wages would always sink to the subsistence level. That is, wages would be just high enough to keep the workers from starving. Malthus and Ricardo thought of themselves as objective social scientists. Yet their teachings were often used by industrial and middle-class interests in England, the Continent, and the United States to justify opposing any kind of government intervention to protect or improve the lot of workers: if workers were poor, it was their own fault, the result of their breeding like rabbits.

In the early nineteenth century, liberal political ideals also became more closely associated with narrow class interests. Early nineteenth-century liberals favored representative government, but they generally wanted property qualifications attached to the right to vote. In practice, this meant limiting the vote to well-to-do aristocratic landowners, substantial businessmen, and successful members of the professions. Workers and peasants as well as the lower middle class of shopkeepers, clerks, and artisans did not own the necessary property and thus could not vote.

As liberalism became increasingly middle class after 1815, some intellectuals and foes of conservatism felt that it did not go nearly far enough. Inspired by memories of the French Revolution and the contemporary example of exuberant Jacksonian democracy in the young American republic, they called for universal voting rights, at least for males. Giving all men the vote, they felt, would allow the masses to join in government and would lead to democracy.

Many people who believed in democracy also believed in the republican form of government. They detested the power of the monarchy, the privileges of the aristocracy, and the great wealth of the upper middle class. These democrats and republicans were more radical than the liberals. Taking for granted much of the liberal program, they sought to go beyond it. Democrats and republicans were also more willing than most liberals to endorse violent upheaval to achieve goals. All of which meant that liberals and radical, democratic republicans could join forces against conservatives only up to a point.

Nationalism

Nationalism was a second radical idea in the years after 1815, an idea destined to have an enormous influence in the modern world. In a summation of this complex ideology, three points stand out. First, nationalism has normally evolved from a real or imagined *cultural* unity, manifesting itself especially in a common language, history, and territory. Second, nationalists have usually sought to turn this cultural unity into *political* reality, so that the territory of each people coincides with its state boundaries. It was this goal that made nationalism so potentially explosive in central and eastern Europe after 1815, when there were either too few states (Austria, Russia, and the Ottoman Empire) or too many (the Italian peninsula and the German Confederation) and when different peoples overlapped and intermingled. Third, modern nationalism had its immediate origins in the French Revolution and the Napoleonic wars. Nationalism was effectively harnessed by the French republic during the Reign of Terror to help repel foreign foes, and all across Europe patriots tried to kindle nationalist flames in the war against Napoleon. Thus by 1815 there were already hints of nationalism's remarkable ability to spread and develop.

Between 1815 and 1850, most people who believed in nationalism also believed in either liberalism or radical, democratic republicanism. In more recent times, however, many governments have been very nationalistic without favoring liberty and democracy. Why, then, was love of liberty almost synonymous with love of nation in the early nineteenth century?

A common faith in the creativity and nobility of the people was perhaps the single most important reason for people's linking these two concepts. Liberals and especially democrats saw the people as the ultimate source of all government. The people (or some of them) elected their officials and governed themselves within a framework of personal liberty. Yet such self-government would be possible only if the people were united by common traditions and common loyalties. In practice, common loyalties rested above all on a common language. Thus liberals and nationalists agreed that a shared language forged the basic unity of a people, a unity that transcended local or provincial interests and even class differences.

Early nationalists usually believed that every nation, like every citizen, has the right to exist in freedom and to develop its character and spirit. They were confident that the independence and freedom of other nations, as in the case of other citizens within a nation, would not lessen the freedom of their own country. Rather, the symphony of nations would promote the harmony and ultimate unity of all peoples. As the French historian Jules Michelet put it in *The People* in 1846, each citizen "learns to recognize his country . . . as a note in the grand concert; through it he himself participates and loves the world." Similarly, the Italian patriot Giuseppe Mazzini believed that "in laboring according to the true principles of our country we are laboring for Humanity." Thus the liberty of the individual and the love of a free nation overlapped greatly in the early nineteenth century.

Nationalism also had a negative side. Even as they talked of serving the cause of humanity, early nationalists stressed the differences between peoples. The German pastor and philosopher Johann Herder (1744–1803) had argued that every people has its own particular spirit and genius, which it expresses through its culture and language. Yet Herder (and others after him) could not define the uniqueness of the French, German, and Slavic peoples without comparing and contrasting one people with another. Thus, even early nationalism developed a strong sense of "we" and "they."

"They" were often the enemy. The leader of the Czech cultural revival, the passionate democrat and nationalist historian Francis Palacký, is a good example of this tendency. In his histories he lauded the achievements of the Czech people, which he characterized as a long struggle against brutal German domination. To this "we—they" outlook, it was all too easy for nationalists to add two other highly volatile ingredients: a sense of national mission and a sense of national superiority. As Mazzini characteristically wrote, "Peoples never stop before they have achieved the ultimate aim of their existence, before having fulfilled their mission." Even Michelet, so alive to the aspirations of other peoples, could not help speaking in 1846 of the "superiority of France"; the principles espoused in the French Revolution had made France the "salvation of mankind."

German and Spanish nationalists had a very different opinion of France. To them the French often seemed as oppressive as the Germans seemed to the Czechs, as hateful as the Russians seemed to the Poles. The despised enemy's mission might seem as oppressive as the American national mission—as the American journalist and strident nationalist John Louis O'Sullivan sketched it in 1845 after the annexation of Texas—seemed to the Mexicans. O'Sullivan wrote that taking land from an "imbecile and distracted Mexico" was a laudable step in the "fulfillment of our manifest destiny to overspread the continent allotted by Providence for the free development of our yearly multiplying millions."[2]

Early nationalism was thus ambiguous. Its main thrust was liberal and democratic. But below the surface lurked ideas of national superiority and national mission, which could lead to aggressive crusades and counter-crusades, as had happened in the French Revolution and in the "wars of liberation" against Napoleon.

Fourier's Utopia The vision of a harmonious planned community freed from capitalism and selfish individualism radiates from this 1847 illustration of Fourier's principles. *(Mary Evans Picture Library)*

French Utopian Socialism

To understand the rise of socialism, one must begin with France. Despite the fact that France lagged far behind Great Britain in developing modern industry, almost all the early socialists were French. Although they differed on many specific points, these French thinkers were acutely aware that the political revolution in France and the rise of modern industry in England had begun a transformation of society. Yet they were disturbed by what they saw. Liberal practices in politics and economics appeared to be fomenting selfish individualism and splitting the community into isolated fragments. There was, they believed, an urgent need for a further reorganization of society to establish cooperation and a new sense of community. Starting from this shared outlook, individual French thinkers went in many different directions. They searched the past, analyzed existing conditions, and fashioned luxurious utopias. Yet certain ideas tied their critiques and visions together.

Early French socialists believed in economic planning. Inspired by the emergency measures of 1793 and 1794 in France, they argued that the government should rationally organize the economy and not depend on destructive competition to do the job. Early socialists also shared an intense desire to help the poor and to protect them from the rich. With passionate moral fervor they preached that the rich and the poor should be more nearly equal economically. Finally, socialists believed that most private property should be abolished and replaced by state or community ownership. Planning, greater economic equality, and state ownership of property: these were the key ideas of early French socialism and of all socialism since.

One of the most influential of these thinkers was a nobleman, Count Henri de Saint-Simon (1760–1825). A curious combination of radical thinker and successful land speculator, Saint-Simon optimistically proclaimed the tremendous possibilities of industrial development: "The age of gold is before us!" The key to progress was proper social organization. Such an arrangement of society required the "parasites"—the court, the aristocracy, lawyers, churchmen—to give way, once and for all, to the "doers"—the leading scientists, engineers, and industrialists. The doers would carefully plan the economy and guide it forward by undertaking vast public works projects and investment banks. Saint-Simon also stressed in highly moralistic terms that every social institution ought to have as its main goal improved conditions for the poor. Saint-Simon's stress on industry and science inspired middle-class industrialists and bankers, like the Pereire brothers, founders of the Crédit Mobilier (Chapter 22).

After 1830, the socialist critique of capitalism became sharper. Charles Fourier (1772–1837), a lonely, saintly man with a tenuous hold on reality, described a socialist utopia in lavish mathematical detail. Hating the urban wage system, Fourier envisaged self-sufficient communities of 1,620 people living communally on five thousand acres devoted to a combination of agriculture and industry. Fourier was also an early proponent of the total emancipation of women, abolition of marriage, and complete sexual freedom. Although Fourier waited in vain each day at noon in his apartment for a wealthy philanthropist to endow his visionary schemes, he was very influential. Several utopian communities were founded along the lines he prescribed, mainly in the United States.

Louis Blanc (1811–1882), a sharp-eyed, intelligent journalist, was much more practical. In his *Organization of Work* (1839), he urged workers to agitate for universal voting rights and to take control of the state peacefully. Blanc believed that the full power of the state should be directed at setting up government-backed workshops and factories to guarantee full employment. The right to work had to become as sacred as any other right. Finally, there was Pierre Joseph Proudhon (1809–1865), a self-educated printer, who wrote a pamphlet in 1840 entitled *What Is Property?* His answer was that it was nothing but theft. Property was profit that was stolen from the worker, who was the source of all wealth. Unlike most socialists, Proudhon feared the power of the state and thus was often considered an anarchist.

Thus a variety of French thinkers blazed the way with utopian socialism in the 1830s and 1840s. Their ideas were very influential, particularly in Paris, where poverty-stricken workers with a revolutionary tradition were attentive students. Yet the economic arguments of the French utopians were weak, and their specific programs usually seemed too fanciful to be taken seriously. To Karl Marx was left the task of establishing firm foundations for modern socialism.

The Birth of Marxian Socialism

In 1848 the thirty-year-old Karl Marx (1818–1883) and the twenty-eight-year-old Friedrich Engels (1820–1895) published the *Communist Manifesto,* the Bible of socialism. The son of a Jewish lawyer who had converted to Christianity, the atheistic young Marx had studied philosophy at the University of Berlin before turning to journalism and economics. He read widely in French socialist thought and was developing his own socialist ideas by the time he was twenty-five.

Early French socialists often appealed to the middle class and the state to help the poor. Marx argued that the interests of the middle class and those of the industrial working class are inevitably opposed to each other. Indeed, according to the *Manifesto,* the "history of all previously existing society is the history of class struggles." In Marx's view, one class had always exploited the other, and with the advent of modern industry, society was split more clearly than ever before: between the middle class—the bourgeoisie—and the modern working class—the proletariat. Moreover, the bourgeoisie had reduced everything to a matter of money and "naked self-interest." "In a

The Marx Family In 1849 the exiled Marx settled in London. There he wrote *Capital,* the weighty exposition of his socialist theories, and worked to organize the working class. With his coauthor and financial supporter Friedrich Engels (left), Marx is shown here with his daughters, ironically a picture of middle-class respectability. *(Culver Pictures)*

word, for exploitation, veiled by religious and political illusions, the bourgeoisie had substituted naked, shameless, direct brutal exploitation."

Just as the bourgeoisie had triumphed over the feudal aristocracy, Marx predicted, the proletariat was destined to conquer the bourgeoisie in a violent revolution. While a tiny minority owned the means of production and grew richer, the ever-poorer proletariat was constantly growing in size and in class consciousness. In this process, the proletariat was aided, according to Marx, by a portion of the bourgeoisie who had gone over to the proletariat and who (like Marx and Engels) "had raised themselves to the level of comprehending theoretically the historical moment." And the critical moment was very near. "Let the ruling classes tremble at a Communist revolution. The proletarians have nothing to lose but their chains. They have a world to win. WORKING MEN OF ALL COUNTRIES, UNITE!" So ends the *Communist Manifesto.*

In brief outline, Marx's ideas may seem to differ only slightly from the wild and improbable ideas of the utopians of his day. Yet whatever one may think of the validity of Marx's analysis, he must be taken seriously. He united sociology, economics, and all human history in a vast and imposing edifice. He synthesized in his socialism not only French utopian schemes but English classical economics and German philosophy—the major intellectual currents of his day. Moreover, after the young Marx fled to England as a penniless political refugee following the revolutions of 1848, he continued to show a rare flair for combining complex theorization with both lively popular writing and practical organizational ability. This combination of theoretical and practical skills contributed greatly to the subsequent diffusion of Marx's socialist synthesis after 1860, as will be shown in Chapter 25.

Marx's debt to England was great. He was the last of the classical economists. Following David Ricardo, who had taught that labor was the source of all value, Marx went on to argue that profits were really wages stolen from the workers. Moreover, Marx incorporated Engels's charges of terrible oppression of the new class of factory workers in England; thus his doctrines seemed to be based on hard facts.

Marx's theory of historical evolution was built on the philosophy of the German Georg Hegel (1770–1831). Hegel believed that history is "ideas in motion": each age is characterized by a dominant set of ideas, which produces opposing ideas and eventually a new synthesis. The idea of being had been dominant initially, for example, and it had produced its antithesis, the idea of nonbeing. This idea in turn had resulted in the synthesis of becoming. History has, therefore, pattern and purpose.

Marx retained Hegel's view of history as a dialectic process of change but made economic relationships between classes the driving force. This dialectic explained the decline of agrarian feudalism and the rise of industrial capitalism. And Marx stressed again and again that the "bourgeoisie, historically, has played a most revolutionary part. . . . During its rule of scarcely one hundred years the bourgeoisie has created more massive and more colossal productive forces than have all preceding generations together." Here was a convincing explanation for people trying to make sense of the dual revolution. Marx's next idea, that it was now the bourgeoisie's turn to give way to the socialism of revolutionary workers, appeared to many the irrefutable capstone of a brilliant interpretation of humanity's long development. Thus Marx pulled together powerful ideas and insights to create one of the great secular religions out of the intellectual ferment of the early nineteenth century.

THE ROMANTIC MOVEMENT

Developing radical concepts of politics and society were accompanied by comparable changes in literature and other arts during the dual revolution. The early nineteenth century marked the acme of the romantic movement, which profoundly influenced the arts and enriched European culture immeasurably.

The romantic movement was in part a revolt against classicism and the Enlightenment. Classicism was essentially a set of artistic rules and standards that went hand in glove with the Enlightenment's belief in rationality, order, and restraint. The classicists believed that the ancient Greeks and Romans had discovered eternally valid aesthetic rules long ago and that playwrights and painters should continue to follow them. Classicists could enforce these rules in the eighteenth century because they dominated the courts and academies for which artists worked.

Forerunners of the romantic movement appeared from about 1750 on. Of these, Rousseau (pages 590–591)—the passionate advocate of feeling, freedom, and natural goodness—was the most influential. Romanticism then crystallized fully in the 1790s, primarily in England and Germany. The French Revolution kindled the belief that radical reconstruction was also possible in cultural and artistic life (even though many early English and German romantics became disillusioned with events in France and turned from liberalism to conservatism in politics). Romanticism gained strength until the 1840s, when realism began to challenge it seriously.

ROMANTICISM

Romanticism was characterized by a belief in emotional exuberance, unrestrained imagination, and spontaneity in both art and personal life. In Germany early romantics of the 1770s and 1780s called themselves the "Storm and Stress" (*Sturm und Drang*) group, and many romantic artists of the early nineteenth century lived lives of tremendous emotional intensity. Suicide, duels to the death, madness, and strange illnesses were not uncommon among leading romantics. Romantic artists typically led bohemian lives, wearing their hair long and uncombed in preference to powdered wigs and living in cold garrets rather than frequenting stiff drawing rooms. They rejected materialism and sought to escape to lofty spiritual heights through their art. Great individualists, the romantics believed the full development of one's unique human potential to be the supreme purpose in life. The romantics were driven by a sense of an unlimited universe and by a yearning for the unattained, the unknown, the unknowable.

Nowhere was the break with classicism more apparent than in romanticism's general conception of nature. Classicism was not particularly interested in nature. In the words of the eighteenth-century English author Samuel Johnson, "A blade of grass is always a blade of grass; men and women are my subjects of inquiry." Nature was portrayed by classicists as beautiful and chaste, like an eighteenth-century formal garden. The romantics, on the other hand, were enchanted by nature. Sometimes they found it awesome and tempestuous, as in Théodore Géricault's painting *The Raft of the Medusa,* which shows the survivors of a shipwreck adrift in a turbulent sea. Others saw nature as a source of spiritual inspiration. As the great English landscape artist John Constable (1776–1837) declared, "Nature is Spirit visible."

Most romantics saw the growth of modern industry as an ugly, brutal attack on their beloved nature and on the human personality. They sought escape—in the unspoiled Lake District of northern England, in exotic North Africa, in an idealized Middle Ages. Yet some romantics found a vast, awesome, terribly moving power in the new industrial landscape. In ironworks and cotton mills they saw the flames of Hell and the evil genius of Satan himself. One of John Martin's last and greatest paintings, *The Great Day of His Wrath* (1850), vividly depicts the last judgment foretold in Revelation VI, "when the

Delacroix: Liberty Leading the People This great romantic painting glorifies the July Revolution in Paris in 1830. Raising high the revolutionary tricolor, Liberty unites the worker, bourgeois, and street child in a righteous crusade against privilege and oppression. *(Louvre, Paris/Giraudon/Art Resource)*

sun became black as sackcloth of hair, and the moon became as blood; and the stars of heaven fell unto the earth." Martin's romantic masterpiece was inspired directly by a journey through the "Black country" of the industrial Midlands in the dead of night. According to Martin's son:

The glow of the furnaces, the red blaze of light, together with the liquid fire, seemed to him truly sublime and awful. He could not imagine anything more terrible even in the regions of everlasting punishment. All he had done or attempted in ideal painting fell far short, very far short, of the fearful sublimity.[3]

Fascinated by color and diversity, the romantic imagination turned toward the study and writing of history with a passion. For romantics, history was not a minor branch of philosophy from which philosophers picked suitable examples to illustrate their teachings. History was beautiful, exciting, and important in its own right. It was the art of change over time—the key to a universe that was now perceived to be organic and dynamic, no longer mechanical and static as it had appeared to the philosophes of the eighteenth-century Enlightenment.

Historical studies supported the development of national aspirations and encouraged entire peoples to seek in the past their special destinies. This trend was especially strong in Germany and eastern Europe. As the famous English historian Lord Acton put it, the growth of historical thinking associated with the romantic movement was a most fateful step in the story of European thought.

Literature

Britain was the first country where romanticism flowered fully in poetry and prose, and the British romantic writers were among the most prominent in Europe. Wordsworth, Coleridge, and Scott were all active by 1800, to be followed shortly by Byron, Shelley, and Keats. All were poets: romanticism found its distinctive voice in poetry, as the Enlightenment had in prose.

A towering leader of English romanticism, William Wordsworth (1770–1850) traveled in France after his graduation from Cambridge. There he fell passionately in love with a French woman, who bore him a daughter. He was deeply influenced by the philosophy of Rousseau and the spirit of the early French Revolution. Back in England, prevented by war and the Terror from returning to France, Wordsworth settled in the countryside with his sister Dorothy and Samuel Taylor Coleridge (1772–1834).

In 1798 the two poets published their *Lyrical Ballads,* one of the most influential literary works in the history of the English language. In defiance of classical rules, Wordsworth and Coleridge abandoned flowery poetic conventions for the language of ordinary speech, simultaneously endowing simple subjects with the loftiest majesty. This twofold rejection of classical practice was at first ignored and then harshly criticized, but by 1830 Wordsworth had triumphed.

One of the best examples of Wordsworth's romantic credo and genius is "Daffodils":

I wandered lonely as a cloud
That floats on high o'er vales and hills,
When all at once I saw a crowd,
A host, of golden daffodils;
Beside the lake, beneath the trees,
Fluttering and dancing in the breeze.

Continuous as the stars that shine
And twinkle on the Milky Way,
They stretched in never-ending line
Along the margin of a bay:
Ten thousand saw I at a glance,
Tossing their heads in sprightly dance.

The waves beside them danced, but they
Out-did the sparkling waves in glee:
A poet could not but be gay,
In such a jocund company:
I gazed—and gazed—but little thought
What wealth the show to me had brought:

For oft, when on my couch I lie
In vacant or in pensive mood,
They flash upon that inward eye
Which is the bliss of solitude;
And then my heart with pleasure fills,
And dances with the daffodils.

Here indeed is simplicity and love of nature in commonplace forms. Here, too, is Wordsworth's romantic conviction that nature has the power to elevate and instruct, especially when interpreted by a high-minded poetic genius. Wordsworth's conception of poetry as the "spontaneous overflow of powerful feeling recollected in tranquility" is well illustrated by the last stanza.

Born in Edinburgh, Walter Scott (1771–1832) personified the romantic movement's fascination with history. Raised on his grandfather's farm, Scott fell under the spell of the old ballads and tales of the Scottish border. He was also deeply influenced by German romanticism, particularly by the immortal poet and dramatist Johann Wolfgang von Goethe (1749–1832). Scott translated Goethe's famous *Götz von Berlichingen,* a play about a sixteenth-century knight who revolted against centralized authority and championed individual freedom—at least in Goethe's romantic drama. A natural storyteller, Scott then composed long narrative poems and a series of historical novels. Scott excelled in faithfully recreating the spirit of bygone ages and great historical events, especially those of Scotland.

At first, the strength of classicism in France inhibited the growth of romanticism there. Then, between 1820 and 1850, the romantic impulse broke through in the poetry and prose of Lamartine, Alfred de Vigny, Victor Hugo, Alexander Dumas, and George Sand. Of these, Victor Hugo (1802–1885) was the greatest in both poetry and prose.

Son of a Napoleonic general, Hugo achieved an amazing range of rhythm, language, and image in his lyric poetry. His powerful novels exemplified the romantic fascination with fantastic characters, strange settings, and human emotions. The hero of Hugo's famous *Hunchback of Notre Dame* (1831) is the great cathedral's deformed bellringer, a "human gargoyle" overlooking the teeming life of fifteenth-century Paris. A great admirer of Shakespeare, whom classical critics had derided as undisciplined and excessive, Hugo also championed romanticism in drama. His play *Hernani* (1830) consciously broke all the old rules, as Hugo renounced his early conservatism and equated freedom in literature with liberty in politics and society. Hugo's political evolution was thus exactly the opposite of Wordsworth's, in whom youthful radicalism gave way to middle-aged caution. As the contrast between the two artists suggests, romanticism was a cultural movement compatible with many political beliefs.

George Sand (1804–1876), a strong-willed and gifted woman, defied the narrow conventions of her time in an unending search for self-fulfillment. After eight years of unhappy marriage in the provinces, she abandoned her dullard of a husband and took her two children to Paris to pursue a career as a writer. There she soon achieved fame and wealth, eventually writing over eighty novels on a variety of romantic and social themes. All were shot through with a typically romantic love of nature and moral idealism. George Sand's striking individualism went far beyond her flamboyant preference for men's clothing and cigars and her notorious affairs with the poet Alfred Musset and the composer Frédéric Chopin, among others. Her semi-autobiographical novel *Lélia* was shockingly modern, delving deeply into her tortuous quest for sexual and personal freedom.

In central and eastern Europe, literary romanticism and early nationalism often reinforced each other. Seeking a unique greatness in every people, well-educated romantics plumbed their own histories and cultures. Like modern anthropologists, they turned their attention to peasant life and transcribed the folk songs, tales, and proverbs that the cosmopolitan Enlightenment had disdained. The brothers Jacob and Wilhelm Grimm were particularly successful at rescuing German fairy tales from oblivion. In the Slavic lands, romantics played a decisive role in converting spoken peasant languages into modern written languages. The greatest of all Russian poets, Alexander Pushkin (1799–1837), rejecting eighteenth-century attempts to force Russian poetry into a classical straitjacket, used his lyric genius to mold the modern literary language.

Art and Music

The greatest and most moving romantic painter in France was Eugène Delacroix (1798–1863), probably the illegitimate son of the French foreign minister Talleyrand. Delacroix was a master of dramatic, colorful scenes that stir the emotions. He was fascinated with remote and exotic subjects, whether lion hunts in Morocco or the languishing, sensuous women of a sultan's harem. Yet he was also a passionate spokesman for freedom. His masterpiece, *Liberty Leading the People,* celebrated the nobility of popular revolution in general and revolution in France in particular.

In England, the most outstanding romantic painters were J. M. W. Turner (1775–1851) and John Constable (1776–1837). Both were fascinated by nature, but their interpretations of it contrasted sharply, aptly symbolizing the tremendous emotional range of the romantic movement. Turner depicted nature's power and terror; wild storms and sinking ships were favorite subjects. Constable painted gentle Wordsworthian landscapes in which human beings are at one with their environment, the comforting countryside of unspoiled rural England (see Color Insert V).

It was in music that romanticism realized most fully and permanently its goals of free expression and emotional intensity. Whereas the composers of the eighteenth century had remained true to well-defined structures, like the classical symphony, the great romantics used a great range of forms to paint a thousand landscapes and evoke a host of powerful emotions. Romantic composers also transformed the small classical orchestra, tripling its size by adding wind instruments, percussion, and more brass and strings. The crashing chords evoking the surge of the masses in Chopin's "Revolutionary" etude, the bottomless despair of the funeral march in Beethoven's Third Symphony, the solemn majesty of a great relig-

Heroes of Romanticism Observed by a portrait of Byron and bust of Beethoven, Liszt plays for friends. From left to right sit Alexander Dumas, George Sand (characteristically wearing men's garb), and Marie d'Agoult, Liszt's mistress. Standing are Victor Hugo, Paganini, and Rossini. *(Bildarchiv Preussischer Kulturbesitz)*

ious event in Schumann's Rhenish Symphony—such were the modern orchestra's musical paintings that plumbed the depths of human feeling.

This range and intensity gave music and musicians much greater prestige than in the past. Music no longer simply complemented a church service or helped a nobleman digest his dinner. Music became a sublime end in itself. It became for many the greatest of the arts, precisely because it achieved the most ecstatic effect and most perfectly realized the endless yearning of the soul. It was worthy of great concert halls and the most dedicated sacrifice. The unbelievable one-in-a-million performer—the great virtuoso who could transport the listener to ecstasy and hysteria—became a cultural hero. The composer Franz Liszt (1811–1886) vowed to do for the piano what Paganini had done for the violin, and he was lionized as the greatest pianist of his age. People swooned for Liszt as they scream for rock stars today.

Though romanticism dominated music until late in the nineteenth century, no composer ever surpassed its first great master, Ludwig van Beethoven

(1770–1827). Extending and breaking open classical forms, Beethoven used contrasting themes and tones to produce dramatic conflict and inspiring resolutions. As the contemporary German novelist Ernst Hoffmann (1776–1822) wrote, "Beethoven's music sets in motion the lever of fear, of awe, of horror, of suffering, and awakens just that infinite longing which is the essence of Romanticism." Beethoven's range was tremendous; his output included symphonies, chamber music, sonatas for violin and piano, masses, an opera, and a great many songs.

At the peak of his fame, in constant demand as a composer and recognized as the leading concert pianist of his day, Beethoven began to lose his hearing. He considered suicide but eventually overcame despair: "I will take fate by the throat; it will not bend me completely to its will."[4] Beethoven continued to pour out immortal music. Among other achievements, he fully exploited for the first time the richness and beauty of the piano. Beethoven never heard much of his later work, including the unforgettable choral finale to the Ninth Symphony, for his last years were silent, spent in total deafness.

REFORMS AND REVOLUTIONS

While the romantic movement was developing, liberal, national, and socialist forces battered against the conservatism of 1815. In some countries, change occurred gradually and peacefully. Elsewhere, pressure built up like steam in a pressure cooker without a safety valve and eventually caused an explosion in 1848. Three important countries—Greece, Great Britain, and France—experienced variations on this basic theme.

National Liberation in Greece

National, liberal revolution, frustrated in Italy and Spain by conservative statesmen, succeeded first after 1815 in Greece. Since the fifteenth century, the Greeks had been living under the domination of the Ottoman Turks. In spite of centuries of foreign rule, the Greeks had survived as a people, united by their language and the Greek orthodox religion. It was perfectly natural that the general growth of national aspirations and a desire for independence would inspire some Greeks in the early nineteenth century. This rising national movement led to the formation of secret societies and then to revolt in 1821, led by Alexander Ypsilanti, a Greek patriot and a general in the Russian army.

The Great Powers, particularly Metternich, were opposed to all revolution, even revolution against the Islamic Turks. They refused to back Ypsilanti and supported the Ottoman Empire. Yet for many Europeans the Greek cause became a holy one. Educated Americans and Europeans were in love with the culture of classical Greece; Russians were stirred by the piety of their Orthodox brethren. Writers and artists, moved by the romantic impulse, responded enthusiastically to the Greek struggle. The flamboyant, radical poet Lord Byron went to Greece and died there in the struggle "that Greece might still be free." Turkish atrocities toward the rebels fanned the fires of European outrage and Greek determination. One of Delacroix's romantic masterpieces memorialized the massacre at Chios, where the Turks slaughtered nearly 100,000 Greeks.

The Greeks, though often quarreling among themselves, battled on against the Turks and hoped for the eventual support of European governments. In 1827 Great Britain, France, and Russia responded to popular demands at home and directed Turkey to accept an armistice. When the Turks refused, the navies of these three powers trapped the Turkish fleet at Navarino and destroyed it. Russia then declared another of its periodic wars of expansion against the Turks. This led to the establishment of a Russian protectorate over much of present-day Rumania, which had also been under Turkish rule. Great Britain, France, and Russia finally declared Greece independent in 1830 and installed a German prince as king of the new country in 1832. In the end the Greeks had won: a small nation had gained its independence in a heroic war against a foreign empire.

Liberal Reform in Great Britain

Eighteenth-century British society had been both flexible and remarkably stable. It was dominated by the landowning aristocracy, but that class was neither closed nor rigidly defined. Successful business and professional people could buy land and become gentlemen, while the common people had more than the usual opportunities of the preindustrial world. Basic civil rights for all were balanced by a tradition of def-

Delacroix: Massacre at Chios The Greek struggle for freedom and independence won the enthusiastic support of liberals, nationalists, and romantics. The Ottoman Turks were seen as cruel oppressors holding back the course of history, as in this powerful masterpiece by Delacroix. *(Louvre/Cliché des Musées Nationaux)*

erence to one's social superiors. Parliament was manipulated by the king and was thoroughly undemocratic. Only about 6 percent of the population could vote for representatives to Parliament, and by the 1780s there was growing interest in some kind of political reform.

But the French Revolution threw the aristocracy into a panic for a generation, making it extremely hostile to any attempts to change the status quo. The Tory party, completely controlled by the landed aristocracy, was particularly fearful of radical movements at home and abroad. Castlereagh initially worked closely with Metternich to restrain France and restore a conservative balance in central Europe. This same intense conservatism motivated the Tory government at home. After 1815, the aristocracy defended its ruling position by repressing every kind of popular protest.

The Prelude to 1848

March 1814	Russia, Prussia, Austria, and Britain form the Quadruple Alliance to defeat France
April 1814	Napoleon abdicates
May–June 1814	Restoration of the Bourbon monarchy; Louis XVIII issues Constitutional Charter providing for civil liberties and representative government
	First Peace of Paris: allies combine leniency with defensive posture toward France
October 1814–June 1815	Congress of Vienna peace settlement: establishes balance-of-power principle and creates the German Confederation
February 1815	Napoleon escapes from Elba and marches on Paris
June 1815	Battle of Waterloo
September 1815	Austria, Prussia, and Russia form the Holy Alliance to repress liberal and revolutionary movements
November 1815	Second Peace of Paris and renewal of Quadruple Alliance: punishes France and establishes the European "congress system"
1819	Carlsbad Decrees: Metternich imposes harsh measures throughout the German Confederation
1820	Revolution in Spain and the Kingdom of the Two Sicilies
	Congress of Troppau: Metternich and Alexander I of Russia proclaim principle of intervention to maintain autocratic regimes
1821	Austria crushes liberal revolution in Naples and restores the Sicilian autocracy
	Greek revolt against the Ottoman Turks
1823	French armies restore the Spanish regime
	United States proclaims the Monroe Doctrine
1824	Reactionary Charles X succeeds Louis XVIII in France
1830	Charles X repudiates the Constitutional Charter; insurrection and collapse of government; Louis Philippe succeeds to the throne and maintains a narrowly liberal regime until 1848
	Greece wins independence from the Ottoman Empire
1832	Reform Bill expands British electorate and encourages the middle class
1839	Louis Blanc, *Organization of Work*
1840	Pierre Joseph Proudhon, *What Is Property?*
1846	Jules Michelet, *The People*
1848	Karl Marx and Friedrich Engels, *The Communist Manifesto*

The first step in this direction was the Corn Law of 1815. During a generation of war with France, the British had been unable to import food. As shortages occurred and agricultural prices skyrocketed, a great deal of marginal land had been brought under cultivation. This development had been a bonanza for the landed aristocracy, whose fat rent rolls became even fatter. Peace meant that grain could be imported again and that the price of wheat and bread would go down. To almost everyone except the aristocracy, lower prices seemed highly desirable. The aristocracy, however, rammed the Corn Law through Parliament. This law prohibited the importation of foreign grain unless the price at home rose above eighty shillings per quarter-ton—a level reached only in time of harvest disaster before 1790. Seldom has a class legislated more selfishly for its own narrow economic advantage.

The Corn Law, coming at a time of widespread unemployment and postwar adjustment, led to protests and demonstrations by urban laborers. They were supported by radical intellectuals, who campaigned for a reformed House of Commons that would serve the nation and not just the aristocracy. In 1817 the Tory government responded by temporarily suspending the traditional rights of peaceable assembly and habeas corpus. Two years later, Parliament passed the infamous Six Acts, which among other things controlled a heavily taxed press and practically eliminated all mass meetings. These acts followed an enormous but orderly protest at Saint Peter's Fields in Manchester, which had been savagely broken up by armed cavalry. Nicknamed the "Battle of Peterloo," in scornful reference to the British victory at Waterloo, this incident expressed the government's determination to repress and stand fast.

Ongoing industrial development was not only creating urban and social problems but also strengthening the upper-middle classes. The new manufacturing and commercial groups insisted on a place for their new wealth alongside the landed wealth of the aristocracy in the framework of political power and social prestige. They called for certain kinds of liberal reform: reform of town government, organization of a new police force, and more rights for Catholics and dissenters. In the 1820s, a less frightened Tory government moved in the direction of better urban administration, greater economic liberalism, and civil equality for Catholics. The prohibition on imports of foreign grain was replaced by a heavy tariff. These actions encouraged the middle classes to press on for reform of Parliament, so they could have a larger say in government and perhaps repeal the revised Corn Law, that symbol of aristocratic domination.

The Whig party, though led like the Tories by great aristocrats, had by tradition been more responsive to commercial and manufacturing interests. In 1830 a Whig ministry introduced "an act to amend the representation of the people of England and Wales." Defeated, then passed by the House of Commons, this reform bill was rejected by the House of Lords. But when in 1832 the Whigs got the king to promise to create enough new peers to pass the law, the House of Lords reluctantly gave in rather than see its snug little club ruined by upstart manufacturers and plutocrats. A mighty surge of popular protest had helped the king and lords make up their minds.

Free-Trade Optimism Appearing in *Punch* in 1846 as the Corn Law was being repealed, this cartoon looked to the future and reflected British self-confidence. Socially and economically advanced Great Britain had no need for protective tariffs. The British economy actually did boom after 1850. *(The British Library)*

The Reform Bill of 1832 had profound significance. The House of Commons had emerged as the all-important legislative body. In the future, an obstructionist House of Lords could always be brought into line by the threat of creating new peers. The new industrial areas of the country gained representation in the Commons, and many old "rotten boroughs"—electoral districts with very few voters that the landed aristocracy had bought and sold—were eliminated.

The redistribution of seats reflected the shift in population to the northern manufacturing counties and the gradual emergence of an urban society. As a result of the Reform Bill of 1832, the number of voters increased about 50 percent. Comfortable middle-class groups in the urban population, as well as some substantial farmers who leased their land, received the vote. Thus the pressures building in Great Britain were successfully—though only temporarily—released. A major reform had been achieved peacefully, without revolution or civil war. More radical reforms within the system appeared difficult but not impossible.

The principal radical program was embodied in the "People's Charter" of 1838 and the Chartist movement (page 720). Partly inspired by the economic distress of the working class, the Chartists' core demand was universal male (not female) suffrage. They saw complete political democracy and rule by the common people as the means to a good and just society. Hundreds of thousands of people signed gigantic petitions calling on Parliament to grant all men the right to vote, first and most seriously in 1839, again in 1842, and yet again in 1848. Parliament rejected all three petitions. In the short run, the working poor failed with their Chartist demands, but they learned a valuable lesson in mass politics.

While calling for universal suffrage, many working-class people joined with middle-class manufacturers in the Anti-Corn Law League, founded in Manchester in 1839. Mass participation made possible a popular crusade against the tariff on imported grain and against the landed aristocracy. People were fired up by dramatic popular orators such as John Bright and Richard Cobden. These fighting liberals argued that lower food prices and more jobs in industry depended on repeal of the Corn Law. Much of the working class agreed. The climax of the movement came in 1845, when Ireland's potato crop failed and famine seemed likely in England. In 1846 the Tory prime minister Robert Peel joined with the Whigs and a minority of his own party to repeal the Corn Law. Thereafter, free trade became almost sacred doctrine in Great Britain.

The following year, the Tories passed a bill designed to help the working classes, but in a different way. This was the Ten Hours Act of 1847, which limited the workday for women and young people in factories to ten hours. Tory aristocrats continued to champion legislation regulating factory conditions. They were competing vigorously with the middle class for the support of the working class. This healthy competition between a still-vigorous aristocracy and a strong middle class was a crucial factor in Great Britain's peaceful evolution. The working classes could make temporary alliances with either competitor to better their own conditions.

The Revolution of 1830 in France

Louis XVIII's Constitutional Charter of 1814—theoretically a gift from the king but actually a response to political pressures—was basically a liberal constitution (page 748). The economic gains of the middle class and the prosperous peasantry were fully protected; great intellectual and artistic freedom was permitted; and a real parliament with upper and lower houses was created. Immediately after Napoleon's abortive Hundred Days, the moderate, worldly-wise king refused to bow to the wishes of die-hard aristocrats like his brother Charles, who wished to sweep away all the revolutionary changes and return to a bygone age of royal absolutism and aristocratic pretension. Instead, Louis appointed as his ministers moderate royalists, who sought and obtained the support of a majority of the representatives elected to the lower Chamber of Deputies between 1816 and Louis's death in 1824.

Louis XVIII's charter was anything but democratic. Only about 100,000 of the wealthiest people out of a total population of 30 million had the right to vote for the deputies who, with the king and his ministers, made the laws of the nation. Nonetheless, the "notable people" who did vote came from very different backgrounds. There were wealthy businessmen, war profiteers, successful professionals, ex-revolutionaries, large landowners from the middle class, Bourbons, and Bonapartists.

The old aristocracy with its pre-1789 mentality was a minority within the voting population. It was this situation that Louis's successor, Charles X (1824–1830), could not abide. Crowned in a lavish, utterly medieval, five-hour ceremony in the cathedral of Rheims in 1824, Charles was a true reactionary. He wanted to re-establish the old order in France. Increasingly blocked by the opposition of the deputies, Charles finally repudiated the Constitutional Charter in an attempted coup in July 1830. He issued decrees stripping much of the wealthy middle class of its voting rights, and he censored the press.

The reaction was an immediate insurrection. In "three glorious days" the government collapsed. Paris boiled with revolutionary excitement, and Charles fled. Then the upper-middle class, which had fomented the revolt, skillfully seated Charles's cousin, Louis Philippe, duke of Orléans, on the vacant throne.

Louis Philippe (1830–1848) accepted the Constitutional Charter of 1814, adopted the red, white, and blue flag of the French Revolution, and admitted that he was merely the "king of the French people." In spite of such symbolic actions, the situation in France remained fundamentally unchanged. As Casimir Périer, a wealthy banker and Louis Philippe's new chief minister, bluntly told a deputy who complained when the vote was extended only from 100,000 to 170,000 citizens: "The trouble with this country is that there are too many people like you who imagine that there has been a revolution in France."[5] The wealthy "notable" elite actually tightened its control as the old aristocracy retreated to the provinces to sulk harmlessly. For the upper-middle class there had been a change in dynasty, in order to protect the status quo and the narrowly liberal institutions of 1815. Republicans, democrats, social reformers, and the poor of Paris were bitterly disappointed. They had made a revolution, but it seemed for naught.

THE REVOLUTIONS OF 1848

In 1848 revolutionary political and social ideologies combined with economic crisis and the romantic impulse to produce a vast upheaval. Only the most advanced and the most backward major countries—reforming Great Britain and immobile Russia—escaped untouched. Governments toppled; monarchs and ministers bowed or fled. National independence, liberal-democratic constitutions, and social reform: the lofty aspirations of a generation seemed at hand. Yet, in the end, the revolutions failed. Why was this so?

A Democratic Republic in France

The late 1840s in Europe were hard economically and tense politically. The potato famine in Ireland in 1845 had echoes on the Continent. Bad harvests jacked up food prices and caused misery and unemployment in the cities. "Prerevolutionary" outbreaks occurred all across Europe: an abortive Polish revolution in the northern part of Austria in 1846, a civil war between radicals and conservatives in Switzerland in 1847, and an armed uprising in Naples, Italy, in January 1848. Revolution was almost universally expected, but it took revolution in Paris—once again—to turn expectations into realities.

From its beginning in 1830, Louis Philippe's "bourgeois monarchy" was characterized by stubborn inaction. There was a glaring lack of social legislation, and politics was dominated by corruption and selfish special interests. The king's chief minister in the 1840s, François Guizot, was complacency personified. Guizot was especially satisfied with the electoral system. Only the rich could vote for deputies, and many of the deputies were docile government bureaucrats. It was the government's stubborn refusal to consider electoral reform that touched off popular revolt in Paris. Barricades went up on the night of February 22, 1848, and by February 24, Louis Philippe had abdicated in favor of his grandson. But the common people in arms would tolerate no more monarchy. This refusal led to the proclamation of a provisional republic, headed by a ten-man executive committee and certified by cries of approval from the revolutionary crowd.

In the flush of victory, there was much about which Parisian revolutionaries could agree. A generation of historians and journalists had praised the First French Republic, and their work had borne fruit: the revolutionaries were firmly committed to a republic as opposed to any form of constitutional monarchy, and they immediately set about drafting a constitution for France's Second Republic. Moreover, they wanted a truly popular and democratic republic, so that the healthy, life-giving forces of the common people—the peasants and the workers—could reform society with wise legislation. In practice, building such a republic meant giving the right to vote to every adult male, and this was quickly done. Revolutionary compassion and sympathy for freedom were expressed in the freeing of all slaves in French colonies, abolition of the death penalty, and the establishment of a ten-hour workday for Paris.

Yet there were profound differences within the revolutionary coalition in Paris. On the one hand there were the moderate, liberal republicans of the middle class. They viewed universal manhood suffrage as the ultimate concession to be made to popular forces and

Daumier: The Legislative Belly Protected by freedom of the press after 1830, French radicals bitterly attacked the do-nothing government of Louis Philippe. Here Daumier savagely ridicules the corruption of the Chamber of Deputies. *(Charles Deering Collection. Courtesy of the Art Institute of Chicago)*

strongly opposed any further radical social measures. On the other hand were the radical republicans. Influenced by the critique of capitalism and unbridled individualism elaborated by a generation of utopian socialists, and appalled by the poverty and misery of the urban poor, the radical republicans were committed to socialism. To be sure, socialism came in many utopian shapes and sizes for the Parisian working poor and their leaders, but that did not make their commitment to it any less real. Finally, wedged in between were individuals like the poet Lamartine and the democrat Ledru-Rollin, who were neither doctrinaire socialists nor stand-pat liberals and who sought to escape an impending tragedy.

Worsening depression and rising unemployment brought these conflicting goals to the fore. Louis Blanc (page 739), who along with a worker named Albert represented the republican socialists in the provisional government, pressed for recognition of a socialist right to work. Blanc asserted that permanent government-sponsored cooperative workshops should be established for workers. Such workshops would be an alternative to capitalist employment and a decisive step toward a new social order.

The moderate republicans wanted no such thing. They were willing to provide only temporary relief. The resulting compromise set up national workshops—soon to become a vast program of pick-and-shovel public works—and established a special commission under Louis Blanc to "study the question." This satisfied no one. As bad as the national workshops were, though, they were better than nothing. An army of desperate poor from the French provinces and even from foreign countries streamed into Paris to sign up. The number enrolled in the workshops soared from 10,000 in March to 120,000 by June, and another 80,000 were trying unsuccessfully to join.

While the workshops in Paris grew, the French masses went to the polls in late April. Voting in most cases for the first time, the people elected to the new

The Revolutions of 1848

February	Revolt in Paris against Louis Philippe's "bourgeois monarchy"; Louis Philippe abdicates; proclamation of a provisional republic
February–June	Establishment and rapid growth of government-sponsored workshops in France
March 3	Hungarians under Kossuth demand autonomy from Austrian Empire
March 13	Uprising of students and workers in Vienna; Metternich flees to London
March 19–21	Frederick William IV of Prussia is forced to salute the bodies of slain revolutionaries in Berlin and agrees to a liberal constitution and merger into a new German state
March 20	Ferdinand I of Austria abolishes serfdom and promises reforms
March 26	Workers in Berlin issue a series of socialist demands
April 22	French voters favor moderate republicans over radicals 5:1
May 15	Parisian socialist workers invade the Constitutional Assembly and unsuccessfully proclaim a new revolutionary state
May 18	Frankfurt Assembly begins writing a new German constitution
June 17	Austrian army crushes working-class revolt in Prague
June 22–26	French government abolishes the national workshops, provoking an uprising
	June Days: republican army defeats rebellious Parisian working class
October	Austrian army besieges and retakes Vienna from students and working-class radicals
December	Conservatives force Ferdinand I of Austria to abdicate in favor of young Francis Joseph
	Frederick William IV disbands Prussian Constituent Assembly and grants Prussia a conservative constitution
	Louis Napoleon wins a landslide victory in French presidential elections
March 1849	Frankfurt Assembly elects Frederick William IV of Prussia emperor of the new German state; Frederick William refuses and reasserts royal authority in Prussia
June–August 1849	Habsburg and Russian forces defeat the Hungarian independence movement

Constituent Assembly about five hundred moderate republicans, three hundred monarchists, and one hundred radicals who professed various brands of socialism. One of the moderate republicans was the author of *Democracy in America,* Alexis de Tocqueville (1805–1859), who had predicted the overthrow of Louis Philippe's government. To this brilliant observer, socialism was the most characteristic aspect of the revolution in Paris.

This socialist revolution had evoked a violent reaction not only among the frightened middle and upper classes but also among the bulk of the population—the peasants. The French peasants owned land, and according to Tocqueville, "private property had become with all those who owned it a sort of bond of fraternity."[6] The countryside, Tocqueville wrote, had been seized with a universal hatred of radical Paris. Returning from Normandy to take his seat in the new Constituent Assembly, Tocqueville saw that a majority of the members were firmly committed to the republic and strongly opposed to the socialists, and he shared their sentiments.

The clash of ideologies—of liberal capitalism and socialism—became a clash of classes and arms after the elections. The new government's executive committee dropped Louis Blanc and thereafter included no representative of the Parisian working class. Fearing that their socialist hopes were about to be dashed, the workers invaded the assembly on May 15 and tried to proclaim a new revolutionary state. But the government was ready and used the middle-class National Guard to squelch this uprising. As the workshops continued to fill and grow more radical, the fearful but powerful propertied classes in the assembly took the offensive. On June 22 the government dissolved the national workshops in Paris, giving the workers the choice of joining the army or going to workshops in the provinces.

The result was a spontaneous and violent uprising. Frustrated in their attempts to create a socialist society, masses of desperate people were now losing even their life-sustaining relief. As a voice from the crowd cried out when the famous astronomer François Arago counseled patience: "Ah, Monsieur Arago, you have never been hungry!"[7] Barricades sprang up in the narrow streets of Paris, and a terrible class war began. Working people fought with the courage of utter desperation, but the government had the army and the support of peasant France. After three terrible "June Days" and the death or injury of more than ten thousand people, the republican army under General Louis Cavaignac stood triumphant in a sea of working-class blood and hatred.

The revolution in France thus ended in spectacular failure. The February coalition of the middle and working classes had in four short months become locked in mortal combat. In place of a generous democratic republic, the Constituent Assembly completed a constitution featuring a strong executive. This allowed Louis Napoleon, nephew of Napoleon Bonaparte, to win a landslide victory in the election of December 1848. The appeal of his great name, as well as the desire of the propertied classes for order at any cost, had produced a semi-authoritarian regime.

The Austrian Empire in 1848

Throughout central Europe, news of the upheaval in France evoked feverish excitement and eventually revolution. Liberals demanded written constitutions, representative government, and greater civil liberties. When governments hesitated, popular revolts followed. Urban workers and students served as the shock troops, but they were allied with middle-class liberals and peasants. In the face of this united front, monarchs collapsed and granted almost everything. The popular revolutionary coalition, having secured great and easy victories, then broke down as it had in France. The traditional forces—the monarchy, the aristocracy, and the regular army—recovered their nerve, reasserted their authority, and took back many though not all of the concessions. Reaction was everywhere victorious.

The revolution in the Austrian Empire began in Hungary. Nationalism had been growing among Hungarians since about 1790, and in 1848 under the leadership of Louis Kossuth, the Hungarians demanded national autonomy, full civil liberties, and universal suffrage. When the monarchy in Vienna hesitated, Viennese students and workers took to the streets on March 13 and added their own demands. Peasant disorders broke out in parts of the empire. The Habsburg emperor Ferdinand I (1835–1848) capitulated and promised reforms and a liberal constitution. Metternich fled in disguise toward London. The old order seemed to be collapsing with unbelievable rapidity.

The coalition of revolutionaries was not completely stable, though. The Austrian Empire was overwhelmingly agricultural, and serfdom still existed. On March 20, as part of its capitulation before upheaval, the monarchy abolished serfdom with its degrading forced labor and feudal services. Peasants throughout the empire felt they had won a victory reminiscent of that in France in 1789. Newly free, men and women of the land lost interest in the political and social questions agitating the cities. The government had in the peasants a potential ally of great importance, especially since, in central Europe as in France, the army was largely composed of peasants.

The coalition of March was also weakened—and ultimately destroyed—by conflicting national aspirations. In March the Hungarian revolutionary leaders pushed through an extremely liberal, almost democratic, constitution granting widespread voting rights and civil liberties and ending feudal obligations. So far, well and good. Yet the Hungarian revolutionaries were also nationalists with a mission. They wanted the ancient Crown of Saint Stephen, with its mosaic of provinces and nationalities, transformed into a unified centralized Hungarian nation. To the minority groups that formed half the population of the kingdom of Hungary—the Croats, the Serbs, and the Rumanians—such unification was completely unacceptable. Each felt entitled to political autonomy and cultural independence. The Habsburg monarchy in Vienna exploited the fears of the minority groups, and they were soon locked in armed combat with the new Hungarian government.

In a somewhat different way, Czech nationalists

Revolutionary Justice in Vienna As part of the conservative resurgence, in October 1848 the Austrian minister of war ordered up reinforcements for an army marching on Hungary. In a last defiant gesture the outraged revolutionaries in Vienna seized the minister and lynched him from a lamppost for treason. The army then reconquered the city in a week of bitter fighting. *(Mary Evans Picture Library)*

based in Bohemia and the city of Prague, led by the Czech historian Palacký, came into conflict with German nationalists. Like the minorities in Hungary, the Czechs saw their struggle for autonomy as a struggle against a dominant group—the Germans. Thus the national aspirations of different peoples in the Austrian Empire came into sharp conflict, and the monarchy was able to play off one group against the other.

Nor was this all. The urban working classes of poor artisans and day laborers were not as radical in the Austrian Empire as they were in France, but then neither were the middle class and lower-middle class. Throughout Austria and the German states, where Metternich's brand of absolutism had so recently ruled supreme, the middle class wanted liberal reform, complete with constitutional monarchy, limited voting rights, and modest social measures. They wanted a central European equivalent of the English Reform Bill of 1832 and the Corn Law repeal of 1846. When the urban poor rose in arms, as they did in the Austrian cities of Vienna, Prague, and Milan and throughout the German Confederation as well, and presented their own demands for universal voting rights and socialist workshops, the prosperous middle classes recoiled in alarm. As in Paris, the union of the urban poor and the middle class was soon a mere memory, and a bad memory at that.

Finally, the conservative aristocratic forces gathered around Emperor Ferdinand I regained their nerve and reasserted their great strength. The archduchess Sophia, a conservative but intelligent and courageous Bavarian princess married to the emperor's brother, provided a rallying point. Deeply ashamed of the emperor's collapse before a "mess of students,"[8] she insisted that Ferdinand, who had no heir, abdicate in favor of her eighteen-year-old son, Francis Joseph. Powerful nobles who held high positions in the government, the army, and the church agreed completely. They organized around Sophia in a secret conspiracy to reverse and crush the revolution.

Their first breakthrough came when one of the most dedicated members of the group, Prince Alfred Windischgrätz, bombarded Prague and savagely crushed a working-class revolt there on June 17. Other Austrian officials and nobles began to lead the minority nationalities of Hungary against the revolutionary government proclaimed by the Hungarian patriots. Another Austrian army reconquered Austria's possessions in northern Italy in late July 1848. Revolution failed as miserably in Italy as everywhere else. At the end of October, the well-equipped, predominantly peasant troops of the regular Austrian army attacked the student and working-class radicals in Vienna and retook the city at the cost of more than four thousand casualties. Thus, the determination of the Austrian aristocracy and the loyalty of its army were the final ingredients in the triumph of reaction and the defeat of revolution.

Only in Hungary were the forces represented by Sophia's son Francis Joseph (1848–1916), crowned emperor of Austria immediately after his eighteenth birthday in December 1848, at first unsuccessful. Yet another determined conservative, Nicholas I of Russia (1825–1855), obligingly lent his iron hand. On June 6, 1849, 130,000 Russian troops poured into Hungary. After bitter fighting—in which the Hungarian army supported the revolutionary Hungarian government—they subdued the country. For a number of years the Habsburgs ruled Hungary as a conquered territory.

Prussia and the Frankfurt Assembly

The rest of the states in the German Confederation generally recapitulated the ebb and flow of developments in France and Austria. The key difference was the additional goal of unifying the thirty-eight states of the German Confederation, with the possible exception of Austria, into a single sovereign nation. Therefore events in Germany were extraordinarily complex, since they were occurring not only in the individual principalities but at the all-German level as well.

After Austria, Prussia was the largest and most influential German kingdom. Prior to 1848, the goal of middle-class Prussian liberals had been to transform absolutist Prussia into a liberal constitutional monarchy. Such a monarchy would then take the lead in merging itself and all the other German states into a liberal unified nation. The agitation following the fall of Louis Philippe encouraged Prussian liberals to press their demands. When they were not granted, the artisans and factory workers in Berlin exploded, joining temporarily with the middle-class liberals in the struggle against the monarchy. The autocratic yet paternalistic Frederick William IV (1840–1861), already displaying the instability that later became insanity, vacillated. Humiliated by the revolutionary

Revolution in Berlin Barricades were erected on March 18 and fierce fighting lasted until dawn. The fury of midnight battle burns with a romantic glow in this contemporary illustration. *(The Bettman Archive)*

crowd, which forced him to salute from his balcony the blood-spattered corpses of workers who had fallen in an uprising on March 18, the nearly hysterical king finally caved in. On March 21 he promised to grant Prussia a liberal constitution and to merge it into a new national German state that was to be created. He appointed two wealthy businessmen from the Rhineland—perfect representatives of moderate liberalism—to form a new government.

The situation might have stabilized at this point if the workers had not wanted much more and the Prussian aristocracy much less. On March 26, the workers issued a series of radical and vaguely socialist demands, which troubled their middle-class allies: universal voting rights, a ministry of labor, a minimum wage, and a ten-hour day. At the same time, a wild-tempered Prussian landowner and aristocrat, Otto von Bismarck, joined the conservative clique gathered around the king to urge counter-revolution. While these tensions in Prussia were growing, an elected assembly arrived in Berlin to write a constitution for the Prussian state.

To add to the complexity of the situation, a self-appointed committee of liberals from various German states successfully called for the formation of a national constituent assembly to begin writing a federal constitution for a unified German state. That body met for the first time on May 18 in Saint Paul's Church in Frankfurt. The Frankfurt National Assembly was a most curious revolutionary body. It was really a serious middle-class body whose 820 members included some 200 lawyers; 100 professors; many doctors, judges, and officials; and 140 businessmen for good measure.

Called together to write a constitution, the learned body was soon absorbed in a battle with Denmark over the provinces of Schleswig and Holstein. Jurisdiction over them was a hopelessly complicated issue from a legal point of view. Britain's Foreign Minister Lord Palmerston once said that only three people had ever understood the Schleswig-Holstein question, and of those one had died, another had gone mad, and he himself had forgotten the answer. The provinces were inhabited primarily by Germans but were ruled by the king of Denmark, although Holstein was a member of the German Confederation. When Frederick VII, the new nationalistic king of Denmark, tried to integrate both provinces into the rest of his state, the Germans there revolted.

Hypnotized by this conflict, the National Assembly at Frankfurt debated ponderously and finally called on the Prussian army to oppose Denmark in the name of the German nation. Prussia responded and began war with Denmark. As the Schleswig-Holstein issue demonstrated, the national ideal was a crucial factor motivating the German middle classes in 1848.

Almost obsessed with the fate of Germans under Danish rule, many members of the Frankfurt assembly also wanted to bring the German-speaking provinces of Austria into the new German state. Yet resurgent Austria resolutely opposed any division of its territory. Once this Austrian action made a "big German state" impossible, the Frankfurt assembly completed drafting a liberal constitution. Finally, in March 1849, the assembly elected King Frederick William of Prussia emperor of the new German national state (minus Austria and Schleswig-Holstein).

By early 1849, however, reaction had been successful almost everywhere. Frederick William reasserted his royal authority, disbanded the Prussian Constituent Assembly, and granted his subjects a limited, essentially conservative, constitution. Reasserting that he ruled by divine right, Frederick William contemptuously refused to accept the "crown from the gutter." The reluctant revolutionaries in Frankfurt had waited too long and acted too timidly.

When Frederick William, who really wanted to be emperor but only on his own authoritarian terms, tried to get the small monarchs of Germany to elect him emperor, Austria balked. Supported by Russia, Austria forced Prussia to renounce all its schemes of unification in late 1850. The German Confederation was re-established. After two turbulent years, the political map of the German states remained unchanged. Attempts to unite the Germans—first in a liberal national state and then in a conservative Prussian empire—had failed completely.

The liberal and nationalistic revolutions of 1848 were abortive. Political, economic, and social pressures that had been building since 1815 exploded dramatically, but very few revolutionary goals were realized. The moderate, nationalistic middle classes were unable to consolidate their initial victories in France or elsewhere in Europe. Instead, they drew back when artisans, factory workers, and radical socialists rose up to present their own much more revolutionary demands. This retreat facilitated the efforts of dedicated aristocrats in central Europe and made possible the crushing of Parisian workers by a coalition of solid bourgeoisie and landowning peasantry in France. A host of fears, a sea of blood, and a torrent of disillusion had drowned the lofty ideals and utopian visions of a generation. The age of romantic revolution was over.

NOTES

1. A. J. May, *The Age of Metternich, 1814–1848,* rev. ed., Holt, Rinehart & Winston, New York, 1963, p. 11.
2. H. Kohn, *Nationalism,* Van Nostrand, New York, 1955, pp. 141–142.
3. Quoted by F. D. Klingender, *Art and the Industrial Revolution,* Paladin, St. Albans, England, 1972, p. 117.
4. Quoted by F. B. Artz, *From the Renaissance to Romanticism: Trends in Style in Art, Literature, and Music, 1300–1830,* University of Chicago Press, Chicago, 1962, pp. 276, 278.
5. Quoted by G. Wright, *France in Modern Times,* Rand McNally, Chicago, 1960, p. 145.
6. A. de Tocqueville, *Recollections,* Columbia University Press, New York, 1949, p. 94.
7. M. Agulhon, *1848,* Editions du Seuil, Paris, 1973, pp. 68–69.

8. Quoted by W. L. Langer, *Political and Social Upheaval, 1832–1852,* Harper & Row, New York, 1969, p. 361.

SUGGESTED READING

All of the works cited in the Notes are highly recommended. May's is a good brief survey, while Kohn has written perceptively on nationalism in many books. Wright's *France in Modern Times* is a lively introduction to French history with stimulating biographical discussions; Langer's is a balanced synthesis with an excellent bibliography. Among general studies, C. Morazé, *The Triumph of the Middle Classes* (1968), a wide-ranging procapitalist interpretation, may be compared with E. J. Hobsbawm's flexible Marxism in *The Age of Revolution, 1789–1848* (1962). For English history, A. Brigg's socially oriented *The Making of Modern England, 1784–1867* (1967) and D. Thomson's *England in the Nineteenth Century, 1815–1914* (1951) are excellent. Restoration France is sympathetically portrayed by G. de Bertier de Sauvigny in *The Bourbon Restoration* (1967). T. Hamerow studies the social implications of the dual revolution in Germany in *Restoration, Revolution, Reaction 1815–1871* (1966), which may be compared to H. Treitschke's bombastic, pro-Prussian *History of Germany in the Nineteenth Century* (1915–1919), a classic of nationalistic history, and L. Snyder, *Roots of German Nationalism* (1978). E. Kedourie, *Nationalism* (1960), is a stimulating critique of the new faith. H. Kissinger, *A World Restored* (1957), offers not only a provocative interpretation of the Congress of Vienna but also insights into the mind of Richard Nixon's famous secretary of state. Compare with H. Nicolson's entertaining *The Congress of Vienna* (1946). On 1848, L. B. Namier's highly critical *1848: The Revolution of the Intellectuals* (1964) and P. Robertson's *Revolutions of 1848: A Social History* (1960) are outstanding. I. Deak, *The Lawful Revolution: Louis Kossuth and the Hungarians, 1848–49* (1979), is a noteworthy study of an interesting figure.

On early socialism and Marxism, there are W. Sewell, Jr.'s *Work and Revolution in France* (1980) and E. Wilson's engrossing survey of nineteenth-century developments, *To the Finland Station* (1953), as well as G. Lichtheim's high-powered *Marxism* (1961) and his *Short History of Socialism* (1970). J. Schumpeter, *Capitalism, Socialism and Democracy* (1947), is magnificent but difficult, a real mind-stretcher. On liberalism, there is R. Heilbroner's entertaining *The Worldly Philosophers* (1967) and G. de Ruggiero's classic *History of European Liberalism* (1959). J. Barzun, *Classic, Romantic and Modern* (1961), skillfully discusses the emergence of romanticism. R. Stromberg, *An Intellectual History of Modern Europe,* 3rd ed. (1981), and F. Baumer, *Modern European Thought: Continuity and Change in Ideas, 1600–1950* (1970), are valuable surveys. The important place of religion in nineteenth-century thought is considered from different perspectives in H. McLeod, *Religion and the People of Western Europe* (1981), and O. Chadwick, *The Secularization of the European Mind in the Nineteenth Century* (1976). Two good church histories with useful bibliographies are J. Altholz, *The Churches in the Nineteenth Century* (1967), and A. Vidler, *The Church in an Age of Revolution: 1789 to the Present Day* (1961).

The thoughtful reader is strongly advised to delve into the incredibly rich writing of contemporaries. J. Bowditch and C. Ramsland, eds., *Voices of the Industrial Revolution* (1961), is an excellent starting point, with well-chosen selections from leading economic thinkers and early socialists. H. Hugo, ed., *The Romantic Reader,* is another fine anthology. Jules Michelet's compassionate masterpiece *The People,* a famous historian's anguished examination of French social divisions on the eve of 1848, draws one into the heart of the period and is highly recommended. Alexis de Tocqueville covers some of the same ground less romantically in his *Recollections,* which may be compared with Karl Marx's white-hot "instant history," *Class Struggles in France, 1848–1850* (1850). Great novels that accurately portray aspects of the times are Victor Hugo, *Les Misérables,* an exciting story of crime and passion among France's poor; Honoré de Balzac, *Cousin Bette* and *Père Goriot;* and Thomas Mann, *Buddenbrooks,* a wonderful historical novel that traces the rise and fall of a prosperous German family over three generations during the nineteenth century.

24

LIFE IN URBAN SOCIETY

THE ERA of intellectual and political upheaval that culminated in the revolutions of 1848 was also an era of rapid urbanization. After 1848 Western political development veered off in a novel and uncharted direction, but the growth of towns and cities rushed forward with undiminished force. Thus Western society was urban and industrial in 1900, as surely as it had been rural and agrarian in 1800. The urbanization of society was both a result of the Industrial Revolution and a reflection of its enormous impact. What was life like in the cities, and how did it change? What did the emergence of urban industrial society mean for rich and poor and in between? How did families cope with the challenges and respond to the opportunities of the developing urban civilization? Finally, what changes in science and thought inspired and gave expression to this new civilization? These are the questions this chapter will investigate.

TAMING THE CITY

The consequences of economic transformation were, from the beginning, more positive than historians have often recognized. Indeed, given the poverty and uncertainty of preindustrial life, the history of industrialization is probably better written in terms of increasing opportunities than of greater hardships. But does not this relatively optimistic view of the consequences of industrialization neglect the quality of life in urban areas? Were not the new industrial towns and cities awful places where people, especially the poor, suffered from bad housing, lack of sanitation, and a sense of hopelessness? Did not these drawbacks more than cancel out higher wages and greater opportunity?

Industry and the Growth of Cities

Since the Middle Ages, European cities had been centers of government, culture, and large-scale commerce. They had also been congested, dirty, and unhealthy. People were packed together almost as tightly as possible within the city limits. The typical city was a "walking city": for all but the wealthiest classes, walking was the only available form of transportation.

Infectious disease spread with deadly speed in cities, and people were always more likely to die in the city than in the countryside. In the larger towns, more people died each year than were born, on the average, and urban populations were able to maintain their numbers only because newcomers were continuously arriving from rural areas. Little could be done to improve these conditions. Given the pervasive poverty, absence of urban transportation, and lack of medical knowledge, the deadly and overcrowded conditions could only be accepted fatalistically. They were the urban equivalents of bad weather and poor crops, the price of urban excitement and opportunity.

Clearly, deplorable urban conditions did not originate with the Industrial Revolution. What the Industrial Revolution did was to reveal those conditions more nakedly than ever before. The steam engine freed industrialists from dependence on the energy of fast-flowing streams and rivers, which meant that by 1800 there was every incentive to build new factories in urban areas. Cities had better shipping facilities and thus better supplies of coal and raw materials. There were also many hands wanting work in the cities, for cities drew people like a magnet. And it was a great advantage for a manufacturer to have other factories nearby to supply his needs and buy his products. Therefore, as industry grew, there was also a rapid expansion of already overcrowded and unhealthy cities.

The challenge of the urban environment was felt first and most acutely in Great Britain. The number of people living in cities of 20,000 or more in England and Wales jumped from 1.5 million in 1801 to 6.3 million in 1851 and reached 15.6 million by 1891. Such cities accounted for 17 percent of the total English population in 1801, 35 percent as early as 1851, and fully 54 percent in 1891. Other countries duplicated the English pattern as they industrialized. An American observer was hardly exaggerating when he wrote in 1899 that "the most remarkable social phenomenon of the present century is the concentration of population in cities"[1] (see Map 24.1).

In the 1820s and 1830s, people in Britain and France began to worry about the condition of their cities. In those years, the populations of a number of

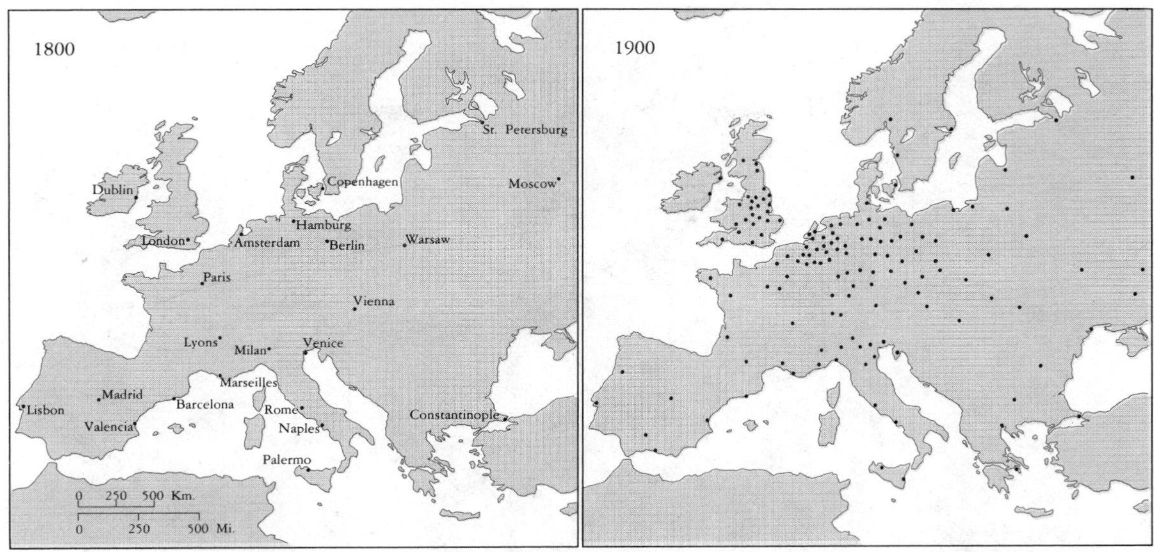

Map 24.1 European Cities of 100,000 or More, 1800 and 1900 There were more large cities in Great Britain in 1900 than in all Europe in 1800.

British cities were increasing by 40 to 70 percent each decade. Manchester, the cotton city, grew by 40 percent between 1811 and 1821, and by 47 percent between 1821 and 1831. The population of the principal Scottish manufacturing city, Glasgow, grew by 30 percent or more each decade between 1801 and 1841. With urban areas expanding at such previously undreamed-of rates, people's traditional fatalistic indifference to overcrowded, unsanitary urban living conditions began to give way to active concern. Something had to be done.

On one point everyone could agree: except on the outskirts, each town and city was using every scrap of land to the fullest extent. Parks and open areas were almost nonexistent. A British parliamentary committee reported in 1833 that "with a rapidly increasing population, lodged for the most part in narrow courts and confined streets, the means of occasional exercise and recreation in fresh air are every day lessened, as inclosures [of vacant areas] take place and buildings spread themselves on every side."[2] Buildings were erected on the smallest possible lots, in order to pack the maximum number of people into a given space. Narrow houses were built wall to wall, in long rows. These row houses had neither front nor back yards, and only a narrow alley in back separated one row from the next. Or buildings were built around tiny courtyards completely enclosed on all four sides. Many people lived in cellars and attics. The tiny rooms within such buildings were often overcrowded. "Six, eight, and even ten occupying one room is anything but uncommon," wrote a doctor from Aberdeen in Scotland for a government investigation in 1842.

These highly concentrated urban populations lived in extremely unsanitary and unhealthy conditions. Open drains and sewers flowed alongside or down the middle of unpaved streets. Due to poor construction and an absence of running water, the sewers often filled with garbage and excrement. Toilet facilities were primitive in the extreme. In parts of Manchester, as many as two hundred people shared a single outhouse. Such privies filled up rapidly, and since they were infrequently emptied, sewage often overflowed and seeped into cellar dwellings.

The extent to which filth lay underfoot and the smell of excrement filled the air is hard to believe; yet it was abundantly documented between 1830 and 1850. One London construction engineer found, for example, that the cellars of two large houses on a major road were "full of night-soil [human excrement], to the depth of three feet, which had been permitted for years to accumulate from the overflow of the cesspools." Moreover, some courtyards in poorer

Filth and Disease This 1852 drawing from *Punch* tells volumes about the unhealthy living conditions of the urban poor. In the foreground children play with a dead rat and a woman scavenges a dungheap. Cheap rooming houses provide shelter for the frightfully overcrowded population. *(The British Library)*

neighborhoods became dunghills, collecting excrement that was sometimes sold as fertilizer. By the 1840s there was among the better-off classes a growing, shocking "realization that, to put it as mildly as possible, millions of English men, women, and children were living in shit."[3]

Who or what was responsible for these awful conditions? The crucial factors were the tremendous pressure of more people coupled with the *total* absence of public transportation. People simply had to jam themselves together if they were to be able to walk to shops and factories. Another factor was that government in Great Britain, both local and national, was slow to provide sanitary facilities and establish adequate building codes. This slow pace was probably attributable more to a need to explore and identify what precisely should be done than to rigid middle-class opposition to government action. Certainly Great Britain had no monopoly on overcrowded and unhealthy urban conditions; may continental cities were every bit as bad.

Most responsible of all was the sad legacy of rural housing conditions in preindustrial society, combined with appalling ignorance. As the author of a recent study concludes, there "were rural slums of a horror not surpassed by the rookeries of London. . . . The evidence shows that the decent cottage was the exception, the hovel the rule."[4] Thus housing was far down on the newcomer's list of priorities, and it is not surprising that many people carried the filth of the mud floor and the dung of the barnyard with them to the city.

Indeed, ordinary people generally took dirt and filth for granted, and some even prized it. As one English miner told an investigator, "I do not think it usual for the lasses [in the coal mines] to wash their bodies; my sisters never wash themselves." As for the men, "their legs and bodies are as black as your hat." When poor people were admitted to English workhouses, they often resisted the required bath. One man protested that it was "equal to robbing him of a great coat which he had had for some years."[5]

The Public Health Movement

Although cleanliness was not next to godliness in most people's eyes, it was becoming so for some reformers. The most famous of these was Edwin Chadwick, one of the commissioners charged with the administration of relief to paupers under the revised Poor Law of 1834. Chadwick was a good *Benthamite* —that is, a follower of the radical philosopher Jeremy Bentham (1748–1832). Bentham had taught that public problems ought to be dealt with on a rational, scientific basis and according to the "greatest good for the greatest number." Applying these principles, Chadwick soon saw that much more than economics was involved in the problems of poverty and the welfare budget. Indeed, he soon became convinced that disease and death actually caused poverty, simply because a sick worker was an unemployed worker and orphaned children were poor children. Most important, Chadwick believed that disease could be prevented by quite literally cleaning up the urban environment. That was his "sanitary idea."

Building on a growing number of medical and sociological studies, Chadwick collected detailed reports from local Poor Law officials on the "sanitary conditions of the laboring population." After three years of investigation, these reports and Chadwick's hard-hitting commentary were published in 1842 to wide publicity. This mass of evidence proved that disease was related to filthy environmental conditions, which were in turn caused largely by lack of drainage, sewers, and garbage collection. Putrefying, smelly excrement was no longer simply disgusting. For reformers like Chadwick, it was a threat to the entire community. It polluted the atmosphere and caused disease.

The key to the energetic action Chadwick proposed was an adequate supply of clean piped water. Such water was essential for personal hygiene, public bathhouses, street cleaning, firefighting, and industry. Chadwick correctly believed that the stinking excrement of communal outhouses could be dependably carried off by water through sewers at less than one-twentieth the cost of removing it by hand. The cheap iron pipes and tile drains of the industrial age would provide running water and sewerage for all sections of town, not just the wealthy ones. In 1848, spurred on by the cholera epidemic of 1846, Chadwick's report became the basis of Great Britain's first public health law, which created a national health board and gave cities broad authority to build modern sanitary systems.

The public health movement won dedicated supporters in the United States, France, and Germany from the 1840s on. As in Great Britain, governments accepted at least limited responsibility for the health of all citizens. Moreover, they adopted increasingly concrete programs of action, programs that broke decisively with the age-old fatalism of urban populations in the face of shockingly high mortality. Thus, despite many people's skepticism about sanitation, European cities were making real progress toward adequate water supplies and sewage systems by the 1860s and 1870s. And city dwellers were beginning to reap the reward of better health.

The Bacterial Revolution

Effective control of communicable disease required more than a clean water supply and good sewers. Victory over disease also required a great leap forward in medical knowledge and biological theory. Reformers like Chadwick were seriously handicapped by the prevailing *miasmatic theory* of disease—the belief that people contract disease when they breathe the bad odors of decay and putrefying excrement; in short, the theory that smells cause disease. The miasmatic theory was a reasonable deduction from empirical observations: cleaning up filth did produce laudable results. Yet the theory was very incomplete.

Keen observation by doctors and public health officials in the 1840s and 1850s pinpointed the role of bad drinking water in the transmission of disease and suggested that contagion was *spread through* filth and not caused by it. Examples of particularly horrid

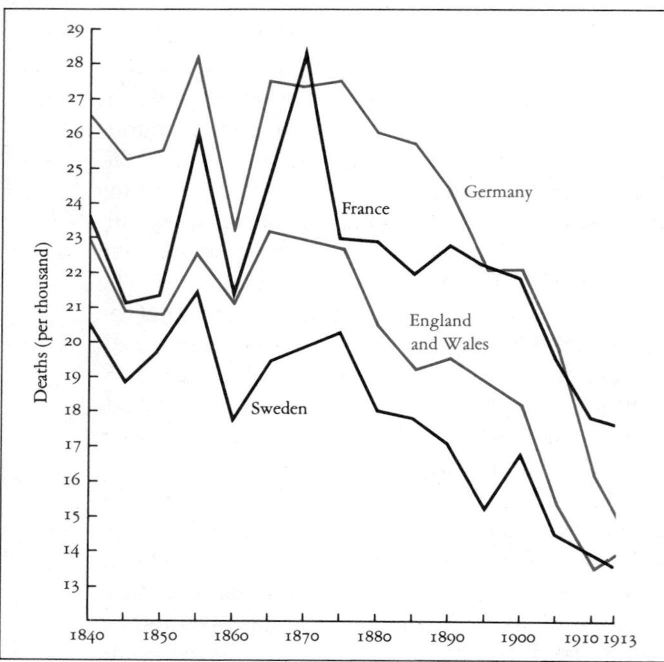

Figure 24.1 The Decline of Death Rates in England and Wales, Germany, France, and Sweden, 1840–1913 A rising standard of living, improvements in public health, and better medical knowledge all contributed to the dramatic decline of death rates in the nineteenth century.

stenches, such as that of the sewage-glutted Thames River at London in 1858, that did not lead to widely feared epidemics also weakened the miasmatic idea. Another factor was the successful merging of anatomical and clinical approaches to medicine between 1800 and 1850, particularly at the University of Paris school of medicine. Doctors there recognized a definite connection between the symptoms of certain illnesses observed at the bedside and the diseased organs seen when the body was dissected at autopsy. Medical research began zeroing in on specific diseases in an attempt to find specific treatments. When an improved theory was developed, progress could be rapid.

The breakthrough was the development of the germ theory of disease by Louis Pasteur (1822–1895). Pasteur was a French chemist by profession, not a physician. After important discoveries about the structure of crystals, he turned in 1854 to the study of fermentation. For ages people had used fermentation to make bread and wine, beer and cheese, but without really understanding what was going on. And from time to time, beer and wine would mysteriously spoil for no apparent reason. As rapidly growing cities provided a vast concentrated demand, large brewers and winemakers were seeking ways to prevent spoilage and financial loss. Responding to their calls for help, Pasteur used his microscope to develop a simple test brewers could use to monitor the fermentation process and avoid spoilage. He then investigated various kinds of fermentation.

Pasteur found that fermentation depended on the growth of living organisms. Moreover, he demonstrated that the activity of these organisms could be suppressed by heating the wine or milk—by *pasteurizing* it. The breathtaking implication was that specific diseases were caused by specific living organisms—germs—and that those organisms could be controlled in people as well as in milk and wine. This theory was confirmed in 1868. After three years of intensive research, Pasteur isolated and controlled parasitic microorganisms that were killing off the silkworms used in France's large silk industry. Once again, scientific research had been stimulated by and had responded to the needs of the emerging industrial society.

By 1870 the work of Pasteur and others had demonstrated the general connection between germs and disease. When, in the middle of the 1870s, the German country doctor Robert Koch and his coworkers developed pure cultures of harmful bacteria and described their life cycles, the dam broke. Over the next twenty years, researchers—mainly Germans—identified the organisms responsible for disease after disease, often identifying several in a single year. At the same time, Pasteur and his colleagues concentrated on modifying and controlling the virulence of disease-producing germs. Building on the example of Edward Jenner's pioneering conquest of smallpox, Pasteur and his team developed a number of effective vaccines. The most famous was his vaccination for rabies in 1885, a crucial step in the development of modern immunology.

Acceptance of the germ theory brought about dramatic improvements in the deadly environment of hospitals and surgery. The English surgeon Joseph Lister (1827–1912) had noticed that patients with simple fractures were much less likely to die than those with compound fractures, in which the skin was broken and internal tissues were exposed to the air. In 1865, when Pasteur showed that the air was full of bacteria, Lister immediately grasped the connection between aerial bacteria and the problem of wound infection. He reasoned that a chemical disinfectant applied to a wound dressing would "destroy the life of the floating particles." Lister's "antiseptic principle" worked wonders. In the 1880s, German surgeons developed the more sophisticated practice of sterilizing not only the wound but everything—hands, instruments, clothing—that entered the operating room.

The achievements of the bacterial revolution coupled with the ever-more-sophisticated public health movement saved millions of lives, particularly after about 1890. Mortality rates began to decline dramatically in European countries (see Figure 24.1), as the awful death sentences of the past—diphtheria, typhoid and typhus, cholera, yellow fever—became vanishing diseases. City dwellers benefited especially from these developments. By 1910 the likelihood of death for people of all ages in urban areas was generally no greater than in rural areas, and sometimes it was less. Particularly striking was the decline in infant mortality in the cities after 1890. In many countries, an urban mother was less likely than a rural mother to see her child die before its first birthday by 1910. A great silent revolution had occurred: the terrible ferocity of death from disease-carrying bacteria in the cities had almost been tamed.

Urban Planning and Public Transportation

Public health was only part of the urban challenge. Overcrowding, bad housing, and lack of transportation could not be solved by sewers and better medicine; yet in these areas, too, important transformations significantly improved the quality of urban life after midcentury.

More effective urban planning was one of the keys to improvement. Earlier urban planning had declined by the early nineteenth century; after 1850 it was revived and extended. France took the lead during the rule of Napoleon III (1848–1870), who sought to stand above class conflict and promote the welfare of all his subjects through government action. He believed that rebuilding much of Paris would provide employment, improve living conditions, and testify to the power and glory of his empire. In the baron Georges Haussmann, an aggressive, impatient Alsatian whom he placed in charge of Paris, Napoleon III found an authoritarian planner capable of bulldozing both buildings and opposition. In twenty years Paris was quite literally transformed (see Map 24.2).

The Paris of 1850 was a labyrinth of narrow, dark streets, the results of desperate overcrowding. In an area of a central city not twice the size of New York's Central Park lived more than one-third of the city's 1 million inhabitants. Terrible slum conditions and extremely high death rates were facts of life. There were few open spaces and only two public parks for the entire metropolis. Public transportation played a very small role in this enormous walking city.

Haussmann and his fellow planners proceeded on many interrelated fronts. With a bold energy that often shocked their contemporaries, they razed old buildings in order to cut broad, straight, tree-lined boulevards through the center of the city as well as in new quarters on the outskirts. These boulevards, designed in part to prevent the easy construction and defense of barricades by revolutionary crowds, also permitted traffic to flow freely. Their construction also demolished some of the worst slums. New streets stimulated the construction of better housing, especially for the middle classes. Small neighborhood parks and open spaces were created throughout the city, and two very large peaks suitable for all kinds of holiday activities were developed on either side of the city. The city also improved its sewers, and a system of aqueducts more than doubled the city's supply of good fresh water.

Haussmann and Napoleon III tried to make Paris a more beautiful city, and to a large extent they succeeded. The broad, straight boulevards, such as those radiating out like the spokes of a wheel from the Arch of Triumph and those centering on the new Opera House, afforded impressive vistas. If for most people Paris remains one of the world's most beautiful and enchanting cities, it is in part because of the transformations of the Second Empire.

The rebuilding of Paris provided a new model for urban planning and stimulated modern urbanism throughout Europe, particularly after 1870. In city after city, public authorities mounted a coordinated attack on many of the interrelated problems of the urban environment. As in Paris, improvements in public health through better water supply and waste disposal often went hand in hand with new boulevard

Apartment Living in Paris This contemporary drawing shows how different social classes lived close together in European cities about 1850. Passing the middle-class family on the first (American second) floor, the economic condition of the tenants declined until one reached abject poverty in the garret. *(Bibliothèque Nationale, Paris)*

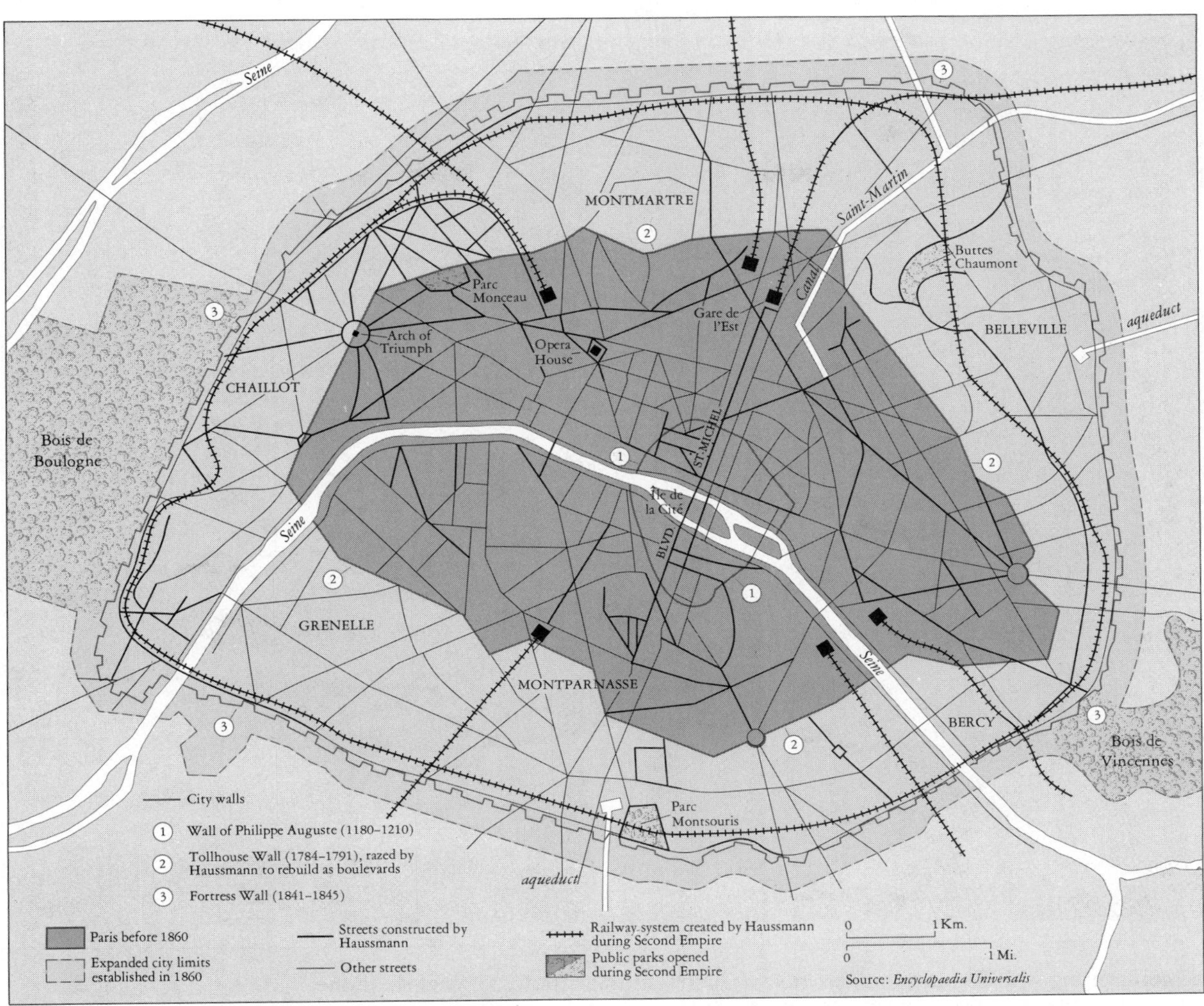

Map 24.2 The Modernization of Paris, ca 1850–1870 Broad boulevards, large parks, and grandiose train stations transformed Paris. The cutting of the new north-south axis—known as the Central Boulevard—was one of Haussmann's most controversial projects. It razed much of Paris's medieval core and filled the Île de la Cité with massive government buildings.

construction. Cities like Vienna and Cologne followed the Parisian example of tearing down old walled fortifications and replacing them with broad, circular boulevards on which office buildings, town halls, theaters, opera houses, and museums were erected. These ring roads and the new boulevards that radiated out from them toward the outskirts eased movement and encouraged urban expansion (see Map 24.2). *Zoning expropriation laws,* which allowed a majority of the owners of land in a given quarter of the city to impose major street or sanitation improvements on a reluctant minority, were an important mechanism of the new urbanism.

The development of mass public transportation was also of great importance in the improvement of urban living conditions. Such transportation came late, but in a powerful rush. In the 1870s, many European cities authorized private companies to operate horse-drawn streetcars, which had been developed in the United States, to carry riders along the growing number of major thoroughfares. Then, in the 1890s, occurred the real revolution: European countries adopted another American transit innovation, the electric streetcar.

Electric streetcars were cheaper, faster, more dependable, and more comfortable than their horse-

Experimenting with Steam Countless inventors sought to adapt steam engines to the demands of urban transit. Yet even the most ingenious steam locomotives, like the one above being introduced in Paris in 1876, remained dirty, noisy, and undependable. And they frightened horses, which toiled on until relieved by electric motors. *(Photo: Caroline Buckler)*

drawn counterparts. Service improved dramatically. Millions of Europeans—workers, shoppers, schoolchildren—hopped on board during the workweek. And on weekends and holidays, streetcars carried millions on happy outings to parks and countryside, racetracks and music halls. In 1886 the horse-drawn streetcars of Austria-Hungary, France, Germany, and Great Britain were carrying about 900 million riders. By 1910 electric streetcar systems in the four countries were carrying 6.7 billion riders.[6] Each man, woman, and child was using public transportation four times as often in 1910 as in 1886.

Good mass transit helped greatly in the struggle for decent housing. Just as the new boulevards and horse-drawn streetcars had facilitated the middle-class move to better housing in the 1860s and 1870s, so electric streetcars gave people of modest means access to new, improved housing after 1890. The still-crowded city was able to expand and become less congested. In England in 1901, only 9 percent of the urban population was "overcrowded" in terms of the official definition of more than two persons per room. On the Continent, many city governments in the early twentieth century were building electric streetcar systems that provided transportation to new public and private housing developments in outlying areas of the city for the working classes. Poor, overcrowded housing, long one of the blackest blots on the urban landscape, was in retreat—another graphic example of the gradual taming of the urban environment.

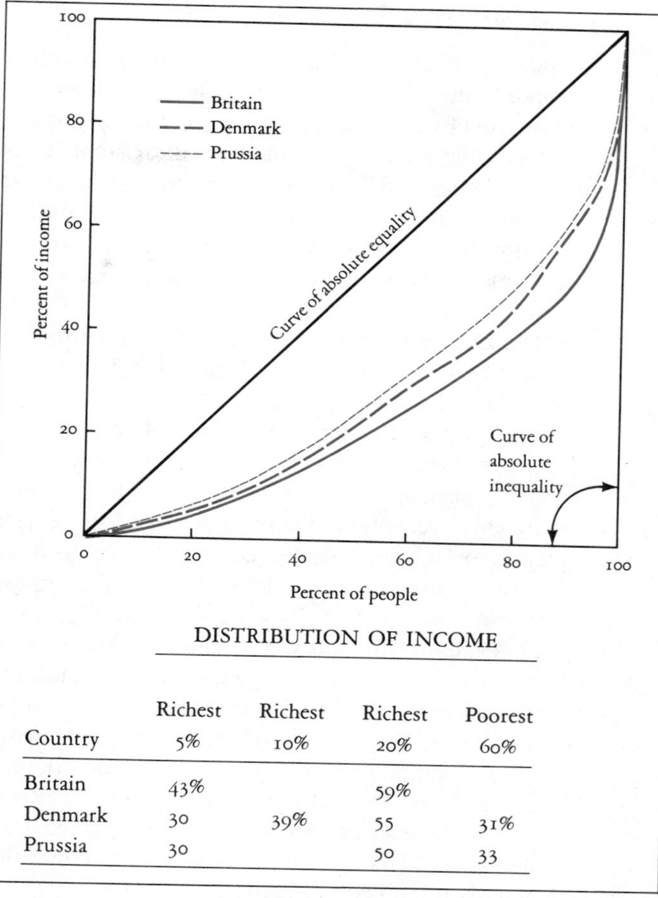

Country	Richest 5%	Richest 10%	Richest 20%	Poorest 60%
Britain	43%		59%	
Denmark	30	39%	55	31%
Prussia	30		50	33

FIGURE 24.2 The Distribution of Income in Britain, Denmark, and Prussia in 1913 The so-called Lorenz curve is useful for showing the degree of economic inequality in a given society. The closer the actual distribution of income lies to the (theoretical) curve of absolute equality, where each 20 percent of the population receives 20 percent of all income, the more incomes are nearly equal. European society was very far from any such equality before World War One. Notice that incomes in Prussia were somewhat more equal than those in Britain. *(Source: S. Kuznets,* Modern Economic Growth, *Yale University Press, New Haven, 1966, pp. 208–209)*

RICH AND POOR AND IN BETWEEN

General improvements in health and in the urban environment had beneficial consequences for all kinds of people. Yet differences in living conditions between social classes remained gigantic.

SOCIAL STRUCTURE

How much had the almost-completed journey to an urban, industrialized world changed the social framework of rich and poor? The first great change was a substantial and undeniable increase in the standard of living for the average person. The real wages of British workers, for example, which had already risen substantially by 1850, almost doubled between 1850 and 1906. Similar unmistakable increases occurred in continental countries as industrial development quickened after 1850. Ordinary people took a great step forward in the centuries-old battle against poverty, reinforcing efforts to improve many aspects of human existence.

There is another side to the income coin, however, and it must be stressed as well. Greater economic rewards for the average person did *not* eliminate poverty, nor did they make the wealth and income of the rich and the poor significantly more equal. In almost every advanced country around 1900, the richest 5 percent of all households in the population received fully one-third of all national income. The richest one-fifth of households received anywhere from 50 to 60 percent of all national income, while the entire bottom four-fifths received only 40 to 50 percent. Moreover, the bottom 30 percent of households received 10 percent or less of all income. These enormous differences are illustrated in Figure 24.2.

The middle classes were smaller than they are today and accounted for only about 20 percent of the population; thus, statistics show that the upper and middle classes alone received more than one-half of all income. The poorest four-fifths—the working classes, including peasants and agricultural laborers—received less altogether than the two richest classes.

And since many wives and teenagers in poor families worked, these figures actually understate the enduring gap between rich and poor. Moreover, income taxes on the wealthy were light or nonexistent. Thus the gap between rich and poor remained enormous at the beginning of the twentieth century. It was probably almost as great as it had been in the age of agriculture and aristocracy, before the Industrial Revolution.

The great gap between rich and poor endured, in part, because industrial and urban development made society more diverse and less unified. By no means did society split into two sharply defined opposing classes, as Marx had predicted. Instead, economic specialization enabled society to produce more effectively and in the process created more new social groups than it destroyed. There developed an almost unlimited range of jobs, skills, and earnings; one group or subclass shaded off into another in a complex, confusing hierarchy. Thus the tiny elite of the very rich and the sizable mass of the dreadfully poor were separated from each other by many subclasses, each filled with individuals struggling to rise or at least to hold their own in the social order. In this atmosphere of competition and hierarchy, neither the middle classes nor the working classes acted as a unified force. The age-old pattern of great economic inequality remained firmly intact.

The Middle Classes

By the beginning of the twentieth century, the diversity and range within the urban middle class were striking. Indeed, it is more meaningful to think of a confederation of middle classes, loosely united by occupations requiring mental rather than physical skill. At the top stood the upper-middle class, composed mainly of the most successful business families from banking, industry, and large-scale commerce. These families were the prime beneficiaries of modern industry and scientific progress. As the incomes of people in the upper-middle class rose and as they progressively lost all traces of radicalism after the trauma of 1848, they were almost irresistibly drawn toward the aristocratic lifestyle.

As the aristocracy had long divided the year between palatial country estates and lavish townhouses during "the season," so the upper-middle class purchased country places or built beach houses for weekend and summer use. (Little wonder that a favorite scenario in late nineteenth-century middle-class novels was a mother and children summering gloriously in the country home, with only sporadic weekend intrusions by a distant, shadowy father.) The number of servants was an important indicator of wealth and standing for the middle class, as it had always been for the aristocracy. Private coaches and carriages, ever an expensive item in the city, were also signs of rising social status. More generally, the rich businessman and certainly his son devoted less time to business and more to "culture" and easy living than was the case in less wealthy or well-established commercial families.

The topmost reaches of the upper-middle class tended to shade off into the old aristocracy to form a new upper class. This was the 5 percent of the population that, as we have seen, received roughly one-third of the national income in European countries before 1914. Much of the aristocracy welcomed this development. Having experienced a sharp decline in its relative income in the course of industrialization, the landed aristocracy had met big business coming up the staircase and was often delighted to trade titles, country homes, and snobbish elegance for good hard cash. Some of the best bargains were made through marriages to American heiresses. Correspondingly, wealthy aristocrats tended increasingly to exploit their agricultural and mineral resources as if they were businessmen. Bismarck was not the only proud nobleman to make a fortune distilling brandy on his estates.

Below the wealthy upper-middle class were much larger, much less wealthy, and increasingly diversified middle-class groups. Here one found the moderately successful industrialists and merchants, as well as professionals in law and medicine. This was the middle-middle class, solid and quite comfortable but lacking great wealth. Below them were independent shopkeepers, small traders, and tiny manufacturers—the lower-middle class. Both of these traditional elements of the middle class expanded modestly in size with economic development.

Meanwhile, the traditional middle class was gaining two particularly important additions. The expansion of industry and technology created a growing demand for experts with specialized knowledge. The most valuable of the specialties became solid middle-class professions. Engineering, for example, emerged from the world of skilled labor as a full-fledged profession of great importance, considerable prestige, and many branches. Architects, chemists, accountants, and surveyors—to name only a few—first achieved professional standing in this period. They established criteria for advanced training and certification and banded together in organizations to promote and defend their interests.

Management of large public and private institutions also emerged as a kind of profession, as governments provided more services and as very large corporations like railroads came into being. Government officials and many private executives were not capitalists in the sense that they owned business enterprises. But public and private managers did have specialized knowledge and the capacity to earn a good living. And they shared most of the values of the business-owning entrepreneurs and the older professionals.

Industrialization also expanded and diversified the lower-middle class. The number of independent, property-owning shopkeepers and small businessmen grew and so did the number of white-collar employees—a mixed group of traveling salesmen, bookkeepers, store managers, and clerks who staffed the offices and branch stores of large corporations. White-collar employees were propertyless and often earned no more than the better-paid skilled or semiskilled workers did. Yet white-collar workers were fiercely committed to the middle class and to the ideal of moving up in society. In the Balkans, for example, clerks let their fingernails grow very long to distinguish themselves from people who worked with their hands. The tie, the suit, and soft clean hands were no-less-subtle marks of class distinction than wages.

Relatively well educated but without complex technical skills, many white-collar groups aimed at achieving professional standing and the accompanying middle-class status. Elementary school teachers largely succeeded in this effort. From being miserably paid part-time workers in the early nineteenth century, teachers rode the wave of mass education to respectable middle-class status and income. Nurses also rose from the lower ranks of unskilled labor to precarious middle-class standing. Dentistry was taken out of the hands of the working-class barbers and placed in the hands of highly trained (and middle-class) professionals.

In spite of their growing occupational diversity and conflicting interests, the middle classes were loosely united by a certain style of life. Food was the largest item in the household budget, for middle-class people liked to eat very well. In France and Italy, the middle classes' love of good eating meant that, even in large cities, activity ground almost to a halt between half past twelve and half past two on weekdays, as husbands and schoolchildren returned home for the midday meal. Around eight in the evening, the serious business of eating was taken up once again.

The English were equally attached to substantial meals, which they ate three times a day if income allowed. The typical English breakfast of bacon and eggs, toast and marmalade, and stewed fruits—not to mention sardines, kidneys, or fresh fish—always astonished French and German travelers, though large-breakfast enthusiasts like the Dutch and Scandinavians were less awed. The European middle classes consumed meat in abundance, and a well-off family might spend fully 10 percent of its substantial earnings on meat alone. In the 1890s, even a very prosperous English family—with an income of, say, $10,000 a year while the average working-class family earned perhaps $400 a year—spent fully a quarter of its income on food and drink.

Spending on food was also great because the dinner party was this class's favored social occasion. A wealthy family might give a lavish party for eight to twelve almost every week, while more modest households would settle for once a month. Throughout middle-class Europe, such dinners were served in the "French manner" (which the French had borrowed from the Russian aristocracy): eight or nine separate courses, from appetizers at the beginning to coffee and liqueurs at the end. In summer, a picnic was in order. But what a picnic! For a party of ten, one English cookbook suggested five pounds of cold salmon, a quarter of lamb, eight pounds of pickled brisket, a beef tongue, a chicken pie, salads, cakes, and six pounds of strawberries. An ordinary family meal normally consisted of only four courses—soup, fish, meat, and dessert.

The middle-class wife could cope with this endless procession of meals, courses, and dishes because she had both servants and money at her disposal. The middle classes were solid members of what some contemporary observers called the "servant-keeping classes." Indeed, the employment of at least one

"A Corner of the Table" With photographic precision this 1904 oil painting by the French academic artist Paul-Emile Chabas (1867–1937) skillfully idealizes the elegance and intimacy of a sumptuous dinner party. *(The Granger Collection)*

enormously helpful full-time maid to cook and clean was the best single sign that a family had crossed the vague line separating the working classes from the middle classes. The greater its income, the greater the number of servants a family employed. The all-purpose servant gave way to a cook and a maid, then to a cook, a maid, and a boy, and so on. A prosperous English family, far up the line with $10,000 a year, in 1900 spent fully one-fourth of its income on a hierarchy of ten servants: a manservant, a cook, a kitchen maid, two housemaids, a serving maid, a governess, a gardner, a coachman, and a stable boy. Domestic servants were the second largest item in the budget of the middle classes. Thus food and servants absorbed about one-half of income at all levels of the middle classes.

Well fed and well served, the middle classes were also well housed by 1900. Many quite prosperous families rented rather than owned their homes. Apartment living, complete with tiny rooms for servants under the eaves of the top floor, was commonplace (outside Great Britain), and wealthy investors and speculative builders found good profits in middle-class housing. By 1900 the middle classes were also quite clothes-conscious. The factory, the sewing machine, and the department store had all helped to reduce the cost and expand the variety of clothing. Middle-class women were particularly attentive to the fickle dictates of fashion.

Education was another growing expense, as middle-class parents tried to provide their children with ever-more-crucial advanced education. The keystones of culture and leisure were books, music, and travel. The long realistic novel, the heroics of Wagner and Verdi, the diligent striving of the dutiful daughter on a piano, and the packaged tour to a foreign country were all sources of middle-class pleasure.

Finally, the middle classes were loosely united by a shared code of expected behavior and morality. This code was strict and demanding. It laid great stress on hard work, self-discipline, and personal achievement. Men and women who fell into crime or poverty were generally assumed to be responsible for their own circumstances. Traditional Christian morality was reaffirmed by this code and preached tirelessly by middle-class people who took pride in their own good conduct and regular church attendance. Drinking and gambling were denounced as vices, sexual purity and fidelity were celebrated as virtues. In short, the middle-class person was supposed to know right from wrong and was expected to act accordingly.

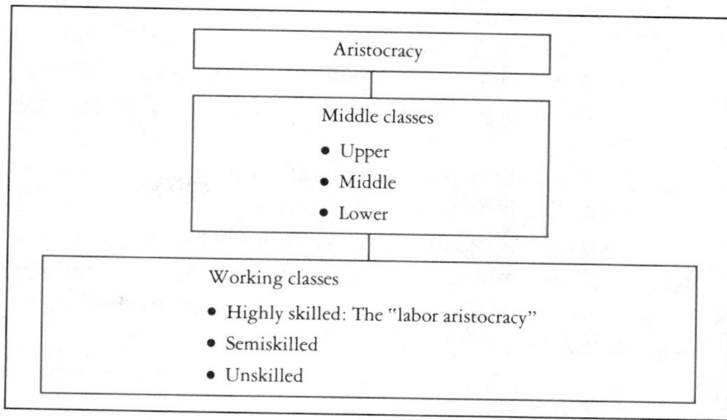

FIGURE 24.3 The Urban Social Hierarchy

THE WORKING CLASSES

About four out of five people belonged to the working classes at the turn of the century. Many members of the working classes—that is, people whose livelihoods depended on physical labor and who did not employ domestic servants—were still small landowning peasants and hired farm hands. This was especially true in eastern Europe. In western and central Europe, however, the typical worker had left the land. In Great Britain, less than 8 percent of the people worked in agriculture, while in rapidly industrializing Germany only one person in four was employed in agriculture and forestry. Even in less-industrialized France, less than half the people depended on the land in 1900.

The urban working classes were even less unified and homogeneous than the middle classes. In the first place, economic development and increased specialization expanded the traditional range of working-class skills, earnings, and experiences. Meanwhile, the old sharp distinction between highly skilled artisans and unskilled manual workers was gradually breaking down. To be sure, highly skilled printers and masons, as well as unskilled dock workers and common laborers, continued to exist. But between these extremes there were ever-more semiskilled groups, many of which were composed of factory workers and machine tenders (see Figure 24.3).

In the second place, skilled, semiskilled, and unskilled workers had widely divergent lifestyles and cultural values, and their differences contributed to a keen sense of social status and hierarchy within the working classes. The result was great variety and limited class unity.

Highly skilled workers, who comprised about 15 percent of the working classes, were a real "labor aristocracy." By 1900 they were earning about £2 a week in Great Britain, or roughly $10 a week and $500 per year. This was only about two-thirds the income of the bottom ranks of the servant-keeping classes. But it was fully twice as much as the earnings of unskilled workers, who averaged about $5 per week, and substantially more than the earnings of semiskilled workers, who averaged perhaps $7 per week. Other European countries had a similar range of earnings.

The most "aristocratic" of the highly skilled workers were construction bosses and factory foremen, men who had risen from the ranks and were fiercely proud of their achievement. The labor aristocracy also included members of the traditional highly skilled handicraft trades that had not been mechanized or placed in factories. These included makers of scientific and musical instruments, cabinetmakers, potters, jewelers, bookbinders, engravers, and printers. This group as a whole was under constant long-term pressure. Irregularly but inexorably, factory methods were being extended to more crafts, and many skilled artisans were being replaced by lower-paid semiskilled factory workers. Traditional woodcarvers and watchmakers virtually disappeared, for example, as the making of furniture and timepieces was taken out of the shop and put into the factory.

At the same time, a contrary movement was occurring. The labor aristocracy was consistently being enlarged by the growing need for highly skilled workers, such as shipbuilders, machine-tool makers, railway locomotive engineers, fine cotton textile spinners, and some metalworkers. Thus, the labor elite was in a state of flux as individuals and whole crafts moved in and out of it.

To maintain their precarious standing, the upper working class adopted distinctive values and straitlaced, almost puritanical, behavior. Like the middle classes, the labor aristocracy was strongly committed to the family and to economic improvement. Families in the upper working class saved money regularly, worried about their children's education, and valued good housing. Despite these similarities, which superficial observers were quick to exaggerate, skilled workers viewed themselves not as aspirants to the middle class but as the pacesetters and natural leaders of all the working classes. Well aware of the poverty and degradation not so far below them, they practiced self-discipline and stern morality.

The upper working class in general frowned on heavy drinking and sexual permissiveness. The organized temperance movement was strong in the countries of northern Europe, such as Great Britain, where a generation advocated tea as the "cup that cheers but does not inebriate." As one German labor aristocrat somberly warned, "the path to the brothel leads through the tavern" and from there quite possibly to drastic decline or total ruin for person and family.[7]

Men and women of the labor aristocracy were quick to find fault with those below them who failed to meet their standards. In 1868 William Lovett, an English labor aristocrat if ever there was one, denounced "this ignorant recklessness and improvidence that produce the swarms of half-starved, neglected, and ignorant children we see in all directions; who mostly grow up to become the burdens and often the pests of society, which the industrious and frugal have to support."[8] Finally, many members of the labor aristocracy had definite political and philosophical beliefs, whether Christian or socialist, or both. Such beliefs further strengthened the stern moral code of the upper working class.

Below the labor aristocracy stood semiskilled and unskilled urban workers. The enormous complexity of this sector of the world of labor is not easily summarized. Workers in the established crafts—carpenters, bricklayers, pipefitters—stood near the top of the semiskilled hierarchy, often flirting with (or having backslid from) the labor elite. A large number of the semiskilled were factory workers, who earned highly variable but relatively good wages and whose relative importance in the labor force was increasing.

The unskilled was the larger group, made up of day laborers such as longshoremen, wagon-driving teamsters, teenagers, and every kind of "helper." Many of these people had real skills and performed valuable services, but they were unorganized and divided, united only by the common fate of meager earnings. The same lack of unity characterized street vendors and market people—self-employed workers who competed savagely with each other and with the established shopkeepers of the lower-middle class.

One of the largest components of the unskilled group was domestic servants, whose numbers grew steadily in the nineteenth century. In advanced Great Britain, for example, one out of every seven employed persons was a domestic servant in 1911. The majority were women; indeed, one out of every three girls in Britain between the ages of fifteen and twenty was a domestic servant. Throughout Europe and America, a great many female domestics in the cities were recent migrants from rural areas. As in earlier times, domestic service was still hard work at low pay with limited personal independence. For the full-time general maid in a lower-middle-class family, there was an unending routine of babysitting, shopping, cooking, and cleaning. In the great households, the girl was at the bottom of a rigid hierarchy; status-conscious butlers and housekeepers were determined to stand almost as far above her as the wealthy master and mistress.

Nonetheless, domestic service had real attractions for "rough country girls" with strong hands and few specialized skills. Marriage prospects were better, or at least more varied, in the city. And though wages were low, they were higher and more regular than in hard agricultural work. Finally, as one London observer noted, young girls and other migrants were drawn to the city by "the contagion of numbers, the sense of something going on, the theaters and the music halls, the brightly lighted streets and busy

Cotton Textile Workers in Germany Factories became larger, faster, and more efficient in the nineteenth century. Compare this cotton mill with that of the early Industrial Revolution on page 715, where women and children are working together. *(Süddeutscher Verlag)*

crowds—all, in short, that makes the difference between the Mile End fair on a Saturday night, and a dark and muddy country lane, with no glimmer of gas and with nothing to do."[9]

Many young domestics from the countryside made a successful transition to working-class wife and mother. Yet, with an unskilled or unemployed husband and a growing family, such a woman often had to join the broad ranks of working women in the "sweated industries." These industries resembled the old putting-out and cottage industries of the eighteenth and early nineteenth centuries. The women normally worked at home, though sometimes together in some loft or garret, for tiny merchant-manufacturers. Paid by the piece and not by the hour, these women (and their young daughters), for whom organization was impossible, earned pitiful wages and lacked any job security.

Some women did hand-decorating of every conceivable kind of object; the majority, however, made clothing, especially after the advent of the sewing machine. Foot-powered sewing machines allowed the poorest wife or widow in the foulest dwelling to rival and eventually supplant the most highly skilled male tailor. By 1900 only a few such tailors lingered on in high-priced "tailor-made" shops. An army of poor women accounted for the bulk of the inexpensive "ready-made" clothes displayed on department store racks and in tiny shops. All of these considerations graphically illustrate the rise and fall of groups and individuals within the working classes.

The urban working classes sought fun and recreation, and they found it. Across the face of Europe, drinking was unquestionably the favorite leisure-time activity of working people. For many middle-class moralists, as well as moralizing historians since,

Servants Seeking Work in Moscow bargained with prospective employers (or their agents) in this special hiring yard just outside the ancient city walls. Moscow's bustling "market for servants" was open every day of the year and was busiest on Sundays. *(University of Illinois, Champaign)*

love of drink has been a curse of the modern age—a sign of social dislocation and popular suffering. Certainly, drinking was deadly serious business. One English slum dweller recalled that "drunkenness was by far the commonest cause of dispute and misery in working class homes. On account of it one saw many a decent family drift down through poverty into total want."[10]

Generally, however, heavy "problem" drinking declined by the late nineteenth century, as it became less and less socially acceptable. This decline reflected in part the firm moral leadership of the upper working class. At the same time, drinking became more public and social, especially as on-the-job drinking, an ancient custom of field laborers and urban artisans, declined. Cafés and pubs became increasingly bright, friendly places. Working-class political activities, both moderate and radical, were also concentrated in taverns and pubs. Moreover, social drinking by married couples and sweethearts became an accepted and widespread practice for the first time. This greater participation by women undoubtedly helped to civilize the world of drink and hard liquor.

The two other leisure-time passions of the working classes were sports and music halls. By the late nineteenth century there had been a great decline in "cruel sports," such as bullbaiting and cockfighting, throughout Europe. Their place was filled by modern spectator sports, of which racing and soccer were the most popular. There was a great deal of gambling on sports events, and for many a workingman the desire to decipher the racing forms was a powerful incentive toward literacy. Music halls and vaudeville theaters, the working-class counterparts of middle-class opera and classical theater, were enormously popular throughout Europe. In the words of one English printer, "It is to the music halls that the vast body of working people look for recreation and entertainment."[11] In 1900 there were more than fifty in London alone. Music-hall audiences were thoroughly mixed, which may account for the fact that drunkenness, sexual intercourse and pregnancy before marriage, marital difficulties, and problems with mothers-in-law were favorite themes of broad jokes and bittersweet songs.

In more serious moments, religion and the Christian churches continued to provide working people with solace and meaning. The eighteenth-century vitality of popular religion in Catholic countries and the Protestant rejuvenation exemplified by German Pietism and English Methodism (pages 661–662)

Sweated Industry About 1900 This moving photograph shows an English family making cheap toys at home for low wages. Women and children were the backbone of sweated industry, and this husband may be filling in while unemployed. *(University of Reading, Institute of Agricultural History and Museum of English Rural Life)*

carried over into the nineteenth century. Indeed, many historians see the early nineteenth century as an age of religious revival. Yet historians also recognize that, by the last two or three decades of the nineteenth century, a considerable decline in both church attendance and church donations was occurring in most European countries. And it seems clear that this decline was greater for the urban working classes than for their rural counterparts or for the middle classes.

What did the decline in working-class church attendance really mean? Some have argued that it accurately reflected a general decline in faith and religious belief. Others disagree, noting correctly that most working-class families still baptized their children and considered themselves Christians. Admitting that more research is necessary, it appears that the urban working classes in Europe did become more secular and less religious in the late nineteenth and early twentieth centuries. They rarely repudiated the Christian religion, but it tended to play a diminishing role in their daily lives.

Part of the reason was that the construction of churches failed to keep up with the rapid growth of urban population, especially in new working-class neighborhoods. Thus the vibrant, materialistic urban environment undermined popular religious impulses, which were poorly served in the cities. Equally important, however, was the fact that throughout the nineteenth century both Catholic and Protestant churches were normally seen as they saw themselves—as conservative institutions defending social order and custom. Therefore, as the European working classes became more politically conscious, as the next chapter will show, they tended to see the established (or quasi-established) "territorial church" as defending what they wished to change and allied with their political opponents. Especially the men of the urban working classes developed vaguely antichurch attitudes, even though they remained neutral or positive toward religion. They tended to regard regular church attendance as "not our kind of thing"—not part of urban working-class culture.

The pattern was different in the United States. There, most churches also preached social conservatism in the nineteenth century. But because church and state had always been separated and because there was always a host of competing denominations and even different religions, working people identified churches much less with the political and social status quo. Instead, individual churches in the United States were often closely identified with an ethnic group rather than with a social class; and churches thrived, in part, as a means of asserting ethnic identity.

THE FAMILY

Urban life wrought many fundamental changes in the family. Although much is still unknown, it seems clear that by the late nineteenth century, the family had stabilized considerably after the disruption of the late eighteenth and early nineteenth centuries. The home became more important for both men and women. The role of women and attitudes toward children underwent substantial change, and adolescence emerged as a distinct stage of life. These are but a few of the transformations that affected all social classes in varying degrees.

Premarital Sex and Marriage

By 1850 the preindustrial pattern of lengthy courtship and mercenary marriage was pretty well dead among the working classes. In its place, the ideal of romantic love had triumphed. As one French observer in a small seaport remarked about 1850: "The young men are constantly letting partners with handsome dowries go begging. When they marry, it's ordinarily for inclination and not for advantage."[12] Couples were ever more likely to come from different, even distant, towns and to be more nearly the same age, further indicating that romantic sentiment was replacing tradition and financial considerations. The calculating practice whereby wealthy old craftsmen took pretty young brides, who as comfortable middle-aged widows later married poor apprentices, was increasingly heard of only in old tales and folk songs.

Economic considerations in marriage long remained much more important to the middle classes than to the working classes. In France, dowries and elaborate legal marriage contracts were standard practice, and marriage was for many families life's most crucial financial transaction. A popular author advised young Frenchmen that "marriage is in general a means of increasing one's credit and one's fortune and of insuring one's success in the world."[13] This preoccupation with money led many middle-class men, in France and elsewhere, to marry late and to choose women considerably younger and less sexually experienced than themselves. These differences between husband and wife became a source of tension in many middle-class marriages.

A young woman of the middle class found her romantic life carefully supervised by her well-meaning mother, who schemed for a proper marriage and guarded her daughter's virginity like the family's credit. After marriage, middle-class morality sternly demanded fidelity.

Middle-class boys were watched, too, but not as vigilantly. By the time they reached late adolescence, they had usually attained considerable sexual experience with maids or prostitutes. With marriage a distant, uncertain possibility, it was all too easy for the young man of the middle classes to turn to the urban underworld of whoredom and sexual exploitation to satisfy his desires.

Sexual experimentation before marriage had also triumphed, as had illegitimacy. There was an "illegitimacy explosion" between 1750 and 1850 (page 641). By the 1840s, as many as one birth in three was occurring outside of wedlock in many large cities. Although poverty and economic uncertainty undoubtedly prevented many lovers from marrying, there were also many among the poor and propertyless who saw little wrong with having illegitimate offspring. As one young Bavarian woman answered happily when asked why she kept having illegitimate children: "It's O.K. to make babies. . . . The king has o.k.'d it!"[14] Thus the pattern of romantic ideals, premarital sexual activity, and widespread illegitimacy was firmly established by midcentury among the urban working classes.

It is hard to know how European couples managed sex, pregnancy, and marriage in the second half of the nineteenth century, because such questions were considered improper both in polite conversation and in public opinion polls. Yet there are many telltale clues. The rising rate of illegitimacy was reversed: more babies were born to married mothers. Some observers have argued that this shift reflected the growth of puritanism and a lessening of sexual permissiveness among the unmarried. This explanation, however, is unconvincing.

The percentage of brides who were pregnant continued to be high and showed little or no tendency to decline. In many parts of urban Europe around 1900, as many as one woman in three was going to the altar an expectant mother. Moreover, unmarried people

Prostitution was commonly known as the "great social evil" because it was so widespread. This young woman probably sold more than flowers. *(Mary Evans Picture Library)*

almost certainly used the cheap condoms and diaphragms the industrial age had made available to prevent pregnancy, at least in predominantly Protestant countries.

Unmarried young people were probably engaging in just as much sexual activity as their parents and grandparents who had created the illegitimacy explosion of 1750 to 1850. But toward the end of the nineteenth century, pregnancy usually meant marriage and the establishment of a two-parent household. This important development reflected the growing respectability of the working classes, as well as their gradual economic improvement. Skipping out was less acceptable, and marriage was less of an economic disaster. Thus the urban working-class couple became more stable, and their stability strengthened the family as an institution.

Prostitution

In Paris alone, 155,000 women were registered as prostitutes between 1871 and 1903, and 750,000 others were suspected of prostitution in the same years. Men of all classes visited prostitutes, but the middle and upper classes supplied much of the motivating cash. Thus, though many middle-class men abided by the publicly professed code of stern puritanical morality, many others indulged their appetites for prostitutes and sexual promiscuity.

My Secret Life, the anonymous eleven-volume autobiography of an English sexual adventurer from the servant-keeping classes, provides a remarkable picture of such a man. Beginning at an early age with a maid, the author becomes progressively obsessed with sex and devotes his life to living his sexual fantasies. In almost every one of his innumerable encounters all across Europe, this man of wealth simply buys his pleasure. Usually meetings are arranged in a businesslike manner: regular and part-time prostitutes quote their prices; working-class girls are corrupted by hot meals and warm baths.

At one point, however, he offers a young girl a sixpence for a kiss and gets it. Learning that the pretty, unskilled working girl earns nine pence a day, he offers her the equivalent of a week's salary for a few moments of fondling. When she finally agrees, he savagely exults that *"her* want was my opportunity."[15] Later he offers more money for more gratification, and when she refuses, he tries unsuccessfully to rape her in a hackney cab. On another occasion he takes a farm worker by force: "Her tears ran down. If I had not committed a rape, it looked uncommonly like one." He then forces his victim to take money to prevent a threatened lawsuit, while the foreman advises the girl to keep quiet and realize that "you be in luck if he likes you."

Obviously atypical in its excesses, the encyclopedic thoroughness of *My Secret Life* does mirror accurately the dark side of sex and class in urban society. Thinking of their wives largely in terms of money and social position, the men of the comfortable classes often purchased sex and even affection from poor girls both before and after marriage. Moreover, the great continuing differences between rich and poor made for every kind of debauchery and sexual exploitation, including the brisk trade in poor virgins that the author of *My Secret Life* particularly relished. Brutal sexist behavior was part of life—a part the sternly moral women (and men) of the upper working class detested and tried to shield their daughters from. For many poor young women, prostitution, like domestic service, was a stage of life. Having passed through it, they went on to marry men of their own class and establish homes and families.

Kinship Ties

Within working-class homes, ties to relatives after marriage—kinship ties—were in general much stronger than superficial social observers have recognized. Most newlyweds tried to live near their parents, though not in the same house. Indeed, for many married couples in the cities, ties to mothers and fathers, uncles and aunts, became more important, and ties to nonrelated acquaintances became weaker.

People turned to their families to help in coping with sickness, unemployment, death, and old age. Although governments were generally providing more welfare services by 1900, the average couple and their children inevitably faced crises. Funerals, for example, were an economic catastrophe, requiring a sudden large outlay for special clothes, carriages, and burial services. Unexpected death or desertion could leave widows and orphans in need of financial aid or perhaps a foster home. Relatives responded to such cries, knowing full well that their time of need and repayment would undoubtedly come.

Relatives were also valuable at less tragic moments. If a couple was very poor, an aged relation often moved in to cook and mind the children so the wife could earn badly needed income outside the home. Sunday dinners and holiday visits were often shared, as was outgrown clothing and useful information. Often the members of a large family group all lived in the same neighborhood.

Women and Family Life

Industrialization and the growth of modern cities brought great changes to the lives of European women. These changes were particularly consequential for married women, and most women did marry in the nineteenth century.

The work of most wives became quite distinct and separate from that of their husbands. Husbands became wage earners in factories and offices, while wives tended to stay home and manage the household and care for the children. The preindustrial pattern among both peasants and cottage workers, in which husbands and wives worked together and divided up household duties and child rearing, declined. Only in a few occupations, such as retail trade, did married couples live where they worked and struggle together to make their mom-and-pop operations a success. Factory employment for married women also declined as the early practice of hiring entire families in the factory disappeared.

As economic conditions improved late in the nineteenth century, married women tended to work outside the home only in poor families. One old English worker recalled that "the boy wanted to get into a position that would enable him to keep a wife and fam-

A Working-Class Home, 1875 Emotional ties within ordinary families grew stronger in the nineteenth century. *(Illustrated London News, LXVI, 1875. Photo courtesy of Boston Public Library)*

ily, as it was considered a thoroughly unsatisfactory state of affairs if the wife had to work to help maintain the home."[16] The ideal was a strict division of labor by sex: the wife as mother and homemaker, the husband as wage earner.

This rigid division of labor meant that married women faced great injustice if they tried to move into the man's world, the world of employment outside the home. Husbands were unsympathetic or hostile. Well-paying jobs were off limits to women, and a woman's wage was almost always less than a man's, even for the same work. No wonder some women rebelled by the second half of the nineteenth century and began the long-continuing fight for equality of the sexes and the rights of women. More generally, rigidly separate roles narrowed women's horizons and fenced in their world.

There was a brighter side to the same coin. As home and children became the wife's main concerns, her control and influence there apparently became increasingly absolute throughout Europe. Among the English working classes, it was the wife who generally determined how the family's money was spent. In many families the husband gave all his earnings to his wife to tend. She returned to him only a small allowance for carfare, beer, tobacco, and union dues. All the major domestic decisions, from the children's schooling and religious instruction to the selection of new furniture or a new apartment, were hers. In France women had even greater power in their assigned domain. One English feminist noted in 1908 that "though legally women occupy a much inferior status than men [in France], in practice they constitute the superior sex. They are the power behind the throne." Another Englishwoman believed that "in most French households, women reign with unchallenged sway."[17]

Women ruled at home partly because running the urban household was a complicated and extremely demanding task. Twice-a-day food shopping, penny pinching, economizing, and the growing crusade against dirt—not to mention child raising—were a full-time occupation. Nor were there any laborsaving appliances to help. The wife also ruled at home because a good deal of her effort was directed toward pampering her husband as he expected. In countless humble households, she saw that he had meat while she ate bread, that he relaxed by the fire while she did the dishes.

The woman's guidance of the household went hand in hand with the increased emotional importance of home and family. The home she ran was idealized as a warm shelter in a hard and impersonal urban world. By the 1820s, one observer of the comfortable middle classes in Marseilles had noted, for example, that "the family father, obliged to occupy himself with difficult business problems during the day, can relax only when he goes home. . . . Family evenings together are for him a time of the purest and most complete happiness."[18]

In time the central place of the family spread down the social scale. For a child of the English slums in the early 1900s,

> *home, however, poor, was the focus of all love and interests, a sure fortress against a hostile world. Songs about its beauties were ever on people's lips. "Home, sweet home," first heard in the 1870s, had become "almost a second national anthem." Few walls in lower-working-class houses lacked "mottoes"—colored strips of paper, about nine inches wide and eighteen inches in length, attesting to domestic joys: EAST, WEST, HOME'S BEST; BLESS OUR HOME; GOD IS MASTER OF THIS HOUSE; HOME IS THE NEST WHERE ALL IS BEST.*[19]

By 1900 home and family were what life was all about for millions of people of all classes.

Women also developed stronger emotional ties to their husbands. Even in the comfortable classes, marriages were increasingly founded on sentiment and sexual attraction rather than on money and calculation. Affection and eroticism became more central to the couple after marriage. Gustave Droz, whose best-seller *Mr., Mrs., and Baby* went through 121 editions between 1866 and 1884, saw love within marriage as the key to human happiness. He condemned men who made marriage sound dull and practical, men who were exhausted by prostitutes and rheumatism and who wanted their young wives to be little angels. He urged women to follow their hearts and marry a man more nearly their own age:

> *A husband who is stately and a little bald is all right, but a young husband who loves you and who drinks out of your glass without ceremony, is better. Let him, if he ruffles your dress a little and places a kiss on your neck as he passes. Let him, if he undresses you after the ball, laughing like a fool. You have fine spiritual qualities, it is true, but your little body is not bad either and when one loves, one loves completely. Behind these follies lies happiness.*[20]

Many French marriage manuals of the late 1800s stressed that women had legitimate sexual needs, such as the "right to orgasm." Perhaps the French were a bit more enlightened in these matters than other nationalities. But the rise of public socializing by couples in cafés and music halls, as well as franker affection within the family, suggest a more erotic, pleasurable intimate life for women throughout Western society. This, too, helped make the woman's role as mother and homemaker acceptable and even satisfying.

Child Raising

One of the most striking signs of deepening emotional ties within the family was the mother's love and concern for her tiny infants. This was a sharp break with the past. It may seem scarcely believable today that the typical mother in preindustrial Western society was very often indifferent toward her baby. This indifference—unwillingness to make real sacrifices for the welfare of the infant—was giving way among the comfortable classes by the later part of the eighteenth century, but the ordinary mother adopted new attitudes only as the nineteenth century progressed. The baby became more important, and women became better mothers.

Mothers increasingly breast-fed their infants, for example, rather than paying wet nurses to do so. Breast-feeding involved sacrifice—a temporary loss of freedom, if nothing else. Yet in an age when there was no good alternative to mother's milk, it saved lives. The surge of maternal feeling also gave rise to a wave of specialized books on child rearing and infant hygiene, such as Droz's phenomenally successful book. Droz urged fathers to get into the act and pitied those "who do not know how to roll around on the carpet, play at being a horse and a great wolf, and undress their baby."[21] Another sign, from France, of increased affection is that fewer illegitimate babies were abandoned as foundlings, especially after about 1850. Moreover, the practice of swaddling disappeared completely. Instead, ordinary mothers allowed their babies freedom of movement and delighted in their spontaneity.

The loving care lavished on infants was matched by greater concern for older children and adolescents. They, too, were wrapped in the strong emotional ties of a more intimate and protective family. For one thing, European women began to limit the number of children they bore, in order to care adequately for those they had. It was evident by the end of the century that the birthrate was declining across Europe, as Figure 24.4 shows, and it continued to do so until after World War Two. The Englishwoman who married in the 1860s, for example, had an average of about six children; her daughter marrying in the 1890s had only four; and her granddaughter marrying in the 1920s had only two or possibly three.

The most important reason for this revolutionary reduction in family size, in which the comfortable and well-educated classes took the lead, was parents' desire to improve their economic and social position and that of their children. Children were no longer an economic asset. By having fewer youngsters, parents could give those they had valuable advantages, from music lessons and summer vacations to long, expensive university educations and suitable dowries. A young German skilled worker with only one child spoke for many in his class when he said, "We want to get ahead, and our daughter should have things better than my wife and sisters did."[22] Thus, the growing tendency of couples in the late nineteenth century to use a variety of contraceptive methods—rhythm, withdrawal, and mechanical devices—certainly reflected increased concern for children.

Indeed, many parents were probably *too* concerned about their children, unwittingly subjecting them to an emotional pressure cooker of almost unbearable intensity. The result was that many children and especially adolescents came to feel trapped and in desperate need of greater independence.

Biological and medical theories led parents to believe that their own emotional characteristics were passed on to their offspring and that they were thus directly responsible for any abnormality in a child. The moment the child was conceived was thought to be of enormous importance. "Never run the risk of conception when you are sick or over-tired or unhappy," wrote one influential American woman.

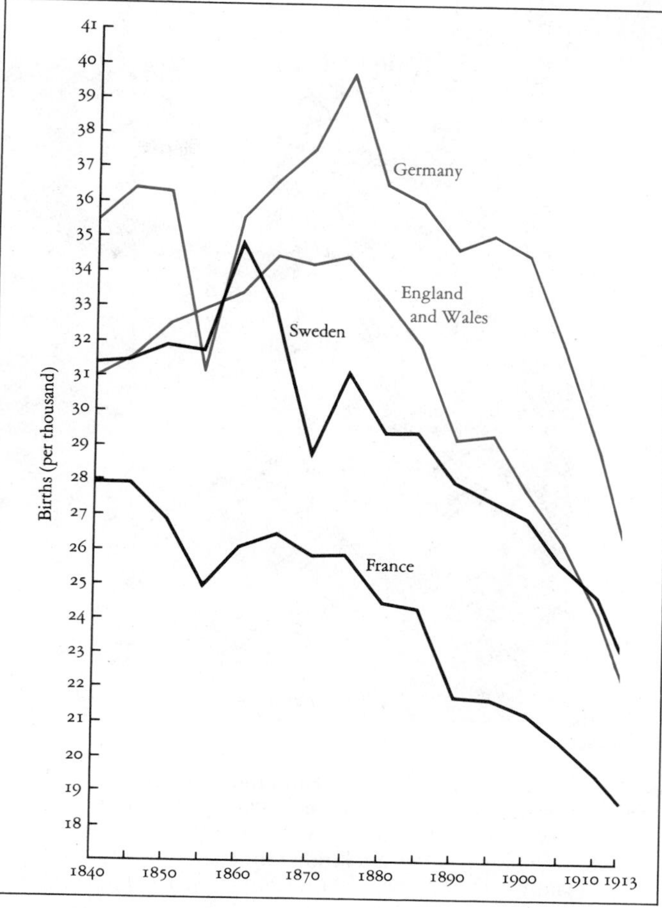

FIGURE 24.4 The Decline of Birthrates in England and Wales, France, Germany, and Sweden, 1840–1913 Women had fewer babies for a variety of reasons, including the fact that their children were increasingly less likely to die before reaching adulthood. Compare with Figure 24.2 on page 771.

"For the bodily condition of the child, its vigor and magnetic qualities, are much affected by conditions ruling this great moment."[23] So might the youthful "sexual excess" of the father curse future generations. Although this was true in the case of syphilis, which could be transmitted to unborn children, the rigid determinism of such views left little scope for the child's individual development.

Another area of excessive parental concern was the sexual behavior of the child. Masturbation was viewed with horror, for it represented an act of independence and even defiance. Diet, clothing, games, and sleeping were carefully regulated. Girls were dis-

The Drawing Room The middle-class ideal of raising cultured, educated, and properly protected young women is captured in this illustration. A serious mother lovingly teaches her youngest child while the older daughters practice their genteel skills. A drawing room was a kind of nineteenth-century family room, mercifully spared the tyranny of television. *(BBC Hulton/The Bettmann Archive)*

couraged from riding horses and bicycling because rhythmic friction simulated masturbation. Boys were dressed in trousers with shallow and widely separated pockets. Between 1850 and 1880, there were surgical operations for children who persisted in masturbating. Thereafter until about 1905, various restraining apparatuses were more often used.

These and less blatant attempts to repress the child's sexuality were a source of unhealthy tension, often made worse by the rigid division of sexual roles within the family. It was widely believed that mother and child love each other easily, but that relations between father and child are necessarily difficult and often tragic. The father was a stranger, his world of business was far removed from the maternal world of spontaneous affection. Moreover, the father was demanding, often expecting the child to succeed where he himself had failed and making his love conditional on achievement. Little wonder that the imaginative literature of the late nineteenth century came to deal with the emotional and destructive elements of father-son relationships. In the Russian Feodor Dostoevsky's great novel *The Brothers Karamazov* (1880–1881), for example, four sons work knowingly or unknowingly to destroy their father. Later, at the murder trial, one of the brothers claims to speak for all mankind and screams out: "Who doesn't wish his father dead?"

Sigmund Freud (1856–1939), the Viennese founder of psychoanalysis, formulated the most striking analysis of the explosive dynamics of the family, particularly the middle-class family in the late nineteenth century. A physician by training, Freud began his career treating mental illness. He noted that the hysteria of his patients appeared to originate in bitter early childhood experiences, wherein the child had been obliged to repress strong feelings. When these painful experiences were recalled and reproduced under hypnosis or through the patient's free association of ideas, the patient could be brought to understand his or her unhappiness and eventually to deal with it.

One of Freud's most influential ideas concerned the Oedipal tensions resulting from the son's instinctive competition with the father for the mother's love and affection. More generally, Freud postulated that much of human behavior is motivated by unconscious emotional needs, whose nature and origins are kept from conscious awareness by various mental devices he called "defense mechanisms." Freud concluded that much unconscious psychological energy is sexual energy, which is in turn repressed and precariously controlled by rational thinking and moral rules. If Freud exaggerated the sexual and familial roots of adult behavior, that exaggeration was itself a reflection of the tremendous emotional intensity of family life in the late nineteenth century.

The working classes probably had more avenues of escape from such tensions than did the middle classes. Unlike the middle-class counterparts, who remained economically dependent on their families until a long education was finished or a proper marriage secured, working-class boys and girls went to work when they reached adolescence. Earning wages on their own, they could bargain with their parents for greater independence within the household by the time they were sixteen or seventeen. If they were unsuccessful, they could and did leave home, to live cheaply as paying lodgers in other working-class homes. Thus, the young person from the working classes broke away from the family more easily when emotional ties became oppressive. In the twentieth century, middle-class youth would follow this lead.

SCIENCE AND THOUGHT

Major changes in Western thought accompanied the emergence of urban society. Two aspects of these complex intellectual developments stand out as especially significant. Scientific knowledge expanded rapidly and came to influence the Western world-view even more profoundly than it had since the Scientific Revolution and the early Enlightenment. And, between about the 1840s and the 1890s, European literature underwent a shift from soaring romanticism to tough-minded realism.

The Triumph of Science

As the pace of scientific advance quickened and as theoretical advances resulted in great practical benefits, science exercised growing influence on human thought. The intellectual achievements of the Scientific Revolution had resulted in few such benefits, and theoretical knowledge had also played a relatively small role in the Industrial Revolution in England. But breakthroughs in industrial technology enormously stimulated basic scientific inquiry, as researchers sought to explain theoretically how such things as steam engines and blast furnaces actually worked. The result was an explosive growth of fundamental scientific discoveries from the 1830s onward. And unlike earlier periods, these theoretical discoveries were increasingly transformed into material improvements for the general population.

A perfect example of the translation of better scientific knowledge into practical human benefits was the work of Pasteur and his followers in biology and the medical sciences. Another was the development of the branch of physics known as *thermodynamics.* Building on Newton's laws of mechanics and on studies of steam engines, thermodynamics investigated the relationship between heat and mechanical energy. By midcentury, physicists had formulated the fundamental laws of thermodynamics, which were then applied to mechanical engineering, chemical processes, and many other fields. The *law of conservation of energy* held that different forms of energy—such as heat, electricity, and magnetism—could be converted but neither created nor destroyed. Nineteenth-century thermodynamics demonstrated that the physical world is governed by firm, unchanging laws.

Chemistry and electricity were two other fields characterized by extremely rapid progress. Chemists devised ways of measuring the atomic weight of different elements, and in 1869 the Russian chemist Dmitri Mendeleev (1834–1907) codified the rules of chemistry in the periodic law and the periodic table. Chemistry was subdivided into many specialized branches, such as *organic chemistry*—the study of the compounds of carbon. Applying theoretical insights gleaned from this new field, researchers in large German chemical companies discovered ways of transforming the dirty, useless coal tar that accumulated in coke ovens into beautiful, expensive synthetic dyes for the world of fashion. The basic discoveries of Michael Faraday (1791–1867) on electromagnetism in the 1830s and 1840s resulted in the first dynamo (generator) and opened the way for the subsequent development of electric motors, electric lights, and electric streetcars.

The triumph of science and technology had at least three significant consequences. First, though ordinary citizens continued to lack detailed scientific knowledge, everyday experience and innumerable popularizers impressed the importance of science on the popular mind.

As science became more prominent in popular thinking, the philosophical implications of science formulated in the Enlightenment spread to broad sections of the population. Natural processes appeared to be determined by rigid laws, leaving little room for either divine intervention or human will. Yet scientific and technical advances had also fed the Enlightenment's optimistic faith in human progress, which now appeared endless and automatic to many middle-class minds.

Finally, the methods of science acquired unrivaled prestige after 1850. For many, the union of careful experiment and abstract theory was the only reliable route to truth and objective reality. The "unscientific" intuitions of poets and the revelations of saints seemed hopelessly inferior.

Social Science and Evolution

From the 1830s onward, many thinkers tried to apply the objective methods of science to the study of society. In some ways these efforts simply perpetuated the critical thinking of the philosophes. Yet there were important differences. The new "social scientists" had access to the massive sets of numerical data that governments had begun to collect, on everything from children to crime, from population to prostitution. In response, they developed new statistical methods to analyze these facts "scientifically" and supposedly to test their theories. And the systems of the leading nineteenth-century social scientists were more unified, all-encompassing, and dogmatic than those of the philosophes. Marx was a prime example (see pages 739–741).

Another extremely influential system builder was the French philosopher Auguste Comte (1798–1857). Initially a disciple of the utopian socialist Saint-Simon (page 739), Comte wrote a six-volume *System of Positive Philosophy* (1830–1842), which was largely overlooked during the romantic era. But when the political failures of 1848 completed the swing to realism, Comte's philosophy came into its own. Its influence has remained great to this day.

Comte postulated that all intellectual activity progresses through predictable stages:

> *The great fundamental law . . . is this:—that each of our leading conceptions—each branch of our knowledge—passes successively through three different theoretical conditions: the Theological, or fictitious; the Metaphysical, or abstract; and the Scientific, or positive . . . The first is the necessary point of departure of human understanding, and the third is the fixed and definitive state. The second is merely a transition.*[24]

By way of example, Comte noted that the prevailing explanation of cosmic patterns had shifted, as knowledge of astronomy developed, from the will of God (the theological) to the will of an orderly Nature (the metaphysical) to the rule of its own unchanging laws (the scientific). Later, this same intellectual progression took place in increasingly complex fields—physics, chemistry, and finally, the study of society. By applying the scientific, positivist method, Comte believed, his new discipline of sociology would soon discover the eternal laws of human relations. This colossal achievement would in turn enable expert social scientists to impose a disciplined harmony and well-being on less-enlightened citizens. Dismissing the "fictions" of traditional religions, Comte became the chief priest of the religion of science and rule by experts.

Comte's stages of knowledge exemplify the nineteenth-century fascination with the idea of evolution and dynamic development. Thinkers in many fields, like the romantic historians and "scientific" Marxists, shared and applied this basic concept. In geology, Charles Lyell (1797–1875) effectively discredited the long-standing view that the earth's surface had been formed by short-lived cataclysms, such as biblical floods and earthquakes. Instead, according to Lyell's principle of uniformitarianism, the same geological processes that are at work today slowly formed the earth's surface over an immensely long time. The evolutionary view of biological development, first proposed by the Greek Anaximander in the sixth century B.C., reemerged in a more modern form in the work of Jean Baptiste Lamarck (1744–1829). Lamarck asserted that all forms of life had

Attracting Females was an integral part of the struggle for survival, according to Darwin. He theorized that those males who were most attractive to females would have the most offspring, like this type of monkey that had developed ornamental hair with devastating sex appeal. Darwin used this illustration in *The Descent of Man* (1871). *(Library of Congress)*

arisen through a long process of continuous adjustment to the demands of the environment.

Lamarck's work was flawed—he believed that characteristics parents acquired in the course of their lives could be inherited by their children—and was not accepted, but it helped prepare the way for Charles Darwin (1809–1882), the most influential of all nineteenth-century evolutionary thinkers. As the official naturalist on a five-year scientific cruise to Latin America and the South Pacific in 1831, Darwin carefully collected specimens of the different animal species he encountered on the voyage. Back in England and convinced by fossil evidence and by his friend Lyell that the earth and life on it were immensely ancient, Darwin came to doubt the general belief in a special divine creation of each species of animals. Instead, he concluded, all life had gradually evolved from a common ancestral origin in an unending "struggle for survival." After long hesitation, Darwin published his research, which immediately attracted wide attention.

Darwin's great originality lay in suggesting precisely *how* biological evolution might have occurred. His theory is summarized in his title—*On the Origin of Species by the Means of Natural Selection* (1859). Decisively influenced by Malthus's gloomy theory that populations naturally grow faster than their food supplies, Darwin argued that chance differences among the members of a given species help some to survive while others died. Thus the variations that prove useful in the struggle for survival are selected naturally and gradually spread to the entire species through reproduction. Darwin did not explain why such variations occurred in the first place, and not until the early twentieth century did the study of genetics and the concept of mutation provide some answers.

As the capstone of already-widespread evolutionary thinking, Darwin's theory had a powerful and many-sided influence on European thought and the European middle classes. Darwin was hailed as the great scientist par excellence, the "Newton of biology," who had revealed once again the powers of objective science. Darwin's findings also reinforced the teachings of secularists like Comte and Marx, who scornfully dismissed religous belief in favor of agnostic or atheistic materialism. In the great cities especially, religion was on the defensive. Finally, many writers applied the theory of biological evolution to human affairs. Herbert Spencer (1820–1903), an English disciple of Auguste Comte, saw the human race as driven forward to ever-greater specialization and progress by the brutal econon ic struggle that efficiently determined the "survival of the fittest." The poor were the ill-fated weak, the prosperous the chosen strong. Understandably, Spencer and other Social Darwinists were especially popular with the upper-middle class.

Realism in Literature

In 1868 Emile Zola (1840–1902), the giant of the realist movement in literature, defended his violently criticized first novel against charges of pornography and corruption of morals. Such accusations were meaningless, Zola claimed: he was only a purely objective scientist using "the modern method, the universal instrument of inquiry of which this age makes such ardent use to open up the future."

I chose characters completely dominated by their nerves and their blood, deprived of free-will, pushed to each action of their lives by the fatality of their flesh. . . . I have simply done on living bodies the work of analysis which surgeons perform on corpses.[25]

Zola's literary manifesto articulated the key themes of realism, which had emerged in the 1840s and continued to dominate Western culture and style until the 1890s. Realist writers believed that literature should depict life exactly as it was. Forsaking poetry for prose and the personal, emotional viewpoint of the romantics for strict, scientific objectivity, the realists simply observed and recorded—content to let the facts speak for themselves.

The major realist writers focused their extraordinary powers of observation on contemporary everyday life. Emphatically rejecting the romantic search for the exotic and the sublime, they energetically pursued the typical and the commonplace. Beginning with a dissection of the middle classes, from which most of them sprang, many realists eventually focused on the working classes, especially the urban working classes, who had been neglected in imaginative literature before this time. They put a microscope to many unexplored and taboo subjects—sex, strikes, violence, alcoholism—and hastened to report that slums and factories teemed with savage behavior. Many shocked middle-class critics denounced realism as ugly sensationalism, wrapped provocatively in pseudoscientific declarations and crude language.

The realists' claims of objectivity did not prevent the elaboration of a definite world-view. Unlike the romantics, who had gloried in individual freedom and an unlimited universe, realists such as Zola were strict determinists. Human beings, like atoms, were components of the physical world, and all human actions were caused by unalterable natural laws. Heredity and environment determined human behavior; good and evil were merely social conventions.

The realist movement began in France, where romanticism had never been completely duminant, and three of its greatest practitioners—Balzac, Flaubert, and Zola—were French. Honoré de Balzac (1799–1850) spent thirty years writing a vastly ambitious panorama of postrevolutionary French life. Known collectively as *The Human Comedy,* this series of nearly one hundred books vividly portrays more than two thousand characters from virtually all sectors of French society. Balzac pictures urban society as grasping, amoral, and brutal, characterized by a Darwinian struggle for wealth and power. In *Père Goriot* (1835), the hero, a poor student from the provinces, eventually surrenders his idealistic integrity to feverish ambition and society's all-pervasive greed.

Madame Bovary (1857), the masterpiece of Gustave Flaubert (1821–1880), is far narrower in scope than Balzac's work but unparalleled in its depth and accuracy of psychological insight. Unsuccessfully prosecuted as an outrage against public morality and religion, Flaubert's carefully crafted novel tells the ordinary, even banal, story of a frustrated middle-class housewife who has an adulterous love affair and is betrayed by her lover. Without moralizing, Flaubert portrays the provincial middle class as petty, smug, and hypocritical.

Zola was most famous for his seamy, animalistic view of working-class life. But he also wrote gripping, carefully researched stories featuring the stock exchange, the big department store, and the army, as well as urban slums and bloody coal strikes. Like many later realists, Zola sympathized with socialism, a sympathy evident in his overpowering *Germinal* (1885).

Realism quickly spread beyond France. In England, Mary Ann Evans (1819–1880), who wrote under the pen name George Eliot, brilliantly achieved a more deeply felt, less sensational kind of realism. "It is the habit of my imagination," George Eliot wrote, "to strive after as full a vision of the medium in which a character moves as one of the character itself." Her great novel *Middlemarch: A Study of Provincial Life* examines masterfully the ways in which people are shaped by their social medium as well as their own inner strivings, conflicts, and moral choices. Thomas Hardy (1840–1928) was more in the Zola tradition. His novels, such as *Tess of the D'Urbervilles* and *Return of the Native,* depicted men and women frustrated and crushed by fate and bad luck.

The greatest Russian realist, Count Leo Tolstoy (1828–1910), combined realism in description and character development with an atypical moralizing, which came to dominate his later work. Tolstoy's greatest work was *War and Peace,* a monumental novel set against the historical background of Napoleon's invasion of Russia in 1812. Tolstoy probes deeply into the lives of a multitude of unforgettable characters, such as the ill-fated Prince Andrei; the shy, fumbling Pierre; and the enchanting, level-headed Natasha. Tolstoy goes to great pains to develop his fatalistic theory of history, which regards free will as an illusion and the achievements of even the greatest leaders as only the channeling of historical necessity. Yet Tolstoy's central message is one that most of the people discussed in this chapter would readily accept: human love, trust, and everyday family ties are life's enduring values.

Thoroughgoing realism (or "naturalism," as it was often called) arrived late in the United States, most arrestingly in the work of Theodore Dreiser (1871–1945). Dreiser's first novel, *Sister Carrie* (1900), the story of an ordinary farm girl who does well going wrong in Chicago, so outraged conventional morality that the publisher withdrew the book. The United States subsequently became a bastion of literary realism in the twentieth century after the movement had faded away in Europe.

The Industrial Revolution had a decisive influence on the urban environment. The populations of towns and cities grew rapidly because it was economically advantageous to locate factories and offices in urban areas. This rapid growth worsened long-standing overcrowding and unhealthy living conditions and posed a frightening challenge for society. Eventually government leaders, city planners, reformers, scientists, and ordinary citizens responded. They took effective action in public health and provided themselves with other badly needed urban services. Gradually they tamed the ferocious savagery of the traditional city.

George Eliot Reared in a strict religious atmosphere against which she later rebelled, Mary Ann Evans accepted scientific attitudes but never lost a strong moral sense of personal responsibility. Her first novels appeared when she was in her early forties. *(National Portrait Gallery, London)*

As urban civilization came to prevail, there were major changes in family life. Especially among the lower classes, family life became more stable, more loving, and less mercenary. These improvements had a price, though. Sex roles for men and women became sharply defined and rigidly separate. Women especially tended to be locked into a subordinate and stereotypic role. Nonetheless, on balance, the quality of family life improved for all family members. Better, more stable family relations reinforced the benefits for the masses of higher real wages, increased social security, political participation, and education.

While the quality of urban and family life improved, the class structure became more complex and diversified than before. Urban society featured many distinct social groups, which existed in a state of constant flux and competition. Thus, the gap between rich and poor remained enormous and really quite traditional in mature urban society, although there were countless gradations between the extremes. Large numbers of poor women in particular continued to labor as workers in sweated industries, as domestic servants, and as prostitutes in order to satisfy the demands of their masters in the servant-keeping classes. Urban society in the late nineteenth century represented a great step forward for humanity, but it remained very unequal.

Inequality was a favorite theme of realist novelists like Balzac and Zola. More generally, literary realism reflected Western society's growing faith in science, progress, and evolutionary thinking. The emergence of urban, industrial civilization accelerated the secularization of the Western world-view.

NOTES

1. A Weber, *The Growth of Cities in the Nineteenth Century,* Columbia University Press, New York, 1899, p. 1.
2. Quoted by W. Ashworth, *The Genesis of Modern British Town Planning,* Routledge & Kegan Paul, London, 1954, p. 17.
3. S. Marcus, "Reading the Illegible," in *The Victorian City: Images and Realities,* ed. H. J. Dyos and Michael Wolff, Routledge & Kegan Paul, London, 1973, 1.266.
4. E. Gauldie, *Cruel Habitations: A History of Working-Class Housing, 1780–1918,* George Allen & Unwin, London, 1974, p. 21.
5. Quoted in E. Chadwick, *Report on the Sanitary Condition of the Labouring Population of Great Britain,* ed. M. W. Flinn, University Press, Edinburgh, 1965 (originally published, 1842). pp. 315–316.
6. J. P. McKay, *Tramways and Trolleys: The Rise of Urban Mass Transport in Europe,* Princeton University Press, Princeton, N.J., 1976, p. 81.
7. Quoted by R. P. Neuman, "The Sexual Question and Social Democracy in Imperial Germany," *Journal of Social History* 7 (Winter 1974):276.
8. Quoted by B. Harrison, "Underneath the Victorians," *Victorian Studies* 10 (March 1967):260.
9. Quoted by J. A. Banks, "The Contagion of Numbers," in Dyos and Wolff, 1.112.
10. R. Roberts, *The Classic Slum: Salford Life in the First Quarter of the Century,* University Press, Manchester, Eng., 1971, p. 95.
11. Quoted by B. Harrison, "Pubs," in Dyos and Wolff, 1.175.
12. Quoted by E. Shorter, *The Making of the Modern Family,* Basic Books, New York, 1975, p. 150.
13. Quoted by T. Zeldin, *France, 1848–1945,* Clarendon Press, Oxford, Eng., 1973, 1.288.
14. Quoted by J. M. Phayer, "Lower-Class Morality: The Case of Bavaria," *Journal of Social History* 8 (Fall 1974):89.
15. Quoted by S. Marcus, *The Other Victorians: A Study of Sexuality and Pornography in Mid-Nineteenth-Century England,* Basic Books, New York, 1966, p. 142,
16. Quoted by G. S. Jones, "Working-Class Culture and Working-Class Politics in London, 1870–1900: Notes on the Remaking of a Working Class," *Journal of Social History* 7 (Summer 1974): 486.
17. Quoted by Zeldin, 1.346.
18. Quoted by Shorter, pp. 230–231.
19. Roberts, p. 35.
20. Quoted by Zeldin, 1.295.
21. Ibid., 1.328
22. Quoted by Neuman, p. 281.
23. Quoted by S. Kern, "Explosive Intimacy: Psychodynamics of the Victorian Family," *History of Childhood Quarterly* 1 (Winter 1974):439.
24. A. Comte, *The Positive Philosophy of Auguste Comte,* trans. H. Martineau, J. Chapman, London, 1853, 1. 1–2.
25. Quoted by G. J. Becker, ed., *Documents of Modern Literary Realism,* Princeton University Press, Princeton, N.J., 1963, p. 159.

ART: A MIRROR OF SOCIETY

Art reveals the interests and values of society and frequently gives intimate and unique glimpses of how people actually lived. In portraits and statues, whether of saints, generals, philosophers, popes, poets, or merchants, it preserves the memory and fame of men and women who shaped society. In paintings, drawings, and carvings, it also shows how people worked, played, relaxed, suffered, and triumphed. Art, therefore, is extremely useful to the historian, especially for periods when written records are scarce. Every work of art and every part of it has meaning and has something of its own to say.

Art also manifests the changes and continuity of European life; as values changed in Europe, so did major artistic themes. In the eighteenth century some artists recalled the Renaissance by choosing to focus on aristocratic lifestyles and interests. Painters like Fragonard (overleaf) developed the rococo style, whose elements reflected the elegant refinement of Enlightenment culture. The romantic artists of the eighteenth and nineteenth centuries, however, rejected materialism and, driven by a sense of an unlimited universe, sought to reach new levels of spiritual understanding through their art. The romantic movement testified to a turbulent Europe caught up in revolutionary change. For these painters, nature replaced rationalism as the proper source of inspiration. Whereas the English landscape artist John Constable saw nature as the manifestation of a beneficent spirit, the nature portrayed by Joseph Turner, England's other great romantic painter, seethed with awesome uncontrollable power. The fury of the sea, a favorite subject, is evident in *Calais Pier* (1806), below. In this early painting the waves roll in higher and higher while black clouds weigh ominously on fishermen setting out to sea. Half sailor and vagabond, Turner lent seascapes unprecedented passion. (Reproduced by Courtesy of the Trustees of The National Gallery, London)

Realism, the next great artistic movement, reflected in part the concern for the working class aroused by the revolutionary failures of 1848. After 1850 social concerns found full expression in the art of realists like Courbet and Degas. Later in the nineteenth century, the impressionists, seeking to capture a given moment as the eye perceives it, gloried in the vibrant diversity of urban society. Though the twentieth century witnessed the disintegration of their faith in science and democracy, the impressionists, by valuing color and abstract design for their own sake, proved the crucial bridge between traditional representational and modern art.

The Swing *(left)* Jean-Honoré Fragonard (1732–1806). The sophistication and frivolity of the eighteenth-century French salon radiate from this delicately naughty work by Fragonard, a brilliant colorist in perfect harmony with the elitist taste of his age. An aging bishop swings a coy beauty, who "accidentally" loses her shoe, allowing her lover an enraptured peek under her petticoat. *(The Wallace Collection)*

The Haywain *(above)* John Constable (1776–1837). Even as the Industrial Revolution was transforming the land, the beauties of the English countryside found their loftiest celebration in the landscapes of John Constable, England's other great romantic painter. In sharp contrast to that of Turner, his nature was peculiarly harmonious, well maintained, and rich in spiritual values. The first artist of importance to paint outdoors, the bright pure colors of this 1821 masterpiece had a powerful impact on young French painters like Delacroix. *(Reproduced by courtesy of the Trustees, The National Gallery, London)*

The Threshing Floor *(below)* Francisco Goya (1746–1828). Until the late nineteenth century, agriculture remained the biggest single employer in most European countries. Most work was still done by hand and often in a community framework. This scene by the independent Spanish master Goya captures the joy of relaxation in the middle of a long day's work. *(Museo del Prado, Spain)*

Woman Ironing *(right, above)* Edgar Degas (1834–1917). After the failure of the revolutions of 1848, European society turned from soaring romanticism to tough-minded realism. The French realist Degas managed to portray the whole range of urban classes and individuals with extraordinary sensitivity and accuracy. In this sympathetic painting a weary woman succumbs to the fatigue and boredom of unskilled labor. *(Cliché des Musées Nationaux-Paris)*

The Stone Breakers *(right, below)* Gustave Courbet (1819–1877). Another famous French painter who rejected "noble ideals" and romantic flights of fancy was Courbet. Socialist and passionate advocate for plain working people, like the stone breakers portrayed here, Courbet believed that art must be firmly rooted in concrete objects and everyday experience. "Show me an angel," he said, "and I will paint it." *(Staatlichen Kunstsammlungen, Dresden)*

Degas

Le Moulin de la Galette à Montmartre *(above)* Auguste Renoir (1841–1919). The painters of the French impressionist school generally affirmed the beauty and value of modern life, reflecting western Europe's nineteenth-century faith in science, progress, and democracy. In this 1876 masterpiece, the joyous Renoir has transformed a popular outdoor dance hall of the urban masses into an enchanted fairyland. Impressionist painters applied colors directly to the canvas without first mixing them, a revolutionary technique that let the eye participate (by itself "mixing" the colors) in this ultimate form of optical realism. *(Cliché des Musées Nationaux-Paris)*

The Boating Party *(above)* Mary Cassatt (1844–1926). Born into a wealthy business family in the United States, Mary Cassatt moved to Paris, where she painted mothers and their children with a sensitivity unequaled in recent times. Here she captures with tender realism an attentive mother and her squirming child on a hot afternoon outing. Cassatt helped many French impressionists by successfully encouraging American collectors to buy their paintings. *(National Gallery of Art, Washington; Chester Dale Collection)*

Square of the Théâtre Français, Afternoon Winter Sun, 1900 *(above)* Camille Pissarro (1830–1803). This painting by the pure impressionist Pissarro captures the excitement and vitality of busy Paris boulevards, which brought all classes together, at least temporarily. The grandiose opera house stands in the distance, connected with France's most distinguished classical theater by the recently completed Avenue of the Opera. *(Courtesy of the Lefevre Gallery, London)*

SUGGESTED READING

All of the books and articles cited in the Notes are highly recommended; each in its own way is an important contribution to social history and life in the urban society. Note that the *Journal of Social History,* which has a strong European orientation, is excellent both for its articles and for its reviews of new books. T. Zeldin, *France, 1848–1945,* 2 vols. (1973, 1977), is a pioneering social history that opens many doors, as is the ambitious synthesis by T. Hamerow, *The Birth of a New Europe: State and Society in the Nineteenth Century* (1983).

On the European city, D. Pickney, *Napoleon III and the Rebuilding of Paris* (1972), is fascinating, as are G. Masur, *Imperial Berlin* (1970), and M. Hamm, ed., *The City in Russian History* (1976). So also are N. Evenson's beautifully illustrated *Paris: A Century of Change, 1878–1978* (1979); D. Grew's authoritative *Town in the Ruhr: A Social History of Bochum, 1860–1914* (1979); and the essays in J. Merriman, ed., *French Cities in the 19th Century: Class, Power, and Urbanization* (1982). D. Olsen's scholarly *Growth of Victorian London* (1978) complements H. Mayhew's wonderful contemporary study, *London Labour and the Labouring Poor* (1861), reprinted recently. M. Crichton's realistic historical novel on organized crime, *The Great Train Robbery* (1976), is excellent. J. J. Tobias, *Urban Crime in Victorian England* (1972), is a lively, scholarly approach to declining criminal activity in the nineteenth century, with a wealth of detail. G. Rosen, *History of Public Health* (1958), is an excellent introduction to medical developments. For society as a whole, J. Burnett, *History of the Cost of Living* (1969), cleverly shows how different classes spent their money, and B. Tuchman, *The Proud Tower* (1966), draws an unforgettable portrait of people and classes before 1914. J. Laver's handsomely illustrated *Manners and Morals in the Age of Optimism, 1848–1914* (1966), investigates the urban underworld and relations between the sexes. Sexual attitudes are also examined by E. Trudgill, *Madonnas and Magdalenas: The Origin and Development of Victorian Sexual Attitudes* (1976); A. McLaren, *Sexuality and Social Order: Birth Control in Nineteenth-Century France* (1982); and J. Phayer, *Sexual Liberation and Religion in Nineteenth Century Europe* (1977).

Women are coming into their own in historical studies. In addition to the general works by Shorter, Wrigley, Stone, and Tilly and Scott cited in Chapter 20, there are a growing number of eye-opening specialized investigations. These include L. Davidoff, *The Best Circles* (1973), on upper-class society types; O. Banks, *Feminism and Family Planning in Victorian England* (1964); and P. Branca, *Women in Europe Since 1750* (1978). L. Holcombe, *Victorian Ladies at Work* (1973), pioneers in examining middle-class women at work. M. Vicinus, ed., *Suffer and Be Still* (1972) and *A Widening Sphere* (1981), are far-ranging collections of essays on women's history, as is R. Bridenthal and C. Koonz, eds., *Becoming Visible: Women in European History* (1976). Feminism is treated perceptively in R. Evans, *The Feminists: Women's Emancipation in Europe, America, and Australia* (1979), and K. Blair, *The Clubwoman as Feminist: True Womanhood Redefined, 1868–1914* (1980). J. Gillis, *Youth and History* (1974), is a good introduction. D. Ransel, ed., *The Family in Imperial Russia* (1978), is an important work on the subject, as is J. Donzelot, *The Policing of Families* (1979), which stresses the loss of family control of all aspects of life to government agencies.

Among studies of special groups, J. Scott, *The Glass-Workers of Carmaux* (1974), is outstanding on skilled French craftsmen, and D. Lockwood, *The Blackcoated Worker* (1958), carefully examines class consciousness in the English lower-middle class. Two fine studies on universities and their professors are S. Rothblatt, *Revolution of the Dons: Cambridge and Society in Victorian England* (1968), and F. Ringer, *The Decline of the German Mandarins* (1969). Servants and their employers receive excellent treatment in T. McBride, *The Domestic Revolution: The Modernization of Household Service in England and France, 1820–1920* (1976), and B. Smith, *Ladies of the Leisure Class: The Bourgeoises of Northern France in the Nineteenth Century* (1981), which may be compared with the innovative study by M. Miller, *The Bon Marché: Bourgeois Culture and the Department Store, 1869–1920* (1981).

On Darwin, M. Ruse, *The Darwinian Revolution* (1979), is a good starting point, as is G. Himmelfarb, *Darwin and the Darwinian Revolution* (1968). O. Chadwick, *The Secularization of the European Mind in the Nineteenth Century* (1976), analyzes the impact of science (and other factors) on religious belief. The masterpieces of the great realist social novelists remain one of the best and most memorable introductions to nineteenth-century culture and thought. In addition to the novels discussed in this chapter, and those cited in the Suggested Reading for Chapters 22 and 23, I. Turgenev's *Fathers and Sons* and Zola's *The Dram-Shop (L'Assommoir)* are especially recommended.

25

THE AGE OF NATIONALISM, 1850–1914

*T*HE REVOLUTIONS OF 1848 closed one era and opened another. Urban industrial society began to take strong hold on the Continent, as it already had in Great Britain. Internationally, the repressive peace and diplomatic stability of Metternich's time was replaced by a period of war and rapid change. In thought and culture, soaring romanticism gave way to tough-minded realism. In the European economy, the hard years of the 1840s were followed by good times and prosperity throughout most of the 1850s and 1860s. Perhaps most important of all, European society progressively found, for better or worse, a new and effective organizing principle, capable of coping with the many-sided challenge of the dual revolution and the emerging urban civilization. That principle was nationalism—dedication to and identification with the nation-state.

The triumph of nationalism in Europe after 1850 is a development of enormous historical significance. It was by no means completely predictable. After all, nationalism had been a powerful force since at least 1789. Yet it had repeatedly failed to realize its goals, most spectacularly so in 1848. Why, then, did nationalism become in one way or another an almost universal faith in Europe between 1850 and 1914? More specifically, how did nationalism evolve so that it appealed not only to predominantly middle-class liberals but to the broad masses of society as well? These are the weighty questions this chapter will seek to answer.

NAPOLEON III IN FRANCE

Early nationalism was at least liberal and idealistic and often democratic and radical as well. The ideas of nationhood and popular sovereignty posed an awesome revolutionary threat to conservatives like Metternich. Yet, from the vantage point of the twentieth century, it is clear that nationalism wears many masks; it may be democratic and radical, as it was for Mazzini and Michelet; but it can also flourish in dictatorial states, which may be conservative, fascist, or communist. Napoleon I's France had already combined national devotion with authoritarian rule. Significantly, it was Napoleon's nephew, Louis Napoleon, who revived and extended this merger. It was he who showed how governments could reconcile popular and conservative forces in an authoritarian nationalism. In doing so, he provided a model for political leaders elsewhere.

THE SECOND REPUBLIC AND LOUIS NAPOLEON

The overwhelming victory of Louis Napoleon Bonaparte in the French presidential elections of December 1848 has long puzzled historians. The nephew of Napoleon I, Louis Napoleon had lived most of his life outside of France and played no part in French politics before 1848. Why did universal manhood suffrage give such an unproven nobody 5.5 million votes, while the runner-up, General Cavaignac of June Days fame, polled only 1.5 million and the other three candidates (including the poet Lamartine) received insignificant support?

The usual explanation is that, though Louis Napoleon had only his great name in common with his uncle, that was enough. According to some historians, the Napoleonic legend—a monument to the power of romanticism between 1820 and 1848—had transformed a dictator into a demigod in the minds of the unsophisticated French masses. Another explanation, popularized by Karl Marx, has stressed the fears of middle-class and peasant property owners in the face of the socialist challenge of urban workers. These classes wanted protection. They wanted a tough cop with a big stick on the beat. They found him in Louis Napoleon, who had indeed served briefly as a special constable in London at the height of the Chartist agitation.

These explanations are not wrong, but there was more to Louis Napoleon's popularity than stupidity and fear. In late 1848, Louis Napoleon had a positive "program" for France, which was to guide him throughout most of his long reign. This program had been elaborated earlier in two pamphlets, *Napoleonic Ideas* and *The Elimination of Poverty,* which Louis Napoleon had written while imprisoned for a farcical attempt to overthrow Louis Philippe's government. The pamphlets had been widely circulated prior to the presidential election.

Louis Napoleon believed that the government should represent the people and that it should also try hard to help them economically. How was this to be done? Parliaments and political parties were not the answer, according to Louis Napoleon. Politicians represented special-interest groups, particularly middle-class ones. When they ran a parliamentary government, they stirred up class hatred because they were not interested in helping the poor. This had occurred under Louis Philippe, and it was occurring again under the Second Republic. The answer was a strong, even authoritarian, national leader, like the first Napoleon, who would serve all the people, rich and poor. This leader would be linked to the people by direct democracy and universal male suffrage. Sovereignty would flow from the entire population to the leader and would not be diluted or corrupted by politicians and legislative bodies.

These political ideas went hand in hand with Louis Napoleon's vision of national unity and social progress. Unlike his uncle, who had reduced unemployment and social tensions by means of foreign wars, Louis Napoleon favored peaceful measures to relieve the awful poverty of the poor. Rather than doing nothing or providing only temporary relief, the state and its leader had a sacred duty to provide jobs and stimulate the economy. All classes would benefit by such action.

Louis Napoleon's political and social ideas were at least vaguely understood by large numbers of French peasants and workers in December 1848. To many common people he appeared to be both a strong man *and* a forward-looking champion of their interests, and that is why they voted for him.

Elected to a four-year term, President Louis Napoleon had to share power with a conservative National Assembly. With some misgivings he signed a bill to increase greatly the role of the Catholic church in primary and secondary education. In France as elsewhere in Europe after 1848, the anxious well-to-do saw religion as a bulwark against radicalism. As one leader of the church in France put it, "There is only one recipe for making those who own nothing believe in property-rights: that is to make them believe in God, who dictated the Ten Commandments and who promises eternal punishment to those who steal."[1] Very reluctantly, Louis Napoleon also signed another conservative law depriving many poor people of the right to vote. He took these conservative measures for two main reasons: he wanted the assembly to vote funds to pay his personal debts, and he wanted it to change the constitution so he could run for a second term.

The assembly did neither. Thus in 1851, Louis Napoleon began to organize a conspiracy with key army officers. On December 2, 1851, he illegally dismissed the assembly and seized power in a coup d'état. There was some armed resistance in Paris and other cities, but the actions of the assembly had left the Second Republic with few defenders. Restoring universal male suffrage, Louis Napoleon called on the French people to legalize his actions as his uncle had done. They did: 92 percent voted to make him a strong president for ten years. A year later, 97 percent agreed in a national plebiscite to make him hereditary emperor. For the third time, and by the greatest margin yet, the authoritarian Louis Napoleon was overwhelmingly elected to lead the French nation.

Napoleon III's Second Empire

Louis Napoleon—now Emperor Napoleon III—experienced both success and failure between 1852 and 1870. His greatest success was with the economy, particularly in the 1850s. His government encouraged the new investment banks and massive railroad construction that were at the heart of the industrial revolution on the Continent. General economic expansion was also fostered by the government's ambitious program of public works, which included the rebuilding of Paris to improve the urban environment. The profits of businessmen soared with prosperity, and the working classes did not fare poorly either. Their wages more than kept up with inflation, and jobs were much easier to find. France's economy benefited from a worldwide economic boom and other external events, such as gold discoveries in California and Australia. Yet the contribution of Napoleon III's economic policies was real all the same.

Louis Napoleon always hoped that economic progress would reduce social and political tensions. This hope was at least partially realized. Until the mid-1860s, there was little active opposition and even considerable support for his government from France's most dissatisfied group, the urban workers. Napoleon III's regulation of pawnshops and his support of credit unions and better housing for the working class were evidence of positive concern in the 1850s. In the 1860s, he granted workers the right to form unions and the right to strike—important economic rights denied by earlier governments.

Rebuilding Paris Expensive and time consuming, boulevard construction in Paris brought massive demolition, considerable slum clearance, and protests of ruin to the old city. In addition to expecting economic benefits, Napoleon III rightly believed that broad boulevards would be harder for revolutionaries to barricade than narrow twisting streets. *(The Mansell Collection)*

At first, political power remained in the hands of the emperor. He alone chose his ministers, and they had great freedom of action. At the same time, Napoleon III restricted but did not abolish the assembly. To be sure, the French parliament in the 1850s had little power. It could not initiate legislation, and it did not control the budget. Parliamentary sessions were not open to the public, and the government permitted only a dry summary of its debates to be published. Yet the members of the assembly were elected by universal male suffrage every six years. In each district the government put up its candidate and permitted opposition candidates, although it restricted speeches and discussions during the electoral campaigns.

Louis Napoleon and his government took the parliamentary elections very seriously. They tried to entice notable people, even those who had opposed the regime, to stand as government candidates in order to expand is base of support. Moreover the government rewarded districts that elected government candidates. It used its officials and appointed mayors to spread the word that the election of the government's candidate was the key to roads, schools, tax rebates, and a thousand other local concerns.

In 1857 and again in 1863, Louis Napoleon's system worked well and produced overwhelming electoral victories. The poet-politician Alphonse de Lamartine was convinced that Louis Napoleon was

France's greatest politician since Talleyrand, and possibly even greater than he. Yet in the course of the 1860s Napoleon III's electoral system gradually disintegrated, for several reasons. France's problems in Italy and the rising power of Prussia led to increasing criticism at home from his Catholic and nationalist supporters. With increasing effectiveness, the middle-class liberals who had always detested his dictatorship continued to denounce his rule as a disgrace to France's republican tradition.

Napoleon was always sensitive to the public mood. Public opinion, he once said, always wins the last victory. Thus in the 1860s, he progressively "liberalized" his empire. He gave the assembly greater powers and the opposition candidates greater freedom, which they used to good advantage. In 1869 the opposition, consisting of republicans, monarchists, and liberals, polled almost 45 percent of the vote.

The following year, a sick and weary Louis Napoleon once again granted France a new constitution, which combined a basically parliamentary regime with a hereditary emperor as chief of state. In a final great plebiscite on the eve of a disastrous war with Prussia, 7.5 million Frenchmen voted in favor of the new constitution, and only 1.5 million opposed it. Napoleon III's attempt to reconcile a strong national state with universal manhood suffrage was still evolving, in a democratic direction.

NATION BUILDING IN ITALY AND GERMANY

Louis Napoleon's triumph in 1848 and his authoritarian rule in the 1850s provided the old ruling classes of Europe with a new model in politics. As the great Swiss historian Jacob Burckhardt later noted,

Louis Napoleon had risked universal suffrage for the elections, and others followed his lead. The conservative streak in the rural populations had been recognized, though no attempt had been made to assess precisely how far it might be extended from the elections to everything and everybody."[2]

To what extent was it possible that the expanding urban middle classes and even the growing working classes might, like people in rural areas, rally to a strong and essentially conservative national state? This was one of the great political questions in the 1850s and 1860s. In central Europe, a resounding and definitive answer came with the national unification of Italy and Germany.

ITALY TO 1850

Italy had never been a united nation prior to 1860. Part of Rome's great empire in ancient times, the Italian peninsula was divided in the Middle Ages into competing city-states, which led the commercial and cultural revival of the West with amazing creativity. A battleground for great powers after 1494, Italy had been reorganized in 1815 at the Congress of Vienna. The rich northern provinces of Lombardy and Venetia were taken by Metternich's Austria. Sardinia and Piedmont were under the rule of an Italian monarch, and Tuscany with its famous capital of Florence shared north central Italy with several smaller states. Central Italy and Rome were ruled by the papacy, which had always considered an independent political existence necessary to fulfill its spiritual mission. Naples and Sicily were ruled, as they had been for almost a hundred years, by a branch of the Bourbons. Metternich was not wrong in dismissing Italy as "a geographical expression" (see Map 25.1).

Between 1815 and 1848, the goal of a unified Italian nation captured the imaginations of increasing numbers of Italians. There were three basic approaches. The first was the radical program of the idealistic patriot Mazzini, who preached a centralized democratic republic based on universal suffrage and the will of the people. The second was that of Gioberti, a Catholic priest, who called for a federation of existing states under the presidency of a progressive pope. Finally, there were those who looked for leadership toward the autocratic kingdom of Sardinia-Piedmont, much as many Germans looked toward Prussia.

The third alternative was strengthened by the failures of 1848, when Austria smashed and discredited Mazzini's republicanism. Almost by accident, Sardinia's monarch Victor Emmanuel retained the liberal constitution granted under duress in March 1848. This constitution provided for a fair degree of civil liberties and real parliamentary government, complete with elections and parliamentary control of taxes. To the Italian middle classes, Sardinia ap-

MAP 25.1 The Unification of Italy, 1859–1870 The leadership of Sardinia-Piedmont and nationalist fervor were decisive factors in the dramatic political unification of the Italian peninsula.

peared to be a liberal, progressive state, ideally suited to achieve the goal of national unification. By contrast, Mazzini's brand of democratic republicanism seemed quixotic and too radical. As for the papacy, the initial cautious support by Pius IX (1846–1878) for unification had given way to fear and hostility after he was temporarily driven from Rome during the upheavals of 1848. For a long generation, the papacy would stand resolutely opposed not only to national unification but to most modern trends. In 1864, in the *Syllabus of Errors,* Pius IX strongly denounced rationalism, socialism, separation of church and state, and religious liberty, denying that "the Roman pontiff can and ought to reconcile and align himself with progress, liberalism, and modern civilization."

Cavour and Garibaldi

Sardinia had the good fortune of being led by a brilliant statesman, Count Camillo Benso di Cavour, the dominant figure in the Sardinian government from 1850 until his death in 1861. Cavour's development was an early sign of the coming tacit alliance between the aristocracy and the solid middle class throughout much of Europe. Beginning as a successful manager of his father's large landed estates in Piedmont, Cavour was also an economic liberal. He turned toward industry and made a substantial fortune in sugar mills, steamships, banks, and railroads. Economically secure, he then entered the world of politics and became chief minister in the liberalized Sardinian monarchy. Cavour's national goals were limited and realistic. Until 1859 he sought unity only for the states of northern and perhaps central Italy in a greatly expanded kingdom of Sardinia. It was not one of his goals to incorporate the papal states or the kingdom of the Two Sicilies, with their very different cultures and governments, into an Italy of all the Italians. Cavour was a moderate nationalist.

In the 1850s Cavour worked to consolidate Sardinia as a liberal state capable of leading northern Italy. His program of highways and railroads, of civil liberties and opposition to clerical privilege, increased support for Sardinia throughout northern Italy. Yet Cavour realized that Sardinia could not drive Austria out of Lombardy and Venetia and unify northern Italy under Victor Emmanuel without the help of a powerful ally. He sought that ally in the person of Napoleon III, who sincerely believed in the general principle of nationality, as well as modest expansion for France.

In a complicated series of diplomatic maneuvers, Cavour in 1854 entered the Crimean War against Russia, on the side of Great Britain and France, and tenaciously worked for a diplomatic alliance with Napoleon III against Austria. Finally he succeeded. In July 1858, Cavour and Napoleon III agreed orally in the utmost secrecy that if Cavour could goad Austria into attacking Sardinia, France would come to Sardinia's "defense."

For a time, Cavour feared that an international congress and a diplomatic compromise would thwart his plans. But in the end, Austria obligingly issued an ultimatum and declared war. Napoleon III came to Sardinia's defense. Then, after the victory of the combined Franco-Sardinian forces, he did a complete about-face. Nauseated by the gore of war and criticized by French Catholics for supporting the pope's declared enemy, Napoleon III abandoned Cavour. He made a compromise peace with the Austrians at Villafranca in July 1859. Sardinia would receive only Lombardy, the area around Milan. The rest of the map of Italy would remain essentially unchanged. Cavour resigned in a rage.

Yet Cavour's plans were salvaged by popular revolts and Italian nationalism. While the war against Austria had raged in the north, dedicated nationalists in central Italy had risen and driven out their rulers. Nationalist fervor seized the urban masses. Large crowds demonstrated, chanting, "Italy and Victor Emmanuel!" and singing passionately, "Foreigners, get out of Italy!" Buoyed up by this enthusiasm, the leaders of the nationalist movement in central Italy ignored the compromise peace of Villafranca and called for fusion with Sardinia. This was not at all what France and the other Great Powers wanted, but the nationalists held firm and eventually had their way. Cavour returned to power in early 1860 and worked out a diplomatic deal with Napoleon III. The people of central Italy voted overwhelmingly to join a greatly enlarged kingdom of Sardinia. Cavour had achieved his original goal of a north Italian state (see Map 25.1).

For superpatriots like Giuseppe Garibaldi (1801–1882), the job of unification was still only half done. The son of a poor sailor, Garibaldi personified the romantic, revolutionary nationalism of Mazzini and 1848. As a lad of seventeen, he had traveled to Rome and been converted to the "New Italy, the Italy of all the Italians." As he later wrote in his *Autobiography,* "The Rome that I beheld with the eyes of youthful imagination was the Rome of the future—the dominant thought of my whole life." Sentenced to death in 1834 for his part in an uprising in Genoa, Garibaldi escaped to South America. For twelve years he led a guerilla band in Uruguay's struggle for independence. "Shipwrecked, ambushed, shot through the neck," he found in a tough young woman, Anna da Silva, a mate and companion in arms. Their first children nearly starved in the jungle while Garibaldi, clad in his long red shirt, fashioned a legend not unlike like that of the Cuban Ché Guevara in recent times. He returned to Italy to fight in 1848 and led a corps of volunteers against Austria in 1859. By the spring of 1860, Garibaldi had emerged as a powerful independent force in Italian politics.

Garibaldi Landing in Sicily With a thousand volunteers the flamboyant Garibaldi conquered the kingdom of the Two Sicilies in 1860 and paved the way for Italian unification. *(Historical Pictures Service, Chicago)*

Partly to use him and partly to get rid of him, Cavour secretly supported Garibaldi's bold plan to "liberate" Sicily. Landing in Sicily in May 1860, Garibaldi's guerrilla band of a thousand "Red Shirts" captured the imagination of the Sicilian peasantry. Outwitting the twenty-thousand-man royal army, the guerrilla leader took Palermo. Then he and his men crossed to the mainland, marched triumphantly toward Naples, and prepared to attack Rome and the pope. But the wily Cavour quickly sent Sardinian forces to occupy most of the Papal States (but not Rome) and to intercept Garibaldi.

Cavour realized that an attack on Rome would bring about war with France, and he also feared Garibaldi's popular appeal. Therefore, he immediately organized a plebiscite in the conquered territories. Despite the urging of some of his more radical supporters, the patriotic Garibaldi did not oppose Cavour, and the people of the south voted to join Sardinia. When Garibaldi and Victor Emmanuel rode through Naples to cheering crowds, they symbolically sealed the union of north and south, of monarch and people.

Cavour had succeeded. He had controlled Garibaldi and had turned popular nationalism in a conservative direction. The new kingdom of Italy, which did not include Venice until 1866 or Rome until 1870, was neither radical nor democratic. Italy was a parliamentary monarchy under Victor Emmanuel, but in accordance with the Sardinian constitution only a small minority of Italians had the right to vote. There was a definite division between the propertied classes and the common people. There was also a great social and cultural gap between the progressive, industrializing north and the stagnant, agrarian south. This gap would increase, since peasant industries in the south would not be able to survive. Italy was united politically. Other divisions remained.

Germany Before Bismarck

In the aftermath of 1848, while Louis Napoleon consolidated his rule and Cavour schemed, the German states were locked in a political stalemate. With Russian diplomatic support, Austria had blocked the halfhearted attempt of Frederick William IV of Prussia (1840–1861) to unify Germany "from above." This action contributed to a growing tension between Austria and Prussia, as each power sought to block the other within the reorganized German Confederation (pages 732 and 756). Stalemate also prevailed in the domestic politics of the individual states, as Austria, Prussia, and the smaller German kingdoms entered a period of reaction and immobility.

At the same time, powerful economic forces were undermining the political status quo. As we have seen, modern industry grew rapidly in Europe throughout the 1850s. Nowhere was this growth more rapid than within the German customs union (Zollverein). Developing gradually under Prussian leadership after 1818 and founded officially in 1834 to stimulate trade and increase the revenues of member states, the customs union had not included Austria. After 1848 it became a crucial factor in the Austro-Prussian rivalry.

Tariff duties were substantially reduced so that Austria's highly protected industry could not bear to join. In retaliation, Austria tried to destroy the Zollverein by inducing the south German states to leave it, but without success. Indeed, by the end of 1853 all the German states except Austria had joined the customs union. A new Germany excluding Austria was becoming an economic reality, and the middle class and business groups were finding solid economic reasons to bolster their idealistic support of national unification. Thus economic developments helped Prussia greatly in its struggle against Austria's traditional supremacy in German affairs.

The national uprising in Italy in 1859 made a profound impression in the German states. In Prussia, great political change and war—perhaps with Austria, perhaps with France—seemed quite possible. The tough-minded William I of Prussia (1858–1888), who had replaced the unstable Frederick William IV as regent in 1858 and became king in 1861, and his top military advisers were convinced of the need for major army reforms. William I wanted to double the size of the regular army. He also wanted to reduce the importance of the reserve militia, a semipopular force created during the Napoleonic wars. William had contempt for the "dirty reservists," those "civilians in uniform," who lacked efficiency and complete obedience. By drafting every young man into the army for three years, the king and his conservative supporters hoped to promote military attitudes in daily life. Of course, reform of the army meant a bigger defense budget and higher taxes.

Prussia had emerged from 1848 with a parliament of sorts, and by 1859 the Prussian parliament was in the hands of the liberal middle class. The middle class, like the landed aristocracy, was overrepresented by the Prussian electoral system, and it wanted society to be less, not more, militaristic. Above all, middle-class representatives wanted to establish once and for all that parliament, not the king, had the ultimate political power. They also wanted to ensure that the army was responsible to the people and not a "state within a state." These demands were popular. The parliament rejected the military budget in 1862, and the liberals triumphed so completely in new elections that the conservatives "could ride to the parliament

Otto von Bismarck A fierce political fighter with a commanding personality and a brilliant mind, Bismarck was devoted to Prussia and its king and aristocracy. Uniforms were worn by civilian officials as well as by soldiers in Prussia. *(Brown Brothers)*

building in a single coach." King William considered abdicating in favor of his more liberal son. In the end, he called on Count Otto von Bismarck to head a ministry and defy the parliament. It was a momentous choice.

Bismarck Takes Command

The most important figure in German history between Luther and Hitler, Otto von Bismarck (1815–1898), has been the object of enormous interest and debate. Like his contemporary Abraham Lincoln, who successfully led the North against the South in a great civil war between 1861 and 1865, Bismarck used military victory to forge a strong, unified national state.

A great hero to some, a great villain to others, Bismarck was above all a master of politics. Born into the Prussian landowning aristocracy, the young Bismark was a wild and tempestuous student, given to duels and drinking. Proud of his Junker heritage—"my fathers have been born and have lived and died in the same rooms for centuries"—and always devoted to his Prussian sovereign, Bismarck had a strong personality and an unbounded desire for power.

Bismarck entered the civil service, which was the only socially acceptable career except the army for a Prussian aristocrat. But he soon found bureaucratic life unbearable and fled to his ancestral estate. The civil servant was like a musician in an orchestra, he said, and "I want to play the tune the way it sounds to me or not at all. . . . My pride bids me command rather than obey."[3] Yet in his drive for power, power for himself and for Prussia, Bismarck was extraordinarily flexible and pragmatic. "One must always have two irons in the fire," he once said. He kept his options open, pursuing one policy and then another as he moved with skill and cunning toward his goal.

Bismarck first honed his political skills as a diplomat. Acquiring a reputation as an ultraconservative in the Prussian assembly in 1848, he fought against Austria as the Prussian ambassador to the German Confederation from 1851 to 1859. Transferred next to St. Petersburg and then to Paris, Bismarck had an excellent opportunity to evaluate Alexander II and Napoleon III at close range. A blunt, expansive talker, especially after a few drinks, Bismarck's basic goal was well known in 1862—to build up Prussia's strength and consolidate Prussia's precarious Great Power status.

To achieve this goal, Bismarck was convinced that Prussia had to control completely the northern, predominantly Protestant part of the German Confederation. He saw three possible paths open before him. He might work with Austria to divide up the smaller German states lying between them. Or he might combine with foreign powers—France and Italy, or even Russia—against Austria. Or he might ally with the forces of German nationalism to defeat and expel Austria from German affairs. Each possibility was explored in many complicated diplomatic maneuvers, but in the end the last path was the one Bismarck took.

That Bismarck would join with the forces of German nationalism to increase Prussia's power seemed unlikely when he took office in 1862. Bismarck's appointment made a strong but unfavorable impression. One of the liberal middle-class members of the Prussian parliament expressed enlightened public opinion throughout Prussia and the other German states: "Bismarck, that is to say: government without budget, rule by the sword in home affairs, and war in foreign affairs. I consider him the most dangerous Minister for Prussia's liberty and happiness."[4]

Bismarck's speeches were a sensation and a scandal. Declaring that the government would rule without parliamentary consent, Bismarck lashed out at the middle-class opposition: "The great questions of the day will not be decided by speeches and resolutions—that was the blunder of 1848 and 1849—but by blood and iron." In 1863 he told the Prussian parliament, "If a compromise cannot be arrived at and a conflict arises, then the conflict becomes a question of power. Whoever has the power then acts according to his opinion." Denounced for this view that "might makes right," Bismarck and the bureaucracy went right on collecting taxes, even though the parliament refused to approve the budget, and reorganized the army. And for four years, from 1862 to 1866, the voters of Prussia continued to express their opposition by sending large liberal majorities to the parliament.

The Austro-Prussian War of 1866

Opposition at home spurred the search for success abroad. The every-knotty question of Schleswig-Holstein provided a welcome opportunity. When the Danish king tried again, as in 1848, to bring the provinces into a centralized Danish state against the will of the German Confederation, Prussia joined Austria in a short and successful war against Denmark in 1864. Then, rather than following nationalist sentiment and allowing the conquered provinces to become another medium-sized independent state within the German Confederation, Bismarck maneuvered Austria into a tricky position. Prussia and Austria agreed to joint administration of the conquered provinces, thereby giving Bismarck a weapon he could use either to force Austria into peacefully accepting Prussian domination in northern Germany or to start a war against Austria.

Bismarck knew that a war with Austria would have to be localized war. He had to be certain that Prussian expansion did not provoke a mighty armed coalition, such as the coalition that had almost crushed Frederick the Great in the eighteenth century. Russia, the great bear to the east, was no problem. Bismarck had already gained Alexander II's gratitude by supporting Russia's repression of a Polish uprising in 1863. Napoleon III—the "sphinx without a riddle," according to Bismarck—was another matter. But Bismarck charmed him into neutrality with vague promises of more territory along the Rhine. Thus, when Austria proved unwilling to give up its historic role in German affairs, Bismarck was in a position to engage in a war of his own making.

The Austro-Prussian War of 1866 lasted only seven weeks. Utilizing railroads to mass troops and the new breechloading needle gun for maximum firepower, the reorganized Prussian army overran northern

Map 25.2 The Unification of Germany, 1866–1871 This map deserves careful study. Note how Prussian expansion, Austrian expulsion from the old German Confederation, and the creation of a new German Empire went hand in hand. Austria lost no territory but Prussia's neighbors in the north suffered grievously or simply disappeared.

Germany and defeated Austria decisively at the battle of Königgrätz in Bohemia. Anticipating Prussia's future needs, Bismarck offered Austria realistic, even generous, peace terms. Austria paid no reparations and lost no territory to Prussia, although Venice was ceded to Italy. But the German Confederation was dissolved, and Austria agreed to withdraw from German affairs. The states north of the Main River were grouped in a new North German Confederation led by an expanded Prussia. The mainly Catholic states of the south were permitted to remain independent, while forming military alliances with Prussia. Bismarck's fundamental goal of Prussian expansion was being realized (see Map 25.2).

The Taming of Parliament

Bismarck had long been convinced that the old order he so ardently defended should make peace—on its own terms—with the liberal middle class and the nationalist movement. Inspired somewhat by Louis Napoleon, he realized that nationalism was not necessarily hostile to conservative, authoritarian government. Moreover, Bismarck believed that, because of the events of 1848, the German middle class could be led to prefer the reality of national unity to a long, uncertain battle for truly liberal institutions. During the constitutional struggle over army reform and parliamentary authority, he had delayed but not abandoned this goal. Thus, during the attack on Austria in 1866, he increasingly identified Prussia's fate with the "national development of Germany."

In the aftermath of victory, Bismarck fashioned a federal constitution for the new North German Confederation. Each state retained its own local government, but the king of Prussia was to be president of the confederation and the chancellor—Bismarck—was to be responsible only to the president. The federal government—William I and Bismarck—controlled the army and foreign affairs. There was also a legislature, consisting of an upper house whose delegates were appointed by the different states and a lower house. Both houses shared equally in the making of laws. Members of the lower house were elected by universal, equal manhood suffrage. With this radical innovation, Bismarck opened the door to popular participation and went over the head of the middle class directly to the people. All the while, however, ultimate power rested as securely as ever in the hands of Prussia and its king and army.

Events within Prussia itself were even more significant than those at the federal level. In the flush of victory, the ultraconservatives expected Bismarck to suspend the Prussian constitution or perhaps abolish the Prussian parliament altogether. Yet he did nothing of the sort. Instead, he held out an olive branch to the parliamentary opposition. Marshaling all his diplomatic skill, Bismarck asked the parliament to pass a special indemnity bill to approve after the fact all of the government's spending between 1862 and 1866. Most of the liberals snatched at the chance to cooperate. For four long years, they had opposed and criticized Bismarck's "illegal" measures. And what had happened? Bismarck, the king, and the army had persevered, and in the end these conservative forces had succeeded beyond the wildest dreams of the liberal middle class. In 1866 German unity was in sight, and the people were going to be allowed to participate actively in the new state. Many liberals repented their "sins" and were overjoyed that Bismarck would forgive them.

"His First Thought" This 1896 cartoon provides a brilliant commentary on German middle-class attitudes. Suddenly crippled, the man's first thought is "Disaster! Now I can no longer be an army reserve officer." Being a part-time junior officer, below the dominant aristocratic career officers, became a great middle-class status symbol. *(Photo: Caroline Buckler)*

None repented more ardently or more typically than Hermann Baumgarten, a mild-mannered, thoroughly decent history professor and member of the liberal opposition. In an essay entitled "A Self Criticism of German Liberalism," he confessed in 1866:

We thought by agitation we could transform Germany. But . . . almost all the elements of our political system have been shown erroneous by the facts themselves. . . . Yet we have experienced a miracle almost without parallel. The victory of our principles would have brought us misery, whereas the defeat of our principles has brought boundless salvation.[5]

The constitutional struggle was over. The German middle class was bowing respectfully before Bismarck and the monarchial authority and aristocratic superiority he represented. They did not stand upright again in the years before 1914.

THE FRANCO-PRUSSIAN WAR OF 1870–1871

The rest of the story of German unification is anticlimactic. In 1867 Bismarck brought the four south German states into the customs union and established a customs parliament. But the south Germans were reluctant to go further because of their different religious and political traditions. Bismarck realized that a patriotic war with France would drive the south German states into his arms. The French obligingly played their part. The apparent issue—whether a distant relative of Prussia's William I (and France's Napoleon III) might become king of Spain—was only a diplomatic pretext. By 1870 the French leaders of the Second Empire, alarmed by their powerful new neighbor on the Rhine, had decided on a war to teach Prussia a lesson.

As soon as war against France began in 1870, Bismarck had the wholehearted support of the south German states. With other governments standing still—Bismark's generosity to Austria in 1866 was paying big dividends—German forces under Prussian leadership decisively defeated Louis Napoleon's armies at Sedan on September 1, 1870. Three days later, French patriots in Paris proclaimed yet another French republic and vowed to continue fighting. But after five months, in January 1871, a starving Paris surrendered, and France went on to accept Bismarck's harsh peace terms. By this time, the south German states had agreed to join a new German Empire. The victorious William I was proclaimed emperor of Germany in the Hall of Mirrors in the palace of Versailles. Europe had a nineteenth-century German "sun king." As in the 1866 constitution, the king of Prussia and his ministers had ultimate power in the new empire, and the lower house of the legislature was elected popularly by universal male suffrage.

The Franco-Prussian War of 1870 to 1871, which Europeans generally saw as a test of nations in a pitiless Darwinian struggle for existence, released an enormous surge of patriotic feeling in Germany. Bismarck's genius, the invincible Prussian army, the solidarity of king and people in a unified nation—these and similar themes were trumpeted endlessly during and after the war. The weakest of the Great Powers in 1862—after Austria, Britain, France, and Russia—Prussia fortified by the other Germans states had become the most powerful state in Europe in less than a decade. Most Germans were enormously proud, enormously relieved. And they were somewhat drunk with success, blissfully imagining themselves the fittest and best of the European species. Semi-authoritarian nationalism had triumphed. Only a few critics remained dedicated to the liberal ideal of truly responsible parliamentary government.

THE MODERNIZATION OF RUSSIA

In Russia, unlike Italy and Germany, there was no need to build a single state out of a jumble of principalities. The vast Russian Empire was a great multinational state. In the early nineteenth century, nationalism there was a subversive ideology, identified with revolution. After 1853, however, old autocratic Russia was in serious trouble. It became clear to Russia's leaders that the country had to embrace the process of modernization.

A vague and often overworked term, *modernization* is a great umbrella under which some writers place most of the major developments of the last two hundred or even five hundred years. Yet defined narrowly—as changes that enable a country to compete effectively with the leading countries at a given time —modernization can be a useful concept. It fits Russia after the Crimean War particularly well.

THE "GREAT REFORMS"

In the 1850s Russia was a poor agrarian society. Industry was little developed, and almost 90 percent of the population lived on the land. Agricultural techniques were backward: the ancient open-field system reigned supreme. Serfdom was still the basic social institution. Bound to the lord on a hereditary basis, the peasant serf was little more than a slave. Individual serfs and serf families were regularly sold, with and without land, in the early nineteenth century. Serfs were obliged to furnish labor services or money payments as the lord saw fit. Moreover, the lord could choose freely among them for army recruits, who had to serve for twenty-five years, and he could punish a serf with deportation to Siberia whenever he wished. Sexual exploitation of female serfs by their lords was common.

Serfdom had become the great moral and political issue for the government by the 1840s, but it might still have lasted many more years had it not been for the Crimean War of 1853 to 1856. The war began as a dispute with France over who should protect certain Christian shrines in the Ottoman Empire. Because the fighting was concentrated in the Crimean peninsula in the Black Sea, Russia's transportation network of rivers and wagons failed to supply the distant Russian armies adequately. France and Great Britain, aided by Sardinia, inflicted a humiliating defeat on Russia.

The military defeat marked a turning point in Russian history. The Russian state had been built on the military, and Russia had not lost a major war for a century and a half. This defeat demonstrated that Russia had fallen behind the rapidly industrializing nations of western Europe in many areas. At the very least, Russia needed railroads, better armaments, and reorganization of the army if it was to maintain its international position. Moreover, the disastrous war had caused hardship and raised the specter of massive peasant rebellion. Reform of serfdom was imperative. And, as the new tsar, Alexander II (1855–1881), told the serf owners, it would be better if reform came from above rather than from below. Military disaster thus forced Alexander II and his ministers along the path of rapid social change and general modernization.

The first and greatest of the reforms was the freeing of the serfs in 1861. Human bondage was abolished forever, and the emancipated peasants received, on the average, about half of the land. Yet they had to pay fairly high prices for their land, and because the land was owned collectively, each peasant village was jointly responsible for the payments of all the families in the village. The government hoped that collective responsibility would strengthen the peasant village as a social unit and prevent the development of a class of landless peasants. In practice, collective ownership and responsibility made it very difficult for individual peasants to improve agricultural methods or leave their villages. Thus the effects of the reform were limited, for it did not encourage peasants to change their old habits and attitudes.

"Farewell," says the triumphant German soldier on the left in this French cartoon. "No, till we meet again," replies the French soldier. "Visits must be returned." German victory and Bismarck's seizure of French territory poisoned Franco-German relations after 1871. *(Photo: Caroline Buckler)*

Most of the later reforms were also halfway measures. In 1864 the government established a new institution of local government, the *zemstvo*. Members of

Novgorod Merchants Drinking Tea This late nineteenth-century photograph suggests how Russian businessmen were slow to abandon traditional dress and attitudes in the face of change. Stern authoritarians in the family circle and staunchly devoted to church and tsar, they were often suspicious of foreigners as well as the lawyers and journalists who claimed to speak for the nation's middle class. *(BBC Hulton/The Bettmann Archive)*

this local assembly were elected by a three-class system of towns, peasant villages, and noble landowners. A zemstvo executive council dealt with local problems. The establishment of the zemstvos marked a significant step toward popular participation, and Russian liberals hoped it would lead to a national parliament. They were soon disappointed. The local zemstvo remained subordinate to the traditional bureaucracy and the local nobility, who were heavily favored by the property-based voting system. More successful was reform of the legal system, which established independent courts and equality before the law. Education was also liberalized somewhat, and censorship was relaxed but not removed.

The Industrialization of Russia

Until the twentieth century, Russia's greatest strides toward modernization were economic rather than political. Industry and transport, both so vital to the military, were transformed in two industrial surges. The first of these came after 1860. The government encouraged and subsidized private railway companies, and construction boomed. In 1860 the empire had only about 1,250 miles of railroads; by 1880 it had about 15,500 miles. The railroads enabled agricultural Russia to export grain and thus earn money for further industrialization. Domestic manufacturing was stimulated, and by the end of the 1870s Russia had a sophisticated and well-developed railway-equipment industry. Industrial suburbs grew up around Moscow and St. Petersburg, and a class of modern factory workers began to take shape.

Industrial development strengthened Russia's military forces and gave rise to territorial expansion to the south and east. Imperial expansion greatly excited many ardent Russian nationalists and superpatriots, who became some of the government's most enthusiastic supporters. Industrial development also contributed mightily to the spread of Marxian thought and the transformation of the Russian revolutionary movement after 1890.

In 1881 Alexander II was assassinated by a small group of terrorists. The era of reform came to an abrupt end, for the new tsar, Alexander III (1881–1894), was a determined reactionary. Russia, and indeed all of Europe, experienced hard times economically in the 1880s. Political modernization remained frozen until 1905, but economic modernization sped forward in the massive industrial surge of the 1890s. As it had after the Crimean War, nationalism played a decisive role. The key leader was Sergei Witte, the tough, competent minister of finance from 1892 to 1903. Early in his career, Witte found in the writings of Friedrich List (page 713) an analysis and a program for action. List had stressed the peril for Germany of remaining behind England in the 1830s and 1840s. Witte saw the same threat of industrial backwardness threatening Russia's power and greatness.

Witte moved forward on several fronts. A railroad manager by training, he believed that railroads were "a very powerful weapon . . . for the direction of the economic development of the country."[6] Therefore, the government built railroads rapidly, doubling the network to 35,000 miles by the end of the century. The gigantic trans-Siberian line connecting Moscow with Vladivostok on the Pacific Ocean 5,000 miles away was Witte's pride, and it was largely completed during his term of office. Following List's advice, Witte raised high protective tariffs to build Russian industry, and he put the country on the gold standard of the "civilized world" in order to strengthen Russian finances.

Building the Trans-Siberian Railroad Constructed largely in the 1890s as part of Witte's industrialization drive, the world's longest railroad facilitated Russian penetration of northern China and Korea. That penetration then led to war with Japan. *(BBC Hulton/The Bettmann Archive)*

Witte's greatest innovation, however, was to use the West to catch up with the West. He aggressively encouraged foreigners to use their abundant capital and advanced technology to build great factories in backward Russia. As he told the tsar, "The inflow of foreign capital is . . . the only way by which our industry will be able to supply our country quickly with abundant and cheap products."[7] This policy was brilliantly successful, especially in southern Russia. There, in the eastern Ukraine, foreign capitalists and their engineers built an enormous and very modern steel and coal industry almost from scratch in little more than a decade. By 1900 only the United States, Germany, and Great Britain were producing more steel than Russia. The Russian petroleum industry had even pulled up alongside that of the United States and was producing and refining half the world's output of oil.

Witte knew how to keep foreigners in line. Once a leading foreign businessman came to him and angrily demanded that the Russian government fulfill a contract it had signed and pay certain debts immediately. Witte asked to see the contract. He read it and then carefully tore it to pieces and threw it in the wastepaper basket without a word of explanation. It was just such a fiercely independent Russia that was catching up with the advanced nations of the West.

The Revolution of 1905

Catching up partly meant vigorous territorial expansion, for this was the age of Western imperialism. By 1903 Russia had established a sphere of influence in Chinese Manchuria and was casting greedy eyes on northern Korea. When the protests of equally imperialistic Japan were ignored, the Japanese launched a surprise attack in February 1904. To the world's amazement, Russia suffered repeated losses, forced in August 1905 to accept a humiliating defeat.

As is often the case, military disaster abroad brought political upheaval at home. The business and professional classes had long wanted to match economic with political modernization. Their minimal goal was to turn the last of Europe's absolutist monarchies into a liberal, representative regime. Factory workers, strategically concentrated in the large cities, had all the grievances of early industrialization and were organized in a radical labor movement. Peasants had gained little from the era of reforms and were suffering from poverty and overpopulation. Finally, nationalist sentiment was emerging among the empire's minorities. The politically and culturally dominant ethnic Russians were only about 45 percent of the population, and by 1900 some intellectuals among the subject nationalities were calling for self-rule and autonomy. Separatist nationalism was strongest among the Polish and Ukrainians. With the army pinned down in Manchuria, all these currents of discontent converged in the revolution of 1905.

The beginning of the revolution pointed up the incompetence of the government. On a Sunday in January 1905, a massive demonstration of workers and their families converged peacefully on the Winter Palace in St. Petersburg to present a petition to the tsar. The workers were led by a trade unionist priest named Father Gapon, who had been secretly supported by the police as a preferable alternative to more radical unions. Carrying icons and respectfully singing "God Save the Tsar," the workers did not know Nicholas II had fled the city. Suddenly troops opened fire, killing and wounding hundreds. The "Bloody Sunday" massacre turned ordinary workers against the tsar and produced a wave of general indignation.

Outlawed political parties came out into the open, and by the summer of 1905 strikes, peasant uprisings, revolts among minority nationalities, and troop mutinies were sweeping the country. The revolutionary surge culminated in October 1905 in a great paralyzing general strike, which forced the government to capitulate. The tsar issued the October Manifesto, which granted full civil rights and promised a popularly elected Duma (parliament) with real legislative power. The Manifesto split the opposition. It satisfied most moderate and liberal demands, but the Social Democrats rejected it and led a bloody workers' uprising in Moscow in December 1905. Frightened middle-class moderates helped the government repress the uprising and survive as a constitutional monarchy.

On the eve of the opening of the first Duma in May 1906, the government issued the new constitution, the Fundamental Laws. The tsar retained great powers. The Duma, elected indirectly by universal male suffrage, and a largely appointive upper house could debate and pass laws, but the tsar had an absolute veto. As in Bismarck's Germany, the emperor appointed his ministers, who did not need to command a majority in the Duma.

The disappointed, predominantly middle-class liberals, the largest group in the newly elected Duma, saw the Fundamental Laws as a great step backwards. Efforts to cooperate with the tsar's ministers soon broke down. The government then dismissed the Duma, only to find that a more hostile and radical opposition was elected in 1907. After three months of deadlock, the second Duma was also dismissed. Thereupon the tsar and his reactionary advisors unilaterally rewrote the electoral law so as to increase greatly the weight of the propertied classes at the expense of workers, peasants, and national minorities.

The new law had the intended effect. With landowners assured half the seats in the Duma, the government finally secured a loyal majority in 1907 and again in 1912. Thus armed, the tough, energetic chief minister, Peter Stolypin, pushed through important agrarian reforms designed to break down collective village ownership of land and to encourage the more enterprising peasants—the so-called wager on the strong. On the eve of the First World War, Russia was partially modernized, a conservative constitutional monarchy with a peasant-based but industrializing economy.

THE RESPONSIVE NATIONAL STATE, 1871–1914

For central and western Europe, the unification of Italy and Germany by "blood and iron" marked the end of a dramatic period of nation building. After 1871 the heartland of Europe was organized in strong national states. Only on the borders of Europe—in Ireland and Russia, in Austria-Hungary and the Balkans—did subject peoples still strive for political unity and independence. Despite national differences, European domestic politics after 1871 had a common framework—the firmly established national state. The common themes within that framework were the emergence of mass politics and growing mass loyalty toward the national state.

For good reason, ordinary people—the masses of an industrializing, urbanizing society—felt increasing loyalty to their governments. More and more people could vote. By 1914 universal manhood suffrage was the rule rather than the exception. This development had as much psychological as political significance. Ordinary men were no longer denied the right to vote because they lacked wealth or education. They counted; they could influence the government to some extent. They could feel that they were becoming "part of the system."

Women began to demand the right to vote. The women's suffrage movement achieved its first success in the western United States, and by 1913 women could vote in twelve states. Europe, too, moved slowly in this direction. In 1914 Norway gave the vote to most women. Elsewhere, women like the English Emmeline Pankhurst were very militant in their demands. They heckled politicians and held public demonstrations. These efforts generally failed before 1914, but they prepared the way for the triumph of the women's suffrage movement immediately after World War One.

As the right to vote spread, politicians and parties in national parliaments represented the people more responsively. Most countries soon had many political parties. The multiparty system meant that parliamentary majorities were built on shifting coalitions, which were unstable but did give parties leverage. They could obtain benefits for their supporters. Governments increasingly passed laws to alleviate general problems and to help specific groups. Governments seemed to care, and they seemed more worthy of support.

The German Empire

Politics in Germany after 1871 reflected many of these developments. The new German Empire was a federal union of Prussia and twenty-four smaller states. Much of the everyday business of government was conducted by the separate states, but there was a strong national government with a chancellor—until 1890, Bismarck—and a popularly elected parliament, called the *Reichstag.* Although Bismarck refused to be bound by a parliamentary majority, he tried nonetheless to maintain such a majority. This situation gave the political parties opportunities. Until 1878 Bismarck relied mainly on the National Liberals, who had rallied to him after 1866. They supported legislation useful for further economic and legal unification of the country.

Less wisely, they backed Bismarck's attack on the Catholic church, the so-called *Kulturkampf,* or "struggle for civilization." Like Bismarck, the middle-class National Liberals were particularly alarmed by Pius IX's declaration of papal infallibility in 1870. That dogma seemed to ask German Catholics to put loyalty to their church above loyalty to their nation. Only in Protestant Prussia did the *Kulturkampf* have even limited success. Catholics throughout the country generally voted for the Catholic Center party, which blocked passage of national laws hostile to the church. Finally in 1878, Bismarck abandoned his attack. Indeed, he and the Catholic Center Party entered into an uneasy but mutually advantageous alliance. The reasons were largely economic.

After a worldwide financial bust in 1873, European agriculture was in an increasingly difficult position. Wheat prices plummeted as cheap grain poured in from the United States, Canada, and Russia. New lands were opening up in North America and Russia, and the combination of railroads and technical improvements in shipping cut freight rates for grain drastically. European peasants with their smaller, less efficient farms could not compete in cereal production, especially in western and southern Germany. The peasantry there was largely Catholic, and the Catholic Center party was thus converted to the cause of higher tariffs to protect the economic interests of its supporters.

The same competitive pressures caused the Protestant Junkers, who owned large estates in eastern Germany, to embrace the cause of higher tariffs. They were joined by some of the iron and steel magnates of the Prussian Rhineland and Westphalia, who had previously been for free trade. With three such influential groups lobbying energetically, Bismarck was happy to go along with a new protective tariff in 1879. In doing so, he won new supporters in parliament—the Center party of the Catholics and the Conservative party of the Prussian landowners—and he held on to most of the National Liberals.

Bismarck had been looking for a way to increase taxes and raise more money for the government. The solution was higher tariffs. Many other governments acted similarly. The 1880s and 1890s saw a widespread return to protectionism. France in particular established very high tariffs to protect agriculture and industry, peasants and manufacturers. Thus the German government and other governments responded to a major economic problem and simultaneously won greater loyalty.

At the same time, Bismarck tried to stop the growth of German socialism because he genuinely feared its revolutionary language and allegiance to a movement transcending the nation state. In 1878, after two attempts on the life of William I by radicals (though not socialists), Bismarck succeeded in ramming through the Reichstag a law repressing socialists. Socialist meetings and publications were strictly controlled. The Social Democratic party was outlawed and driven underground. However, German socialists displayed a discipline and organization worthy of the Prussian army itself. Bismarck had to try another tack.

Thus Bismarck's state pioneered with social measures designed to win the support of working-class people. In 1883 he pushed through the parliament the first of several modern social security laws to help wage earners. The laws of 1883 and 1884 established national sickness and accident insurance; the law of 1889 established old-age pensions and retirement benefits. Henceforth sick, injured, and retired workers could look forward to regular weekly benefits from the state. This national social security system, paid for through compulsory contributions by wage earners and employers as well as grants from the state, was the first of its kind anywhere. It was to be fifty years before similar measures would be taken in the United States. Bismarck's social security system did not wean workers from socialism, but it did protect them from some of the uncertainties of the complex urban industrial world. This enormously significant development was a product of political competition and governmental efforts to win popular support.

Increasingly, the great issues in German domestic politics were socialism and the Marxian Social Democratic party. In 1890 the new emperor, the young, idealistic, and unstable William II (1888–1918), opposed Bismarck's attempt to renew the law outlawing the Social Democratic party. Eager to rule in his own right, as well as to earn the support of the workers, William II forced Bismarck to resign. After the "dropping of the pilot," German foreign policy changed profoundly and mostly for the worse, but the government did pass new laws to aid workers and to legalize socialist political activity.

Yet William II was no more successful than Bismarck in getting workers to renounce socialism. In-

Bismarck and William II Shown here visiting Bismarck's country estate in 1888, shortly after he became emperor of Germany (and king of Prussia), the young and impetuous William II soon quarrelled with his chief minister. Determined to rule, not merely to reign, his dismissal of Bismarck in 1890 was a fatal decision. *(Bildarchiv Preussicher Kulturbesitz)*

deed, socialist ideas spread rapidly, and more and more Social Democrats were elected to the parliament in the 1890s. After opposing a colonial war in German Southwest Africa in 1906 and thus suffering important losses in the general elections of 1907, the German Social Democratic party broadened its base in the years before World War One. In the elections of 1912, the party scored a great victory, becoming the largest single party in the Reichstag. The "revolutionary" socialists were, however, becoming less and less revolutionary in Germany. In the years before World War One, the strength of socialist opposition to greater military spending and imperialist expansion declined greatly. German socialists marched under the national banner.

Republican France

In 1871 France seemed hopelessly divided once again. The patriotic republicans who proclaimed the Third Republic in Paris after the military disaster at Sedan refused to admit defeat. They defended Paris with great heroism for weeks, living off rats and zoo animals, until they were quite literally starved into submission by German armies in January 1871. When national elections then sent a large majority of conservatives and monarchists to the National Assembly, the traumatized Parisians exploded and proclaimed the Paris Commune in March 1871. Vaguely radical, the leaders of the Commune wanted to govern Paris without interference by the conservative

Civil War in France When the French army invaded Paris, the Communards retaliated by placing hostages before firing squads, as this photograph reveals. The conquering army replied by summarily executing many prisoners and deporting others. Atrocities on both sides nurtured a tradition of class conflict that has often plagued modern France. *(BBC Hulton/The Bettmann Archive)*

French countryside. The National Assembly, led by the aging politician Adolphe Thiers, would hear none of it. The Assembly ordered the French army into Paris and brutally crushed the Commune. Twenty thousand people died in the fighting. As in June 1848, it was Paris against the provinces, French against French.

Out of this tragedy France slowly formed a new national unity, achieving considerable stability before 1914. How is one to account for this? Luck played a part. Until 1875 the monarchists in the "republican" National Assembly had a majority but could not agree who should be king. The compromise Bourbon candidate refused to rule except under the white flag of his ancestors—a completely unacceptable condition. In the meantime, Thiers' slaying of the radical Commune and his other firm measures showed the fearful provinces and the middle class that the Third Republic might be moderate and socially conservative. France therefore retained the republic, though reluctantly. As President Thiers cautiously said, it was "the government which divides us least."

Another stabilizing factor was the skill and determination of the moderate republican leaders in the early years. The most famous of these was Léon Gambetta, the son of an Italian grocer, a warm, easygoing, unsuccessful lawyer turned professional politician. A master of emerging mass politics, Gambetta combined eloquence with the personal touch as he preached a republic of truly equal opportunity. Gambetta was also instrumental in establishing absolute parliamentary supremacy between 1877 and 1879, when the somewhat autocratic president Marie Edmé MacMahon was forced to resign. By 1879 the great majority of members of both the upper and the lower houses of parliament were republicans. Although these republicans were split among many parliamentary groups and later among several parties—a situation that led to constant coalition politics and the rapid turnover of ministers—the Third Republic had firm foundations after almost a decade.

The moderate republicans sought to preserve their creation by winning the hearts and minds of the next generation. Trade unions were fully legalized, and France acquired a colonial empire. More important, under the leadership of Jules Ferry, the moderate republicans of small towns and villages passed a series of laws between 1879 and 1886 establishing free compulsory elementary education for both girls and boys. At the same time, they greatly expanded the state system of public tax-supported schools. Thus France shared fully in the general expansion of public education, which served as a critical nation-building tool throughout the Western world in the late nineteenth century.

In France most elementary and much secondary education had traditionally been in the parochial schools of the Catholic church, which had long been hostile to republics and to much of secular life. Free compulsory elementary education in France became secular republican education. The pledge of allegiance and the national anthem replaced the catechism and the "Ave Maria." Militant young elementary teachers carried the ideology of patriotic republicanism into every corner of France. In their classes, they sought to win the loyalty of the young citizens to the republic, so that France would never again vote en masse for dictators like the two Napoleons.

Although these educational reforms disturbed French Catholics, many of them rallied to the republic in the 1890s. The limited acceptance of the modern world by the more liberal Pope Leo XIII (1878–1903) eased tensions between church and state. Unfortunately, the Dreyfus affair changed all that.

Alfred Dreyfus, a Jewish captain in the French army, was falsely accused and convicted of treason. His family never doubted his innocence and fought unceasingly to reopen the case, enlisting the support of prominent republicans and intellectuals such as the novelist Emile Zola. In 1898 and 1899, the case split France apart. On one side was the army, which had manufactured evidence against Dreyfus, joined by anti-Semites and most of the Catholic establishment. On the other side stood the civil libertarians and most of the more radical republicans.

This battle, which eventually led to Dreyfus's being declared innocent, revived republican feeling against the church. Between 1901 and 1905, the government severed all ties between the state and the Catholic church, after centuries of close relations. The salaries of priests and bishops were no longer paid by the government, and all churches were given to local committees of lay Catholics. Catholic schools were put completely on their own financially, and in a short time they lost a third of their students. The state school system's power of indoctrination was greatly strengthened. In France, only the growing socialist movement, with its very different and thoroughly secular ideology, stood in opposition to patriotic, republican nationalism.

Great Britain and Ireland

Britain in the late nineteenth century has often been seen as a shining example of peaceful and successful political evolution. Germany was stuck with a manipulated parliament that gave an irresponsible emperor too much power; France had a quarrelsome parliament that gave its presidents too little power. Great Britain, in contrast, seemed to enjoy an effective two-party parliament that skillfully guided the country from classical liberalism to full-fledged democracy with hardly a misstep.

This view of Great Britain is not so much wrong as incomplete. After the right to vote was granted to males of the solid middle class in 1832, opinion leaders and politicians wrestled long and hard with the uncertainties of a further extension of the franchise. In his famous "Essay on Liberty," published in

THE SPREAD OF NATIONALISM IN EUROPE, 1850–1914

1851	Louis Napoleon dismisses French National Assembly in coup d'état
1852–1870	Second Empire in France
1853–1856	Crimean War
1859	Mill, *Essay on Liberty*
1859–1870	Unification of Italy
1861	Abolition of serfdom in Russia
1862–1890	Bismarck's reign of power in German affairs
1864–1871	First Socialist International
1866	Prussia wins decisive victory in Austro-Prussian War
1866–1871	Unification of the German Empire
1867	Magyar nobility increases its power by restoring the constitution of 1848 in Hungary, thereby further dividing the Austro-Hungarian Empire
	Marx, *Das Capital*
	Second Reform Act passed by British parliament
1870–1871	Prussia wins decisive victory in Franco-Prussian War; William I proclaimed emperor of a united Germany
1871	Paris Commune
1871–1914	Third Republic in France
1878	Suppression of Social Democrats in Germany
1881	Assassination of Tsar Alexander II
1883–1889	Enactment of social security laws in Germany
1884	Third Reform Act passed by British parliament
1889–1914	Second Socialist International
1890	Repeal of anti–Social Democrat law in Germany
1892–1903	Witte directs modernization of Russian economy
1904–1905	Japan wins decisive victory in Russo-Japanese War
1905	Revolution in Russia: Tsar Nicholas II forced to issue the October Manifesto promising a popularly elected Duma
1906–1914	Liberal reform in Great Britain
1907–1912	Stolypin's agrarian reforms in Russia
1912	German Social Democratic party becomes largest party in the German Reichstag
1914	Irish Home Rule bill passed by British parliament but immediately suspended with outbreak of First World War

1859, the philosopher John Stuart Mill (1806–1873), the leading heir to the Benthamite tradition (page 765), probed the problem of how to protect the rights of individuals and minorities in the emerging age of mass electoral participation. Mill pleaded eloquently for the practical and moral value inherent in safeguarding individual differences and unpopular opinions. In 1867 Benjamin Disraeli and the Conservatives extended the vote to all middle-class males and the best-paid workers. The son of a Jewish stockbroker, himself a novelist and urban dandy, the ever-fascinating Disraeli (1804–1881) was willing to risk this "leap in the dark" in order to gain new supporters. The Conservative party, he believed, needed to broaden its traditional base of aristocratic and landed support if it was to survive. After 1867 English political parties and electoral campaigns became more modern, and the "lower orders" appeared to vote as responsibly as their "betters." Hence the Third Reform Bill of 1884 gave the vote to almost every adult male.

While the House of Commons was drifting toward democracy, the House of Lords was content to slumber nobly. Between 1901 and 1910, however, that bastion of aristocratic conservatism tried to reassert itself. Acting as supreme court of the land, it ruled against labor unions in two important decisions. And after the Liberal party came to power in 1906, the Lords vetoed several measures passed by the Commons, including the so-called People's Budget. The Lords finally capitulated, as they had done in 1832, when the king threatened to create enough new peers to pass the bill.

Aristocratic conservatism yielded to popular democracy, once and for all. The result was that extensive social welfare measures, slow to come to Great Britain, were passed in a spectacular rush between 1906 and 1914. During those years, the Liberal party, inspired by the fiery Welshman David Lloyd George (1863–1945), substantially raised taxes on the rich as part of the People's Budget. This income helped the government pay for national health insurance, unemployment benefits, old-age pensions, and a host of other social measures. The state was integrating the urban masses socially as well as politically.

This record of accomplishment was only part of the story, though. On the eve of World War One, the ever-emotional, ever-unanswered question of Ireland brought Great Britain to the brink of civil war. In the 1840s, Ireland had been decimated by famine, which fueled an Irish revolutionary movement. Thereafter, the English slowly granted concessions, such as the abolition of the privileges of the Anglican church and rights for Irish peasants. The Liberal prime minister William Gladstone (1809–1898), who had proclaimed twenty years earlier that "my mission is to pacify Ireland," introduced bills to give Ireland self-government in 1886 and in 1893. They failed to pass. After two decades of relative quiet, Irish nationalists in the British Parliament saw their chance. They supported the Liberals in their battle for the People's Budget and received passage of a home-rule bill for Ireland in return.

Thus Ireland, the emerald isle, achieved self-government—but not quite, for Ireland is composed of two peoples. As much as the Irish Catholic majority in the southern counties wanted home rule, precisely that much did the Irish Protestants of the northern countries of Ulster come to oppose it. Motivated by the accumulated fears and hostilities of generations, the Protestants of Ulster refused to submerge themselves in a Catholic Ireland, just as Irish Catholics had refused to submit to a Protestant Britain.

The Ulsterites vowed to resist home rule in northern Ireland. By December 1913, they had raised 100,000 armed volunteers, and they were supported by much of English public opinion. Thus in 1914, the Liberals in the House of Lords introduced a compromise home-rule law that did not apply to the northern counties. This bill, which openly betrayed promises made to Irish nationalists, was rejected and in September the original home-rule plan was passed but simultaneously suspended for the duration of the hostilities. The momentous Irish question had been overtaken by earth-shattering world war in August 1914.

Irish developments illustrated once again the power of national feeling and national movements in the nineteenth century. Moreover, they were proof that governments could not elicit greater loyalty unless they could capture and control that elemental current of national feeling. Though Great Britain had much going for it—power, Parliament, prosperity—none of these availed in the face of the conflicting nationalisms espoused by Catholics and Protestants in northern Ireland. Similarly, progressive Sweden was

Magyar Nationalism flourished in Buda and Pest, built on opposite sides of the Danube and merged together in 1872. A whole series of splendid new buildings rose up, reflecting the desire of Hungarians to make Budapest a truly great capital city. *(Historical Pictures Service, Chicago)*

powerless to stop the growth of the Norwegian national movement, which culminated in Norway's breaking away from Sweden and becoming a fully independent nation in 1905. In this light, one can also see how hopeless was the case of the Ottoman Empire in Europe in the later nineteenth century. It was only a matter of time before the Serbs, Bulgarians, and Rumanians would break away, and they did.

The Austro-Hungarian Empire

The dilemma of conflicting nationalisms in Ireland also helps one appreciate how desperate the situation in the Austro-Hungarian Empire had become by the early twentieth century. In 1849 Magyar nationalism had driven Hungarian patriots to declare an independent Hungarian republic, which was savagely crushed by Russian and Austrian armies (pages 754–756). Throughout the 1850s, Hungary was ruled as a conquered territory, and Emperor Francis Joseph and his bureaucracy tried hard to centralize the state and germanize the language and culture of the different nationalities.

Then, in the wake of defeat by Prussia in 1866, a weakened Austria was forced to strike a compromise and establish the so-called dual monarchy. The empire was divided in two and the nationalistic Magyars gained virtual independence for Hungary. Henceforth each half of the empire agreed to deal with its own "barbarians"—its own minorities—as it saw fit. The two states were joined only by a shared monarch and common ministries for finance, defense, and foreign affairs. After 1867 the disintegrating force of competing nationalisms continued unabated, for both Austria and Hungary had several "Irelands" within their borders.

In Austria, ethnic Germans were only one-third of the population, and by the late 1890s many Germans saw their traditional dominance threatened by Czechs, Poles, and other Slavs. A particularly emotional and divisive issue in the Austrian parliament was the language used in government and elementary education at the local level. From 1900 to 1914, the parliament was so divided that ministries generally could not obtain a majority and ruled instead by decree. Efforts by both conservatives and socialists to defuse national antagonisms by stressing economic issues cutting across ethnic lines—which led to the introduction of universal male suffrage in 1907—proved largely unsuccessful.

One aspect of such national antagonisms was anti-Semitism, which was particlarly virulent in Austria. The Jewish populations of Austrian cities grew very rapidly after Jews obtained full legal equality in 1867, reaching 10 percent of the population of Vienna by 1900. Many Jewish businessmen were quite successful in banking and retail trade, while Jewish artists, intellectuals, and scientists, like the world-famous Sigmund Freud, played a major role in making Vienna a leading center of European culture and modern thought. When extremists charged the Jews with controlling the economy and corrupting German culture with alien ideas and ultramodern art, anxious Germans of all classes tended to listen. The popular mayor of Vienna from 1897 to 1910, Dr. Karl Lueger, combined anti-Semitic rhetoric with calls for "Christian socialism" and municipal ownership of basic services. Lueger appealed especially to the German lower-middle class—and to an unsuccessful young artist named Adolf Hitler.

In Hungary, the Magyar nobility in 1867 restored the constitution of 1848 and used it to dominate both the Magyar peasantry and the minority populations until 1914. Only the wealthiest one-fourth of adult males had the right to vote, making the parliament the creature of the Magyar elite. Laws promoting use of the Magyar (Hungarian) language in schools and government were rammed through and bitterly resented, especially by the Croatians and Rumanians. While Magyar extremists campaigned loudly for total separation from Austria, the radical leaders of the subject nationalities dreamed in turn of independence from Hungary. Unlike most major countries, which harnessed nationalism to strengthen the state after 1871, the Austro-Hungarian Empire was progressively weakened and destroyed by it.

MARXISM AND THE SOCIALIST MOVEMENT

Nationalism served, for better or worse, as a new unifying principle. But what about socialism? Did the rapid growth of socialist parties, which were generally Marxian parties, dedicated to an international proletarian revolution, mean that national states had failed to gain the support of workers? Certainly, many prosperous and conservative citizens were greatly troubled by the socialist movement. And many historians have portrayed the years before 1914 as a time of increasing conflict between revolutionary socialism on the one hand and a nationalist alliance between conservative aristocracy and the prosperous middle class on the other. This question requires close examination.

The Socialist International

The growth of socialist parties after 1871 was phenomenal. Neither Bismarck's antisocialist laws nor his extensive social security system checked the growth of the German Social Democratic party, which espoused the Marxian ideology. By 1912 it had attracted millions of followers and was the largest party in the parliament. Socialist parties also grew in other countries, though nowhere else with quite such success. In 1883 Russian exiles in Switzerland founded a Russian Social Democratic party, which grew rapidly in the 1890s and thereafter, despite internal disputes. In France, various socialist parties reemerged in the 1880s after the carnage of the Commune. Most of them were finally unified in a single, increasingly powerful Marxian party, called the French Section of the Workers International, in 1905. Belgium and Austria-Hungary also had strong socialist parties of the Marxian persuasion.

As the name of the French party suggests, Marxian socialist parties were eventually linked together in an international organization. As early as 1848, Marx had laid out his intellectual system in the *Communist Manifesto* (pages 739–740). He had declared that "the working men have no country," and he had urged proletarians of all nations to unite against their governments. Joining the flood of radicals and republicans who fled continental Europe for England and America after the revolutions of 1848, Marx settled in London. Poor and depressed, he lived on his meager earnings as a journalist and on the gifts of his friend Engels. Marx never stopped thinking of revolution. Digging deeply into economics and history, he concluded that revolution follows economic crisis and tried to prove it in *Critique of Political Economy* (1859) and his greatest theoretical work, *Capital* (1867).

The bookish Marx also excelled as a practical organizer. In 1864 he played an important role in founding the First International of socialists—the International Working Men's Association. In the following years, he battled successfully to control the organization and used its annual meetings as a means of spreading his realistic, "scientific" doctrines of inevitable socialist revolution. Then Marx enthusiastically embraced the passionate, vaguely radical patriotism of the Paris Commune and its terrible conflict with the French National Assembly as a giant step toward socialist revolution. This impetuous action frightened many of his early supporters, especially the more moderate British labor leaders. The First International collapsed.

Yet international proletarian solidarity remained an important objective for Marxists. In 1889, as the individual parties in different countries grew stronger, socialist leaders came together to form the Second International, which lasted until 1914. Although the International was only a federation of various national socialist parties, it had great psychological impact. Every three years, delegates from the different parties met to interpret Marxian doctrines and plan coordinated action. May 1—May Day—was declared an annual international one-day strike, a day of marches and demonstrations. A permanent executive for the International was established. Many feared and many others rejoiced in the growing power of socialism and the Second International.

Unions and Revisionism

Was socialism really radical and revolutionary in these years? On the whole, it was not. Indeed, as socialist parties grew and attracted large numbers of members, they looked more and more toward gradual change and steady improvement for the working class, less and less toward revolution. The mainstream of European socialism became militantly moderate; that is, they increasingly combined radical rhetoric with sober action.

Workers themselves were progressively less inclined to follow radical programs. There were several reasons for this. As workers gained the right to vote and to participate politically in the nation-state, their attention focused more on elections than on revolutions. And as workers won real, tangible benefits, this furthered the process. Workers were not immune to patriotic education and indoctrination during military service, however ardently socialist intellectuals might wish the contrary. Nor were workers a unified social group, as demonstrated in Chapter 24.

Perhaps most important of all, workers' standard of living rose substantially after 1850 as the promise of the Industrial Revolution was at least partially realized. In Great Britain, for example, workers could buy almost twice as much with their wages in 1906 as in 1850, and most of the increase came after 1870. Workers experienced similar increases in most continental countries after 1850, though much less strikingly in late-developing Russia. Improvement in the standard of living was much more than merely a matter of higher wages. The quality of life improved dramatically in urban areas. For all these reasons, workers tended more and more to become militantly moderate: they demanded gains, but they were less likely to take to the barricades in pursuit of them.

The growth of labor unions reinforced this trend toward moderation. In the early stages of industrialization, modern unions were generally prohibited by law. A famous law of the French Revolution had declared all guilds and unions illegal in the name of "liberty" in 1791. In Great Britain, attempts by workers to unite were considered criminal conspiracies after 1799. Other countries had similar laws, and these obviously hampered union development. In France, for example, about two hundred workers were imprisoned each year between 1825 and 1847 for taking part in illegal combinations. Unions were considered subversive bodies, only to be hounded and crushed.

From this sad position workers struggled to escape. Great Britain led the way in 1824 and 1825, when unions won the right to exist but (generally) not the right to strike. After the collapse of Robert Owen's attempt to form one big union in the 1830s (page 720), new and more practical kinds of unions appeared. Limited primarily to highly skilled workers such as machinists and carpenters, the "new model unions" avoided both radical politics and costly strikes. Instead, their sober, respectable leaders concentrated

Socialist Clubs helped spread Marxian doctrines among the working classes. There workers (and intellectuals) from different backgrounds debated the fine points and developed a sense of solidarity. *(Historical Pictures Service, Chicago)*

on winning better wages and hours for their members through collective bargaining and compromise. This approach helped pave the way to full acceptance in Britain in the 1870s, when unions won the right to strike without being held legally liable for the financial damage inflicted on employers. After 1890 unions for unskilled workers developed, and between 1901 and 1906, the legal position of British unions was further strengthened.

Germany was the most industrialized, socialized, and unionized continental country by 1914. German unions were not granted important rights until 1869, and until the antisocialist law was repealed in 1890, they were frequently harassed by the government as socialist fronts. Nor were socialist leaders particularly interested in union activity, believing as they did in the iron law of low wages and the need for political revolution. The result was that, as late as 1895, there were only about 270,000 union members in a male industrial work force of nearly 8 million. Then, with German industrialization still storming ahead and almost all legal harassment eliminated, union membership skyrocketed to roughly 3 million in 1912.

This great expansion both reflected and influenced the changing character of German unions. Increasingly, unions in Germany focused on concrete bread-and-butter issues—wages, hours, working conditions—rather than on instilling pure socialist doctrine. Genuine collective bargaining, long opposed by socialist intellectuals as a "sellout," was officially recognized as desirable by the German Trade Union Congress in 1899. When employers proved unwilling to bargain, a series of strikes forced them to change their minds.

Between 1906 and 1913, successful collective bargaining was gaining a prominent place in German industrial relations. In 1913 alone, over ten thousand collective bargaining agreements affecting 1.25 million workers were signed. Further gradual improvement, not revolution, was becoming the primary objective of the German trade union movement.

The German trade unions and their leaders were —in fact, if not in name—thoroughgoing revisionists. *Revisionism*—that most awful of sins in the eyes of militant Marxists in the twentieth century—was an effort by various socialists to update Marxian doctrines to reflect the realities of the time. Thus the socialist Edward Bernstein argued in 1899 in his *Evolutionary Socialism* that Marx's predictions of ever-greater poverty for workers and ever-greater concentration of wealth in ever-fewer hands had been proven false. Therefore, Bernstein suggested, socialists should reform their doctrines and tactics. They should combine with other progressive forces to win gradual evolutionary gains for workers through legislation, unions, and further economic development. These views were formally denounced as heresy by the German Social Democratic party and later by the entire Second International. Nevertheless, the revisionist, gradualist approach continued to gain the tacit acceptance of many German socialists, particularly in the trade unions.

Moderation found followers elsewhere. In France, the great humanist and socialist leader Jean Jaurès formally repudiated revisionist doctrines in order to establish a unified socialist party, but he remained at heart a gradualist. Questions of revolutionary versus gradualist policies split Russian Marxists.

Socialist parties before 1914 had clear-cut national characteristics. Russians and socialists in the Austro-Hungarian Empire tended to be the most radical. The German party talked revolution and practiced reformism, greatly influenced by its enormous trade union movement. The French party talked revolution and tried to practice it, unrestrained by a trade union movement that was both very weak and very radical. In England, the socialist but non-Marxian Labour party, reflecting the well-established union movement, was formally committed to gradual reform. In Spain and Italy, Marxian socialism was very weak. There anarchism, seeking to smash the state rather than the bourgeoisie, dominated radical thought and action.

In short, socialist policies and doctrines varied from country to country. Socialism itself was to a large extent "nationalized" behind the imposing façade of international unity. This helps explain why, when war came in 1914, socialist leaders almost without exception supported their governments.

From the mid-nineteenth century on, Western society became nationalistic as well as urban and industrial. Nation-states and strong-minded national leaders gradually enlisted widespread support and gave men and women a sense of belonging. Even socialism became increasingly national in orientation, gathering strength as a champion of working-class interests in domestic politics. Yet, while nationalism served to unite peoples, it also drove them apart. Though most obvious in Austria-Hungary and Ireland, this was in a real sense true for all of Western civilization. For the universal national faith, which reduced social tensions within states, promoted a bitter, almost Darwinian competition between states and thus ominously threatened the progress and unity it had helped to build.

NOTES

1. Quoted by G. Wright, *France in Modern Times*, Rand McNally, Chicago, 1960, p. 179.
2. J. Burckhardt, *Reflections on History*, G. Allen & Unwin, London, 1943, p. 165.
3. Quoted by O. Pflanze, *Bismarck and the Development of Germany: The Period of Unification, 1815–1871*, Princeton University Press, Princeton, N.J., 1963, p. 60.
4. Quoted by E. Eyck, *Bismarck and the German Empire*, W. W. Norton, New York, 1964, p. 59.
5. Quoted by H. Kohn, *The Mind of Germany: The Education of a Nation*, Charles Scribner's Sons & Macmillan, New York, 1960, pp. 156–161.
6. Quoted by T. von Laue, *Sergei Witte and the Industrialization of Russia*, Columbia University Press, New York, 1963, p. 78.
7. Quoted by J. P. McKay, *Pioneers for Profit: Foreign Entrepreneurship and Russian Industrialization, 1885–1913*, Chicago University Press, Chicago, 1970, p. 11.

SUGGESTED READING

In addition to the general works mentioned in the Suggested Reading for Chapter 23, which treat the entire nineteenth century, G. Craig, *Germany, 1866–1945* (1980), and B. Moore, *Social Origins of Dictatorship and Democracy* (1966), are outstanding.

Among specialized works of high quality, R. Williams, *Gaslight and Shadows* (1957), brings the world of Napoleon III vibrantly alive, while Karl Marx's *The Eighteenth Brumaire of Louis Napoleon* is a famous denunciation of the coup d'état. The engaging collective biography by R. Shattuck, *The Banquet Years* (1968), captures the spirit of artistic and intellectual Paris at the end of the century. E. Weber, *Peasants into Frenchmen* (1976), stresses the role of education and modern communications in the transformation of rural France after 1870. E. Thomas, *The Women Incendiaries* (1966), examines radical women in the Paris Commune. G. Chapman, *The Dreyfus Case: A Reassessment* (1955), and D. Johnson, *France and the Dreyfus Affair* (1967), are careful examinations of the famous case. In *Jean Barois,* Nobel Prize winner R. M. Du Gard accurately recreates in novel form the Dreyfus affair, and Emile Zola's novel *The Debacle* treats the Franco-Prussian War realistically.

D. M. Smith has written widely on Italy, and his *Garibaldi* (1956) and *Italy: A Modern History,* rev. ed. (1969) are recommended. P. Schroeder, *Austria, Great Britain and the Crimean War* (1972), is an outstanding and highly original diplomatic study. In addition to the important studies on Bismarck and Germany by Pflanze, Eyck, and Kohn cited in the Notes, F. Stern, *Gold and Iron* (1977), is a fascinating examination of relations between Bismarck and his financial adviser, the Jewish banker Bleichröder. G. Iggers, *The German Conception of History* (1968); K. D. Barkin, *The Controversy Over German Industrialization, 1890–1902* (1970); and E. Spencer, *Management and Labor in Imperial Germany: Ruhr Industrialists as Employers* (1984), are valuable in-depth investigations. H. Glasser, ed., *The German Mind in the Nineteenth Century* (1981), is an outstanding anthology, as is P. Mendes-Flohr, *The Jew in the Modern World: A Documentary History* (1980). C. Schorske, *Fin de Siècle Vienna: Politics and Culture* (1980), and P. Gay, *Freud, Jews, and Other Germans* (1978), are brilliant on aspects of modern culture. R. Kann, *The Multinational Empire,* 2 vols. (1950, 1964), probes the intricacies of the nationality problem in Austria-Hungary, while S. Stavrianos has written extensively on southeastern Europe, including *The Balkans, 1815–1914* (1963).

In addition to the studies on Russian industrial development by von Laue and McKay cited in the Notes, W. Blackwell, *The Industrialization of Russia,* 2nd. ed. (1982), and A. Rieber, *Merchants and Entrepreneurs in Imperial Russia* (1982), are recommended. Among fine studies on Russian social development and modernization, T. Emmons, *The Russian Landed Gentry and the Peasant Emancipation of 1861* (1968); R. Zelnik, *Labor and Society in Tsarist Russia, 1855–1870* (1971); R. Johnson, *Peasant and Proletarian: The Working Class of Moscow at the End of the Nineteenth Century* (1979); and H. Troyat, *Daily Life in Russia Under the Last Tsar* (1962), are particularly noteworthy. W. E. Mosse, *Alexander II and the Modernization of Russia* (1958), provides a good discussion of midcentury reforms, while C. Black, ed., *The Transformation of Russian Society* (1960), offers a collection of essays on Russian modernization. I. Turgenev's great novel *Fathers and Sons* probes the age-old conflict of generations as well as nineteenth-century Russian revolutionary thought.

G. Dangerfield, *The Strange Death of Liberal England* (1961), brilliantly examines social tensions in Ireland as well as Englishwomen's struggle for the vote before 1914. W. Arnstein convincingly shows how the Victorian aristocracy survived and even flourished in nineteenth-century Britain in F. Jaher, ed., *The Rich, the Well-Born, and the Powerful* (1973), an interesting collection of essays on social elites in history. The theme of aristocratic strength and survival is expanded in A. Mayer's provocative *Persistence of the Old Regime: Europe to the Great War* (1981).

On late-nineteenth-century socialism, C. Schorske, *German Social Democracy, 1905–1917* (1955), is a modern classic. V. Lidtke, *The Outlawed Party* (1966), ably treats the German socialists between 1878 and 1890. H. Goldberg, *The Life of Jean Jaurès* (1962), is a sympathetic account of the great French socialist leader. P. Stearns, who has written several books on European labor history, considers radical labor leaders in *Revolutionary Syndicalism and French Labor* (1971). M. Hanagan, *The Logic of Solidarity* (1980), examines the working class in three French towns between 1870 and 1914.

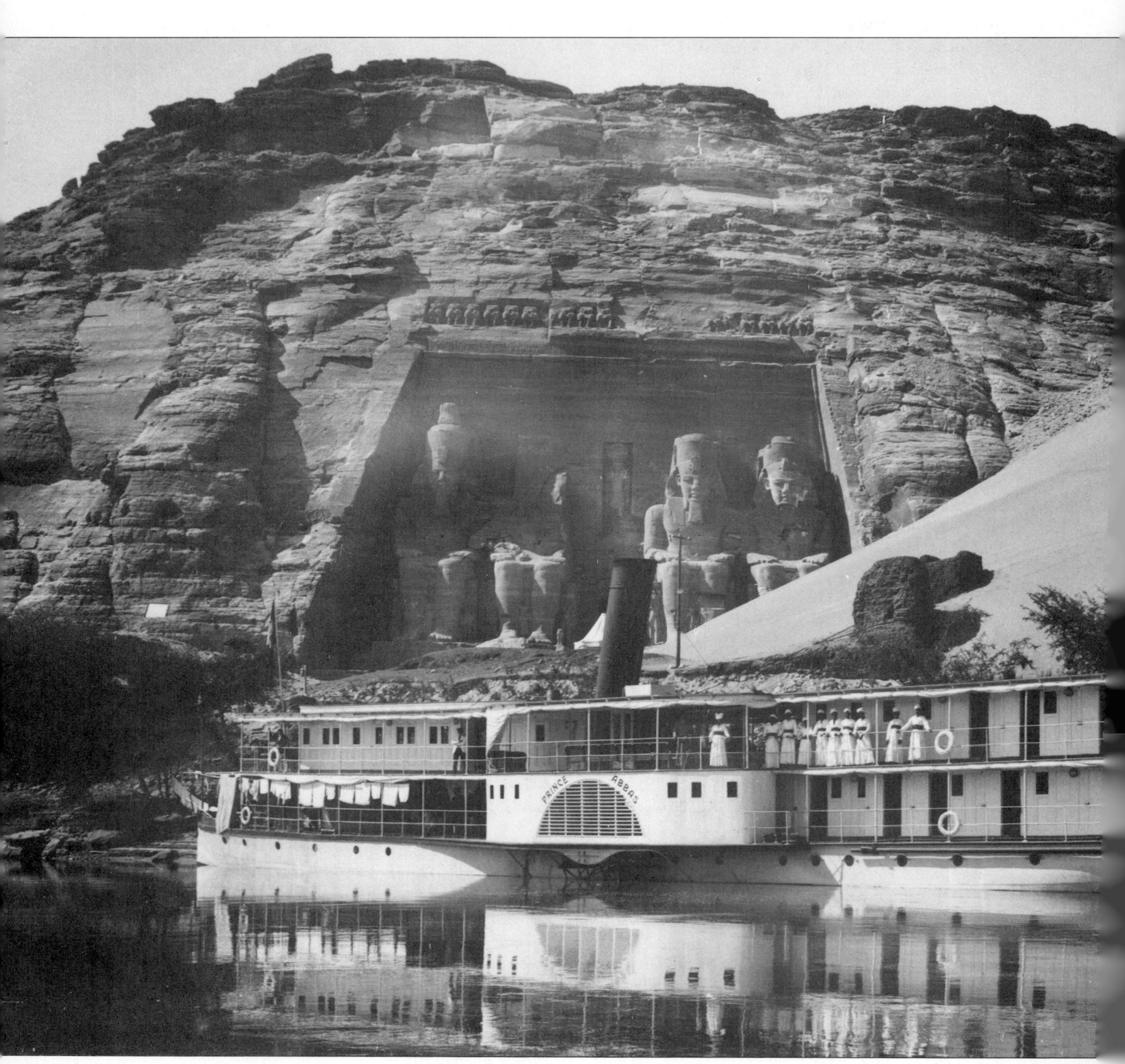
PRINCE ABBAS

26

THE WEST AND THE WORLD

HILE BOTH NATIONALISM and urban life were transforming Western society, Western society itself was reshaping the world. At the peak of its power and pride, the West entered the third and most dynamic phase of the aggressive expansion that began with the Crusades and continued with the great discoveries and the rise of seaborne colonial empires. An ever-growing stream of products, people, and ideas flowed out of Europe in the nineteenth century. Hardly any corner of the globe was left untouched. The most spectacular manifestations of Western expansion came in the late nineteenth century, when the leading European nations established or enlarged their far-flung political empires. The political annexation of territory in the 1880s—the "new imperialism," as it is often called by historians—was the capstone of a profound underlying economic and technological process. How and why did this many-sided, epoch-making expansion occur, and what were some of its consequences for the West and the rest of the world? This chapter will focus on these questions.

BUILDING A WORLD ECONOMY

The Industrial Revolution created, first in Great Britain and then in continental Europe and North America, a growing and tremendously dynamic economic system. In the course of the nineteenth century, that system was extended across the face of the earth. Much of this extension into non-Western areas was peaceful and beneficial for all concerned, for the West had many products and techniques the rest of the world desired. If peaceful methods failed, however, Europeans did not stand on ceremony. They used their superior military power to force non-Western nations to open their doors to trade and investment.

Trade and Communications

Commerce between nations has always been a powerful stimulus to economic development. Never was this more true than in the nineteenth century, when world trade grew prodigiously. As Figure 26.1 shows, world trade grew modestly until about 1840, and then it took off. After a slowdown in the last years of the century, another surge lasted until World War One. The value of world trade in 1913 was roughly *twenty-five* times what it had been in 1800. This figure actually understates growth, since average prices of both manufactured goods and raw materials were substantially *lower* in 1913 than in 1800. In a general way, the enormous increase in international commerce summed up the growth of an interlocking world economy, centered in and directed by Europe.

Great Britain played a key role in using trade to tie all corners of the world together economically. In 1815 Britain already had a colonial empire, for India, Canada, Australia, and other scattered areas remained British possessions after American independence. The technological breakthroughs of the Industrial Revolution allowed Britain to manufacture cotton textiles, iron, and other goods more cheaply and to far outstrip domestic demand for such products. By 1820 Britain was exporting half of its cotton textiles, for example. As European nations and the United States erected protective tariff barriers and began to industrialize, British cotton-textile manufacturers aggressively sought and found other foreign markets. In 1820 Europe bought half of Britain's cotton-textile exports and India bought only 6 percent. By 1850 India bought 25 percent and Europe only 16 percent of a much larger total.

Moreover, after the repeal of the Corn Laws in 1846, Britain's commitment to free trade was unswerving. The decisive argument in the battle against tariffs on imported grain had been, "We must give, if we mean honestly to receive, and buy as well as sell." Until 1914 Britain thus remained the world's emporium, where not only agricultural products and raw materials but also manufactured goods entered freely. Free access to the enormous market of Britain and its empire stimulated business activities around the world.

The growth of trade was facilitated by the conquest of distance. The earliest railroad construction occurred in Europe (including Russia) and in America north of the Rio Grande; other parts of the globe saw the building of rail lines after 1860. By 1920 more than one-quarter of the world's railroads were in Latin America, Asia, Africa, and Australia. Wherever railroads were built, they drastically reduced transportation costs, opened new economic opportunities, and called forth new skills and attitudes. Moreover, in the areas of massive European settlement—North America and Australia—they were built in advance of the population and provided a means of settling the land.

The power of steam revolutionized transportation by sea as well as by land. In 1807 inhabitants of the Hudson Valley in New York saw the "Devil on the way to Albany in a saw-mill," as Robert Fulton's steamship *Clermont* traveled 150 miles upstream in thirty-two hours. Steam power, long used to drive paddle-wheelers on rivers, particularly in Russia and North America, finally began to supplant sails on the oceans of the world in the late 1860s. Lighter, stronger, cheap steel replaced iron, which had replaced wood. Screw propellers superseded paddle wheels, while mighty compound steam engines cut fuel consumption by half. Passenger and freight rates tumbled, and the intercontinental shipment of low-priced raw materials became feasible. In addition to the large passenger liners and freighters of the great shipping companies, there were innumerable independent tramp steamers searching endlessly for cargo around the world.

An account of an actual voyage by a typical tramp freighter will highlight nineteenth-century developments in global trade. The ship left England in 1910, carrying rails and general freight to western Australia. From there, it carried lumber to Melbourne in southeastern Australia, where it took on harvester combines for Argentina. In Buenos Aires it loaded wheat for Calcutta, and in Calcutta it took on jute for New York. From New York it carried a variety of industrial products to Australia, before returning to England with lead, wool, and wheat after a voyage of approximately 72,000 miles to six continents in seventeen months.

The revolution in land and sea transportation helped European pioneers to open up vast new territories and to produce agricultural products and raw materials there for sale in Europe. Moreover, the development of refrigerated railway cars and, from the 1880s, refrigerator ships enabled first Argentina and then the United States, Australia, and New Zealand to ship mountains of chilled or frozen beef and mutton to European (mainly British) consumers. From Asia, Africa, and Latin America came not only the traditional tropical products—spices, tea, sugar, coffee—but new raw materials for industry, such as jute, rubber, cotton, and coconut oil.

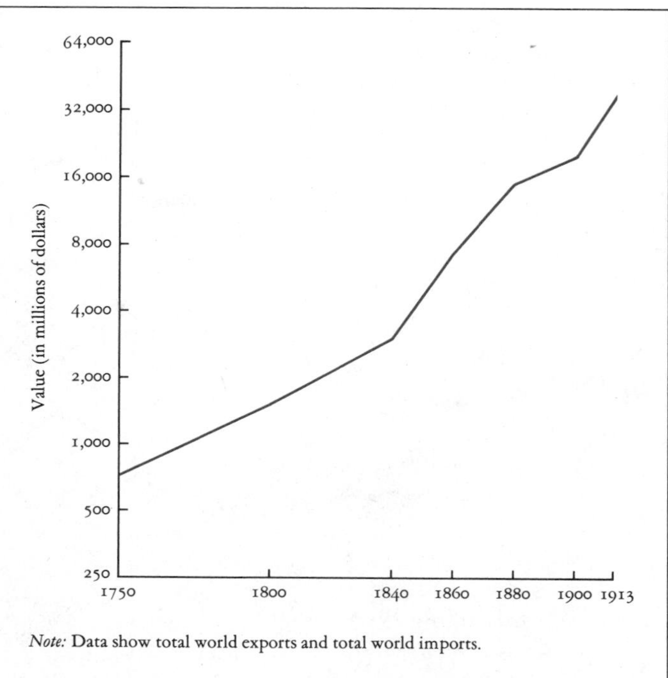

FIGURE 26.1 The Growth of World Trade, 1750–1913 in 1913 Dollars The expansion of international commerce encouraged and reflected Western economic development in the nineteenth century. *(Source: W. Woodruff,* Impact of Western Man: A Study of Europe's Role in the World Economy. *St. Martin's Press, New York, 1967, p. 313 and references cited therein.)*

Intercontinental trade was enormously facilitated by the Suez and Panama canals. Of great importance, too, was large and continuous investment in modern port facilities, which made loading and unloading cheaper, faster, and more dependable. Finally, transoceanic telegraph cables inaugurated rapid communications among the financial centers of the world. While a British tramp freighter steamed from Calcutta to New York, a broker in London was arranging, by telegram, for it to carry an American cargo to Australia. World commodity prices were also instantaneously conveyed by the same network of communications.

In surveying these dramatic and impressive developments, one must remember that, in terms of value, most *trade* (as opposed to most *shipping*) was among European nations, the United States, and Canada. It was not between Europe and the colonial-tropical lands of Africa, Asia, and Latin America. For example, Britain and Germany, both great world traders, carried on a very large and profitable trade with each

The Opening of the Suez Canal in 1869 revolutionized communications between Europe and Asia. This drawing shows opening-day ceremonies. *(BBC Hulton/The Bettmann Archive)*

other before World War One. Between 1900 and 1913, Britain's second-best customer in the entire world (after India) was Germany, and Britain was Germany's largest single customer. Germany sold twice as much to Britain alone as to all of Africa and Asia combined. Before 1914 world trade was centered in the prosperous, tightly integrated European economy.

Foreign Investment

The growth of trade and the conquest of distance encouraged the expanding European economy to make massive foreign investments. Beginning about 1840, European capitalists started to invest large sums in foreign lands. They did not stop until the outbreak of World War One in 1914. By that year, Europeans had invested more than $40 billion abroad. Great Britain, France, and Germany were the principal investing countries, although by 1913 the United States was emerging as a substantial foreign investor. The sums involved were enormous (see Map 26.1). In the decade before 1914, Great Britain was investing 7 percent of its annual national income abroad, or slightly more than it was investing in its entire domestic economy. The great gap between rich and poor meant that the wealthy and moderately well-to-do could and did send great sums abroad in search of interest and dividends.

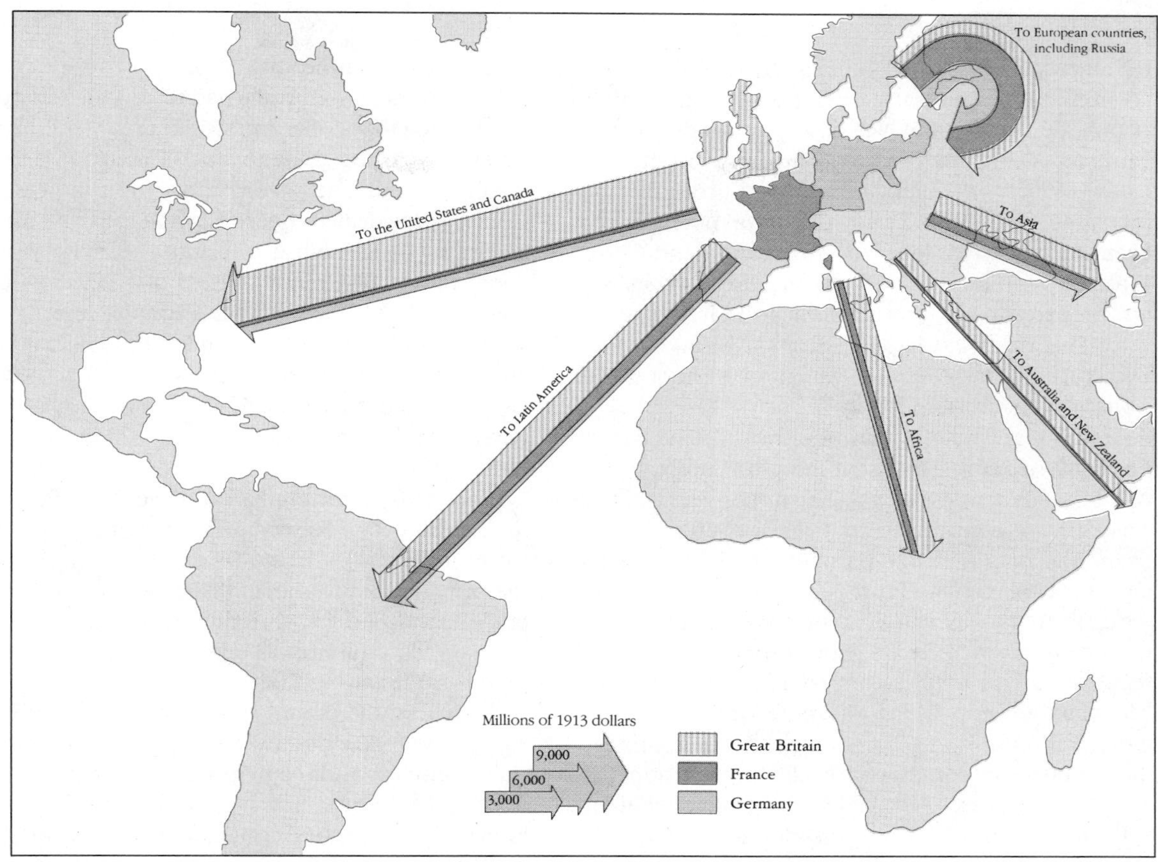

MAP 26.1 European Investment to 1914 Foreign investment grew rapidly after 1850, and Britain, France, and Germany were the major investing nations. As shown, most European investment was not directed to the area seized by the "new imperialism."

Contrary to what many people assume, most of the capital exported did *not* go to European colonies or protectorates in Asia and Africa. About three-quarters of total European investment went to other European countries, the United States and Canada, Australia and New Zealand, and Latin America. The reason was simple: Europe found its most profitable opportunities for investment in construction of the railroads, ports, and utilities that were necessary to settle and develop those almost-vacant lands. By loaning money for a railroad in Argentina or in Canada's prairie provinces, for example, Europeans not only collected interest but also enabled white settlers to buy European rails and locomotives, developed sources of cheap wheat, and opened still more territory for European settlement. Much of this investment—such as in American railroads, fully a third of whose capital in 1890 was European, or in Russian railroads, which drew heavily on loans from France—was peaceful and mutually beneficial. The victims were native American Indians and Australian aborigines, who were decimated by the diseases, liquor, and guns of an aggressively expanding Western society.

THE OPENING OF CHINA AND JAPAN

Europe's relatively peaceful developuent of robust offshoots in sparsely populated North America, Australia, and much of Latin America absorbed huge quantities of goods, investments, and migrants. From a Western point of view, that was the most important aspect of Europe's global thrust. Yet Europe's economic and cultural penetration of old, densely populated civilizations was also profoundly significant, especially for the non-European peoples affected by it. With such civilizations Europeans also increased their trade and profit. Moreover, as had been the case ever since Vasco da Gama and Christopher Columbus, the expanding Western society was prepared to use force to attain its desires, if necessary. This was what happened in China and Japan, two crucial examples of the general pattern of intrusion into non-Western lands.

Traditional Chinese civilization was self-sufficient. For centuries China had sent more to Europe in the way of goods and inventions than it received, and this was still the case in the eighteenth century. Europeans and the English in particular had developed a taste for Chinese tea, but they had to pay for it with hard silver since China was supremely uninterested in European wares. Trade with Europe was carefully regulated by the Chinese imperial government—the Manchu dynasty—which was more interested in isolating and controlling the strange "sea barbarians" than in pursuing commercial exchange. The imperial government refused to establish diplomatic relations with the "inferior" European states, and it required all foreign merchants to live in the southern city of Canton and to buy and sell only from the local merchant monopoly. Practices considered harmful to Chinese interests, such as the sale of opium and the export of silver from China, were strictly forbidden.

For years the little community of foreign merchants in Canton had to accept the Chinese system. By the 1820s, however, the dominant group, the British, was flexing its muscles. Moreover, in the smoking of opium—that "destructive and ensnaring vice" denounced by Chinese decrees—they had found something the Chinese really wanted. Grown legally in British-occupied India, opium was smuggled into China by means of fast ships and bribed officials. The more this rich trade developed, the greedier British merchants became and the more they resented the patriotic attempts of the Chinese government to stem the tide of drug addiction. By 1836 the aggressive goal of the British merchants in Canton was an independent British colony in China and "safe and unrestricted liberty" in trade. They pressured the British government to take decisive action and enlisted the support of British manufacturers with visions of vast Chinese markets to be opened.

At the same time, the Manchu government decided that the opium trade had to be stamped out. It was ruining the people and stripping the empire of its silver, which was going to British merchants to pay for the opium. The government began to prosecute Chinese drug dealers vigorously and in 1839 sent special envoy Lin Tse-hsü to Canton. Lin Tse-hsü ordered the foreign merchants to obey China's laws, "for our great unified Manchu Empire regards itself as responsible for the habits and morals of its subjects and cannot rest content to see any of them become victims of a deadly poison."[1] The British merchants refused and were expelled, whereupon war soon broke out.

Using troops from India and in control of the seas, the British occupied several coastal cities and forced China to surrender. In the Treaty of Nanking in 1842, the imperial government was forced to cede the island of Hong Kong to Britain forever, pay an indemnity of $100 million, and open up four large cities to foreign trade with low tariffs.

Thereafter the opium trade flourished, and Hong Kong developed rapidly as an Anglo-Chinese enclave. China continued to nurture illusions of superiority and isolation, however, and refused to accept foreign diplomats to Peking, the imperial capital. Finally, there was a second round of foreign attack between 1856 and 1860, culminating in the occupation of Peking by seventeen thousand British and French troops and the intentional burning of the emperor's summer palace. Another round of harsh treaties gave European merchants and missionaries greater privileges and protection. Thus did Europeans use military aggression to blow a hole in the wall of Chinese seclusion and open the country to foreign trade and foreign ideas.

China's neighbor, Japan, had its own highly distinctive civilization and even less use for Westerners. European traders and missionaries first arrived in Japan in the sixteenth century. By 1640 Japan had reacted quite negatively to their presence. The government decided to seal off the country from all European influences, in order to preserve its traditional culture and society. It ruthlessly persecuted Japanese Christians and expelled all but a few Dutch merchants, who were virtually imprisoned in a single port and rigidly controlled. When American and British whaling ships began to appear off Japanese coasts almost two hundred years later, the policy of exclusion was still in effect. An order of 1825 com-

East Meets West This painting gives a Japanese view of the first audience of the American Consul and his staff with the shogun, Japan's hereditary military governor, in 1859. The Americans appear strange and ill at ease. *(Bradley Smith)*

manded Japanese officials to "drive away foreign vessels without second thought."[2]

Japan's unbending isolation seemed hostile and barbaric to the West, particularly to the United States. It complicated the practical problems of shipwrecked American sailors and provisioning of whaling ships and China traders sailing in the eastern Pacific. It also thwarted the hope of trade and profit. Also, Americans shared the self-confidence and dynamism of expanding Western society. They had taken California from Mexico in 1848, and Americans felt destined to play a great role in the Pacific. It seemed, therefore, the United States' duty to force the Japanese to share their ports and behave like a "civilized" nation.

After several unsuccessful American attempts to establish commercial relations with Japan, Commodore Matthew Perry steamed into Edo (now Tokyo) Bay in 1853 and demanded diplomatic negotiations with the emperor. Japan entered a grave crisis. Some Japanese warriors urged resistance, but senior officials realized how defenseless their cities were against naval bombardment. Shocked and humiliated, they reluctantly signed a treaty with the United States that opened two ports and permitted trade. Over the next five years, more treaties spelled out the rights and privileges of the Western nations and their merchants in Japan. Japan was "opened." What the British had done in China with war, the Americans had done in Japan with the threat of war.

Western Penetration of Egypt

Egypt's experience illustrates not only the explosive power of the expanding European economy and society but also their seductive appeal in non-Western lands. Of great importance in African and Middle Eastern history, the ancient land of the pharaohs had since 525 B.C. been ruled by a succession of foreigners, most recently by the Ottoman Turks. In 1798 French armies under young General Napoleon Bonaparte invaded the Egyptian part of the Ottoman Empire and occupied the territory for three years. Into the power vacuum left by the French withdrawal stepped an extraordinary Albanian-born Turkish general, Mohammed Ali (1769–1849).

First appointed governor of Egypt by the Turkish sultan, Mohammed Ali soon disposed of his political rivals and set out to build his own state on the strength of a large, powerful army organized along European lines. He drafted for the first time the illiterate, despised peasant masses of Egypt, and he hired French and Italian army officers to train these raw recruits and their Turkish officers. The government was also reformed, new lands were cultivated, and communications were improved. By the time of his death in 1849, Mohammed Ali had established a strong and virtually independent Egyptian state, to be ruled by his family on an hereditary basis within the Turkish empire.

Mohammed Ali's policies of modernization attracted large numbers of Europeans to the banks of the Nile. As one Arab sheik of the Ottoman Empire remarked in the 1830s, "Englishmen are like ants; if one finds a bit of meat, hundreds follow."[3] The port city of Alexandria had more than fifty thousand Europeans by 1864, most of them Italians, Greeks, French, and English. Europeans served not only as army officers but also as engineers, doctors, high government officials, and policemen. Others found their "meat" in trade, finance, and shipping. This was particularly true after 1863, when Mohammed Ali's grandson Ismail began his sixteen-year rule as Egypt's *khedive,* or "prince."

Educated at France's leading military academy, Ismail was a westernizing autocrat. He dreamed of using European technology and capital to modernize Egypt quickly and build a vast empire in northwest Africa. The large irrigation networks he promoted caused cotton production and exports to Europe to boom. Ismail also borrowed large sums to install modern communications, and with his support the Suez Canal was completed by a French company in 1869. The Arabic of the masses rather than the Turkish of the conquerors became the official language, and young Egyptians educated in Europe helped spread new skills and new ideas in the bureaucracy. Cairo acquired modern boulevards, Western hotels, and an opera house. As Ismail proudly declared: "My country is no longer in Africa, we now form part of Europe."[4]

Yet Ismail was too impatient and too reckless. His projects were enormously expensive, and the sale of his stock in the Suez Canal to the British government did not relieve the situation. By 1876 Egypt owed foreign bondholders a colossal $450 million and could not pay the interest on its debt. Rather than let Egypt go bankrupt and repudiate its loans, as had some Latin American countries and U.S. state governments in the early nineteenth century, the governments of France and Great Britain intervened politically in support of the European bankers who held the Egyptian bonds. They forced Ismail to appoint French and British commissioners to oversee Egyptian finances, in order that the Egyptian debt would be paid in full. This was a momentous decision. It implied direct European political control and was a sharp break with the previous pattern of trade investment, and relatively peaceful economic and cultural penetration. Some English critics denounced this action as naked aggression, cloaked in hypocrisy about guarding the Suez Canal, the "life line to India."

Foreign financial control evoked a violent nationalistic reaction among Egyptian religious leaders, young intellectuals, and army officers. In 1879, under the leadership of Colonel Ahmed Arabi, they formed the Egyptian Nationalist party. Continuing diplomatic pressure, which forced Ismail to abdicate in favor of his weak son Tewfiq (1879–1892), resulted in bloody anti-European riots in Alexandria in 1882. A number of Europeans were killed, and Tewfiq and his court had to flee to British ships for safety. When the British fleet bombarded Alexandria, more riots swept the country, and Colonel Arabi declared that "an irreconcilable war existed between the Egyptians and the English." But a British expeditionary force decimated Arabi's forces and occupied all of Egypt.

The British said their occupation was temporary, but British armies remained in Egypt until 1956. They maintained the façade of the khedive's government as an autonomous province of the Ottoman

British Influence in Egypt was pervasive after 1882. In this unusual photograph from 1890, Scottish soldiers swarm over the ancient and mysterious Great Sphinx like school children on an outing. *(BBC Hulton/The Bettmann Archive)*

Empire, but the khedive was a mere puppet. The able British consul general Evelyn Baring, later Lord Cromer, ruled the country after 1883. Once a vocal opponent of involvement in Egypt, Baring was a paternalistic reformer who had come to believe that "without European interference and initiative reform is impossible here." Baring's rule did result in better conditions for peasants and tax reforms, while foreign bondholders tranquilly clipped their coupons and Egyptian nationalists nursed their injured pride.

In Egypt, Baring and the British reluctantly but spectacularly provided a new model for European expansion in densely populated lands. Such expansion was based on military force, political domination, and a self-justifying ideology of beneficial reform. This model was to predominate until 1914.

THE GREAT MIGRATION

A poignant human drama was interwoven with economic expansion: literally millions of people picked up stakes and left their ancestral lands in the course of history's greatest migration. To millions of ordinary people, for whom the opening of China and the interest on the Egyptian debt had not the slightest significance, this great movement was the central experience in the saga of Western expansion. It was, in part, because of this great migration that the West's impact on the world in the nineteenth century was so many-sided, affecting far more than just economic matters.

Ellis Island in New York's harbor was the main entry point into the United States after 1892. For millions of migrants the first frightening experience in the new land was being inspected and processed through its crowded "pens." *(Culver Pictures)*

THE PRESSURE OF POPULATION

In the early eighteenth century, the growth of European population entered its third and decisive stage, which continued unabated until the twentieth century (page 618). Birthrates eventually declined in the nineteenth century, but so did death rates, mainly because of the rising standard of living and secondarily because of the medical revolution. Thus the population of Europe (including Asiatic Russia) more than doubled, from approximately 188 million in 1800 to roughly 432 million in 1900.

These figures actually understate Europe's population explosion, for between 1815 and 1932 more than 60 million people left Europe. These migrants went primarily to the "areas of European settlement"—North and South America, Australia, New Zealand, and Siberia—where they contributed to a rapid growth of numbers. The population of North America (the United States and Canada) alone grew from 6 million to 81 million between 1800 and 1900 because of continuous immigration and the high fertility rates of North American women. Since population grew more slowly in Africa and Asia than in Europe, as Figure 26.2 shows, Europeans and people of European origin jumped from about 22 percent of the world's total to about 38 percent on the eve of World War One.

The growing number of Europeans provided further impetus for Western expansion. It was a driving force behind emigration. As in the eighteenth century, the rapid increase in numbers put pressure on the land and led to land hunger and relative overpopulation in area after area. In most countries, migration increased twenty years after a rapid growth in population, as many children of the baby boom grew up, saw little available land and few opportunities, and migrated. This pattern was especially prevalent when rapid population increase predated extensive industrial development, which offered the best long-term hope of creating jobs within the country and reducing poverty. Thus millions of country folk went abroad, as well as to nearby cities, in search of work and economic opportunity. The case of the Irish, who left en masse for Britain during the Industrial Revolution and for the United States after the potato famine, was extreme but not unique.

Before looking at the people who migrated, let us consider three facts. First, the number of men and women who left Europe increased steadily until

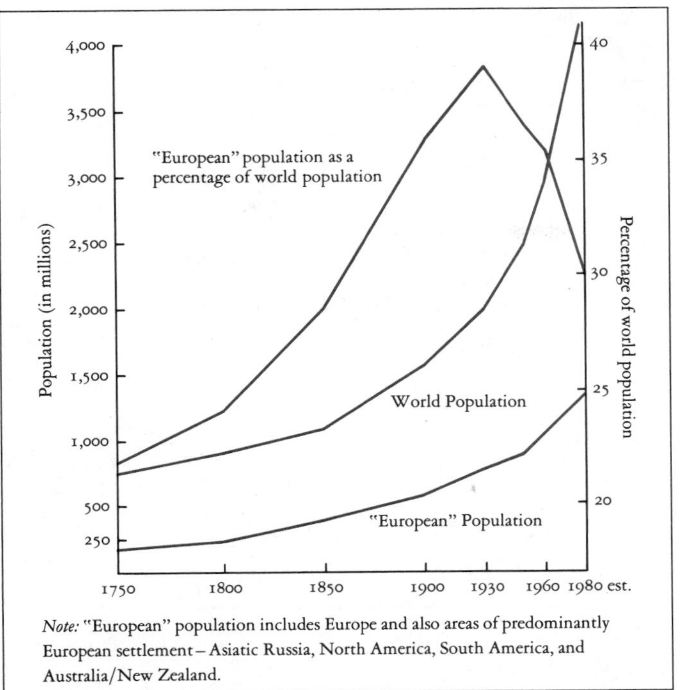

FIGURE 26.2 The Increase of European and World Populations, 1750–1980 *(Sources: W. Woodruff,* Impact of Western Man: A Study of Europe's Role in the World Economy. *St. Martin's Press, New York, 1967, p. 103; United Nations,* Statistical Yearbook, 1982, *1985, pp. 2–3.)*

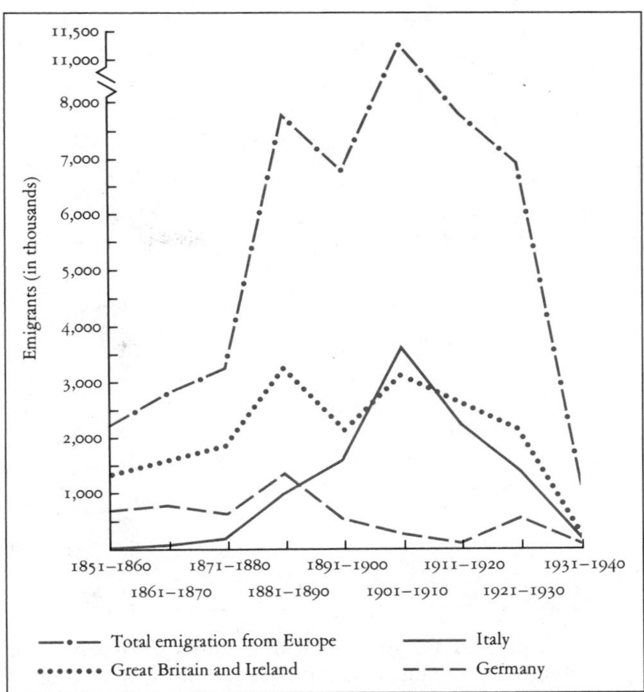

FIGURE 26.3 Emigration from Europe by Decades, 1851–1940 *(Source: W. Woodruff,* Impact of Western Man: A Study of Europe's Role in the World Economy. *St. Martin's Press, New York, 1967, pp. 106–107 and references cited therein.)*

World War One. As Figure 26.3 shows, more than 11 million left in the first decade of the twentieth century, over five times the number departing in the 1850s. The outflow of migrants was clearly an enduring characteristic of European society for the entire period.

Second, different countries had very different patterns of movement. As Figure 26.3 also shows, people left Britain and Ireland (which are not distinguished in the British figures) in large numbers from the 1840s on. This emigration reflected not only rural poverty but also the movement of skilled, industrial technicians and the preferences shown to British migrants in the British Empire. Ultimately, about one-third of all European migrants between 1840 and 1920 came from the British Isles. German migration was quite different. It grew irregularly after about 1830, reaching a first peak in the early 1850s and another in the early 1880s. Thereafter it declined rapidly, for Germany's rapid industrialization was providing adequate jobs at home. This pattern contrasted sharply with that of Italy. More and more Italians left the country right up to 1914, reflecting severe problems in Italian villages and relatively slow industrial growth. In sum, migration patterns mirrored social and economic conditions in the various European countries and provinces.

Third, although the United States absorbed the largest number of European migrants, only slightly more than half went to the United States. Asiatic Russia, Canada, Argentina, Brazil, and Australia also attracted large numbers, as Figure 26.4 shows. Moreover, migrants accounted for a larger proportion of the total population in Argentina, Brazil, and Canada than in the United States. Between 1900 and 1910, for example, new arrivals represented 3 percent of Argentina's population each year, as opposed to only 1 percent for the United States. The common American assumption that European migration meant migration to the United States is quite inaccurate.

European Migrants

What kind of people left Europe, and what were their reasons for doing so? Most were poor people from rural areas, though seldom from the poorest classes. Indeed, the European migrant was most often a small

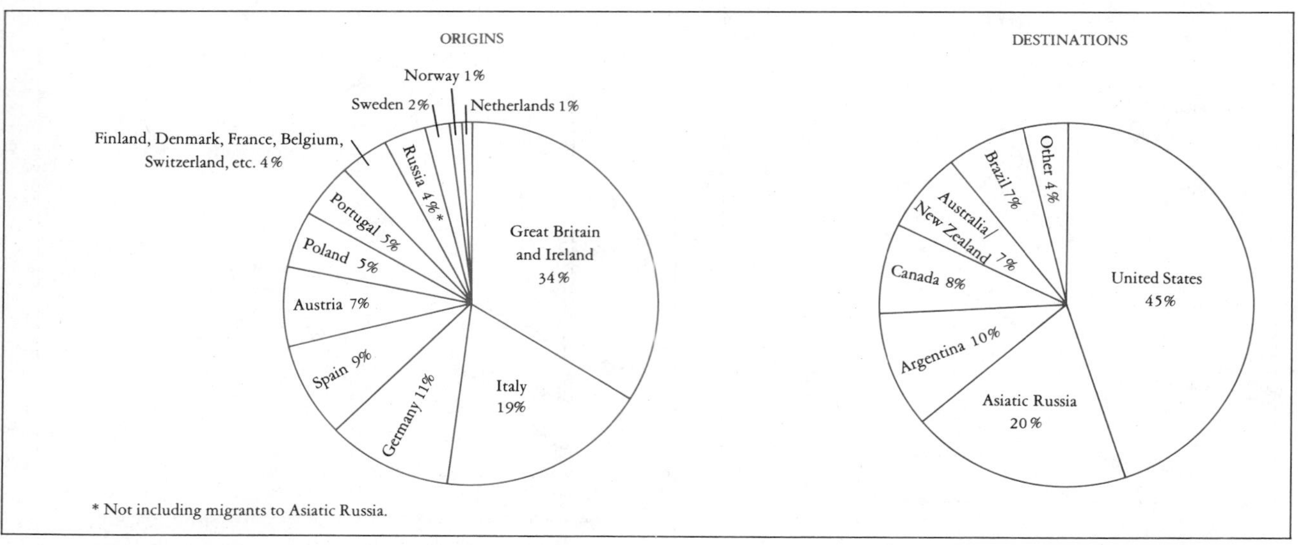

FIGURE 26.4 Origin and Destination of European Emigrants, 1851–1960 *(Source: W. Woodruff,* Impact of Western Man: A Study of Europe's Role in the World Economy. *St. Martin's Press, New York, 1967, pp. 108–109 and references cited therein.)*

peasant landowner or a village craftsman, whose traditional way of life was threatened by too little land, estate agriculture, and cheap, factory-made goods. German peasants who left the Rhineland and southwestern Germany between 1830 and 1854, for example, felt trapped by what Friedrich List called the "dwarf economy," with its tiny landholdings and declining craft industries. Selling out and moving to buy much cheaper land in the American Midwest became a common response. Contrary to what is often said, the European migrant was generally not a desperately impoverished landless peasant or urban proletarian, but an energetic small farmer or skilled artisan trying hard to stay ahead of poverty.

Determined to maintain or improve their status, migrants were a great asset to the countries that received them. This was doubly so because the vast majority were young and very often unmarried. Fully two-thirds of those admitted to the United States were under thirty-one years of age, and 90 percent were under forty. They came in the prime of life and were ready to work hard in the new land, at least for a time.

Many Europeans, especially by the end of the nineteenth century, were truly migrants as opposed to immigrants—that is, they returned home after some time abroad. One in two migrants to Argentina, and probably one in three to the United States, eventually returned to their native land. The likelihood of repatriation varied greatly by nationality. Seven out of eight people who migrated from the Balkans to the United States in the late nineteenth century returned to their countries. At the other extreme, only one person in ten from Ireland and only one in twenty among eastern European Jews returned to the country of origin.

Once again, the possibility of buying land in the old country was of central importance. Land in Ireland (as well as in England and Scotland) was tightly held by large, often-absentee landowners, and little land was available for purchase. In Russia, Jews were left in relative peace until the assassination of Alexander II by non-Jewish terrorists in 1881 brought a new tsar and an official policy of pogroms and savage discrimination. Russia's 5 million Jews were already confined to the market towns and small cities of the so-called Pale of Settlement, where they worked as artisans and petty traders. Most land was held by non-Jews. When, therefore, Russian Jewish artisans began in the 1880s to escape both factory competition and oppression by migrating—a migration that eventually totaled 2 million people—it was basically a once-and-for-all departure. Non-Jewish migrants from Russia, who constituted a majority of those leaving the tsar's empire after 1905, had access to land and thus returned much more frequently to their peasant villages in central Russia, Poland, and the Ukraine.

The mass movement of Italians illustrates many of the characteristics of European migration. As late as the 1880s, which was for Italians as for Russian Jews the first decade of substantial exodus, three in every four Italians depended on agriculture. With the influx of cheap North American wheat, the long-standing problems of the Italian village became more acute. And since industry was not advancing fast enough to provide jobs for the rapidly growing population, many Italians began to leave their country for economic reasons. Most Italian migrants were not landless laborers from areas dominated by large estates; such people tended to stay in Italy and turned increasingly toward radical politics. Instead, most were small landowning peasants, whose standard of living was falling because of rural overpopulation and agricultural depression. Migration provided them both an escape valve and a possible source of income to buy more land.

Many Italians went to the United States, but before 1900 more went to Argentina and Brazil. Indeed, two out of three migrants to those two developing countries came from Italy. In Brazil, the large coffee planters, faced with the collapse of black slavery, attracted Italians to their plantations with subsidized travel and promises of relatively high wages.

Many Italians had no intention of settling abroad permanently. Some called themselves "swallows": after harvesting their own wheat and flax in Italy, they "flew" to Argentina to harvest wheat between December and April. Returning to Italy for the spring planting, they repeated the exhausting process.

Cheap Land in distant North America was an irresistible magnet for millions of Europeans. *The Modern Ship of the Plains* by Rufus Zogbaum portrays with sympathy the long journey by rail to the farming frontier in the 1880s. *(Library of Congress)*

This was a very hard life, but a frugal worker could save $250 to $300 in the course of a season. A one-way passage from Latin America to Italy usually cost only $25 to $30, and sometimes as little as $8. Italian migrants also dominated the building trades and the architectural profession in Latin America and succeeded in giving a thoroughly Italian character to many Latin American cities.

Other Italians migrated to other European countries. France was a favorite destination. In 1911 the Italian-born population of France was roughly a third as large as that in the United States.

Ties of family and friendship played a crucial role in the movement of peoples. There are many examples of people from a given province or village settling together in rural enclaves or tight-knit urban neighborhoods thousands of miles away. Very often a strong individual—a businessman, a religious leader—would blaze the way and others would follow.

Many landless young European men and women were spurred to leave by a spirit of revolt and independence. In Sweden and in Norway, in Jewish Russia and in Italy, these young people felt frustrated by the small privileged classes, who often controlled both church and government and resisted demands for change and greater opportunity. Many a young Norwegian seconded the passionate cry of their national poet, Bjørnson: "Forth will I! Forth! I will be crushed and consumed if I stay."[5]

Many young Jews wholeheartedly agreed with a spokesman of Kiev's Jewish community in 1882, who declared, "Our human dignity is being trampled upon, our wives and daughters are being dishonored, we are looted and pillaged: either we get decent human rights or else let us go wherever our eyes may lead us."[6] Thus, for many, migration was a radical way to "get out from under." Migration slowed down when the people won basic political and social reforms, such as the right to vote and social security.

Asian Migrants

Not all migration was from Europe. A substantial number of Chinese, Japanese, Indians, and Filipinos—to name only four key groups—responded to rural hardship with temporary or permanent migration. At least 3 million Asians (as opposed to more than 60 million Europeans) moved abroad before 1920. Most went as indentured laborers to work under incredibly difficult conditions on the plantations or in the goldfields of Latin America, southern Asia, Africa, California, Hawaii, and Australia. White estate owners very often used Asians to replace or supplement blacks after the suppression of the slave trade.

In the 1840s, for example, there was a strong demand for field hands in Cuba, and the Spanish government actively recruited Chinese laborers. They came under eight-year contracts, were paid about twenty-five cents a day, and were fed potatoes and salted beef. Between 1853 and 1873, when such migration was stopped, more than 130,000 Chinese laborers went to Cuba. The majority spent their lives as virtual slaves. The great landlords of Peru also brought in more than 100,000 workers from China in the nineteenth century, and there were similar movements of Asians elsewhere.

Such migration from Asia would undoubtedly have grown to much greater proportions if planters and mine owners in search of cheap labor had had their way. But they did not. Asians fled the plantations and goldfields as soon as possible, seeking greater opportunities in trade and towns. There they came into conflict with other brown-skinned peoples—such as in Malaya and East Africa—and with white settlers in areas of European settlement.

These settlers demanded a halt to Asian migration. One Australian brutally summed up the typical view: "The Chinaman knows nothing about Caucasian civilization. . . . In fact, a Chinaman is a mere dumb animal . . . and could never be anything else. It would be less objectionable to drive a flock of sheep to the poll than to allow Chinamen to vote. The sheep at all events would be harmless."[7] By the 1880s Americans and Australians were building "great white walls"—discriminatory laws designed to keep Asians out. Thus a final, crucial factor in the migrations before 1914 was the general policy of "whites only" in the open lands of possible permanent settlement. Racism meant that Asian migration was always of secondary importance in the world of expanding European society.

WESTERN IMPERIALISM

The expansion of Western society reached its apex between about 1880 and 1914. In those years, the leading European nations not only continued to send massive streams of migrants, money, and manufac-

The Chinese Exclusion Act This vicious cartoon from a San Francisco newspaper celebrates American anti-migration laws. Americans and Europeans generally shared the same attitudes regarding the non-Western world. *(Photo: Caroline Buckler)*

tured goods around the world, but also rushed to create or enlarge vast *political* empires abroad. This political empire building contrasted sharply with the economic penetration of non-Western territories between 1816 and 1880, which had left a China or a Japan "opened" but politically independent. By contrast, the empires of the late nineteenth century recalled the old European colonial empires of the seventeenth and eighteenth centuries and led contemporaries to speak of the new imperialism.

Characterized by a frantic rush to plant the flag over as many people and as much territory as possible, the new imperialism had momentous consequences. It resulted in new tensions among competing European states, and it led to wars and rumors of war with non-European powers. The new imperialism was aimed primarily at Africa and Asia. It put millions of black, brown, and tan peoples directly under the rule of whites. How and why did whites come to rule these peoples?

The Scramble for Africa

The most spectacular manifestation of the new imperialism was the seizure of Africa, which broke sharply with previous patterns and fascinated contemporary Europeans and Americans.

As late as 1880, European nations controlled only 10 percent of the African continent, and their possessions were hardly increasing. The French had begun conquering Algeria in 1830, and within fifty years substantial numbers of French, Italian, and Spanish colonists had settled among the overwhelming Arab majority.

At the other end of the continent, in South Africa, the British had taken possession of the Dutch settlements at Capetown during the wars with Napoleon I. This takeover had led disgruntled Dutch cattlemen and farmers in 1835 to make their so-called Great Trek into the interior, where they fought the Zulu and Kaffir peoples for land. After 1853, while British colonies like Canada and Australia were beginning to evolve toward self-government, the Boers (as the Dutch in South Africa were called) proclaimed their political independence and defended it against British armies. By 1880 Dutch and British settlers, who detested each other, had wrested control of much of South Africa from the Zulus and Kaffirs.

European trading posts and forts dating back to the Age of Discovery and the slave trade dotted the coast of West Africa. The Portuguese proudly but ineffectively held their old possessions in Angola and Mozambique. Elsewhere, over the great mass of the continent, Europeans did not rule.

Between 1880 and 1900, the situation changed drastically. Britain, France, Germany, and Italy scrambled for African possessions as if their lives depended on it. By 1900 nearly the whole continent had been carved up and placed under European rule: only Ethiopia in northeast Africa and Liberia on the west African coast remained independent. Even the Dutch settler republics of southern Africa were conquered by the British in the bloody Boer War (1899–1902). In the years before 1914, the European powers tightened their control and established colonial governments to rule their gigantic empires (see Map 26.2).

In the complexity of the European seizure of Africa, certain events and individuals stand out. Of enormous importance was the British occupation of Egypt, which established the new model of formal political control. There was also the role of Leopold II of Belgium (1865–1909), an energetic, strong-willed monarch with a lust for distant territory. "The sea bathes our coast, the world lies before us," he had exclaimed in 1861. "Steam and electricity have annihilated distance, and all the non-appropriated lands on the surface of the globe can become the field of our operations and of our success."[8] By 1876 Leopold was focusing on central Africa. Subsequently he formed a financial syndicate under his personal control to send H. M. Stanley, a sensation-seeking journalist and part-time explorer, to the Congo basin. Stanley established trading stations, signed "treaties" with African chiefs, and planted Leopold's flag. Leopold's actions alarmed the French, who quickly sent out an expedition under Pierre de Brazza. In 1880 de Brazza signed a treaty of protection with the chief of the large Teke tribe and began to establish a French protectorate on the north bank of the Congo River.

Map 26.2 The Partition of Africa European nations carved up Africa after 1880 and built vast political empires.

Leopold's buccaneering intrusion into the Congo area raised the question of the political fate of black Africa—Africa south of the Sahara. By the time the British successfully invaded and occupied Egypt, the richest and most developed land in Africa in 1882, Europe had caught "African fever." There was a gold-rush mentality, and the race for territory was on.

To lay down some basic rules for this new and dangerous game of imperialist competition, Jules Ferry of France and Bismarck of Germany arranged an international conference on Africa in Berlin in 1884 and 1885. The conference established the principle that European claims to African territory had to rest on "effective occupation" in order to be recognized by other states. This principle was very important. It meant that Europeans would push relentlessly into interior regions from all sides and that no single European power would be able to claim the entire continent. The conference recognized Leopold's personal rule over a neutral Congo Free State and declared all of the Congo basin a free-trade zone. The conference also agreed to work to stop slavery and the slave trade in Africa.

The Berlin conference coincided with Germany's sudden emergence as an imperial power. Prior to about 1880, Bismarck, like many European leaders at the time, had seen little value in colonies. Colonies reminded him, he said, of a poor but proud nobleman who wore a fur coat when he could not afford a shirt underneath. Then, in 1884 and 1885, as political agitation for expansion increased, Bismarck did an abrupt about-face, and Germany established protectorates over a number of small African kingdoms and tribes in Togo, Cameroon, South West Africa, and later in East Africa.

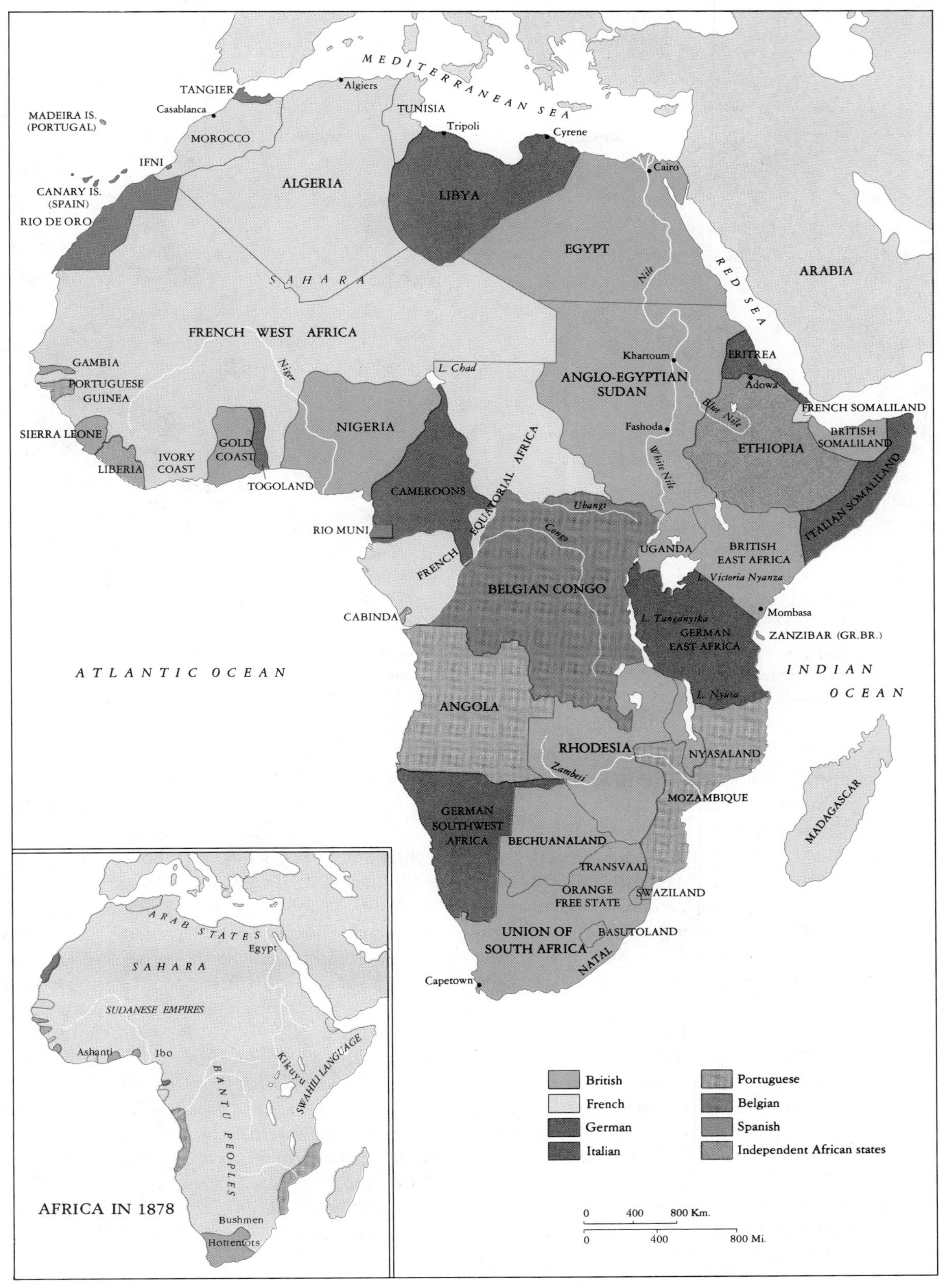
MEDITERRANEAN SEA
TANGIER
Algiers
MADEIRA IS. (PORTUGAL)
Casablanca
TUNISIA
Tripoli
Cyrene
MOROCCO
IFNI
CANARY IS. (SPAIN)
ALGERIA
LIBYA
Cairo
RIO DE ORO
EGYPT
SAHARA
Nile
RED SEA
ARABIA
FRENCH WEST AFRICA
GAMBIA
PORTUGUESE GUINEA
Niger
L. Chad
Khartoum
ERITREA
ANGLO-EGYPTIAN SUDAN
Adowa
FRENCH SOMALILAND
SIERRA LEONE
NIGERIA
Fashoda
Blue Nile
BRITISH SOMALILAND
LIBERIA
IVORY COAST
GOLD COAST
TOGOLAND
FRENCH EQUATORIAL AFRICA
White Nile
ETHIOPIA
CAMEROONS
Ubangi
ITALIAN SOMALILAND
RIO MUNI
Congo
UGANDA
BRITISH EAST AFRICA
L. Victoria Nyanza
BELGIAN CONGO
CABINDA
L. Tanganyika
GERMAN EAST AFRICA
Mombasa
ZANZIBAR (GR.BR.)
ATLANTIC OCEAN
INDIAN OCEAN
L. Nyasa
ANGOLA
RHODESIA
NYASALAND
Zambesi
MOZAMBIQUE
GERMAN SOUTHWEST AFRICA
BECHUANALAND
MADAGASCAR
TRANSVAAL
ORANGE FREE STATE
SWAZILAND
UNION OF SOUTH AFRICA
BASUTOLAND
NATAL
Capetown
ARAB STATES
Egypt
SAHARA
SUDANESE EMPIRES
Ashanti
Ibo
Kikuyu
SWAHILI LANGUAGE
BANTU PEOPLES
Bushmen
Hottentots
AFRICA IN 1878
British
French
German
Italian
Portuguese
Belgian
Spanish
Independent African states
0 400 800 Km.
0 400 800 Mi.

Omdurman, 1898 The military superiority of the Europeans made it impossible for these brave tribesmen to defend their homeland. Thus the Sudan was conquered and one million square miles were added to the British empire. *(The Mansell Collection)*

In acquiring colonies, Bismarck cooperated against the British with France's Jules Ferry, who was as ardent for empire as he was for education. With Bismarck's tacit approval, the French pressed vigorously southward from Algeria, eastward from their old forts on the Senegal coast, and northward from de Brazza's newly formed protectorate on the Congo River. The object of these three thrusts was Lake Chad, a malaria-infested swamp on the edge of the Sahara Desert.

Meanwhile, the British began enlarging their west African enclaves and impatiently pushing northward from the Cape Colony and westward from Zanzibar. Their thrust southward from Egypt was blocked in the Sudan by fiercely independent Muslims, who massacred a British force at Khartoum in 1885.

A decade later, another British force under General Horatio H. Kitchener moved cautiously and more successfully up the Nile River, building a railroad to supply arms and reinforcements as it went. Finally, in 1898, these British troops met their foe at Omdurman, where Muslim tribesmen charged time and time again only to be cut down by the recently invented machine gun. For one smug participant, the young British officer Winston Churchill, it was "like a pantomime scene" in a play. "These extraordinary foreign figures . . . march up one by one from the darkness of Barbarism to the footlights of civilization . . . and their conquerors, taking their possessions, forget even their names. Nor will history record such trash." For another more somber English observer, "It was not a battle but an execution. The bodies were not in heaps . . . but they spread evenly over acres and acres."[9] In the end, eleven thousand fanatical Muslim tribesmen lay dead, while only twenty-eight Britons had been killed.

Continuing up the Nile after the battle of Omdurman, Kitchener's armies found that a small French force had already occupied the village Fashoda. Locked in imperial competition ever since Britain had occupied Egypt, France had tried to beat the British to one of Africa's last unclaimed areas—the upper reaches of the Nile. The result was a serious diplomatic crisis, and even the threat of war. Eventually, wracked by the Dreyfus affair (see page 817) and unwilling to fight, France backed down and withdrew its forces.

The reconquest of the Sudan exemplifies the general process of empire building in Africa. The fate of the Muslim force at Omdurman was eventually inflicted on all native peoples who resisted European rule: they were blown away by vastly superior military force. But however much the European powers squabbled for territory and privilege around the world, they always had the sense to stop short of actually fighting each other for it. Imperial ambitions were not worth a great European war.

Imperialism in Asia

Although the sudden division of Africa was more spectacular, Europeans also extended their political control in Asia. In 1815 the Dutch ruled little more than the island of Java in the East Indies. Thereafter they gradually brought almost all of the three-thousand-mile archipelago under their political authority, though—in good imperialist fashion—they had to share some of the spoils with Britain and Germany. In the critical decade of the 1880s, the French under the leadership of Jules Ferry took Indochina. India, Japan, and China also experienced a profound imperialist impact (see Map 26.3).

Two other great imperialist powers, Russia and the United States, also acquired rich territories in Asia. Russia, whose history since the later Middle Ages has been marked by almost continuous expansion, moved steadily forward on two fronts throughout the nineteenth century. Russians conquered Muslim areas to the south in the Caucasus and in central Asia and also proceeded to nibble greedily on China's outlying provinces in the Far East, especially in the 1890s.

The United States' great conquest was the Philippines, taken from Spain in 1898 after the Spanish-American War. When it quickly became clear that the United States had no intention of granting independence, Philippine patriots rose in revolt and were suppressed only after long, bitter fighting. (Not until 1933 was a timetable for independence established.) Some Americans protested the taking of the Philippines, but to no avail. Thus another great Western power joined the imperialist ranks in Asia.

Causes of the New Imperialism

Many factors contributed to the late nineteenth-century rush for territory and empire, which was in turn one aspect of Western society's generalized expansion in the age of industry and nationalism. Little wonder that controversies have raged over interpretation of the new imperialism, especially since authors of every persuasion have often exaggerated particular aspects in an attempt to prove their own theories. Yet despite complexity and controversy, basic causes are clearly identifiable.

Economic motives played an important role in the extension of political empires, especially the British Empire. By the late 1870s, France, Germany, and the United States were industrializing rapidly behind rising tariff barriers. Great Britain was losing its early lead and facing increasingly tough competition in foreign markets. In this new economic situation, Britain came to value old possessions, such as India and Canada, more highly. The days when a leading free-trader like Richard Cobden could denounce the "bloodstained fetish of Empire" and statesman Benjamin Disraeli could call colonies a "millstone round our necks" came to an abrupt end. When continental powers began to grab any and all unclaimed territory in the 1880s, the British followed suit immediately. They feared that France and Germany would seal off their empires with high tariffs and restrictions and that future economic opportunities would be lost forever.

Actually, the overall economic gains of the new imperialism proved quite limited before 1914. The new colonies were simply too poor to buy much, and they offered few immediately profitable investments. Nonetheless, even the poorest, most barren desert was jealously prized, and no territory was ever abandoned. Colonies became important for political and diplomatic reasons. Each leading country saw colonies as crucial to national security, military power, and international prestige. For instance, safeguarding the Suez Canal played a key role in the British occupation of Egypt, and protecting Egypt in turn led to the bloody reconquest of the Sudan. National security was a major factor in the United States' decision

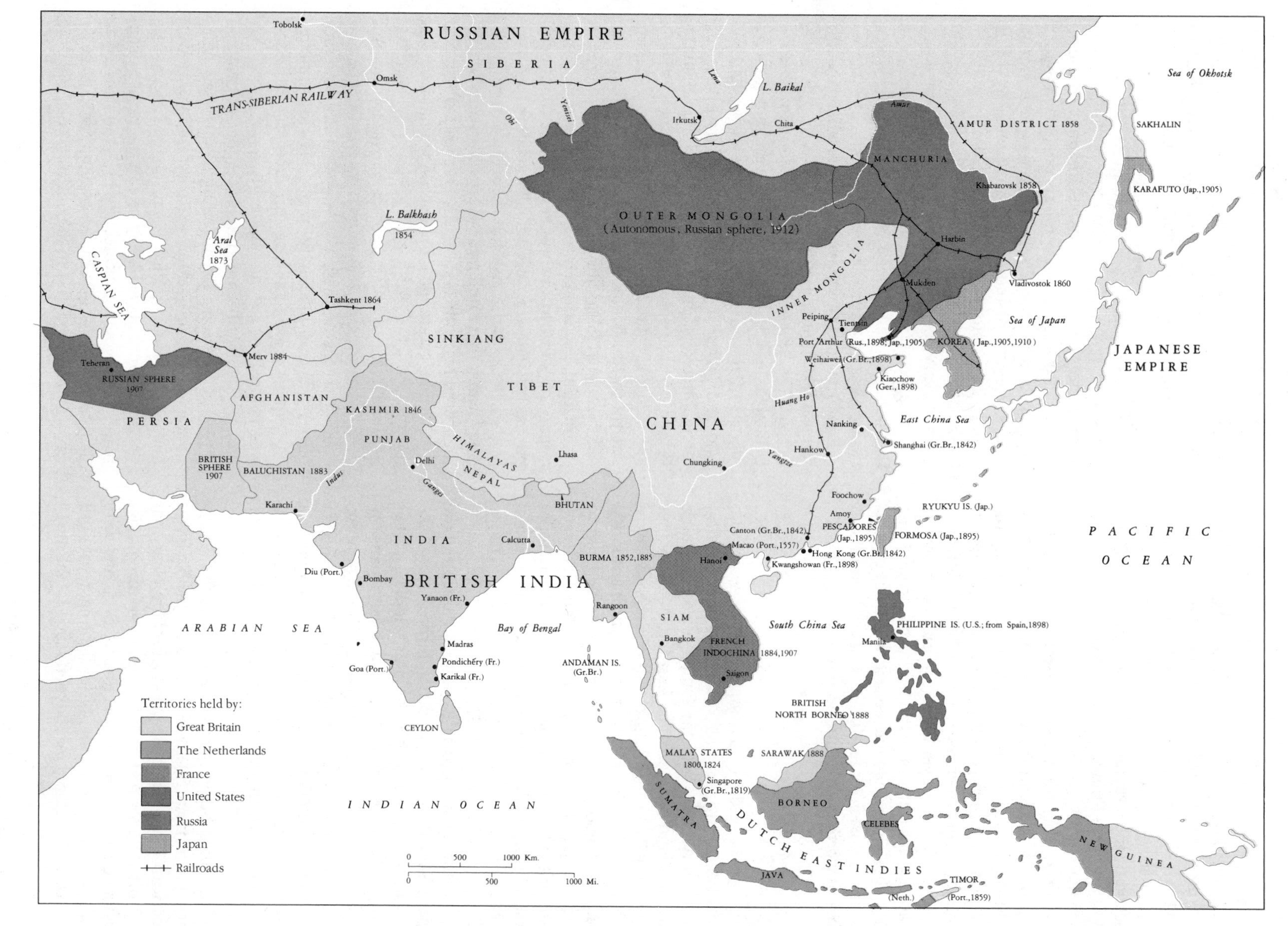

RUSSIAN EMPIRE
SIBERIA
Tobolsk
Omsk
TRANS-SIBERIAN RAILWAY
Obi
Yenisei
Lena
L. Baikal
Irkutsk
Chita
Amur
AMUR DISTRICT 1858
Sea of Okhotsk
SAKHALIN
KARAFUTO (Jap.,1905)
MANCHURIA
Khabarovsk 1858
Harbin
Mukden
Vladivostok 1860
Sea of Japan
JAPANESE EMPIRE
OUTER MONGOLIA
(Autonomous, Russian sphere, 1912)
INNER MONGOLIA
Peiping
Tientsin
Port Arthur (Rus.,1898; Jap.,1905)
KOREA (Jap.,1905,1910)
Weihaiwei (Gr.Br.,1898)
Kiaochow (Ger.,1898)
Huang Ho
Nanking
East China Sea
Shanghai (Gr.Br.,1842)
Hankow
Yangtze
CHINA
Chungking
Foochow
Amoy
RYUKYU IS. (Jap.)
PESCADORES (Jap.,1895)
FORMOSA (Jap.,1895)
Canton (Gr.Br.,1842)
Macao (Port.,1557)
Hong Kong (Gr.Br.,1842)
Kwangshowan (Fr.,1898)
PACIFIC OCEAN
L. Balkhash
1854
Aral Sea
1873
CASPIAN SEA
Tashkent 1864
Merv 1884
Teheran
RUSSIAN SPHERE 1907
PERSIA
AFGHANISTAN
SINKIANG
TIBET
KASHMIR 1846
PUNJAB
HIMALAYAS
Lhasa
Delhi
NEPAL
BRITISH SPHERE 1907
BALUCHISTAN 1883
Indus
Ganges
Karachi
BHUTAN
INDIA
Calcutta
BURMA 1852,1885
Hanoi
Diu (Port.)
Bombay
BRITISH INDIA
Yanaon (Fr.)
Rangoon
SIAM
South China Sea
PHILIPPINE IS. (U.S.; from Spain,1898)
Manila
ARABIAN SEA
Bay of Bengal
Madras
Bangkok
FRENCH INDOCHINA 1884,1907
Goa (Port.)
Pondichéry (Fr.)
Karikal (Fr.)
ANDAMAN IS. (Gr.Br.)
Saigon
CEYLON
BRITISH NORTH BORNEO 1888
MALAY STATES 1800,1824
SARAWAK 1888
Singapore (Gr.Br.,1819)
BORNEO
SUMATRA
CELEBES
INDIAN OCEAN
DUTCH EAST INDIES
NEW GUINEA
JAVA
TIMOR
(Neth.)
(Port.,1859)
Territories held by:
Great Britain
The Netherlands
France
United States
Russia
Japan
Railroads
0 500 1000 Km.
0 500 1000 Mi.

MAP 26.3 Asia in 1914 India remained under British rule while China precariously preserved its political independence.

to establish firm control over the Panama Canal Zone in 1903. Far-flung possessions guaranteed ever-growing navies the safe havens and the dependable coaling stations they needed in time of crisis or war.

Many people were convinced that colonies were essential to great nations. "There has never been a great power without great colonies," wrote one French publicist in 1877. "Every virile people has established colonial power," echoed the famous nationalist historian of Germany, Heinrich von Treitschke. "All great nations in the fullness of their strength have desired to set their mark upon barbarian lands and those who fail to participate in this great rivalry will play a pitiable role in time to come."[10]

Treitschke's harsh statement reflects not only the increasing aggressiveness of European nationalism after Bismarck's wars of German unification but also social Darwinian theories of brutal competition between races. As one prominent English economist argued, the "strongest nation has always been conquering the weaker . . . and the strongest tend to be best." Thus European nations, which were seen as racially distinct parts of the dominant white race, had to seize colonies to show they were strong and virile. Moreover, since racial struggle was nature's inescapable law, the conquest of inferior peoples was just. "The path of progress is strewn with the wreck . . . of inferior races," wrote one professor in 1900. "Yet these dead peoples are, in very truth, the stepping stones on which mankind has risen to the higher intellectual and deeper emotional life of to-day."[11] Social Darwinism and racial doctrines fostered imperial expansion.

Finally, certain special-interest groups in each country were powerful agents of expansion. Shipping companies wanted lucrative subsidies. White settlers on dangerous, turbulent frontiers constantly demanded more land and greater protection. Missionaries and humanitarians wanted to spread religion and stop the slave trade. Explorers and adventurers sought knowledge and excitement. Military men and colonial officials, whose role has often been overlooked by writers on imperialism, foresaw rapid advancement and high-paid positions in growing empires. The actions of such groups and the determined individuals who led them thrust the course of empire forward.

Western society did not rest the case for empire solely on naked conquest and a Darwinian racial struggle, or on power politics and the need for naval bases on every ocean. In order to satisfy their consciences and answer their critics, imperialists developed additional arguments.

A favorite idea was that Europeans could and should "civilize" more primitive nonwhites. According to this view, nonwhites would eventually receive the benefits of modern economies, cities, advanced medicine, and higher standards of living. In time, they might be ready for self-government and Western democracy. Thus the French spoke of their sacred "civilizing mission." Rudyard Kipling (1865–1936), who wrote masterfully of Anglo-Indian life and was perhaps the most influential writer of the 1890s, exhorted Europeans to unselfish service in distant lands:

Take up the White Man's Burden—
Send forth the best ye breed—
Go bind your sons to exile
To serve your captives' need,
To wait in heavy harness,
On fluttered folk and wild—
Your new-caught, sullen peoples
Half-devil and half-child.[12]

Many Americans accepted the ideology of the white man's burden. It was an important factor in the decision to rule rather than liberate the Philippines after the Spanish-American War. Like their European counterparts, these Americans sincerely believed that their civilization had reached unprecedented height and that they had unique benefits to bestow on all "less-advanced" peoples. Another argument was that imperial government protected natives from tribal warfare as well as cruder forms of exploitation by white settlers and businessmen.

Peace and stability under European control also permitted the spread of Christianity—the "true" religion. In Africa, Catholic and Protestant missionaries competed with Islam south of the Sahara, seeking converts and building schools to spread the Gospel.

"The Administration of Justice" In this 1895 illustration from a popular magazine, a Belgian official, flanked by native soldiers, settles a tribal dispute in the Congo State. This flattering view of Europe's "civilizing mission" suggests how imperial rule rested on more than just brute force. *(BBC Hulton/The Bettmann Archive)*

Many Africans' first real contact with whites was in mission schools. As late as 1942, for example, 97 percent of Nigeria's student population was in mission schools. Some peoples, like the Ibos in Nigeria, became highly christianized.

Such occasional successes in black Africa contrasted with the general failure of missionary efforts in India, China, and the Islamic world. There, Christians often preached in vain to peoples with ancient, complex religious beliefs. Yet the number of Christian believers around the world did increase substantially in the nineteenth century, and missionary groups kept trying. Unfortunately, "many missionaries had drunk at the well of European racism," and this probably prevented them from doing better.[13]

Critics of Imperialism

The expansion of empire aroused sharp, even bitter, critics. A forceful attack was delivered in 1902, after the unpopular Boer War, by the radical English economist J. A. Hobson (1858–1940) in his *Imperialism,* a work that influenced Lenin and others. Hobson contended that the rush to acquire colonies was due to the economic needs of unregulated capitalism, particularly the need of the rich to find outlets for their surplus capital. Yet, Hobson argued, imperial possessions do not pay off economically for the country as a whole. Only unscrupulous special-interest groups profit from them, at the expense of both the European taxpayer and the natives. Moreover, the quest for empire diverts attention from domestic reform and closing the gap between rich and poor. These and similar arguments were not very persuasive. Most people then (and now) believed that imperialism was economically profitable for the homeland, and a broad and genuine enthusiasm for empire developed among the masses.

Hobson and many other critics struck home, however, with their moral condemnation of whites imperiously ruling nonwhites. They rebelled against crude Social Darwinian thought. "O Evolution, what crimes are committed in thy name!" cried one foe. Another sardonically coined a new beatitude: "Blessed are the strong, for they shall prey on the weak."[14] Kipling and his kind were lampooned as racist bullies, whose rule rested on brutality, racial contempt, and the Maxim machine gun. Henry Labouchère, a member of Parliament and prominent spokesman for this position, mocked Kipling's famous poem:

Pile on the Brown Man's burden!
And if ye rouse his hate,
Meet his old-fashioned reasons
With Maxims up to date,
With shells and Dum-Dum bullets
A hundred times plain
The Brown Man's loss must never
Imply the White Man's gain.[15]

In *Heart of Darkness,* the Polish-born novelist Joseph Conrad (1857–1924) castigated the "pure selfishness" of Europeans in "civilizing" Africa; the main character, once a liberal scholar, turns into a savage brute.

Critics charged Europeans with applying a degrading double standard and failing to live up to their own noble ideals. At home, Europeans had won or were winning representative government, individual liberties, and a certain equality of opportunity. In their empires, Europeans imposed military dictatorships on Africans and Asians, forced them to work involuntarily, almost like slaves, and discriminated against them shamelessly. Only by renouncing imperialism, its critics insisted, and giving captive peoples the freedoms Western society had struggled for since the French Revolution, would Europeans be worthy of their traditions. Europeans who denounced the imperialist tide provided colonial peoples with a Western ideology of liberation.

RESPONSES TO WESTERN IMPERIALISM

To consider the great surge of European expansion from the Western point of view is to see only half the story. It is time to try to examine what foreign domination and imperialism meant to those who were ruled.

To peoples in Africa and Asia, Western expansion represented a profoundly disruptive assault. Everywhere it threatened traditional ruling classes, traditional economies, and traditional ways of life. Christian missionaries and European secular ideologies challenged established beliefs and values. Non-Western peoples experienced a crisis of identity, a crisis made all the more painful by the power and arrogance of the white intruders.

The initial response of African and Asian rulers was to try to drive the unwelcome foreigners away. This was the case in China, Japan, and the upper Sudan, as we have seen. Violent antiforeign reactions exploded elsewhere again and again, but the superior military technology of the industrialized West almost invariably prevailed. Beaten in battle, many Africans and Asians concentrated on preserving their cultural traditions at all costs. Others found themselves forced to reconsider their initial hostility. Some (like Ismail of Egypt) concluded that the West was indeed superior in some ways and that it was therefore necessary to reform their societies and copy European achievements. Thus it is possible to think of responses to the Western impact as a spectrum, with "traditionalists" at one end, "westernizers" or "modernizers" at the other, and many shades of opinion in between. Both before and after European domination, the struggle among these groups was often intense. With time, however, the modernizers tended to gain the upper hand.

When the power of both the traditionalists and the modernizers was thoroughly shattered by superior force, the great majority of Asians and Africans accepted imperial rule. Political participation in non-Western lands was historically limited to small elites, and the masses were used to doing what their rulers told them. In these circumstances Europeans, clothed in power and convinced of their righteousness, governed smoothly and effectively. They received considerable support from both traditionalists —local chiefs, landowners, religious leaders—and

The Spread of Western Imperialism

1800–1913	World trade increases 25-fold
1816–1880	European economic penetration of non-Western countries
1835	Great Trek: Boers proclaim independence from Great Britain in the South African hinterland
1840s	European capitalists begin large-scale foreign investment
1842	Treaty of Nanking: Manchu government of China cedes Hong Kong to Great Britain
1846	Repeal of Corn Laws: Great Britain declares its strong support of free trade
1848	British defeat of last independent native state in India
1853	Perry's arrival in Tokyo: Japan opened to European influence
1857–1858	Great Rebellion in India
1858–1863	Anti-foreign reaction in Japan
1867	Meiji Restoration in Japan: adoption of Western reforms
1869	Completion of Suez Canal
1871	Abolition of feudal domains in Japan
1876	Ismail, khedive of Egypt, appoints British and French commissioners to oversee government finances
1880	Establishment of French protectorate on the northern bank of the Congo
1880–1900	European powers intensify their "scramble for Africa"
1882	British occupation of Egypt
1883	Formation of the Indian National Congress
1884–1885	International conference on Africa in Berlin: European powers require "effective occupation"; Germany acquires protectorates in Togo, Cameroon, South West Africa, and East Africa; Belgium acquires the Congo Free State
1890	Establishment of an authoritarian constitution in Japan
1893	France completes its acquisition of Indochina
1894	Sino-Japanese War: Japan acquires Formosa
1898	Battle of Omdurman: under Kitchener, British forces reconquer the Sudan Spanish-American War: United States acquires the Philippines "Hundred Days of Reform" in China
1899–1902	Boer War: British defeat Dutch settlers in South Africa
1900–1903	The Boxer Rebellion in China
1903	American occupation of the Panama Canal zone
1904–1905	Russo-Japanese War: Japan wins protectorate over Port Arthur in China
1910	Japanese annexation of Korea
1912	Fall of Manchu dynasty in China

Senegalese Scouts, 1913 Europeans recruited large numbers of native soldiers to expand and enforce their rule in Africa and Asia. Senegalese scouts were the pride of the French army in black Africa. *(Roger-Viollet)*

modernizers—the Western-educated professional classes and civil servants.

Nevertheless, imperial rule was in many ways a hollow shell built on sand. Support for European rule among the conforming and accepting millions was shallow and weak. Thus the conforming masses followed with greater or lesser enthusiasm a few determined personalities who came to oppose the Europeans. Such leaders always arose, both when Europeans ruled directly and when they manipulated native governments, for at least two basic reasons.

First, the nonconformists—the eventual anti-imperialist leaders—developed a burning desire for human dignity. They came to feel that such dignity was incompatible with foreign rule with its smirks and smiles, its paternalism and condescension. Second, potential leaders found in the Western world the ideologies and justification for their protest. They discovered liberalism with its credo of civil liberty and political self-determination. They echoed the demands of anti-imperialists in Europe and America that the West live up to its own ideals.

More important, they found themselves attracted to modern nationalism, which asserted that every people had the right to control its own destiny. After 1917 anti-imperialist revolt would find another weapon in Lenin's version of Marxian socialism. Thus the anti-imperialist search for dignity drew strength from Western culture, as is apparent in the development of three major Asian countries—India, Japan, and China.

Empire in India

India was the jewel of the British Empire, and no colonial area experienced a more profound British impact. Unlike Japan and China, which maintained a real or precarious independence, and unlike African territories, which were annexed by Europeans only at the end of the nineteenth century, India was ruled more or less absolutely by Britain for a very long time.

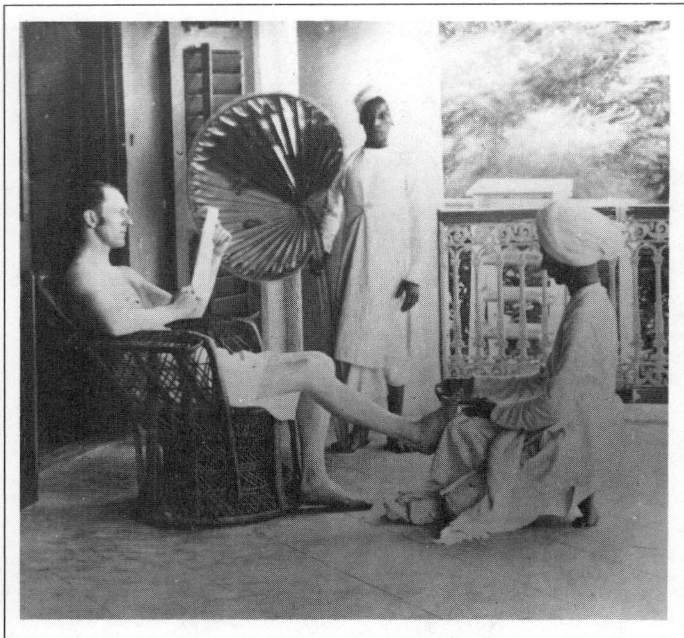

The British in India This photo suggests not only the incredible power and luxury of the British ruling class in India but its confidence and self-satisfaction as well. As one British viceroy said: "We are all British gentlemen engaged in the magnificent work of governing an inferior race." *(BBC Hulton/The Bettmann Archive)*

Arriving in India on the heels of the Portuguese in the seventeenth century, the British East India Company had conquered the last independent native state by 1848. The last "traditional" response to European rule—the attempt by the established ruling classes to drive the white man out by military force—was broken in India in 1857 and 1858. Those were the years of the Great Rebellion (which the British called a "mutiny"), when an insurrection by Muslim and Hindu mercenaries in the British army spread throughout northern and central India before it was finally crushed, primarily by loyal native troops from southern India. Thereafter Britain ruled India directly. India illustrates, therefore, for better and for worse, what generations of European domination might produce.

After 1858 India was ruled by the British Parliament in London and administered by a tiny, all-white civil service in India. In 1900 this elite consisted of fewer than 3,500 top officials, for a population of 300 million. The white elite, backed by white officers and native troops, was competent and generally well disposed toward the welfare of the Indian peasant masses. Yet it practiced strict job discrimination and social segregation, and most of its members quite frankly considered the jumble of Indian peoples and castes to be racially inferior. As Lord Kitchener, one of the most distinguished top military commanders of India, stated:

> *It is this consciousness of the inherent superiority of the European which has won for us India. However well educated and clever a native may be, and however brave he may prove himself, I believe that no rank we can bestow on him would cause him to be considered an equal of the British officer.*[16]

When, for example, the British Parliament in 1883 was considering a major bill to allow Indian judges to try white Europeans in India, the British community rose in protest and defeated the measure. The idea that they might be judged by Indians was inconceivable to Europeans, for it was clear to the Europeans that the empire in India rested squarely on racial inequality.

In spite of (perhaps even because of) their strong feelings of racial and cultural superiority, the British acted energetically and introduced many desirable changes to India. Realizing that they needed well-educated Indians to serve as skilled subordinates in the government and army, the British established a modern system of progressive secondary education, in which all instruction was in English. Thus, through education and government service the British offered some Indians excellent opportunities for both economic and social advancement. High-caste Hindus were particularly quick to respond and emerged as skillful intermediaries between the British rulers and the Indian people—a new elite profoundly influenced by Western thought and culture.

This new bureaucratic elite played a crucial role in modern economic development, which was a second result of British rule. Irrigation projects for agriculture, the world's third largest railroad network for good communications, and large tea and jute plantations geared to the world economy were all developed. Unfortunately, the lot of the Indian masses improved little, for the increase in production was quite literally eaten up by population increase.

Finally, with a well-educated, English-speaking Indian bureaucracy and modern communications, the British created a unified, powerful state. They placed under the same general system of law and administration the different Hindu and Muslim peoples and the vanquished kingdoms of the entire subcontinent —groups that had fought each other for centuries during the Middle Ages and had been repeatedly conquered by Muslim and Mongol invaders. It was as if Europe, with its many states and varieties of Christianity, had been conquered and united in a single great empire.

In spite of these achievements, the decisive reaction to European rule was the rise of nationalism among the Indian elite. No matter how anglicized and necessary a member of the educated classes became, he or she could never become the white ruler's equal. The top jobs, the best clubs, the modern hotels, and even certain railroad compartments were sealed off to brown-skinned men and women. The peasant masses might accept such inequality as the latest version of age-old oppression, but the well-educated, English-speaking elite eventually could not. For the elite, racial discrimination meant not only injured pride but bitter injustice. It flagrantly contradicted those cherished Western concepts of human rights and equality. Moreover, it was based on dictatorship, no matter how benign.

By 1883, when educated Indians came together to found the predominantly Hindu Indian National Congress, demands were increasing for the equality and self-government Britain enjoyed and had already granted white-settler colonies, such as Canada and Australia. By 1907, emboldened in part by Japan's success (see the next section), the radicals in the Indian National Congress were calling for complete independence. Even the moderates were demanding home rule for India through an elected parliament. Although there were sharp divisions between Hindus and Muslims, Indians were finding an answer to the foreign challenge. The common heritage of British rule and Western ideals, along with the reform and revitalization of the Hindu religion, had created a genuine movement for national independence.

The Examples of Japan

When Commodore Perry arrived in Japan in 1853 with his crude but effective gunboat diplomacy, Japan was a complex feudal society. At the top stood a figurehead emperor, but for more than two hundred years, real power had been in the hands of a hereditary military governor, the *shogun.* With the help of a warrior nobility known as *samurai,* the shogun governed a country of hardworking, productive peasants and city dwellers. Often poor and restless, the intensely proud samurai were deeply humiliated by the sudden American intrusion and the unequal treaties with Western countries. When foreign diplomats and merchants began to settle in Yokohama, radical samurai reacted with a wave of antiforeign terrorism and antigovernment assassinations between 1858 and 1863. The imperialist response was swift and unambiguous. An allied fleet of American, British, Dutch, and French warships demolished key forts, which further weakened the power and prestige of the shogun's government. Then, in 1867, a coalition led by patriotic samurai seized control of the government with hardly any bloodshed and restored the political power of the emperor. This was the Meiji Restoration, a great turning point in Japanese development.

The immediate, all-important goal of the new government was to meet the foreign threat. The battle cry of the Meiji reformers was "enrich the state and strengthen the armed forces." Yet how was this to be done? In an about-face that was one of history's most remarkable chapters, the young but well-trained, idealistic but flexible, leaders of Meiji Japan dropped their antiforeign attacks. Convinced that Western civilization was indeed superior in its military and industrial aspects, they initiated from above a series of measures to reform Japan along modern lines. They were convinced that "Japan must be reborn with America its mother and France its father."[17] In the broadest sense, the Meiji leaders tried to harness the power inherent in Europe's dual revolution, in order to protect their country and catch up with the West.

In 1871 the new leaders abolished the old feudal structure of aristocratic, decentralized government and formed a strong unified state. Following the example of the French Revolution, they dismantled the four-class legal system and declared social equality. They decreed freedom of movement in a country where traveling abroad had been a most serious crime. They created a free, competitive, government-stimulated economy. Japan began to build railroads and modern factories. Thus the new generation adopted many principles of a free, liberal society; and, as in Europe, such freedom resulted in a tremendously creative release of human energy.

Yet the overriding concern of Japan's political leadership was always a powerful state, and to achieve this, more than liberalism was borrowed

The Modernization of Japan Soon after it reluctantly opened its doors to foreigners, Japan built its first railroad, sketched here by a native artist. *(Historical Pictures Service, Chicago)*

from the West. A powerful modern navy was created, and the army was completely reorganized along French and German lines, with three-year military service for all males and a professional officer corps. This army of draftees effectively put down disturbances in the countryside, and in 1877 it was used to crush a major rebellion by feudal elements protesting the loss of their privileges. Japan also borrowed rapidly and adopted skillfully the West's science and modern technology, particularly in industry, medicine, and education. Many Japanese were encouraged to study abroad, and the government paid large salaries to attract foreign experts. These experts were always carefully controlled, though, and replaced by trained Japanese as soon as possible.

By 1890, when the new state was firmly established, the wholesale borrowing of the early restoration had given way to more selective emphasis on those things foreign that were in keeping with Japanese tradition. Following the model of the German Empire, Japan established an authoritarian constitution and rejected democracy. The power of the emperor and his ministers was vast, that of the legislature limited.

Japan successfully copied the imperialism of Western society. Expansion not only proved that Japan was strong; it also cemented the nation together in a great mission. Having "opened" Korea with the gunboat diplomacy of imperialism in 1876, Japan decisively defeated China in a war over Korea in 1894 and took Formosa. In the next years, Japan competed aggressively with the leading European powers for influence and territory in China, particularly Manchuria. There Japanese and Russian imperialism met and collided. In 1904 Japan attacked Russia without warning, and after a bloody war, Japan emerged with a valuable foothold in China, Russia's former protectorate over Port Arthur (see Map 26.3). By 1910, when it annexed Korea, Japan was a major imperial power, continuously expanding its influence in China in spite of sharp protests from its distant Pacific neighbor, the United States.

Japan became the first non-Western country to use an ancient love of country to transform itself and thereby meet the many-sided challenge of Western expansion. Moreover, Japan demonstrated convincingly that a modern Asian nation could defeat and humble a great Western power. Many Chinese nationalists were fascinated by Japan's achievement. A group of patriots in French-ruled southern Vietnam sent Vietnamese students to Japan to learn the island empire's secret of success. Japan provided patriots in Asia and Africa with an inspiring example of national recovery and liberation.

Toward Revolution in China

In 1860 the two-hundred-year-old Manchu dynasty in China appeared on the verge of collapse. Efforts to repel the foreigner had failed, and rebellion and chaos wracked the country. Yet the government drew on its traditional strengths and made a surprising comeback that lasted more than thirty years.

The Hatred of Foreigners burns in the eyes of this Chinese prisoner condemned to death for murdering foreign missionaries in the aftermath of the Sino-Japanese war. Both his face and crime foretell the fury of the Boxer Rebellion. *(BBC Hulton/The Bettmann Archive)*

Two factors were crucial in this reversal. First, the traditional ruling groups temporarily produced new and effective leadership. Loyal scholar-statesmen and generals quelled disturbances like the great Tai Ping rebellion. A truly remarkable woman, the empress dowager Tzu Hsi, governed in the name of her young son and combined shrewd insight with vigorous action to revitalize the bureaucracy.

Second, destructive foreign aggression lessened, for the Europeans had obtained their primary goal of commercial and diplomatic relations. Indeed, some Europeans contributed to the dynasty's recovery. A talented Irishman effectively reorganized China's customs office and increased the government tax receipts, while a sympathetic American diplomat represented China in foreign lands and helped strengthen the central government. Such efforts dovetailed with the dynasty's efforts to adopt some aspects of Western government and technology while maintaining traditional Chinese values and beliefs.

The parallel movement toward domestic reform and limited cooperation with the West collapsed under the blows of Japanese imperialism. The Sino-Japanese war of 1894–1895 and the subsequent harsh peace treaty revealed China's helplessness in the face of aggression, triggering a rush for foreign concessions and protectorates in China. At its high point in 1898, it appeared that the European powers might actually divide China among themselves, as they had recently divided Africa. Probably only the jealousy each nation felt toward its imperial competitors saved China from partition, although the United States' Open Door policy, which opposed formal annexation of Chinese territory, may have helped tip the balance. In any event, the tempo and impact of foreign penetration greatly accelerated after 1894.

So, too, did the intensity and radicalism of the Chinese reaction. Like the men of the Meiji Restoration, some modernizers saw salvation in Western institutions. In 1898 the government launched a desperate "hundred days of reform" in an attempt to meet the foreign challenge. More radical reformers like the revolutionary Sun Yat-sen (1866–1925), who came from the peasantry and was educated in Hawaii by Christian missionaries, sought to overthrow the dynasty altogether, and establish a republic.

On the other side, some traditionalists turned back toward ancient practices, political conservatism, and fanatical hatred of the "foreign devils." "Protect the country, destroy the foreigner" was their simple motto. Such conservative, antiforeign patriots had often clashed with foreign missionaries, whom they charged with undermining reverence for ancestors and thereby threatening the Chinese family and the entire society. In the agony of defeat and unwanted reforms, secret societies like the Boxers rebelled. In northeastern China, more than two hundred foreign missionaries and several thousand Chinese Christians were killed. Once again, the imperialist response was swift and harsh. Peking was occupied and plundered by foreign armies. A heavy indemnity was imposed.

The years after the Boxer Rebellion (1900–1903) were ever more troubled. Anarchy and foreign influence spread, as the power and prestige of the Manchu dynasty declined still further. Antiforeign, antigovernment revolutionary groups agitated and plotted. Finally, in 1912, a spontaneous uprising topped the Manchu dynasty. After thousands of years of emperors and empires, a loose coalition of revolutionaries proclaimed a Western-style republic and called for an elected parliament. The transformation of China under the impact of expanding Western society entered a new phase, and the end was not in sight.

In the nineteenth century the West entered the third and most dynamic phase of is centuries-old expansion into non-Western lands. In so doing, Western nations forged an integrated world economy, sent forth millions of emigrants, and established political influence in Asia and vast political empires in Africa. The reasons for this culminating surge were many, but the economic thrust of robust industrial capitalism, an ever-growing lead in technology, and the competitive pressures of European nationalism were particularly important.

Western expansion had far-reaching consequences. For the first time in human history, the world became in many ways a single unit. Moreover, European expansion diffused the ideas and techniques of a highly developed civilization. Yet the West relied on force to conquer and rule, and it treated non-Western peoples as racial inferiors. Thus non-Western elites, often armed with Western doctrines, gradually responded to the Western challenge. They launched a national, anti-imperialist struggle for dignity, genuine independence, and modernization. This struggle would emerge as a central drama of world history after the great European civil war of 1914 to 1918, which reduced the West's technological advantage and shattered its self-confidence and complacent moral superiority.

NOTES

1. Quoted by A. Waley, *The Opium War Through Chinese Eyes,* Macmillan, New York, 1958, p. 29.
2. Quoted by J. W. Hall, *Japan, from Prehistory to Modern Times,* Delacorte Press, New York, 1970, p. 250.
3. Quoted by R. Hallett, *Africa to 1875,* University of Michigan Press, Ann Arbor, 1970, p. 109.
4. Quoted by Earl of Cromer, *Modern Egypt,* London, 1911, p. 48.
5. Quoted by T. Blegen, *Norwegian Migration to America,* Norwegian-American Historical Association, Northfield, Minn., 1940, 2.468.
6. Quoted by I. Howe, *World of Our Fathers,* Harcourt Brace Jovanovich, New York, 1976, p. 25.
7. Quoted by C. A. Price, *The Great White Walls Are Built: Restrictive Immigration to North America and Australia, 1836–1888,* Australian National University Press, Canberra, 1974, p. 175.
8. Quoted by W. L. Langer, *European Alliances and Alignments, 1871–1890,* Vintage Books, New York, 1931, p. 290.
9. Quoted by J. Ellis, *The Social History of the Machine Gun,* Pantheon Books, New York, 1975, pp. 86, 101.
10. Quoted by G. H. Nadel and P. Curtis, eds., *Imperialism and Colonialism,* Macmillan, New York, 1964, p. 94.

11. Quoted by W. L. Langer, *The Diplomacy of Imperialism,* 2nd ed., Knopf, New York, 1951, pp. 86, 88.
12. Rudyard Kipling, *The Five Nations,* London, 1903, quoted by the permission of Mrs. George Bambridge, Methuen & Company, and Doubleday & Company, Inc.
13. E. H. Berman, "African Responses to Christian Mission Education," *African Studies Review* 17:3 (1974):530.
14. Quoted in Langer, *Diplomacy of Imperialism,* p. 88.
15. Quoted by Ellis, pp. 99–100.
16. Quoted by K. M. Panikkar, *Asia and Western Dominance,* George Allen & Unwin, London, 1959, p. 116.
17. Quoted by Hall, p. 289.

SUGGESTED READING

Hall and Hallett, cited in the Notes, are excellent introductions to the histories of Japan and Africa. A. Waley, also cited in the Notes, has written extensively and well on China. K. Latourette, *The Chinese: Their History and Culture,* rev. ed. (1964), is a fine survey with many suggestions for further reading. Howe and Blegen, cited in the Notes, provide dramatic accounts of Jewish and Norwegian migration to the United States. Most other migrant groups have also found their historians: M. Walker, *Germany and the Emigration, 1816–1885* (1964), and W. Adams, *Ireland and Irish Emigration to the New World* (reissued 1967), are outstanding. Langer's volumes consider the diplomatic aspects of imperialism in exhaustive detail. Ellis's well-illustrated study of the machine gun is fascinating, as is Price on the restriction of Asian migration to Australia. All these works are cited in the Notes.

General surveys of European expansion in a broad perspective include R. Betts, *Europe Overseas* (1968); A. Thornton, *Imperialism in the 20th Century* (1977); T. Smith, *The Patterns of Imperialism* (1981); and W. Woodruff, *Impact of Western Man* (1967), which has an extensive bibliography. D. K. Fieldhouse has also written two fine surveys, *Economics and Empire, 1830–1914* (1970) and *Colonialism, 1870–1945* (1981). G. Barraclough, *An Introduction to Contemporary History* (1964), argues powerfully that Western imperialism and the non-Western reaction to it have been crucial in world history since about 1890. J. A. Hobson's classic *Imperialism* (1902) is readily available, and the Marxist-Leninist case is effectively presented in V. G. Kieran, *Marxism and Imperialism* (1975). Two excellent anthologies on the problem of European expansion are G. Nadel and P. Curtis, eds., *Imperialism and Colonialism* (1964), and H. Wright, ed., *The "New Imperialism,"* rev. ed. (1975).

Britain's leading position in European imperialism is examined in a lively way by B. Porter, *The Lion's Share* (1976); J. Morris, *Pax Britannica* (1968); and D. Judd, *The Victorian Empire* (1970), a stunning pictorial history. B. Semmel has written widely on the intellectual foundations of English expansion, as in *The Rise of Free Trade Imperialism* (1970). J. Gallegher and R. Robinson, *Africa and the Victorians: The Climax of Imperialism* (1961), is an influential reassessment. H. Brunschwig, *French Colonialism, 1871–1914* (1966), and W. Baumgart, *Imperialism: The Idea and Reality of British and French Colonial Expansion* (1982), are well-balanced studies. A. Moorehead, *The White Nile* (1971), tells the fascinating story of the European exploration of the mysterious upper Nile. Volumes 5 and 6 of K. Latourette, *History of the Expansion of Christianity,* 7 vols. (1937–1945), examines the powerful impulse for missionary work in non-European areas. D. Headrick stresses Western technological superiority in *Tools of Empire* (1981).

Two unusual and provocative studies on personal relations between European rulers and non-European subjects are D. Mannoni, *Prospero and Caliban: The Psychology of Colonialization* (1964), and F. Fanon, *Wretched of the Earth* (1965), a bitter attack on white racism by a black psychologist active in the Algerian revolution. Novels also bring the psychological and human dimensions of imperialism alive. H. Rider Haggard, *King Solomon's Mines,* portrays the powerful appeal of adventure in exotic lands, while Rudyard Kipling, the greatest writer of European expansion, is at his stirring best in *Kim* and *Soldiers Three.* Joseph Conrad unforgettably probes European motives in *Heart of Darkness,* while André Gide, *The Immoralist,* closely examines European moral corruption in North Africa.

27

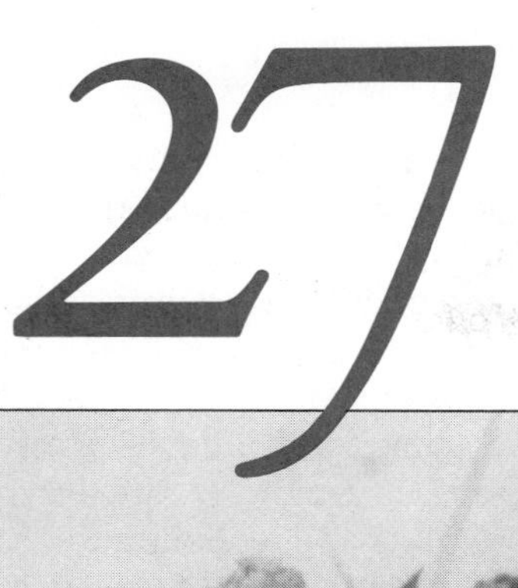

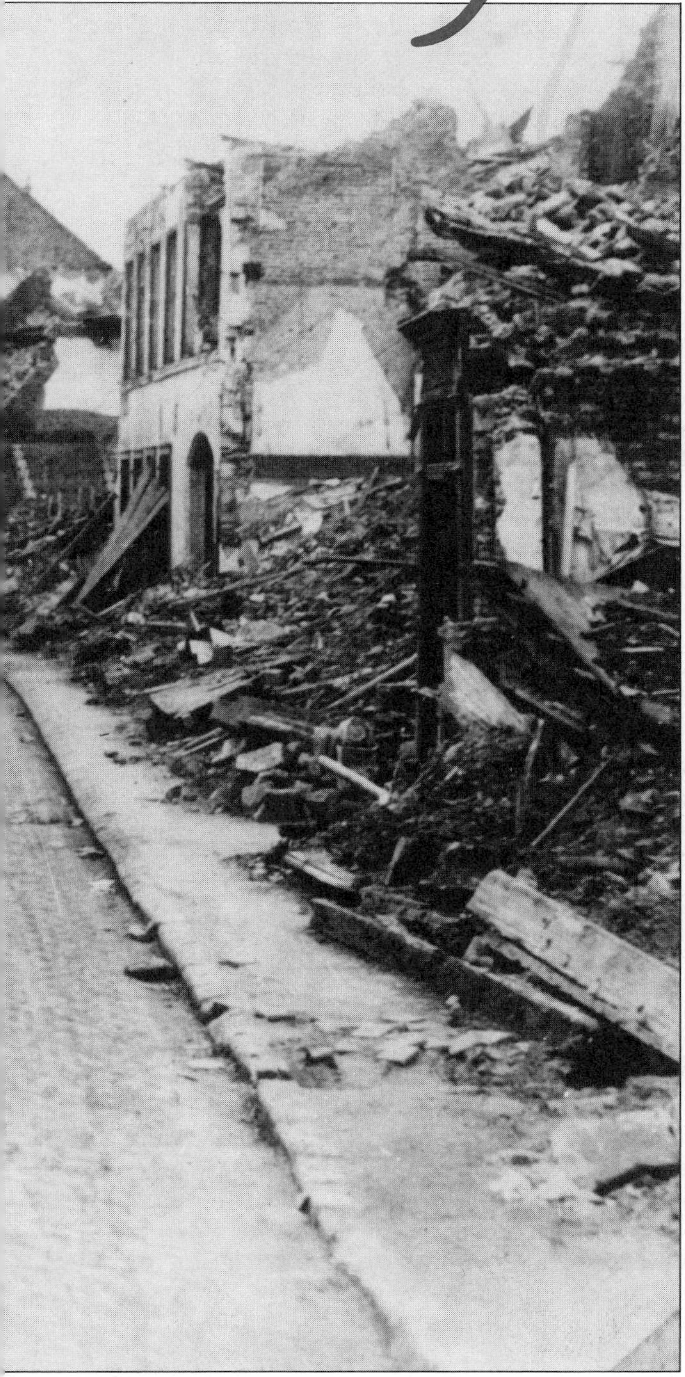

THE GREAT BREAK: WAR AND REVOLUTION

IN THE SUMMER OF 1914 the nations of Europe went willingly to war. They believed they had no other choice. Moreover, both peoples and governments confidently expected a short war leading to a decisive victory. Such a war, they believed, would "clear the air," and European society would go on as before.

These expectations were almost totally mistaken. The First World War was long, indecisive, and tremendously destructive. To the shell-shocked generation of survivors, it was known simply as the Great War: the war of unprecedented scope and intensity. From today's perspective it is clear that the First World War marked a great break in the course of Western historical development since the French and Industrial Revolutions. A noted British political scientist has gone so far as to say that even in victorious and relatively fortunate Great Britain, the First World War was *the* great turning point in government and society, "as in everything else in modern British history. . . . There's a much greater difference between the Britain of 1914 and, say, 1920, than between the Britain of 1920 and today."[1]

This is a strong statement, but it contains much truth, for all of Europe as well as for Britain. It suggests three questions this chapter will try to answer. What caused the Great War? How and why did war and revolution have such enormous and destructive consequences? And where in the trauma and bloodshed were formed elements of today's world, many of which people now accept and even cherish?

THE FIRST WORLD WAR

The First World War was so long and destructive because it involved all the Great Powers and because it quickly degenerated into a senseless military stalemate. Like two evenly matched boxers in a championship bout, each side tried to wear down its opponent. There was no referee to call a draw, only the blind hammering of a life-or-death struggle.

The Bismarckian System of Alliances

The Franco-Prussian War and the foundation of the German Empire opened a new era in international relations. France was decisively defeated in 1871 and forced to pay a large war indemnity and give up Alsace-Lorraine. In ten short years, from 1862 to 1871, Bismarck had made Prussia-Germany—traditionally the weakest of the Great Powers—the most powerful nation in Europe (pages 804–808). Had Bismarck been a Napoleon I or a Hitler, for whom no gain was ever sufficient, continued expansion would no doubt sooner or later have raised a powerful coalition against the new German Empire. Yet he was not. As Bismarck never tired of repeating after 1871, Germany was a "satisfied" power. Germany had no territorial ambitions and only wanted peace in Europe.

But how was peace to be preserved? The most serious threat to peace came from the east, from Austria-Hungary and from Russia. Those two enormous multinational empires had many conflicting interests, particularly in the Balkans, where the Ottoman Empire—the "sick man of Europe"—was ebbing fast. There was a real threat that Germany might be dragged into a great war between the two rival empires. Bismarck's solution was a system of alliances (Figure 27.1) to restrain both Russia and Austria-Hungary, to prevent conflict between them, and to isolate a hostile France.

A first step was the creation in 1873 of the conservative Three Emperors' League, which linked the monarchs of Austria-Hungary, Germany, and Russia in an alliance against radical movements. In 1877 and 1878, when Russia's victories over the Ottoman Empire threatened the balance of Austrian and Russian interests in the Balkans and the balance of British and Russian interests in the Middle East, Bismarck played the role of sincere peacemaker. At the Congress of Berlin in 1878, he saw that Austria obtained the right to "occupy and administer" the Ottoman provinces of Bosnia and Herzegovnia to counterbalance Russian gains, while independent Balkan states were also carved from the disintegrating Ottoman Empire.

Bismarck's balancing efforts at the Congress of Berlin infuriated Russian nationalists, which led Bismarck to conclude a defensive military alliance with Austria against Russia in 1879. Motivated by tensions with France, Italy joined Germany and Austria in 1882, thereby forming the Triple Alliance.

Bismarck continued to work for peace in eastern Europe, seeking to neutralize tensions between Austria-Hungary and Russia. In 1881 he capitalized on their mutual fears and cajoled them both into a secret

The Congress of Berlin, 1878 With the Austrian representative on his right and with other participants looking on, Bismarck the mediator symbolically seals the hard-won agreement by shaking hands with the chief Russian negotiator. The Great Powers often relied on such special conferences to settle their international disputes. *(The Bettmann Archive)*

alliance with Germany. This Alliance of the Three Emperors lasted until 1887. It established the principle of cooperation among all three powers in any further division of the Ottoman Empire, while each state pledged friendly neutrality in case one of the three found itself at war with a fourth power (except the Ottoman Empire).

Bismarck also maintained good relations with Britain and Italy, while cooperating with France in Africa but keeping France isolated in Europe. In 1887 Russia declined to renew the Alliance of the Three Emperors because of new tensions in the Balkans. Bismarck craftily substituted a Russian-German Reinsurance Treaty, by which both states promised neutrality if the other were attacked.

Bismarck's accomplishments in foreign policy after 1871 were great. For almost a generation, he maintained German leadership in international affairs, and he worked successfully for peace by managing conflicts and by restraining Austria-Hungary and Russia with defensive alliances.

The Rival Blocs

In 1890 the young, impetuous emperor William II dismissed Bismarck, in part because of the chancellor's friendly policy toward Russia since the 1870s. William then adamantly refused to renew the Russian-German Reinsurance Treaty, in spite of Russian willingness to do so. This fateful departure in foreign affairs prompted long-isolated republican France to court absolutist Russia, offering loans, arms, and friendship. In both countries there were enthusiastic public demonstrations, and in St. Petersburg the autocratic Alexander III stood bareheaded on a French battleship while a band played the "Marseillaise," the hymn of the Revolution. A preliminary agreement between the two countries was reached in 1891, and in early 1894 France and Russia became military allies. This alliance (Figure 27.1) was to remain in effect as long as the Triple Alliance of Austria, Germany, and Italy: continental Europe was dangerously divided into two rival blocs.

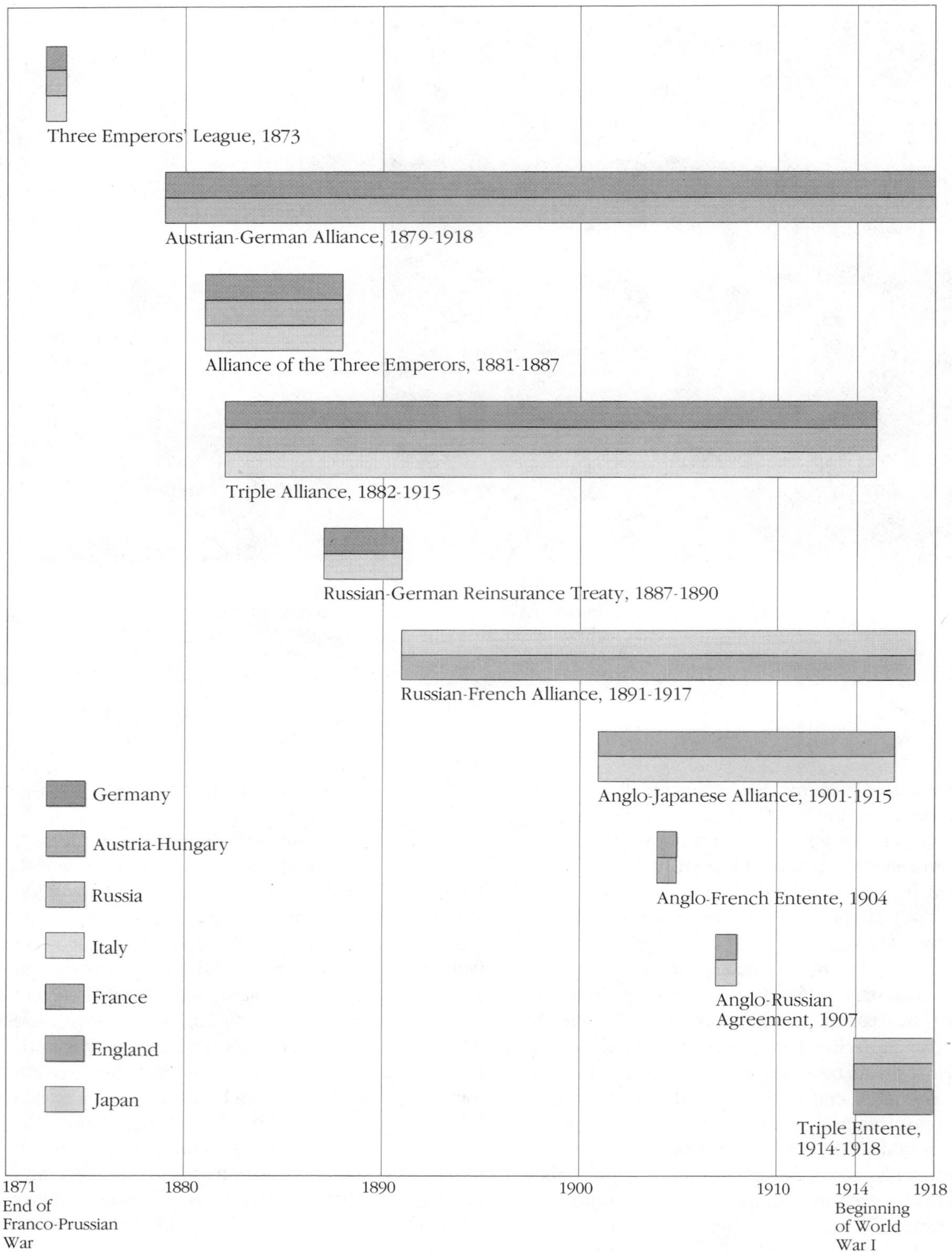

Three Emperors' League, 1873
Austrian-German Alliance, 1879-1918
Alliance of the Three Emperors, 1881-1887
Triple Alliance, 1882-1915
Russian-German Reinsurance Treaty, 1887-1890
Russian-French Alliance, 1891-1917
Anglo-Japanese Alliance, 1901-1915
Anglo-French Entente, 1904
Anglo-Russian Agreement, 1907
Triple Entente, 1914-1918
Germany
Austria-Hungary
Russia
Italy
France
England
Japan
1871 End of Franco-Prussian War
1880
1890
1900
1910
1914 Beginning of World War I
1918

FIGURE 27.1 The Alliance System After 1871 Bismarck's subtle diplomacy maintained reasonably good relations among the eastern monarchies—Germany, Russia, and Austria-Hungary—and kept France isolated. The situation changed dramatically in 1891, when the Russian-French Alliance divided the Great Powers into two fairly equal military blocs.

The policy of Great Britain became increasingly crucial. Long content with "splendid isolation" and no permanent alliances, Britain after 1891 was the only uncommitted Great Power. Could Britain afford to remain isolated, or would it feel compelled to take sides? Alliance with France or Russia certainly seemed highly unlikely. With its vast and rapidly expanding empire, Britain was often in serious conflict with these countries around the world in the heyday of imperialism.

Britain also squabbled with Germany, for Emperor William II was a master of tactless public statements, and Britain found Germany's pursuit of greater world power after about 1897 vaguely disquieting. Nevertheless, many Germans and some Britons believed that their statesmen would eventually formalize the "natural alliance" they felt already united the advanced, racially related Germanic and Anglo-Saxon peoples. Alas, such an understanding never materialized. Instead, the generally good relations that has prevailed between Prussia and Great Britain ever since the mid-eighteenth century, and certainly under Bismarck, gave way to a bitter Anglo-German rivalry.

There were several reasons for this tragic development. The hard-fought Boer War (1899–1902) between the British and the tiny Dutch republics of South Africa had a major impact on British policy. British statesmen saw that Britain was overextended around the world. The Boer War also brought into the open widespread anti-British feeling, as editorial writers in many nations denounced the latest manifestation of British imperialism. There was even talk of Germany, Austria, France, and Russia forming a grand alliance against the bloated but insatiable British Empire. Therefore British statesmen prudently set about shoring up their exposed position with alliance and agreements.

Britain improved its often-strained relations with the United States and in 1902 concluded a formal alliance with Japan (Figure 27.1). Britain then responded favorably to the advances of France's skillful foreign minister, Théophile Delcassé, who wanted better relations with Britain and was willing to accept British rule in Egypt in return for British support of French plans to dominate Morocco. The resulting Anglo-French Entente of 1904 (Figure 27.1) settled all outstanding colonial disputes between Britain and France.

Frustrated by Britain's turn toward France in 1904, Germany decided to test the strength of the entente and drive Britain and France apart. First Germany threatened and bullied France into dismissing Delcassé. However, rather than accept the typical territorial payoff of imperial competition—a slice of French jungle in Africa or a port in Morocco—in return for French primacy in Morocco, the Germans foolishly rattled their swords in 1905. They insisted on an international conference on the whole Moroccan question without presenting precise or reasonable demands. Germany's crude bullying forced France and Britain closer together, and Germany left the Algeciras Conference of 1906 empty-handed and isolated (except for Austria-Hungary).

The result of the Moroccan crisis and the Algeciras Conference was something of a diplomatic revolution. Britain, France, Russia, and even the United States began to see Germany as a potential threat, which might seek to dominate all Europe. At the same time, German leaders began to see sinister plots to "encircle" Germany and block its development as a world power. In 1907 Russia, battered by the disastrous war with Japan and the revolution of 1905, agreed to settle its quarrels with Great Britain in Persia and central Asia with a special Anglo-Russian Agreement (Figure 27.1). As a result of that agreement, Germany's blustering paranoia increased and so did Britain's thinly disguised hostility.

Germany's decision to add a large, enormously expensive fleet of big-gun battleships to its already expanding navy also heightened tensions after 1907. German nationalists, led by the all-too-persuasive Admiral Tirpitz, saw a large navy as the legitimate mark of a great world power. But British leaders like Lloyd George saw it as a detestable military challenge, which forced them to spend the "People's Budget" on battleships rather than on social welfare. As Germany's rapid industrial growth allowed it to overcome Britain's early lead, economic rivalry also contributed to distrust and hostility between the two

German Warships Under Full Steam As this impressive row of ships on maneuvers in 1911 suggests, Germany did succeed in building a large modern navy. But Britain was equally determined to maintain its naval superiority, and the spiraling arms race helped poison relations between the two countries. *(Süddeutscher Verlag)*

nations. Unscrupulous journalists and special-interest groups in both countries portrayed healthy competition in foreign trade and investment as a form of economic welfare.

Many educated shapers of public opinion and ordinary people in Britain and Germany were increasingly locked in a fateful "love-hate" relationship between the two countries. Proud nationalists in both countries simultaneously admired and feared the power and accomplishments of their nearly equal rival. In 1909 the mass-circulation London *Daily Mail* hysterically informed its readers in a series of reports that "Germany is deliberately preparing to destroy the British Empire."[2] By then, Britain was psychologically, if not officially, in the Franco-Russian camp. The leading nations of Europe were divided into two hostile blocs, both ill prepared to deal with upheaval on Europe's southeastern frontier.

The Outbreak of War

In the early years of this century, war in the Balkans was as inevitable as anything can be in human history. The reason was simple: nationalism was destroying the Ottoman Empire and threatening to break up the Austro-Hungarian Empire. The only questions were what kinds of wars would occur and where they would lead.

Greece had long before led the struggle for national liberation, winning its independence in 1832. In 1875 widespread nationalist rebellion in the Ottoman Empire had resulted in Turkish repression, Russian intervention, and Great Power tensions. Bismarck had helped resolve this crisis at the 1878 Congress of Berlin, which worked out the partial division of Turkish possessions in Europe. Austria-Hungary obtained the right to "occupy and adminis-

Map 27.1 The Balkans After the Congress of Berlin, 1878 The Ottoman Empire suffered large territorial losses but remained a power in the Balkans.

Map 27.2 The Balkans in 1914 Ethnic boundaries did not follow political boundaries, and Serbian national aspirations threatened Austria-Hungary.

ter" Bosnia and Herzegovina. Serbia and Rumania won independence, and a part of Bulgaria won local autonomy. The Ottoman Empire retained important Balkan holdings, for Austria-Hungary and Russia each feared the other's domination of totally independent states in the area (see Map 27.1).

After 1878 the siren call of imperialism lured European energies, particularly Russian energies, away from the Balkans. This division helped preserve the fragile balance of interests in southeastern Europe. By 1903, however, Balkan nationalism was on the rise once again. Serbia led the way, becoming openly hostile toward both Austria-Hungary and the Ottoman Empire. The Serbs, a Slavic people, looked to Slavic Russia for support of their national aspirations. To block Serbian expansion and to take advantage of Russia's weakness after the revolution of 1905, Austria in 1908 formally annexed Bosnia and Herzegovina with their predominantly Serbian populations. The kingdom of Serbia erupted in rage but could do nothing without Russian support.

Then in 1912, in the First Balkan War, Serbia turned southward. With Greece and Bulgaria it took Macedonia from the Ottoman Empire and then quarreled with its ally Bulgaria over the spoils of victory—a dispute that led in 1913 to the Second Balkan War. Austria intervened in 1913 and forced Serbia to give up Albania. After centuries, nationalism had finally destroyed the Ottoman Empire in Europe. This sudden but long-awaited event elated the Balkan nationalists and dismayed the leaders of multinational Austria-Hungary. The former hoped and the latter feared that Austria might be next to be broken apart.

Within this tense context, Archduke Francis Ferdinand, heir to the Austrian and Hungarian thrones, and his wife Sophie were assassinated by Bosnian revolutionaries on June 28, 1914, during a state visit to the Bosnian capital of Sarajevo. The assassins were closely connected to the ultranationalist Serbian society The Black Hand. This revolutionary group was secretly supported by members of the Serbian government and was dedicated to uniting all Serbians in a single state. Although the leaders of Austria-Hungary did not and could not know all the details of Serbia's involvement in the assassination plot, they concluded after some hesitation that Serbia had to be severely punished once and for all. After a month of maneuvering, Austria-Hungary presented Serbia with an unconditional ultimatum, on July 23.

The Serbian government had just forty-eight hours in which to agree to cease all subversion in Austria and all anti-Austrian propaganda in Serbia. Moreover, a thorough investigation of all aspects of the assassination at Sarajevo was to be undertaken in Serbia by a joint commission of Serbian and Austrian officials. These demands amounted to control of the Serbian state. When Serbia replied moderately but evasively, Austria began to mobilize and then declared war on Serbia on July 28. Thus a desperate multinational Austria-Hungary deliberately chose war in a last-ditch attempt to stem the rising tide of hostile nationalism. The "Third Balkan War" had begun (see Map 27.2).

Of prime importance in Austria-Hungary's fateful decision was Germany's unconditional support. Emperor William II and his chancellor Theobald von Bethmann-Hollweg gave Austria-Hungary a "blank check" and urged aggressive measures in early July, even though they realized that war between Austria and Russia was the most probable result. They knew Russian pan-Slavs saw Russia not only as the protector, but also as the eventual liberator, of southern Slavs. As one pan-Slav had said much earlier, "Austria can hold her part of the Slavonian mass as long as Turkey holds hers and vice versa."[3] At the very least a resurgent Russia could not stand by, as in the Bosnian crisis, and simply watch the Serbs be crushed. Yet Bethmann-Hollweg apparently hoped that while Russia (and therefore France) would go to war, Great Britain would remain neutral, unwilling to fight for "Russian aggression" in the distant Balkans. After all, Britain had reached only "friendly understandings" with France and Russia on colonial questions and had no alliance with either power.

In fact, the diplomatic situation was already out of control. Military plans and timetables began to dictate policy. Russia, a vast country, would require much longer to mobilize its armies than Germany and Austria-Hungary. On July 28, as Austrian armies bombarded Belgrade, Tsar Nicholas II ordered a partial mobilization against Austria-Hungary. Almost immediately he found that this was impossible. All the complicated mobilization plans of the Russian general staff had assumed a war with both Austria *and* Germany: Russia could not mobilize against one without mobilizing against the other. On July 29, therefore, Russia ordered full mobilization and in effect declared general war. For, as the French general Goisdeffre had said to the agreeing Russian tsar when the Franco-Russian military convention was being negotiated in 1892, "mobilization is a declaration of war."[4]

The same tragic subordination of political considerations to military strategy descended on Germany. The German general staff had also thought only in terms of a two-front war. Their plan for war—the Schlieffen plan, the work of Count Alfred von Schlieffen, chief of the German general staff from 1891 to 1906 and a professional military man—called for knocking out France first with a lightning attack through neutral Belgium before turning on Russia.

Thus, on August 2, 1914, General Helmuth von Moltke, "acting under a dictate of self-preservation," demanded that Belgium permit German armies to pass through its territory. Belgium, whose neutrality was solemnly guaranteed by all the great states including Prussia, refused. Germany attacked. Thus Germany's terrible, politically disastrous response to a war in the Balkans was an all-out invasion of France by way of the plains of neutral Belgium on August 3. In the face of this act of aggression, Great Britain declared war on Germany the following day. The First World War had begun.

Reflections on the Origins of the War

Although few events in history have aroused such interest and controversy as the coming of the First World War, the question of immediate causes and responsibilities can be answered with considerable certainty. Austria-Hungary deliberately started the "Third Balkan War." A war for the right to survive was Austria-Hungary's desperate, if understandable, response to the aggressive, yet understandable, revolutionary drive of Serbian nationalists to unify their people in a single state. In spite of Russian intervention in the quarrel, it is clear from the beginning of the crisis that Germany not only pushed and goaded Austria-Hungary but was also responsible for turning a little war into the Great War by means of its sledgehammer attack on Belgium and France.

After Bismarck's resignation in 1890, German leaders lost control of the international system. They felt increasingly that Germany's status as a world power was declining while that of Britain, France, Russia, and the United States was growing. Indeed, the powers of what officially became in August 1914 the Triple Entente—Great Britain, France, and Russia—were checking Germany's vague but real aspirations, as well as working to strangle Austria-Hungary, Germany's only real ally. Germany's aggression in 1914 reflected the failure of all European statesmen, not just German leaders, to incorporate Bismarck's mighty empire permanently and peacefully into the international system.

There were other underlying causes. The new overseas expansion—imperialism—did not play a direct role, since the European powers always settled their colonial conflicts peacefully. Yet the easy imperialist victories did contribute to a general European overconfidence and reinforced national rivalries. In this respect it was influential.

The triumph of nationalism was a crucial underlying precondition of the Great War. Nationalism was at the heart of the Balkan wars, in the form of Serbian aspirations and the grandiose pan-German versus pan-Slavic racism of some fanatics. Nationalism drove the spiraling arms race. More generally, as shown in Chapter 25, the aristocracy and middle classes arrived at nationalistic compromises, while ordinary people looked toward increasingly responsive states for psychological and material well-being.

Broad popular commitment to "my country right or wrong" weakened groups that thought in terms of international communities and consequences. Thus the big international bankers, who were frightened by the prospect of war in July 1914, and the extreme-left socialists, who believed that the enemy was at home and not abroad, were equally out of step with national feeling.

Finally, the wealthy governing classes underestimated the risk of war in 1914. They had forgotten that great wars and great social revolutions very often go together in history. Metternich's alliance of conservative forces in support of international peace and the domestic status quo had become only a distant memory.

The First Battle of the Marne

When the Germans invaded Belgium in August 1914, they and everyone else believed that the war would be short, for urban society rested on the food and raw materials of the world economy: "The boys will be home by Christmas." The Belgian army heroically defended its homeland, however, and fell back in good order to join a rapidly landed British army corps near the Franco-Belgian border. This action complicated the original Schlieffen plan of concentrating German armies on the right wing and boldly capturing Paris in a vast encircling movement. Moreover, the German left wing in Lorraine failed to retreat, thwarting the plan to suck French armies into Germany and then annihilate them. Instead, by the end of August dead-tired German soldiers were advancing along an enormous front in the scorching summer heat. The neatly designed prewar plan to surround Paris from the north and west had been thrown into confusion.

French armies totaling 1 million, reinforced by more than 100,000 British troops, had retreated in orderly fashion before Germany's 1.5 million men in the field. Under the leadership of the steel-nerved General Joseph Joffre, the French attacked a gap in the German line at the Battle of the Marne on September 6. For three days, France threw everything into the attack. At one point, the French government desperately requisitioned all the taxis of Paris to rush reserves to the troops at the front. Finally, the Germans fell back. Paris and France had been miraculously saved.

Stalemate and Slaughter

The attempts of French and British armies to turn the German retreat into a rout were unsuccessful, and so were moves by both sides to outflank each other in northern France. As a result, both sides began to dig trenches to protect themselves from machine gun fire. By November 1914, an unbroken line of trenches extended from the Belgian ports through

Preparing the Attack The great offenses of the First World War required the mobilization of men and material on an unprecedented scale. This photo shows American troops moving up. *(U.S. Army Signal Corps)*

northern France past the fortress of Verdun and on to the Swiss frontier.

In the face of this unexpected stalemate, slaughter on the western front began in earnest. The defenders on both sides dug in behind rows of trenches, mines, and barbed wire. For days and even weeks ceaseless shelling by heavy artillery supposedly "softened up" the enemy in a given area (and also signaled the coming attack). Then young draftees and their junior officers went "over the top" of the trenches in frontal attacks on the enemy's line.

The cost in lives was staggering, the gains in territory minuscule. The massive French and British offensives during 1915 never gained more than three miles of blood-soaked earth from the enemy. In the Battle of the Somme in the summer of 1916, the British and French gained an insignificant 125 square miles at the cost of 600,000 dead or wounded, while the Germans lost half a million men. That same year, the unsuccessful German campaign against Verdun cost 700,000 lives on both sides. The British poet Siegfried Sassoon (1886–1967) wrote of the Somme offensive: "I am staring at a sunlit picture of Hell."

Terrible 1917 saw General Robert Nievelle's French army almost destroyed in a grand spring attack at Champagne, while at Passchendaele in the fall, the British traded 400,000 casualties for fifty square miles of Belgian Flanders. The hero of Erich Remarque's great novel *All Quiet on the Western Front* (1929) describes one such attack:

The Fruits of War The extent of carnage, the emotional damage, and the physical destruction were equally unprecedented. Once great cathedrals standing in ruin symbolized the disaster. *(UPI/Bettmann Newsphotos)*

We see men living with their skulls blown open; we see soldiers run with their two feet cut off. . . . Still the little piece of convulsed earth in which we lie is held. We have yielded no more than a few hundred yards of it as a prize to the enemy. But on every yard there lies a dead man.

Such was war on the western front.

The war of the trenches shattered an entire generation of young men. Millions who could have provided political creativity and leadership after the war were forever missing. Moreover, those who lived through the holocaust were maimed, shell-shocked, embittered, and profoundly disillusioned. The young soldiers went to war believing in the world of their leaders and elders, the pre-1914 world of order, progress, and patriotism. Then, in Remarque's words, the "first bombardment showed us our mistake, and under it the world as they had taught it to us broke in pieces." For many, the sacrifice and comradeship of the battlefield became life's crucial experience, an experience that "soft" civilians could never understand. A chasm opened up between veterans and civilians, making the difficult postwar reconstruction all the more difficult.

The Widening War

On the eastern front, slaughter did not degenerate into suicidal trench warfare. With the outbreak of the war, the "Russian steamroller" immediately moved

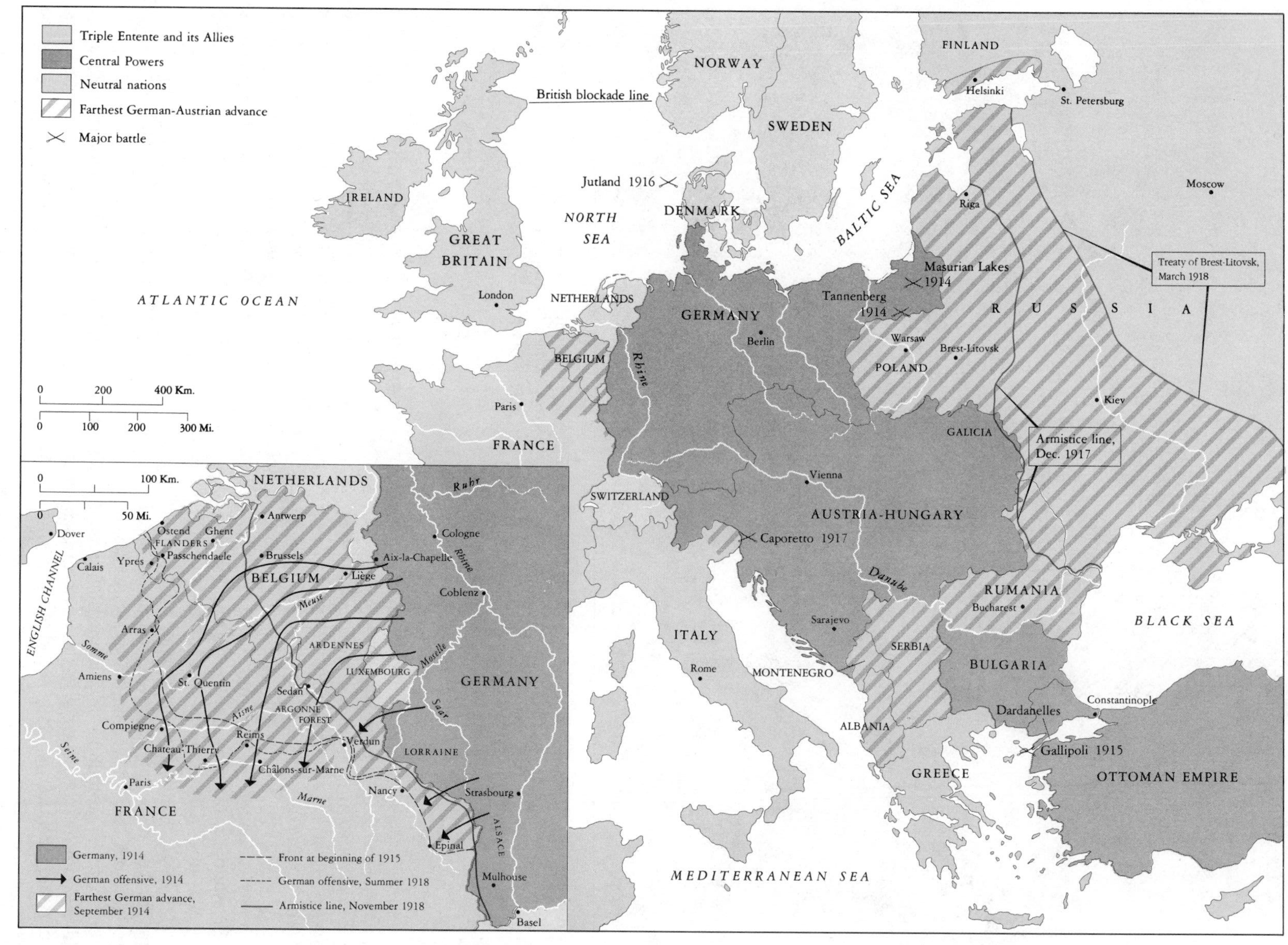
Triple Entente and its Allies
Central Powers
Neutral nations
Farthest German-Austrian advance
Major battle
British blockade line
0 200 400 Km.
0 100 200 300 Mi.
ATLANTIC OCEAN
IRELAND
GREAT BRITAIN
London
NORTH SEA
Jutland 1916
NORWAY
SWEDEN
FINLAND
Helsinki
St. Petersburg
Moscow
DENMARK
BALTIC SEA
Riga
Masurian Lakes 1914
Tannenberg 1914
Treaty of Brest-Litovsk, March 1918
RUSSIA
NETHERLANDS
BELGIUM
Paris
FRANCE
GERMANY
Berlin
Warsaw
Brest-Litovsk
POLAND
Kiev
Rhine
GALICIA
Armistice line, Dec. 1917
SWITZERLAND
Vienna
AUSTRIA-HUNGARY
Caporetto 1917
Danube
RUMANIA
Bucharest
BLACK SEA
ITALY
Rome
Sarajevo
MONTENEGRO
SERBIA
BULGARIA
ALBANIA
Constantinople
Dardanelles
Gallipoli 1915
GREECE
OTTOMAN EMPIRE
MEDITERRANEAN SEA
0 100 Km.
0 50 Mi.
NETHERLANDS
Dover
ENGLISH CHANNEL
Calais
Ostend
Ghent
FLANDERS
Ypres
Passchendaele
Antwerp
Brussels
BELGIUM
Liège
Aix-la-Chapelle
Cologne
Ruhr
Rhine
Coblenz
Meuse
Arras
Somme
Amiens
ARDENNES
LUXEMBOURG
Moselle
St. Quentin
Sedan
ARGONNE FOREST
GERMANY
Saar
Compiegne
Aisne
Reims
Verdun
Seine
Chateau-Thierry
Châlons-sur-Marne
LORRAINE
Paris
Marne
Nancy
Strasbourg
FRANCE
Epinal
ALSACE
Mulhouse
Basel
Germany, 1914
German offensive, 1914
Farthest German advance, September 1914
Front at beginning of 1915
German offensive, Summer 1918
Armistice line, November 1918

Map 27.3 The First World War in Europe The trench war on the western front was concentrated in Belgium and northern France, while the war in the east encompassed an enormous territory.

into eastern Germany. Very badly damaged by the Germans under Generals Paul von Hindenburg and Erich Ludendorff at the battles of Tannenberg and the Masurian Lakes in August and September 1914, Russia never threatened Germany again. On the Austrian front, enormous armies seesawed back and forth, suffering enormous losses. Austro-Hungarian armies were repulsed twice by little Serbia in bitter fighting. But with the help of German forces, they reversed the Russian advances of 1914 and forced the Russians to retreat deep into their own territory in the eastern campaign of 1915. A staggering 2.5 million Russians were killed, wounded, or taken prisoner that year.

These changing tides of victory and defeat brought neutral countries into the war (see Map 27.3). Italy, a member of the Triple Alliance since 1882, had declared its neutrality in 1914 on the grounds that Austria had launched a war of aggression. Then, in May 1915, Italy joined the Triple Entente of Great Britain, France, and Russia in return for promises of Austrian territory. Bulgaria allied with Austria and Germany, now known as the Central Powers, in September 1915 in order to settle old scores with Serbia.

The entry of Italy and Bulgaria in 1915 was part of a general widening of the war. The Balkans, with the exception of Greece, came to be occupied by the Central Powers, and British forces were badly defeated in 1915 trying to take the Dardanelles from Turkey, Germany's ally. More successful was the entente's attempt to incite Arab nationalists against their Turkish overlords. An enigmatic British colonel, soon known to millions as Lawrence of Arabia, aroused the Arab princes to revolt in early 1917. In 1918 British armies from Egypt smashed the Ottoman Empire once and for all. In their Middle East campaign, the British drew on forces from Australia, New Zealand, and India. Contrary to German hopes, the colonial subjects of the British (and French) did not revolt but loyally supported their foreign masters. Instead, the European war extended around the globe as Great Britain, France, and Japan seized Germany's colonies.

A crucial development in the expanding conflict came in April 1917, when the United States declared war on Germany. American intervention grew out of the war at sea, sympathy for the entente, and the increasing desperation of total war. At the beginning of the war, Britain and France had established a total naval blockade to strangle the Central Powers and prevent deliveries of food and raw materials from overseas. No neutral ship was permitted to sail to Germany with any cargo. The blockade annoyed Americans, but effective propaganda over German atrocities in occupied Belgium and lush profits from selling war supplies to Britain and France blunted American indignation.

Moreover, in early 1915 Germany launched a counter-blockade using the murderously effective submarine, a new weapon that violated traditional niceties of fair warning under international law. In May 1915, after sinking about ninety ships in the British war zone, a German submarine sank the British passenger liner *Lusitania,* which was also carrying arms and munitions. More than a thousand lives, among them 139 Americans, were lost. President Woodrow Wilson protested vigorously. Germany was forced to relax its submarine warfare for almost two years; the alternative was almost certain war with the United States.

Early in 1917, the German military command—confident that improved submarines could starve their island enemy, Britain, into submission before the United States could come to its rescue—resumed unrestricted submarine warfare. Like the invasion of Belgium, this was a reckless gamble. British shipping losses reached staggering proportions, though by late 1917 naval strategists came up with the inevitable effective response: the convoy system for safe transatlantic shipping. In the meantime, the embattled President Wilson had told a sympathetic Congress and people that the "German submarine warfare against commerce is a warfare against mankind." Thus the last uncommitted great nation, as fresh and enthusiastic as Europe had been in 1914, entered the world war in April 1917, almost three years after it began. Eventually the United States was to tip the balance in favor of Great Britain and France.

THE HOME FRONT

Before looking at the last year of the Great War, let us turn our attention to the people on the home front. The people behind the lines were tremendously involved in the titanic struggle. War's impact on them was no less massive than on the men crouched in the trenches.

Mobilizing for Total War

In August 1914 most people had greeted the outbreak of hostilities enthusiastically. In every country, the masses believed that their nation was in the right and defending itself from aggression. With the exception of a few extreme left-wingers, even socialists supported the war. Tough standby plans to imprison socialist leaders and break general strikes protesting the war proved quite unnecessary in 1914. In Germany, for example, the trade unions voted not to strike, and socialists in the parliament voted money for war credits in order to counter the threat of Russian despotism. A German socialist volunteered for the front, explaining to fellow members of the Reichstag that "to shed one's blood for the fatherland is not difficult: it is enveloped in romantic heroism."[5] Everywhere the patriotic support of the masses and the working class contributed to national unity and an energetic war effort.

By mid-October generals and politicians began to realize that more than patriotism would be needed to win the war, whose end was not in sight. Each country experienced a relentless, desperate demand for men and weapons. In France, for example, the generals found themselves needing 100,000 heavy artillery shells a day, as opposed to the 12,000 they had anticipated using. This enormous quantity had to come from a French steel industry that had lost three-fourths of its iron resources in the first days of the war, when Germany seized the mines of French Lorraine. Each belligerent quickly faced countless shortages, for prewar Europe had depended on foreign trade and a great international division of labor. In each country economic life and organization had to change and change fast to keep the war machine from sputtering to a stop. And change they did.

In each country a government of national unity began to plan and control economic and social life in order to wage "total war." Free-market capitalism was abandoned, at least "for the duration." Instead, government planning boards established priorities and decided what was to be produced and consumed. Rationing, price and wage controls, and even restrictions on workers' freedom of movement were imposed by government. Only through such regimentation could a country make the greatest possible military effort. Thus, though there were national variations, the great nations all moved toward planned economies commanded by the established political leadership.

This revolutionary development would burn deeply into the twentieth-century consciousness. The planned economy of total war released the tremendous energies first harnessed by the French under Robespierre during the French Revolution. Total war, however, was based on tremendously productive industrial economies not confined to a single nation. The result was an effective—and therefore destructive—war effort on all sides.

Moreover, the economy of total war blurred the old distinction between soldiers on the battlefield and civilians at home. As President Wilson told Americans shortly after the United States entered the war, there were no armies in the struggle in the traditional sense. Rather, "there are entire nations armed. Thus the men [and women] who remain to till the soil and man the factories are not less a part of the army than the men beneath the battle flags."[6] The war was a war of whole peoples and entire populations, and the loser would be the society that cracked first.

Finally, however awful the war was, the ability of governments to manage and control highly complicated economies strengthened the cause of socialism. With the First World War, socialism became for the first time a realistic economic blueprint rather than a utopian program.

Germany illustrates the general trend. It also went furthest in developing a planned economy to wage total war. As soon as war began, Walter Rathenau, the talented, foresighted Jewish industrialist in charge of Germany's largest electrical company, convinced the government to set up a War Raw Materials Board to ration and distribute raw materials. Under Rathenau's direction, every useful material from foreign oil to barnyard manure was inventoried and rationed. Moreover, the board launched successful attempts to produce substitutes, such as synthetic rubber and synthetic nitrates. Without the spectacular double achievement of discovering a way to "fix" nitrogen present in the air and then of producing synthetic nitrates in enormous quantity, the blockaded German war machine would have stalled in a matter of months.

Food was also rationed in accordance with physical need. Men and women doing hard manual work were given extra rations. During the last two years of the war, only children and expectant mothers received milk rations. Sometimes mistakes were made that would have been funny if they had not been tragic. In early 1915, German authorities calculated that greedy pigs were eating food that hungry people needed, and ordered a "hog massacre" only to find that there were too few pigs left to eat an abundant potato crop. Germany also failed to tax the war profits of private firms heavily enough. This contributed to massive deficit financing, inflation, the growth of a black market, and the eventual re-emergence of class conflict.

Following the terrible battles of Verdun and the Somme in 1916, the military leaders Hindenburg and Ludendorff became the real rulers of Germany, and they decreed the ultimate mobilization for total war. Germany, said Hindenburg, could win only "if all the treasures of our soil that agriculture and industry can produce are used exclusively for the conduct of War. . . . All other considerations must come second."[7] This goal, they believed, required that every German man, woman, and child be drafted into the service of the war. Thus, in December 1916, the military leaders rammed through the parliament the Auxiliary Service Law, which required all males between seventeen and sixty to work only at jobs considered critical to the war effort.

Waging Total War A British war plant strains to meet the insatiable demand for trench-smashing heavy artillery shells. Quite typically, many of these defense workers are women. *(By courtesy of the Trustees of the Imperial War Museum)*

Although women and children were not specifically mentioned, this forced-labor law was also aimed at them. Many women already worked in war factories, mines, and steel mills, where they labored like men at the heaviest and most dangerous jobs. With the passage of the Auxiliary Service Law, many more women followed. Children were organized by their teachers into garbage brigades to collect every scrap of useful materials: grease strained from dishwater, coffee grounds, waste paper, tin cans, metal door knockers, bottles, rags, hair, bones, and so forth, as well as acorns, chestnuts, pinecones, and rotting leaves. Potatoes gave way to turnips, and people averaged little more than a thousand calories a day. Thus in Germany total war led to the establishment of history's first "totalitarian" society, and war production increased while some people literally starved to death.

Great Britain mobilized for total war less rapidly and less completely than Germany, for it could import materials from its empire and from the United States. By 1915, however, a serious shortage of shells led to the establishment of a Ministry of Munitions under David Lloyd George. The ministry organized private industry to produce for the war, controlled profits, allocated labor, fixed wage rates, and settled labor disputes. By December 1916, when Lloyd George became prime minister, the British economy was largely planned and regulated. More than two hundred factories and 90 percent of all imports were bought and allocated directly by the state. Subsequently, even food was strictly rationed, while war production continued to soar. Great Britain had followed successfully in Germany's footsteps.

The Social Impact

The social impact of total war was no less profound than the economic, though again there were important national variations. The millions of men at the front and the insatiable needs of the military created a tremendous demand for workers. Jobs were available for everyone. This situation had seldom if ever been seen before 1914, when unemployment and poverty had been facts of urban life. The exceptional demand for labor brought about momentous changes.

One such change was greater power and prestige for labor unions. Having proved their loyalty in August 1914, labor unions became an indispensable partner of government and private industry in the planned war economy. Unions cooperated with war governments on work rules, wages, and production schedules in return for real participation in important decisions. This entry of labor leaders and unions into policy-making councils paralleled the entry of socialist leaders into the war governments.

The role of women changed dramatically. In every country, large numbers of women left home and domestic service to work in industry, transportation, and offices. By 1917 women formed fully 43 percent of the labor force in Russia. The number of women driving buses and streetcars increased tenfold in Great Britain. Moreover, women became highly visible—not only as munitions workers but as bank tellers, mail carriers, even policewomen.

At first, the male-dominated unions were hostile to women moving into new occupations, believing that their presence would lower wages and change work rules. But government pressure and the principle of equal pay for equal work (at least until the end of the war) overcame these objections. Women also served as nurses and doctors at the front. In general, the war greatly expanded the range of women's activities and changed attitudes toward them. As a direct result of their many-sided war effort, Britain, Germany, and Austria granted women the right to vote immediately after the war. Women also showed a growing spirit of independence during the war, as they started to bob their hair, shorten their skirts, and smoke in public.

War also promoted great social equality, blurring class distinctions and lessening the gap between rich and poor. This blurring was most apparent in Great Britain, where wartime hardship was never extreme. In fact, the bottom third of the population generally lived *better* than ever before, for the poorest gained most from the severe shortage of labor. The English writer Robert Roberts recalled how his parents' tiny grocery store in the slums of Manchester thrived as never before during the war, when people who had scrimped to buy bread and soup bones were able to afford fancy cakes and thick steaks. In 1924 a British government study revealed that the distribution of income had indeed shifted in favor of the poorest; only half as many families lived in severe poverty as in 1911, even though total production of goods had not increased. In continental countries greater equality was reflected in full employment, rationing according to physical needs, and a sharing of hardships.

Wartime Propaganda was skillful and effective. The poster on the left spurred men to volunteer bravely for military service before the draft was introduced in Britain in 1916. The grim warrior on the right calls on French men and women at home to unite as firmly as the soldiers at the front against defeatist plots in 1918. *(The Trustees of the Imperial War Museum)*

There, too, society became more uniform and more egalitarian, in spite of some war profiteering.

Finally, death itself had no respect for traditional social distinctions. It savagely decimated the young aristocratic officers who led the charge, and it fell heavily on the mass of drafted peasants and unskilled workers who followed. Yet death often spared the aristocrats of labor, the skilled workers and foremen. Their lives were too valuable to squander at the front, for they were needed to train and direct the newly recruited women and older unskilled men laboring valiantly in war plants at home.

Growing Political Tensions

During the first two years of war, most soldiers and civilians supported their governments. Even in Austria-Hungary—the most vulnerable of the belligerents, with its competing nationalities—loyalty to the state and monarchy remained astonishingly strong through 1916. Belief in a just cause, patriotic nationalism, the planned economy, and a sharing of burdens united peoples behind their various national leaders. Furthermore, each government did its best to control public opinion to bolster morale. Newspa-

The Easter Rebellion, 1916 Irish nationalists rose but were suppressed by overwhelming military force. Shelling by British gunboats devastated central Dublin, shown here. *(BBC Hulton/The Bettmann Archive)*

pers, letters, and public addresses were rigorously censored. Good news was overstated; bad news was repressed or distorted.

Each government used both crude and subtle propaganda to maintain popular support. German propaganda hysterically pictured black soldiers from France's African empire raping German women, while German atrocities in Belgium and elsewhere were ceaselessly recounted and exaggerated by the French and British. Patriotic posters and slogans, slanted news and biased editorials inflamed national hatreds and helped sustain superhuman efforts.

By the spring of 1916, however, people were beginning to crack under the strain of total war. In April 1916, Irish nationalists in Dublin tried to take advantage of this situation and rose up against British rule in their great Easter Rebellion. A week of bitter fighting passed before the rebels were crushed and their leaders executed. Strikes and protest marches over inadequate food began to flare up on every home front. Soldiers' morale began to decline. Italian troops mutinied. Numerous French units refused to fight after General Nivelle's disastrous offensive of May 1917. Only tough military justice and a tacit agreement with his troops that there would be no more grand offensives enabled the new general in chief, Henri-Philippe Pétain, to restore order. A rising tide of war-weariness and defeatism also swept France's civilian population before Georges Clemenceau emerged as a ruthless and effective wartime leader in November 1917. Clemenceau established a virtual dictatorship, pouncing on strikers and jailing without trial journalists and politicians who dared to suggest a compromise peace with Germany.

The strains were worse for the Central Powers. In October 1916, the chief minister of Austria was assassinated by a young socialist crying, "Down with Absolutism! We want peace!"[8] The following month, when the feeble old Emperor Francis Joseph died sixty-eight years after his mother Sophia had pushed him onto the throne in 1848 (page 756), a symbol of unity disappeared. In spite of absolute censorship, political dissatisfaction and conflicts among nationalities grew. In April 1917, Austria's chief minister summed up the situation in the gloomiest possible terms. The country and army were exhausted. Another winter of war would bring revolution and disintegration. "If the monarchs of the Central Powers cannot make peace in the coming months," he wrote, "it will be made for them by their peoples."[9] Both

The Fruits of War This photo shows how, in desperation, the people of Vienna decimated the city's beloved forest to get a little firewood to heat their homes. Economic collapse weighed heavily on all classes. *(Bildarchiv d. Osterreichische Nationalbibliothek)*

Czech and Yugoslav leaders demanded autonomous democratic states for their peoples. The allied blockade kept tightening; people were starving.

The strain of total war and the Auxiliary Service Law was also evident in Germany. In the winter of 1916 to 1917, Germany's military position appeared increasingly desperate. Stalemates and losses in the west were matched by temporary Russian advances in the east: hence the military's insistence on the all-or-nothing gamble of unrestricted submarine warfare when the entente refused in December 1916 to consider peace on terms that were favorable to the Central Powers.

Also, the national political unity of the first two years of war was collapsing as the social conflict of prewar Germany re-emerged. A growing minority of socialists in the parliament began to vote against war credits, calling for a compromise "peace without annexations or reparations." In July 1917, a coalition of socialists and Catholics passed a resolution in the parliament to that effect. Such a peace was unthinkable for conservatives and military leaders. So also was the surge in revolutionary agitation and strikes by war-weary workers that occurred in early 1917. When the bread ration was further reduced in April, more than 200,000 workers struck and demonstrated for a week in Berlin, returning to work only under the threat of prison and military discipline. Thus militaristic Germany, like its ally Austria-Hungary (and its enemy France), was beginning to crack in 1917. Yet its was Russia that collapsed first and saved the Central Powers, for a time.

THE RUSSIAN REVOLUTION

The Russian Revolution of 1917 was one of modern history's most momentous events. Directly related to the growing tensions of World War One, its significance went far beyond the wartime agonies of a single European nation. The Russian Revolution opened a new era. For some it was Marx's socialist vision come true; for others, it was the triumph of dictatorship. To all, it presented a radically new prototype of state and society.

THE FALL OF IMPERIAL RUSSIA

Like its allies and its enemies, Russia embraced war with patriotic enthusiasm in 1914. At the Winter Palace, while throngs of people knelt and sang "God Save the Tsar," Tsar Nicholas II (1894–1917) repeated the oath Alexander I had made in 1812 and vowed never to make peace as long as the enemy stood on Russian soil. Russia's lower house, the Duma, voted war credits. Conservatives anticipated expansion in the Balkans, while liberals and most socialists believed alliance with Britain and France would bring democratic reforms. For a moment, Russia was united.

Soon, however, the strains of war began to take their toll. The unprecedented artillery barrages used up Russia's supplies of shells and ammunition, and better-equipped German armies inflicted terrible losses. For a time in 1915, substantial members of Russian soldiers were sent to the front without rifles; they were told to find their arms among the dead. There were 2 million Russian casualties in 1915 alone. Morale declined among soldiers and civilians. Nonetheless, Russia's battered peasant army did not collapse but continued to fight courageously until early 1917.

Under the shock of defeat, Russia moved toward full mobilization on the home front. The Duma and organs of local government took the lead, setting up special committees to coordinate defense, industry, transportation, and agriculture. These efforts improved the military situation, and Russian factories produced more than twice as many shells in 1916 as in 1915. Yet there were many failures, and Russia mobilized less effectively for total war than the other warring nations.

The great problem was leadership. Under the constitution resulting from the revolution of 1905 (pages 812–813), the tsar had retained complete control over the bureaucracy and the army. Legislation proposed by the Duma, which was weighted in favor of the wealthy and conservative classes, was subject to the tsar's veto. Moreover, Nicholas II fervently wished to maintain the sacred inheritance of supreme royal power, which with the Orthodox church was for him the key to Russia's greatness. A kindly, slightly stupid man, of whom a friend said he "would have been an ideal country gentleman, devoting his life to wife and children, his farms and his sport," Nicholas failed to form a close partnership with his citizens in order to fight the war more effectively. He relied instead on the old bureaucratic apparatus, distrusting the moderate Duma, rejecting popular involvement, and resisting calls to share power.

As a result the Duma, the educated middle classes, and the masses became increasingly critical of the tsar's leadership. Following Nicholas's belated dismissal of the incompetent minister of war, demands for more democratic and responsive government exploded in the Duma in the summer of 1915. "From the beginning of the war," declared one young liberal, "public opinion has understood the character and magnitude of the struggle; it has understood that short of organizing the whole country for war, victory is impossible. But the Government has rejected every offer of help with disdain."[10] In September, parties ranging from conservative to moderate socialist formed the Progressive Bloc, which called for a completely new government responsible to the Duma instead of the tsar. In answer, Nicholas temporarily adjourned the Duma and announced that he was traveling to the front in order to lead and rally Russia's armies.

His departure was a fatal turning point. With the tsar in the field with the troops, control of the government was taken over by the hysterical empress, Tsarina Alexandra, and a debauched adventurer, the monk Rasputin. A minor German princess and granddaughter of England's Queen Victoria, Nicholas's wife was a devoted mother with a sick child, a strong-willed woman with a hatred of parliaments. Having constantly urged her husband to rule absolutely, Alexandra tried to do so herself in his absence. She seated and unseated the top ministers. Her most trusted adviser was "our Friend Grigori," an uneducated Siberian preacher who was appropriately nicknamed Rasputin—the "Degenerate."

Rasputin began his career with a sect noted for mixing sexual orgies with religious ecstasies, and his influence rested on mysterious healing powers. Alexis, Alexandra's fifth child and heir to the throne, suffered from a rare disease, hemophilia. The tiniest cut meant uncontrollable bleeding, terrible pain, and possible death. Medical science could do nothing. Only Rasputin could miraculously stop the bleeding, perhaps through hypnosis. The empress's faith in Rasputin was limitless. "Believe more in our Friend," she wrote her husband in 1916. "He lives for you and Russia." In this atmosphere of unreality, the government slid steadily toward revolution.

In a desperate attempt to right the situation and end unfounded rumors that Rasputin was the empress's lover, three members of the high aristocracy murdered Rasputin in December 1916. The empress went into semipermanent shock, her mind haunted by the dead man's prophecy: "If I die or you desert me, in six months you will lose your son and your throne."[11] Food shortages in the cities worsened, morale declined. On March 8, women in Petrograd (formerly St. Petersburg) calling for bread started riots, which spontaneously spread to the factories and throughout the city. From the front the tsar ordered the troops to restore order, but discipline broke down and the soldiers joined the revolutionary crowd. The Duma responded by declaring a provisional government on March 12, 1917. Three days later, Nicholas abdicated without protest.

Family Portrait With husband Nicholas II standing behind, the beautiful but tense Alexandra shows one of her daughters, who could not inherit the Russian throne, to her grandmother, Queen Victoria of England, and Victoria's son, the future Edward VII. European monarchs were closely related by blood and breeding before 1914. *(Nicholas A. de Basily Collection, Hoover Institution)*

The Provisional Government

The March revolution was the result of an unplanned uprising of hungry, angry people in the capital, but it was joyfully accepted throughout the country. The patriotic upper and middle classes rejoiced at the prospect of a more determined and effective war effort, while workers happily anticipated better wages and more food. All classes and political parties called for liberty and democracy. They were not disappointed. As Lenin said, Russia became the freest country in the world. After generations of arbitrary authoritarianism, the provisional government quickly established equality before the law; freedom of religion, speech, and assembly; the right of unions to organize and strike; and the rest of the classic liberal program.

Yet both the liberal and moderate socialist leaders of the provisional government rejected social revolution. The reorganized government formed in May 1917, which included the fiery agrarian socialist Alexander Kerensky, refused to confiscate large landholdings and give them to peasants, fearing that such drastic action in the countryside would only complete the disintegration of Russia's peasant army. For the patriotic Kerensky, as for other moderate socialists, the continuation of war was still the all-important national duty. There would be plenty of time for land reform later, and thus all the government's efforts were directed toward a last offensive in July. Human suffering and war-weariness grew, sapping the limited strength of the provisional government.

From its first day, the provisional government had to share power with a formidable rival—the Petrograd Soviet (or council) of Workers' and Soldiers' Deputies. Modeled on the revolutionary soviets of 1905, the Petrograd Soviet was a huge, fluctuating mass meeting of two to three thousand workers, soldiers, and socialist intellectuals. Seeing itself as a true grass-roots revolutionary democracy, this counter- or half-government suspiciously watched the provisional government and issued its own radical orders, further weakening the provisional government. The most famous of these orders was Army Order No. 1, issued to all Russian military forces as the provisional government was forming.

Order No. 1 stripped officers of their authority and placed power in the hands of elected committees of common soldiers. Designed primarily to protect the revolution from some counter-revolutionary Bonaparte on horseback, Army Order No. 1 instead led to a total collapse of army discipline. Many an officer was hanged for his sins. Meanwhile, following the foolhardy summer offensive, masses of peasant soldiers began "voting with their feet," to use Lenin's graphic phrase. That is, they began returning to their villages to help their families get a share of the land, land that peasants were simply seizing as they settled old scores in a great agrarian upheaval. All across the country, liberty was turning into anarchy in the summer of 1917. It was an unparalleled opportunity for the most radical and most talented of Russia's many socialist leaders, Vladimir Ilyich Lenin (1870–1924).

Lenin and the Bolshevik Revolution

From his youth, Lenin's whole life was dedicated to the cause of revolution. Born into the middle class, the seventeen-year-old Lenin became an implacable enemy of imperial Russia when his older brother was executed for plotting to kill the tsar in 1887. As a law student he began searching for a revolutionary faith. He found it in Marxian socialism, which began to win converts among radical intellectuals as industrialization surged forward in Russia in the 1890s. Exiled to Siberia for three years because of socialist agitation, Lenin studied Marxist doctrines with religious intensity. After his release, the young priest of socialism joined fellow believers in western Europe. There he lived for seventeen years and developed his own revolutionary interpretations of the body of Marxian thought.

Three interrelated ideas were central for Lenin. First, turning to the early fire-breathing Marx of 1848 and the *Communist Manifesto* for inspiration, Lenin stressed that capitalism could be destroyed only by violent revolution. He tirelessly denounced all revisionist theories of a peaceful evolution to socialism as betraying Marx's message of unending class conflict. Lenin's second, more original, idea was that, under certain conditions, a socialist revolution was possible even in a relatively backward country like Russia. Though capitalism was not fully developed there and the industrial working class was small, the peasants were poor and thus potential revolutionaries.

Lenin believed that at a given moment revolution was determined more by human leadership than by vast historical laws. Thus Lenin's third basic idea: the necessity of a highly disciplined workers' party, strictly controlled by a dedicated elite of intellectuals and full-time revolutionaries like Lenin himself. Unlike ordinary workers and trade union officials, this elite would never be seduced by short-term gains. It would not stop until revolution brought it to power.

Lenin's theories and methods did not go unchallenged by other Russian Marxists. At the meetings of the Russian Social Democratic Labor party in London in 1903, matters came to a head. Lenin demanded a small, disciplined, elitist party, while his opponents wanted a more democratic party with mass membership. The Russian party of Marxian socialism promptly split into two rival factions. Lenin's camp was called *Bolsheviks,* or "Majority group"; his opponents were *Mensheviks,* or "Minority group." Lenin's majority did not last, but Lenin did not care. He kept the fine-sounding name Bolshevik and developed the party he wanted: tough, disciplined, revolutionary.

Unlike most socialists, Lenin did not rally round the national flag in 1914. Observing events from neutral Switzerland, he saw the war as a product of imperialistic rivalries and a marvelous opportunity for class war and socialist upheaval. The March revolution was, Lenin felt, a step in that direction. Since propaganda and internal subversion were accepted weapons of total war, the German government graciously provided the impatient Lenin, his wife, and about twenty trusted colleagues with safe passage across Germany and back into Russia in April 1917. The Germans hoped that Lenin would undermine the sagging war effort of the world's freest society. They were not disappointed.

Mass Demonstrations in Petrograd in June 1917 showed a surge of working-class support for the Bolsheviks. In this photo a few banners of the Mensheviks and other moderate socialists are drowned in a sea of Bolshevik slogans. *(Sovfoto)*

Arriving triumphantly at Petrograd's Finland Station on April 3, Lenin attacked at once. To the great astonishment of the local Bolsheviks, he rejected all cooperation with the "bourgeois" provisional government of the liberals and moderate socialists. His slogans were radical in the extreme: "All power to the Soviets." "All land to the peasants." "Stop the war now." Never a slave to Marxist determinism, the brilliant but not unduly intellectual Lenin was a superb tactician. The moment was now.

Yet Lenin almost overplayed his hand. An attempt by the Bolsheviks to seize power in July collapsed, and Lenin fled and went into hiding. He was charged with being a German agent, and indeed he and the Bolsheviks were getting money from Germany.[12] But no matter. Intrigue between Kerensky, who became prime minister in July, and his commander in chief General Lavr Kornilov, a popular war hero "with the heart of a lion and the brains of a sheep," resulted in Kornilov's leading a feeble attack against the provisional government in September. In the face of this rightist "counter-revolutionary" threat, the Bolsheviks were rearmed and redeemed. Kornilov's forces disintegrated, but Kerensky lost all credit with the army, the only force that might have saved him and democratic government in Russia.

The Russian Revolution

1914	Russia enthusiastically enters the First World War
1915	Two million Russian casualties
	Progressive Bloc calls for a new government responsible to the Duma rather than to the tsar
	Tsar Nicholas adjourns the Duma and departs for the front; control of the government falls to Alexandra and Rasputin
December 1916	Murder of Rasputin
March 8, 1917	Bread riots in Petrograd (St. Petersburg)
March 12, 1917	Duma declares a provisional government
March 15, 1917	Tsar Nicholas abdicates without protest
April 3, 1917	Lenin returns from exile and denounces the provisional government
May 1917	Reorganized provisional government, including Kerensky, continues the war
	Petrograd Soviet issues Army Order no. 1, granting military power to committees of common soldiers
Summer 1917	Agrarian upheavals: peasants seize estates, peasant soldiers desert the army to participate
October 1917	Bolsheviks gain a majority in the Petrograd Soviet
November 6, 1917	Bolsheviks seize power; Lenin heads the new "provisional workers' and peasants' government"
November 1917	Lenin ratifies peasant seizure of land and worker control of factories; all banks nationalized
January 1918	Lenin permanently disbands the Constituent Assembly
February 1918	Lenin convinces the Bolshevik Central Committee to accept a humiliating peace with Germany in order to pursue the revolution
March 1918	Treaty of Brest-Litovsk: Russia loses one-third of its population
	Trotsky as war commissar begins to rebuild the Russian army
	Government moves from Petrograd to Moscow
1918–1920	Great Civil War
Summer 1918	Eighteen competing regional governments; White armies oppose the Bolshevik revolution
1919	White armies on the offensive but divided politically; they receive little benefit from Allied intervention
1920	Lenin and Red armies victorious, retaking Belorussia and the Ukraine

Vladimir Lenin Dramatically displaying both his burning determination and his skill as a revolutionary orator, Lenin addresses the victorious May Day celebration of 1918 in Moscow's Red Square. *(Culver Pictures)*

Trotsky and the Seizure of Power

Throughout the summer, the Bolsheviks had appealed very effectively to the workers and soldiers of Petrograd, markedly increasing their popular support. Party membership had soared from 50,000 to 240,000 and in October the Bolsheviks gained a fragile majority in the Petrograd Soviet. Moreover, Lenin had found a strong right arm—Leon Trotsky, the second most important person in the Russian Revolution.

A spellbinding revolutionary orator and independent radical Marxist, Trotsky (1877–1940) supported Lenin wholeheartedly in 1917. It was he who brilliantly executed the Bolshevik seizure of power. Painting a vivid but untruthful picture of German and counter-revolutionary plots, Trotsky first convinced the Petrograd Soviet to form a special Military-Revolutionary Committee in October and make him its leader. Military power in the capital passed into Bolshevik hands. Trotsky's second master stroke was to insist that the Bolsheviks reduce opposition to their coup by taking power in the name, not of the Bolsheviks, but of the more popular and democratic soviets, which were meeting in Petrograd from all over Russia in early November. On the night of November 6, militants from Trotsky's committee joined with trusty Bolshevik soldiers to seize government buildings and pounce on members of the provisional government. Then on to the congress of soviets! There a Bolshevik majority—roughly 390 of 650 turbulent delegates—declared that all power had passed to the soviets and named Lenin head of the new government.

The Bolsheviks came to power for three key reasons. First, by late 1917 democracy had given way to anarchy: power was there for those who would take it. Second, in Lenin and Trotsky the Bolsheviks had an utterly determined and truly superior leadership, which both the tsarist government and the provisional government lacked. Third, in 1917 the Bolsheviks succeeded in appealing to many soldiers and urban workers, people who were exhausted by war and eager for socialism. With time, many workers would become bitterly disappointed, but for the moment they had good reason to believe they had won what they wanted.

Dictatorship and Civil War

History is full of short-lived coups and unsuccessful revolutions. The truly monumental accomplishment of Lenin, Trotsky, and the rest of the Bolsheviks was not taking power but keeping it. In the next four years, the Bolsheviks went on to conquer the chaos they had helped to create, and they began to build their kind of dictatorial socialist society. The conspirators became conquerors. How was this done?

Lenin had the genius to profit from developments over which he and the Bolsheviks had no control. Since summer, a peasant revolution had been sweeping across Russia, as the tillers of the soil invaded and divided among themselves the great and not-so-great estates of the landlords and the church. Peasant seizure of the land—a Russian 1789—was not very Marxist, but it was quite unstoppable in 1917. Thus Lenin's first law, which supposedly gave land to the peasants, actually merely approved what peasants were already doing. Urban workers' great demand in November was direct control of individual factories by local workers' committees. This, too, Lenin ratified with a decree in November.

Unlike many of his colleagues, Lenin acknowledged that Russia had lost the war with Germany, that the Russian army had ceased to exist, and that the only realistic goal was peace at any price. The price was very high. Germany demanded in December 1917 that the Soviet government give up all its western territories. These areas were inhabited by Poles, Finns, Lithuanians, and other non-Russians—all those peoples who had been conquered by the tsars over three centuries and put into the "prison-house of nationalities," as Lenin had earlier called the Russian Empire.

At first, Lenin's fellow Bolsheviks would not accept such great territorial losses. But when German armies resumed their unopposed march into Russia in February 1918, Lenin had his way in a very close vote in the Central Committee of the party. "Not even his greatest enemy can deny that at this moment Lenin towered like a giant over his Bolshevik colleagues."[13] A third of old Russia's population was sliced away by the German meat ax in the Treaty of Brest-Litovsk in March 1918. With peace, Lenin had escaped the certain disaster of continued war and could uncompromisingly pursue his goal of absolute political power for the Bolsheviks—now renamed Communists—within Russia.

In November 1917, the Bolsheviks had cleverly proclaimed their regime only a "provisional workers' and peasants' government," promising that a freely elected Constituent Assembly would draw up a new constitution. But the freest elections in Russia's history—both before and after 1917—produced a stunning setback for the Bolsheviks, who won less than one-fourth of the elected delegates. The Socialist Revolutionaries—the peasants' party—had a clear majority. The Constituent Assembly met for only one day, on January 18, 1918. It was then permanently disbanded by Bolshevik soldiers acting under Lenin's orders. Thus, even before the peace with Germany, Lenin was forming a one-party government.

The destruction of the democratically elected Constituent Assembly helped feed the flames of civil war. People who had risen up for self-rule in November saw that once again they were getting dictatorship from the capital. For the next three years, "Long live the [democratic] soviets; down with the Bolsheviks" was to be a popular slogan. The officers of the old army took the lead in organizing the so-called White opposition to the Bolsheviks in southern Russia and the Ukraine, in Siberia, and to the west of Petrograd. The Whites came from many social groups and were united only by their hatred of the Bolsheviks—the Reds.

By the summer of 1918, fully eighteen self-proclaimed regional governments—several of which represented minority nationalities—competed with Lenin's Bolsheviks in Moscow. By the end of the year, White armies were on the attack. In October 1919, it appeared they might triumph, as they closed in on Lenin's government from three sides. Yet they did not. By the spring of 1920, the White armies had been almost completely defeated, and the Bolshevik Red Army had retaken Belorussia and the Ukraine. The following year, the Communists also reconquered the independent nationalist governments of the Caucasus. The civil war was over; Lenin had won.

Lenin and the Bolsheviks won for several reasons. Strategically, they controlled the center, while the Whites were always on the fringes and disunited. Moreover, the poorly defined political program of the Whites was vaguely conservative, and it did not unite all the foes of the Bolsheviks under a progressive, democratic banner. For example, the most gifted of the White generals, the nationalistic General Anton Denikin, refused to call for a democratic republic and a federation of nationalities, although he knew that doing so would help his cause. Most important, the Communists quickly developed a better army, an army for which the divided Whites were no match.

Once again, Trotsky's leadership was decisive. The Bolshevik's had preached democracy in the army and elected officers in 1917. But beginning in March 1918, Trotsky as war commissar re-established the draft and the most drastic discipline for the newly formed Red Army. Soldiers deserting or disobeying an order were summarily shot. Moreover, Trotsky made effective use of former tsarist army officers, who were actively recruited and given unprecedented powers of discipline over their troops. In short, Trotsky formed a disciplined and effective fighting force.

The Bolsheviks also mobilized the home front. Establishing "war communism"—the application of the total war concept to a civil conflict—they seized grain from peasants, introduced rationing, nationalized all banks and industry, and required everyone to work. Although these measures contributed to a breakdown of normal economic activity, they also served to maintain labor discipline and to keep the Red Army supplied.

"Revolutionary terror" also contributed to the Communist victory. The old tsarist secret police was re-established as the Cheka, which hunted down and executed thousands of real or supposed foes, like the tsar's family and other "class enemies." At one point, shortly after the government moved from Petrograd to Moscow in March 1918, a circus clown in Moscow was making fun of the Bolsheviks to an appreciative audience. Chekists in the crowd quickly pulled out their guns and shot several laughing people. Moreover, people were shot or threatened with being shot for minor nonpolitical failures. The terror caused by the secret police became a tool of the government. The Cheka sowed fear, and fear silenced opposition.

Finally, foreign military intervention in the civil war ended up helping the Communists. After Lenin made peace with Germany, the Allies (the Americans, British, and Japanese) sent troops to Archangel and Vladivostok to prevent war materiel they had sent the provisional government from being captured by the Germans. After the Soviet government nationalized all foreign-owned factories without compensation and refused to pay all of Russia's foreign debts, Western governments and particularly France began to support White armies. Yet these efforts were small and halfhearted. In 1919 Western peoples were sick of war, and few Western politicians believed in a military crusade against the Bolsheviks. Thus Allied intervention in the civil war did not aid the Whites effectively, though it did permit the Communists to appeal to the patriotic nationalism of ethnic Russians, which was particularly strong among former tsarist army officers. Allied intervention was both too little and too much.

The Russian Revolution and the Bolshevik triumph was, then, one of the reasons why the First World War was such a great turning point in modern history. A radically new government, based on socialism and one-party dictatorship, came to power in a great European state, maintained power, and eagerly encouraged worldwide revolution. Although halfheartedly constitutional monarchy in Russia was undoubtedly headed for some kind of political crisis before 1914, it is hard to imagine the triumph of the most radical proponents of change and reform except in a situation of total collapse. That was precisely what happened to Russia in the First World War.

THE PEACE SETTLEMENT

In 1918 the guns of world war finally fell silent. After winning great concessions from Lenin in the Treaty of Brest-Litovsk in March 1918, the Germans launched their last major attack against France. Yet this offensive failed like those before it. With breathtaking rapidity, the United States, Great Britain, and France decisively defeated Germany militarily. Then, as civil war spread in Russia and as chaos engulfed much of eastern Europe, the victorious Western Allies came together in Paris to establish a lasting peace.

The Fall of Monarchy Entitled simply "November 1918," this eloquent drawing from a popular German magazine shows the crowns of Europe scattered like driftwood after the final wave of war and revolution. *(Photo: Caroline Buckler)*

Expectations were high; optimism was almost unlimited. The Allies labored intensively and soon worked out terms for peace with Germany and for the creation of the peace-keeping League of Nations. Nevertheless, the hopes of peoples and politicians were soon disappointed, for the peace settlement of 1919 turned out to be a terrible failure. Rather than creating conditions for peace, it sowed the seeds of another war. Surely this was the ultimate tragedy of the Great War, a war that directly and indirectly cost $332 billion and left 10 million dead and another 20 million wounded. How did it happen? Why was the peace settlement unsuccessful?

The End of the War

In early 1917, the strain of total war was showing everywhere. After the Russian Revolution in March, there were major strikes in Germany. In July a coalition of moderates passed a "peace resolution" in the German parliament, calling for peace without territorial annexations. To counter this moderation born of war-weariness, the German military established a virtual dictatorship and aggressively exploited the collapse of Russian armies after the Bolshevik Revolution. Victory in the east having quieted German moderates, General Ludendorff and company fell on France once more in the great spring offensive of 1918. For a time, German armies pushed forward, coming within thirty-five miles of Paris. But Ludendorff's exhausted, overextended forces never broke through. They were decisively stopped in July at the second battle of the Marne, where 140,000 fresh American soldiers saw action. Adding 2 million men in arms to the war effort by August, the late but massive American intervention decisively tipped the scales in favor of Allied victory.

By September, British, French, and American armies were advancing steadily on all fronts, and a panicky General Ludendorff realized that Germany had lost the war. Yet he insolently insisted that moderate politicians shoulder the shame of defeat, and on October 4, the emperor formed a new, more liberal German government to sue for peace. As negotiations over an armistice dragged on, an angry and frustrated German people finally rose up. On November 3, sailors in Kiel mutinied, and throughout northern Germany, soldiers and workers began to establish revolutionary councils on the Russian soviet model. The same day, Austria-Hungary surrendered to the Allies and began breaking apart. Revolution broke out in Germany, and masses of workers demonstrated for peace in Berlin. With army discipline collapsing, the emperor was forced to abdicate and fled to Holland. Socialist leaders in Berlin proclaimed a German republic on November 9 and simultaneously agreed to tough Allied terms of surrender. The armistice went into effect November 11, 1918. The war was over.

Revolution in Germany

Military defeat brought political revolution to Germany and Austria-Hungary, as it had to Russia. In Austria-Hungary, the revolution was primarily nationalistic and republican in character. Having started the war to preserve an antinationalist dynastic state, the Habsburg Empire had perished in the attempt. In its place, independent Austrian, Hungarian, and Czechoslovakian republics were pro-

Rosa Luxemburg Shown here addressing a party congress, Rosa Luxemburg played a leading role in the socialist movement until her death in 1919. A brilliant theorist, she scorned moderate socialism and stressed the revolutionary character of Marxism. *(Süddeutscher Verlag)*

claimed, while a greatly expanded Serbian monarchy united the south Slavs and took the name of Yugoslavia. The prospect of firmly establishing the new national states overrode class considerations for most people in east central Europe.

The German Revolution of November 1918 resembled the Russian Revolution of March 1917. In both cases, a genuine popular uprising toppled an authoritarian monarchy and established a liberal provisional republic. In both countries, liberals and moderate socialists took control of the central government, while workers' and soldiers' councils formed a counter-government. In Germany, however, the moderate socialists won and the Lenin-like radical revolutionaries in the councils lost. In communist terms, the liberal, republican revolution in Germany in 1918 was only half a revolution: a bourgeois political revolution without a communist second installment. It was Russia without Lenin's Bolshevik triumph.

There were several reasons for the German outcome. The great majority of Marxian socialist leaders in the Social Democratic party were, as before the war, really pink and not red. They wanted to establish real political democracy and civil liberties, and they favored the gradual elimination of capitalism. They were also German nationalists, appalled by the prospect of civil war and revolutionary terror. Moreover, there was much less popular support among workers and soldiers for the extreme radicals than in Russia. Nor did the German peasantry, which already had most of the land, at least in western Germany, provide the elemental force that has driven all great modern revolutions, from the French to the Chinese.

Of crucial importance also was the fact that the moderate German Social Democrats, unlike Kerensky and company, accepted defeat and ended the war the day they took power. This act ended the decline in morale among soldiers and prevented the

The Treaty of Versailles was signed in the magnificent Hall of Mirrors, part of the vast palace that Louis XIV had built to celebrate his glory. The Allies did not allow Germany to participate in the negotiation of the treaty. *(National Archives, Washington)*

regular army with its conservative officer corps from disintegrating. When radicals, headed by Karl Liebknecht and Rosa Luxemburg and their supporters in the councils, tried to seize control of the government in Berlin in January, the moderate socialists called on the army to crush the uprising. Liebknecht and Luxemburg were arrested and then brutally murdered by army leaders, which caused the radicals in the Social Democratic party to break away in anger and form a pro-Lenin German Communist party shortly thereafter. Finally, even if the moderate socialists had followed Liebknecht and Luxemburg on the Leninist path, it is very unlikely they would have succeeded. Civil war in Germany would certainly have followed, and the Allies, who were already occupying western Germany according to the terms of the armistice, would have marched on to Berlin and ruled Germany directly. Historians have often been unduly hard on Germany's moderate socialists.

The Treaty of Versailles

The peace conference opened in Paris in January 1919 with seventy delegates representing twenty-seven victorious nations. There were great expectations. A young British diplomat later wrote that the victors "were convinced that they would never commit the blunders and iniquities of the Congress of Vienna [of 1815]." Then the "misguided, reactionary, pathetic aristocrats" had cynically shuffled populations; now "we believed in nationalism, we believed in the self-determination of peoples." Indeed, "we were journeying to Paris . . . to found a new order in Europe. We were preparing not Peace only, but Eternal Peace."[14] The general optimism and idealism had been greatly strengthened by President Wilson's January 1918 peace proposal, the Fourteen Points, which stressed national self-determination and the rights of small countries.

The real powers at the conference were the United States, Great Britain, and France, for Germany was not allowed to participate, and Russia was locked in civil war and did not attend. Italy was considered part of the Big Four, but its role was quite secondary. Almost immediately the three great allies began to quarrel. President Wilson, who was wildly cheered by European crowds as the spokesman for a new idealistic and democratic international cooperation, was almost obsessed with creating a League of Nations. Wilson insisted that this question come first, for he passionately believed that only a permanent international organization could protect member states from aggression and avert future wars. Wilson had his way, although Lloyd George of Great Britain and especially Clemenceau of France were unenthusiastic. They were primarily concerned with punishing Germany.

Playing on British nationalism, Lloyd George had already won a smashing electoral victory in December on the popular platform of making Germany pay for the war. "We shall," he promised, "squeeze the orange until the pips squeak." Personally inclined to make a somewhat moderate peace with Germany, Lloyd George was to a considerable extent a captive of demands for a total victory worthy of the sacrifices of total war against a totally depraved enemy. As Rudyard Kipling summed up the general British feeling at the end of the war, the Germans were "a people with the heart of beasts."[15]

France's Georges Clemenceau, "the Tiger" who had broken wartime defeatism and led his country to victory, wholeheartedly agreed. Like most French people, Clemenceau wanted old-fashioned revenge. He also wanted lasting security for France. This, he believed, required the creation of a buffer state between France and Germany, the permanent demilitarization of Germany, and vast German reparations. He feared that sooner or later Germany with its 60 million people would attack France with its 40 million, unless the Germans were permanently weakened. Moreover, France had no English Channel (or Atlantic Ocean) as a reassuring barrier against German aggression. Wilson, supported by Lloyd George, would hear none of it. Clemenceau's demands seemed vindictive, violating morality and the principle of national self-determination. By April the conference was deadlocked on the German question, and Wilson packed his bags to go home.

Clemenceau's obsession with security reflected his anxiety about France's long-term weakness. In the end, convinced that France should not break with its allies because France could not afford to face Germany alone in the future, he agreed to a compromise. He gave up the French demand for a Rhineland buffer state in return for a formal defensive alliance with the United States and Great Britain. Under the terms of this alliance, both Wilson and Lloyd George promised that their countries would come to France's aid in the event of a German attack. Thus Clemenceau appeared to win his goal of French security, as Wilson had won his of a permanent international organization. The Allies moved quickly to finish the peace settlement, believing that necessary adjustments would later be possible within the dual framework of a strong Western alliance and the League of Nations (see Map 27.4).

The Treaty of Versailles between the Allies and Germany was the key to the settlement, and the terms were not unreasonable as a first step toward reestablishing international order. (Had Germany won, it seems certain that France and Belgium would have been treated with greater severity, as Russia had been at Brest-Litovsk.) Germany's colonies were given to France, Britain, and Japan as League of Nations mandates. Germany's territorial losses within Europe were minor, thanks to Wilson. Alsace-Lorraine was returned to France. Parts of Germany inhabited primarily by Poles were ceded to the new Polish state, in keeping with the principle of national self-determination. Predominantly German Danzig was also placed within the Polish tariff lines, but as a self-governing city under League of Nations protection. Germany had to limit its army to 100,000 men and agree to build no military fortifications in the Rhineland.

More harshly, the Allies declared that Germany (with Austria) was responsible for the war and had therefore to pay reparations equal to all civilian damages caused by the war. This unfortunate and much-criticized clause expressed inescapable popular demands for German blood, but the actual figure was not set and there was the clear possibility that reparations might be set at a reasonable level in the future, when tempers had cooled.

When presented with the treaty, the German government protested vigorously. But there was no alternative, especially in that Germany was still starving

MAP 27.4 Shattered Empires and Territorial Changes After World War One The Great War brought tremendous changes in eastern Europe. New nations were established, and a dangerous power vacuum was created between Germany and Soviet Russia.

because the Allies had not yet lifted their naval blockade. On June 28, 1919, German representatives of the ruling moderate Social Democrats and the Catholic party signed the treaty in the Sun King's Hall of Mirrors at Versailles, where Bismarck's empire had been joyously proclaimed almost fifty years before.

Separate peace treaties were concluded with the other defeated powers—Austria, Hungary, Bulgaria, and Turkey. For the most part, these treaties merely ratified the existing situation in east central Europe following the breakup of the Austro-Hungarian Empire. Like Austria, Hungary was a particularly big loser, as its "captive" nationalities (and some interspersed Hungarians) were ceded to Rumania, Czechoslovakia, Poland, and Yugoslavia. Italy got some Austrian territory. The Turkish empire was broken up. France received Lebanon and Syria, while Britain took Iraq and Palestine, which was to include a Jewish national homeland first promised by Britain in 1917. Officially League of Nations mandates, these acquisitions of the Western powers were one of the more imperialistic elements of the peace settlement. Another was mandating Germany's holdings in China to Japan. The age of Western imperialism lived on. National self-determination remained a reality only for Europeans and their offspring.

American Rejection of the Versailles Treaty

The rapidly concluded peace settlement of early 1919 was not perfect, but within the context of war-shattered Europe it was an acceptable beginning. The principle of national self-determination, which had played such a large role in starting the war, was accepted and served as an organizing framework. Germany had been punished but not dismembered. A new world organization complemented a traditional defensive alliance of satisfied powers. The serious remaining problems could be worked out in the future. Moreover, Allied leaders had seen speed as essential for another reason: they detested Lenin and feared that his Bolshevik Revolution might spread. They realized that their best answer to Lenin's unending calls for worldwide upheaval was peace and tranquillity for war-weary peoples.

There were, however, two great interrelated obstacles to such peace: Germany and the United States. Plagued by communist uprisings, reactionary plots, and popular disillusionment with losing the war at the last minute, Germany's moderate socialists and their liberal and Catholic supporters faced an enormous challenge. Like French republicans after 1871, they needed time (and luck) if they were to establish firmly a peaceful and democratic republic. Progress in this direction required understanding yet firm treatment of Germany by the victorious Western Allies, and particularly by the United States.

However, the United States Senate and, to a lesser extent, the American people rejected Wilson's handiwork. Republican senators led by Henry Cabot Lodge refused to ratify the Treaty of Versailles without changes in the articles creating the League of Nations. The key issue was the league's power—more apparent than real—to require member states to take collective action against aggression.

Lodge and others believed that this requirement gave away Congress's constitutional right to declare war. No doubt Wilson would have been wise to accept some reservations. But, in failing health, Wilson with narrow-minded self-righteousness rejected all attempts at compromise. He instructed loyal Democratic senators to vote against any reservations whatsoever to the Treaty of Versailles. In doing so, Wilson assured that the treaty was never ratified by the United States in any form and that the United States never joined the League of Nations. Moreover, the Senate refused to ratify Wilson's defensive alliance with France and Great Britain. America turned its back on Europe.

Perhaps understandable in the light of American traditions and the volatility of mass politics, the Wilson-Lodge fiasco and the new-found gospel of isolationism nevertheless represented a tragic and cowardly renunciation of America's responsibility. Using America's action as an excuse, Great Britain, too, refused to ratify its defensive alliance with France. Bitterly betrayed by its allies, France stood alone. Very shortly, France was to take actions against Germany that would feed the fires of German resentment and seriously undermine democratic forces in the new republic. The great hopes of early 1919 were turning to ashes by the end of the year. The Western alliance had collapsed, and a grandiose plan for permanent peace had given way to a fragile truce. For this and for what came later, the United States must share a large part of the guilt.

Why did World War One have such revolutionary consequences? Why was it such a great break with the past? World War One was, first of all, a war of committed peoples. In France, Britain, and Germany in particular, governments drew on genuine popular support. This support reflected not only the diplomatic origins of the war but also the way western European society had been effectively unified under the nationalist banner in the later nineteenth century. The relentlessness of total war helps explain why so many died, why so many were crippled physically and psychologically, and why Western civilization would in so many ways never be the same again. More concretely, the war swept away monarchs and multinational empires. National self-determination apparently triumphed, not only in Austria-Hungary but in much of Russia's western borderlands as well. Except in Ireland and parts of Soviet Russia, the revolutionary dream of national unity, born of the French Revolution, had finally come true.

Two other revolutions were products of the war. In Russia, the Bolsheviks established a radical regime, smashed existing capitalist institutions, and stayed in power with a new kind of authoritarian rule. Whether the new Russian regime was truly Marxian or socialist was questionable, but it indisputably posed a powerful, ongoing revolutionary challenge in Europe and Europe's colonial empires.

More subtle, but quite universal in its impact, was an administrative revolution. This revolution, born of the need to mobilize entire societies and economies for total war, greatly increased the power of government. And after the guns grew still, government planning and wholesale involvement in economic and social life did not disappear in Europe. Liberal market capitalism and a well-integrated world economy were among the many casualties of the administrative revolution, and greater social equality was everywhere one of its results. Thus, even in European countries where a communist takeover never came close to occurring, society still experienced a great revolution.

Finally, the "war to end war" did not bring peace but only a fragile truce: in the West the Allies failed to maintain their wartime solidarity. Germany remained unrepentant and would soon have more grievances to nurse. Moreover, the victory of national self-determination in eastern Europe created a power vacuum between a still-powerful Germany and a potentially mighty communist Russia. A vast area lay open to military aggression from two sides.

NOTES

1. M. Beloff, *U.S. News and World Report,* March 8, 1976, p. 53.
2. Quoted by J. Remak, *The Origins of World War I,* Holt, Rinehart & Winston, New York, 1967, p. 84.
3. Quoted by W. E. Mosse, *Alexander II and the Modernization of Russia,* Collier Books, New York, 1962, pp. 125–126.
4. Quoted by Remak, p. 123.
5. Quoted by J. E. Rodes, *The Quest for Unity: Modern Germany 1848–1970,* Holt, Rinehart & Winston, New York, 1971, p. 178.
6. Quoted by F. P. Chambers, *The War Behind the War, 1914–1918,* Faber & Faber, London, 1939, p. 444.
7. Ibid., p. 168.
8. Quoted by R. O. Paxton, *Europe in the Twentieth Century,* Harcourt Brace Jovanovich, New York, 1975, p. 109.
9. Quoted by Chambers, p. 378.
10. Ibid., . 110.
11. Ibid., pp. 302, 304.
12. A. B. Ulam, *The Bolsheviks,* Collier Books, New York, 1968, p. 349.
13. Ibid., p. 405.
14. H. Nicolson, *Peacemaking 1919,* Grosset & Dunlap Universal Library, New York, 1965, pp. 8, 31–32.
15. Ibid., p. 24.

SUGGESTED READING

O. Hale, *The Great Illusion, 1900–1914* (1971), is a thorough account of the prewar era. Both J. Remak, *The Origins of World War I* (1967), and L. Lafore, *The Long Fuse* (1971), are highly recommended studies of the causes of the First World War. A. J. P. Taylor, *The Struggle for Mastery in Europe, 1848–1919* (1954), is an outstanding survey of diplomatic developments with an exhaustive bibliography. V. Steiner, *Britain and the Origins of the First World War* (1978), and G. Kennan, *The Decline of Bismarck's European Order: Franco-Russian Relations, 1875–1890* (1979), are also major contributions. K. Jarausch's *The Enigmatic Chancellor* (1973) is an important recent study on Bethmann-Hollweg and German policy in 1914. C. Falls, *The Great War* (1961), is the best brief introduction to military aspects of the war. B. Tuchman, *The Guns of August* (1962), is a marvelous account of the dramatic first month of the war and the beginning of military stalemate. G. Ritter provides an able study in *The Schlieffen Plan* (1958). A. J. P. Taylor, *The First World War* (1963), is a strikingly illustrated history of the war, and A. Horne, *The Price of Glory: Verdun 1916* (1979), is a moving account of the famous siege. J. Ellis, *Eye-Deep in Hell* (1976), is a vivid account of trench warfare.

F. L. Carsten, *War Against War* (1982), considers radical movements in Britain and Germany. The best single volume on the home fronts is still F. Chambers, *The War Behind the War, 1914–1918* (1939). Chambers drew heavily on the many fine books on the social and economic impact of the war in different countries published by the Carnegie Endowment for International Peace under the general editorship of J. T. Shotwell. A Marwick, *The Deluge* (1970), is a lively account of war and society in Britain, while G. Feldman, *Army, Industry, and Labor in Germany, 1914–1918* (1966), shows the impact of total war and military dictatorship on Germany. Two excellent collections of essays, J. Roth, ed., *World War I* (1967), and R. Albrecht-Carrié, ed., *The Meaning of the First World War* (1965), deftly probe the enormous consequences of the war for people and society. The debate over Germany's guilt and aggression, which has been reopened in recent years, may be best approached through G. Feldman, ed., *German Imperialism, 1914–1918* (1972), and A. Hillgruber, *Germany and the Two World Wars* (1981). M. Fainsod, *International Socialism and the World War* (1935), ably discusses the splits between radical and moderate socialists during the conflict. In addition to Erich Maria Remarque's great novel *All Quiet on the Western Front,* Henri Barbusse, *Under Fire* (1917), and Jules Romains, *Verdun* (1939), are highly recommended for their fictional yet realistic recreations of the war. P. Fussell, *The Great War and Modern Memory* (1975), probes all the powerful literature inspired by the war.

A. Ulam's *The Bolsheviks* (1968), which focuses on Lenin, is a masterful introduction to the Russian Revolution, as is B. Wolfe, *Three Who Made a Revolution* (1955), a collective biography of Lenin, Trotsky, and Stalin. R. Conquest, *V. I. Lenin* (1972), is a good short biography. Leon Trotsky himself wrote the colorful and exciting *History of the Russian Revolution* (1932), which may be compared with the classic eyewitness account of the young, pro-Bolshevik American John Reed, *Ten Days That Shook the World* (1919). R. Daniels, *Red October* (1969), provides a clear account of the Bolshevik seizure of power, and R. Pipes, *The Formation of the Soviet Union* (1968), is recommended for its excellent treatment of the nationality problem during the revolution. A. Wildman, *The End of the Russian Imperial Army* (1980), is a fine account of the soldiers' revolt, and G. Leggett, *The Cheka: Lenin's Secret Police* (1981), shows revolutionary terror in action. Boris Pasternak's justly celebrated *Doctor Zhivago* is a great historical novel of the revolutionary era. R. Massie, *Nicholas and Alexandra* (1971), is a moving popular biography of Russia's last royal family and the terrible health problem of the heir to the throne. H. Nicolson, *Peacemaking 1919* (1965), captures the spirit of the Versailles settlement. T. Bailey, *Woodrow Wilson and the Lost Peace* (1963), and W. Widenor, *Henry Cabot Lodge and the Search for an American Foreign Policy* (1981), are also highly recommended. A. Mayer provocatively stresses the influence of domestic social tensions and widespread fear of further communist revolt in *The Politics and Diplomacy of Peacemaking* (1969).

28

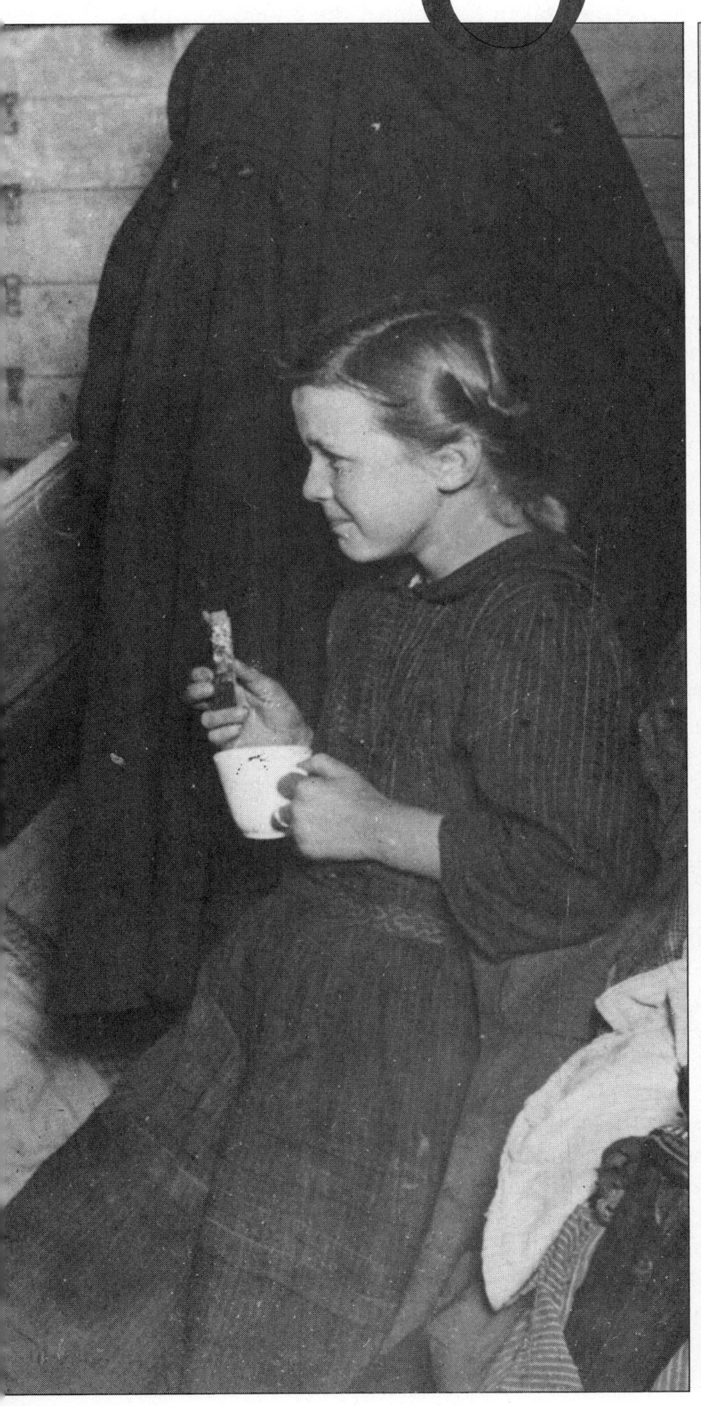

THE AGE OF ANXIETY

HEN *ALLIED DIPLOMATS* met in Paris in early 1919 with their optimistic plans for building a lasting peace, most people looked forward to happier times. They hoped that life would return to normal. They hoped that once again life would make sense in the familiar prewar terms of peace, prosperity, and progress. These hopes were in vain. The Great Break—the First World War and the Russian Revolution—had mangled too many things beyond repair. Life would no longer fit neatly into the old molds.

Instead, great numbers of men and women felt themselves increasingly adrift in a strange, uncertain, and uncontrollable world. They saw themselves living in an age of anxiety, an age of continuous crisis, which lasted until at least the early 1950s. In almost every area of human experience, people went searching for ways to put meaning back into life. What did the doubts and searching mean for Western thought, art, and culture? How did political leaders try to reestablish real peace and prosperity between 1919 and 1939? And why did they fail? These are questions this chapter will explore.

UNCERTAINTY IN MODERN THOUGHT

A complex revolution in thought and ideas was under way before the First World War, but only small, unusual groups were aware of it. After the war, new and upsetting ideas began to spread through the entire population. Western society began to question and even abandon many cherished values and beliefs that had guided it since the eighteenth-century Enlightenment and the nineteenth-century triumph of industrial development, scientific advances, and evolutionary thought.

Before 1914 most people still believed in progress, reason, and the rights of the individual. Progress was a daily reality, apparent in the rising standard of living, the taming of the city, and the steady increase in popular education. Such developments also encouraged the comforting belief in the logical universe of Newtonian physics, as well as faith in the ability of a rational human mind to understand that universe through intellectual investigation. And just as there were laws of science, so were there laws of society that rational human beings could discover and then wisely act on. Finally, the rights of the individual were not just taken for granted, they were actually increasing. Well-established rights were gradually spreading to women and workers, and new "social rights" like old-age pensions were emerging. In short, before World War One, most Europeans had a moderately optimistic view of the world, and with good reason.

From the 1880s on, however, a small band of serious thinkers and creative writers began to attack these well-worn optimistic ideas. These critics rejected the general faith in progress and the power of the rational human mind. One of the most influential of them was the German philosopher Friedrich Nietzsche (1844–1900).

Nietzsche believed that Western civilization had lost its creativity and decayed into mediocrity. Christianity's "slave morality" had glorified weakness and humility. Furthermore, human beings in the West had overstressed rational thinking at the expense of passion and emotion. Nietzsche viewed the pillars of conventional morality—reason, democracy, progress, respectability—as outworn social and psychological constructs whose influence was suffocating creativity. The only hope of revival was for a few superior individuals to free themselves from the humdrum thinking of the masses and embrace life passionately. Such individuals would become true heroes, supermen capable of leading the dumb herd of inferior men and women. Nietzsche also condemned both political democracy and greater social equality.

The growing dissatisfaction with established ideas before 1914 was apparent in other thinkers. In the 1890s, the French philosophy professor Henri Bergson (1859–1941) convinced many young people through his writing that immediate experience and intuition are as important as rational and scientific thinking for understanding reality. Indeed, according to Bergson, a religious experience or a mystical poem is often more accessible to human comprehension than a scientific law or a mathematical equation.

Another thinker who agreed about the limits of rational thinking was the French socialist Georges Sorel (1847–1922). Sorel frankly characterized

Marxian socialism as an inspiring but unprovable religion rather than a rational scientific truth. Socialism would come to power, he believed, through a great, violent strike of all working people, which would miraculously shatter capitalist society. Sorel rejected democracy and believed that the masses of the new socialist society would have to be tightly controlled by a small revolutionary elite.

In the years after 1918, a growing chorus of thinkers, creative writers, and scientists echoed and enlarged on the themes first expressed by the small band of critics between 1880 and 1914. Many prophets of doom bore witness to the decline and decay of Western civilization. The experience of history's most destructive war suggested to many that human beings certainly were a pack of violent, irrational animals quite capable of tearing the individual and his or her rights to shreds. There was growing pessimism and a general crisis of the mind. People did not know what to think. This disorientation was particularly acute in the 1930s, when the rapid rise of harsh dictatorships and the Great Depression transformed old certainties into bitter illusions.

No one expressed this state of uncertainty better than the French poet and critic Paul Valéry (1871–1945) in the early 1920s. Speaking of the "crisis of the mind," Valéry noted that Europe was looking at its future with dark foreboding:

The storm has died away, and still we are restless, uneasy, as if the storm were about to break. Almost all the affairs of men remain in a terrible uncertainty. We think of what has disappeared, and we are almost destroyed by what has been destroyed; we do not know what will be born, and we fear the future, not without reason. . . . Doubt and disorder are in us and with us. There is no thinking man, however shrewd or learned he may be, who can hope to dominate this anxiety, to escape from this impression of darkness.[1]

In the midst of economic, political, and social disruptions Valéry saw the "cruelly injured mind," besieged by doubts and suffering from anxieties. This was the general intellectual crisis of the twentieth century, which touched almost every field of thought. The implications of new discoveries and ideas in physics, psychology, philosophy, and literature played a central role in this crisis, disturbing "thinking people" everywhere.

The New Physics

Ever since the scientific revolution of the seventeenth century, scientific advances and their implications have greatly influenced the beliefs of thinking people. By the late nineteenth century, science was one of the main pillars supporting Western society's optimistic and rationalistic view of the world. The Darwinian concept of evolution had been accepted and assimilated in most intellectual circles. Progressive minds believed that science, unlike religion and philosophical speculation, was based on hard facts and controlled experiments. Science seemed to have achieved an unerring and almost completed picture of reality. Unchanging natural laws seemed to determine physical processes and permit useful solutions to more and more problems. All this was comforting, especially to people who were no longer committed to traditional religious beliefs. And all this was challenged by the new physics.

An important first step toward the new physics was the discovery at the end of the century that atoms were not like hard, permanent little billiard balls. They were actually composed of many far smaller, fast-moving particles, such as electrons and protons. The Polish-born physicist Marie Curie (1867–1934) and her French husband discovered that radium constantly emits subatomic particles and thus does not have a constant atomic weight. Building on this and other work in radiation, the German physicist Max Planck (1858–1947) showed in 1900 that subatomic energy is emitted in uneven little spurts, which Planck called "quanta," and not in a steady stream as previously believed. Planck's discovery called into question the old sharp distinction between matter and energy; the implication was that matter and energy might be different forms of the same thing. The old view of atoms as the stable, basic building blocks of nature, with a different kind of unbreakable atom for each of the ninety-two chemical elements, was badly shaken.

In 1905 the German-born Jewish genius Albert Einstein (1879–1955) went further than the Curies and Planck in challenging Newtonian physics. His famous theory of special relativity postulated that time and space are not absolute, but relative to the viewpoint of the observer. To clarify Einstein's idea, consider a person riding on a train. From the viewpoint of an observer outside the train, the passenger's

"The War, as I Saw It" This was the title of a series of grotesque drawings that appeared in 1920 in *Simplicissimus,* Germany's leading satirical magazine. Nothing shows better the terrible impact of World War One than this profoundly disturbing example of expressionist art. *(Photo: Caroline Buckler)*

net speed is exactly the same whether the passenger is walking or sitting. From the passenger's viewpoint, walking to the restaurant car is different from sitting in a seat. The closed framework of Newtonian physics was quite limited compared to that of Einsteinian physics, which unified an apparently infinite universe with the incredibly small, fast-moving subatomic world. Moreover, Einstein's theory stated clearly that matter and energy are interchangeable and that all matter contains enormous levels of potential energy.

The 1920s opened the "heroic age of physics," in the apt words of one of its leading pioneers, Ernest Rutherford (1871–1937). Breakthrough followed breakthrough. In 1919 Rutherford showed that the atom could be split. By 1944 seven subatomic particles had been identified, of which the most important was the neutron. The neutron's capacity to pass through other atoms allowed for even more intense experimental bombardment of matter, leading to chain reactions of unbelievable force. This was the road to the atomic bomb.

Although few nonscientists understood the revolution in physics, the implications of the new theories and discoveries, as presented by newspapers and popular writers, were disturbing to millions of men and women in the 1920s and 1930s. The new universe was strange and troubling. It lacked any absolute objective reality. Everything was "relative," that is, dependent on the observer's frame of reference. Moreover, the universe was uncertain and undetermined, without stable building blocks. In 1927 the German physicist Werner Heisenberg (1901–1976) formulated the "principle of uncertainty." Heisenberg's principle postulates that, because it is impossible to know the position and speed of an individual electron, it is therefore impossible to predict its behavior. Instead of Newton's dependable, rational laws, there seemed to be only tendencies and probabilities in an extraordinarily complex and uncertain universe.

Moreover, a universe described by abstract mathematical symbols seemed to have little to do with human experience and human problems. When, for example, Max Planck was asked what science could contribute to resolving conflicts of values, his response was simple: "Science is not qualified to speak to this question." Physics, the queen of the sciences, no longer provided people easy, optimistic answers—or, for that matter, any answers at all.

Freudian Psychology

With physics presenting an uncertain universe so unrelated to ordinary human experience, questions regarding the power and potential of the human mind assumed special significance. The findings and speculations of the leading psychologist, Sigmund Freud (page 786), were particularly disturbing.

Before Freud, poets and mystics had probed the unconscious and irrational aspects of human behavior. But most professional, "scientific" psychologists assumed that a single, unified conscious mind processed sense experiences in a rational and logical way. Human behavior in turn was the result of rational calculation—of "thinking"—by the conscious mind. Basing his insights on the analysis of dreams and of hysteria, Freud developed a very different view of the human psyche beginning in the late 1880s.

According to Freud, human behavior is basically irrational. The key to understanding the mind is the primitive irrational unconscious, which he called the id. The unconscious is driven by sexual, aggressive, and pleasure-seeking desires and is locked in a constant battle with the other parts of the mind: the rationalizing conscious (the ego), which mediates what a person *can* do, and ingrained moral values (the superego), which tell what a person *should* do. Human behavior is a product of fragile compromise between instinctual drives and the controls of rational thinking and moral values. Since the instinctual drives are extremely powerful, the ever-present danger for individuals and whole societies is that unacknowledged drives will overwhelm the control mechanisms in a violent, distorted way. Yet Freud also agreed with Nietzsche that the mechanisms of rational thinking and traditional moral values can be too strong. They can repress sexual desires too effectively, crippling individuals and entire peoples with guilt and neurotic fears.

Freudian psychology and clinical psychiatry had become an international movement by 1910, but only after 1918 did they receive popular attention, especially in the Protestant countries of northern Europe and in the United States. Many opponents and even some enthusiasts interpreted Freud as saying that the first requirement for mental health is an uninhibited sex life. Thus, after the First World War, the popular interpretation of Freud reflected and en-

Freud's Consulting Room in Vienna Freud developed his theories as a therapist while treating mental disorders. He sat in the armchair on the left. His patients lay on the couch and gazed away from him, in part because Freud could not bear being watched all day long. *(Photograph by Edmund Engelman)*

couraged growing sexual experimentation, particularly among middle-class women. For more serious students, the psychology of Freud and his followers drastically undermined the old, easy optimism about the rational and progressive nature of the human mind.

Philosophy: Logical Empiricism and Existentialism

The intellectual crisis of the twentieth century was fully reflected in philosophy, but in two very different ways. In English-speaking countries, the main development was the acceptance of logical empiricism (or logical positivism) in university circles. In continental countries, where esoteric and remote logical empiricism has never won many converts, the primary development in philosophy was existentialism.

Logical empiricism was truly revolutionary. It quite simply rejected most of the concerns of traditional philosophy, from the existence of God to the meaning of happiness, as nonsense and hot air. This outlook began primarily with the Austrian philosopher Ludwig Wittgenstein (1889–1951), who later emigrated to England, where he trained numerous disciples.

Wittgenstein argued in his pugnacious *Tractatus Logico-Philosophicus (Essay on Logical Philosophy)* in 1922 that philosophy is only the logical clarification of thoughts, and therefore the study of language, which expresses thoughts. The great philosophical issues of the ages—God, freedom, morality, and so on—are quite literally senseless, a great waste of time, for statements about them can neither be tested by scientific experiments nor demonstrated by the logic of mathematics. Statements about such matters reflect only the personal preferences of a given individual. As Wittgenstein put it in the famous last sentence of his work: "Of what one cannot speak, of that one must keep silent." Logical empiricism, which has remained dominant in England and the United States to this day, drastically reduced the scope of philosophical inquiry. Anxious people could find few if any answers in this direction.

Highly diverse and even contradictory, *existential* thinkers were loosely united in a courageous search for moral values in a world of terror and uncertainty. Theirs were true voices of the age of anxiety.

Most existential thinkers in the twentieth century have been atheists. Like Nietzsche, who had already proclaimed that "God is dead," they did not believe a supreme being had established humanity's fundamental nature and given life its meaning. In the words of the famous French existentialist Jean-Paul Sartre (1905–1980), human beings simply exist: "They turn up, appear on the scene." Only after they "turn up" do they seek to define themselves. Honest human beings are terribly alone, for there is no God to help them. They are hounded by despair and the meaninglessness of life. The crisis of the existential thinker epitomized the modern intellectual crisis—the shattering of traditional beliefs in God, reason, and progress.

Existentialists did recognize that human beings, unless they kill themselves, must act. Indeed, in the words of Sartre, "man is condemned to be free." There is, therefore, the possibility—indeed, the necessity—of giving meaning to life through actions, of defining oneself through choices. To do so, individuals must become "engaged" and choose their own actions courageously, consistently, and in full awareness of their inescapable responsibility for their own behavior. In the end, existentialists argued, human beings can overcome the absurdity that existentialists saw in life.

Modern existentialism developed first in Germany in the 1920s , when the philosophers Martin Heidegger and Carl Jaspers found a sympathetic audience among disillusioned postwar university students. But it was in France during the years immediately after World War Two that existentialism came of age. The terrible conditions of the war reinforced the existential view of life and the existential approach to it. On the one hand, the armies of the German dictator Hitler had conquered most of Europe and unleashed a hideous reign of barbarism. On the other, men and women had more than ever to define themselves by their actions. Specifically, each individual had to choose whether to join the Resistance against Hitler or to accept and even abet tyranny. The writings of Sartre, who along with Albert Camus (1913–1960), was the leading French existentialist and himself active in the Resistance, became enormously influential. He and his colleagues offered a powerful answer to profound moral issues and the contemporary crisis.

The Revival of Christianity

Christianity and religion in general had been on the defensive in intellectual circles since the Enlightenment, especially during the late nineteenth century. The loss of faith in human reason and in continual progress now led to a renewed interest in the Christian view of the world in the twentieth century. A number of thinkers and theologians began to revitalize the fundamentals of Christianity, especially after World War One. They had a powerful impact on society. Sometimes described as Christian existentialists because they shared the loneliness and despair of atheistic existentialists, they revived the tradition of Saint Augustine. They stressed human beings' sinful nature, the need for faith, and the mystery of God's forgiveness.

This development was a break with the late nineteenth century. In the years before 1914, some theologians, especially Protestant theologians, had felt the need to interpret Christian doctrine and the Bible so that they did not seem to contradict science, evolution, and common sense. Christ was therefore seen primarily as the greatest moral teacher, and the "supernatural" aspects of his divinity were strenuously played down. An important if extreme example of this tendency was the young Albert Schweitzer's *Quest of the Historical Jesus* (1906). A theologian and later a famous medical missionary and musician of note, Schweitzer (1875–1965) argued that Christ while on earth was a completely natural man whose teachings had been only temporary rules to prepare himself and his disciples for the end of the world, which they were erroneously expecting. In short, some modern theologians were embarrassed by the miraculous, unscientific aspects of Christianity and turned away from them.

The revival of fundamental Christian belief after World War One was fed by rediscovery of the work of the nineteenth-century Danish religious philosopher Søren Kierkegaard (1813–1855), whose ideas became extremely influential. Kierkegaard had rejected formalistic religion and denounced the worldliness of the Danish Lutheran church. He had eventually resolved his personal anguish over his imperfect nature by making a total religious commitment to a remote and majestic God.

Similar ideas were brilliantly developed by the Swiss Protestant theologian Karl Barth (1886–1968), whose many influential writings after 1920 sought to re-create the religious intensity of the Reformation. For Barth, the basic fact about human beings is that they are imperfect, sinful creatures, whose reason and will are hopelessly flawed. Religious truth is therefore made known to human beings only through God's grace. People have to accept God's word and the supernatural revelation of Jesus Christ with awe, trust, and obedience. Lowly mortals should not expect to "reason out" God and his ways.

Among Catholics, the leading existential Christian thinker was Gabriel Marcel (1889–1973). Born into a cultivated French family, where his atheistic father was "gratefully aware of all that . . . art owed to Catholicism but regarded Catholic thought itself as obsolete and tainted with absurd superstitions,"[2] Marcel found in the Catholic church an answer to what he called the postwar "broken world." Catholicism and religious belief provided the hope, humanity, honesty, and piety for which he hungered. Flexible and gentle, Marcel and his countryman Jacques Maritain (1882–1973) denounced anti-Semitism and supported closer ties with non-Catholics.

After 1914 religion became much more relevant and meaningful to thinking people than it was before the war. In addition to Marcel and Maritain, many other illustrious individuals turned to religion between about 1920 and 1950. The poets T. S. Eliot and W. H. Auden, the novelists Evelyn Waugh and Aldous Huxley, the historian Arnold Toynbee, the Oxford professor C. S. Lewis, the psychoanalyst Karl Stern, and the physicist Max Planck were all either converted to religion or attracted to it for the first time. Religion, often of a despairing, existential variety, was one meaningful answer to terror and anxiety. As another famous Roman Catholic convert, English novelist Graham Greene, wrote: "One began to believe in heaven because one believed in hell."[3]

Twentieth-Century Literature

Literature articulated the general intellectual climate of pessimism, relativism, and alienation. Novelists developed new techniques to express new realities. The great nineteenth-century novelists had typically written as all-knowing narrators, describing realistic characters and their relationship to an understandable if sometimes harsh society. In the twentieth century, most major writers adopted the limited, often confused viewpoint of a single individual. Like Freud, these novelists focused their attention on the complexity and irrationality of the human mind, where feelings, memories, and desires are forever scrambled. The great French novelist Marcel Proust (1871–1922), in his semi-autobiographical *Remembrance of Things Past* (1913–1922), recalled bittersweet memories of childhood and youthful love and tried to discover their innermost meaning. To do so, Proust lived like a hermit in a soundproof Paris apartment for ten years, withdrawing from the present to dwell on the past.

Serious novelists also used the "stream-of-consciousness" technique to explore the psyche. In *Jacob's Room* (1922), Virginia Woolf (1882–1941) turned the novel into a series of internal monologues, in which ideas and emotions from different periods of time bubble up as randomly as from a patient on a psychoanalyst's couch. William Faulkner (1897–1963), perhaps America's greatest twentieth-century novelist, used the same technique in *The Sound and the Fury,* much of whose intense drama is confusedly seen through the eyes of an idiot. The most famous stream-of-consciousness novel—and surely the most disturbing novel of its generations—is *Ulysses,* which the Irish novelist James Joyce (1882–1941) published in 1922. Into *Ulysses'* account of an ordinary day in the life of an ordinary man, Joyce weaves an extended ironic parallel between his hero's aimless wanderings through the streets and pubs of Dublin and the adventures of Homer's hero Ulysses on his way home from Troy. Abandoning conventional grammar and blending foreign words, puns, bits of knowledge, and scraps of memory together in bewildering confusion, the language of *Ulysses* is intended to mirror modern life itself: a gigantic riddle waiting to be unraveled.

As creative writers turned their attention from society to the individual and from realism to psychological relativity, they rejected the idea of progress.

Some even described "anti-utopias," nightmare visions of things to come. In 1918 an obscure German high school teacher named Oswald Spengler (1880–1936) published *Decline of the West,* which quickly became an international sensation. According to Spengler, every culture experiences a life cycle of growth and decline. Western civilization, in Spengler's opinion, was in its old age, and death was approaching in the form of conquest by the yellow race. T. S. Eliot (1888–1965), in his famous poem *The Waste Land* (1922), depicted a world of growing desolation, although after his conversion to Anglo-Catholicism in 1927, Eliot came to hope cautiously for humanity's salvation. No such hope appeared in the work of Franz Kafka (1883–1924), whose novels *The Trial* and *The Castle,* as well as several of his greatest short stories, portray helpless individuals crushed by inexplicably hostile forces. The German-Jewish Kafka died young, at forty-one, and so did not see the world of his nightmares materialize in the Nazi state.

The Englishman George Orwell (1903–1950), however, had seen both that reality and its Stalinist counterpart by 1949 when he wrote perhaps the ultimate in anti-utopian literature: *1984.* The action is set in the future, in 1984. Big Brother—the dictator—and his totalitarian state use a new kind of language, sophisticated technology, and psychological terror to strip a weak individual of his last shred of human dignity. As the supremely self-confident chief of the Thought Police tells the tortured, broken, and framed Winston Smith: "If you want a picture of the future, imagine a boot stamping on a human face—forever."[4] A phenomenal best-seller, *1984* spoke to millions of people in the closing years of the age of anxiety.

Virginia Woolf grew up in a famous literary family to become a leading member of England's intellectual aristocracy. Her novels captured sensations like impressionist paintings, and her home attracted a circle of artists and writers known as the Bloomsbury Group. *(BBC Hulton/The Bettmann Archive)*

MODERN ART AND MUSIC

Throughout the twentieth century, there has been considerable unity in the arts. The "modernism" of the immediate prewar years and the 1920s is still strikingly modern. Manifestations of modernism in art, architecture, and music have of course been highly varied, just as in physics, psychology, and philosophy; yet there are resemblances, for artists, scientists, and original thinkers partake of the same culture. Creative artists rejected old forms and old values. Modernism in art and music meant constant experimentation and a search for new kinds of expression. And though many people find the modern visions of the arts strange, disturbing, and even ugly, the twentieth century, so dismal in many respects, will probably stand as one of Western civilization's great artistic eras.

Architecture and Design

Modernism in the arts was loosely unified by a revolution in architecture. The architectural revolution not only gave the other arts striking new settings, it intended nothing less than to transform the physical framework of the urban society according to a new

Frank Lloyd Wright: The "Falling Water" House Often considered Wright's masterpiece, Falling Water combines modern architectural concepts with close attention to a spectacular site. Anchored to a high rock ledge by means of reinforced concrete, the house soars out over a cascading waterfall at Bear Run in western Pennsylvania. Built in 1937 for a Pittsburgh businessman, Falling Water is now open to the public and attracts 70,000 visitors each year. *(Western Pennsylvania Conservancy/Art Resource)*

principle: *functionalism.* Buildings, like industrial products, should be useful and "functional": that is, they should serve, as well as possible, the purpose for which they were made. Thus, architects and designers had to work with engineers, town planners, and even sanitation experts. Moreover, they had to throw away useless ornamentation and find beauty and aesthetic pleasure in the clean lines of practical constructions and efficient machinery. The Viennese pioneer Adolf Loos (1870–1933) quite typically equated ornamentation with crime, and the Franco-Swiss genius Le Corbusier (1887–1965) insisted that "a house is a machine for living in."[5]

The United States, with its rapid urban growth and lack of rigid building traditions, pioneered in the new architecture. In the 1890s, the Chicago school of architects, led by Louis H. Sullivan (1856–1924), used cheap steel, reinforced concrete, and electric elevators to build skyscrapers and office buildings lacking almost any exterior ornamentation. In the first decade of the twentieth century, Sullivan's student Frank Lloyd Wright (1869–1959) built a series of radically new and truly modern houses featuring low lines, open interiors, and mass-produced building materials. Europeans were inspired by these efforts and by such other American examples of functional construction as the massive, unadorned grain elevators of the Midwest.

Around 1905, when the first really modern buildings were going up in Europe, architectural leadership shifted to the German-speaking countries and remained there until Hitler took power in 1933. In

1911 the twenty-eight-year-old Walter Gropius (1883–1969) broke sharply with the past in his design of the Fagus shoe factory at Alfeld, Germany. A clean, light, elegant building of glass and iron, Gropius's new factory represented a jump right into the middle of the century.

After the First World War, the new German republic gave Gropius the authority to merge the schools of fine and applied arts at Weimar into a single, interdisciplinary school, the Bauhaus. In spite of intense criticism from conservative politicians and university professors, the Bauhaus brought together many leading modern architects, artists, designers, and theatrical innovators, who worked as an effective, inspired team. Throwing out traditional teaching methods, they combined the study of fine art, such as painting and sculpture, with the study of applied art in the crafts of printing, weaving, and furniture making. Throughout the 1920s, the Bauhaus, with its stress on functionalism and good design for everyday life, attracted enthusiastic students from all over the world. It had a great and continuing impact.

Along with Gropius, the architect and town planner Le Corbusier had a revolutionary influence on the development of modern architecture. Often drawing his inspiration from industrial forms, such as ocean liners, automobiles, and airplanes, Le Corbusier designed houses with flat roofs, open interior spaces, and clear, clean lines. His famous Savoy Villa at Poissy rested on concrete pillars and seemed to float on air. A true visionary, Le Corbusier sketched plans for a city of the future, with tall buildings surrounded by playgrounds and parks.

Another leader in the modern or "international" style was Ludwig Mies van der Rohe (1886–1969), who followed Gropius as director of the Bauhaus in 1930 and emigrated to the United States in 1937. His classic Lake Shore Apartments in Chicago, built between 1948 and 1951, symbolize the triumph of steel-frame and glass-wall modern architecture, which had grown out of Sullivan's skyscrapers and German functionalism in the great building boom after the Second World War.

Modern Painting

Modern painting grew out of a revolt against French impressionism (see Color Insert V). The *impressionism* of Monet, Renoir, and Pissarro was, in part, a kind of "superrealism." Leaving exact copying of objects to photography, these artists sought to capture the momentary overall feeling, or impression, of light falling on a real-life scene before their eyes. By 1890, when impressionism was finally established, a few artists known as *post-impressionists,* or *expressionists,* were already striking out in new directions. After 1905 art took on an abstract, nonrepresentational character, which it has generally retained to the present.

Though individualistic in their styles, post-impressionists were united in their desire to know and depict worlds other than the visible world of fact. Like the early nineteenth-century romantics, they wanted to portray unseen, inner worlds of emotion and imagination. Like modern novelists, they wanted to express a complicated psychological view of reality as well as an overwhelming emotional intensity. In *The Starry Night* (1889), for example, the great Dutch expressionist Vincent van Gogh (1853–1890) painted the vision of his mind's eye. Flaming cypress trees, exploding stars, and a cometlike Milky Way swirl together in one great cosmic rhythm (see Color Insert V). Paul Gauguin (1848–1903), the French stockbroker-turned-painter, pioneered in expressionist techniques, though he used them to infuse his work with tranquillity and mysticism. In 1891 he fled to the South Pacific in search of unspoiled beauty and a primitive way of life. Gauguin believed that the form and design of a picture was important in itself and that the painter need not try to represent objects on canvas as the eye actually saw them.

Fascination with form, as opposed to light, was characteristic of post-impressionism and expressionism (see Color Insert VI). Paul Cézanne (1839–1906), who had a profound influence on twentieth-century painting, was particularly committed to form and ordered design. He told a young painter, "You must see in nature the cylinder, the sphere, and the cone."[6] As Cézanne's later work became increasingly abstract and nonrepresentational, it also moved away from the traditional three-dimensional perspective toward the two-dimensional plane, which has characterized so much of modern art. The expressionism of a group of painters led by Henri Matisse (1869–1954) was so extreme that an exhibition of their work in Paris in 1905 prompted shocked critics to call them *les fauves* —"the wild beasts." Matisse and his followers were primarily concerned, not with real objects, but with the arrangement of color, line, and form as an end in itself.

Picasso: Guernica In this rich, complex work a shrieking woman falls from a burning house on the far right. On the left a woman holds a dead child, while toward the center are fragments of a warrior and a screaming horse pierced by a spear. Picasso has used only the mournful colors of black, white, and gray. *(Pablo Picasso, Guernica [1937, May–early June]. Oil on canvas. © SPADEM, Paris/VAGA, New York, 1982)*

In 1907 a young Spaniard in Paris, Pablo Picasso (1881–1973), founded another movement—cubism. Cubism concentrated on a complex geometry of zigzagging lines and sharp-angled, overlapping planes. About three years later came the ultimate stage in the development of abstract, nonrepresentational art. Artists such as the Russian-born Wassily Kandinsky (1866–1944) turned away from nature completely. "The observer," said Kandinsky, "must learn to look at [my] pictures . . . as form and color combinations . . . as a representation of *mood* and not as a representation of *objects*."[7] On the eve of the First World War, extreme expressionism and abstract painting were developing rapidly not only in Paris but also in Russia and Germany. Modern art had become international.

In the 1920s and 1930s, the artistic movements of the prewar years were extended and consolidated. The most notable new developments were dadaism and surrealism. Dadaism attacked all accepted standards of art and behavior, delighting in outrageous conduct. Its name, from the French word *dada,* meaning "hobbyhorse," is deliberately nonsensical. A famous example of dadaism was a reproduction of Leonardo da Vinci's *Mona Lisa* in which the famous woman with the mysterious smile sports a mustache and is ridiculed with an obscene inscription. After 1924 many dadaists were attracted to surrealism, which became very influential in art in the late 1920s and 1930s. Surrealism was inspired to a great extent by Freudian psychology. Surrealists painted a fantastic world of wild dreams and complex symbols, where watches melted and giant metronomes beat time in precisely drawn but impossible alien landscapes.

Refusing to depict ordinary visual reality, surrealist painters made powerful statements about the age of anxiety. Picasso's twenty-six-foot-long mural *Guernica* (1937) masterfully unites several powerful strands in twentieth-century art. Inspired by the Spanish civil war, the painting commemorates the bombing of the ancient Spanish town of Guernica by fascist planes, an attack that took the lives of a thousand people—one out of every eight inhabitants—in a single night of terror. Combining the free distortion of expressionism, the overlapping planes of cubism, and the surrealist fascination with grotesque subject matter, *Guernica* is what Picasso meant it to be: an unforgettable attack on "brutality and darkness."

Modern Music

Developments in modern music were strikingly parallel to those in painting. Composers, too, were attracted by the emotional intensity of expressionism. The ballet *The Rite of Spring* by Igor Stravinsky (1882–1971) practically caused a riot when it was first performed in Paris in 1913 by Sergei Diaghilev's famous Russian dance company. The combination of pulsating, barbaric rhythms from the orchestra pit and an earthy representation of lovemaking by the dancers on the stage seemed a shocking, almost pornographic enactment of a primitive fertility rite.

After the experience of the First World War, when irrationality and violence seemed to pervade the human experience, expressionism in opera and ballet flourished. One of the most famous and powerful examples is the opera *Wozzeck* by Alban Berg (1885–1935), first performed in Berlin in 1925. Blending a half-sung, half-spoken kind of dialogue with harsh, atonal music, *Wozzeck* is a gruesome tale of a soldier driven by Kafka-like inner terrors and vague suspicions of unfaithfulness to murder his mistress.

Some composers turned their backs on long-established musical conventions. As abstract painters arranged lines and color but did not draw identifiable objects, so modern composers arranged sounds without creating recognizable harmonies. Led by the Viennese composer Arnold Schönberg (1874–1951), they abandoned traditional harmony and tonality. The musical notes in a given piece were no longer united and organized by a key; instead they were independent and unrelated. Schönberg's twelve-tone music of the 1920s arranged all twelve notes of the scale in an abstract, mathematical pattern, or "tone row." This pattern sounded like no pattern at all to the ordinary listener and could be detected only by a highly trained eye studying the musical score. Accustomed to the harmonies of classical and romantic music, audiences generally resisted modern atonal music. Only after the Second World War did it begin to win acceptance.

MOVIES AND RADIO

Until after World War Two at the earliest, these revolutionary changes in art and music appealed mainly to a minority of "highbrows" and not to the general public. That public was primarily and enthusiastically wrapped up in movies and radio. The long-declining traditional arts and amusements of people in villages and small towns almost vanished, replaced by standardized, commercial entertainment.

Moving pictures were first shown as a popular novelty in naughty peepshows—"What the Butler Saw"—and penny arcades in the 1890s, especially in Paris. The first movie houses date from an experiment in Los Angeles in 1902. They quickly attracted large audiences and led to the production of short, silent action films like the eight-minute *Great Train Robbery* of 1903. American directors and businessmen then set up "movie factories," at first in the New York area and after 1910 in Los Angeles. These factories churned out two short films each week. On the eve of the First World War full-length feature films like the Italian *Quo Vadis* and the American *Birth of a Nation,* coupled with improvements in the quality of pictures, suggested the screen's vast possibilities.

During the First World War the United States became the dominant force in the rapidly expanding silent-film industry. In the 1920s, Mack Sennett (1884–1960) and his zany Keystone Cops specialized in short, slapstick comedies noted for frantic automobile chases, custard-pie battles, and gorgeous bathing beauties. Screen stars such as Mary Pickford and Lillian Gish, Douglas Fairbanks and Rudolph Valentino became household names, with their own "fan clubs." Yet Charlie Chaplin (1889–1978), a funny little Englishman working in Hollywood, was unquestionably the king of the "silver screen" in the 1920s. In his enormously popular role as a lonely tramp, complete with baggy trousers, battered derby, and an awkward, shuffling walk, Chaplin symbolized the "gay spirit of laughter in a cruel, crazy world."[8] Chaplin also demonstrated that, in the hands of a genius, the new medium could combine mass entertainment and artistic accomplishment.

The early 1920s was also the great age of German films. Protected and developed during the war, the

Matinee Idols Fresh and winsome, Canadian-born Mary Pickford was affectionately known as "America's Sweetheart." Starring in sentimental romances like *Poor Little Rich Girl,* she reigned over Hollywood with her husband Douglas Fairbanks. Dark and handsome, Italian-born Rudolph Valentino, shown here in the stirring *Four Horsemen of the Apocalypse,* was Hollywood's original "Latin lover." *(The New York Public Library Picture Collection)*

large German studios excelled in bizarre expressionist dramas, beginning with *The Cabinet of Dr. Caligari* in 1919. Unfortunately, their period of creativity was short-lived. By 1926 American money was drawing the leading German talents to Hollywood and consolidating America's international domination. Film making was big business, and European theater owners were forced to book whole blocks of American films to get the few pictures they really wanted. This system put European producers at a great disadvantage until "talkies" permitted a revival of national film industries in the 1930s, particularly in France.

Whether foreign or domestic, motion pictures became the main entertainment of the masses until after the Second World War. In Great Britain one in every four adults went to the movies twice a week in the late 1930s, and two in five went once a week. Continental countries had similar figures. The greatest appeal of motion pictures was that they offered ordinary people a temporary escape from the hard realities of everyday life. For an hour or two the moviegoer could flee the world of international tensions, uncertainty, unemployment, and personal frustrations. The appeal of escapist entertainment was especially strong during the Great Depression.

Millions flocked to musical comedies featuring glittering stars such as Ginger Rogers and Fred Astaire and to the fanciful cartoons of Mickey Mouse and his friends.

Radio became possible with the transatlantic "wireless" communication of Guglielmo Marconi (1874–1937) in 1901 and the development of the vacuum tube in 1904, which permitted the transmission of speech and music. But only in 1920 were the first major public broadcasts of special events made in Great Britain and the United States. Lord Northcliffe, who had pioneered in journalism with the inexpensive, mass-circulation *Daily Mail,* sponsored a broadcast of "only one artist . . . the world's very best, the soprano Nellie Melba."[9] Singing from London in English, Italian, and French, Melba was heard simultaneously all over Europe on June 16, 1920. This historic event captured the public's imagination. The meteoric career of radio was launched.

Every major country quickly established national broadcasting networks. In the United States, such networks were privately owned and financed by advertising. In Great Britain, Parliament set up an independent, high-minded public corporation, the British Broadcasting Corporation (BBC), which was supported by licensing fees. Elsewhere in Europe, the typical pattern was direct control by the government.

Whatever the institutional framework, radio became popular and influential. By the late 1930s, more than three out of every four households in both democratic Great Britain and dictatorial Germany had at least one cheap, mass-produced radio. In other European countries, radio ownership was not quite so widespread, but the new medium was no less important.

Radio in unscrupulous hands was particularly well suited for political propaganda. Dictators like Mussolini and Hitler controlled the airwaves and could reach enormous national audiences with their frequent, dramatic speeches. In democratic countries, politicians such as President Franklin Roosevelt and Prime Minister Stanley Baldwin effectively used informal "fireside chats" to bolster their support.

Motion pictures also became powerful tools of indoctrination, especially in countries with dictatorial regimes. Lenin himself encouraged the development of Soviet film making, believing that the new medium was essential to the social and ideological transformation of the country. Beginning in the mid-1920s, a series of epic films, the most famous of which were directed by Sergei Eisenstein (1898–1948), brilliantly dramatized the communist view of Russian history.

In Germany, Hitler turned to a young and immensely talented woman film maker, Leni Riefenstahl (b. 1902), for a masterpiece of documentary propaganda, *The Triumph of the Will,* based on the Nazi party rally at Nuremberg in 1934. Riefenstahl combined stunning aerial photography, joyful crowds welcoming Hitler, and mass processions of young Nazi fanatics. Her film was a brilliant and all-too-powerful documentary of Germany's "Nazi rebirth." The new media of mass culture were clearly potentially dangerous instruments of political manipulation.

THE SEARCH FOR PEACE AND POLITICAL STABILITY

The Versailles settlement had established a shaky truce, not a solid peace. Within the general context of intellectual crisis and revolutionary artistic experimentation, politicians and statesmen struggled to create a stable international order.

The pursuit of real and lasting peace proved difficult. Germany hated the Treaty of Versailles, France was fearful and isolated. Britain was undependable, and the United States had turned its back on European problems. Eastern Europe was in ferment, and no one could predict the future of communist Russia. Moreover, the international economic situation was poor and greatly complicated by war debts and disrupted patterns of trade. Yet for a time, from 1925 to late 1929, it appeared that peace and stability were within reach. When the subsequent collapse of the 1930s mocked these hopes, the disillusionment of liberals in the democracies was intensified.

GERMANY AND THE WESTERN POWERS

Germany was the key to lasting peace. Only under the pressure of the Allies' naval blockade and threat to extend their military occupation from the Rhineland to the rest of the country had Germany's new republican government signed the Treaty of Versailles in June 1919. To Germans of all political parties, the treaty represented a harsh, dictated peace, to be revised or repudiated as soon as possible. The treaty had neither broken nor reduced Germany, which was potentially still the strongest country in Europe. Thus the treaty had fallen between two stools: too harsh for a peace of reconciliation, too soft for a peace of conquest.

Moreover, with ominous implications for the future, France and Great Britain did not see eye to eye on Germany. By the end of 1919, France wanted to stress the harsh elements in the Treaty of Versailles. Most of the war in the west had been fought on French soil, and much of rich, industrialized, northern France had been devastated. The expected costs of reconstruction were staggering; like Great Britain, France had also borrowed large sums from the United States during the war, which had to be repaid. Thus French politicians believed that massive reparations from Germany were a vital economic necessity. Moreover, if the Germans had to suffer to make the payments, the French would not be overly concerned. Having compromised with President Wilson only to be betrayed by America's failure to ratify the treaty, many French leaders saw strict implementation of all provisions of the Treaty of Versailles as France's last best hope. Large reparation payments could hold Germany down indefinitely, and France would realize its goal of security.

The British soon felt differently. Prewar Germany had been Great Britain's second-best market in the entire world, and after the war a healthy, prosperous Germany appeared to be essential to the British economy. Indeed, many English people agreed with the analysis of the young English economist John Maynard Keynes (1883–1946), who eloquently denounced the Treaty of Versailles in his famous *Economic Consequences of the Peace* (1919). According to Keynes's interpretation, astronomical reparations and harsh economic measures would indeed reduce Germany to the position of an impoverished second-rate power, but such impoverishment would increase economic hardship in all countries. Only a complete revision of the foolish treaty could save Germany—and Europe. Keynes's attack exploded like a bombshell and became very influential. It stirred deep guilt feelings about Germany in the English-speaking world, feelings that often paralyzed English and American leaders in their relations with Germany and its leaders between the First and Second World Wars.

The British were also suspicious of France's army—momentarily the largest in Europe—and France's foreign policy. Ever since 1890, France had looked to Russia as a powerful ally against Germany. But with Russia hostile and socialist, and with Britain and the United States unwilling to make any firm commitments, France turned to the newly formed states of eastern Europe for diplomatic support. In 1921 France signed a mutual defense pact with Poland and associated itself closely with the so-called Little Entente, an alliance that joined Czechoslovakia, Rumania, and Yugoslavia against defeated and bitter Hungary. The British and the French were also on cool terms because of conflicts relating to their League of Nations mandates in the Middle East.

While French and British leaders drifted in different directions, the Allied reparations commission completed its work. In April 1921, it announced that Germany had to pay the enormous sum of 132 billion gold marks ($33 billion), payable in annual installments of 2.5 billion gold marks. Facing possible occupation of more of its territory, the young German republic, which had been founded in Weimar but moved back to Berlin, made its first payment in 1921. Then in 1922, wracked by rapid inflation and political assassinations, and motivated by hostility and arrogance as well, the Weimar Republic announced its inability to pay more. It proposed a moratorium on reparations for three years, with the clear implication that thereafter reparations would either be drastically reduced or eliminated entirely.

The British were willing to accept this offer, but the French were not. Led by their tough-minded, legalistic prime minister, Raymond Poincaré, they decided they either had to call Germany's bluff or see the entire peace settlement dissolve to France's great disadvantage. So, despite strong British protests, France and its ally Belgium decided to pursue a firm policy. In early January 1923, French and Belgian armies began to occupy the Ruhr district, the heartland of industrial Germany, creating the most serious international crisis of the 1920s.

The Occupation of the Ruhr

The strategy of Poincaré and his French supporters was simple. Since Germany would not pay reparations in hard currency or gold, France and Belgium would collect reparations in kind—coal, steel, and

"Hands Off the Ruhr" The French occupation of the Ruhr to collect reparations payments raised a storm of patriotic protest, including this anti-French poster of 1923. *(Internationaal Institut voor Sociale Geschiedenis)*

The Fruits of Germany's Inflation In the end, currency had value only as waste paper. Here bank notes are being purchased by the bail for paper mills, along with old rags *(Lumpen)* and bones *(Knochen)*. *(Archiv für Kunst u. Geschichte/Katherine Young)*

machinery. If forcible collection proved impossible, France would use occupation to paralyze Germany and force it to accept the Treaty of Versailles.

Strengthened by a wave of patriotism, the German government ordered the people of the Ruhr to stop working and start resisting—passively—the French occupation. The coal mines and steel mills of the Ruhr grew silent, leaving 10 percent of Germany's total population in need of relief. The French answer to passive resistance was to seal off, not only the Ruhr, but the entire Rhineland from the rest of Germany, permitting only enough food to prevent starvation. They also revived plans for a separate state in the Rhineland.

By the summer of 1923, France and Germany were engaged in a great test of wills. As the German government had anticipated, French armies could not collect reparations from striking workers at gunpoint. But French occupation was indeed paralyzing Germany and its economy, for the Ruhr district normally produced 80 percent of Germany's steel and coal. Moreover, the occupation of the Ruhr turned rapid German inflation into runaway inflation. Faced with the need to support the striking Ruhr workers and their employers, the German government began to print money to pay its bills. Prices soared. People went to the store with a big bag of paper money; they returned home with a handful of groceries. German money rapidly lost all value, and so did anything else with a stated fixed value.

Runaway inflation brought about a social revolution. The accumulated savings of many retired and middle-class people were wiped out. The old middle-class virtues of thrift, caution, and self-reliance were cruelly mocked by catastrophic inflation. People told themselves that nothing had real value any more, not even money. The German middle and lower-middle classes felt cheated and burned with resentment. Many hated and blamed the Western governments, their own government, big business, the Jews, the workers, the communists for their misfortune. They were psychologically prepared to follow radical leaders in a moment of crisis.

In August 1923, as the mark fell and political unrest grew throughout Germany, Gustav Stresemann assumed leadership of the government. Stresemann adopted a compromising attitude. He called off passive resistance in the Ruhr and in October agreed in principle to pay reparations, but asked for a re-examination of Germany's ability to pay. Poincaré accepted. His hard line was becoming increasingly unpopular with French citizens, and it was hated in Britain and the United States. Moreover, occupation was dreadfully expensive, and France's own currency was beginning to lose value on foreign exchange markets.

More generally, in both Germany and France power was finally passing to the moderates, who realized that continued confrontation was a destructive, no-win situation. Thus, after five long years of hostility and tension culminating in a kind of undeclared war in the Ruhr in 1923, Germany and France decided to give compromise and cooperation a try. The British, and even the Americans, were willing to help. The first step was a reasonable compromise on the reparations question.

Hope in Foreign Affairs, 1924–1929

The Reparations Commission appointed an international committee of financial experts headed by an American banker, Charles G. Dawes, to re-examine reparations from a broad perspective. The committee made a series of recommendations known as the Dawes Plan (1924), which was accepted by France, Germany, and Britain. German reparations were reduced and placed on a sliding scale, like an income tax, whereby yearly payments depended on the level of German economic prosperity. The Dawes Plan also recommended large loans to Germany, loans that could come only from the United States. These loans were to help Stresemann's government put its new currency on a firm basis and promote German recovery. In short, Germany would get private loans from the United States and pay reparations to France and Britain, thus enabling those countries to repay the large sums they owed the United States.

This circular flow of international payments was complicated and risky. For a time, though, it worked. The German republic experienced a spectacular economic recovery. By 1929 Germany's wealth and income were 50 percent greater than in 1913. With prosperity and large, continuous inflows of American capital, Germany easily paid about $1.3 billion in reparations in 1927 and 1928, enabling France and Britain to pay the United States. In 1929 the Young Plan, named after an American businessman, further reduced German reparations and formalized the link between German reparations and French-British debts to the United States. In this way the Americans, who did not have armies but who did have money, belatedly played a part in the general economic settlement, which though far from ideal facilitated the worldwide recovery of the late 1920s.

The economic settlement was matched by a political settlement. In 1925 the leaders of Europe signed a number of agreements at Locarno, Switzerland. Stresemann, who guided German's foreign policy until his death in 1929, had suggested a treaty with France's conciliatory Aristide Briand, who had returned to office in 1924 after French voters rejected the bellicose Poincaré. By this treaty Germany and France solemnly pledged to accept their common border, and both Britain and Italy agreed to fight either country if it invaded the other. Stresemann also agreed to settle boundary disputes with Poland and Czechoslovakia by peaceful means, and France promised those countries military aid if they were attacked by Germany. For their efforts Stresemann and Briand shared the Nobel Peace Prize in 1926. The effect of the treaties of Locarno was far-reaching. For several years, a "spirit of Locarno" gave Europeans a sense of growing security and stability in international affairs.

Hopes were strengthened by other developments. In 1926 Germany joined the League of Nations, where Stresemann continued his "peace offensive."

In 1928 fifteen countries signed the Kellogg-Briand Pact, which "condemned and renounced war as an instrument of national policy." The signing states agreed to settle international disputes peacefully. Often seen as idealistic nonsense because it made no provisions for action in case war actually occurred, the pact was nevertheless a hopeful step. It grew out of a suggestion by Briand that France and the United States renounce the possibility of war between their two countries. Briand was gently and subtly trying to draw the United States back into involvement with Europe. When Secretary of State Frank B. Kellogg proposed a multinational pact, Briand appeared close to success. Thus the cautious optimism of the late 1920s also rested on the hope that the United States would accept its responsibilities as a great world power and consequently contribute to European stability.

Hope in Democratic Government

Domestic politics also offered reason to hope. During the occupation of the Ruhr and the great inflation, republican government in Germany had appeared on the verge of collapse. In 1923 communists momentarily entered provincial governments, and in November an obscure nobody named Adolf Hitler leaped on a table in a beer hall in Munich and proclaimed a "national socialist revolution." But Hitler's plot was poorly organized and easily crushed, and Hitler was sentenced to prison, where he outlined his theories and program in his book *Mein Kampf* (*My Struggle*). Throughout the 1920s, Hitler's National Socialist party attracted support only from a few fanatical anti-Semites, ultranationalists, and disgruntled ex-servicemen. In 1928 his party had an insignificant twelve seats in the national parliament. Indeed, after 1923 democracy seemed to take root in Weimar Germany. A new currency was established, and the economy boomed.

The moderate businessmen who tended to dominate the various German coalition governments were convinced that economic prosperity demanded good relations with the Western powers, and they supported parliamentary government at home. Stresemann himself was a man of this class, and he was the key figure in every government until his death in 1929. Elections were held regularly, and republican democracy appeared to have growing support among a majority of the German people.

There were, however, sharp political divisions in the country. Many unrepentant nationalists and monarchists populated the right and the army. Germany's Communists were noisy and active on the left. The Communists, directed from Moscow, reserved their greatest hatred and sharpest barbs for their cousins the Social Democrats, whom they endlessly accused of betraying the revolution. The working classes were divided politically, but most supported the nonrevolutionary but socialist Social Democrats.

The situation in France had numerous similarities to that in Germany. Communists and Socialists battled for the support of the workers. After 1924 the democratically elected government rested mainly in the hands of coalitions of moderates, and business interests were well represented. France's great accomplishment was rapid rebuilding of its war-torn northern region. The expense of this undertaking led, however, to a large deficit and substantial inflation. By early 1926, the franc had fallen to 10 percent of its prewar value, causing a severe crisis. Poincaré was recalled to office, while Briand remained minister for foreign affairs. The Poincaré government proceeded to slash spending and raise taxes, restoring confidence in the economy. The franc was "saved," stabilized at about one-fifth of its prewar value. Good times prevailed until 1930.

Despite its political shortcomings, France attracted artists and writers from all over the world in the 1920s. Much of the intellectual and artistic ferment of the times flourished in Paris. As the writer Gertrude Stein (1874–1946), a leader of the large colony of American expatriates living in Paris, later recalled: "Paris was where the twentieth century was."[10] More generally, France appealed to foreigners and the French as a harmonious combination of small businesses and family farms, of bold innovation and solid traditions.

Britain, too, faced challenges after 1920. The wartime trend toward greater social equality continued, however, helping to maintain social harmony. The great problem was unemployment. Many of Britain's best markets had been lost during the war. In June 1921, almost 2.2 million people—23 percent of the labor force—were out of work, and throughout the 1920s unemployment hovered around 12 percent. Yet the state provided unemployment benefits of equal size to all those without jobs and supplemented those payments with subsidized housing, medical

An American in Paris The young Josephine Baker suddenly became a star when she brought an exotic African eroticism to French music halls in 1925. American blacks and Africans had a powerful impact on entertainment in Europe in the 1920s and 1930s. *(BBC Hulton/The Bettmann Archive)*

aid, and increased old-age pensions. These and other measures kept living standards from seriously declining, defused class tensions, and pointed the way toward the welfare state Britain established after World War Two.

Relative social harmony was accompanied by the rise of the Labour party as a determined champion of the working classes and of greater social equality. Committed to the kind of moderate, "revisionist" socialism that had emerged before World War One (pages 818–819), the Labour party replaced the Liberal party as the main opposition to the Conservatives. The new prominence of the Labour party reflected the decline of old liberal ideals of competitive capitalism, limited government control, and individual responsibility. In 1924 and 1929, the Labour party under Ramsay MacDonald governed the country with the support of the smaller Liberal party. Yet Labour moved toward socialism gradually and democratically, so that the middle classes were not overly frightened as the working classes won new benefits.

The Conservatives under Stanley Baldwin showed

the same compromising spirit on social issues. The last line of Baldwin's greatest speech in March 1925 summarized his international and domestic programs: "Give us peace in our time, O Lord." Thus, in spite of such conflicts as the 1926 strike by hard-pressed coal miners, which ended in an unsuccessful general strike, social unrest in Britain was limited in the 1920s and in the 1930s as well. In 1922 Britain granted southern, Catholic Ireland full autonomy after a bitter guerrilla war, thus removing another source of prewar friction. In summary, developments in both international relations and in the domestic politics of the leading democracies gave cause for cautious optimism in the late 1920s.

THE GREAT DEPRESSION, 1929–1939

Like the Great War, the Great Depression must be spelled with capital letters. Economic depression was nothing new. Depressions occurred throughout the nineteenth century with predictable regularity, as they recur in the form of recessions and slumps to this day. What was new about this depression was its severity and duration. It struck with ever-greater intensity from 1929 to 1933, and recovery was uneven and slow. Only with the Second World War did the depression disappear in much of the world (see Map 28.1).

The social and political consequences of prolonged economic collapse were enormous. The depression shattered the fragile optimism of political leaders in the late 1920s. Mass unemployment made insecurity a reality for millions of ordinary people, who had paid little attention to the intellectual crisis or to new directions in art and ideas. In desperation, people looked for leaders who would "do something." They were willing to support radical attempts to deal with the crisis by both democratic leaders and dictators.

The Economic Crisis

There is no agreement among historians and economists about why the Great Depression was so deep and lasted so long. Thus, it is best to trace the course of the great collapse before trying to identify what caused it.

Though economic activity was already declining moderately in many countries by early 1929, the crash of the stock market in the United States in October of that year really started the Great Depression. The American stock market boom, which had seen stock prices double between early 1928 and September 1929, was built on borrowed money. Many wealthy investors, speculators, and people of modest means had bought stocks by paying only a small fraction of the total purchase price and borrowing the remainder from their stockbrokers. Such buying "on margin" was extremely dangerous. When prices started falling, the hard-pressed margin buyers either had to put up more money, which was often impossible, or sell their shares to pay off their brokers. Thus thousands of people started selling all at once. The result was a financial panic. Countless investors and speculators were wiped out in a matter of days or weeks.

The general economic consequences were swift and severe. Stripped of their wealth and confidence, battered investors and their fellow citizens started buying fewer goods. Production began to slow down, and unemployment began to rise. Soon the entire American economy was caught in a vicious, spiraling decline.

The financial panic in the United States triggered a worldwide financial crisis, and that crisis resulted in a drastic decline in production in country after country. Throughout the 1920s American bankers and investors had lent large amounts of capital not only to Germany but to many countries. Many of these loans were short term, and once panic broke, New York bankers began recalling them. Gold reserves thus began to flow out of European countries, particularly Germany and Austria, toward the United States. It became very hard for European businessmen to borrow money, and the panicky public began to withdraw its savings from the banks. These banking problems eventually led to the crash of the largest bank in Austria in 1931 and then to general financial chaos. The recall of private loans by American bankers also accelerated the collapse in world prices, as businessmen around the world dumped industrial goods and agricultural commodities in a frantic attempt to get cash to pay what they owed.

The financial crisis led to a general crisis of production: between 1929 and 1933, world output of goods fell by an estimated 38 percent. As this happened, each country turned inward and tried to go it alone.

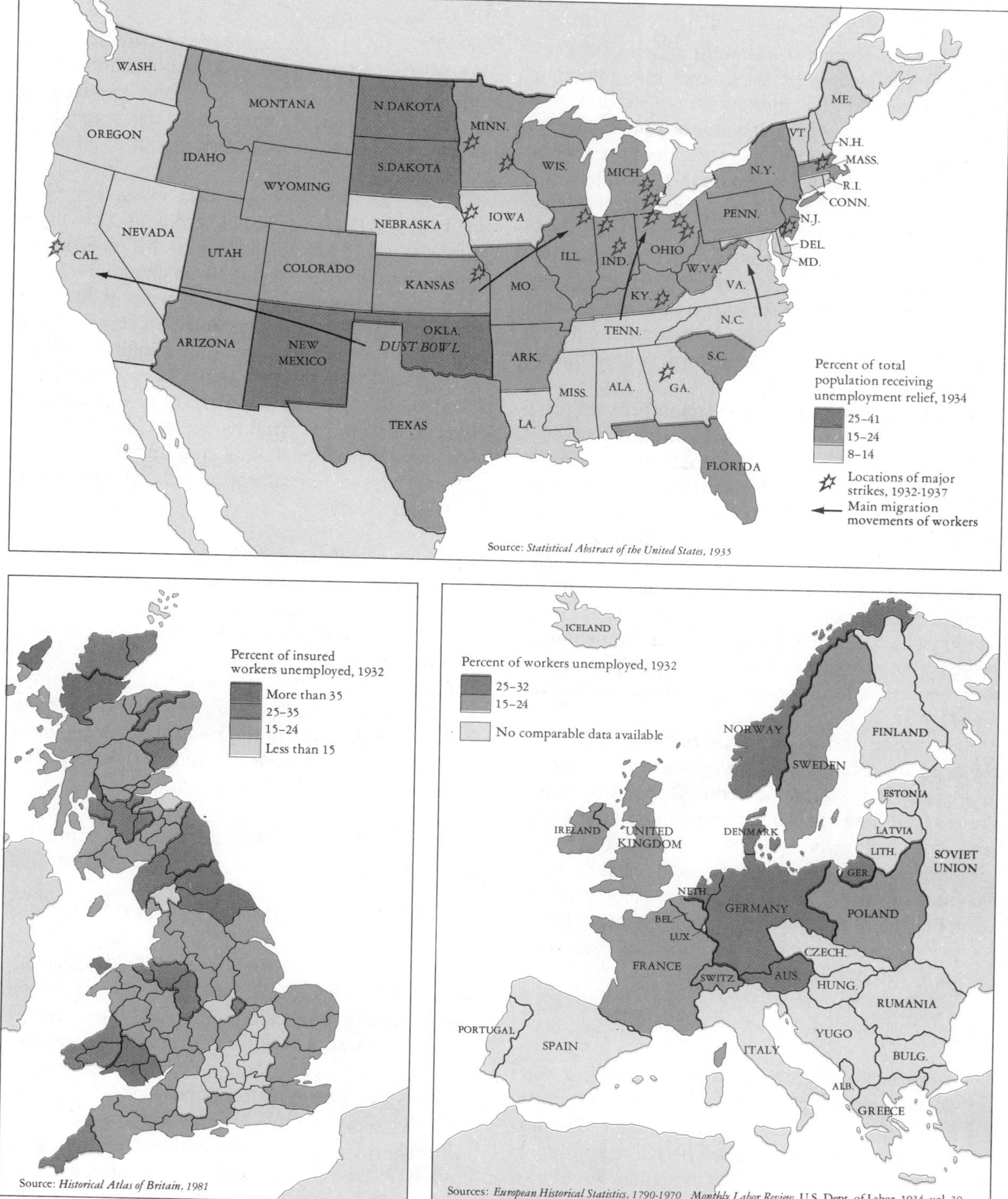

Map 28.1 The Great Depression in the United States, Britain, and Europe National and regional differences were substantial. Germany, industrial northern Britain, and the American Middle West were particularly hard-hit.

In 1931, for example, Britain went off the gold standard, refusing to convert bank notes into gold, and reduced the value of its money. Britain's goal was to make its goods cheaper and therefore more salable in the world market. But because more than twenty nations, including the United States in 1934, also went off the gold standard, no country gained a real advantage. Similarly, country after country followed the example of the United States when it raised protective tariffs to their highest levels ever in 1930 and tried to seal off shrinking national markets for American producers only. Within this context of fragmented and destructive economic nationalism, recovery finally began in 1933.

Although opinions differ, two factors probably best explain the relentless slide to the bottom from 1929 to early 1933. First, the international economy lacked a leadership able to maintain stability when the crisis came. Specifically, as a noted American economic historian concludes, the seriously weakened British, the traditional leaders of the world economy, "couldn't and the United States wouldn't" stabilize the international economic system in 1929.[11] The United States, which had momentarily played a positive role after the occupation of the Ruhr, cut back its international lending and erected high tariffs.

The second factor was poor national economic policy in almost every country. Governments generally cut their budgets and reduced spending when they should have run large deficits in an attempt to stimulate their economies. Since World War Two, such a "counter-cyclical policy," advocated by John Maynard Keynes, has become a well-established weapon against depression. But in the 1930s Keynes's prescription was generally regarded with horror by orthodox economists.

Mass Unemployment

The need for large-scale government spending was tied to mass unemployment. As the financial crisis led to cuts in production, workers lost their jobs and had little money to buy goods. This led to still more cuts in production and still more unemployment, until millions were out of work. In Britain, unemployment had averaged 12 percent in the 1920s; between 1930 and 1935, it averaged more than 18 percent. Far worse was the case of the United States, where unemployment had averaged only 5 percent in the 1920s. In 1932 unemployment soared to about *one-third* of the entire labor force: 14 million people were out of work (see Map 28.1). Only by pumping new money into the economy could the government increase demand and break the vicious cycle of decline.

Along with its economic effects, mass unemployment posed a great social problem that mere numbers cannot adequately express. Millions of people lost their spirit and dignity in an apparently hopeless search for work. Homes and ways of life were disrupted in millions of personal tragedies. Young people postponed marriages they could not afford, and birthrates fell sharply. There was an increase in suicide and mental illness. Poverty or the threat of poverty became a grinding reality. In 1932 the workers of Manchester, England, appealed to their city officials—a typical appeal echoed throughout the Western world:

> *We tell you that thousands of people . . . are in desperate straits. We tell you that men, women, and children are going hungry. . . . We tell you that great numbers are being rendered distraught through the stress and worry of trying to exist without work. . . .*
>
> *If you do not do this—if you do not provide useful work for the unemployed—what, we ask, is your alternative? Do not imagine that this colossal tragedy of unemployment is going on endlessly without some fateful catastrophe. Hungry men are angry men.*[12]

Mass unemployment was a terrible time bomb preparing to explode.

The New Deal in the United States

Of all the major industrial countries, only Germany was harder hit by the Great Depression, or reacted more radically to it, than the United States. Depression was so traumatic in the United States because the 1920s had been a period of complacent prosperity. The Great Depression and the response to it was a major turning point in American history.

President Herbert Hoover and his administration initially reacted to the stock market crash and economic decline with dogged optimism and limited action. In May 1930, Hoover told a group of business and farm leaders, "I am convinced that we have now passed the worst and with continued unity of effort we shall rapidly recover." When, however, the full force of the financial crisis struck Europe in the summer of 1931 and boomeranged back to the United States, people's worst fears became reality. Banks failed; unemployment soared. In 1932 industrial production fell to about 50 percent of its level in 1929. In these tragic circumstances Franklin Delano Roosevelt, an inspiring wheelchair aristocrat previously crippled by polio, won a landslide electoral victory with grand but vague promises of a "New Deal for the forgotten man."

Roosevelt's basic goal was to reform capitalism in order to preserve it. In his words, "A frank examination of the profit system in the spring of 1933 showed it to be in collapse; but substantially everybody in the United States, in public office and out of public office, from the very rich to the very poor, was as determined as was my Administration to save it."[13] Roosevelt rejected socialism and government ownership of industry in 1933. To right the situation, he chose forceful government intervention in the economy.

In this choice, Roosevelt and his advisers were greatly influenced by American experience in World War One. During the wartime emergency, the American economy had been thoroughly planned and regulated. Roosevelt and his "brain trust" of advisers adopted similar policies to restore prosperity and reduce social inequality. Roosevelt was flexible, pragmatic, and willing to experiment. Government intervention and experimentation were combined in some of the New Deal's most significant measures.

The most ambitious attempt to control and plan the economy was the National Recovery Administration (NRA), established by Congress right after Roosevelt took office. The key idea behind the NRA was to reduce competition and fix prices and wages for everyone's benefit. This goal required government, business, and labor to hammer out detailed regulations for each industry. Along with this kind of national planning in the private sector of the economy, the government believed it could sponsor enough public works projects to assure recovery. Because the NRA broke with the cherished American tradition of free competition and aroused conflicts among businessmen, consumers, and bureaucrats, it did not work well. By the time the NRA was declared unconstitutional in 1935, Roosevelt and the New Deal were already moving away from government efforts to plan and control the entire economy.

Instead, Roosevelt and his advisers attacked the key problem of mass unemployment directly. The federal government accepted the responsibility of employing directly as many people as financially possible, something Hoover had consistently rejected. Thus, when it became clear in late 1933 that the initial program of public works was too small, new agencies were created to undertake a vast range of projects.

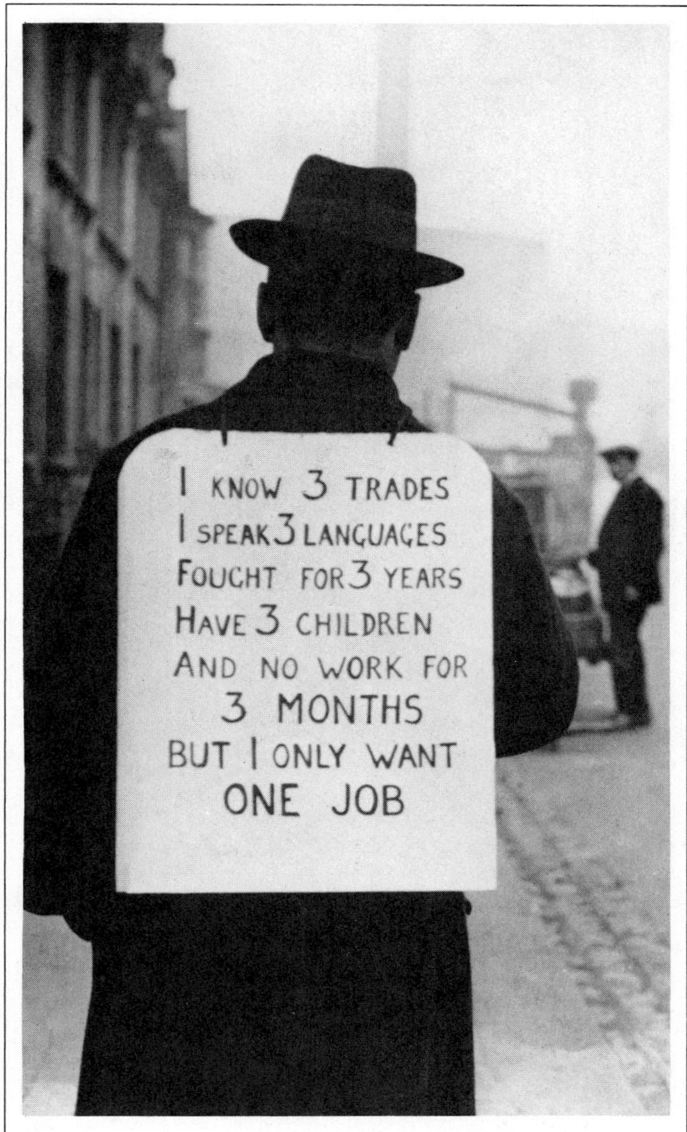

Middle-Class Unemployment An English office worker's unusual sandwich board poignantly summarizes the bitter despair of the unemployed in the 1930s. *(BBC Hulton/The Bettmann Archive)*

San Francisco, 1934 Standing on the corner, waiting for something to do: this classic photograph by Dorothea Lange captures the frustration and waste of unemployment in the Depression years. *(Dorothea Lange, The Oakland Museum)*

The most famous of these was the Works Progress Administration (WPA), set up in 1935. At its peak in late 1938, this government agency employed more than 3 million individuals. One-fifth of the entire labor force worked for the WPA at some point in the 1930s. To this day thousands of public buildings, bridges, and highways built by the WPA stand as monuments to energetic government efforts to provide people with meaningful work. The WPA was enormously popular in a nation long schooled in self-reliance and the work ethic. The hope of a job with the government helped check the threat of social revolution in the United States.

Other social measures aimed in the same direction. Following the path blazed by Germany's Bismarck in the 1880s, the U.S. government in 1935 established a national social security system, with old-age pensions and unemployment benefits, to protect many workers against some of life's uncertainties. The National Labor Relations Act of 1935 gave union organizers the green light by declaring collective bargaining to be the policy of the United States. Following some bitter strikes, such as the sit-down strike at General Motors in early 1937, union membership more than doubled, from 4 million in 1935 to 9 million in 1940. In general, between 1935 and 1938 government rulings and social reforms chipped away at the privileges of the wealthy and tried to help ordinary people.

Yet, despite its undeniable accomplishments in social reform, the New Deal was only partly successful as a response to the Great Depression. At the height of the recovery, in May 1937, 7 million workers were still unemployed. The economic situation then worsened seriously in the recession of 1937 and 1938. Production fell sharply, and although unemployment never again reached the 15 million mark of 1933, it hit 11 million in 1938 and was still a staggering 10 million when war broke out in Europe in September 1939.

The New Deal never did pull the United States out of the Depression. This failure frustrated Americans then, and it is still puzzling today. Perhaps, as some have claimed, Roosevelt should have used his enormous popularity and prestige in 1933 to nationalize the banks, the railroads, and some heavy industry, so that national economic planning could have been successful. On the other hand, Roosevelt's sharp attack on big business and the wealthy after 1935 had popular appeal but also damaged business confidence and made the great capitalists uncooperative. Given the low level of profit and the underutilization of many factories, however, it is questionable whether business would have behaved much differently even if the New Deal had catered to it.

Finally, it is often argued that the New Deal did not put enough money into the economy through deficit financing. Like his predecessors in the White House, Roosevelt was attached to the ideal of the balanced budget. His largest deficit was only $4.4 billion in 1936. Compare this figure with deficits of $21.5 billion in 1942 and $57.4 billion in 1943, when the nation was prosperously engaged in total war and unemployment had vanished. By 1945 many

ART: A MIRROR OF SOCIETY

Art reveals the interests and values of society and frequently gives intimate and unique glimpses of how people actually lived. In portraits and statues, whether of saints, generals, philosophers, popes, poets, or merchants, it preserves the memory and fame of men and women who shaped society. In paintings, drawings, and carvings, it also shows how people worked, played, relaxed, suffered, and triumphed. Art, therefore, is extremely useful to the historian, especially when written records are scarce. Every work of art and every part of it has meaning and has something of its own to say.

Art also manifests the changes and continuity of European life; as values changed in Europe, so did major artistic themes. In the nineteenth century, the impressionists, seeking to capture a given moment as the eye perceives it, gloried in the vibrant diversity of urban society. In their wholehearted embrace of modern life, they reflected western Europe's faith in science, progress, and democracy in the late nineteenth century. Though the twentieth century witnessed the dissipation of such optimism, the impressionists, by valuing color and abstract design for their own sake, served as the crucial bridge between traditional representational and modern art. The career of Cézanne (overleaf), in particular, exemplifies this artistic progression: after rejecting as too light and frivolous his early impressionistic work, Cézanne adopted a style characterized by greater form and solidity.

Artists of the early and mid-twentieth century anticipated and then gave poignant expression to the anxieties and terrors that have plagued modern times. Some continued Cézanne's experimentation with form, a process that found its ultimate expression in cubism. The cubist works of artists like Picasso reflect the distorted and multiple viewpoints of a society that lacked nineteenth-century certitudes. Others such as Gustave Klimt (also represented here) retreated from realistic depiction by conveying their ideas and emotions indirectly through symbols. Still other artists participated in the movement known as expressionism, which emphasized the subjective portrayal of inner experience. In *The Dance of Life,* below, Edvard Munch, a leading proponent of expressionism, tries to show the whole range of human emotions at once. Solitary figures struggling fitfully with terror and uncertainty—a favorite twentieth-century theme—dominate Munch's work. Here the girl in white represents innocence, the tense women in black stand for mourning and rejection, and the women in red evoke the joy of passing pleasure. (Nasjonalgalleriet, Oslo.)

The Card Players *(above)* Paul Cézanne (1839–1906). An immensely important and revolutionary painter, Cézanne rejected his early impressionistic style as too light and delicate. In this 1892 masterpiece he shows the dignity of all human existence and experience, no matter how ordinary or commonplace. One can also sense the devotion to form and solidity that made Cézanne the father of modern abstract painting. *(The Metropolitan Museum of Art: Bequest of Stephen C. Clark, 1960)*

The Starry Night *(above)* Vincent van Gogh (1853–1890). The distorted visions of van Gogh anticipated the widespread tension and torment that marked the age of anxiety. The tragic Dutchman absorbed impressionism in Paris, but under the burning sun of southern France he went beyond portraying the world of external reality. He feverishly painted his own inner world of intense emotion and wild imagination, thereby contributing greatly to modern expressionism. *(Museum of Modern Art, New York. Acquired through the Lillie P. Bliss Bequest)*

Judith I *(left)* Gustave Klimt (1862–1918). Men (and women) were firm believers in the elemental power of female seduction at the beginning of this century. This 1901 painting by a leading Viennese symbolist retells the biblical story of Judith, who slept with a Babylonian general for many nights in order to cut off his head and save her people. The symbolists' fascination with exotic sensations harkened back to romanticism. *(Osterreichische Galerie, Vienna)*

The Three Dancers *(right)* Pablo Picasso (1881–1973). A child prodigy, Picasso turned from realism to the fractured, shifting, multiple point of view known as cubism. With this immensely influential innovation Picasso shattered the continuity of composition that had prevailed since the Renaissance, and merged time and space in the relativity of an Einsteinian world. In this 1925 painting Picasso mourns in rage a friend's death through the frenzied contortions and cruciform image of the dancers. *(Tate Gallery, London/S.P.A.D.E.M., Paris/V.A.G.A., New York)*

Birthday *(above)* Marc Chagall (1889–1985). No modern artist has expressed more joyfully the enduring mystery of love than the highly original, Russian-born Jewish painter Chagall. In this 1915 painting the prospect of a birthday bouquet from his beloved Bella sends the young husband soaring in bliss. Love and fantasy go hand in hand, Chagall seems to say. *(Solomon R. Guggenheim Museum, New York; Photo: Carmelo Guadagno)*

The Grand Constructors *(right)* Fernard Léger (1881–1955). The twentieth-century fascination with urban life, the machine, and workers dominate the work of Léger. Like most ordinary people, Léger is thoroughly enchanted with the creations of technology and mass culture. Yet the robot-like action of the workers in this 1950 picture also suggests that dehumanization often accompanies our modern marvels. *(Musée National Fernand Léger, Bot/S.P.A.D.E.M., Paris/V.A.G.A., New York)*

50

Christmas Night *(left)* Henri Matisse (1869–1954). In his youth Matisse led avant-garde artists who delighted in breaking with tradition and shocking the public. This joyous design for a church stained-glass window, however, glows with cultural continuity and the spiritual peace of the artist's last years. Its beauty inspired by that of medieval masterpieces (see insert II), Matisse's stained-glass window proclaims the good tidings of Christmas to our time. *(Museum of Modern Art, New York. Gift of Time, Inc.)*

economists concluded that the New Deal's deficit-financed public works had been too small a step in the right direction. These Keynesian views were to be very influential in economic policy in Europe and America after the Second World War.

The Scandinavian Response to Depression

Of all the Western democracies, the Scandinavian countries under Socialist leadership responded most successfully to the challenge of the Great Depression. Having grown steadily in the late nineteenth century, Socialists became the largest political party in Sweden and then in Norway after the First World War. In the 1920s they passed important social reform legislation for both peasants and workers, gained practical administrative experience, and developed a unique kind of socialism. Flexible and nonrevolutionary, Scandinavian socialism grew out of a strong tradition of cooperative community action. Even before 1900, Scandinavian agricultural cooperatives had shown how individual peasant families could join together for everyone's benefit. Labor leaders and capitalists were also inclined to work together.

When the economic crisis struck in 1929, Socialist governments in Scandinavia built on this pattern of cooperative social action. Sweden in particular pioneered in the use of large-scale deficits to finance public works and thereby maintain production and employment. Scandinavian governments also increased social welfare benefits, from old-age pensions and unemployment insurance to subsidized housing and maternity allowances. All this spending required a large bureaucracy and high taxes, first on the rich and then on practically everyone. Yet both private and cooperative enterprise thrived, as did democracy. Some observers saw Scandinavia's welfare socialism as an appealing "middle way" between sick capitalism and cruel communism or fascism.

Recovery and Reform in Britain and France

In Britain, MacDonald's Labour government and then, after 1931, the Conservative-dominated coalition government followed orthodox economic theory. The budget was balanced, but unemployed workers received barely enough welfare to live. Despite government lethargy, the economy recovered considerably after 1932. By 1937 total production was about 20 percent higher than in 1929. In fact, for Britain the years after 1932 were actually somewhat better than the 1920s had been, quite the opposite of the situation in the United States and France.

This good, but by no means brilliant, performance reflected the gradual reorientation of the Britain economy. After going off the gold standard in 1931 and establishing protective tariffs in 1932, Britain concentrated increasingly on the national rather than the international market. The old export industries of the Industrial Revolution, such as textiles and coal, continued to decline, but the new industries like automobiles and electrical appliances grew in response to British home demand. Moreover, low interest rates encouraged a housing boom. By the end of the decade there were highly visible differences between the old, depressed industrial areas of the north and the new, growing areas of the south. These developments encouraged Britain to look inward and avoid unpleasant foreign questions.

Because France was relatively less industrialized and more isolated from the world economy, the Great Depression came late. But once the depression hit France, it stayed and stayed. Decline was steady until 1935, and the short-lived recovery never brought production or employment back up to predepression levels. Economic stagnation both reflected and heightened an ongoing political crisis. There was no stability in government. As before 1914, the French parliament was made up of many political parties, which could never cooperate for very long. In 1933, for example, five coalition cabinets formed and fell in rapid succession.

The French lost the underlying unity that had made governmental instability bearable before 1914. Fascist-type organizations agitated against parliamentary democracy and looked to Mussolini's Italy and Hitler's Germany for inspiration. In February 1934, French fascists and semifascists rioted and threatened to overturn the republic. At the same time the Communist party and many workers opposed to the existing system were looking to Stalin's Russia for guidance. The vital center of moderate republicanism was sapped from both sides.

Frightened by the growing strength of the Fascists at home and abroad, the Communists, the Socialists, and the Radicals formed an alliance—the Popular Front—for the national elections of May 1936. Their clear victory reflected the trend toward polarization.

The number of Communists in the parliament jumped dramatically from 10 to 72, while the Socialists, led by Léon Blum, became the strongest party in France with 146 seats. The really quite moderate Radicals slipped badly, and the conservatives lost ground to the semifascists.

In the next few months, Blum's Popular Front government made the first and only real attempt to deal with the social and economic problems of the 1930s in France. Inspired by Roosevelt's New Deal, the Popular Front encouraged the union movement and launched a far-reaching program of social reform, complete with paid vacations and a forty-hour workweek. Popular with workers and the lower-middle class, these measures were quickly sabotaged by rapid inflation and cries of revolution from fascists and frightened conservatives. Wealthy people sneaked their money out of the country, labor unrest grew, and France entered a severe financial crisis. Blum was forced to announce a "breathing spell" in social reform.

The fires of political dissension were also fanned by civil war in Spain. The Communists demanded that France support the Spanish republicans, while many French conservatives would gladly have joined Hitler and Mussolini in aiding the attack of Spanish fascists. Extremism grew, and France itself was within sight of civil war. Blum was forced to resign in June 1937, and the Popular Front quickly collapsed. An anxious and divided France drifted aimlessly once again, preoccupied by Hitler and German rearmament.

After the First World War, Western society entered a complex and difficult era—truly an age of anxiety. Intellectual life underwent a crisis marked by pessimism, uncertainty, and fascination with irrational forces. Rejection of old forms and ceaseless experimentation characterized art and music, while motion pictures and radio provided a new, standardized entertainment for the masses. Intellectual and artistic developments that had been confined to small avant-garde groups before 1914 gained wider currency along with the insecure state of mind they expressed.

Politics and economics were similarly disrupted. In the 1920s, statesmen groped to create an enduring peace and rebuild the prewar prosperity, and for a brief period late in the decade, they even seemed to have succeeded. Then the Great Depression shattered the fragile stability. Uncertainty returned with redoubled force in the 1930s. The international economy collapsed, and unemployment struck millions. The democracies turned inward as they sought to cope with massive domestic problems and widespread disillusionment. Generally speaking, they were not very successful. The old liberal ideals of individual rights and responsibilities, elected government, and economic freedom seemed ineffective and outmoded to many, even when they managed to survive. And in many countries they were abandoned completely.

NOTES

1. P. Valéry, *Variety,* trans. Malcolm Cowley, Harcourt, Brace, New York, 1927, pp. 27–28.
2. G. Marcel, as quoted by S. Hughes, *The Obstructed Path: French Social Thought in the Years of Desperation, 1930–1960,* Harper & Row, New York, 1967, p. 82.
3. G. Greene, *Another Mexico,* Viking Press, New York, 1939, p. 3.
4. G. Orwell, *1984,* New American Library, New York, p. 220.
5. C. E. Jeanneret-Gris (Le Corbusier), *Towards a New Architecture,* J. Rodker, London, 1931, p. 15.
6. Quoted by A. H. Barr, Jr., *What Is Modern Painting?,* 9th ed., Museum of Modern Art, New York, 1966, p. 27.
7. Ibid., p. 25.
8. R. Graves and A. Hodge, *The Long Week End: A Social History of Great Britain, 1918–1939,* Macmillan, New York, 1941, p. 131.
9. Quoted by A. Briggs, *The Birth of Broadcasting,* Oxford University Press, London, 1961, 1.47.
10. Quoted by R. J. Sontag, *A Broken World, 1919–1939,* Harper & Row, New York, 1971, p. 129.
11. C. P. Kindleberger, *The World in Depression, 1929–1939,* University of California Press, Berkeley, 1973, p. 292.
12. Quoted by S. B. Clough et al., eds., *Economic History of Europe: Twentieth Century,* Harper & Row, New York, 1968, pp. 243–245.

13. Quoted by D. Dillard, *Economic Development of the North Atlantic Community,* Prentice-Hall, Englewood Cliffs, N.J., 1967, p. 591.

SUGGESTED READING

Among general works, R. Sontag, *A Broken World, 1919–1939* (1971), and E. Wiskema, *Europe of the Dictators, 1919–1945* (1966), are particularly recommended. The former has an excellent bibliography. A. Bullock, ed., *The Twentieth Century* (1971), is a lavish visual feast combined with penetrating essays on major developments since 1900. Two excellent accounts of contemporary history—one with a liberal and the other with a conservative point of view—are R. Paxton, *Europe in the Twentieth Century* (1975), and P. Johnson, *Modern Times: The World from the Twenties to the Eighties* (1983). Crucial changes in thought before and after World War One are discussed in three rewarding intellectual histories: G. Masur, *Prophets of Yesterday* (1961); H. S. Hughes, *Consciousness and Society* (1956); and M. Biddiss, *Age of the Masses: Ideas and Society Since 1870* (1977). R. Stromberg, *European Intellectual History Since 1789,* 4th ed. (1986), and F. Baumer, *Modern European Thought: Continuity and Change in Ideas, 1600–1950* (1970), are recommended general surveys.

J. Rewald, *The History of Impressionism,* rev. ed. (1961) and *Post-Impressionism* (1956), are excellent, as are the works of A. H. Barr, Jr., cited in the Notes. P. Collaer, *A History of Modern Music* (1961), and H. R. Hitchcock, *Architecture: 19th and 20th Centuries* (1958), are good introductions, while T. Wolfe, *From Bauhaus to My House* (1981), is a lively critique of modern architecture. L. Barnett, *The Universe and Dr. Einstein* (1952), is a fascinating study of the new physics. P. Rieff, *Freud* (1956), and M. White, ed., *The Age of Analysis* (1955), open up basic questions of twentieth-century psychology and philosophy. P. Gay, *Weimar Culture* (1970), is a brilliant exploration of the many-sided artistic renaissance in Germany in the 1920s. M. Marrus, ed., *Emergence of Leisure* (1974), is a pioneering inquiry into an important aspect of mass culture. H. Daniels-Rops, *A Fight for God,* 2 vols. (1966), is a sympathetic history of the Catholic church between 1870 and 1939.

C. Maier, *Recasting Bourgeois Europe* (1975), is an ambitious comparative study of social classes and conflicts in France, Germany, and Italy after World War One. R. Wohl, *The Generation of 1914* (1979); R. Kuisel, *Capital and State in Modern France: Renovation and Economic Management* (1982); and W. McDougall, *France's Rhineland Diplomacy, 1914–1924* (1978), are three more important studies on aspects of the postwar challenge. M. Childs, *Sweden: The Middle Way* (1961), applauds Sweden's efforts at social reform. W. Neuman, *The Balance of Power in the Interwar Years, 1919–1939* (1968), perceptively examines international politics after the Locarno treaties of 1925. In addition to the contemporary works discussed in the text, the crisis of the interwar period comes alive in R. Crossman, ed., *The God That Failed* (1950), in which famous Western writers tell why they were attracted to and later repelled by communism; Ortega y Gassett's renowned *The Revolt of the Masses* (1932); and F. A. Hayek's *The Road to Serfdom* (1944), a famous warning of the dangers to democratic freedoms.

In addition to C. Kindleberger's excellent study of the Great Depression cited in the Notes, there is J. Galbraith's very lively and understandable account of the stock market collapse, *The Great Crash* (1955). J. Garraty, *Unemployment in History* (1978), is noteworthy, though novels best portray the human tragedy of economic decline. W. Holtby, *South Riding* (1936), and W. Greenwood, *Love on the Dole* (1933), are moving stories of the Great Depression in England; H. Fallada, *Little Man, What Now?* (1932), is the classic counterpart for Germany. Also highly recommended as commentaries on English life between the wars are R. Graves, *Goodbye to All That,* rev. ed. (1957), and G. Orwell, *The Road to Wigan Pier* (1972). Among French novelists, André Gide painstakingly examines the French middle class and its values in *The Counterfeiters,* while Albert Camus, the greatest of the existential novelists, is at his unforgettable best in *The Stranger* and *The Plague.*

29

DICTATORSHIPS AND THE SECOND WORLD WAR

THE ERA OF ANXIETY and economic depression was also a time of growing strength for political dictatorship. Popularly elected governments and basic civil liberties declined drastically in Europe. On the eve of the Second World War, liberal democratic government survived only in Great Britain, France, the Low Countries, the Scandinavian nations, and neutral Switzerland. Elsewhere in Europe, various kinds of "strong men" ruled. Dictatorship seemed the wave of the future. Thus the decline in liberal political institutions and the intellectual crisis were related elements in the general crisis of European civilization.

The era of dictatorship is a highly disturbing chapter in the history of Western civilization. The key development was not simply the resurgence of dictatorship but the rise of a new kind of tyranny—the modern totalitarian state. Modern totalitarianism reached its fullest realization in Communist Russia and Nazi Germany in the 1930s. Stalin and Hitler mobilized their peoples for enormous undertakings and ruled with unprecedented severity.

Today we want to believe that the era of totalitarian dictatorship was a terrible accident, that Stalin's slave labor camps and Hitler's gas chambers "can't happen again." But one cannot be sure: it was all very recent and very powerful. What was the nature of the twentieth-century totalitarian state? How did totalitarianism affect ordinary people, and why did it lead to another world war? These are the questions this chapter will seek to answer.

AUTHORITARIAN AND TOTALITARIAN STATES

The modern totalitarian state differed from the old-fashioned authoritarian state. Completely rejecting liberal values and drawing on the experience of total war, the totalitarian state exercised much greater control over the masses and mobilized them for constant action. The nature of this control may be examined by comparing the old and new forms of dictatorship in a general way, before entering the strange worlds of Stalin's Russia and Hitler's Germany.

Conservative Authoritarianism

The traditional form of antidemocratic government in European history has been conservative authoritarianism. Like Catherine the Great in Russia and Metternich in Austria, the leaders of such governments have tried to prevent major changes that would undermine the existing social order. To do so, they have relied on obedient bureaucracies, vigilant police departments, and trustworthy armies. Popular participation in government has been forbidden or else severely limited to such natural allies as landlords, bureaucrats, and high church officials. Liberals, democrats, and socialists have been persecuted as radicals, often to find themselves in jail or exile.

Yet old-fashioned authoritarian governments were limited in their power and in their objectives. Lacking modern technology and communications, they had not the power to control many aspects of their subjects' lives. Nor did they wish to do so. Preoccupied with the goal of mere survival, these governments' demands were largely limited to taxes, army recruits, and passive acceptance. As long as the people did not try to change the system, they often had considerable personal independence.

After the First World War, this kind of authoritarian government revived, especially in the less-developed eastern part of Europe. There, the parliamentary regimes that had been founded on the wreckage of empires in 1918 fell one by one. By early 1938 only economically and socially advanced Czechoslovakia remained true to liberal political ideals. Conservative dictators also took over in Spain and Portugal.

There were several reasons for this development. These lands lacked a strong tradition of self-government, with its necessary restraint and compromise. Moreover, many of these new states were torn by ethnic conflicts that threatened their very existence. Dictatorship appealed to nationalists and military leaders as a way to repress such tensions and preserve national unity. Large landowners and the church were still powerful forces in these largely agrarian areas, and they often looked to dictators to save them from progressive land reform or communist agrarian upheaval. So did some members of the middle class, which was small and weak in eastern Europe. Finally, though some kind of democracy managed to stagger through the 1920s in Austria, Bulgaria, Rumania, Greece, Estonia, and Latvia, the Great Depression delivered the final blow in those countries in 1936.

Nazi Mass Rally, 1936 This picture captures the spirit of modern totalitarianism. The uniformed members of the Nazi party have willingly merged themselves into a single force and await the command of the godlike leader. *(Wide World Photos)*

Although some of the authoritarian regimes adopted certain Hitlerian and fascist characteristics in the 1930s, their general aims were not totalitarian. They were concerned more with maintaining the status quo than with forcing society into rapid change or war. This tradition lives on today, especially in some of the military dictatorships in Latin America.

Hungary was a good example of conservative authoritarianism. In the chaos of collapse in 1919, Béla Kun formed a Lenin-like government, but communism in Hungary was soon crushed by foreign troops, large landowners, and hostile peasants. Thereafter, a combination of great and medium-sized landowners instituted a semi-authoritarian regime, which maintained the status quo in the 1920s. Hungary had a parliament, but elections were carefully controlled. The peasants did not have the right to vote, and an upper house representing the landed aristocracy was re-established. There was no land reform, no major social change. In the 1930s, the Hungarian government remained conservative and nationalistic. Increasingly, it was opposed by a Nazi-like fascist movement, the Arrow Cross, which demanded radical reform and totalitarian measures.

Another example of conservative authoritarianism was newly independent Poland, where democratic government was overturned in 1926 when General Joseph Pilsudski established a military dictatorship. Poland was torn by bitter party politics and sandwiched between Russia and Germany. Pilsudski silenced opposition and tried to build a strong state. His principal supporters were the army, major industrialists, and dedicated nationalists.

In Yugoslavia, King Alexander (1921–1934) proclaimed a centralized dictatorship in 1929 to prevent ethnic rivalries among Serbs, Croats, and Slovenes from tearing the country apart. An old-style authoritarian, Alexander crushed democracy, jailed separatists, and ruled through the bureaucracy.

Another example of conservative authoritarianism was Portugal, at the westernmost end of the European peninsula. Constantly shaken by military coups and uprisings after a republican revolution in 1910, very poor and backward Portugal finally got a strong dictator in Antonio de Oliveira Salazar in 1932. A devout Catholic, Salazar gave the church the strongest possible position in the country, while controlling the press and outlawing most political activity. Yet there was no attempt to mobilize the masses or to accomplish great projects. The traditional society was firmly maintained, and that was enough.

Modern Totalitarianism

Although both are dictatorships, modern totalitarianism and conservative authoritarianism differ. They may be thought of as two distinct types of political organization that in practice sometimes share certain elements.

Modern totalitarianism burst on the scene with the revolutionary total war effort of 1914 to 1918. The war called forth a tendency to subordinate all institutions and all classes to one supreme objective: victory. Nothing, absolutely nothing, had equal value. People were called to make ever-greater sacrifices, and their personal freedom was constantly reduced by ever-greater government control. As the outstanding French thinker Elie Halévy put it in 1936, the varieties of modern totalitarian tyranny—fascism, nazism, and communism—may be thought of as "feuding brothers" with a common father, the nature of modern war.[1]

The crucial experience of World War One was carried further by Lenin and the Bolsheviks during the Russian civil war. Lenin showed how a dedicated minority could make a total effort and achieve victory over a less-determined majority. Lenin also demonstrated how institutions and human rights might be subordinated to the needs of a single group—the Communist party—and its leader, Lenin. Thus Lenin provided a model for single-party dictatorship, and he inspired imitators.

Building on its immediate origins in World War One and the Russian civil war, modern totalitarianism reached maturity in the 1930s in Stalinist Russia and Nazi Germany. Both had several fundamental characteristics of modern totalitarianism.

Armed with modern technology and communications, the true totalitarian state began as a dictatorship exercising complete political power, but it did not stop there. Increasingly, the state took over and tried to control just as completely the economic, social, intellectual, and cultural aspects of life. Although such unlimited control could not be fully realized, the individual's freedom of action was greatly reduced. Deviation from the norm even in art or family behavior could become a crime. In theory, nothing was politically neutral, nothing was outside the scope of the state.

This grandiose vision of total state control broke decisively not only with conservative authoritarianism but also with nineteenth-century liberalism and democracy. Indeed, totalitarianism was a radical revolt against liberalism. Liberalism sought to limit the power of the state and protect the sacred rights of the individual. Moreover, liberals stood for rationality, harmony, peaceful progress, and a strong middle class. All of that disgusted totalitarians as sentimental slop. They believed in will power, preached conflict, and worshiped violence. They believed that the individual was infinitely less valuable than the state and that there were no lasting rights, only temporary rewards for loyal and effective service. Only a single powerful leader and a single party, both unrestrained by law or tradition, determined the destiny of the totalitarian state.

Unlike old-fashioned authoritarianism, modern totalitarianism was based not on an elite but on the masses. As in the First World War, the totalitarian state sought and sometimes won the support and even the love of ordinary people. Modern totalitarianism built on politically alert masses, on people who had already become engaged in the political process, most notably through commitment to nationalism and socialism. Its character as a mass movement gave totalitarianism much of its elemental force.

The final shared characteristic of real totalitarian states was their boundless dynamism. The totalitarian society was a fully mobilized society, a society moving toward some goal. It was never content merely to survive, like an old-fashioned military dictatorship or a decaying democracy. Paradoxically, totalitarian regimes never reached their goals. Or, more precisely, as soon as one goal was achieved at the cost of enormous sacrifice, another arose at the leader's command to take its place. Thus totalitarianism was in the end a *permanent* revolution, an *unfinished* revolution, in which rapid, profound change imposed from on high went on forever.

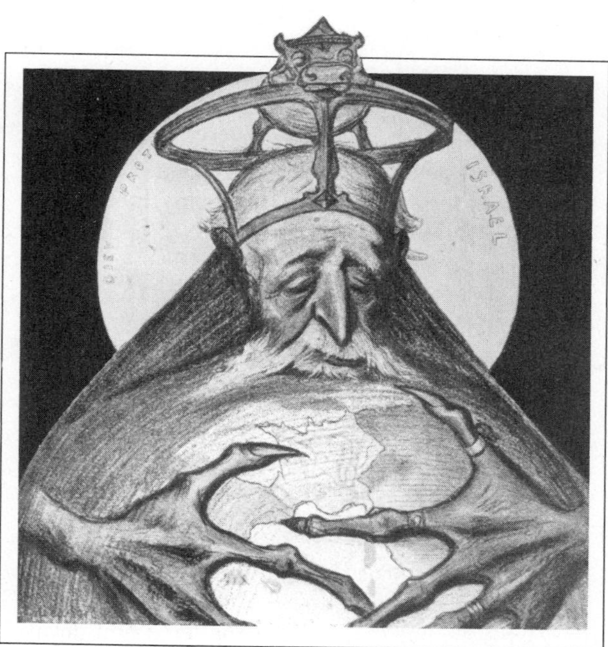

Vicious Anti-Semitism was visible in all European countries before World War One. This 1898 French cartoon shows the Jewish banker Rothschild worshipping gold and exploiting the whole world. Jews were also denounced as revolutionary socialists intent upon destroying private property and the middle class. *(Historical Pictures Service, Chicago)*

Totalitarianism of the Left and the Right

The two most-developed totalitarian states—Stalin's Communist Russia and Hitler's Nazi Germany—shared all the central characteristics of totalitarianism. But although those regimes may seem more alike than not, there were at least two major differences between them.

Communism as practiced in Soviet Russia grew out of Marxian socialism. Nazism in Germany grew out of extreme nationalism and racism. This distinction meant that private property and the middle class received very different treatment in the two states. In Soviet Russia, the socialist program of the radical left was realized: all large holdings of private property were taken over by the state, and the middle class lost its wealth and status. In Germany, big landowners and industrialists on the conservative right were sharply criticized but managed to maintain their private wealth. This difference in property and class relations has led some scholars to speak of "totalitarianism of the left"—Stalinist Russia—and "totalitarianism of the right"—Nazi Germany.

More important were the differing possibilities for regeneration. Socialism, with its concetn for social justice and human progress, is linked to the living core of Western civilization and the Judeo-Christian tradition. Stalin's communism was an ugly perversion of socialism, but even in its darkest moments it had the potential for reforming itself and creating a more humane society. Nazism, however, had no such potential. Based on the claptrap phobias of anticapitalism, anti-Semitism, and racism, its elements could be found in many a European city before the First World War. Totally negative and devoid of even perverted truth, it promised only destruction and never rebirth.

STALIN'S RUSSIA

Lenin established the basic outlines of a modern totalitarian dictatorship in Russia after the Bolshevik Revolution and during the civil war. Joseph Stalin (1879–1953) finished the job. A master of political infighting, Stalin cautiously consolidated his power and eliminated his enemies in the mid-1920s. Then in 1928, as undisputed leader of the ruling Communist party, he launched the first five-year plan—the "revolution from above," as he so aptly termed it.

The five-year plans were extremely ambitious. Often incorrectly considered a mere set of economic measures to speed up Soviet Russia's industrial development, the five-year plans actually marked the beginning of a renewed attempt to mobilize and transform Soviet society along socialist lines. The goal was to create a new way of life and to generate new attitudes and new loyalties. The means Stalin and the small Communist party elite chose were constant propaganda, enormous sacrifice, and unlimited violence and state control. Thus the Soviet Union in the 1930s became a dynamic, modern totalitarian state.

From Lenin to Stalin

By spring 1921, Lenin and the Bolsheviks had won the civil war, but they ruled a shattered and devastated land. Many farms were in ruins, and food supplies were exhausted. In southern Russia, drought combined with the ravages of war to produce the worst famine in generations. By 1920, according to the government, from 50 to 90 percent of the population in seventeen provinces was starving. Industrial production also broke down completely. In 1921, for example, output of steel and cotton textiles was only about 4 percent of what it had been in 1913. The revolutionary Trotsky later wrote that the "collapse of the productive forces surpassed anything of the kind history had ever seen. The country, and the government with it, were at the very edge of the abyss."[2] The Bolsheviks had destroyed the economy as well as their foes.

In the face of economic disintegration and rioting by peasants and workers, as well as an open rebellion by previously pro-Bolshevik sailors at Kronstadt, which had to be quelled with machine guns, the tough but ever-flexible Lenin changed course. In March 1921, he announced the New Economic Policy (NEP), which re-established limited economic freedom in an attempt to rebuild agriculture and industry. During the civil war, the Communists had simply seized grain without payment. Lenin in 1921 substituted a grain tax on the country's peasant producers, who were permitted to sell their surpluses in free markets. Peasants were also encouraged to buy as many goods as they could afford from private traders and small handicraft manufacturers, both of whom were allowed to reappear. Heavy industry, railroads, and banks, however, remained wholly nationalized. Thus NEP saw only a limited restoration of capitalism.

Lenin's New Economic Policy was shrewd and successful, from two points of view. Politically, it was a necessary but temporary compromise with Russia's overwhelming peasant majority. Flushed with victory after their revolutionary gains of 1917, the peasants would have fought to hold onto their land. With fond hopes of immediate worldwide revolution fading by 1921, Lenin realized that his government was not strong enough to take it from them. As he had accepted Germany's harsh terms at Brest-Litovsk in 1918, Lenin made a deal with the only force capable of overturning his government.

Economically, NEP brought rapid recovery. In 1926 industrial output had surpassed the level of 1913, and Russian peasants were producing almost as much grain as before the war. Counting shorter hours and increased social benefits, workers were living somewhat better than they had in the past.

As the economy recovered and the government somewhat relaxed its censorship and repression, an intense struggle for power began in the inner circles of the Communist party, for Lenin had left no chosen successor when he died in 1924. The principal contenders were the stolid Stalin and the flamboyant Trotsky.

The son of a shoemaker, Joseph Dzhugashvili—later known as Stalin—studied for the priesthood but was expelled from his theological seminary, probably for rude rebelliousness. By 1903 he had joined the Bolsheviks. In the years before the First World War, he engaged in many revolutionary activities in the Transcaucasian area of southern Russia, including a daring bank robbery to get money for the Bolsheviks. This raid gained Lenin's attention and approval. Ethnically a Georgian and not a Russian, Stalin in his early writings focused on the oppression of minority peoples in the Russian Empire. Stalin was a good organizer but a poor speaker and writer, with no experience outside of Russia.

Leon Trotsky, a great and inspiring leader who had planned the 1917 takeover (pages 883–884) and then created the victorious Red Army, appeared to have all the advantages. Yet it was Stalin who succeeded Lenin. Stalin won because he was more effective at gaining the all-important support of the party, the only genuine source of power in the one-party state.

Lenin and Stalin in 1922 Lenin re-established limited economic freedom throughout Russia in 1921, but he ran the country and the Communist party in an increasingly authoritarian way. Stalin carried the process much further and eventually built a regime based on harsh dictatorship. *(Sovfoto)*

Rising to general secretary of the party's Central Committee just before Lenin's first stroke in 1922, Stalin used his office to win friends and allies with jobs and promises. Stalin also won recognition as commissar of nationalities, a key position in which he governed many of Russia's minorities.

The "practical" Stalin also won because he appeared better able than the brilliant Trotsky to relate Marxist teaching to Russian realities in the 1920s. First, as commissar of nationalities, he built on Lenin's idea of granting minority groups a certain degree of freedom in culture and language while maintaining rigorous political control through carefully selected local Communists. Stalin could loudly claim, therefore, to have found a way to solve the ancient problem of ethnic demands for independence in the multinational state. And of course he did.

Second, Stalin developed a theory of "socialism in one country," which was more appealing to the majority of Communists than Trotsky's doctrine of "permanent revolution." Stalin argued that Russia had the ability to build socialism on its own. Trotsky maintained that socialism in Russia could succeed only if revolution occurred quickly throughout Europe. To many communists, Trotsky's views seemed to sell Russia short and to promise risky conflicts with capitalist countries by recklessly encouraging revolutionary movements around the world. Stalin's willingness to break with NEP and push socialism at home appealed to young militants. In short, Stalin's theory of socialism in one country provided many in the party with a glimmer of hope in the midst of the capitalist-appearing NEP, which they had come to detest.

With cunning skill Stalin gradually achieved absolute power between 1922 and 1927. First he allied with Trotsky's personal enemies to crush Trotsky, who was expelled from the Soviet Union in 1929 and eventually was murdered in Mexico in 1940, undoubtedly on Stalin's order. Stalin then aligned with the moderates, who wanted to go slow at home, to suppress Trotsky's radical followers. Finally, having defeated all the radicals, he turned against his allies, the moderates, and destroyed them as well. Stalin's final triumph came at the Party Congress of December 1927, which condemned all "deviation from the general party line" formulated by Stalin. The dictator was then ready to launch his "revolution from above"—the real Russian revolution for millions of ordinary citizens.

The Five-Year Plans

The Party Congress of 1927, which ratified Stalin's seizure of power, marked the end of the New Economic Policy and the beginning of the era of socialist five-year plans. The first five-year plan had staggering economic objectives. In just five years, total industrial output was to increase by 250 percent. Heavy industry, the preferred sector, was to grow even faster; steel production, for example, was to jump almost 300 percent. Agricultural production was slated to increase by 150 percent, and one-fifth of Russia's peasants were scheduled to give up their private plots and join socialist collective farms. In spite of warnings from moderate Communists that these goals were unrealistic, Stalin raised them higher as the plan got under way. By 1930 a whirlwind of economic and social change was sweeping the country.

Stalin unleashed his "second revolution" for a variety of interrelated reasons. There were, first of all, ideological considerations. Like Lenin, Stalin and his militant supporters were deeply committed to socialism as they understood it. Since the country had recovered economically and their rule was secure, they burned to stamp out NEP's private traders, independent artisans, and few well-to-do peasants. Purely economic motivations were also important. Although the economy had recovered, it seemed to have stalled in 1927 and 1928. A new socialist offensive seemed necessary if industry and agriculture were to grow rapidly.

Political considerations were most important. Internationally, there was the old problem, remaining from prerevolutionary times, of catching up with the advanced and presumably hostile capitalist nations of the West. As Stalin said in 1931, when he pressed for ever-greater speed and sacrifice: "We are fifty or a hundred years behind the advanced countries. We must make good this distance in ten years. Either we do it, or we shall go under."[3]

Domestically, there was what Communist writers of the 1920s called the "cursed problem"—the problem of the Russian peasants. For centuries, Russian peasants had wanted to own the land, and finally they had it. Sooner or later, the Communists reasoned, the peasants would become conservative little capitalists and pose a threat to the regime. Therefore, Stalin decided on a preventive war against the peasantry, in order to bring it under the absolute control of the state.

That war was *collectivization*—the forcible consolidation of individual peasant farms into large, state-controlled enterprises. Beginning in 1929, peasants all over the Soviet Union were ordered to give up their land and animals and to become members of collective farms, although they continued to live in their own homes. As for the *kulaks,* the better-off peasants, Stalin instructed party workers to "liquidate them as a class." Stripped of their land and livestock, the kulaks were generally not even permitted to join the collective farms. Many starved or were deported to forced-labor camps for "re-education."

Since almost all peasants were in fact poor, the term *kulak* soon meant any peasant who opposed the new system. Whole villages were often attacked. One conscience-stricken colonel in the secret police confessed to a foreign journalist: "I am an old Bolshevik. I worked in the underground against the Tsar and then I fought in the Civil War. Did I do all that in order that I should now surround villages with machineguns and order my men to fire indiscriminately into crowds of peasants? Oh, no, no!"[4]

Forced collectivization of the peasants led to economic and human disaster. Large numbers of peasants slaughtered their animals and burned their crops in sullen, hopeless protest. Between 1929 and 1933, the number of horses, cattle, sheep, and goats in the Soviet Union fell by at least half. Nor were the state-controlled collective farms more productive. The output of grain barely increased between 1928 and 1938, when it was almost identical to that of 1913. Communist economists had expected collectivized agriculture to pay for new factories. Instead, the state had to invest heavily in agriculture, building thousands of tractors to replace slaughtered draft horses. Collectivized agriculture was unable to make any substantial financial contribution to Soviet industrial development in the first five-year plan. The human dimension of the tragedy was shocking. Collectivization created man-made famine in 1932 and 1933, and many perished. Indeed, Stalin confided to Churchill at Yalta in 1945 that 10 million people had died in the course of collectivization.

Yet collectivization was a political victory of sorts. By the end of 1932, fully 60 percent of Russian peasant families had been herded onto collective farms; by 1938, 93 percent. Regimented and indoctrinated as employees of an all-powerful state, the peasants were no longer even a potential political threat to Stalin and the Communist party. Moreover, the state was assured of grain for bread for urban workers, who were much more important politically than the peasants. Collective farmers had to meet their grain quotas first and worry about feeding themselves second. Many collectivized peasants drew much of their own food from tiny, grudgingly tolerated garden plots that they worked in their off hours. No wonder some peasants joked, with that grim humor peculiar to the totalitarian society, that the initials then used by the Communist party actually stood for "The Second Serfdom, That of the Bolsheviks."

The industrial side of the five-year plans was more successful—indeed, quite spectacular. The output of industry doubled in the first five-year plan and doubled again in the second. Soviet industry produced about four times as much in 1937 as it had in 1928. No other major country had ever achieved such rapid industrial growth. Heavy industry led the way; consumer industry grew quite slowly. Steel production—a near-obsession with Stalin, whose name fittingly meant "man of steel" in Russian—increased roughly 500 percent between 1928 and 1937. A new heavy industrial complex was built almost from scratch in western Siberia. Industrial growth also went hand in hand with urban development. Cities rose where nomadic tribes had grazed their flocks. More than 25 million people migrated to cities during the 1930s.

The great industrialization drive, concentrated between 1928 and 1937, was an awe-inspiring achievement purchased at enormous sacrifice. The sudden creation of dozens of new factories required a great increase in investment and a sharp decrease in consumption. Few nations had ever invested more than one-sixth of their yearly net national income. Soviet planners decreed that more that one-third of net income go for investment. This meant that only two-thirds of everything being produced could be consumed by the people *and* the increasingly voracious military. The money was collected from the people by means of heavy, hidden sales taxes.

There was, therefore, no improvement in the average standard of living. Indeed, the most careful studies show that the average nonfarm wage apparently purchased only about *half* as many goods in 1932 as in 1928. After 1932 real wages rose slowly, so that in 1937 workers could buy about 60 percent of what they had bought in 1928. Thus rapid industrial development went with an unprecedented decline in the standard of living for ordinary people.

Two other factors contributed importantly to rapid industrialization: firm labor discipline and foreign engineers. Between 1930 and 1932, trade unions lost most of their power. The government could assign workers to any job anywhere in the country, and individuals could not move without the permission of the police. When factory managers needed more hands, they called on their counterparts on the collective farms, who sent them millions of "unneeded" peasants over the years.

Foreign engineers were hired to plan and construct many of the new factories. Highly skilled American engineers, hungry for work in the depression years, were particularly important until newly trained Soviet experts began to replace them after 1932. The gigantic mills of the new Siberian steel industry were modeled on America's best. Those modern mills were eloquent testimony to the ability of Stalin's planners to harness even the skill and technology of capitalist countries to promote the surge of socialist industry.

Life in Stalinist Society

The aim of Stalin's five-year plans was to create a new kind of society and human personality, as well as a strong industrial economy and a powerful army. Stalin and his helpers were good Marxian economic determinists. Once everything was owned by the state, they believed, a socialist society and a new kind of human being would inevitably emerge. They were by no means totally successful, but they did build a new society, whose broad outlines exist to this day. For the people, life in Stalinist society had both good and bad aspects.

The most frightening aspect of Stalinist society was brutal, unrestrained police terrorism. First directed primarily against the peasants after 1929, terror was increasingly turned on leading Communists, powerful administrators, and ordinary people for no apparent reason. As one Soviet woman later recalled: "We all trembled because there was no way of getting out of it. Even a Communist himself can be caught. To avoid trouble became an exception."[5] A climate of fear fell on the land.

In the early 1930s, the top members of the party and government were Stalin's obedient servants, but there was some grumbling in the party. At a small gathering in November 1932, even Stalin's wife complained bitterly about the misery of the people. Stalin showered her with insults, and she died that same night, apparently by her own hand. In late 1934 Stalin's number-two man, Sergei Kirov, was suddenly and mysteriously murdered. Although Stalin himself probably ordered Kirov's murder, he used the incident to launch a reign of terror.

In August 1936 sixteen prominent old Bolsheviks confessed to all manner of plots against Stalin in spectacular public trials in Moscow. Then, in 1937, lesser party officials and newer henchmen were arrested. In addition to party members, union officials, managers, intellectuals, army officers, and countless ordinary citizens were struck down. Local units of the secret police were even ordered to arrest a certain percentage of the people in their district. In all, at least 8 million people were probably arrested, and millions never returned from prisons and forced labor camps.

Stalin's mass purges were truly baffling, and many explanations have been given for them. Possibly Stalin believed that the old Communists, like the peasants under NEP, were a potential threat to be wiped out in a preventive attack. Yet why did leading Communists willingly confess to crimes they could not possibly have committed? Their lives had been devoted to the party and the socialist revolution. In the words of the German novelist Arthur Koestler, they probably confessed "in order to do a last service to the Party," the party they loved even when it was wrong. Some of them were subjected to torture and brainwashing. It has been argued that the purges indicate that Stalin was sadistic or insane, for his bloodbath greatly weakened the government and the army. Others see the terror as an aspect of the fully developed totalitarian state, which must by its nature always be fighting real or imaginary enemies. At the least, the mass purges were a message to the people: no one was secure. Everyone had to serve the party and its leader with redoubled devotion.

Another aspect of life in the 1930s was constant propaganda and indoctrination. Party activists lectured workers in factories and peasants on collective farms, while newspapers, films, and radio broadcasts endlessly recounted socialist achievements and capitalist plots. Art and literature became highly political. Whereas the 1920s had seen considerable experimentation in modern art and theater, the intellectual elite were ordered by Stalin to become "engineers of human minds." Writers and artists who could effectively combine genuine creativity and political propaganda became the darlings of the regime. They often lived better than top members of the political elite. It became increasingly important for the successful writer and artist to glorify Russian nationalism. Russian history was rewritten so that early tsars like Ivan the Terrible and Peter the Great became worthy forerunners of the greatest Russian leader of all—Stalin.

Adult Education Illiteracy, especially among women, was a serious problem after the Russian Revolution. This early photo shows how adults successfully learned to read and write throughout the Soviet Union. *(Sovfoto/Eastfoto)*

Stalin seldom appeared in public, but his presence was everywhere—in portraits, statues, books, and quotations from his "sacred" writings. Although the government persecuted religion and turned churches into "museums of atheism," the state had both an earthly religion and a high priest—Marxian socialism and Joseph Stalin.

Life was hard in Stalin's Soviet Russia. The standard of living declined substantially in the 1930s. The masses of people lived primarily on black bread and wore old, shabby clothing. There were constant shortages in the stores, although very heavily taxed vodka was always readily available. A shortage of housing was a particularly serious problem. Millions were moving into the cities, but the government built few new apartments. In 1940 there were approximately 4 people per room in every urban dwelling, as opposed to 2.7 per room in 1926. A relatively lucky family received one room for all its members and shared both a kitchen and a toilet with others on the floor. Less-fortunate workers, kulaks, and class enemies built scrap-lumber shacks or underground dugouts in shantytowns.

Life was hard, but by no means hopeless. Idealism and ideology had real appeal for many Russians, who saw themselves heroically building the world's first socialist society while capitalism crumbled in the West. This optimistic belief in the future of Soviet Russia also attracted many disillusioned Western liberals to communism in the 1930s.

On a more practical level, Soviet workers did receive some important social benefits, such as old-age pensions, free medical services, free education, and day-care centers for children. Unemployment was almost unknown. Finally, there was the possibility of personal advancement.

The keys to improving one's position were specialized skills and technical education. Rapid industrialization required massive numbers of trained experts, such as skilled workers, engineers, and plant managers. Thus the state provided tremendous incentives to those who could serve its needs. It paid the mass of unskilled workers and collective farmers very low wages, but it dangled high salaries and many special privileges before its growing technical and managerial elite. This elite joined with the political and artistic elites in a new upper class, whose members were rich, powerful, and insecure, especially during the purges. Yet the possible gains of moving up outweighed the risks. Millions struggled bravely in universities, institutes, and night schools for the all-important specialized education. One young man summed it up: "In Soviet Russia there is no capital except education. If a person does not want to become a collective farmer or just a cleaning woman, the only means you have to get something is through education."[6]

Women in Soviet Russia

Women's lives were radically altered by Stalinist society. Marxists had traditionally believed that both capitalism and the middle-class husband exploited women. The Russian Revolution of 1917 immediately proclaimed complete equality of rights for women. In the 1920s, divorce and abortion were made very easy, and women were urged to work outside the home and liberate themselves sexually. A prominent and influential Bolshevik feminist, Alexandra Kollontai, went so far as to declare that the sexual act had no more significance than "drinking a glass of water." This observation drew a sharp rebuke from the rathet prudish Lenin, who said that "no sane man would lie down to drink from a puddle in the gutter or even drink from a dirty glass."[7] After Stalin came to power, sexual and familial liberation was played down, and the most lasting changes for women involved work and education.

The changes were truly revolutionary. Young women were constantly told that they must be fully equal with men, that they could and should do anything men could do. Russian peasant women had long experienced the equality of backbreaking physical labor in the countryside, and they continued to enjoy that equality on collective farms. With the advent of the five-year plans, millions of women also began to toil in factories and on heavy construction, building dams, roads, and steel mills in summer heat and winter frost. Yet most of the opportunities open to men through education were also opened to women. Determined women pursued their studies and entered the ranks of the better-paid specialists in industry and science. Medicine practically became a woman's profession. By 1950, 75 percent of all doctors in Soviet Russia were women.

Thus Stalinist society gave women great opportunities but demanded great sacrifices as well. The vast majority of women simply *had* to work outside the home. Wages were so low that it was almost impossible for a family or couple to live only on the husband's earnings. Moreover, the full-time working woman had a heavy burden of household tasks in her off hours, for most Soviet men in the 1930s still considered the home and the children the woman's responsibility. Finally, rapid change and economic hardship led to many broken families, creating further physical, emotional, and mental strains for women. In any event, the often-neglected human resource of women was ruthlessly mobilized in Stalinist society. This, too, was an aspect of the Soviet totalitarian state.

MUSSOLINI'S ITALY

Before turning to Hitler's Germany, it is necessary to look briefly at Mussolini's role in Italy. Like all the other emerging dictators, Mussolini hated liberalism, and he destroyed it in Italy. But that was not all. Mussolini and his supporters were the first to call themselves "fascists"—revolutionaries determined to create a certain kind of totalitarian state. As Mussolini's famous slogan of 1926 put it: "Everything in the state, nothing outside the state, nothing against the state." But Mussolini in power, unlike Stalin and Hitler, did not in fact create a real totalitarian state.

His dictatorship was rather an instructive hybrid, a halfway house between conservative authoritarianism and modern totalitarianism.

THE SEIZURE OF POWER

Before the First World War, Italy was a liberal state moving gradually toward democracy. But there were serious problems. Much of the Italian population was still poor, and class differences were extreme. Many peasants were more attached to their villages and local interests than to the national state. Moreover, the papacy and many devout Catholics, as well as the socialists, were strongly opposed to the heirs of Cavour and Garibaldi, middle-class lawyers and politicians who ran the country largely for their own benefit. Relations between church and state were often tense.

The war worsened the political situation. Having fought on the side of the Allies almost exclusively for purposes of territorial expansion, Italian nationalists were bitterly disappointed with Italy's modest gains at Versailles. Workers and peasants also felt cheated: to win their support during the war, the government had promised social and land reform, which it did not deliver after the war.

Encouraged by the Russian Revolution of 1917, radical workers and peasants began occupying factories and seizing land in 1920. These actions scared and radicalized the property-owning classes. The Italian middle classes were already in an ugly mood, having suffered from inflation during the war. Moreover, after the war, the pope lifted his ban on participation by Catholics in Italian politics, and a strong Catholic party quickly emerged. Thus by 1922 almost all the major groups in Italian society were opposed—though for different reasons—to the liberal parliamentary government.

Into these cross-currents of unrest and frustration stepped the blustering, bullying Benito Mussolini (1883–1945). Son of a village schoolteacher and a poor blacksmith, Mussolini began his political career as a Socialist leader and radical newspaper editor before World War One. In 1914, powerfully influenced by antiliberal cults of violent action, the young Mussolini urged that Italy join the Allies, for which he was expelled from the Italian Socialist party by its antiwar majority. Later Mussolini fought at the front and was wounded in 1917. Returning home, he began organizing bitter war veterans like himself into a band of Fascists—from the Italian word for "a union of forces."

At first, Mussolini's program was a radical combination of nationalist and socialist demands, including territorial expansion, benefits for workers, and land reform for peasants. As such, it competed with the better-organized Socialist party and failed to get off the ground. When Mussolini saw that his violent verbal assaults on the rival Socialists won him growing support from the frightened middle class, he shifted gears in 1920. In thought and action, Mussolini was a striking example of the turbulence of the age of anxiety.

Mussolini and his growing private army of Black Shirts began to grow violent. Typically, a band of Fascist toughs would roar off in trucks at night and swoop down on a few isolated Socialist organizers, beating them up and force-feeding them almost deadly doses of castor oil. Few people were killed, but Socialist newspapers, union halls, and local Socialist party headquarters were destroyed. Mussolini's toughs pushed Communists and Socialists out of the city governments of northern Italy.

Mussolini, a skillful politician, refused to become a puppet of frightened conservatives and capitalists. He allowed his followers to convince themselves that they were not just opposing the "reds," but making a real revolution of their own. Many believed that they were not only destroying parliamentary government, but forming a strong, dynamic movement that would help the little people against the established interests.

With the government breaking down in 1922, largely because of the chaos created by his direct-action bands, Mussolini stepped forward as the savior of order and property. Striking a conservative note in his speeches and gaining the sympathetic neutrality of army leaders, Mussolini demanded the resignation of the existing government and his own appointment by the king. In October 1922, to force matters a large group of Fascists marched on Rome to threaten the king and force him to call on Mussolini. The threat worked. Victor Emmanuel III (1900–1946), who had no love for the old liberal politicians, asked Mussolini to form a new cabinet. Thus, after widespread violence and a threat of armed uprising, Mussolini seized power "legally." He was immediately granted dictatorial authority for one year by the king and the parliament.

Mussolini loved to swagger and bluster. Here he strikes a theatrical pose while reviewing his troops in Rome. *(BBC Hulton/The Bettmann Archive)*

The Regime in Action

Mussolini became dictator on the strength of Italians' rejection of parliamentary government, coupled with fears of Russian-style revolution. Yet what he intended to do with his power was by no means clear until 1924. Some of his dedicated supporters pressed for a "second revolution." Mussolini's ministers, however, included old Conservatives, Moderates, and even two reform-minded Socialists. A new electoral law was passed giving two-thirds of the representatives in the parliament to the party that won the most votes, which allowed the Fascists and their allies to win an overwhelming majority in 1924. Shortly thereafter, five of Mussolini's Fascist thugs kidnapped and murdered Giacomo Matteotti, the young leader of the Socialists in the parliament. In the face of this outrage, the opposition demanded that Mussolini's armed squads be dissolved and all violence be banned.

Although he may or may not have ordered Matteotti's murder, Mussolini stood at the crossroads of a severe political crisis. After some hesitation, he charged forward. Declaring his desire to "make the nation Fascist," he imposed a series of repressive measures. Freedom of the press was abolished, elections were fixed, and the government ruled by decree. Mussolini arrested his political opponents, disbanded all independent labor unions, and put dedicated Fascists in control of Italy's schools. Moreover, he created a Fascist youth movement, Fascist labor unions, and many other Fascist organizations. By the end of 1926, Italy was a one-party dictatorship under Mussolini's unquestioned leadership.

Yet Mussolini did not complete the establishment of a modern totalitarian state. His Fascist party never became all-powerful. It never destroyed the old power structure, as the Communists did in Soviet Russia, or succeeded in dominating it, as the Nazis did in Germany. Membership in the Fascist party was more a sign of an Italian's respectability than a commitment to radical change. Interested primarily in personal power, Mussolini was content to compromise with the old conservative classes that controlled the army, the economy, and the state. He never tried to purge these classes or even move very vigorously against them. He controlled and propagandized labor, but left big business to regulate itself, profitably and securely. There was no land reform.

Mussolini also came to draw on the support of the Catholic church. In the Lateran Agreement of 1929, he recognized the Vatican as a tiny independent state, and he agreed to give the church heavy financial support. The pope expressed his satisfaction and urged Italians to support Mussolini's government.

Nothing better illustrates Mussolini's unwillingness to harness everyone and everything for dynamic action than his treatment of women. He abolished divorce and told women to stay at home and produce children. To promote that goal, he decreed a special tax on bachelors in 1934. In 1938 women were limited by law to a maximum of 10 percent of the better-paying jobs in industry and government. Italian women, as women, appear not to have changed their attitudes or behavior in any important way under Fascist rule.

It is also noteworthy that Mussolini's government did not persecute Jews until late in the Second World War, when Italy was under Nazi control. Nor did Mussolini establish a truly ruthless police state. Only twenty-three political prisoners were condemned to death between 1926 and 1944. In spite of much pompous posing by the chauvinist leader and in spite of mass meetings, salutes, and a certain copying of Hitler's aggression in foreign policy after 1933, Mussolini's Italy—though undemocratic—was never really totalitarian.

Adolf Hitler A lonely, unsuccessful misfit before 1914, Hitler found his mission during World War One and its aftermath. He emerged as a spellbinding speaker and a master of the politics of hate and violence. *(UPI/Bettmann Newsphotos)*

HITLER'S GERMANY

The most frightening totalitarian state was Nazi Germany. A product of Hitler's evil genius as well as of Germany's social and political situation and the general attack on liberalism and rationality in the age of anxiety, Nazi Germany emerged rapidly after Hitler came to power in 1933. The Nazis quickly smashed or took over most independent organizations, mobilized the economy, and began brutally persecuting the Jewish population. From the start, all major decisions were in the hands of the aggressive dictator Adolf Hitler.

The Roots of Nazism

Nazism grew out of many complex developments, of which the most influential were extreme nationalism and racism. These two ideas captured the mind of the young Hitler, and it was he who dominated Nazism for as long as it lasted.

Born the fourth child of a successful Austrian customs official and an indulgent mother, Adolf Hitler (1889–1945) spent his childhood happily in small towns in Austria. A good student in grade school, Hitler did poorly on reaching high school and dropped out at age fourteen after the death of his father. After four years of unfocused loafing, Hitler finally left for Vienna to become an artist. Denied admission to the Imperial Academy of Fine Arts because he lacked talent, the dejected Hitler stayed on in Vienna. There he lived a comfortable, lazy life on his generous orphan's pension and found most of the perverted beliefs that guided his life.

In Vienna Hitler soaked up extreme German nationalism, which was particularly strong there. Austro-German nationalists, as if to compensate for their declining position in the Austro-Hungarian Empire, believed Germans to be a superior people and the natural rulers of central Europe. They often advocated union with Germany and violent expulsion of "inferior" peoples as the means of maintaining German domination of the Austro-Hungarian Empire.

Hitler was deeply impressed by Vienna's mayor, Karl Lueger, whom he called the "mightiest mayor of all times." Lueger claimed to be a "Christian socialist." With the help of the Catholic trade unions, he had succeeded in winning the support of the little people of Vienna for an attack on capitalism and liberalism, which he held responsible for un-Christian behavior and excessive individualism. A master of mass politics in the urban world, Lueger showed Hitler the enormous potential of anticapitalist and antiliberal propaganda.

From Lueger and others, Hitler eagerly absorbed virulent anti-Semitism, racism, and hatred of Slavs. He was particularly inspired by the racist ravings of an ex-monk named Lanz von Liebenfels. Preaching the crudest, most exaggerated distortions of the Darwinian theory of survival, Liebenfels stressed the superiority of Germanic races, the inevitability of racial conflict, and the inferiority of the Jews. Liebenfels even anticipated the breeding and extermination policies of the Nazi state. He claimed that the master race had to multiply its numbers by means of polygamy and breeding stations, while it systematically sterilized and liquidated inferior races. Anti-Semitism and racism became Hitler's most passionate convictions, his explanation for everything. He believed inferior races—the Slavs and the Jews in particular—were responsible for Austria's woes. The Jews, he claimed, directed an international conspiracy of finance capitalism and Marxian socialism against German culture, German unity, and the German race. Hitler's belief was totally irrational, but he never doubted it.

Although he moved to Munich in 1913 to avoid being drafted in the Austrian army, the lonely Hitler greeted the outbreak of the First World War as a salvation. He later wrote in his autobiography, *Mein Kampf,* that, "overcome by passionate enthusiasm, I fell to my knees and thanked heaven out of an overflowing heart." The struggle and discipline of war gave life meaning, and Hitler served bravely as a dispatch carrier on the western front.

When Germany was suddenly defeated in 1918, Hitler's world was shattered. Not only was he a fanatical nationalist, but war was his reason for living. Convinced that Jews and Marxists had "stabbed Germany in the back," he vowed to fight on. And in the bitterness and uncertainty of postwar Germany, his wild speeches began to attract attention.

In late 1919 Hitler joined a tiny extremist group in Munich called the German Workers' party. In addition to denouncing Jews, Marxists, and democrats, the German Workers' party promised unity under a uniquely German "national socialism," which would abolish the injustices of capitalism and create a mighty "people's community." By 1921 Hitler had gained absolute control of this small but growing party. Moreover, Hitler was already a master of mass propaganda and political showmanship. Party members sported badges and uniforms, gave victory salutes, and marched like robots through the streets of Munich. But Hitler's most effective tool was the mass rally, a kind of political revival meeting. Songs, slogans, and demonstrations built up the tension until Hitler finally arrived. He then often worked his audience into a frenzy with wild, demagogic attacks on the Versailles treaty, the Jews, the war profiteers, and Germany's Weimar Republic.

Party membership multiplied tenfold after early 1922. In late 1923, when the Weimar Republic seemed on the verge of collapse, Hitler decided on an armed uprising in Munich. Inspired by Mussolini's recent easy victory, Hitler had found an ally in General Ludendorff of First World War fame. After Hitler had overthrown the Bavarian government, Ludendorff was supposed to march on Berlin with Hitler's support. The plot was poorly organized, however, and it was crushed by the police, backed up by the army, in less than a day. Hitler was arrested, tried, and sentenced to five years in prison. He had failed for the moment. But Nazism had been born, and it did not die.

Hitler's Road to Power

At his trial, Hitler violently denounced the Weimar Republic and skillfully presented his own program. In doing so he gained enormous publicity and attention. Moreover, he learned from his unsuccessful

"Hitler, Our Last Hope" So reads the very effective Nazi campaign poster, which is attracting attention with its gaunt and haggard faces. By 1932 almost half of all Germans, like these in Berlin, had come to agree. *(Bildarchiv Preussischer Kulturbesitz)*

revolt. Hitler concluded that he had to undermine rather than overthrow the government, that he had to use its tolerant democratic framework to intimidate the opposition and come to power through electoral competition. He forced his more violent supporters to accept his new strategy. Finally, Hitler used his brief prison term—he was released in less than a year—to dictate *Mein Kampf.* There he expounded on his basic themes—"race," with the stress on anti-Semitism; "living space," with a sweeping vision of war and conquered territory; and the leader-dictator (*Führer*) with unlimited, arbitary power. Hitler's followers had their bible.

In the years of prosperity and relative stability between 1924 and 1929, Hitler concentrated on building his National Socialist German Workers' party, or Nazi party. By 1928 the party had a hundred thousand highly disciplined members under Hitler's absolute control. To appeal to the middle class, Hitler de-emphasized the anticapitalist elements of national socialism and vowed to fight Bolshevism.

The Nazis were still a small splinter group in 1928, when they received only 2.6 percent of the vote in the general elections and twelve Nazis won seats in the parliament. There the Nazi deputies pursued the legal strategy of using democracy to destroy democracy. As Hitler's talented future minister of propaganda Joseph Goebbels (1897–1945) explained in 1928 in the party newspaper: "We become Reichstag deputies in order to paralyze the spirit of Weimar with its own aid. . . . We come as enemies! As the wolf breaks into the sheepfold, so we come."[8]

In 1929 the Great Depression began striking down economic prosperity, one of the barriers that had kept the wolf at bay. Unemployment jumped from 1.3 million in 1929 to 5 million in 1930; that year Germany had almost as many unemployed as all the other countries of Europe combined. Industrial production fell by one-half between 1929 and 1932. By the end of 1932, an incredible 43 percent of the labor force was unemployed, and it was estimated that only one in every three union members was working full time. No factor contributed more to Hitler's success than the economic crisis. Never very interested in economics before, Hitler began promising German voters economic as well as political and military salvation.

Hitler focused his promises on the middle and lower-middle class—small businessmen, office workers, artisans, and peasants. Already disillusioned by the great inflation of 1923, these people were seized by panic as bankruptcies increased, unemployment soared, and the dreaded Communists made dramatic election gains. The middle and lower-middle classes deserted the Conservative and Moderate parties for the Nazis in great numbers.

The Nazis also appealed strongly to German youth. Indeed, in some ways the Nazi movement was a mass movement of young Germans. Hitler himself was only forty in 1929, and he and most of his top aides were much younger than other leading German politicians. "National Socialism is the organized will of the youth," proclaimed the official Nazi slogan, and the battle cry of Gregor Strasser, a leading Nazi organizer, was, "Make way, you old ones."[9] In 1931 almost 40 percent of Nazi party members were under thirty, compared to 20 percent of Social Democrats. Two-thirds of Nazi members were under forty. National recovery, exciting and rapid change, and personal advancement: these were the appeals of Nazism to millions of German youths.

In the election of 1930, the Nazis won 6.5 million votes and 107 seats, which made them second in strength only to the Social Democrats, the moderate socialists. The economic situation continued to deteriorate, and Hitler kept promising he would bring recovery. In 1932 the Nazi vote leaped to 14.5 million, and the Nazis became the largest party in the Reichstag.

Another reason Hitler came to power was the breakdown of democratic government as early as May 1930. Unable to gain support of a majority in the Reichstag, Chancellor (chief minister) Heinrich Brüning convinced the president, the aging war hero General Hindenburg, to authorize rule by decree. The Weimar Republic's constitution permitted such rule in emergency situations, but the rather authoritarian, self-righteous Brüning intended to use it indefinitely. Moreover, Brüning was determined to overcome the economic crisis by cutting back government spending and ruthlessly forcing down prices and wages. Brüning's ultraorthodox policies not only intensified the economic collapse in Germany, they also convinced the lower-middle classes that the country's republican leaders were stupid and corrupt. These classes were pleased rather than dismayed by Hitler's attacks on the republican system. After President Hindenburg forced Brüning to resign in May 1932, the new government headed by Franz von Papen continued to rule by decree.

The continuation of the struggle between the Social Democrats and Communists, right up until the moment Hitler took power, was another aspect of the breakdown of democratic government. The Communists foolishly refused to cooperate with the Social Democrats, even though the two parties together outnumbered the Nazis in the Reichstag, even after the elections of 1932. German Communists (and the complacent Stalin) were blinded by their ideology and their hatred of the Socialists. They were certain that Hitler's rise represented the last agonies of monopoly capitalism and that a Communist revolution would quickly follow his taking power. The Socialist leaders pleaded, even at the Russian embassy, for at least a temporary alliance with the Communists to block Hitler, but to no avail. Perhaps the Weimar Republic was already too far gone, but this disunity on the left was undoubtedly another nail in its coffin.

Finally, there was Hitler's skill as a politician. A master of mass propaganda and psychology, he had written in *Mein Kampf* that the masses were the "driving force of the most important changes in this world" and were themselves driven by hysterical fanaticism and not by knowledge. To arouse such hysterical fanaticism, he believed that all propaganda had to be limited to a few simple, endlessly repeated

The Mobilization of Young People was a prime objective of the Nazi leadership. Here boys in a Nazi youth group, some of whom are only children, are disciplined and conditioned to devote themselves to the regime. *(BBC Hulton/The Bettmann Archive)*

slogans. Thus, in the terrible economic and political crisis, he harangued vast audiences with passionate, irrational oratory. Men moaned and women cried, seized by emotion. And many uncertain individuals, surrounded by thousands of entranced listeners, found security and a sense of belonging.

At the same time, Hitler excelled at dirty, backroom politics. That, in fact, brought him to power. In 1932 he cleverly succeeded in gaining the support of key people in the army and big business. These people thought they could use Hitler for their own advantage, to get increased military spending, fat contracts, and tough measures against workers. Conservative and nationalistic politicians like Papen thought similarly. They thus accepted Hitler's demand to join the government only if he became chancellor. There would be only two other National Socialists and nine solid Conservatives as ministers, and in such a coalition government, they reasoned, Hitler could be used and controlled. On January 30, 1933, Hitler was legally appointed chancellor by President Hindenburg.

The Nazi State and Society

Hitler moved rapidly and skillfully to establish an unshakable dictatorship. His first step was to continue using terror and threats to gain more power while maintaining legal appearances. He immediately called for new elections and applied the enormous power of the government to restrict his opponents. In the midst of a violent electoral campaign, the Reichstag building was partly destroyed by fire. Although the Nazis themselves may have set the fire, Hitler screamed that the Communist party was responsible. On the strength of this accusation, he convinced President Hindenburg to sign dictatorial emergency acts that practically abolished freedom of speech and assembly, in addition to most personal liberties.

When the Nazis won only 44 percent of the vote in the elections, Hitler immediately outlawed the Communist party and arrested its parliamentary representatives. Then, on March 23, 1933, the Nazis pushed through the Reichstag the so-called Enabling Act, which gave Hitler absolute dictatorial power for four years. Only the Social Democrats voted against this bill, for Hitler had successfully blackmailed the Center party by threatening to attack the Catholic church.

Armed with the Enabling Act, Hitler and the Nazis moved to smash or control all independent organizations. Meanwhile, Hitler and his propagandists constantly proclaimed that their revolution was legal and constitutional. This deceitful stress on legality, coupled with the divide-and-conquer technique, disarmed the opposition until it was too late for effective resistance.

The systematic subjugation of independent organizations and the creation of a totalitarian state had massive repercussions. The Social Democrat and Center parties were soon dissolved, and Germany became a one-party state. Only the Nazi party was legal. Elections were farces. The Reichstag was jokingly referred to as the most expensive glee club in the country, for its only function was to sing hymns of praise to the Führer. Hitler and the Nazis took over the government bureaucracy intact, installing many Nazis in top positions. At the same time, they created a series of overlapping Nazi party organizations, responsible solely to Hitler. Thus Hitler had both an established bureaucracy for normal business and a private, personal "party government" for special duties.

In the economic sphere, strikes were forbidden and labor unions were abolished, replaced by a Nazi Labor Front. Professional people—doctors and lawyers, teachers and engineers—also saw their previously independent organizations swallowed up in Nazi associations. Nor did the Nazis neglect cultural and intellectual life. Publishing houses were put under Nazi control, and universities and writers were quickly brought into line. Democratic, socialist, and Jewish literature was put on ever-growing blacklists. Passionate students and pitiful professors burned forbidden books in public squares. Modern art and architecture were ruthlessly prohibited. Life became violently anti-intellectual. As Hitler's cynical minister of propaganda, Joseph Goebbels, put it: "When I hear the word 'culture' I reach for my gun."[10] By 1934 a totalitarian state characterized by frightening dynamism and obedience to Hitler was already largely in place.

By 1934 only the army retained independence, and Hitler moved brutally and skillfully to establish his control there, too. He realized that the army, as well as big business, was suspicious of the Nazi storm troopers (the SA), the quasi-military band of 3 million toughs in brown shirts who had fought Communists and beaten up Jews before the Nazis took power. These unruly storm troopers expected top positions in the army and even talked of a "second revolution" against capitalism. Needing the support of the army and big business, Hitler decided that the SA leaders had to be eliminated. On the night of June 30, 1934, he struck.

Hitler's elite personal guard—the SS—arrested and shot without trial roughly a thousand SA leaders and assorted political enemies. While his propagandists spread lies about SA conspiracies, the army leaders and President Hindenburg responded to the purge with congratulatory telegrams. Shortly thereafter, the army leaders swore a binding oath of "unquestioning obedience . . . to the Leader of the German State and People, Adolf Hitler." The purge of the SA was another decisive step toward unlimited totalitarian terror. The SS, the elite guard that had loyally murdered the SA leaders, grew rapidly. Under its methodical, inhuman leader, Heinrich Himmler (1900–1945), the SS joined with the political police, the Gestapo, to expand its network of special courts and concentration camps. Nobody was safe.

From the beginning, the Jews were a special object of Nazi persecution. By the end of 1934, most Jewish lawyers, doctors, professors, civil servants, and musicians had lost their jobs and right to practice their professions. In 1935 the infamous Nuremberg Laws classified as Jewish anyone having one or more Jewish grandparents and deprived Jews of all rights of citizenship. By 1938 roughly one-quarter of Germany's half-million Jews had emigrated, sacrificing almost all their property in order to leave Germany.

Following the assassination of a German diplomat in Paris by a young Jewish boy trying desperately to strike out at persecution, the attack on the Jews accelerated. A well-organized wave of violence destroyed homes, synagogues, and businesses, after which German Jews were rounded up and made to pay for the damage. It became very difficult for Jews to leave Germany. Some Germans privately opposed these outrages, but most went along or looked the other way. Although this lack of response partly reflected the individual's helplessness in the totalitarian state, it was also a sign of the strong popular support Hitler's government enjoyed.

Hitler's Popularity

Hitler had promised the masses economic recovery —"work and bread"—and he delivered. Breaking with Brüning's do-nothing policies, Hitler immediately launched a large public works program to pull Germany out of the depression. Work began on superhighways, offices, gigantic sports stadia, and public housing. In 1936, as Germany rearmed rapidly, government spending began to concentrate on the military. The result was that unemployment dropped steadily, from 6 million in January 1933 to about 1 million in late 1936. By 1938 there was a shortage of workers, and women eventually took many jobs previously denied them by the antifeminist Nazis. Thus everyone had work, and between 1932 and 1938 the standard of living for the average employed worker rose more than 20 percent. The profits of business also increased. For millions of people, economic recovery was tangible evidence in their daily lives that the excitement and dynamism of Nazi rule were based on more than show.

For the masses of ordinary German citizens, who were not Jews, Slavs, gypsies, Jehovah's Witnesses, or Communists, Hitler's government meant greater equality and exceptional opportunities. It must be remembered that in 1933 the position of the traditional German elites—the landed aristocracy, the wealthy capitalists, and the well-educated professional classes —was still very strong. Barriers between classes were generally high. Hitler's rule introduced vast changes in this pattern. For example, stiff educational requirements, which favored the well-to-do, were greatly relaxed. The new Nazi elite was composed largely of young and poorly educated dropouts, rootless lower-middle-class people like Hitler, who rose to the top with breathtaking speed.

More generally, the Nazis, like the Russian Communists, tolerated privilege and wealth only as long as they served the needs of the party. Big business was constantly ordered around, to the point that "probably never in peacetime has an ostensibly capitalist economy been directed as non- and even anti-capitalistically as the German economy between 1933 and 1939."[11] Hitler brought about a kind of social revolution, which was enthusiastically embraced by millions of modest middle- and lower-middle-class people and even by many workers.

Hitler's extreme nationalism, which had helped him gain power, continued to appeal to Germans after 1933. Ever since the wars against Napoleon, many Germans had believed in a special mission for a superior German nation. The successes of Bismarck had furthered such feelings, and near-victory in World War One made nationalists eager for re-

Events Leading to World War Two

1919	Treaty of Versailles
	J. M. Keynes, *Economic Consequences of the Peace*
1919–1920	U.S. Senate rejects the Treaty of Versailles
1921	Germany is billed $35 billion in reparations
1922	Mussolini seizes power in Italy
	Germany proposes a moratorium on reparations
January 1923	France and Belgium occupy the Ruhr
	Germany orders passive resistance to the occupation
October 1923	Stresemann agrees to reparations with re-examination of Germany's ability to pay
1924	Dawes Plan: German reparations reduced and put on a sliding scale; large U.S. loans to Germany recommended to promote German recovery; occupation of the Ruhr ends
	Adolf Hitler, *Mein Kampf*
1924–1929	Spectacular German economic recovery; circular flow of international funds enables sizable reparations payments
1925	Treaties of Locarno promote European security and stability
1926	Germany joins the League of Nations
1928	Kellogg-Briand Pact renounces war as an instrument of international affairs
1929	Young Plan further reduces German reparations
	Crash of U.S. stock market
1929–1933	Depths of the Great Depression
1931	Japan invades Manchuria
1932	Nazis become the largest party in the Reichstag
January 1933	Hitler appointed chancellor
March 1933	Reichstag passes the Enabling Act, granting Hitler absolute dictatorial power
October 1933	Germany withdraws from the League of Nations
July 1934	Nazis murder Austrian chancellor
March 1935	Hitler announces German rearmament
June 1935	Anglo-German naval agreement
October 1935	Mussolini invades Ethiopia and receives Hitler's support
1935	Nuremburg Laws deprive Jews of all rights of citizenship
March 1936	German armies move unopposed into the demilitarized Rhineland
July 1936	Outbreak of civil war in Spain
1937	Japan invades China
	Rome-Berlin Axis
March 1938	Germany annexes Austria
September 1938	Munich Conference: Britain and France agree to German seizure of the Sudetenland from Czechoslovakia
March 1939	Germany occupies the rest of Czechoslovakia; the end of appeasement in Britain
August 1939	Russo-German nonaggression pact
September 1, 1939	Germany invades Poland
September 3, 1939	Britain and France declare war on Germany

newed expansion in the 1920s. Thus, when Hitler went from one foreign triumph to another and a great German empire seemed within reach, the majority of the population was delighted and praised the Führer's actions.

By no means all Germans supported Hitler, however, and a number of German groups actively resisted him after 1933. Tens of thousands of political enemies were imprisoned, and thousands were executed. Opponents of the Nazis pursued different goals, and under totalitarian conditions they were never unified, which helps account for their ultimate lack of success. In the first years of Hitler's rule, the principal resisters were the Communists and the Social Democrats in the trade unions. But the expansion of the SS system of terror after 1935 smashed most of these leftists. A second group of opponents arose in the Catholic and Protestant churches. However, their efforts were directly primarily at preserving genuine religious life, not at overthrowing Hitler. Finally, in 1938 (and again in 1942–1944), some high-ranking army officers, who feared the consequences of Hitler's reckless aggression, plotted against him, unsuccessfully.

NAZI EXPANSION AND THE SECOND WORLD WAR

Although economic recovery and increased opportunities for social advancement won Hitler support, they were only by-products of Nazi totalitarianism. The guiding concepts of Nazism remained space and race—the territorial expansion of the superior German race. As Germany regained its economic strength and as independent organizations were brought under control, Hitler formed alliances with other dictators and began expanding. German expansion was facilitated by the uncertain, divided, pacific Western democracies, which tried to buy off Hitler to avoid war. Yet war was inevitable, in both the West and the East, for Hitler's ambitions were essentially unlimited. On both war fronts the Nazi soldiers scored enormous successes until late 1942, establishing a horrifyingly vast empire of death and destruction.

AGGRESSION AND APPEASEMENT, 1933–1939

Hitler's tactics in international politics after 1933 strikingly resembled those he used in domestic politics between 1924 and 1933. When Hitler was weak, he righteously proclaimed that he intended to overturn the "unjust system" established by the treaties of Versailles and Locarno—but only by legal means. As he grew stronger, and as other leaders showed their willingness to compromise, he increased his demands and finally began attacking his independent neighbors (see Map 29.1).

Hitler realized that his aggressive policies had to be carefully camouflaged at first, for Germany's army was limited by the Treaty of Versailles to only a hundred thousand men. As he told a group of army commanders in February 1933, the early stages of his policy of "conquest of new living space in the East and its ruthless Germanization" had serious dangers. If France had real leaders, Hitler said, "it will not give us time but attack us, presumably with its eastern satellites."[12] Thus Hitler loudly proclaimed his peaceful intentions to all the world. Nevertheless, he felt strong enough to walk out of a sixty-nation disarmament conference and withdraw from the League of Nations in October 1933. Stresemann's policy of peaceful cooperation was dead; the Nazi determination to rearm was out in the open.

Following this action, which met with widespread approval at home, Hitler moved to incorporate independent Austria into a Greater Germany. Austrian Nazis climaxed an attempted overthrow by murdering the Austrian chancellor in July 1934. They were unable to take power, however, because a worried Mussolini, who had initially greeted Hitler as a fascist little brother, massed his troops on the Brenner Pass and threatened to fight. When, in March 1935, Hitler established a general military draft and declared the "unequal" disarmament clauses of the Treaty of Versailles null and void, other countries appeared to understand the danger. With France taking the lead, Italy and Great Britain protested strongly and warned against future aggressive actions.

Yet the emerging united front against Hitler quickly collapsed. Of crucial importance, Britain adopted a policy of appeasement, granting Hitler everything he could reasonably want (and more) in order to avoid war. The first step was an Anglo-German naval agreement in June 1935, which broke

MAP 29.1 The Growth of Nazi Germany, 1933–1939 Until March 1939, Hitler brought ethnic Germans into the Nazi state; then he turned on the Slavic peoples he had always hated.

Germany's isolation. The second step came in March 1936, when Hitler suddenly marched his armies into the demilitarized Rhineland, brazenly violating the treaties of Versailles and Locarno. This was the last good chance to stop the Nazis, for Hitler had ordered his troops to retreat if France resisted militarily. But an uncertain France would not move without British support, and the occupation of German soil by German armies seemed right and just to Britain. Its strategic position greatly improved, Germany had handed France a tremendous psychological defeat.

British appeasement, which practically dictated French policy, lasted far into 1939. It was motivated by British feelings of guilt toward Germany and the pacifism of a population still horrified by the memory of the First World War. Like many Germans,

Cartoonist David Low's biting criticism of appeasing leaders appeared shortly after Hitler remilitarized the Rhineland. Appeasement also appealed to millions of ordinary citizens, who wanted to avoid at any cost another great war. *(Cartoon by David Low supplied by permission of* The London Standard*)*

British statesmen seriously underestimated Hitler. They believed that they could use him to stop Russian communism. A leading member of Britain's government personally told Hitler in November 1937 that it was his conviction that Hitler "not only had accomplished great things in Germany itself, but that through the total destruction of Communism in his own country . . . Germany rightly had to be considered as a Western bulwark against Communism."[13] Such rigid anticommunist feelings made an alliance between the Western powers and Stalin against Hitler very unlikely.

As Britain and France opted for appeasement and Russia watched all developments suspiciously, Hitler found powerful allies. In 1935 the bombastic Mussolini decided that imperial expansion was needed to revitalize fascism. From Italian colonies on the east coast of Africa he attacked the independent African kingdom of Ethiopia. The Western powers and the League of Nations piously condemned Italian aggression, which angered Mussolini, without saving Ethiopia from defeat. Hitler, who had secretly supplied Ethiopia with arms to heat up the conflict, supported Italy energetically and thereby overcame Mussolini's lingering doubts about the Nazis. The result was an agreement on close cooperation in 1936 between Italy and Germany, the so-called Rome-Berlin Axis. Japan, which had been expanding into Manchuria since 1931, soon joined the alliance between Italy and Germany.

At the same time, Germany and Italy intervened in the long, complicated Spanish civil war, where their support eventually helped General Francisco Franco's fascist movement defeat republican Spain. Spain's only official aid came from Soviet Russia, for public opinion in Britain and especially in France was hopelessly divided on the Spanish question.

By late 1937, as he was proclaiming his peaceful intentions to the British and their gullible prime minister, Neville Chamberlain, Hitler told his generals his real plans. His "unshakable decision" was to crush Austria and Czechoslovakia at the earliest possible moment, as the first step in his long-contemplated drive to the east for "living space." By threatening Austria with invasion, Hitler forced the Austrian chancellor in March 1938 to put local Nazis in control of the government. The next day, German armies moved in unopposed, and Austria became two more provinces of Greater Germany (see Map 29.1).

Simultaneously, Hitler began demanding that the pro-Nazi, German-speaking minority of western Czechoslovakia—the Sudetenland—be turned over to Germany. Yet democratic Czechoslovakia was prepared to defend itself. Moreover, France had been Czechoslovakia's ally since 1924; and if France fought, Soviet Russia was pledged to help. As war appeared inevitable—for Hitler had already told the leader of the Sudeten Germans that "we must always ask so much we cannot be satisfied"—appeasement triumphed again. In September 1938, Chamberlain flew to Germany three times in fourteen days. In these negotiations, to which Russia was deliberately not invited, Chamberlain and the French agreed with Hitler that the Sudetenland should be ceded to Germany immediately. Returning to London from the Munich Conference, Chamberlain told cheering crowds that he had secured "peace with honor . . . peace for our time." Sold out by the Western powers, Czechoslovakia gave in.

Confirmed once again in his opinion of the Western democracies as weak and racially degenerate, Hitler accelerated his aggression. In a shocking violation of his solemn assurances that the Sudetenland was his last territorial demand, Hitler's armies occupied the Czech lands in March 1939, while Slovakia became a puppet state. The effect on Western public opinion was electrifying. For the first time, there was no possible rationale of self-determination for Nazi aggression, since Hitler was seizing Czechs and Slovaks as captive peoples. Thus, when Hitler used the question of German minorities in Danzig as a pretext to smash Poland, a suddenly militant Chamberlain declared that Britain and France would fight if Hitler attacked his eastern neighbor. Hitler did not take these warnings seriously, and he pressed on.

In an about-face that stunned the world, Hitler offered and Stalin signed a ten-year Russo-German nonaggression pact in August 1939, whereby each dictator promised to remain neutral if the other became involved in war. Even more startling was the attached secret protocol, which ruthlessly divided eastern Europe into German and Russian zones, "in the event of a political territorial reorganization." Although this top-secret protocol sealing the destruction of Poland and the Baltic states became known only after the war, the nonaggression pact itself was enough to make Britain and France cry treachery, for they too had been negotiating with Stalin. But Stalin had remained distrustful of Western intentions. Moreover, Britain and France had offered him military risk without gain, while Hitler had offered territorial gain without risk. For Hitler, everything was set. He told his generals on the day of the nonaggression pact: "My only fear is that at the last moment some dirty dog will come up with a mediation plan." On September 1, 1939, German armies and warplanes smashed into Poland from three sides. Two days later, finally true to their word, Britain and France declared war on Germany. The Second World War had begun.

Hitler's Empire, 1939–1942

Using planes, tanks, and trucks in the first example of the *Blitzkrieg,* or "lightning war," Hitler's armies crushed Poland in four weeks. While Soviet Russia quickly took its part of the booty—the eastern half of Poland and the Baltic states of Lithuania, Estonia, Latvia—French and British armies dug in in the west. They expected another war of attrition and economic blockade.

In spring 1940, the lightning war struck again. After quickly occupying Denmark, Norway, and Holland, German motorized columns broke through southern Belgium, split the Franco-British forces, and trapped the entire British army on the beaches of Dunkirk. By heroic efforts the British managed to withdraw their troops but not their equipment to England.

France was taken by the Nazis. The aging marshal Henri-Philippe Pétain formed a new French government—the so-called Vichy government—to accept defeat, and German armies occupied most of France. By July 1940, Hitler ruled practically all of western continental Europe; Italy was an ally; and the Soviet Union a friendly neutral. Only Britain, led by the uncompromising Winston Churchill (1874–1965), remained unconquered. Churchill proved to be one of history's greatest wartime leaders, rallying his fellow citizens with stirring speeches, infectious confidence, and bulldog determination.

Germany sought to gain control of the air, the necessary first step for an amphibious invasion of Britain. In the Battle of Britain, up to a thousand German planes attacked British airfields and key factories in a single day, dueling with British defenders high in the skies. Losses were heavy on both sides. Then in September Hitler angrily and foolishly changed his strategy, turning from military objectives to indiscriminate bombing of British cities in an attempt to break British morale. British factories increased production of their excellent fighter planes; antiaircraft defense improved with the help of radar; and the heavily bombed people of London defiantly dug in. In September–October 1940, Britain was beating Germany three to one in the air war. There was no possibility of immediate German invasion of Britain.

In these circumstances, the most reasonable German strategy would have been to attack Britain through the eastern Mediterranean, taking Egypt and the Suez Canal and pinching off Britain's supply of oil. Moreover, Mussolini's early defeats in Greece had drawn Hitler into the Balkans, where Germany quickly conquered Greece and Yugoslavia while forcing Hungary, Rumania and Bulgaria into alliances with Germany by April 1941. This reinforced the logic of a thrust into the eastern Mediterranean. But Hitler was not a reasonable person. His lifetime obsession with a vast eastern European empire for the master race irrationally dictated policy. By late 1940, he had already decided on his next move, and in June 1941, German armies suddenly attacked the Soviet Union along a vast front. With Britain still unconquered, Hitler's decision was a wild, irrational gamble, epitomizing the violent, unlimited ambitions of modern totalitarianism.

Faithfully fulfilling all his obligations under the Nazi-Soviet Pact and even ignoring warnings of impending invasion, Stalin was caught off guard. Nazi armies moved like lightning across the Russian steppe. By October 1941, Leningrad was practically surrounded, Moscow beseiged, and most of the Ukraine conquered; yet the Russians did not collapse. When a severe winter struck German armies outfitted in summer uniforms, the invaders were stopped.

While Hitler's armies dramatically expanded the war in Europe, his Japanese allies did the same in Asia. Engaged in a general but undeclared war against China since 1937, Japan's rulers had increasingly come into diplomatic conflict with the Pacific Basin's other great power, the United States. When the Japanese occupied French Indochina in July 1941, the United States retaliated by cutting off sales of vital rubber, scrap iron, oil, and aviation fuel. Tension mounted further, and on December 7, 1941, Japan attacked the U.S. naval base at Pearl Harbor in Hawaii. Hitler immediately declared war on the United States, even though his treaty obligations with Japan did not require him to initiate this course of action.

As Japanese forces advanced swiftly into southeast Asia after the crippling surprise attack at Pearl Harbor, Hitler and his European allies continued the two-front war against the Soviet Union and Great Britain. Not until late 1942 did the Nazis suffer their first major defeats, as will be shown in Chapter 30. In the meantime, Hitler ruled a vast European empire stretching from the outskirts of Moscow to the English Channel. Hitler and the top Nazi leadership began building their "New Order," and they continued their efforts until their final collapse in 1945. In doing so, they showed what Nazi victory would have meant.

Hitler's New Order was based firmly on the guiding principle of Nazi totalitarianism: racial imperialism. Within this New Order, the Nordic peoples—the Dutch, the Norwegians, and Danes—received preferential treatment, for they were racially related to the Germans. The French, an "inferior" Latin people, occupied the middle position. They were heavily taxed to support the Nazi war effort, but were tolerated as a race. Once Nazi reverses began to mount in late 1942, however, all the occupied territories of western and northern Europe were exploited with increasing intensity. Material shortages and both mental and physical suffering afflicted millions of people.

Slavs in the conquered territories to the east were treated with harsh hatred as "subhumans." At the height of his success in 1941 to 1942, Hitler painted for his intimate circle the fantastic details of a vast eastern colonial empire, where the Poles, Ukrainians, and Russians would be enslaved and forced to die

Prelude to Murder This photo captures the terrible inhumanity of Nazi racism. Frightened and bewildered families from the soon-to-be destroyed Warsaw ghetto are being forced out of their homes by German soldiers for deportation to concentration camps. There they face murder in the gas chambers. *(Collection Viollet)*

out, while Germanic peasants resettled their abandoned lands. Himmler and the elite corps of SS volunteers struggled loyally, sometimes against the German army, to implement part of this general program even before victory was secured. In parts of Poland, the SS arrested and evacuated Polish peasants to create a German "mass settlement space." Polish workers and Russian prisoners of war were transported to Germany, where they did most of the heavy labor and were systematically worked to death. The conditions of Russian slave labor in Germany were so harsh that four out of five Russian prisoners did not survive the war.

Finally, Jews were condemned to extermination, along with gypsies, Jehovah's Witnesses, and captured Communists. By 1939 German Jews had lost all their civil rights, and after the fall of Warsaw the Nazis began deporting them to Poland. There they and Jews from all over Europe were concentrated in ghettos, compelled to wear the Jewish star, and turned into slave laborers. But by 1941, Himmler's SS was carrying out the "final solution of the Jewish question"—the murder of every single Jew. All over Hitler's empire, Jews were arrested, packed like cattle onto freight trains, and dispatched to extermination camps.

There the victims were taken by force or deception to "shower rooms," which were actually gas chambers. These gas chambers, first perfected in the quiet, efficient execution of 70,000 mentally ill Germans between 1938 and 1941, permitted rapid, hideous, and thoroughly bureaucratized mass murder. For fifteen to twenty minutes there came the terrible screams and gasping sobs of men, women, and children choking to death on poison gas. Then, only silence. Special camp workers quickly tore the victims' gold teeth from their jaws and cut off their hair for use as chair stuffings. The bodies were then cremated, or sometimes boiled for oil to make soap, while the bones were crushed to produce fertilizers. At Auschwitz, the most infamous of the Nazi death factories, as many as 12,000 human beings were slaughtered each day. On the turbulent Russian front, the SS death squads forced the Jewish population to dig giant pits, which became mass graves as the victims were lined up on the edge and cut down by machine guns. The extermination of the European Jews was the ultimate monstrosity of Nazi racism and racial imperialism. By 1945, 6 million Jews had been murdered in cold blood.

The tremendous practical and spiritual maladies of the age of anxiety led in many lands to the rise of dictatorships. Many of these dictatorships were variations on conservative authoritarianism, but there was also a fateful innovation—the modern totalitarian regime, most fully developed in Communist Russia and Nazi Germany. The totalitarian regimes utterly rejected the liberalism of the nineteenth century. Inspired by the lessons of total war and Lenin's one-party rule, they tried to subordinate everything to the state. Although some areas of life escaped them, state control increased to a staggering, unprecedented degree. The totalitarian regimes trampled on basic human rights with unrestrained brutality and police terror. Moreover, they were armed with the weapons of modern technology, rendering opposition almost impossible.

Both Communist Russia and Nazi Germany tried to gain the *willing* support of their populations. Monopolizing the means of expression and communication, they claimed to represent the masses and to be building new, more equal societies. Many people believed them. Both regimes also won enthusiastic supporters by offering tough, ruthless people from modest backgrounds enormous rewards for loyal and effective service. Thus these totalitarian dictatorships rested on considerable genuine popular support, as well as on police terror. This combination gave them their awesome power and dynamism. That dynamism was, however, channeled in quite different directions. Stalin and the Communist party aimed at building their kind of socialism and the new socialist personality at home. Hitler and the Nazi elite aimed at unlimited territorial and racial aggression on behalf of a master race; domestic recovery was only a means to that end. Unlimited aggression made war inevitable, first with the Western democracies and then with Germany's totalitarian neighbor. It plunged Europe into the ultimate nightmare.

NOTES

1. E. Halévy, *The Era of Tyrannies,* Doubleday, Garden City, N.Y., 1965, pp. 265–316, esp. p. 300.

2. Quoted by P. C. Roberts, " 'War Communism': A Re-examination," *Slavic Review* 29 (June 1970): 257.
3. Quoted by A. G. Mazour, *Soviet Economic Development: Operation Outstrip, 1921–1965,* Van Nostrand, Princeton, N.J., 1967, p. 130.
4. Quoted by I. Deutscher, *Stalin: A Political Biography,* 2nd ed., Oxford University Press, New York, 1967, p. 325.
5. Quoted by H. K. Geiger, *The Family in Soviet Russia,* Harvard University Press, Cambridge, 1968, p. 123.
6. Ibid., p. 156.
7. Quoted by B. Rosenthal, "Women in the Russian Revolution and After," in *Becoming Visible: Women in European History,* ed., R. Bridenthal and C. Koonz, Houghton Mifflin, Boston, 1976, p. 383.
8. Quoted by K. D. Bracher, in T. Eschenburg et al., *The Path to Dictatorship, 1918–1933,* Doubleday, Garden City, N.Y., 1966, p. 117.
9. Quoted by K. D. Bracher, *The German Dictatorship: The Origins, Structure and Effects of National Socialism,* Praeger, New York, 1970, pp. 146–147.
10. Quoted by R. Stromberg, *An Intellectual History of Modern Europe,* Appleton-Century-Crofts, New York, 1966, p. 393.
11. D. Schoenbaum, *Hitler's Social Revolution: Class and Status in Nazi Germany, 1933–1939,* Doubleday, Garden City, N.Y., 1967, p. 114.
12. Quoted by Bracher, *German Dictatorship,* p. 289.
13. Ibid, p. 306.

SUGGESTED READING

The historical literature on totalitarian dictatorships is rich and fascinating. H. Arendt, *The Origins of Totalitarianism* (1951), is a challenging interpretation. E. Weber, *Varieties of Fascism* (1964), stresses the radical social aspirations of fascist movements all across Europe. F. L. Carsten, *The Rise of Fascism,* rev. ed. (1982), and W. Laqueur, ed., *Fascism* (1976), are also recommended.

Richard Stites, *The Women's Liberation Movement in Russia: Feminism, Nihilism, and Bolshevism, 1860–1930* (1978); S. Fitzpatrick, *Cultural Revolution in Russia, 1928–1931* (1978); K. Geiger, *The Family in Soviet Russia* (1968); and I. Deutscher, *Stalin: A Political Biography* (1967), are all highly recommended, as is Deutscher's sympathetic three-volume study of Trotsky. S. Cohen, *Bukharin and the Bolshevik Revolution* (1973), examines the leading spokesman of moderate communism, who was destroyed by Stalin. R. Conquest, *The Great Terror* (1968), is an excellent account of Stalin's purges of the 1930s. A. Solzhenitsyn, *The Gulag Archipelago* (1964), passionately condemns Soviet police terror, which Solzhenitsyn tracks back to Lenin. A. Koestler, *Darkness at Noon* (1956), is a famous fictional account of Stalin's trials of the Old Bolsheviks. R. Medvedev, *Let History Judge* (1972), is a penetrating and highly recommended history of Stalinism by a Russian dissident. Three other remarkable books are J. Scott, *Behind the Urals* (1942, 1973), an eyewitness account of an American steelworker in Russia in the 1930s; S. Alliluyeva, *Twenty Letters to a Friend* (1967), the amazing reflections of Stalin's daughter, who has twice chosen to live in the United States; and M. Fainsod, *Smolensk Under Soviet Rule* (1958), a unique study based on Communist records captured first by the Germans and then by the Americans.

E. R. Tannebaum, *The Fascist Experience* (1972), is an excellent study of Italian culture and society under Mussolini. I. Silone, *Bread and Wine* (1937), is a moving novel by a famous opponent of dictatorship in Italy. Two excellent books on Spain are H. Thomas, *The Spanish Civil War* (1961), and E. Malefakis, *Agrarian Reform and Peasant Revolution in Spain* (1970). In the area of foreign relations, G. Kennan, *Russia and the West Under Lenin and Stalin* (1961), is justly famous, while A. L. Rowse, *Appeasement* (1961), powerfully denounces the policies of the appeasers. R. Paxton, *Vichy France* (1973), tells a controversial story extremely well, and J. Lukac, *The Last European War* (1976), skillfully —and infuriatingly—argues that victory by Hitler could have saved Europe from both Russian and American domination.

On Germany, F. Stern, *The Politics of Cultural Despair* (1963), and G. Mosse, *The Crisis of German Ideology* (1964), are excellent complementary studies on the origins of Nazism. The best single work on Hitler's Germany is K. Bracher, *The German Dictatorship: The Origins, Structure and Effects of National Socialism* (1970), while W. Shirer, *The Rise and Fall of the Third Reich* (1960), is the best-selling account of an American journalist who experienced Nazi Germany firsthand. J.

Fest, *Hitler* (1974), and A. Bullock, *Hitler* (1953), are engrossing biographies of the Führer. In addition to *Mein Kampf, Hitler's Secret Conversations, 1941–1944* (1953) reveals the dictator's wild dreams and beliefs. Among countless special studies, E. Kogon, *The Theory and Practice of Hell* (1958), is a chilling examination of the concentration camps; M. Mayer, *They Thought They Were Free* (1955), probes the minds of ten ordinary Nazis and why they believed Hitler was their liberator; and A. Speer, *Inside the Third Reich* (1970), contains the fascinating recollections of Hitler's wizard of the armaments industry. G. Mosse, *Toward the Final Solution* (1978), is a powerful history of European racism, and L. Dawidowicz, *The War Against the Jews, 1933–1945* (1975), is a superb account of the Holocaust. Jørgen Haestrup, *Europe Ablaze* (1978), is a monumental account of wartime resistance movements throughout Europe, and *The Diary of Anne Frank* is a remarkable personal account of a young Jewish girl in hiding during the Nazi occupation of Holland.

30

THE RECOVERY OF EUROPE AND THE AMERICAS

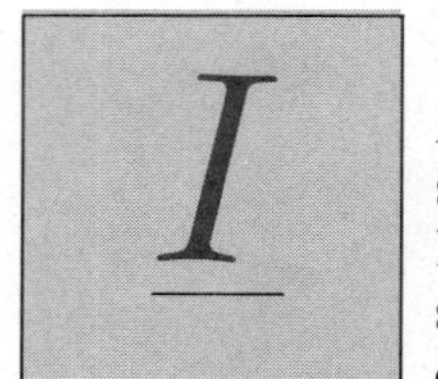

N *1942,* when Hitler's empire stretched across Europe and the Nazi "New Order" was taking shape, Western civilization was in danger of dying. A terrible, triumphant barbarism was striking at the hard-won accomplishments and uneven progress of many generations. From this low point, European society staged a truly astonishing recovery.

The Nazis and their allies were utterly defeated. Battered western Europe then experienced a great renaissance in the postwar era, which lasted into the late 1960s. The western hemisphere, with its strong European heritage, also made exemplary progress. Soviet Russia eventually became more humane and less totalitarian. Yet there was also a tragic setback. The Grand Alliance against Hitler gave way to an apparently endless cold war, in which conflict between East and West threatened world peace and troubled domestic politics.

How and why did Europe recover from the depths of despair in one of the most extraordinary periods of rebirth in its long history? What were the causes of the cold war, the most disappointing development of the postwar era? These are some of the more important questions this chapter will seek to answer.

ALLIED VICTORY AND THE COLD WAR, 1942–1950

The recovery of Western society depended on the defeat of the Nazis and their Italian, Balkan, and Japanese allies. On this point the twenty-six allied nations, led by Britain, the United States, and Soviet Russia, were firmly agreed. The Grand Alliance—to use Winston Churchill's favorite term—functioned quite effectively in military terms to achieve this overwhelming objective. By the summer of 1943, the tide of battle had turned, and Allied victory was only a matter of time.

Yet victory was flawed. The Allies could not cooperate politically when it came to peacemaking. Motivated by different goals and hounded by misunderstandings, the United States and Soviet Russia soon found themselves at loggerheads. By the end of 1947, Europe was rigidly divided. It was West versus East in the cold war.

THE GRAND ALLIANCE

Chance, rather than choice, brought together the anti-Axis coalition. Stalin had been cooperating fully with Hitler between August 1939 and June 1941, and only the Japanese attack on Pearl Harbor in December 1941 and Hitler's immediate declaration of war had overwhelmed powerful isolationism in the United States. The Allies' first task was to try to overcome their mutual suspicions and build an unshakable alliance on the quicksand of accident. By means of two interrelated policies they succeeded.

First, President Roosevelt accepted Churchill's contention that the United States should concentrate first on defeating Hitler. Only after victory in Europe would the United States turn toward the Pacific for an all-out attack on Japan, the lesser threat. Therefore, the United States promised and sent large amounts of military aid to Britain and Russia, and American and British forces in each combat zone were tightly integrated under a single commander. America's policy of "Europe first" helped solidify the anti-Hitler coalition.

Second, within the European framework, the Americans and the British put immediate military needs first. They consistently postponed tough political questions relating to the eventual peace settlement. Thus, in December 1941 and again in May 1942, Stalin asked the United States and Britain to agree to Russia's moving its western border of 1938 farther west at the expense of Poland, in effect ratifying the gains Stalin had made from his deal with Hitler in 1939.

Stalin's request ran counter to the moralistic Anglo-American Atlantic Charter of August 1941. In good Wilsonian fashion, the Atlantic Charter had called for peace without territorial expansion or secret agreements, and free elections and self-determination for all liberated nations. Stalin thus received only a military alliance and no postwar commitments in 1942. Yet the United States and Britain did not try to take advantage of Russia's precarious position in 1942, promising an invasion of continental Europe as soon as possible. They feared that hard bargaining would anger Stalin and encourage him to consider making a separate peace with Hitler.

Both sides found it advantageous to paper over their long-standing differences by stressing military operations and the total defeat of the Axis. At a January 1943 conference in Casablanca, Morocco, to plan a massive Allied offensive, Churchill and Roosevelt adopted the principle of the "unconditional surrender" of Germany and Japan. Stalin agreed to it shortly thereafter. The policy of unconditional surrender had profound implications. It cemented the Grand Alliance, denying Hitler any hope of dividing his foes. It probably also discouraged Germans and Japanese who might have tried to overthrow their dictators in order to make a compromise peace. And, most important, it meant that Russian and Anglo-American armies would almost certainly come together to divide all of Germany, and all of Europe, among themselves.

The military resources of the Grand Alliance were awesome. The strengths of the United States were its mighty industry, its large population, and its national unity. Even before Pearl Harbor, President Roosevelt had called America the "arsenal of democracy" and given military aid to Britain and Russia. Now the United States geared up rapidly for all-out war production and drew heavily on a generally cooperative Latin America for resources. It not only equipped its own armies but eventually gave its allies about $50 billion of arms and equipment. Britain received by far the most, but about one-fifth of the total went to Russia in the form of badly needed trucks, planes, and munitions.

Too strong to lose and too weak to win when it stood alone, Britain, too, continued to make a great contribution. The British economy was totally and effectively mobilized, and the sharing of burdens through rationing and heavy taxes on war profits maintained social harmony. Moreover, as 1942 wore on, Britain could increasingly draw on the enormous physical and human resources of its empire and the United States. By early 1943, the Americans and the British combined small aircraft carriers with radar-guided bombers to rid the Atlantic of German submarines. Britain, the impregnable floating fortress, became a gigantic front-line staging area for the decisive blow to the heart of Germany.

As for Soviet Russia, so great was its strength that it might well have defeated Germany without Western help. In the face of the German advance, whole factories and populations were successfully evacuated to eastern Russia and Siberia. There, war production was reorganized and expanded, and the Red Army was increasingly well supplied. The Red Army was

The Siege of Leningrad lasted almost three years, but the Russians heroically defended their city, which was never taken. These women are sawing poles for anti-tank defenses beside a bomb-battered building on what was once Leningrad's most stylish thoroughfare. *(Sovfoto)*

also well led, for a new generation of talented military leaders quickly arose to replace those so recently purged. Most important of all, Stalin drew on the massive support and heroic determination of the Soviet people. Broad-based Russian nationalism, as opposed to narrow communist ideology, became the powerful unifying force in what was appropriately called the "Great Patriotic War of the Fatherland."

Finally, the United States, Britain, and Soviet Russia were not alone. They had the resources of much of the world at their command. And, to a greater or lesser extent, they were aided by a growing resistance movement against the Nazis throughout Europe, even in Germany. Thus, although Ukrainian peasants often welcomed the Germans as liberators, the barbaric occupation policies of the Nazis quickly drove them to join and support behind-the-lines guerrilla forces. More generally, after Russia was invaded in June 1941, Communists throughout Europe took the lead in the underground resistance,

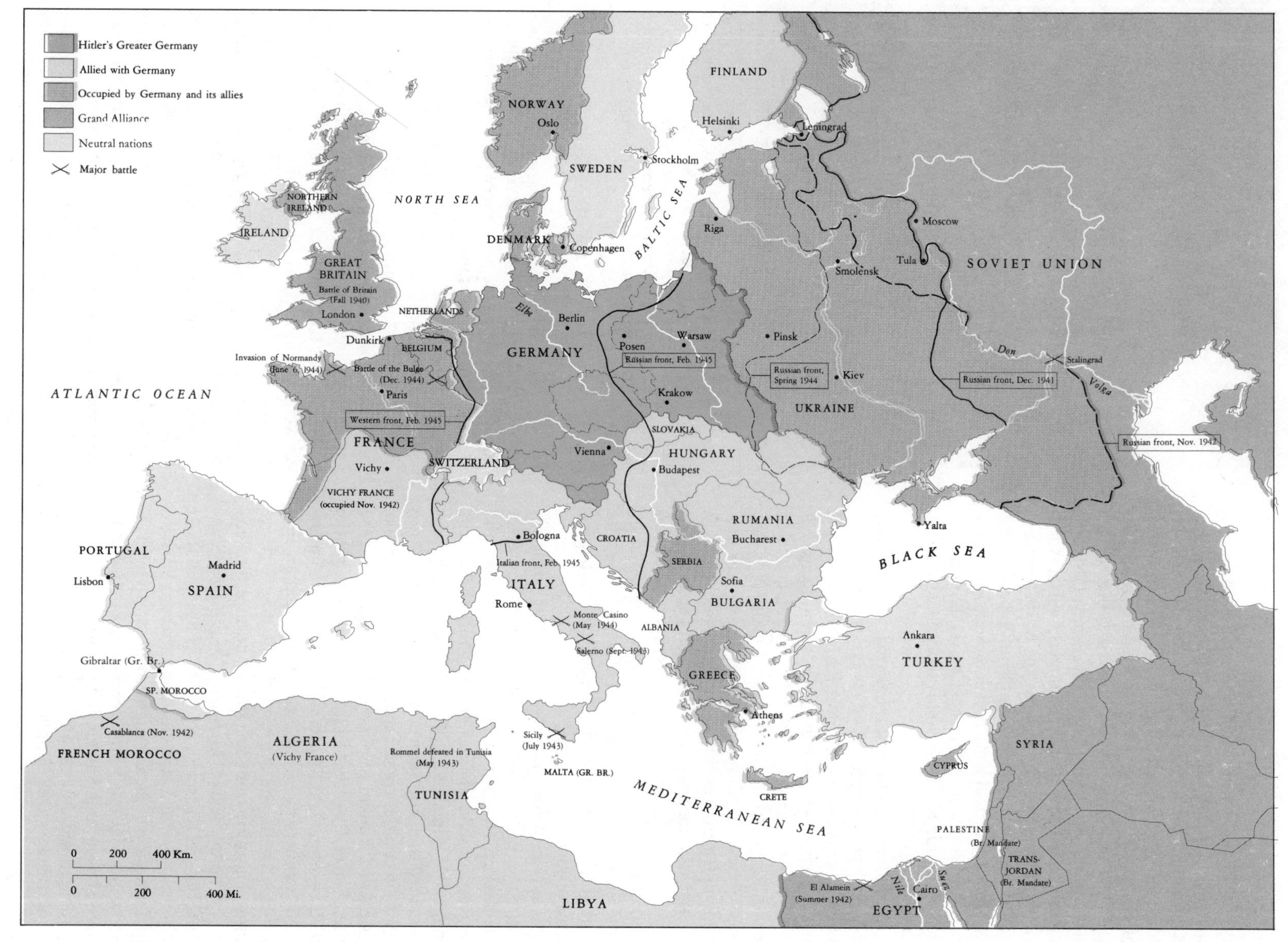

Hitler's Greater Germany
Allied with Germany
Occupied by Germany and its allies
Grand Alliance
Neutral nations
Major battle
NORTH SEA
ATLANTIC OCEAN
BALTIC SEA
BLACK SEA
MEDITERRANEAN SEA
NORWAY
Oslo
SWEDEN
Stockholm
FINLAND
Helsinki
Leningrad
DENMARK
Copenhagen
NORTHERN IRELAND
IRELAND
GREAT BRITAIN
Battle of Britain (Fall 1940)
London
NETHERLANDS
BELGIUM
Dunkirk
Invasion of Normandy (June 6, 1944)
Battle of the Bulge (Dec. 1944)
Paris
Western front, Feb. 1945
FRANCE
Vichy
VICHY FRANCE (occupied Nov. 1942)
SWITZERLAND
GERMANY
Elbe
Berlin
Posen
Warsaw
Russian front, Feb. 1945
Krakow
Riga
Smolensk
Moscow
Tula
SOVIET UNION
Pinsk
Russian front, Spring 1944
Kiev
UKRAINE
Don
Stalingrad
Russian front, Dec. 1941
Volga
Russian front, Nov. 1942
SLOVAKIA
HUNGARY
Budapest
Vienna
RUMANIA
Bucharest
CROATIA
SERBIA
Sofia
BULGARIA
ALBANIA
GREECE
Athens
CRETE
Yalta
Ankara
TURKEY
CYPRUS
SYRIA
PALESTINE (Br. Mandate)
TRANS-JORDAN (Br. Mandate)
Suez
Nile
Cairo
EGYPT
El Alamein (Summer 1942)
PORTUGAL
Lisbon
Madrid
SPAIN
Gibraltar (Gr. Br.)
SP. MOROCCO
Casablanca (Nov. 1942)
FRENCH MOROCCO
ALGERIA (Vichy France)
Rommel defeated in Tunisia (May 1943)
TUNISIA
LIBYA
Bologna
Italian front, Feb. 1945
ITALY
Rome
Monte Casino (May 1944)
Salerno (Sept. 1943)
Sicily (July 1943)
MALTA (GR. BR.)
0 200 400 Km.
0 200 400 Mi.

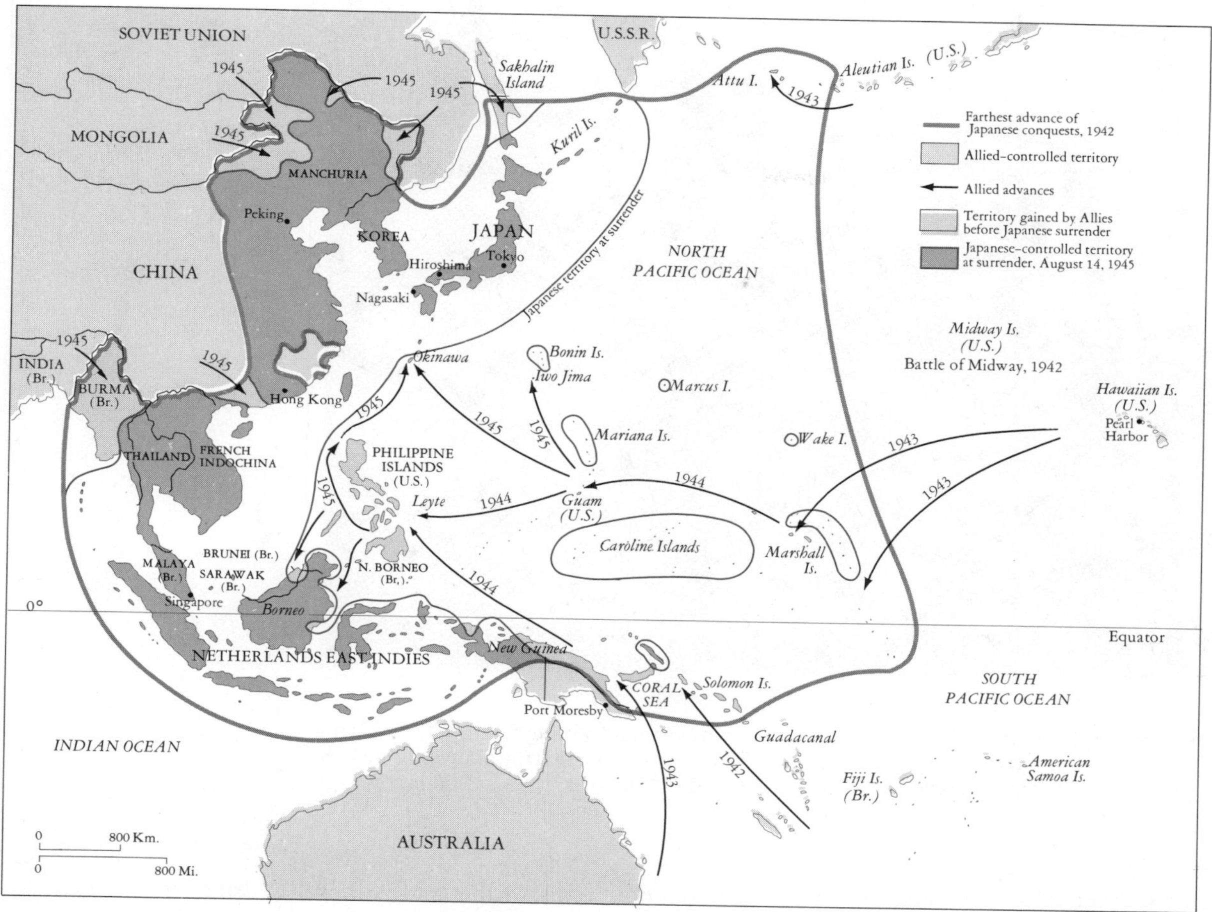

MAP 30.1 World War Two in Europe The map shows the extent of Hitler's empire at its height, before the battle of Stalingrad in late 1942, and the subsequent advances of the Allies until Germany surrendered on May 7, 1945.

MAP 30.2 World War Two in the Pacific Japanese forces also overran an enormous territory in 1942, which the Allies slowly recaptured in a long bitter struggle. As this map shows, Japan still held a large Asian empire in August 1945, when the unprecedented devastation of atomic warfare suddenly forced it to surrender.

joined by a growing number of patriots and Christians. Anti-Nazi leaders from occupied countries established governments-in-exile in London, like that of the "Free French" under the intensely proud General Charles de Gaulle. These governments gathered valuable secret information from resistance fighters and even organized armies to help defeat Hitler.

The Tide of Battle

Barely halted at the gates of Moscow and Leningrad in 1941, the Germans renewed their Russian offensive in July 1942. This time they drove toward the southern city of Stalingrad, in an attempt to cripple communications and seize the crucial oil fields of Baku. Reaching Stalingrad, the Germans slowly occupied most of the ruined city in a month of incredibly savage house-to-house fighting.

Then, in November 1942, Soviet armies counterattacked. They rolled over Rumanian and Italian troops to the north and south of Stalingrad, quickly closing the trap and surrounding the entire German Sixth Army of 300,000 men. The surrounded Germans were systematically destroyed, until by the end of January 1943 only 123,000 soldiers were left to surrender. Hitler, who had refused to allow a retreat,

B-17 Pilots These American women are returning from a training flight in their Flying Fortress, nicknamed "Pistol Packin' Mama." Women pilots ferried the planes for the U.S. Air Corps in support missions during the second World War. *(U.S. Air Force Photo)*

had suffered a catastrophic defeat. In the summer of 1943, the larger, better-equipped Soviet armies took the offensive and began moving forward (see Map 30.1).

In late 1942 the tide also turned in the Pacific and North Africa. By early summer 1942, Japan had established a great empire in east Asia (see Map 30.2). Unlike the Nazis, the Japanese made clever appeals to local nationalists, who hated European imperial domination and preferred Japan's so-called Greater Asian Co-Prosperity Sphere.

Then, in the Battle of the Coral Sea in May 1942, Allied naval and air power stopped the Japanese advance and also relieved Australia from the threat of invasion. This victory was followed by the Battle of Midway Island, in which American pilots sank all four of the attacking Japanese aircraft carriers and established American naval superiority in the Pacific. In August 1942, American marines attacked Guadalcanal in the Solomon Islands. Badly hampered by the policy of "Europe first"—only 15 percent of Allied resources were going to fight the war in the Pacific in early 1943—the Americans, under General Douglas MacArthur and Admiral Chester Nimitz, and the Australians nevertheless began "island hopping" toward Japan. Japanese forces were on the defensive.

In North Africa, the war had been seesawing back and forth since 1940. In May 1942, combined German and Italian armies, under the brilliant General Erwin Rommel, attacked British-occupied Egypt and the Suez Canal for the second time. After a rapid advance, they were finally defeated by British forces at the Battle of El Alamein, only seventy miles from Alexandria. In October, the British counter-attacked in Egypt, and almost immediately thereafter, an Anglo-American force landed in Morocco and Algeria. These French possessions, which were under the control of Pétain's Vichy French goverment, quickly went over to the Allies.

Having driven the Axis powers from North Africa by the spring of 1943, Allied forces maintained the initiative by invading Sicily and then mainland Italy. Mussolini was deposed by a war-weary people, and the new Italian government publicly accepted unconditional surrender in September 1943. Italy, it seemed, was liberated. Yet Mussolini was rescued by

War in the Pacific A Japanese ship burns off the coast of New Guinea as an attacking B-25 roars overhead. The lights along the shoreline are fires caused by United States bombers. *(Air Force Photo)*

German commandos in a daring raid and put at the head of a puppet government. German armies seized Rome and all of northern Italy. Fighting continued in Italy.

Indeed, bitter fighting continued in Europe for almost two years. Germany, less fully mobilized for war than Britain in 1941, applied itself to total war in 1942 and enlisted millions of prisoners of war and slave laborers from all across occupied Europe in that effort. Between early 1942 and July 1944, German war production actually tripled. Although British and American bombing raids killed many German civilians, they were surprisingly ineffective from a military point of view. Also, German resistance against Hitler failed. After an unsuccessful attempt on Hitler's life in July 1944, thousands of Germans were brutally liquidated by SS fanatics. Terrorized at home and frightened by the prospect of unconditional surrender, the Germans fought on with suicidal stoicism.

On June 6, 1944, American and British forces under General Dwight Eisenhower landed on the beaches of Normandy in history's greatest naval invasion. Having tricked the Germans into believing that the attack would come near the Belgian border, the Allies secured a foothold on the coast of Normandy. In a hundred dramatic days, more than 2 million men and almost a half-million vehicles pushed inland and broke through German lines. Rejecting proposals to strike straight at Berlin in a massive attack, Eisenhower moved forward cautiously on a broad front. Not until March 1945 did American troops cross the Rhine and enter Germany.

The Russians, who had been advancing steadily since July 1943, reached the outskirts of Warsaw by August 1944. For the next six months they moved southward into Rumania, Hungary, and Yugoslavia. In January 1945, Red armies again moved westward through Poland, and on April 26 they met American forces on the Elbe River. The Allies had closed their vise on Nazi Germany and overrun Europe. As Soviet forces fought their way into Berlin, Hitler committed suicide in his bunker, and on May 7 German commanders capitulated.

Three months later the United States dropped atomic bombs on Hiroshima and Nagasaki. Mass

Hiroshima, August 1945 A single atomic bomb leveled 90 percent of this major city and claimed 130,000 casualties. Hiroshima has never regained its earlier prosperity. *(U.S. Army Air Forces)*

bombing of cities and civilians, one of the terrible new practices of World War Two, had ended in the final nightmare—unprecedented human destruction in a single blinding flash. The Japanese surrendered. The Second World War, which had claimed the lives of more than 50 million soldiers and civilians, was over.

The Origins of the Cold War

Total victory was not followed by genuine peace. The most powerful allies—Soviet Russia and the United States—began to quarrel as soon as the unifying threat of Nazi Germany disappeared. Though the hostility between the eastern and western superpowers was a tragic disappointment for millions of people, it was not really surprising. It grew sadly but logically out of military developments, wartime agreements, and long-standing political and ideological differences.

The conference Stalin, Roosevelt, and Churchill had held in the Iranian capital of Teheran in November 1943 was of crucial importance in determining subsequent events. There, the Big Three had jovially reaffirmed their determination to crush Germany and searched for the appropriate military strategy. Churchill, fearful of the military dangers of a direct attack and anxious to protect Britain's political interests in the eastern Mediterranean, argued that American and British forces should follow up their North African and Italian campaigns with an indirect attack on Germany through the Balkans. Roosevelt, however, agreed with Stalin that an American-British frontal assault through France would be better. This agreement was part of Roosevelt's general effort to meet Stalin's wartime demands whenever possible. As Roosevelt reportedly told his friend William Bullitt, formerly American ambassador to the Soviet Union, before the Teheran conference, "I have just a hunch that Stalin doesn't want anything but security

The Big Three In 1945 a triumphant Winston Churchill, ailing Franklin Roosevelt, and determined Joseph Stalin met at Yalta in southern Russia to plan for peace. Cooperation soon gave way to bitter hostility. *(National Archives, Washington)*

for his country, and I think that if I give him everything I possibly can and ask nothing from him in return, *noblesse oblige,* he won't try to annex anything and will work for a world of democracy and peace."[1]

At Teheran, the Normandy invasion had been set for the spring of 1944. Although military considerations probably largely dictated this decision, it had momentous political implications: it meant that the Russian and the American-British armies would come together in defeated Germany along a north-south line and that only Russian troops would liberate eastern Europe. Thus the basic shape of postwar Europe was already emerging. Real differences over questions like Poland were carefully ignored.

When the Big Three met again at Yalta on the Black Sea in southern Russia in February 1945, rapidly advancing Soviet armies were within one hundred miles of Berlin. The Red Army had occupied not only Poland but also Bulgaria, Rumania, Hungary, part of Yugoslavia, and much of Czechoslovakia. The temporarily stalled American-British forces had yet to cross the Rhine into Germany. Moreover, the United States was far from defeating Japan. Indeed, it was believed that the invasion and occupation of Japan would cost a million American casualties—an estimate that led to the subsequent decision to drop atomic bombs in order to save American lives. In short, Russia's position was strong and America's weak.

There was little the increasingly sick and apprehensive Roosevelt could do but double his bet on Stalin's peaceful intentions. It was agreed at Yalta that Germany would be divided into zones of occupation and would pay heavy reparations to the Soviet Union in the form of agricultural and industrial goods, though many details remained unsettled. At American insistence, Stalin agreed to declare war on Japan after Germany was defeated. He also agreed to join the proposed United Nations, which the Americans believed would help preserve peace after the war; it was founded in April 1945 in San Francisco. For Poland and eastern Europe—"that Pandora's Box of infinite troubles," according to American Secretary of State Cordell Hull—the Big Three struggled to reach an ambiguous compromise at Yalta: East European governments were to be freely elected but pro-Russian. As Churchill put it at the time, "The Poles will have their future in their own hands, with the single limitation that they must honestly follow in harmony with their allies, a policy friendly to Russia."[2]

The Yalta compromise over eastern Europe broke down almost immediately. Even before the Yalta Conference, Bulgaria and Poland were in the hands of Communists, who arrived home in the baggage of the Red Army. Minor concesssions to non-Communist groups thereafter did not change this situation. Elsewhere in eastern Europe, pro-Russian "coalition" governments of several parties were formed, but the key ministerial posts were reserved for Moscow-trained Communists.

At the postwar Potsdam Conference of July 1945, the long-ignored differences over eastern Europe finally surged to the fore. The compromising Roosevelt had died and been succeeded by the more determined President Harry Truman, who demanded immediate free elections throughout eastern Europe. Stalin refused pointblank. "A freely elected government in any of these East European countries would be anti-Soviet," he admitted simply, "and that we cannot allow."[3]

Here, then, is the key to the much-debated origins of the cold war. American ideals, pumped up by the crusade against Hitler, and American politics, heavily influenced by millions of voters from eastern Europe, demanded free elections in Soviet-occupied eastern Europe. On the other hand, Stalin, who had lived through two enormously destructive German invasions, wanted absolute military security from Germany and its potential Eastern allies, once and for all. Suspicious by nature, he believed that only Communist states could truly be devoted allies, and he feared that free elections would result in independent and quite possibly hostile governments on his western border. Moreover, by the middle of 1945 there was no way short of war that the United States and its Western allies could really influence developments in eastern Europe, and war was out of the question. Stalin was bound to have his way.

West Versus East

The American response to Stalin's exaggerated conception of security was to "get tough." In May 1945, Truman abruptly cut off all aid to Russia. In October, he declared that the United States would never recognize any government established by force against the free will of its people. In March 1946, former British Prime Minister Churchill ominously informed an American audience that an "iron curtain" had fallen across the continent, dividing Germany and all of Europe into two antagonistic camps. Soon emotional, moralistic denunciations of Stalin and Communist Russia re-emerged as part of American political life. Yet the United States also responded to the popular desire to "bring the boys home" and demobilized with incredible speed, though some historians have argued that American leaders believed that the atomic bomb gave the United States all the power it needed. When the war against Japan ended in September 1945, there were 12 million Americans in the armed forces; by 1947 there were only 1.5 million, as opposed to 6 million for Soviet Russia. "Getting tough" really meant "talking tough."

Stalin's agents quickly reheated the "ideological struggle against capitalist imperialism." Moreover, the large, well-organized Communist parties of France and Italy obediently started to uncover American plots to take over Europe and aggressively challenged their own governments with violent criticisms and large strikes. The Soviet Union also put pressure on Iran and Turkey, and while Greek Communists battled Greek royalists, another bitter civil war raged in China. By the spring of 1947, it appeared to many Americans that Stalin wanted much more than just puppet regimes in Soviet-occupied eastern Europe. He seemed determined to export communism by subversion throughout Europe and around the world.

The American response to this challenge was the Truman Doctrine, which was aimed at "containing" communism to areas already occupied by the Red Army. Truman told Congress in March 1947: "I believe it must be the policy of the United States to support free people who are resisting attempted subjugation by armed minorities or by outside pressure." To begin, Truman asked Congress for military aid to Greece and Turkey. Then in June, Secretary of State George C. Marshall offered Europe economic aid—the "Marshall Plan"—to help it rebuild.

The Berlin Air Lift Standing in the rubble of their bombed-out city, a German crowd in the American sector awaits the arrival of a U.S. transport plane flying in over the Soviet blockade in 1948. The crisis over Berlin was a dramatic indication of growing tensions among the Allies, which resulted in the division of Europe into two hostile camps. *(Walter Sanders,* Life © *Time Inc.)*

Stalin refused Marshall Plan assistance for all of eastern Europe. He purged the last remaining non-Communist elements from the coalition governments of eastern Europe and established Soviet-style, one-party Communist dictatorships. The seizure of power in Czechoslovakia in February 1948 was particularly brutal and antidemocratic, and it greatly strengthened Western fears of limitless Communist expansion, beginning with Germany. Thus, when Stalin blocked all traffic through the Soviet zone of Germany to the former capital of Berlin, which had also been divided into sectors at the end of the war by the occupying powers, the Western allies responded firmly but not provocatively. Hundreds of planes began flying over the Russian roadblocks around the clock, supplying provisions to the people of West Berlin and thwarting Soviet efforts to swallow them up. After 324 days, the Russians backed down: containment seemed to work. In 1949, therefore, the United States formed an anti-Soviet military alliance of western governments, the North Atlantic Treaty Organization (NATO); in response, Stalin tightened his hold on his satellites, later united in the Warsaw Pact. Europe was divided into two hostile blocs.

In late 1949, the Communists triumphed in China, frightening and infuriating many Americans, who saw an all-powerful worldwide communist conspiracy extending even into the upper reaches of the American government. When the Russian-backed Communist forces of northern Korea invaded southern Korea in 1950, President Truman's response was swift. American-led United Nations armies intervened. The cold war had spread around the world and become very hot.

It seems clear that the rapid descent from victorious Grand Alliance to bitter cold war was intimately connected with the tragic fate of eastern Europe. When the eastern European power vacuum after 1932 had lured Nazi racist imperialism, the appeasing Western democracies had quite mistakenly done nothing. They had, however, had one telling insight: how, they had asked themselves, could they unite with Stalin to stop Hitler without giving Stalin great gains on his western borders? After Hitler's invasion of Soviet Russia, the Western powers preferred to ignore this question and hope for the best. But when Stalin later began to claim the spoils of victory, a helpless but moralistic United States refused to cooperate and professed outrage. One cannot help but feel that Western opposition immediately after the war came too late and quite possibly encouraged even more aggressive measures by the always-suspicious Stalin. And it helped explode the quarrel over eastern Europe into a global confrontation, which became institutionalized and lasts to this day despite intermittent periods of relaxation.

THE WESTERN EUROPEAN RENAISSANCE

As the cold war divided Europe into two blocs, the future appeared bleak on both sides of the Iron Curtain. Economic conditions were the worst in generations, and millions of people lived on the verge of starvation. Politically, Europe was weak and divided, a battleground for cold war ambitions. Moreover, long-cherished European empires were crumbling in the face of Asian and African nationalism. Yet Europe recovered, and the Western nations led the way. In less than a generation, western Europe achieved unprecedented economic prosperity and regained much of its traditional prominence in world affairs. It was an amazing rebirth—a true renaissance.

The Postwar Challenge

After the war, economic conditions in western Europe were terrible. Simply finding enough to eat was a real problem. Runaway inflation and black markets testified to severe shortages and hardship. The bread ration in Paris in 1946 was little more than it had been in 1942 under the Nazi occupation. Rationing of bread had to be introduced in Britain in 1946 for the first time. Both France and Italy produced only about half as much in 1946 as before the war. Many people believed that Europe was quite simply finished. The prominent British historian Arnold Toynbee felt that, at best, western Europeans might seek to civilize the crude but all-powerful Americans, somewhat as the ancient Greeks had civilized their Roman conquerors.

Suffering was most intense in defeated Germany. The major territorial change of the war had moved Soviet Russia's border far to the west. Poland was in turn compensated for this loss to Russia with land taken from Germany (see Map 30.3). To solidify these boundary changes, 13 million people were driven from their homes in eastern Germany (and other eastern countries) and forced to resettle in a greatly reduced Germany. The Russians were also seizing factories and equipment as reparations, even tearing up railroad tracks and sending the rails to the Soviet Union. The command "Come here, woman," from a Russian soldier was the sound of terror, the prelude to many a rape.

In 1945 and 1946, conditions were not much better in the Western zones. There was the same soul-numbing devastation. Walking through Munich, a survivor wrote that

You could often see for miles, and then you went through canyons, as in the mountains, the rubble towering up on both sides. . . . I wandered like a sleepwalker through this wasteland. . . . There was no city. There was only the ghost, the feeling, the sensation of a devastated, stunned wasteland. The creatures in this wasteland resembled ghosts. . . . Their faces were without expression, their eyes sunken and listless. . . . A huge solitude and despair seized me.[4]

The Western allies also treated the German population with great severity at first. By February 1946, the average daily diet of a German in the Ruhr had been reduced to two slices of bread, a pat of margarine, a spoonful of porridge, and two small potatoes. Countless Germans sold many of their possessions to American soldiers to buy food. Cigarettes replaced worthless money as currency. The winter of 1946 to 1947 was one of the coldest in memory, and there were widespread signs of actual starvation. By the spring of 1947, refugee-clogged, hungry, prostrate

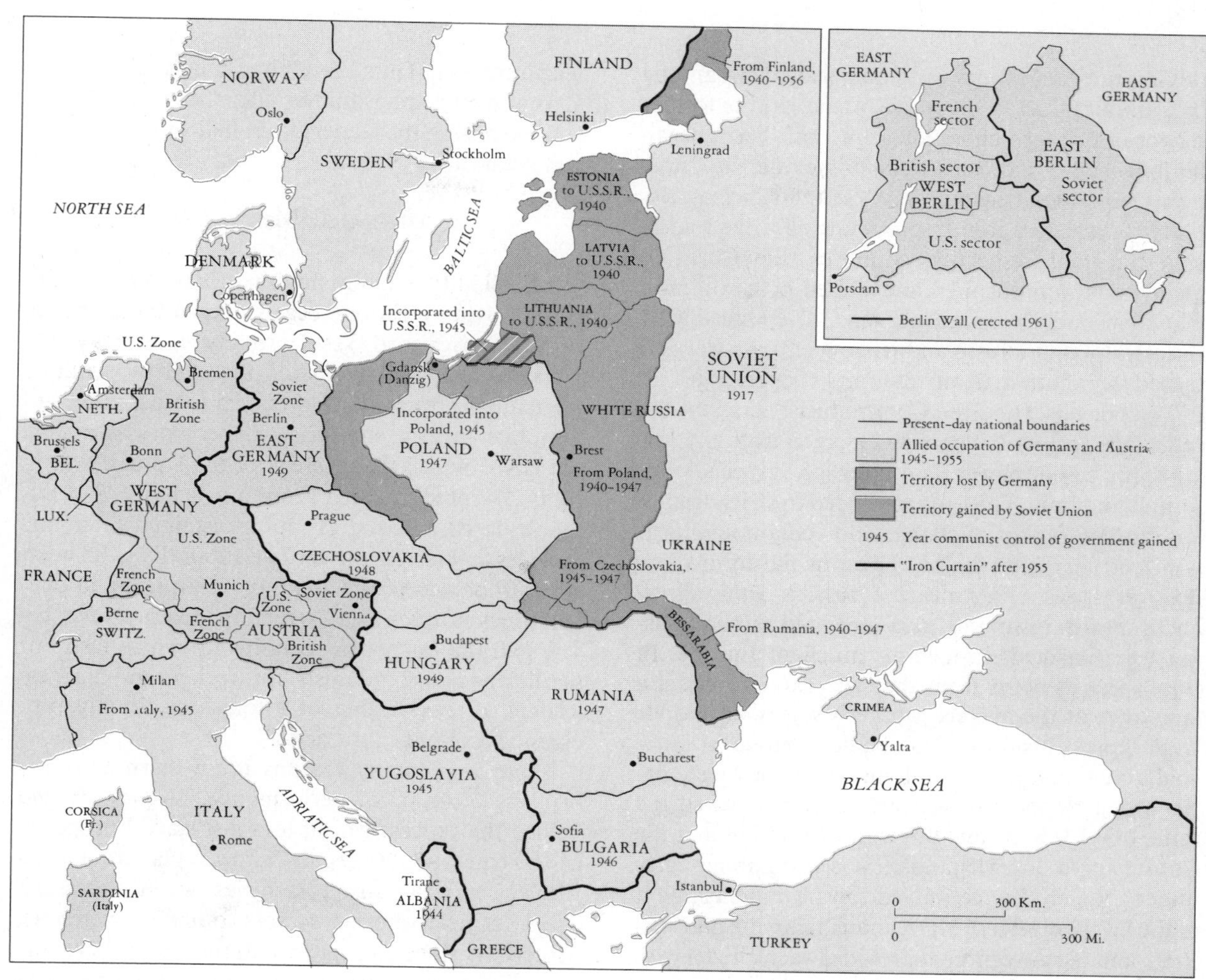

MAP 30.3 Europe After World War Two Both the Soviet Union and Poland took land from Germany, which the Allies partitioned into occupation zones. Those zones subsequently formed the basis of the East and the West German states, as the Iron Curtain fell to divide both Germany and Europe.

Germany was on the verge of total collapse and threatening to drag down the rest of Europe.

Yet western Europe was not finished. The Nazi occupation and the war had discredited old ideas and old leaders. All over Europe, many people were willing to change and experiment in hopes of building a new and better Europe out of the rubble. New groups and new leaders were coming to the fore to guide these aspirations. Progressive Catholics and revitalized Catholic political parties—the Christian Democrats—were particularly influential.

In Italy the Christian Democrats emerged as the leading party in the first postwar elections in 1946, and in early 1948 they won an absolute majority in the parliament in a landslide victory. Their very able leader was Alcide De Gasperi, a courageous antifascist and former Vatican librarian, firmly committed to political democracy, economic reconstruction, and moderate social reform. In France, too, the Catholic party provided some of the best postwar leaders, like Robert Schuman. This was particularly true after January 1946, when General De Gaulle, the inspiring wartime leader of the Free French, resigned after having re-established the free and democratic Fourth Republic. As Germany was partitioned by the cold war, a radically purified Federal Republic of Germany found new and able leadership among its Catholics. In 1949 Konrad Adenauer, the former mayor of Cologne and a long-time anti-Nazi, began his long, highly successful democratic rule; the Christian Democrats became West Germany's majority party for a generation. In providing effective leadership for their respective countries, the Christian Democrats were inspired and united by a common Christian and European heritage. They steadfastly rejected totalitarianism and narrow nationalism and placed their faith in democracy and cooperation.

The Socialists and the Communists, active in the resistance against Hitler, also emerged from the war with increased power and prestige, especially in France and Italy. They, too, provided fresh leadership and pushed for social change and economic reform with considerable success. Thus, in the immediate postwar years, welfare measures such as family allowances, health insurance, and increased public housing were enacted throughout much of Europe. In Italy social benefits from the state came to equal a large part of the average worker's wages. In France large banks, insurance companies, public utilities, coal mines, and the Renault auto company were nationalized by the government. Britain followed the same trend. The voters threw out Churchill and the Conservatives in 1945, and the socialist Labour party under Clement Attlee moved toward establishment of the "welfare state." Many industries were nationalized, and the government provided each citizen with free medical service and taxed the middle and upper classes heavily. Thus, all across Europe, social reform complemented political transformation, providing solid foundations for a great European renaissance.

The United States also provided strong and creative leadership. Frightened by fears of Soviet expansion, the United States provided western Europe with both massive economic aid and ongoing military protection. Economic aid was channeled through the Marshall Plan, which required that the participating countries coordinate their efforts for maximum effectiveness and which led to the establishment of the Organization of European Economic Cooperation (OEEC). Over the next five years, the United States furnished foreign countries roughly $22.5 billion, of which seven-eighths was in the form of outright gifts rather than loans. Military protection was provided through NATO, established as a regional alliance for self-defense and featuring American troops stationed permanently in Europe as well as the American nuclear umbrella. Thus the United States assumed its international responsibilities after the Second World War, exercising the leadership it had shunned in the tragic years after 1919.

Economic "Miracles"

As Marshall Plan aid poured in, the battered economies of western Europe began to turn the corner in 1948. Impoverished West Germany led the way with a spectacular advance after the Allies permitted Adenauer's government to reform the currency and stimulate private enterprise. Other countries were not far behind. The outbreak of the Korean War in 1950 further stimulated economic activity, and Europe entered a period of rapid, sustained economic progress that lasted into the late 1960s. By 1963 western Europe was producing more than two-and-one-half times as much as it had before the war. Never before had the European economy grown so fast. For politicians and economists, for workers and business leaders, it was a time of astonishing, loudly proclaimed economic "miracles."

There were many reasons for western Europe's brilliant economic performance. American aid helped the process get off to a fast start. Europe received equipment to repair damaged plants and even whole new specialized factories when necessary. Thus, critical shortages were quickly overcome. Moreover, since European nations coordinated the distribution of American aid, many barriers to European trade and cooperation were quickly dropped. Aid from the United States helped, therefore, to promote both a resurgence of economic liberalism with its healthy competition and an international division of labor.

As in most of the world, economic growth became a basic objective of all western European governments, for leaders and voters were determined to avoid a return to the dangerous and demoralizing stagnation of the 1930s. Governments generally accepted Keynesian economics (see page 918) and sought to stimulate their economies, and some also adopted a number of imaginative strategies. Those in Germany and France were particularly successful and influential.

Under Minister of Economy Ludwig Erhard, a roly-poly, cigar-smoking ex-professor, postwar West Germany broke decisively with the totally regulated, strait-jacketed Nazi economy. Erhard bet on the free-

Berlin Digs Out What was once a great newspaper building stands as a ghostly gutted-out shell in this altogether typical postwar scene from 1945. But the previously impassable street has been partially cleared of rubble and traffic has begun to move again. In the midst of ruins life refuses to die. *(U.S. Army Signal Corps)*

market economy, while maintaining the extensive social welfare network inherited from the Hitler era. He and his teachers believed, not only that capitalism was more efficient, but also that political and social freedom could thrive only if there were real economic freedom. Erhard's first step was to reform the currency and abolish rationing and price controls in 1948. He boldly declared, "The only ration coupon is the Mark."[5] At first, profits jumped sharply, prompting businessmen to quickly employ more people and produce more. By the late 1950s, Germany had a prospering economy and full employment, a strong currency and stable prices. Germany's success aroused renewed respect for free-market capitalism and encouraged freer trade among other European nations.

In France the major innovation was a new kind of planning. Under the guidance of Jean Monnet, an economic pragmatist and apostle of European unity, a planning commission set ambitious but flexible goals for the French economy. It used Marshall aid money and the nationalized banks to funnel money into key industries, several of which were state owned. At the same time, the planning commission and the French bureaucracy encouraged private enterprise to "think big." The often-cautious French business community responded, investing heavily in new equipment and modern factories. Thus France combined flexible planning and a "mixed" state and private economy to achieve the most rapid economic development in its long history. Throughout the 1950s and 1960s, there was hardly any unemployment in France. The average person's standard of living improved dramatically. France, too, was an economic "miracle."

Other factors also contributed to western Europe's economic boom. In most countries after the war, there were large numbers of men and women ready to work hard for low wages and the hope of a better future. Germany had millions of impoverished refugees, while France and Italy still had millions of poor peasants. Expanding industries in those countries thus had a great asset to draw on. More fully urbanized Britain had no such rural labor pool; this lack, along with a welfare socialism that stressed "fair shares" rather than rapid growth, helps account for its fairly poor postwar economic performance.

In 1945 impoverished Europe was still rich in the sense that it had the human skills of an advanced industrial society. Skilled workers, engineers, managers, and professionals knew what could and should be done, and they did it.

Many consumer products had been invented or perfected since the late 1920s, but few Europeans had been able to buy them during the depression and war. In 1945 the electric refrigerator, the washing machine, and the automobile were rare luxuries. There was, therefore, a great potential demand, which the economic system moved to satisfy.

Finally, ever since 1919 the nations of Europe had suffered from high tariffs and small national markets, which made for small and therefore inefficient factories. In the postwar era European countries junked many of these economic barriers and gradually created a large unified market—the Common Market. This action, which stimulated the economy, was part of the postwar search for a new European unity.

Toward European Unity

Western Europe's political recovery was spectacular. Republics were re-established in France, West Germany, and Italy. Constitutional monarchs were restored in Belgium, Holland, and Norway. These democratic governments took root once again and thrived. To be sure, only West Germany established a two-party system on the British-American model; states like France and Italy returned to multiparty politics and shifting parliamentary coalitions. Yet the middle-of-the-road parties—primarily the Christian Democrats and the Socialists—dominated and provided continuing leadership. National self-determination was accompanied by civil liberties and great individual freedom. All of this was itself an extraordinary achievement.

Even more remarkable was the still-unfinished, still-continuing movement toward a united Europe. The Christian Democrats with their shared Catholic heritage were particularly committed to "building Europe," and other groups shared their dedication. Many Europeans believed that narrow, exaggerated nationalism had been a fundamental cause of both world wars, and that only through unity could European conflict be avoided in the future. Many western Europeans also realized how very weak their countries were in comparison with the United States and the Soviet Union, the two superpowers that had divided Europe from outside and made it into a cold war battleground. Thus, the cold war encouraged some visionaries to seek a new "European nation," a superpower capable of controlling western Europe's destiny and reasserting its influence in world affairs.

Map 30.4 European Alliance Systems After the Cold War divided Europe into two hostile military alliances, six Western European countries formed the Common Market in 1957. The Common Market grew later to include most of Western Europe, while the Communist states organized their own economic association—COMECON.

The close cooperation among European states required by the Marshall Plan led to the creation of both the OEEC and the Council of Europe in 1948. European federalists hoped that the Council of Europe would quickly evolve into a true European parliament with sovereign rights, but this did not happen. Britain, with its empire and its "special relationship" with the United States, consistently opposed giving any real political power—any sovereignty—to the council. Many old-fashioned continental nationalists and communists felt similarly. The Council of Europe became little more than a multinational debating society.

Frustrated in the direct political approach, European federalists turned toward economics. As one of them explained, "Politics and economics are closely related. Let us try, then, for progress in economic matters. Let us suppress those obstacles of an economic nature which divide and compartmentalize the nations of Europe."[6] In this they were quite successful.

Two far-seeing French statesmen, the planner Jean Monnet and Foreign Minister Robert Schuman, courageously took the lead in 1950. The Schuman Plan called for a special international organization to control and integrate all European steel and coal production. West Germany, Italy, Belgium, the Netherlands, and Luxembourg accepted the French idea in 1952; the British would have none of it. The immediate economic goal—a single competitive market without national tariffs or quotas—was rapidly realized. By 1958 coal and steel moved as freely among

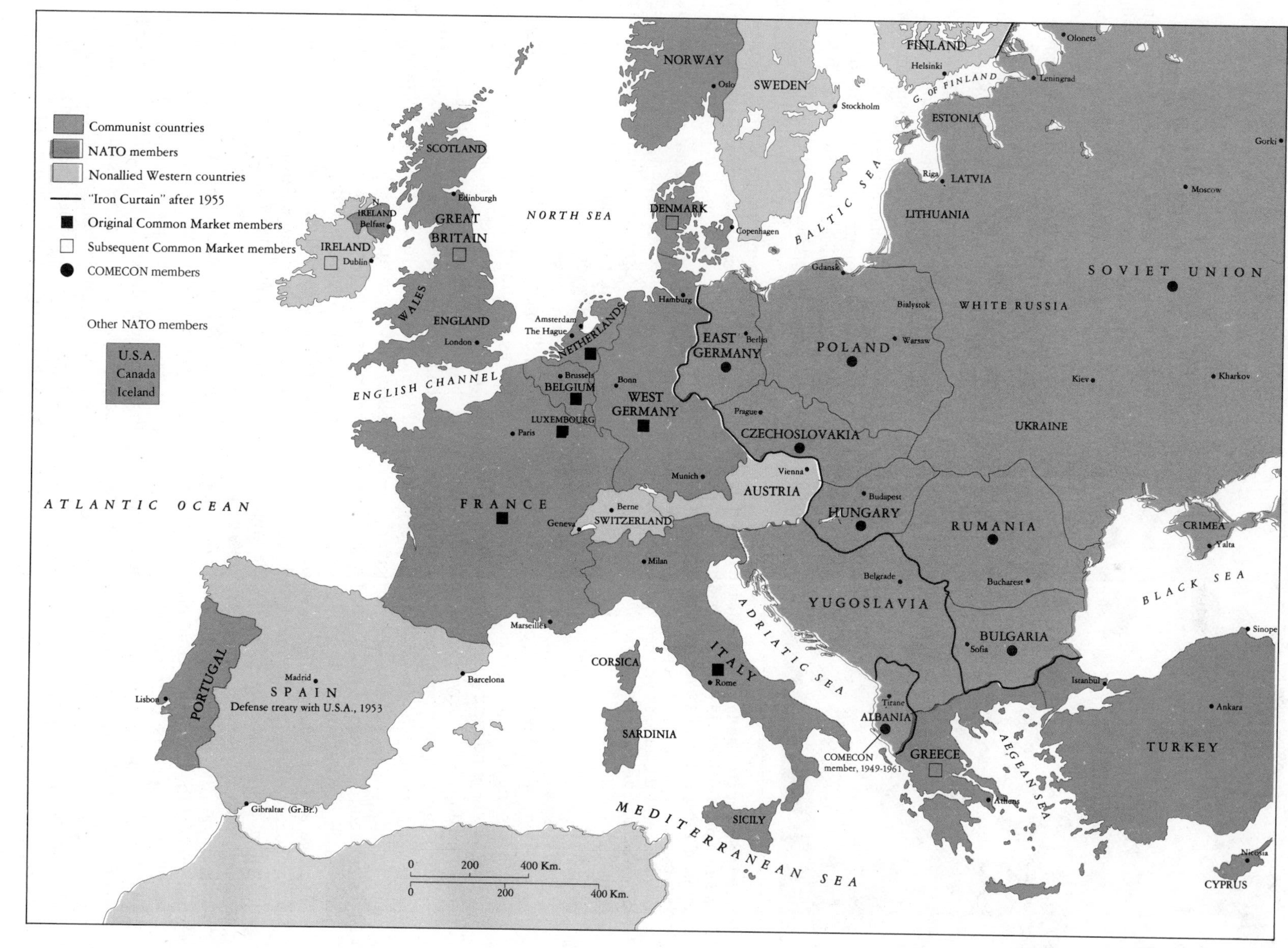
Communist countries
NATO members
Nonallied Western countries
"Iron Curtain" after 1955
Original Common Market members
Subsequent Common Market members
COMECON members
Other NATO members
U.S.A.
Canada
Iceland
NORWAY
Oslo
SWEDEN
Stockholm
FINLAND
Helsinki
G. OF FINLAND
Leningrad
Olonets
ESTONIA
Riga
LATVIA
LITHUANIA
Gorki
Moscow
SOVIET UNION
WHITE RUSSIA
Bialystok
Warsaw
POLAND
Kiev
Kharkov
UKRAINE
SCOTLAND
Edinburgh
N. IRELAND
Belfast
IRELAND
Dublin
GREAT BRITAIN
WALES
ENGLAND
London
NORTH SEA
DENMARK
Copenhagen
BALTIC SEA
Gdansk
Hamburg
EAST GERMANY
Berlin
Amsterdam
The Hague
NETHERLANDS
Brussels
BELGIUM
LUXEMBOURG
Bonn
WEST GERMANY
Paris
ENGLISH CHANNEL
Prague
CZECHOSLOVAKIA
Munich
Vienna
AUSTRIA
Budapest
HUNGARY
RUMANIA
Bucharest
CRIMEA
Yalta
BLACK SEA
ATLANTIC OCEAN
FRANCE
Geneva
Berne
SWITZERLAND
Milan
Belgrade
YUGOSLAVIA
BULGARIA
Sofia
Sinope
Istanbul
Ankara
TURKEY
ADRIATIC SEA
Tirane
ALBANIA
COMECON member, 1949-1961
GREECE
AEGEAN SEA
Athens
Marseilles
CORSICA
ITALY
Rome
SARDINIA
SICILY
PORTUGAL
Lisbon
Madrid
SPAIN
Defense treaty with U.S.A., 1953
Barcelona
Gibraltar (Gr.Br.)
MEDITERRANEAN SEA
0
200
400 Km.
0
200
400 Km.
Nicosia
CYPRUS

French President De Gaulle and his wife bid farewell to President and Mrs. Kennedy at the presidential palace in Paris in 1961. A proud statesman who never forgot the snubs received from his American and British allies during the war, De Gaulle challenged American leadership in Western Europe. *(Wide World Photos)*

the six nations of the European Coal and Steel Community as among the states of the United States. The more far-reaching political goal was to bind the six member nations so closely together economically that war among them would become unthinkable and virtually impossible. This brilliant strategy did much to reduce tragic old rivalries, particularly that of France and Germany, which practically disappeared in the postwar era.

The coal and steel community was so successful that it encouraged further technical and economic cooperation among "the Six." In 1957 the same six nations formed Euratom to pursue joint research in atomic energy; they also signed the Treaty of Rome, which created the European Economic Community, generally known as the Common Market (see Map 30.4). The first goal of the treaty was gradual reduction of all tariffs among the Six to create a large free-trade area. Others were the free movement of capital and labor and common economic policies and institutions.

An epoch-making stride toward unity, the Common Market was a tremendous success. Tariffs were rapidly reduced, and the European economy was stimulated. Companies and regions specialized in what they did best. Western Europe was being united in a single market almost as large as that of the United States. Many medium-sized American companies rushed to Europe, for a single modern factory in, say, Belgium or southern Italy had a vast potential market of 170 million customers.

The development of the Common Market fired imaginations and encouraged hopes of rapid progress toward political as well as economic union. In the 1960s, however, these hopes were frustrated by a resurgence of more traditional nationalism. Once again, France took the lead. Mired in a bitter colonial war in Algeria, the country turned in 1958 to General De Gaulle, who established the Fifth French Republic and ruled as its president until 1969. A towering giant both literally and figuratively, De Gaulle was the last of the bigger-than-life wartime leaders. A complex man who aroused a strong and sometimes negative response, especially in the United States, De Gaulle was at heart a romantic nationalist dedicated to reasserting France's greatness and glory. Once he had resolved the Algerian conflict, he labored to re-create a powerful, truly independent France, which would lead and even dictate to the other Common Market states.

De Gaulle personified the political resurgence of the leading nations of western Europe, as well as declining fears of the Soviet Union in the 1960s. Viewing the United States as the main threat to genuine French (and European) independence, he withdrew all French military forces from the "American-controlled" NATO command, which had to move from Paris to Brussels. De Gaulle tried to create financial difficulties for the United States by demanding gold for the American dollars France had accumulated. France also developed its own nuclear weapons. Within the Common Market, De Gaulle in 1963 and again in 1967 vetoed the application of the pro-American British, who were having second thoughts and wanted to join. More generally, he refused to permit the scheduled advent of majority rule within the Common Market, and he forced his partners to accept many of his views. Thus, throughout the 1960s the Common Market thrived economically, but it did not transcend deep-seated nationalism and remained a union of sovereign states.

Decolonialization

The postwar era saw the total collapse of colonial empires. Between 1947 and 1962, almost every colonial territory gained independence. Europe's long expansion, which had reached a high point in the late nineteenth century, was completely reversed (see Map 30.5). The spectacular collapse of Western political empires fully reflected old Europe's eclipsed power after 1945. Yet the new nations of Asia and Africa have been so deeply influenced by Western ideas and achievements that the "westernization" of the world has continued to rush forward.

Modern nationalism, with its demands for political self-determination and racial equality, spread from intellectuals to the masses in virtually every colonial territory after the First World War. Economic suffering created bitter popular resentment, and thousands of colonial subjects had been unwillingly drafted into French and British armies. Nationalist leaders stepped up their demands. By 1919 one high-ranking British official mournfully wrote: "A wave of unrest is sweeping over the Empire, as over the rest of the world. Almost every day brings some disturbance or other at our Imperial outposts."[7] The Russian Revolution also encouraged the growth of nationalism, and Soviet Russia verbally and militarily supported nationalist independence movements.

Furthermore, European empires had been based on an enormous power differential between the rulers and the ruled, a difference that had declined almost to the vanishing point by 1945. Not only was western Europe poor and battered immediately after the war, but Japan had demonstrated that whites were not invincible. With its political power and moral authority in tatters, Europe's only choice was either to submit gracefully or to enter into risky wars of reconquest.

Most Europeans regarded their empires very differently after 1945 than before 1914, or even before 1939. Empire had rested on self-confidence and a sense of righteousness; Europeans had believed their superiority to be not only technical and military but spiritual and moral as well. The horrors of the Second World War and the near-destruction of Western civilization destroyed such complacent arrogance and gave opponents of imperialism the upper hand in Europe. After 1945 most Europeans were willing to let go of their colonies more or less voluntarily and to concentrate on rebuilding at home.

India played a key role in decolonialization and the end of empire. India was Britain's oldest, largest, and most lucrative nonwhite possession, and Britain had by far the largest colonial empire. Nationalist opposition to British rule coalesced after the First World War under the leadership of the British-educated lawyer Mahatma Gandhi (1869–1948), who preached nonviolent "noncooperation" against the British. Indian intellectuals effectively argued the old liberal case for equality and self-determination. In response, Britain's rulers gradually introduced political reforms and limited self-government. When the war ended, independence followed very rapidly. The new Labour government was determined to leave India; radicals and socialists had always opposed imperialism, and the heavy cost of governing India had become an intolerable financial burden. The obstacle posed by conflict between India's Hindu and Muslim populations was resolved in 1947 by creating two states, predominantly Hindu India and Muslim Pakistan.

If Indian nationalism drew on Western parliamentary liberalism, Chinese nationalism developed and triumphed in the framework of Marxist-Leninist totalitarianism. In the turbulent early 1920s, a broad alliance of nationalist forces within the Russian-supported *Kuomintang*—the National People's party—was dedicated to unifying China and abolishing European concessions. But in 1927 Chiang Kai-shek (1887–1975), the successor to Sun Yat-Sen (page 856) and the leader of the Kuomintang, broke with his more radical Communist allies, headed by Mao Tse-tung.

In 1931 Mao Tse-tung (1893–1976) led his followers on an incredible five-thousand-mile march to remote northern China and dug in. Even war against the Japanese army of occupation could not force Mao and Chiang to cooperate. By late 1945 the longstanding quarrel erupted in civil war. Stalin gave Mao some aid, and the Americans gave Chiang much more. Winning the support of the peasantry by promising to expropriate the big landowners, the tougher, better-organized Communists forced the Nationalists to withdraw to the island of Taiwan in 1949.

Mao and the Communists united China's 550 million inhabitants in a strong centralized state, expelled foreigners, and began building a new society along Soviet lines, with mass arrests, forced-labor camps, and ceaseless propaganda. The peasantry was collectivized, and the inevitable five-year plans concentrated quite successfully on the expansion of heavy industry.

Most Asian countries followed the pattern of either India or China. Britain quickly gave Sri Lanka (Ceylon) and Burma independence in 1948; the Philippines became independent of the United States in 1946. The Dutch attempt to reconquer the Netherlands East Indies was unsuccessful, and in 1949 Indonesia emerged independent.

The French similarly sought to re-establish colonial rule in Indochina, but despite American aid, they were defeated in 1954 by forces under the Communist and nationalist guerrilla leader Ho Chi Minh (1890–1969), supported by Russia and China. At the subsequent international peace conference in Geneva, French Indochina gained independence. Vietnam was divided into two hostile zones, one communist and one anticommunist, pending unification on the basis of internationally supervised free elections. But the elections were never held, and civil war soon broke out between the North and the South.

In Africa, Arab nationalism was an important factor in the ending of empire. Sharing a common language and culture, Arab nationalists were also loosely united by their opposition to the colonial powers and to the migration of Jewish refugees to Palestine. The British, whose occupation policies in Palestine were condemned by Arabs and Jews, by Russians and Americans, announced their withdrawal from Palestine in 1948. The United Nations voted for the creation of two states, one Arab and one Jewish. The Arab countries immediately attacked the new Jewish nation and suffered a humiliating defeat. In the course of the fighting, thousands of Arab refugees fled from the territory that became the Jewish state of Israel.

Many of these Arab refugees refused to accept defeat. They vowed to fight on, for generations if necessary, until the state of Israel was destroyed or until they established their own independent Palestinian

Map 30.5 The New States in Africa and Asia Divided primarily along religious lines into two states, British India led the way to political independence in 1947. Most African territories achieved statehood by the mid-1960s, as European empires passed away, unlamented.

Chinese Red Guards line up before a giant picture of Mao Tse-tung in about 1967. They are waving the "Little Red Book," which contains a collection of Mao's slogans and teachings. *(Wide World Photos)*

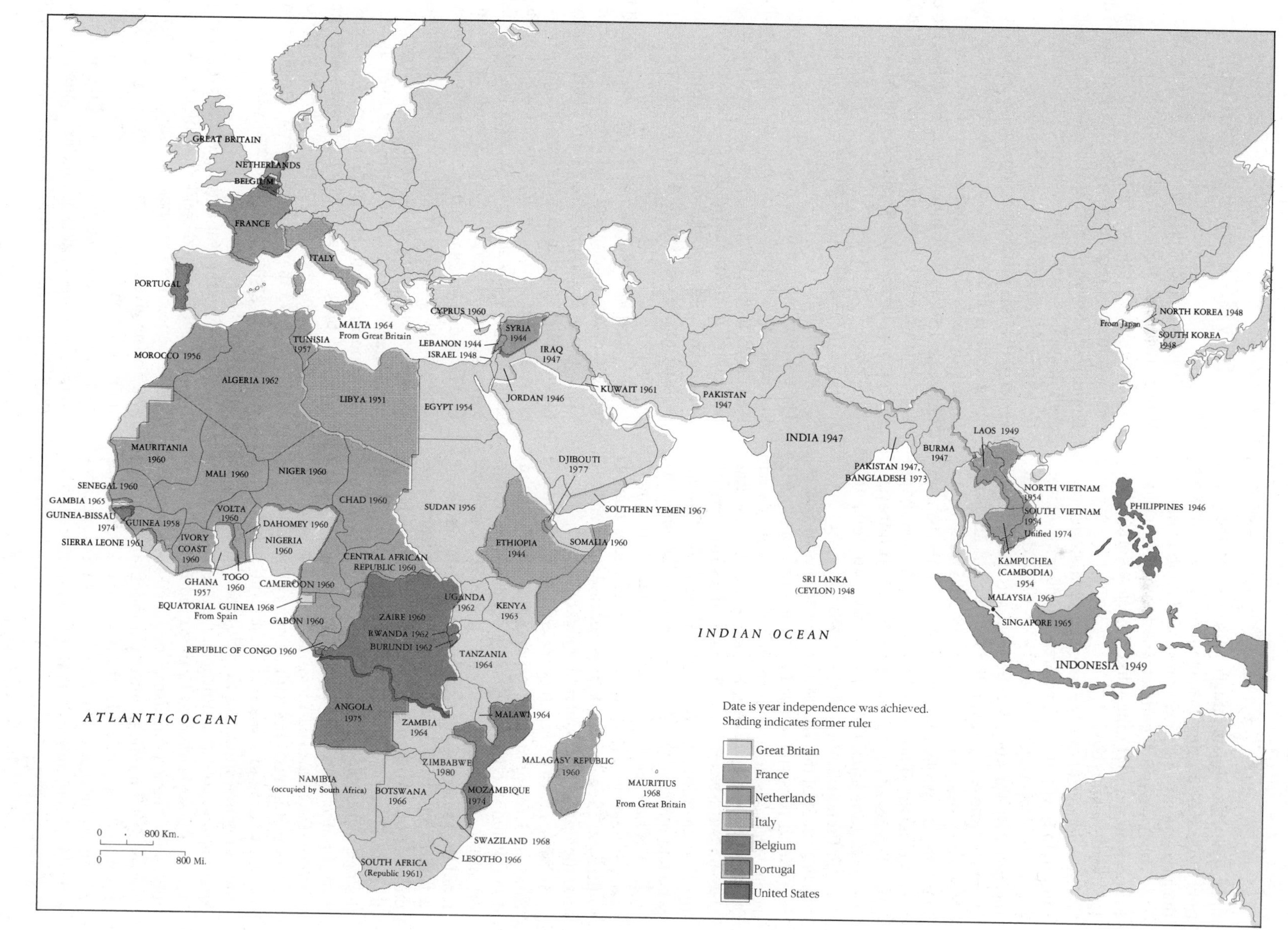

GREAT BRITAIN
NETHERLANDS
BELGIUM
FRANCE
ITALY
PORTUGAL
CYPRUS 1960
MALTA 1964
From Great Britain
SYRIA 1944
LEBANON 1944
ISRAEL 1948
IRAQ 1947
JORDAN 1946
KUWAIT 1961
TUNISIA 1957
MOROCCO 1956
ALGERIA 1962
LIBYA 1951
EGYPT 1954
MAURITANIA 1960
MALI 1960
NIGER 1960
SENEGAL 1960
GAMBIA 1965
GUINEA-BISSAU 1974
GUINEA 1958
SIERRA LEONE 1961
IVORY COAST 1960
VOLTA 1960
GHANA 1957
TOGO 1960
DAHOMEY 1960
NIGERIA 1960
CHAD 1960
SUDAN 1956
DJIBOUTI 1977
SOUTHERN YEMEN 1967
ETHIOPIA 1944
SOMALIA 1960
CENTRAL AFRICAN REPUBLIC 1960
CAMEROON 1960
EQUATORIAL GUINEA 1968
From Spain
GABON 1960
REPUBLIC OF CONGO 1960
ZAIRE 1960
RWANDA 1962
BURUNDI 1962
UGANDA 1962
KENYA 1963
TANZANIA 1964
ANGOLA 1975
ZAMBIA 1964
MALAWI 1964
ZIMBABWE 1980
NAMIBIA
(occupied by South Africa)
BOTSWANA 1966
MOZAMBIQUE 1974
MALAGASY REPUBLIC 1960
MAURITIUS 1968
From Great Britain
SWAZILAND 1968
LESOTHO 1966
SOUTH AFRICA
(Republic 1961)
ATLANTIC OCEAN
0 800 Km.
0 800 Mi.
PAKISTAN 1947
INDIA 1947
PAKISTAN 1947,
BANGLADESH 1973
SRI LANKA
(CEYLON) 1948
BURMA 1947
LAOS 1949
NORTH VIETNAM 1954
SOUTH VIETNAM 1954
Unified 1974
KAMPUCHEA
(CAMBODIA)
1954
MALAYSIA 1963
SINGAPORE 1965
INDONESIA 1949
PHILIPPINES 1946
NORTH KOREA 1948
From Japan
SOUTH KOREA 1948
INDIAN OCEAN
Date is year independence was achieved.
Shading indicates former ruler
Great Britain
France
Netherlands
Italy
Belgium
Portugal
United States

state. The Palestinian refugees also sought the support of existing Arab states, claiming that Israel was the great enemy of Arab interests and Arab nationalism. The Arab-Israeli conflict was destined to outlive the postwar era, enduring—like Soviet-American antagonism—to this day.

The Arab defeat in 1948 triggered a nationalist revolution in Egypt in 1952, where a young army officer named Gamal Abdel Nasser (1918–1970) drove out the pro-Western king. In 1956 Nasser abruptly nationalized the Suez Canal, the last symbol and substance of Western power in the Middle East. Infuriated, the British and French, along with the Israelis, invaded Egypt. This was, however, to be the dying gasp of imperial power: the moralistic, anti-imperialist Americans joined with the Russians to force the British, French, and Israelis to withdraw.

The failure of the Western powers to unseat Nasser in 1956 in turn encouraged Arab nationalists in Algeria. Algeria's large French population considered Algeria an integral part of France. It was this feeling that made the ensuing war so bitter and so atypical of decolonialization. In the end, General De Gaulle, who had returned to power as part of a movement to keep Algeria French, accepted the principle of Algerian self-determination. In 1962, after more than a century of French rule, Algeria became independent and the European population quickly fled.

In most of Africa south of the Sahara, decolonialization proceeded much more smoothly. Beginning in 1957, Britain's colonies won independence with little or no bloodshed. In 1960 the clever De Gaulle offered the leaders of French black Africa the choice of a total break with France or immediate independence within a kind of French commonwealth. Heavily dependent on France for economic aid and technology, all but one of the new states chose association with France. Throughout the 1960s France (and its western European partners) successfully used economic and cultural ties with former colonies, such as special trading privileges with the Common Market and heavy investment in French-based education, to maintain a powerful European presence in black Africa. Radicals charged France (and Europe generally) with "neocolonialism," designed to perpetuate European economic domination indefinitely. In any event, enduring aid and influence in black Africa was an important manifestation of western Europe's political recovery and even of its possible emergence as a genuine superpower.

SOVIET EASTERN EUROPE

While western Europe surged ahead economically, regaining political independence as American influence gradually waned, eastern Europe followed a different path. Soviet Russia first tightened its grip on the "liberated" nations of eastern Europe under Stalin and then refused to let go. Economic recovery in eastern Europe proceeded, therefore, along Soviet lines, and political and social developments were largely determined by changes in the Soviet Union. Thus one must look primarily at Soviet Russia to understand the achievements and failures of eastern European peoples after the Second World War.

Stalin's Last Years

The unwillingness of the United States to accept what Stalin did to territories occupied by the triumphant Red Army was at least partly responsible for the outbreak and institutionalization of the cold war. Yet Americans were not the only ones who felt disappointed and even betrayed by Stalin's postwar actions.

The Great Patriotic War of the Fatherland had fostered Russian nationalism and a relaxation of totalitarian terror. It also produced a rare but real unity between Soviet rulers and most Russian people. When an American correspondent asked a distinguished sixty-year-old Jewish scientist, who had decided to leave Russia for Israel in 1972, what had been the best period in Russian history, he received a startling answer: the Second World War. The scientist explained: "At that time we all felt closer to our government than at any other time in our lives. It was not *their* country then, but *our* country. . . . It was not *their* war, but *our* war."[8] Having made such a heroic war effort, the vast majority of the Soviet people hoped in 1945 that a grateful party and government would grant greater freedom and democracy. Such hopes were soon crushed.

Even before the war ended, Stalin was moving his country back toward rigid dictatorship. As early as 1944, the leading members of the Communist party were being given a new motivating slogan: "The war on Fascism ends, the war on capitalism begins."[9] By early 1946, Stalin was publicly singing the old tune that war was inevitable as long as capitalism existed. Stalin's invention of a new foreign foe was mainly an

Lenin Avenue, Volgograd Devastated Stalingrad was completely rebuilt and then renamed Volgograd as part of Khrushchev's de-Stalinization campaign. Seen here are the massive apartment blocks, the gigantic boulevard, and the stress on public transportation as opposed to private automobiles, which are all quite characteristic of Soviet urban style. *(Sovfoto/Eastfoto)*

excuse for re-establishing totalitarian measures, for the totalitarian state cannot live without enemies. Unfortunately, as dissident Russian historians have argued, Stalin's language at home and his actions in eastern Europe were so crudely extreme that he managed to turn an imaginary threat into a real one, as the cold war took hold.

One of Stalin's first postwar goals was to repress the millions of Soviet citizens who were outside Soviet borders when the war ended. Many had been captured by the Nazis; others were ordinary civilians who had been living abroad. Many were opposed to Stalin; some had fought for the Germans. Determined to hush up the fact that large numbers of Soviet citizens hated his regime so much that they had willingly supported the Germans and refused to go home, Stalin demanded that all these "traitors" be returned to him. At Yalta, Roosevelt and Churchill agreed, and they kept their word. American and British military commanders refused to recognize the right of political asylum under any circumstances.

Roughly 2 million people were delivered to Stalin against their will. Most were immediately arrested and sent to forced-labor camps, where about 50 percent perished. The revival of many forced-labor camps, which had accounted for roughly one-sixth of all new construction in Soviet Russia before the war, was further stimulated by large-scale purges of many people who had never left the Soviet Union, particularly in 1945 and 1946.

Culture and art were also purged. Rigid anti-Western ideological conformity was reimposed in violent campaigns led by Stalin's trusted henchman, Andrei Zhdanov. Zhdanov denounced many artists, including the composers Sergei Prokofiev and Dimitri Shostakovich and the outstanding film director Sergei Eisenstein. The great poet Anna Akhmatova was condemned as "a harlot and nun who mixes harlotry and prayer" and, like many others, driven out of the writers' union, which practically ensured that her work would not be published. In 1949 Stalin launched a savage verbal attack on Soviet Jews, who were accused of being pro-Western and antisocialist.

In the political realm, Stalin reasserted the Communist party's complete control of the government and his absolute mastery of the party. Five-year plans were reintroduced to cope with the enormous task of economic reconstruction. Once again, heavy and military industry were given top priority, and consumer goods, housing, and still-collectivized agriculture were neglected. Everyday life was very hard: in 1952 the wages of ordinary people still bought 25 to 40 percent *less* than in 1928. In short, it was the 1930s all over again in Soviet Russia, although police terror was less intense than during that era's purges.

Stalin's prime postwar innovation was to export the Stalinist system to the countries of eastern Europe. The Communist parties of eastern Europe had established one-party states by 1948, thanks to the help of the Red Army and the Russian secret police. Rigid ideological indoctrination, attacks on religion, and a lack of civil liberties were soon facts of life. Industry was nationalized, and the middle class was stripped of its possessions. Economic life was then faithfully recast in the Stalinist mold. Forced industrialization, with five-year plans and a stress on heavy industry, lurched forward without regard for human costs. For the sake of ideological uniformity, agriculture had to be collectivized; this process went much faster in Bulgaria and Czechoslovakia than in Hungary and Poland. Finally, the satellite countries were forced to trade heavily with Soviet Russia on very unfavorable terms, as traditional economic ties with western Europe were forcibly severed.

Only Josip Tito (1892–1980), the popular resistance leader and Communist chief of Yugoslavia, was able to resist Russian economic exploitation successfully. Tito openly broke with Stalin in 1948, and since there was no Russian army in Yugoslavia, he got away with it. Tito's successful proclamation of Communist independence led the infuriated and humiliated Stalin to purge the Communist parties of eastern Europe. Hundreds of thousands who had joined the party after the war were expelled. Popular Communist leaders who, like Tito, had led the resistance against Germany, were made to star in reruns of the great show trials of the 1930s, complete with charges of treason, unbelievable confessions, and merciless executions. Thus did history repeat itself as Stalin sought to create absolutely obedient instruments of domination in eastern Europe.

Reform and De-Stalinization

In 1953 the aging Stalin finally died, and a new era slowly began in Soviet eastern Europe. Even as they struggled for power, Stalin's heirs realized that change and reform were necessary. There was, first of all, widespread fear and hatred of Stalin's political terrorism, which had struck both high and low with its endless purges and unjust arrests. Even Stalin's secret-police chief, Lavrenti Beria, publicly favored a relaxation of controls in an unsuccessful attempt to seize power. Beria was arrested and shot, after which the power of the secret police was curbed and many of its infamous forced-labor camps were gradually closed. Change was also necessary for economic reasons. Agriculture was in bad shape, and shortages of consumer goods were discouraging hard work and initiative. Finally, Stalin's aggressive foreign policy had led directly to an ongoing American commitment to western Europe and a strong Western alliance. Soviet Russia was isolated and contained.

On the question of just how much change should be permitted, the Communist leadership was badly split. The conservatives led by Stalin's long-time foreign minister, the stone-faced Vyacheslav Molotov, wanted to make as few changes as possible. The reformers, led by Nikita Khrushchev, argued for major innovations. Khrushchev (1894–1971), who had joined the party as an uneducated coal miner in 1918 at twenty-four and had risen steadily to a high-level position in the 1930s, was emerging as the new ruler by 1955.

To strengthen his position and that of his fellow reformers within the party, Khrushchev launched an all-out attack on Stalin and his crimes at a closed session of the Twentieth Party Congress in 1956. In gory detail he described to the startled Communist delegates how Stalin had tortured and murdered thousands of loyal Communists, how he had trusted Hitler completely and bungled the country's defense, and how he had "supported the glorification of his own person with all conceivable methods." For hours Soviet Russia's top leader delivered an attack whose content would previously have been dismissed as "anti-Communist hysteria" in many circles throughout the Western world.

Khrushchev's "secret speech" was read to Communist party meetings throughout the country and strengthened the reform movement. The liberalization—or "de-Stalinization," as it was called in the West—of Soviet Russia was genuine. The Communist party jealously maintained its monopoly on political power, but Khrushchev shook it up and brought in new blood. The economy was made more responsive to the needs and even some of the desires of the people, as some resources were shifted from heavy industry and the military toward consumer goods and agriculture. Stalinist controls over workers were relaxed, and independent courts rather than the secret police judged and punished nonpolitical crimes.

Russia's very low standard of living finally began to improve and continued to rise throughout the 1960s. By 1970 Russians were able to buy twice as much food, three times as much clothing, and twelve times as many appliances as in 1950. (Even so, the standard of living in Soviet Russia was only about half that of the wealthier western European countries in 1970 and well below that of east European countries as well.)

De-Stalinization created great ferment among writers and intellectuals, who hungered for cultural freedom. The poet Boris Pasternak (1890–1960), who survived the Stalinist years by turning his talents to translating Shakespeare, finished his great novel *Doctor Zhivago* in 1956. Published in the West but not in Russia, *Doctor Zhivago* is both a literary masterpiece and a powerful challenge to communism. It tells the story of a prerevolutionary intellectual who rejects the violence and brutality of the revolution of 1917 and the Stalinist years. Even as he is destroyed, he triumphs because of his humanity and Christian spirit. Pasternak was forced by Khrushchev himself to refuse the Nobel prize in 1958—but he was not shot. Other talented writers followed Pasternak's lead, and courageous editors let the sparks fly.

The writer Alexander Solzhenitsyn (b. 1918) created a sensation when his *One Day in the Life of Ivan Denisovich* was published in Russia in 1962. Solzhenitsyn's novel portrays in grim detail life in a Stalinist concentration camp—a life to which Solzhenitsyn himself had been unjustly condemned—and is a damning indictment of the Stalinist past.

Khrushchev also de-Stalinized Soviet foreign policy. "Peaceful coexistence" with capitalism was possible, he argued, and great wars were not inevitable. Khrushchev made positive concessions, meeting with U.S. President Dwight Eisenhower at the first summit meeting since Potsdam and agreeing in 1955 to real independence for a neutral Austria after ten long years of Allied occupation. Thus there was considerable relaxation of cold war tensions between 1955 and 1957. At the same time, Khrushchev began wooing the new nations of Asia and Africa—even if they were not communist—with promises and aid. He also proclaimed that there could be different paths to socialism, thus calling a halt to the little cold war with Tito's Yugoslavia.

De-Stalinization stimulated rebelliousness in the eastern European satellites. Having suffered in silence under Stalin, Communist reformers and the masses were quickly emboldened to seek much greater liberty and national independence. Poland took the lead in March 1956: riots there resulted in the release of more than nine thousand political prisoners, including the previously purged Wladyslaw Gomulka. Taking charge of the government, Gomulka skillfully managed to win greater autonomy for Poland while calming anti-Russian feeling.

Hungary experienced a real and very tragic revolution. Led by students and workers—the classic urban revolutionaries—the people of Budapest installed a liberal Communist reformer as their new chief in October 1956. Soviet troops were forced to leave the country. One-party rule was abolished, and the new government promised free elections, freedom of expression, and massive social changes. Worst of all from the Russian point of view, the new government declared Hungarian neutrality and renounced Hungary's military alliance with Moscow. As in 1849, the Russian answer was to invade Hungary with a large army and to crush, once again, a national, democratic revolution.

Fighting was bitter until the end, for the Hungarians hoped that the United States would fulfill its earlier propaganda promises and come to their aid. When this did not occur because of American unwillingness to risk a general war, the people of eastern Europe realized that their only hope was to strive for small domestic gains while following Russia obediently in foreign affairs. This cautious approach produced some results. In Poland, for example, the peasants were not collectivized, and Catholics were allowed to practice their faith. Thus eastern Europe profited, however modestly, from Khrushchev's policy of de-Stalinization and could hope for still greater freedom in the future.

The Fall of Khrushchev

In October 1962, a remarkable poem entitled "Stalin's Heirs," by the popular young poet Yevgeny Yevtushenko (b. 1933), appeared in *Pravda,* the official newspaper of the Communist party and the most important one in Soviet Russia. Yevtushenko wrote:

Some of his heirs are in retirement pruning their rose-
bushes,
and secretly thinking that their time will come again.
Others even attack Stalin from the rostrum but at
home, at night-time, think back to bygone days.[10]

Like Solzhenitsyn's novel about Stalin's concentration camps, published a month later, this very political poem was authorized by Communist party boss Khrushchev himself. It was part of his last, desperate offensive against the many well-entrenched conservative Stalinists in the party and government, who were indeed "secretly thinking that their time will come again." And it did.

Within two years Khrushchev had fallen in a bloodless palace revolution. Under Leonid Brezhnev (1906–1982), Soviet Russia began a period of limited "re-Stalinization." The basic reason for this development was that Khrushchev's Communist colleagues saw de-Stalinization as a dangerous, two-sided threat. How could Khrushchev denounce the dead dictator without eventually denouncing and perhaps even arresting his still-powerful henchmen? In a heated secret debate in 1957, when the conservatives had tried without success to depose the menacing reformer, Khrushchev had pointed at two of Stalin's most devoted followers, Molotov and Kaganovich, and exclaimed: "Your hands are stained with the blood of our party leaders and of innumerable innocent Bolsheviks!" "So are yours!" Molotov and Kaganovich shouted back at him. "Yes, so are mine," Khrushchev replied. "I admit this. But during the purges I was merely carrying out your order. . . . I was not responsible. You were."[11] Moreover, the widening campaign of de-Stalinization posed a clear threat to the dictatorial authority of the party. It was producing growing, perhaps uncontrollable, criticism of the whole Communist system. The party had to tighten up while there was still time. It was clear that Khrushchev had to go.

Another reason for conservative opposition was Khrushchev's foreign policy. Although he scored some diplomatic victories, notably with Egypt and India, Khrushchev's policy toward the West was highly erratic and ultimately unsuccessful. In 1958 he ordered the Western allies to evacuate West Berlin within six months, which led only to a reaffirmation of allied unity and to Khrushchev's backing down. Then in 1961, as relations with Communist China deteriorated dramatically, Khrushchev ordered the East Germans to build a wall between East and West Berlin, thereby sealing off West Berlin in clear violation of existing access agreements between the Great Powers. The recently elected U.S. president, John F. Kennedy, acquiesced. Emboldened and seeing a chance to change the balance of military power decisively, Khrushchev ordered missiles with nuclear warheads installed in Fidel Castro's Communist Cuba. President Kennedy countered with a naval blockade of Cuba, and after a tense diplomatic crisis, Khrushchev was forced to remove the Russian missiles in return for American pledges not to disturb Castro's regime. Khrushchev looked like a bumbling buffoon; his influence, already slipping, declined rapidly after the Cuban fiasco.

After Brezhnev and his supporters took over in 1964, they started talking cautiously of Stalin's "good points" and ignoring his crimes. Their praise of the whole Stalinist era, with its rapid industrialization and wartime victories, informed Soviet citizens that no fundamental break with the past had occurred at home. Russian leaders also launched a massive arms buildup, determined never to suffer Khrushchev's humiliation in the face of American nuclear superiority. And they began building the large navy and air force necessary for intervention in faraway places, like Cuba, around the globe. Yet Brezhnev and company proceeded cautiously in the mid-1960s. They avoided direct confrontation with the United States and seemed more solidly committed to peaceful coexistence than the deposed Khrushchev—to the great relief of people in the West.

THE WESTERN HEMISPHERE

One way to think of what historians used to call the New World is as a vigorous offshoot of Western civilization, an offshoot that has gradually developed its own characteristics while retaining European roots. From this perspective, one can see many illuminating parallels and divergences in the histories of Europe and the Americas. So it was after the Second World War. The western hemisphere experienced a many-faceted postwar recovery, somewhat similar to that of Europe, though it began earlier, especially in Latin America.

Postwar Prosperity in the United States

The Second World War cured the depression in the United States and brought about the greatest boom in American history. Unemployment practically vanished, as millions of new workers, half of them women, found jobs. Personal income doubled and the well-being of Americans increased dramatically. Yet the experience of the 1930s weighed heavily on people's minds, feeding fears that peace would bring renewed depression.

In fact, conversion to a peacetime economy went smoothly, marred only by a spurt of inflation accompanying the removal of government controls. Moreover, the U.S. economy continued to advance fairly steadily for a long generation. Though cold-war fears marked American relations with the rest of the world, economic prosperity satisfied at home.

This helps explain why postwar domestic politics consisted largely of modest adjustments to the status quo until the 1960s. After a flurry of unpopular postwar strikes, a conservative Republican Congress chopped away at the power of labor unions by means of the Taft-Hartley Act of 1947. But Truman's upset victory in 1948 demonstrated that Americans had no interest in undoing Roosevelt's social and economic reforms. The Congress proceeded to increase social security benefits, subsidize middle- and lower-class housing, and raise the minimum wage. These and other liberal measures consolidated the New Deal. But true innovations, whether in health or civil rights, were rejected, and in 1952 the Republican party and the voters turned to General Eisenhower, a national hero and self-described moderate.

The federal government's only major new undertaking during the "Eisenhower years" was the interstate highway system, a suitable symbol of the basic satisfaction of the vast majority. Some Americans feared that the United States was becoming a "blocked society," obsessed with stability and incapable of wholesome change. This feeling contributed in 1960 to the election of the young, attractive John F. Kennedy, who promised to "get the country moving again." President Kennedy captured the popular imagination with his flair and rhetoric, revitalized the old Roosevelt coalition, and modestly expanded existing liberal legislation before he was struck down by an assassin's bullet in 1963.

The Civil Rights Revolution

Belatedly and reluctantly, complacent postwar America experienced a genuine social revolution: after a long and sometimes bloody struggle, blacks (and their white supporters) threw off a deeply entrenched system of segregation, discrimination, and repression. This movement for civil rights advanced on several fronts. Eloquent lawyers from the National Association for the Advancement of Colored People (NAACP) challenged school segregation in the courts and in 1954 won a landmark decision in the Supreme Court that "separate educational facilities are inherently unequal." While state and local governments in the South were refusing to comply, blacks were effectively challenging institutionalized inequality with bus boycotts, sit-ins, and demonstrations. As Martin Luther King told the white power structure, "We will not hate you, but we will not obey your evil laws."[12]

Blacks also used their growing political power in key northern states to gain the support of the liberal wing of the Democratic party. All these efforts culminated after the liberal landslide that elected Lyndon Johnson in 1964. The Civil Rights Act of 1964 categorically prohibited discrimination in public services and on the job. In the follow-up Voting Rights Act of 1965, the federal government firmly guaranteed all blacks the right to vote. By the 1970s, substantial numbers of blacks had been elected to public and private office throughout the southern states, proof positive that dramatic changes had occurred in American race relations.

Black voters and political leaders enthusiastically supported the accompanying surge of new liberal social legislation in the mid-1960s. President Johnson, reviving the New Deal approach of his early congressional years, solemnly declared "unconditional war on poverty." Congress and the administration created a host of antipoverty projects, such as the domestic peace corps, free preschools for slum children, and community-action programs. Although these programs were directed to all poor Americans—the majority of whom are white—they were also intended to extend greater equality for blacks to the realm of economics. More generally, the United States promoted in the mid-1960s the kind of fundamental social reform that western Europe had em-

The March on Washington in August 1963 marked a dramatic climax in the civil rights struggle. More than 200,000 people gathered at the Lincoln Memorial to hear the young Martin Luther King deliver his greatest address, his "I have a dream" speech. *(UPI/ Bettmann Newsphotos)*

braced immediately after World War Two. The United States became much more of a welfare state, as government spending for social benefits rose dramatically and approached European levels.

Economic Nationalism in Latin America

Although the countries of Latin America share a European heritage, specifically a Spanish-Portuguese heritage, their striking differences make it difficult to generalize meaningfully about modern Latin American history. Yet a growing economic nationalism seems unmistakable. As the early nineteenth century saw Spanish and Portuguese colonies win wars of political independence, recent history has been an ongoing quest for genuine economic independence through local control and industrialization, which has sometimes brought Latin American countries into sharp conflict with Europe and the United States.

To understand the rise of economic nationalism, one must remember that Latin American countries developed as producers of foodstuffs and raw materials, which were exported to Europe and the United States in return for manufactured goods and capital investment. This exchange was mutually beneficial, especially in the later nineteenth century, and the countries that participated most actively, like Argentina and southern Brazil, became the wealthiest and most advanced. There was, however, a heavy price to pay. Latin America became very dependent on foreign markets, products, and investments. Industry did not develop and large landowners profited most, further enhancing their social and political power.

The old international division of labor, disrupted by the First World War but re-established in the 1920s, was finally destroyed by the Great Depression—a historical turning point as critical for Latin America as for the United States. Prices and exports of Latin American commodities collapsed as Europe and the United States drastically reduced their purchases and raised tariffs to protect domestic procedures. With foreign sales plummeting, Latin American countries could not buy industrial goods abroad. Latin America suffered the full force of the global economic crisis.

The result in the larger, more important Latin American countries was a profound shift in the direction of economic nationalism after 1930. The more popularly based governments worked to reduce foreign influence and gain control of their own economies and natural resources. They energetically promoted national industry by means of high tariffs, government grants, and even state enterprise. They favored the lower-middle and urban working classes with social benefits and higher wages in order to increase their purchasing power and gain their support. These efforts at recovery were fairly successful. By the late 1940s, the factories of Argentina, Brazil, and Chile could generally satisfy domestic consumer demand for the products of light industry. In the 1950s, some countries began moving into heavy industry. Economic nationalism and the rise of industry are particularly striking in the two largest and most influential countries, Mexico and Brazil, which together account for half the population of Latin America.

MEXICO. Overthrowing the elitist, upper-class rule of the tyrant Porfirio Díaz, the spasmodic, often-chaotic Mexican Revolution of 1910 culminated in 1917 in a new constitution. This radical nationalistic document called for universal suffrage, massive land reform, benefits for labor, and strict control of foreign capital. Actual progress was quite modest until 1934, when a charismatic young Indian from a poor family, Lazaro Cárdenas, became president and dramatically revived the languishing revolution. Under Cárdenas, many large estates were divided up among small farmers or returned undivided to Indian communities.

Meanwhile, because foreign capitalists were being discouraged, Mexican businessmen built many small factories and managed to thrive. The government also championed the cause of industrial workers. In 1938, when Mexican workers became locked in a bitter dispute with British and American oil companies, Cárdenas nationalized the petroleum industry—to the astonishment of a world unaccustomed to such actions. Finally, the 1930s saw the flowering of a distinctive Mexican culture, which proudly embraced its long-despised Indian past and gloried in the modern national revolution.

In 1940 the official, semiauthoritarian party that has governed Mexico continuously since the revolution selected the first of a series of more moderate presidents. Steadfast in their radical, occasionally anti-American rhetoric, these presidents used the full power of the state to promote industrialization through a judicious mixture of public, private, and even foreign enterprise. The Mexican economy grew rapidly, at about 6 percent per year from the early 1940s and the late 1960s, with the upper and middle classes reaping the lion's share of the benefits.

BRAZIL. After the fall of Brazil's monarchy in 1889, politics was largely dominated by the coffee barons and by regional rivalries. These rivalries and deteriorating economic conditions allowed a military revolt led by Getulio Vargas, governor of one of Brazil's larger states, to seize control of the federal government in 1930. Vargas, who proved to be a consummate politician, fragmented the opposition and established a mild dictatorship that lasted until 1945. Vargas's rule was generally popular, combining as it did effective economic nationalism and moderate social reform.

Somewhat like President Franklin Roosevelt in the United States, Vargas decisively tipped the balance of political power away from the Brazilian states to the ever-expanding federal government, which became a truly national government for the first time. Vargas and his allies also set out to industrialize Brazil and gain economic independence. While the national coffee board used mountains of surplus coffee beans to fire railroad locomotives, the government supported Brazilian manufacturers with high tariffs, gen-

José Clemente Orozco (1883–1949) was one of the great and committed painters of the Mexican Revolution. Orozco believed that art should reflect the "new order of things" and inspire the common people—the workers and the peasants. This vibrant central mural in the National Palace in Mexico City, one of Orozco's many great wall paintings, depicts a brutal Spanish conquest and a liberating revolution. *(Reproduction authorized by The Instituto Nacional de Bellas Artes)*

erous loans, and labor peace. This probusiness policy did not prevent new social legislation: workers received shorter hours, pensions, health and accident insurance, paid vacations, and other benefits. Finally, Vargas shrewdly upheld the nationalist cause in his relations with the giant to the north. Early in the Second World War, for example, he traded U.S. military bases in Brazil for American construction of Brazil's first huge steel-making complex. By 1945, when the authoritarian Vargas fell in a bloodless military coup that called for greater political liberty, Brazil was modernizing rapidly.

Modernization continued for the next fifteen years. The economy boomed. Presidential politics were re-established, while the military kept a watchful eye for extremism among the civilian politicians. Economic nationalism was especially vigorous under the flamboyant President Kubitschek (1956–1960), a doctor of German-Czech descent. The government borrowed heavily from international bankers to promote industry and built the extravagant new capital of Brasília in the midst of a wilderness. When Brazil's creditors demanded more conservative policies to stem inflation, Kubitschek delighted the nationalists with his firm and successful refusal. His slogan was "Fifty Years' Progress in Five," and he seemed to mean it.

The Brazilian and Mexican formula of national economic development, varying degrees of electoral competition, and social reform was shared by some other Latin American countries, notably Argentina and Chile. By the late 1950s, optimism was widespread, if cautious. Economic and social progress seemed to promise less violent, more democratic politics. These expectations were profoundly shakened by the Cuban revolution.

The Cuban Revolution

Although many aspects of the Cuban revolution are obscured by controversy, certain background conditions are clear. First, after achieving independence in 1898, Cuba was for many years virtually an American protectorate. The Cuban constitution gave the United States the legal right to intervene in Cuban affairs, a right that was frequently exercised until Roosevelt renounced it in 1934. Second, and partly because the American army had often been the real power, Cuba's political institutions were weak and its politicians were extraordinarily corrupt. Under the strongman Fulgencio Batista, an opportunistic ex-sergeant who controlled the government almost continually from 1933 to 1958, graft and outright looting were a way of life. Third, Cuba was one of Latin America's most prosperous and advanced countries by the 1950s, but its sugar-and-tourist economy was dependent on the United States. Finally, the enormous differences between rich and poor in Cuba were typical of Latin America. But Cuba also had a strong Communist party, which was highly unusual.

Fidel Castro, a magnetic leader with the gift of oratory and a flair for propaganda, managed to unify anti-Batista elements in a revolutionary front. When Castro's guerrilla forces triumphed in late 1958, the new government's goals were unclear. Castro had promised a "real" revolution but had always laughed at charges that he was a communist. As the regime consolidated its power in 1959 and 1960, it became increasingly clear that "real" meant "communist" in Castro's mind. Wealthy Cubans, who owned three-quarters of the sugar industry and many profitable businesses, fled to Miami. Soon the middle class began to follow.

Meanwhile, relations with the Eisenhower administration—which had indirectly supported Castro by refusing to sell arms to Batista after March 1958—deteriorated rapidly. Thus, in April 1961, newly elected President Kennedy went ahead with a pre-existing CIA plan to use Cuban exiles to topple Castro. But the Kennedy administration lost its nerve and abandoned the exiles as soon as they were put ashore at the Bay of Pigs. This doomed the invasion, and the exiles were quickly captured, to be ransomed later for $60 million.

The Bay of Pigs invasion—a triumph for Castro and a humiliating, roundly criticized fiasco for the United States—had significant consequences. It freed Castro to build his version of a communist society, and he did. Political life in Cuba featured "anti-imperialism," an alliance with the Soviet bloc, the dictatorship of the party, and a vigorously promoted Castro cult. Revolutionary enthusiasm was genuine among party activists, much of Cuba's youth, and some of the masses some of the time. Prisons and emigration silenced opposition. The economy was characterized by all-pervasive state ownership, collective farms, and Soviet trade and aid. Early efforts to industrialize ran aground, and sugar production at pre-Castro levels continued to dominate the economy.

Socially, the regime pursued equality and the creation of a new socialist personality. In short, revolutionary totalitarianism came to the Americas.

The failure of the United States' halfhearted effort to derail Castro probably encouraged Khrushchev to start putting nuclear missiles in Cuba, leading directly to the most serious East-West crisis since the Korean war. And, although the Russians backed down (page 982), Castro's survival heightened both hopes and fears that the Cuban revolution could spread throughout Latin America. As leftists were emboldened to try guerrilla warfare, conservatives became more rigid and suspicious of calls for change. In the United States, fear of communism aroused heightened cold war–style interest in Latin America. Using the Organization of American States to isolate Cuba, the United States in 1961 pledged $10 billion in aid over ten years to a new hemispheric "Alliance for Progress." The alliance was intended to promote long-term economic development and social reform, which American liberals typically assumed would immunize Latin America from the Cuban disease.

U.S. aid did contribute modestly to continued Latin America economic development in the 1960s, although population growth canceled out two-thirds of the increase on a per capita basis. Democratic social reforms—the other half of the Alliance for Progress formula—proceeded slowly, however. Instead, the period following the Cuban revolution saw the rise of extremism and a revival of conservative authoritarianism in Latin America. These developments marked the turbulent beginnings of a new era in the late 1960s.

The recovery of Europe and the Americas during and after World War Two is one of the most remarkable chapters in the long, uneven course of Western civilization. Although the dangerous tensions of the cold war frustrated fond hopes for a truly peaceful international order, the transition from imperialism to decolonialization proceeded rapidly, surprisingly smoothly, and without serious damage to western Europe. Instead, genuine political democracy gained unprecedented strength in the West, and economic progress quickened the pace of ongoing social and cultural transformation. Thus the tremendous promise inherent in Western society's fateful embrace of the "dual revolution," which had begun in France and England in the late eighteenth century and which had momentarily halted the agonies of the Great Depression and the horrors of Nazi totalitarianism, was largely if perhaps only temporarily realized in the shining achievements of the postwar era.

NOTES

1. William Bullitt, "How We Won the War and Lost the Peace," *Life,* XXV (30 August 1948): 94.
2. Quoted by N. Graebner, *Cold War Diplomacy, 1945–1960,* Van Nostrand, Princeton, N.J., 1962, p. d17.
3. Ibid.
4. Quoted by F. Prinz, ed., *Trümmerzeit in Munchen,* Münchner Stadtmuseum, Munich, 1984, p. 273; trans. by J. Buckler.
5. Quoted in J. Hennessy, *Economic "Miracles,"* André Deutsch, London, 1964, p. 5.
6. P. Van Zeeland, in *European Integration,* ed. C. G. Haines, John Hopkins Press, Baltimore, 1957, p. xi.
7. Lord Milner, quoted by R. von Albertini, "The Impact of Two World Wars on the Decline of Colonialism," *Journal of Contemporary History* 4 (January 1969):17.
8. Quoted by H. Smith, *The Russians,* Quadrangle/New York Times, New York, 1976, p. 303.
9. Quoted by D. Treadgold, *Twentieth Century Russia,* Houghton Mifflin, Boston, 5th ed., 1981, p. 442.
10. Quoted by M. Tatu, *Power in the Kremlin: From Khrushchev to Kosygin,* Viking Press, New York, 1968, p. 248.
11. Quoted by I. Deutscher, in *Soviet Society,* ed. A. Inkeles and K. Geiger, Houghton Mifflin, Boston, 1961, p. 41.
12. Quoted by S. E. Morison et al., *A Concise History of the American Republic,* Oxford University Press, New York, 1977, p. 697.

SUGGESTED READING

G. Wright, *The Ordeal of Total War, 1939–1945* (1968), is the best comprehensive study on World War Two, while B. H. Liddell Hart, *The History of the Second*

World War (1971), is a good overview of military developments. Three dramatic studies of special aspects of the war are A. Dallin, *German Rule in Russia, 1941–1945* (1957), which analyzes the effects of Nazi occupation policies on the Soviet population; L. Collins and D. La Pierre, *Is Paris Burning?* (1965), a best-selling account of the liberation of Paris and Hitler's plans to destroy the city; and J. Toland, *The Last 100 Days* (1966), a lively account of the end of the war. Great leaders and matchless stylists, Winston Churchill and Charles de Gaulle have both written histories of the war in the form of memoirs. Other interesting memoirs are those of Harry Truman (1958); Dwight Eisenhower, *Crusade in Europe* (1948); and Dean Acheson, *Present at the Creation* (1969), a beautifully written defense of American foreign policy in the early cold war. W. A. Williams, *The Tragedy of American Diplomacy* (1962), and W. La Feber, *America, Russia, and the Cold War* (1967), claim, on the contrary, that the United States was primarily responsible for the conflict with the Soviet Union. Two other important studies focusing on American policy are J. Gaddis, *The United States and the Origins of the Cold War* (1972), and D. Yergin, *Shattered Peace: The Origins of the Cold War and the National Security Council* (1977). A. Fontaine, a French journalist, provides a balanced general approach in his *History of the Cold War,* 2 vols. (1968). V. Mastny's thorough investigation of Stalin's war aims, *Russia's Road to the Cold War* (1979), is highly recommended.

R. Mayne, *The Recovery of Europe, 1945–1973,* rev. ed. (1973), and N. Luxenburg, *Europe Since World War II,* rev. ed. (1979), are recommended general surveys, as are two important works: W. Laqueur, *Europe Since Hitler,* rev. ed. (1982), and P. Johnson, *Modern Times: The World from the Twenties to the Eighties* (1983). T. White, *Fire in the Ashes* (1953), is a vivid view of European resurgence and Marshall Plan aid by an outstanding journalist. Postwar economic and technological developments are carefully analyzed by D. S. Landes, *The Unbound Prometheus: Technological Change and Industrial Development in Western Europe from 1750 to the Present* (1969). A Shonfield, *Modern Capitalism* (1965), provides an engaging, optimistic assessment of the growing importance of government investment and planning in European economic life. F. R. Willis, *France, Germany, and the New Europe, 1945–1967* (1968), is useful for postwar European diplomacy. Three outstanding works on France are J. Ardagh, *The New French Revolution* (1969), which puts the momentous social changes since 1945 in human terms; G. Wright, *Rural Revolution in France: The Peasantry in the Twentieth Century* (1964); and D. L. Hanley et al., eds., *France: Politics and Society Since 1945* (1979). R. Dahrendorf, *Society and Democracy in Germany* (1971), and H. S. Hughes, *The United States and Italy* (1968), are excellent introductions to recent German and Italian history. A. Marwick, *British Society Since 1945* (1982), and A. H. Halsey, *Change in British Society,* 2nd ed. (1981), are good on postwar developments.

H. Seton-Watson, *The East European Revolution* (1965), is a good history of the communization of eastern Europe, and S. Fischer-Galati, ed., *Eastern Europe in the Sixties* (1963), discusses major developments. P. Zinner, *National Communism and Popular Revolt in Eastern Europe* (1956) and *Revolution in Hungary* (1962), are excellent on the tragic events of 1956. Z. Brzezinski, *The Soviet Bloc: Unity and Conflict* (1967), is a major inquiry. W. Connor, *Socialism, Politics and Equality: Hierarchy and Change in Eastern Europe and the USSR* (1979), and J. Hough and M. Fainsod, *How the Soviet Union is Governed* (1978), are important general studies. A. Amalrik, *Will the Soviet Union Survive Until 1984?* (1970), is a fascinating interpretation of contemporary Soviet society and politics by a Russian who paid for his criticism with prison and exile. A. Lee, *Russian Journal* (1981), and H. Smith, *The Russians* (1976), are excellent journalistic yet comprehensive reports by perceptive American observers.

R. von Albertini, *Decolonialization* (1971), is a good history of the decline and fall of European empires. The tremendous economic problems of the newly independent countries of Asia and Africa are discussed sympathetically by B. Ward, *Rich Nations and Poor Nations* (1962), and R. Heilbroner, *The Great Ascent* (1953). Two excellent general studies on Latin America are J. E. Fagg, *Latin America: A General History,* 3rd ed. (1977), and R. J. Shafer, *A History of Latin America* (1978). Both contain detailed suggestions for further reading.

31

LIFE IN THE POSTWAR ERA

HILE EUROPE staged its astonishing political and economic recovery from the Nazi nightmare, the patterns of everyday life and the structure of Western society were changing no less rapidly and remarkably. Epoch-making inventions and new technologies—the atomic bomb, television, computers, jet planes, and contraceptive pills, to name only a few—profoundly affected human existence. Important groups in society formulated new attitudes and demands, which were reflected in such diverse phenomena as the ever-expanding role of government, the revolt of youth in the late 1960s, and the women's movement. Rapid social change was clearly a fact of life in the Western world.

It was by no means easy to make sense out of all these changes while they were happening. Many "revolutions" and "crises" proved to be merely passing fads, sensationally ballyhooed by the media one day and forgotten the next. Some genuinely critical developments, such as those involving the family, were complex and contradictory, making it hard to understand what was really happening, much less explain why. Yet, by the 1980s, the great changes in social structure and everyday life that took place after the Second World War were coming into sharper focus. Above all, the historian was gaining vital perspective, for it became increasingly clear that the years from about 1968 to 1974 marked the end of the postwar period, as shall be seen in Chapter 32. Thus the startling postwar renaissance emerged in its turn as a separate era in the long evolution of the West, an era with its own distinctive social characteristics but still linked to what came before and after.

How, then, did Western society and everyday life change in the postwar era, and why? What did these changes mean to people? These are the questions this chapter will seek to answer.

SCIENCE AND TECHNOLOGY

Ever since the scientific revolution of the seventeenth century and the Industrial Revolution at the end of the eighteenth century, scientific and technical developments have powerfully influenced attitudes, society, and everyday life. Never was this influence stronger than after about 1940. Fantastic pipe dreams of science fiction a brief century ago became realities. Submarines passed under the North Pole, and astronauts walked on the moon. Skilled surgeons replaced their patients' failing arteries with plastic tubing. Millions of people around the world simultaneously watched a historic event on television. The list of wonders seemed endless.

The reason science and technology proved so productive and influential was that, for the first time in history, they were effectively joined together on a massive scale. This union of "pure theoretical" science with "applied" science or "practical" technology had already made possible striking achievements in the late nineteenth century in some select fields, most notably organic chemistry, electricity, and preventive medicine. Generally, however, the separation of science and technology still predominated in the late 1930s. Most scientists were university professors, who were little interested in such practical matters as building better machines and inventing new products. Such problems were the concern of tinkering technicians and engineers, who were to a large extent trained on the job. Their accomplishments and discoveries owed more to careful observation and trial-and-error experimentation than to theoretical science.

During World War Two, however, scientists and technicians increasingly marched to the sound of the same drummer. Both scientific research and technical expertise began to be directed at difficult but highly practical military problems. The result was a number of spectacular breakthroughs, such as radar and the atomic bomb, which had immediate wartime applications. After the war, this close cooperation between pure science and applied technology continued with equal success. Indeed, the line between science and technology became harder and harder to draw.

The consequences of the new, intimate link between science and technology were enormous. Seventeenth-century propagandists for science, such as Francis Bacon, had predicted that scientific knowledge of nature would give human beings the power to control the physical world. With such control, they believed, it would be possible to create material abundance and genuine well-being. The successful union of science and technology created new industries and spurred rapid economic growth after 1945, making this prediction finally come true for the great majority of people in Europe and North America in the postwar era.

At the same time, however, the unprecedented success of science in controlling and changing the physical environment produced unexpected and unwanted side effects. Chemical fertilizers poisoned rivers in addition to producing bumper crops. A great good like the virtual elimination of malaria-carrying mosquitoes by DDT dramatically lowered the death rate in tropical lands, but it also contributed to a population explosion in those areas. The list of such unwelcome side effects became very long. By the late 1960s, concern about the undesirable results of technological change had brought into being a vigorous environmental movement. The ability of science and technology to control and alter nature was increasingly seen as a two-edged sword, which had to be wielded with great care and responsibility.

The Stimulus of World War Two

Just before the outbreak of World War Two, a young Irish scientist and Communist named John Desmond Bernal wrote a book entitled *The Social Function of Science.* Bernal argued that the central government should be the source of funds for scientific research and that these funds should be granted on the basis of the expected social and political benefits. Most scientists were horrified by Bernal's proposals, which were contradictory to their cherished ideals. Scientists were committed to designing their own research without regard for its immediate usefulness. As late as 1937, the great physicist Ernest Rutherford could state that the work he and his colleagues were doing in nuclear physics at Cambridge University had no conceivable practical value for anyone, and he expressed delight that such was the case. Nor did university scientists concern themselves with government grants, since many had independent incomes to help finance their still-inexpensive experiments.

The Second World War changed this pattern. Pure science lost its impractical innocence. Most leading university scientists went to work on top-secret projects to help their governments fight the war. The development of radar by British scientists was a particularly important outcome of this new kind of sharply focused research.

Lord Rutherford The great British physicist Ernest Rutherford split the atom in 1919 with a small device he could hold in his hands. Here he is seen with a colleague in Cambridge University's renowned Cavendish Laboratory in 1932, when pure science was still relatively small-scale and unconcerned with practical applications. *(Cavendish Laboratory, University of Cambridge)*

As early as 1934, the British Air Ministry set up a committee of scientists and engineers to study the problem of air defense systematically. A leading British expert's calculations on radio waves suggested that the idea of a "death ray" so powerful it could destroy an attacking enemy aircraft was nonsense, but that detection of enemy aircraft by radio waves was theoretically possible. Radio waves emitted at intervals by a transmitter on the ground would bounce off flying aircraft, and a companion receiver on the ground would hear this echo and detect the approaching plane. Experiments went forward, and by 1939 the British had installed a very primitive radar system along the southern and eastern coasts of England.

Immediately after the outbreak of war with Germany in September 1939, the British military enlisted leading academic scientists in an all-out effort to improve the radar system. The basic problem was developing a high-powered transmitter capable of sending very short wavelengths, which could be precisely focused in a beam sweeping the sky like a searchlight. In summer 1940, British physicists made the dramatic technical breakthrough that solved this problem of short-wave transmission. The new and radically improved radar system, which was quickly installed, played a key role in Britain's victory in the battle for air supremacy in the fall of 1940. During the war, many different types of radar were developed—for fighter planes, for bombers, for detection of submarines.

After 1945, war-born microwave technology generated endless applications, especially in telecommunications. Microwave transmission very conveniently carried long-distance telephone conversations, television programs, and messages to and from satellites.

The air war also greatly stimulated the development of jet aircraft and computers. Although the first jet engines were built in the mid-1930s, large-scale government-directed research did not begin until immediately before the war. The challenge was to build a new kind of engine—a jet engine—capable of burning the low-grade "leftovers" of petroleum refining, thereby helping to overcome the desperate shortage of aviation fuel. The task proved extremely difficult and expensive. Only toward the end of the war did fast, high-flying jet fighters become a reality. Quickly adopted for both military and peacetime purposes after the war, jet airplanes contributed to the enormous expansion of commercial aviation in the 1950s.

The problems of air defense also spurred further research on electronic computers, which had barely come into existence before 1939. Computers calculated the complex mathematical relationships between fast-moving planes and antiaircraft shells, to increase the likelihood of a hit.

Wartime needs led to many other major technical breakthroughs. Germany had little oil and was almost completely cut off from foreign supplies. But Germany's scientists and engineers found ways to turn coal into gasoline so that the German war machine did not sputter to a halt.

The most spectacular result of directed scientific research during the war was the atomic bomb. In August 1939, Albert Einstein wrote to President Franklin Roosevelt, stating that recent work in physics suggested that

> *it may become possible to set up a nuclear chain reaction in a large mass of uranium, by which vast amounts of power and large quantities of new radium-like elements would be generated. . . . This new phenomenon would also lead to the construction of bombs, and it is conceivable—though much less certain—that extremely powerful bombs of a new type may thus be constructed.*[1]

This letter and ongoing experiments by nuclear physicists led to the top-secret Manhattan Project and the decision to build the atomic bomb.

The American government spared no expense to turn a theoretical possibility into a practical reality. A mammoth crash program went forward in several universities and special laboratories, the most important of which was the newly created laboratory at Los Alamos in the wilds of New Mexico. The Los Alamos laboratory was masterfully directed from 1942 by J. Robert Oppenheimer (1904–1967), a professor and theoretical physicist. Its sole objective was to design and build an atomic bomb. Toward that end Oppenheimer assembled a team of brilliant American and European scientists and managed to get them to cooperate effectively. After three years of intensive effort, the first atomic bomb was successfully tested in July 1945. In August 1945, two bombs were dropped on Hiroshima and Nagasaki, ending the war with Japan.

Atomic Weapons were the ultimate in state-directed scientific research. In this awesome photo the mushroom cloud of an American atomic bomb rises over the Pacific island of Bikini. *(Joint Army Navy Task Force)*

The atomic bomb showed the world both the awesome power and the heavy moral responsibilities of modern science and its high priests. As one of Oppenheimer's troubled colleagues exclaimed while he watched the first mushroom cloud rise over the American desert: "We are all sons-of-bitches now!"[2]

The Rise of Big Science

The spectacular results of directed research during World War Two inspired a new model for science—"Big Science." By combining theoretical work with sophisticated engineering in a large organization, Big Science could attack extremely difficult problems. Solution of these problems led to new and better products for consumers and to new and better weapons for the military. In any event, the assumption was that almost any conceivable technical goal might be attained. Big Science was extremely expensive. Indeed, its appetite for funds was so great that it could be financed only by governments and large corporations. Thus the ties between science and taxpaying society grew very close.

Science became so "big" largely because its equipment grew ever more complex and expensive. Because many advances depended directly on better instruments, the trend toward bigness went on unabated. This trend was particularly pronounced in atomic physics, perhaps the most prestigious and influential area of modern science. When Rutherford first "split the atom" in 1919, his equipment cost only a few dollars. In the 1930s, the price of an accelerator, or "atom smasher," reached $10,000, and the accelerators used in high-energy experiments while the atomic bomb was being built were in the $100,000 range. By 1960, however, when the western European nations pooled their resources in the European Council for Nuclear Research (CERN) to build an accelerator outside of Geneva—an accelerator with power in billions rather than millions of electron volts—the cost had jumped to $30 million. These big accelerators did an amazingly good job of prying atoms apart, and over two hundred different particles have been identified so far. Yet new answers produced new questions, and the logic of ever-more-sophisticated observations demanded ever-more-powerful and ever-more-costly accelerators in the postwar period.

Astronomers followed physicists in the ways of Big Science. Their new eye was the radio telescope, which picked up radio emissions rather than light. In the 1960s the largest of these costly radio telescopes sat atop a mountain and had a bowl a thousand feet wide to focus the radio signals from space. Aeronautical research and development also attained mammoth proportions. The cost of the Anglo-French *Concorde,* the first supersonic passenger airliner, went into the billions. Even ordinary science became big and expensive by historical standards. The least costly laboratory capable of doing useful research in either pure or applied science required around $200,000 a year in the 1960s.

Populous, victorious, and wealthy, the United States took the lead in Big Science after World War Two. Between 1945 and 1965, spending on scientific research and development in the United States grew five times as fast as the national income. By 1965 fully 3 percent of all income in the United States was spent on science. While large American corporations maintained impressive research laboratories, fully three-quarters of all funds spent on scientific research and development in the United States was coming from the government by 1965. It was generally accepted that government should finance science heavily. One wit pointed out that by the mid-1960s the "science policy" of the supposedly conservative Republican party in the United States was almost identical to that of the supposedly revolutionary Communist party of the Soviet Union.

One of the reasons for the similarity was that science was not demobilized in either country after the war. Indeed, scientists remained a critical part of every major military establishment and, after 1945 as during World War Two, a large portion of all scientific research went for "defense." Jet bombers gave way to rockets, battleships were overtaken by submarines with nuclear warheads, and spy planes were replaced with spy satellites. All such new weapons demanded breakthroughs no less remarkable than those of radar and the first atomic bomb. After 1945, roughly one-quarter of all men and women trained in science and engineering in the West—and perhaps more in the Soviet Union—were employed full-time in the production of weapons to kill other humans.

The Apollo Program Astronauts Neil Armstrong, Michael Collins, and Edwin Aldrin, Jr., took off from Florida on July 16, 1969 in the Apollo II spacecraft. Astronaut Armstrong was the first man to set foot on the moon, four days later, on July 20. His footprint in the lunar dust brought to reality another fantasy of science fiction. The astronauts splashed down in the Pacific Ocean, and recovery was made by the U.S.S. *Hornet* on July 24. *(National Aeronautics and Space Administration)*

Sophisticated science, lavish government spending, and military needs all came together in the space race of the 1960s—the most sensational example of Big Science in action after the creation of the atomic bomb. In 1957 the Russians used long-range rockets developed in their nuclear weapons program to put a satellite in orbit. In 1961 they sent the world's first cosmonaut circling the globe. Breaking with President Eisenhower's opposition to an expensive space program, President Kennedy made an all-out U.S. commitment to catch up with the Russians and land a manned spacecraft on the moon "before the decade was out." Harnessing pure science, applied technology, and up to $5 billion a year, the Apollo Program achieved its ambitious objective in 1969. Four more moon landings followed by 1972.

The rapid expansion of government-financed research in the United States attracted many of Europe's best scientists during the 1950s and 1960s. Thoughtful Europeans lamented this "brain drain." In his best seller *The American Challenge* (1967), the French journalist Jean-Jacques Servan-Schreiber

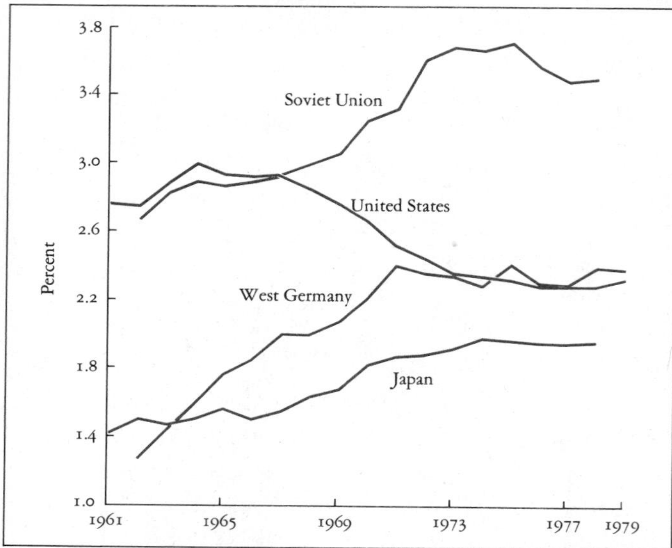

FIGURE 31.1 Research and Development Expenditures as a Percentage of GNP in the United States, Soviet Union, West Germany, and Japan, 1961–1979 While the United States spent less of its national income on research and development after the early 1960s, European nations and Japan spent more. This helped Europe and Japan narrow or even close the technological gap that had existed after the end of World War Two. *(Source: Data Resources, Inc.)*

warned that Europe was falling hopelessly behind the United States in science and technology. The only hope was to copy American patterns of research before the United States achieved an absolute stranglehold on computers, jet aircraft, atomic energy, and indeed most of the vital dynamic sectors of the late twentieth-century economy.

In fact, a revitalized Europe was already responding to the American challenge. European countries were beginning to pool their efforts and spend more on science and engineering, as they concentrated on big projects like the *Concorde* supersonic passenger airliner and the peaceful uses of atomic energy. Thus European countries created their own Big Science. By 1974 many European nations were devoting a substantial percentage of their income to research and development and were in the process of achieving equality with the United States in many fields of scientific endeavor (see Figure 31.1).

THE LIFE OF SCIENTISTS AND TECHNOLOGISTS

The rise of Big Science and of close ties between science and technology greatly altered the lives of scientists. The scientific community grew much larger than ever before: of all the scientists who have ever lived, nine out of ten are still alive today. The astonishing fact is that the number of scientists has been doubling every fifteen years for the past three centuries. There were, therefore, about four times as many scientists in 1975 as in 1945, just as there were a *million times* as many scientists as there were in 1670. Scientists, technologists, engineers, and medical specialists counted in modern society, in part because there were so many of them.

One important consequence of the bigness of science was its high degree of specialization. With close to a hundred thousand scientific journals being published by the 1970s, no one could possibly master a broad field like physics or medicine. Instead, a field like physics was constantly dividing and subdividing into new specialties and subdisciplines. The fifty or one hundred men and women who were truly abreast of the latest developments in a highly specialized field formed an international "invisible college." Cooperating and competing, communicating through special journals and conferences, the leading members of these invisible colleges kept the problems of the subdiscipline under constant attack. Thus intense specialization undoubtedly increased the rates at which both basic knowledge was acquired and practical applications were made.

Highly specialized modern scientists and technologists normally had to work as members of a team. The problems and equipment of Big Science were simply too complicated and expensive for a person to work effectively as an individual researcher. The collaborative "team" character of much of modern scientific research—members of invisible colleges were typically the leaders of such teams—completely changed the work and lifestyle of modern scientists. Old-fashioned, prewar scientists were like professional golfers—lonely individuals who had to make all the shots themselves. Modern scientists and technologists were more like players on American professional football teams. There were owners and directors, coaches and assistant coaches, overpaid stars and unsung heroes, veterans and rookies, kickoff specialists and substitutes, trainers and water boys.

James Watson and Harry Crick won the 1962 Nobel Prize in Medicine. Their pathbreaking work on DNA, the molecule of heredity, helped open exciting possibilities for gene-splicing and biological engineering. *(UPI/Bettmann Newsphotos)*

If this parallel seems fanciful, consider the research group of Luis Alvarez at the high-energy physics Radiation Laboratory of the University of California at Berkeley in the late 1960s. This group consisted of more than two hundred people. At the top were Alvarez and about twenty Ph.D.'s, followed by twenty graduate research assistants and fourteen full-time engineers. Almost fifty people were categorized as "technical leadership"—computer programmers, equipment operators, and so on. Finally, there were more than a hundred "technical assistants"—primarily scanners who analyzed photographs showing the tracks of particles after various collisions. A laboratory like that of CERN outside Geneva resembled a small city of several thousand people—scientists, technicians, and every kind of support personnel. A great deal of modern science and technology went on, therefore, in large, well-defined bureaucratic organizations. The individual was very often a small cog in a great machine, a member of a scientific army.

The advent of large-scale scientific bureaucracies led to the emergence of a new group, science managers and research administrators. Such managers generally had scientific backgrounds, but their main tasks were scheduling research, managing people, and seeking money from politicians or financial committees of large corporations. This last function was particularly important, for there were limits to what even the wealthiest governments and corporations would spend for research. Competition for funds was always intense, even in the fat 1960s.

Many science managers were government bureaucrats. These managers doled out funds and "refereed" the scientific teams that were actually playing on the field. Was the *Concorde* supersonic jet too noisy to land in New York City? Did saccharin cause cancer, and should it be banned? The list of potential questions was endless. Beginning in the late 1960s, the number of such referees and the penalties they were imposing seemed to explode, driven forward by public alarm about undesirable side effects of technological advance. More generally, the growth of the scientific bureaucracy suggested how scientists and technologists permeated the entire society and many aspects of life.

Two other changes in the lives of scientists should be noted briefly. One was the difficulty of appraising an individual's contribution to a collaborative team effort. Who deserved the real credit (or blame) for a paper coauthored by a group of twenty-five physicists? Even in a field like chemistry, which remained relatively "small" in its research techniques, more than two-thirds of all papers had two or more authors by the 1970s. Questions of proper recognition within the team effort were thus very complicated and preoccupying to modern scientists.

A second, related change was that modern science became highly, even brutally, competitive. This competitiveness is well depicted in Nobel Prize winner James Watson's fascinating book *The Double Helix,* which tells how in 1953 Watson and an Englishman, Francis Crick, discovered the structure of DNA, the molecule of heredity. A brash young American Ph.D. in his twenties, Watson seemed almost obsessed by the idea that some other research team would find the solution first and thereby deprive him of the fame and fortune he desperately wanted. With so many thousands of like-minded researchers in the wealthy countries of the world, it was hardly surprising that scientific and technical knowledge rushed forward in the postwar era.

TOWARD A NEW SOCIETY

The prodigious expansion of science and technology greatly affected the peoples of the Western world. By creating new products and vastly improved methods of manufacturing and farming, it fueled rapid economic growth and rising standards of living. Moreover, especially in Europe, scientific and technological progress, combined with economic prosperity, went a long way toward creating a whole new society after World War Two.

This new society was given many catchy titles. Some called it the "technocratic society," a society of highly trained specialists and experts. For others, fascinated by the great increase in personal wealth, it was the "affluent society" or the "consumer society." For those struck by the profusion of government-provided social services, it was simply the "welfare state." For still others, it was the "permissive society," where established codes of conduct no longer prevailed. In fact, Western society in the postwar era was all of these: technocratic, affluent, welfare-oriented, and permissive. These characteristics reflected changes in the class structure and indicated undeniable social progress.

THE CHANGING CLASS STRUCTURE

After 1945 European society became more mobile and more democratic. Old class barriers relaxed, and class distinctions became fuzzier.

Changes in the structure of the middle class, directly related to the expansion of science and technology, were particularly influential in the general drift toward a less rigid class structure. The model for the middle class in the nineteenth and early twentieth centuries was the independent, self-employed individual who owned a business or practiced a liberal profession like law or medicine. Many businesses and professional partnerships were tightly held family firms. Marriage into such a family often provided the best opportunity for an outsider to rise to the top. Ownership of property—usually inherited property—and strong family ties were often the keys to wealth and standing within the middle class.

This traditional pattern, which first changed in the United States and the Soviet Union (for very different reasons) before the Second World War, declined drastically in western Europe after 1945. A new breed of managers and experts rose to replace traditional property owners as the leaders of the middle class. Within large bureaucratic corporations and government, men and women increasingly advanced as individuals and on the basis of merit (and luck). Ability to serve the needs of a large organization, which usually depended on special expertise, largely replaced inherited property and family connections in determining an individual's social position in the middle and upper-middle class. Social mobility, both upward and downward, increased. At the same time, the middle class grew massively and became harder to define.

There were a number of reasons for these developments. Rapid industrial and technological expansion created in large corporations and government agen-

A Modern Manager Despite considerable discrimination, women were increasingly found in the expanding middle class of salaried experts after World War Two, working in business, science, and technology. *(Niépce-Rapho)*

cies a powerful demand for technologists and managers capable of responding effectively to an ever-more-complicated world. This growing army of specialists—the backbone of the new middle class—could be led effectively only by like-minded individuals, of whom only a few at best could come from the old owning families.

Second, the old propertied middle class lost control of many of its formerly family-owned businesses. Even very wealthy families had to call on the general investing public for capital, and heavy inheritance taxes forced sales of stock, further diluting family influence. Many small businesses (including family farms) simply passed out of existence, and their ex-owners joined the ranks of salaried employees. In Germany in 1950, for example, 33 percent of the labor force was self-employed and 20 percent was white-collar workers. By 1962 the percentages for these two groups were exactly reversed. Moreover, the wave of nationalization in western and eastern Europe after the Second World War automatically replaced capitalist owners with salaried managers and civil servants in state-owned companies.

Top managers and ranking civil servants therefore represented the model for a new middle class of salaried specialists. Well paid and highly trained, often with backgrounds in science or engineering or accounting, these experts increasingly came from all social classes, even the working class. Pragmatic and realistic, they were primarily concerned with efficiency and practical solutions to concrete problems. Generally, they were not very interested in the old ideological debates about capitalism and socialism, confidently assuming that their skills were indispensable in either system or any combination of the two.

Indeed, the new middle class of experts and managers was an international class, not much different in socialist eastern Europe than in capitalist western Europe and North America. Everywhere successful managers and technocrats passed on the opportunity for all-important advanced education to their children, but only in rare instances could they pass on the positions they had attained. Thus the new middle class, which was based largely on specialized skills and high levels of education, was more open, democratic, and insecure than the old propertied middle class.

The structure of the traditional lower classes also became more flexible and open. There was a mass exodus from farms and the countryside. One of the most traditional and least mobile groups in European society drastically declined: after 1945 the number of peasants declined by more than 50 percent in almost every European country. Meanwhile, because of rapid technological change, the industrial working class ceased to expand, stabilizing at slightly less than one-half of the labor force in wealthy advanced countries. Job opportunities for white-collar and service employees, however, expanded rapidly. Such employees bore a greater resemblance to the new middle class of salaried specialists than to industrial workers, who were themselves better educated and more specialized. Developments within the lower classes contributed, therefore, to the breakdown of rigid social divisions.

Social Security Reforms and Rising Affluence

While the demands of modern technology and big bureaucracies broke down rigid class divisions, European governments, with their new and revitalized political leadership (pages 968–970), reduced class tensions with a series of social security reforms. Many of these reforms simply strengthened social security measures first pioneered in Bismarck's Germany before World War One. Unemployment and sickness benefits were increased and extended, as were retirement benefits and old-age pensions. Other programs were new.

Britain's Labour government took the lead immediately after the Second World War in establishing a comprehensive national health system; other European governments followed the British example. Depending on the system, patients either received completely free medical care or paid only a very small portion of the total cost.

Most countries also introduced family allowances —direct government grants to parents to help them raise their children. Lower-paid workers generally received the largest allowances, and the rate per child often kept increasing until the third or fourth child. These allowances helped many poor families make ends meet. Most European governments also gave maternity grants and built inexpensive public housing for low-income families and individuals. Other social welfare programs ranged from cash bonuses for getting married in Belgium and Switzerland to subsidized vacations for housewives in Sweden.

It would be wrong to think that the expansion of social security services after World War Two provided for every human need "from cradle to grave," as early advocates of the welfare state hoped and its critics feared. But these social reforms did provide a humane floor of well-being, below which very few individuals could fall in the advanced countries of northern and western Europe. (Social benefits were greatest in the wealthiest nations, such as Sweden, West Germany, Britain, and less in poorer areas of southern and eastern Europe.)

These reforms also promoted greater social and economic equality. They were expensive, paid for in part by high taxes on the rich. In Britain, for example, where social security benefits for the population at large and taxes on the rich have both become quite high, the top 5 percent of the population received about 14 percent of national income after taxes in 1957, as opposed to fully 43 percent in 1913. Thus extensive welfare measures leveled society both by raising the floor and by lowering the ceiling.

The rising standard of living and the spread of standardized, mass-produced consumer goods also worked to level Western society. A hundred years ago, food and drink cost roughly two-thirds of the average family's income in western and northern Europe; by the mid-1960s, they took only about one-third to two-fifths of that family's income. Consumption of traditional staples like bread and potatoes actually declined almost everywhere in Europe after 1945; yet because incomes have risen rapidly, people eat more meat, fish, and dairy products. The long-elusive goal of adequate and good food was attained almost universally in advanced countries.

But progress introduced new problems. People in Europe and North America were eating too much rather than too little, giving rise to an endless proliferation of diet foods and diet fads. Another problem was that modern consumers often appeared remarkably ignorant of basic nutrition. They stuffed themselves with candy, soft drinks, French fries, and spongy white bread, and frequently got poor value for their money. Finally, the traditional pleasures of eating good food well prepared suffered catastrophic declines in the postwar age of fast-food franchises and mass-produced, hopelessly standardized burgers and buns.

The phenomenal expansion of the automobile industry exemplified even more strikingly the emergence of the consumer society. In the United States, automobile ownership was commonplace far down the social scale by the mid-1920s, whereas only the rich could generally afford cars in Europe before the Second World War. In 1948 there were only 5 million cars in western Europe, and most ordinary people dreamed at most of stepping up from a bicycle to a motorcycle. With the development of cheaper, mass-produced cars, this situation changed rapidly. By 1957 the number of cars had increased to 15 million, and automobiles had become a standard item of middle-class consumption. By 1965 the number of cars in western Europe had tripled again to 44 million, and car ownership had come well within the range of better-paid workers.

Europeans took great pleasure in the products of the "gadget revolution" as well. Like Americans, Europeans filled their houses and apartments with washing machines, vacuum cleaners, refrigerators, dishwashers, radios, TVs, and stereos. The purchase of these and other consumer goods was greatly facilitated by installment purchasing, which allowed people to buy on credit. Before World War Two, Europeans had rarely bought "on time." But with the expansion of social security safeguards, reducing the need to accumulate savings for hard times, ordinary people were increasingly willing to take on debt. This change had far-reaching consequences.

Household appliances became necessities for most families. Middle-class women had to do much of their own housework, for young girls avoided domestic service like the plague. Moreover, more women than ever before worked outside the home, and they needed machines to help do household chores as quickly as possible. The power tools of "do-it-yourself" work also became something of a necessity, for few dependable artisans were available for household repairs.

Leisure and recreation occupied an important place in consumer societies. Indeed, with incomes rising and the workweek shrinking from roughly forty-eight hours right after the war to about forty-one hours by the early 1970s, leisure became big business. In addition to ever-popular soccer matches and horse races, movies, and a growing addiction to television, individuals had at their disposal a vast range of commercialized hobbies, most of which could soak up a lot of cash. Newsstands were full of specialized magazines about everything from hunting and photography to knitting and antique collecting. Interest in "culture," as measured by attendance at concerts and exhibitions, also increased. Even so, the commercialization of leisure through standardized manufactured products was striking.

The most astonishing leisure-time development in the consumer society was the blossoming of mass travel and tourism. Before the Second World War, travel for pleasure and relaxation remained a rather aristocratic pastime. Most people had neither the time nor the money for it. But with month-long paid vacations required by law in most European countries, and widespread automobile ownership, beaches and ski resorts came within the reach of the middle class and many workers. At certain times of year, hordes of Europeans surged to the sea or the mountains, and woe to the traveler who had not made arrangements well in advance. By the late 1960s packaged tours with cheap group flights and bargain hotel accommodations had made even distant lands easily accessible. One-fifth of West Germany's population traveled abroad each year. A French company, the Club Méditerranée, grew rich building imitation Tahitian paradises around the world. At Swedish nudist colonies on secluded west African beaches, secreta-

Sports Fans developed fierce tribal loyalties, finding comradeship and a sense of belonging cheering for their teams. Here Liverpool's famous rooting section goes wild with delight after its team clinches the English soccer championship in 1977. Soccer matches have occasionally degenerated into pitched battles between rival fans. *(Wide World Photos)*

ries and salesmen from Stockholm fleetingly worshiped the sun in the middle of the long northern winter. Truly, consumerism had come of age.

Renewed Discontent and the Student Revolt

For twenty years after 1945, Europeans were largely preoccupied with the possibilities of economic progress and consumerism. The more democratic class structure also helped to reduce social tension, and ideological conflict went out of style. In the late 1960s, however, sharp criticism and discontent reemerged. It was a common complaint that Europeans were richer but neither happier nor better. Social conflicts re-emerged.

Simmering discontent in eastern Europe was not hard to understand. The gradual improvement in the standard of living stood in stark contrast to the ongoing lack of freedom in political and intellectual life and made that lack of freedom all the more distasteful. As will be shown in the next chapter, such dissatisfaction found eloquent expression once again, despite the refinement of techniques of repression in eastern Europe and the willingness of the Soviet Union to crush reform efforts in Czechoslovakia with military might in 1968.

The reappearance of discontent in western Europe was not so easily explained. From the mid-1950s on, western European society was prosperous, democratic, and permissive. Yet this did not prevent growing hostility to the existing order among some children of the new society. Radical students in particular rejected the materialism of their parents and claimed that the new society was repressive and badly flawed. Though these criticisms and the movements they sparked were often ridiculed by the older generation, they reflected some real problems of youth, education, and a society of specialists. They deserve closer attention.

In contrast to the United States, high school and university educations in Europe were limited for centuries to a small elite. That elite consisted mainly of young men and women from the well-to-do classes, along with a sprinkling of scholarship students from humble origins. Whereas 22 percent of the American population was going on to some form of higher education in 1950, only 3 to 4 percent of west European youths were doing so. Moreover, European education was still directed toward traditional fields: literature, law, medicine, and pure science. Its basic goal was to pass on culture and pure science to an elite, and with the exception of law and medicine, applied training for specialists was not considered very important.

After World War Two, public education in western Europe began to change dramatically. Enrollments exploded. By 1960 there were at least three times as many students going to some kind of university as there had been before the war, and the number continued to rise sharply until the 1970s. Holland had ten thousand university students in 1938 and a hundred thousand in 1960. In France 14 percent of young people went to a university in 1965, as opposed to 4.5 percent in 1950. With an increase in scholarships and a growing awareness that higher education was the key to success, European universities became more democratic, opening their doors to more students from the lower-middle and lower classes. Finally, in response to the prodigious expansion of science and technology, the curriculum gradually changed. All sorts of new, "practical" fields —from computer science to business administration —appeared alongside the earlier liberal arts and sciences.

The rapid expansion of higher education created problems as well as opportunities for students. Classes were badly overcrowded, and there was little contact with professors. Competition for grades became intense. Moreover, although more "practical" areas of study were added, they were added less quickly than many students wanted. Thus many students felt that they were not getting the kind of education they needed for the modern world and that basic university reforms were absolutely necessary. The emergence of a distinctive "youth culture" also brought students into conflict with those symbols of the older generation and parental authority—professors and school officials.

These tensions within the exploding university population came to a head in the late 1960s and early 1970s. Following in the footsteps of their American counterparts, who pioneered with large-scale student protests in the mid-1960s, European university students rose to challenge their university administrations and even their governments. The most far-reaching of these revolts occurred in France in 1968.

Student Protest in Paris These rock-throwing students in the Latin Quarter of Paris are trying to force educational reforms, or even to topple De Gaulle's government. Throughout May 1968 students clashed repeatedly with France's tough riot police in bloody street fighting. *(Bruno Barbey/Magnum Photos, Inc.)*

It began at the stark new University of Nanterre in the gloomy industrial suburbs of Paris. Students demanded both changes in the curriculum and a real voice in running the university. The movement spread to the hallowed halls of the medieval Sorbonne in the heart of Paris. Students occupied buildings and took over the university. This takeover led to violent clashes with police, who were ordered in to break up a demonstration that was fast becoming an uprising.

The student radicals appealed to France's industrial workers for help. Rank-and-file workers ignored the advice of their cautious union officials, and a more or less spontaneous general strike spread across France in May 1968. It seemed certain that President De Gaulle's Fifth Republic would collapse. In fact, De Gaulle stiffened, declaring he was in favor of reforms but would oppose "bedwetting." Securing the firm support of French army commanders in West Germany, he moved troops toward Paris and called for new elections. Thoroughly frightened by the protest-turned-upheaval and fearful that a successful revolution could lead only to an eventual Communist takeover, the masses of France voted for a return to law and order. De Gaulle and his party scored the biggest electoral victory in modern French history, and the mini-revolution collapsed.

Yet the proud De Gaulle and the confident, if old-fashioned, national political revival he represented had been cruelly mocked. In 1969 a tired and discouraged President De Gaulle resigned over a minor issue, and within a year he was dead. For much of the older generation in France, and indeed throughout western Europe, the student revolution of 1968 signaled the end of illusions and the end of an era. Social stability and material progress had resulted in conflict and uncertainty. Under such conditions, all schemes for western European equality with the external superpowers—the United States and the Soviet Union—would have an air of unreality.

The student protest of the 1960s, which peaked in 1968 but echoed well into the 1970s, was due to more than overcrowded classrooms and outdated courses. It reflected a rebirth of romantic revolutionary idealism, which repudiated the quest for ever more consumer goods as stupid and destructive. Student radicalism was also related to the Vietnam War, which led many students in Europe and America to convince themselves that Western civilization was immoral and imperialistic. Finally, the students of the late 1960s were a completely new generation: they had never known anything but prosperity and tranquillity, and they had grown bored with both.

The student revolt was also motivated by new perceptions about the new society of highly trained experts. Some reflective young people feared that universities would soon do nothing but turn out docile technocrats both to stock and to serve "the establishment." Others saw the class of highly trained specialists they expected to enter as the new exploited class in society. The remedy to this situation, both groups believed, was "participation"—the democratization of decision making *within* large, specialized bureaucratic organizations. Only in this way would such organizations serve real human needs and not merely exploit the individual and the environment. Thus the often unrealistic and undisciplined student radicals tried to answer a vital question: how was the complex new society of specialized experts to be made humane and responsive?

WOMEN AND THE FAMILY

The growing emancipation of women in Europe and North America was unquestionably one of the most important developments after the Second World War. This development gathered speed in the 1960s and reached a climax in the mid-1970s. Women demanded and won new rights. Having shared fully in the postwar education revolution, women were better educated than ever before. They took advantage of the need for trained experts in a more fluid society and moved into areas of employment formerly closed to them. Married women in particular became much more likely to work outside the home than they were a few short years earlier. Women no longer had to fatalistically accept childbearing and childrearing, for if they wished they could use modern techniques of contraception to control the number and spacing of their offspring. In short, women became more equal and independent, less confined and stereotyped. A major transformation was in process.

The changing position of women altered the modern family. Since the emancipation of women is still incomplete, it is impossible to say for certain whether some major revolution has occurred within the family. Nevertheless, as women today consolidate and expand the breakthroughs of the 1960s and early 1970s, it seems clear that the family has experienced some fundamental reorientations at the very least. This becomes apparent if we examine women's traditional role in the home and then women's new roles outside the home in the postwar era.

Marriage and Motherhood

Before the Industrial Revolution, most men and women married late, and substantial numbers never married at all. Once a woman was married, though, she normally bore several children, of whom a third to a half would not survive to adulthood. Moreover, many women died in childbirth. With the growth of industry and urban society, people began to marry earlier, and fewer remained unmarried. As industrial development led to higher incomes and better diets, more children survived to adulthood, and population grew rapidly in the nineteenth century. By the late nineteenth century, contraception within marriage was spreading.

In the twentieth century, and especially after World War Two, these trends continued. In the postwar era, women continued to marry earlier. In Sweden, for example, the average age of first marriage dropped steadily from twenty-six in the early 1940s to twenty-three in the late 1960s. Moreover, more than nine out of ten women were marrying at least once, usually in their early twenties. Marriage was never more in vogue than in the generation after the Second World War. The triumph of romantic attraction over financial calculation seemed complete, and perhaps never before had young couples expected so much emotional satisfaction from matrimony.

After marrying early, the typical woman in Europe, the United States, and Canada had her children quickly. Whereas women in the more distant past very often had children as long as they were fertile, women in Europe and North America were having about 80 percent of their children before they were thirty. As for family size, the "baby boom" that lasted several years after 1945 made for fairly rapid population growth of 1 to 1.5 percent per year in many European countries. In the 1960s, however, the long-term decline in birthrates resumed. Surveys in northern and western Europe began to reveal that most women believed that two instead of three children were ideal.

Women must have 2.1 children on the average if total population is to remain constant over the long term. Indeed, the number of births fell so sharply in the 1960s that total population practically stopped growing in many European countries. By the mid-1970s, more people were dying each year than were being born in Austria, East Germany, West Germany, and Luxembourg, where total numbers actually declined. The United States followed the same trend; the birthrate declined from 25 per thousand in 1957 to 15 per thousand in 1973, and it recovered slightly thereafter only because the baby boomers were reaching childbearing age, not because individual women were having more children. Since the American death rate has remained practically unchanged, the rate of population growth from natural increase (that is, excluding immigration) dropped by two-thirds, from 1.5 percent to .6 percent per year between the 1950s and the 1970s. The population of Africa, Asia, and Latin America was still growing very rapidly from natural increase, but that was certainly not true for most European countries and countries of predominantly European ancestry.

The culmination of the trends toward early almost-universal marriage and small family size in wealthy societies had revolutionary implications for women. An examination of these implications suggests why the emancipation of women—sooner or later—was almost assuredly built into the structure of modern life.

The main point is that motherhood occupied a much smaller portion of a woman's life than at the beginning of this century. The average woman's life expectancy at birth increased from about fifty years in 1900 to about seventy-five years in 1970. At the same time, women were increasingly compressing childbearing into the decade between their twentieth and thirtieth birthdays, instead of bearing children until they were in their late thirties. By the early 1970s about half of Western women, and more than half in some nations, were having their last baby by the age of twenty-six or twenty-seven. When the youngest child trooped off to kindergarten, the average mother still had more than forty years of life in front of her.

This was a momentous change. Throughout history, most married women had been defined to a considerable extent as mothers. Motherhood was very demanding: pregnancy followed pregnancy, and there were many children to nurse, guide, and bury. Now, however, the years devoted to having babies and caring for young children represented at most a seventh of the average woman's life. Motherhood had become a relatively short phase in most women's total life span. Perhaps a good deal of the frustration that many women felt in the 1960s and 1970s was due to the fact that their traditional role as mothers no longer absorbed the energies of a lifetime, and new roles in the male-dominated world outside the family were opening up slowly.

A related revolutionary change for women was that the age-old biological link between sexual intercourse and motherhood was severed. As is well known, beginning in the early 1960s many women chose to gain effective control over pregnancy with oral contraceptives and intrauterine devices. They no longer relied on undependable males and their undependable methods. Less well known are certain physiological facts, which help explain why many women in the advanced countries did elect to practice birth control at some point in their lives.

Women in the postwar era were capable of having children for many more years than their forebears. The age of *menarche*—the age at which girls begin to menstruate and become fertile—had dropped from about seventeen years in the early nineteenth century to about thirteen years by the 1970s. At the same time, the age at onset of menopause rose. At the beginning of the eighteenth century, menopause occurred at about age thirty-six, on average; it now occurred at about fifty. These physiological changes over time are poorly understood, but they were apparently due to better diets and living standards, which also substantially increased people's height and size. In any event, many modern women chose to separate their sexual lives from their awesome reproductive power, which had increased with the lengthening of the time in which they were capable of

A Modern Family This scene sums up some important changes taking place within the family in the postwar era. The young father feeds and talks with the baby, while the student-mother concentrates on the education essential for successful employment. *(Niépce-Rapho)*

bearing children. In doing so, these women became free to pursue sensual pleasure for its own sake. The consequences of this revolutionary development will continue to work themselves out for a long time.

Women at Work

For centuries before the Industrial Revolution, ordinary women were highly productive members of society. They often labored for years before marriage to accumulate the necessary dowry. Once married, women worked hard on farms and in home industries while bearing and caring for their large families. With the growth of modern industry and large cities, young women continued to work as wage earners. But once a poor woman married, she typically stopped working in a factory or a shop, struggling instead to earn money at home by practicing some low-paid craft as she looked after her children. In the middle classes, it was a rare and tough-minded woman who worked outside the home for wages, although charity work was socially acceptable.

Since the beginning of the twentieth century and especially after World War Two, the situation has changed dramatically once again. Opportunities for women of modest means to earn cash income within the home practically disappeared. Piano teachers, novelists, and part-time typists still worked at home as independent contractors, but the ever-greater complexity of the modern wage-based economy and its sophisticated technology meant that almost all would-be wage earners had to turn elsewhere. Moreover, motherhood took less and less time, so that the full-time mother-housewife had less and less eco-

Day-Care Centers have gradually developed to meet the needs of working women. This center at a Chicago high school is open to children of teachers and of teen-aged mothers who are continuing their schooling. *(Wide World Photos)*

nomic value for families. Thus the reduction of home-centered work and child care resulted in a sharp rise across Europe and North America in the number of married women who were full-time wage earners.

In communist countries, the trend went the furthest. In the Soviet Union, most married women worked outside the home; there women accounted for almost half of all employed persons in the postwar era. In noncommunist western Europe and North America there was a good deal of variety, depending on whether married women had traditionally worked outside the home, as in France or Sweden, or stayed at home, as in Belgium and Switzerland. Nevertheless, the percentage of married women who worked rose sharply in all countries, from a range of roughly 20 to 25 percent in 1950 to a range of 35 to 60 percent in the 1970s. This rise was particularly dramatic in the United States, where married women were twice as likely to be employed in 1979 as they were in 1952.

The dramatic growth of employment among married women was a development whose ultimate effects are still unknown. Nevertheless, it seems clear that the rising employment of married women was a powerful force in the drive for women's equality and emancipation. Take the critical matter of widespread discrimination between men and women in pay, occupation, and advancement. The young unmarried woman of eighty years ago generally accepted such injustices. She thought of them as temporary nuisances and looked forward to marriage and motherhood for fulfillment. In the postwar era, a married wage earner in her thirties developed a totally different perspective. Employment became a permanent condition within which she, like her male counterpart, sought not only income but psychological satisfaction as well. Sexism and discrimination quickly became increasingly loathsome and evoked that sense of injustice that drives revolutions and reforms. The "movement" spread, winning converts among the young and newly awakened.

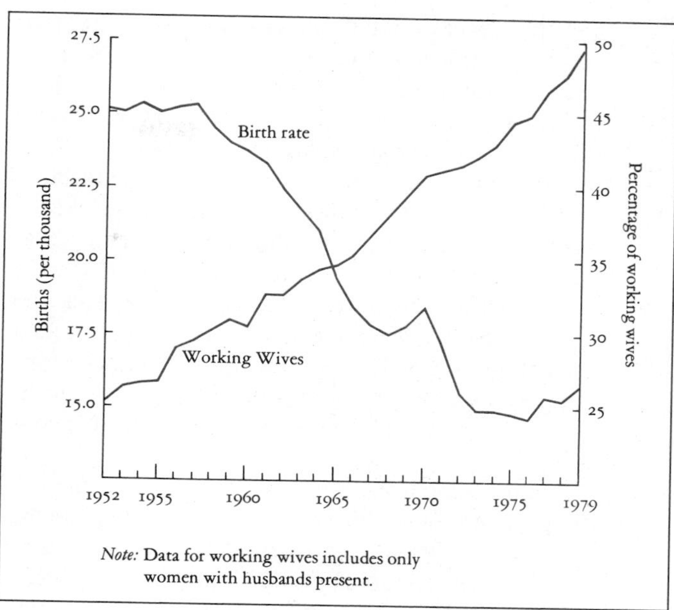

FIGURE 31.2 The Decline of the Birthrate and the Increase of Working Wives in the United States, 1952–1979 The challenge of working away from home encouraged American wives to prefer fewer children and helped to lower the birthrate.

Rising employment for married women was a factor in the decline of the birthrate (see Figure 31.2). Women who worked had significantly fewer children than women of the same age who did not. Moreover, survey research showed that young women who had worked and intended to work again revised downward the number of children they expected to have after the first lovable but time-consuming baby was born. One reason was obvious: raising a family while holding down a full-time job was a tremendous challenge and often resulted in the woman being grossly overworked. The fatiguing, often frustrating multiple demands of job, motherhood, and marriage simply became more manageable with fewer children.

Another reason for the decline of the birthrate was that motherhood interrupted a woman's career. The majority of women in Western countries preferred or were forced to accept—interpretations varied—staying at home for a minimum of two or three years while their children were small. The longer the break in employment, the more a woman's career suffered. Women consistently earned less than men partly because they were employed less continuously and thus did not keep moving steadily up the bureaucratic ladders of large organizations.

Because most Western countries did little to help women in the problem of re-employment after their children were a little older, some women came to advocate the pattern of career and family typically found in communist eastern Europe. There, women were usually employed continuously until they retired. There were no career-complicating interruptions for extended mothering. Instead, a woman in a communist country received as her right up to three months of maternity leave to care for her newborn infant and recover her strength. Then she returned to her job, leaving her baby in the care of a state-run nursery or, more frequently, a retired relative or neighbor. By the 1970s some western European countries were beginning to provide well-defined maternity leaves as part of their social security systems. The United States lagged far behind in this area.

What the increasing numbers of career-minded women with independent, self-assertive spirits meant for marriage and relations between the sexes was by no means clear. As we have seen, marriage remained an almost universal experience. Moreover, the decline of informal village and neighborhood socializing with the advent of the automobile and suburban living made most wives and husbands more dependent than ever on their mates (and their children) for their emotional needs. Never was more being demanded from hearth and home.

The great increase in life expectancy for males and females by itself made marriage more stable, at least in one sense. The average couple was living together for forty years before the death of one dissolved the union, as opposed to less than twenty years together at the beginning of the century. And husbands were slowly getting the message that the old rule of leaving the dishes and diapers exclusively to wives needed rewriting, especially in two-income families. In short, the nuclear family showed great strength, adapting itself once again to changing values and changing conditions.

At the same time, contrary trends clearly emerged in the late 1960s, which carried over strongly into the 1970s and 1980s. Everywhere the divorce rate kept moving up: it doubled in the United States between 1970 and 1980. Nearly everywhere in Western countries, except in southern Europe, over one-quarter of marriages ended in divorce by the early 1980s: in Sweden, it was one in two. Studies of marriage consistently showed that working women were considerably more likely to get divorced than nonworking women. The independent working woman could more easily afford to leave if dissatisfied, while the no-income career housewife was more nearly locked into her situation.

Beginning in the very late 1960s, the marriage rate also began to plunge in a number of Western countries, and it continued to decline throughout the 1970s before stabilizing in the 1980s. Both women and men married progressively later, and those who never married grew as a portion of the population. As the number of singles grew, there was also a considerable increase in the number of unmarried couples living together, reminiscent of patterns among the European working classes in the early days of industrialization. Some observers argued that young women and men were only postponing marriage because of less robust economic conditions. Others contended that marriage, after its long rise, was finally in retreat in the face of growing careerism and acceptance of new, less structured relations between (and within) the sexes. More fundamentally, falling birthrates, more married women in the workplace, later marriage, and increased divorce (and remarriage) rates were all related to the growing emancipation of women. They were all part of a complicated constellation of striking changes, which strongly suggested that a major break with the past had already taken place in marriage patterns and family relationships.

This chapter has examined the major postwar social changes that accompanied the political recovery and economic expansion discussed in Chapter 30. These social changes were profound. Science combined with technology, often under government direction, to fulfill the loftiest hopes of its enthusiasts and achieve amazing success. The triumphs of applied science contributed not only to economic expansion but also to a more fluid, less antagonistic class structure, in which specialized education was the high road to advancement, regardless of political system. Within the prosperous, increasingly technocratic society, women asserted themselves. Beginning in the 1960s, they moved increasingly into the labor market and gave birth to fewer children. In doing so, women began striking off in a new direction, which has continued to this day. Their greater commitment to employment and decision to raise fewer children—a social pattern in sharp contrast to that of the late 1940s and 1950s—foretold the more general break in Western history that occurred shortly thereafter, as will be shown in Chapter 32.

NOTES

1. Quoted by J. Ziman, *The Force of Knowledge: The Scientific Dimension of Society,* Cambridge University Press, Cambridge, Eng., 1976, p. 128.
2. Quoted by S. Toulmin, *The Twentieth Century: A Promethean Age,* ed. A. Bullock, Thames & Hudson, London, 1971, p. 294.

SUGGESTED READING

J. Ziman, *The Force of Knowledge: The Scientific Dimension of Society* (1976), which has an excellent bibliography, is a penetrating look at science by a leading physicist. C. P. Snow, *The Two Cultures and the Scientific Revolution,* rev. ed. (1963), explores the gap between scientists and nonscientists in a widely discussed book. A Toffler, *Future Shock* (1970), is an interesting but exaggerated best-seller, which claims that many contemporary psychological problems are due to overly rapid technical and scientific development. J. Ellul, *The Technological Society* (1964), is also highly critical of technical progress, while D. S. Landes, *The Unbound Prometheus: Technological Change and Industrial Development in Western Europe from 1750 to the Present* (1969), remains enthusiastic. Two more stimulating works on technology are J. J. Servan-Schreiber, *The World Challenge* (1981), and H. Jacoby, *The Bureaucratization of the World* (1973).

In addition to studies cited in the Suggested Reading for Chapter 30, A. Simpson, *The New Europeans* (1968), is a good guide to contemporary Western society. Two engaging books on recent intellectual developments are J. Barzun, *The House of Intellect* (1959), and R. Stromberg, *After Everything: Western Intellectual History Since 1945* (1970). L. Wylie, *Village in the Vaucluse,* rev. ed. (1964), and P. J. Hélias, *The Horse of Pride* (1980), provide fascinating pictures of life in the French village. A. Kriegel, *The French Communists* (1972) and *Eurocommunism* (1978), are also recommended. A. Touraine, *The May Movement* (1971), is sympathetic toward the French student revolt, while the noted sociologist R. Aron, *The Elusive Revolution* (1969), is highly critical. F. Zweig, *The Worker in an Affluent Society* (1961), probes family life and economic circumstances in the British working class on the basis of extensive interviews. R. E. Tyrrell, ed., *The Future That Doesn't Work* (1977), is a polemical but absorbing attack on British socialism. W. Hollstein, *Europe in the Making* (1973), is a fervent plea to integrate Europe by a former top official of the Common Market. The magazines *Encounter, Commentary,* and *The Economist* often carry interesting articles on major social and political trends, as do *Time* and *Newsweek.*

E. Sullerot, *Women, Society and Change* (1971), is an outstanding introduction to women's evolving role. R. Patia, ed., *Women in the Modern World* (1967), compares women's situations in many countries. Two other influential books on women and their new awareness are S. de Beauvoir, *The Second Sex* (1962), and B. Friedan, *The Feminine Mystique* (1963). These may be compared with C. Lasch, *Haven in a Heartless World* (1977), and A. Cherlin, *Marriage, Divorce, Remarriage* (1981), which interpret changes in the American family.

32

THE RECENT PAST, 1968 TO THE PRESENT

SOMETIME DURING the late 1960s or early 1970s, the postwar era came to an end. With fits and starts, a new age opened, as postwar certitudes like domestic political stability, social harmony, and continuous economic improvement evaporated. In any event, that is how this historian reads the most recent past. Others may form different judgments, for we are simply too close to the postwar era to gain vital perspective on the period that has succeeded it. As Voltaire once said, "The man who ventures to write contemporary history must expect to be attacked for everything he has said and everything he has not said."[1]

Yet the historian must take a stand. We have already examined some indications of the end of the postwar era. Fundamental changes within the family, featuring new roles for women, gathered momentum in the late 1960s. The minirevolution of 1968 was a fundamental turning point in recent French history, symptomatic of a general rebirth of political instability and even crisis in several leading nations. Major changes in East-West relations also marked a real, if more ambiguous, turning point. Most important of all, the astonishing postwar economic advance, unparalleled in its rapidity and consistency, came to an abrupt halt. Old, almost forgotten, problems like high unemployment, expensive energy, and international monetary instability suddenly re-emerged. Throughout the Western world, the general mood changed; stylish opinion leaders traded in facile optimism for equally superficial pessimism. There was clearly no going back to the buoyant self-confidence of the postwar era.

In an attempt to make sense out of a turbulent recent past, which merges with an uncertain present, this chapter will focus on three questions of fundamental importance. First, why, after a generation, did the world economy shift into reverse gear, and what were some of the social consequences of that shift? Second, what were the most striking political developments within the nations of the Atlantic alliance? Specifically, how did West Germany take the initiative in trying to negotiate an enduring reconciliation with its Communist neighbors, and why did the United States enter into a time of troubles before seeking to reassert its strength and leadership in the 1980s? Third, how did these changes interact with the evolution of the Soviet bloc? Finally, the chapter will close with some reflections on the future.

THE TROUBLED ECONOMY

The energy crisis looms large in the sudden transition from almost automatic postwar growth to serious economic difficulties in the 1970s and 1980s. The first surge in oil prices in 1973 stunned the international economy, and the second surge in 1979 led to the deepest recession since the 1930s. The collapse of the postwar monetary system in 1971 and the rapid accumulation of international debts also caused heavy long-term damage. The social consequences of harder times were profound and many-sided.

Money and Oil

During the Second World War, British and American statesmen were convinced that international financial disorder after 1918 had contributed mightily to economic problems, the Great Depression, and renewed global warfare. They were determined not to repeat their mistakes, and in the Bretton Woods Agreement of 1944, they laid the foundations for a new international monetary system, which proved instrumental in the unprecedented postwar boom.

The new system, operating through the World Bank and the International Monetary Fund, was based on the American dollar, which was supposed to be "as good as gold" because foreign governments could always exchange dollars for gold at $35 an ounce. The United States proceeded to make needed dollars readily available to the rest of the world, first by giving Marshall Plan aid to Europe and then by constantly spending more abroad than it earned in the 1950s and 1960s. However, by early 1971, the United States had overspent to the point where it had only $11 billion in gold left in Fort Knox and Europe had accumulated 50 billion American dollars. The result was a classic, long-overdue "run on the bank" in 1971, as foreigners panicked and raced to exchange their dollars for gold. President Richard Nixon was forced to stop the sale of American gold. The price of gold then soared on world markets, and the value of the dollar declined. Moreover, fixed rates of exchange were abandoned, and all major currencies began to fluctuate rapidly against each other. The American dollar, for example, lost 40 percent of its value against the German mark between February

An OPEC Meeting Begins As this picture suggests, the Organization of Petroleum Exporting Countries (OPEC) took on many aspects of an international political alliance, through which ministers of member states met periodically to fix the price of world trade's most vital commodity. The OPEC alliance rode high in the 1970s as the industrialized nations failed to make a concerted response. *(Wide World Photos)*

and March 1973. Great uncertainty replaced postwar predictability in international finance, which also complicated trade and foreign investment.

Even more serious was the dramatic reversal in the price and availability of energy. As described in Chapter 22, coal-fired steam engines broke the bottleneck of chronically inadequate energy in the late eighteenth-century economy, making possible the Industrial Revolution and improved living standards in the nineteenth century. In the twentieth century, petroleum proved its worth, and the great postwar boom was fueled by cheap oil, especially in western Europe. Cheap oil from the Middle East permitted energy-intensive industries—automobiles, chemicals, and electric power—to expand rapidly and lead other sectors of the economy forward. More generally, cheap oil and cheap energy encouraged businesses to invest massively in machinery and improved technology. This investment enabled workers to produce more—quite typically, productivity per worker in the United States grew handsomely at more than 3 percent a year between 1950 and 1973

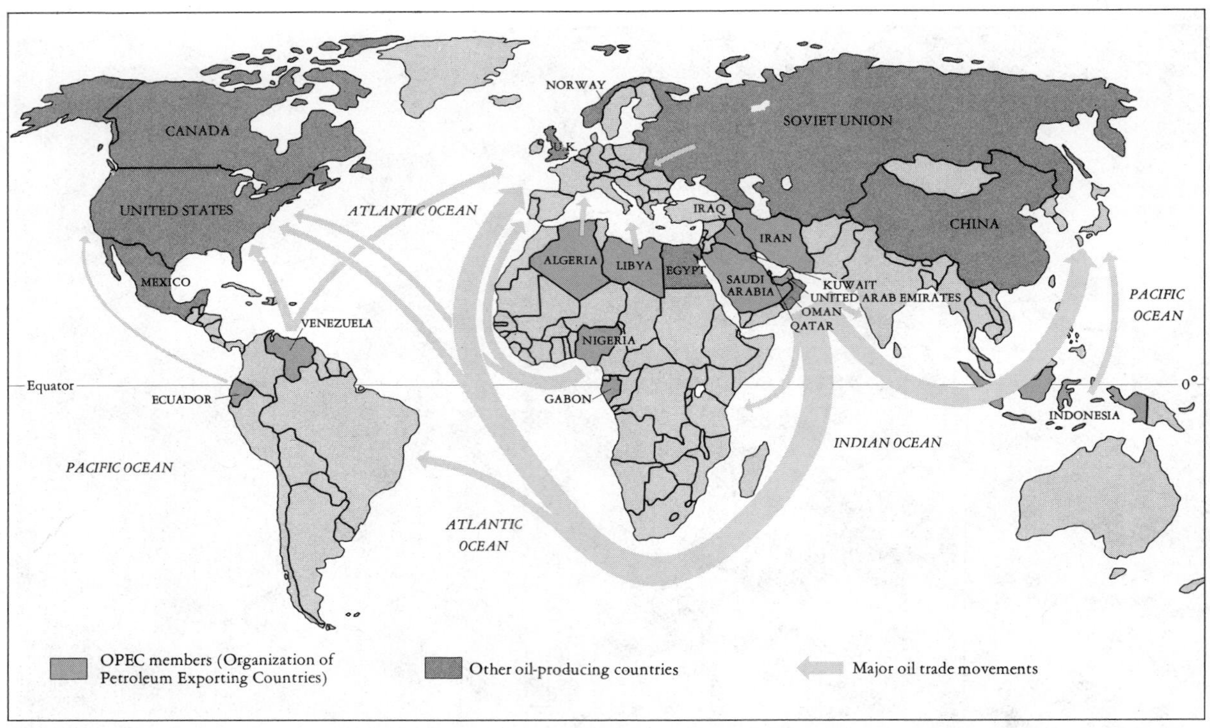

MAP 32.1 OPEC and the World Oil Trade Though much of the world depends on imported oil, Western Europe and Japan are OPEC's biggest customers. What major oil exporters remain outside of OPEC?

—and allowed a steady rise in the standard of living without much inflation.

In the 1950s and 1960s, the main oil-exporting countries, grouped together in the Arab-dominated Organization of Petroleum Exporting Countries (OPEC), had watched the price of crude oil decline consistently compared to the price of manufactured goods, as the Western oil companies vigorously expanded production and kept prices low to win users of coal to petroleum (see Map 32.1). The Egyptian leader Nasser argued that Arab countries should manipulate oil prices to further increase their revenues and also to strike at Israel and its Western allies. But Egypt lacked oil and Nasser failed. Colonel Muammar Khadafy of Libya proved more successful. He won important concessions from Western nations and oil companies in the early 1970s, and his example activated the OPEC countries. In 1971 OPEC for the first time presented a united front against the oil companies and obtained a solid price increase. The stage was set for the revolution in energy prices during the fourth Arab-Israeli war in October 1973.

The war began on the solemn sabbath celebration of Yom Kippur, or the Day of Atonement, the holiest day in the Jewish calendar. Egypt and Syria launched a surprise attack on an unsuspecting Israel, breaking through defense positions and destroying a large part of the Israeli air force. In response to urgent pleas, the United States airlifted $2.2 billion of its most sophisticated weapons to Israel, which accepted a cease-fire after its successful counterattack had encircled much of the Egyptian army. Surprisingly, the Yom Kippur War eventually led to peace between Egypt and Israel. Egypt's initial military victories greatly enhanced the power and prestige of General Anwar Sadat (1918–1981), Nasser's successor. This advantage enabled the realistic Sadat to achieve in 1979 the negotiated settlement with Israel that he had long desired.

In the first days of the war, the Arab (and non-

The Egyptian-Israeli Peace Treaty of 1979 is celebrated by the men who made it possible, Egypt's President Anwar al-Sadat, U.S. President Jimmy Carter, and Israeli Prime Minister Menachem Begin. Egypt recognized Israel's right to exist and established normal diplomatic relations, while Israel agreed to withdraw from Egyptian territory occupied in the Six-Day War of 1967. *(National Archives and Records Administration)*

Arab) oil producers in OPEC placed an embargo on oil shipments to the United States and the Netherlands, in retaliation for their support of Israel. They also cut production and raised prices by 70 percent, ostensibly to prevent Europe from sharing oil with the United States. In reality, greed and a desire for revenge against the West took over: a second increase in December, after the cease-fire, meant that crude oil prices quadrupled in less than a year. It was widely realized that OPEC's brutal action was economically destructive, but the world's major powers did nothing. The Soviet Union was a great oil exporter and benefited directly, while a cautious western Europe looked to the United States for leadership. But the United States was immobilized, its attention absorbed by the Watergate crisis (see page 1026). Thus governments, companies, and individuals were left to deal piecemeal and manage as best they could with the so-called oil shock—a "shock" that was really an earthquake.

Inflation, Debt, and Unemployment

Coming close on the heels of upheaval in the international monetary system, the price revolution in energy sources plunged the world into its worst economic decline since the 1930s. The energy-intensive industries that had driven the economy up in the 1950s and 1960s now dragged it down in the mid-1970s. Yet, while industrial output fell, soaring energy costs sent prices surging. "Stagflation"—the unexpected combination of economic stagnation and rapid inflation—appeared, to bedevil the public and baffle economists. Unemployment rose, while productivity and living standards declined.

But no cycle lasts forever, and by 1976 a modest recovery was in progress. People were learning to save energy, turning down thermostats, and buying smaller cars. Optimists argued that the challenge of redesigning life styles to cope with expensive energy actually represented a great opportunity.

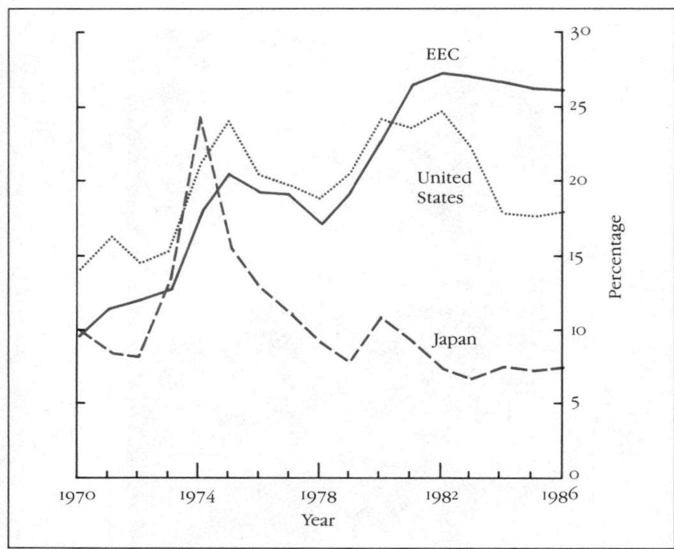

FIGURE 32.1 The Misery Index, 1970–1985 Combining rates of unemployment and inflation provided a simple but effective measure of economic hardship. This particular index represents the sum of two times the unemployment rate plus the inflation rate, reflecting the widespread belief that joblessness causes more suffering than higher prices. EEC = European Economic Community, or Common Market countries. *(Source: OECD data, as given in* The Economist, *June 15, 1985, p. 69.)*

Iran's Islamic revolution in 1978 and 1979 confounded these hopes, at least in the short run. Iranian oil production collapsed, OPEC again doubled the price of crude oil, and the world economy succumbed to its second oil shock. Once again, unemployment and inflation rose dramatically before another recovery began in 1982, driven by a reversal in oil prices, falling interest rates, and large U.S. trade and budget deficits. But the recovery was very uneven. In the summer of 1985, the unemployment rate in western Europe rose to its highest levels since the Great Depression. Fully 19 million people were unemployed.

Many means were devised in the 1970s to measure the troubled economy, but perhaps none was more telling than the "misery index." First used with considerable effect by candidate Jimmy Carter in the 1976 U.S. presidential debates, the misery index combined rates of inflation and unemployment in a single, powerfully emotional number. Figure 32.1 presents a comparison of misery indexes for the United States and the Common Market countries between 1970 and 1985. As may be seen, "misery" increased on both sides of the Atlantic, but the increase was substantially greater in western Europe. This helps explain why these hard times—often referred to by Europeans simply as "the crisis"—probably had an even greater psychological impact on Europeans than on Americans.

Nor was the Soviet bloc spared. Both the Soviet Union and the satellite states of its eastern European empire did less and less well: annual rates of economic growth fell from 6 to 7 percent in the late 1960s to 2 to 3 percent in 1980. This performance was no worse than that of most Western countries, but it mocked the long-standing propaganda boast to "catch and surpass the capitalistic West," which was quietly dropped in favor of less humorous slogans.

The revolution in energy prices had major consequences for economic and political relations between East bloc members. Eastern Europe is generally poor in energy resources, especially petroleum, whereas the Soviet Union has enormous gas deposits and is the world's largest oil producer. Thus the explosion of oil prices greatly increased the economic leverage of the Soviet Union over eastern Europe, and it strengthened trade ties within Comecon, the economic "club" formed by the Soviet Union and its allies. The Russians supplied more desperately needed oil and raw materials, and they took in return the pick of eastern European manufacturers. Eastern European hopes of closer commercial (and cultural) ties with their Western neighbors necessarily faded.

Debts and deficits piled up quickly in the troubled economy of the 1970s and 1980s. In the first place, the price hikes of 1973 required a massive global transfer of wealth to the OPEC countries from both rich and poor nations. Like individual consumers suddenly faced with a financial emergency, countries scrambled to borrow to pay their greatly increased fuel bills. Poor countries, especially, turned to the big private international banks. These banks received deposits—the so-called petrodollars—from OPEC members and lent them back out to poor countries so that these nations could pay their oil bills. This circular flow averted total collapse. But there was a high price to pay in the form of a rapid expansion of international debt, which bounded higher after the second oil shock and posed a serious long-term threat to the world economy in the 1980s.

Rich nations also went on a borrowing binge. Almost everywhere they ran up big debts to pay for imported oil and also to maintain social welfare services, as their economies declined and tax receipts fell. Even West Germany, justly famous for its commitment to low inflation and sound money, ran up a huge increase. By 1981 interest on Germany's national debt consumed one quarter of all government spending and was the largest single item in Germany's budget.

Western consumers also joined the race for ever-higher levels of debt. Borrowing to buy before prices rose seemed smart in the 1970s, and that attitude carried over into the 1980s. Like burgeoning government debt, a record-high level of consumer debt was a two-edged sword. It sustained current economic activity but quite possibly posed serious repayment problems, an appropriately ambiguous reflection of the troubled economy.

Some Social Consequences

The most pervasive consequences of recent economic stagnation was probably psychological and attitudinal. Optimism gave way to pessimism; romantic utopianism yielded to sober realism. This drastic change in mood—a complete surprise only to those who had never studied history—affected states, institutions, and individuals in countless ways.

To be sure, there were heartbreaking human tragedies—lost jobs, bankruptcies, and mental breakdowns. But, on the whole, the welfare system fashioned in the postwar era prevented mass suffering and degradation. Extended benefits for the unemployed, pensions for the aged, free medical care for the needy, surplus food and special allowances for parents with children—all these and a host of lesser supports did their part. The responsive, socially concerned national state undoubtedly contributed to the preservation of political stability and democracy in the face of economic difficulties, difficulties that might have brought revolution and dictatorship in earlier times.

The energetic response of governments to social needs helps explain the sharp increase in total government spending in most countries during the 1970s and 1980s. In 1982 western European governments spent an average of more than one-half of gross national income, as compared to only 37 percent fifteen years earlier. In the United States, the combined share of federal, state, and local governments rose from 31 to 35 percent in the same years. The role of government in everyday life became more important.

In all countries, people were much more willing to see their governments increase spending than raise taxes. This imbalance contributed to the rapid growth of budget deficits, national debts, and inflation discussed earlier. By the late 1970s, a powerful reaction to government's ever-increasing role set in, and Western governments were gradually forced to introduce austerity measures to slow the seemingly inexorable growth of public spending and the welfare state. The partially successful efforts of Margaret Thatcher in Britain and Ronald Reagan in the United States to limit the growth of social programs absorbed the attention of the English-speaking world, but François Mitterrand of France was the temporary exception who proved the general rule. After his election as president in 1981, Mitterrand led his Socialist party and Communist allies on a vast program of nationalization and public investment designed to spend France out of economic stagnation. By 1983 this attempt had clearly failed. Mitterrand's Socialist government was then compelled to impose a wide variety of austerity measures fully worthy of Reagan and Thatcher, until elections in 1986 brought a conservative coalition to power by a narrow margin.

When governments were eventually forced to restrain spending, Big Science was often singled out for cuts, unless its ties to the military were very direct. The problems of CERN were a good example. Formed to pool western European efforts in high-energy particle physics (page 996), CERN succeeded admirably in stealing the lead from the United States in this exciting but esoteric and uncommercial field. But the costs were so enormous—$400 million for construction of the latest electron-smashing accelerator—that some governments, such as Great Britain's, were budgeting 10 percent of all their spending for scientific research on particle physics alone. In the 1980s, CERN was increasingly attacked as an extravagant misallocation of scarce resources at a time when new fields, such as computers and genetic research, were bursting with scientific opportunities that offered mouth-watering commercial applications. More generally, tighter funding for Big Science accelerated the ongoing computer revolution. That

"The New Poor" Economic crisis and prolonged unemployment in the early 1980s reduced many from modest affluence to harsh poverty, creating a class of new poor. This photo captures that human tragedy. After two years of unemployment, this homeless French office worker must sleep each night in a makeshift shelter for the destitute. *(Dennis Stock/Magnum)*

revolution thrived on the diffusion of unprecedented computational and informational capacity to small research groups and private businesses, which were both cause and effect of the revolution itself.

Individuals felt the impact of austerity even earlier, for unlike governments, they could not pay their bills by printing money and going ever further into debt. The energy crisis forced them to re-examine not only their fuel bills, but the whole pattern of self-indulgent materialism in the postwar era as well. The result was a leaner, tougher lifestyle, featuring more attention to nutrition and a passion for exercise. Correspondingly, there was less blind reliance on medical science for good health and a growing awareness that individuals must accept a large portion of the responsibility for illness and disease. More people began to realize that they could substantially increase their life spans simply by eating regular meals, sleeping seven or eight hours each night, exercising two or three times a week, maintaining moderate weight, forgoing smoking, and using alcohol only in moderation. A forty-five-year-old American male who practiced three or fewer of these habits could expect to live to be sixty-seven; one who adhered to five or six could expect to live eleven more years, to age seventy-eight.

Yet it was the very real threat of unemployment that probably had the most profound impact. A good job promised pride and well-being, while the most generous unemployment benefits only prevented catastrophe. The increased focus on jobs continued the 1960s trend of more married women working. It also encouraged both men and women to postpone marriage until they had put their careers on a firm foundation, so that the age of marriage rose sharply for both sexes in many Western countries.

Indeed, the employment question seemed to shape

the outlook of a whole generation. The students of the 1980s were serious, practical, and often conservative. As one young woman at a French university told a reporter in 1985, "Jobs are the big worry now, so everyone wants to learn something practical." In France, as elsewhere, it was an astonishing shift from the romantic visions and political activism of the late 1960s. Speaking of the French student revolution of 1968, another undergraduate handed down a tough judgment for the same reporter. "It was a search for a Utopia that can't exist. It just doesn't mean a thing to us anymore."[2]

THE ATLANTIC ALLIANCE

Forged in the late 1940s to rebuild Europe and prevent possible Soviet expansion beyond the iron curtain, the Atlantic alliance remained an enduring reality in the face of economic difficulties. But the alliance was neither static nor monolithic, and its evolution reflected major developments within the member states. Those in West Germany and the United States were of critical importance.

Germany and the European Settlement

The turning points of history are sometimes captured in dramatic moments rich in symbolism. So it was in December 1970, when West German Chancellor Willy Brandt flew to Poland for the signing of a historic treaty of reconciliation. Brandt laid a wreath at the tomb of the Polish unknown soldier and another at the monument commemorating the armed uprising of Warsaw's Jewish ghetto against occupying Nazi armies, after which the ghetto was totally destroyed and the Jewish survivors sent to the gas chambers. Standing before the ghetto memorial, a somber Brandt fell to his knees and knelt as if in prayer. "I wanted," Brandt said later, "to ask pardon in the name of our people for a million-fold crime which was committed in the misused name of the Germans."[3]

Brandt's gesture at the Warsaw ghetto memorial and the treaty with Poland were part of his policy of reconciliation with eastern Europe, which aimed at nothing less than a comprehensive peace settlement for central Europe and a new resolution of the "German question." That weighty question had first burst on the European scene with the modern nationalism of the French Revolution. How could fragmented Germany achieve political unity, and what role would a powerful, unified Germany play in the international order? "Resolved" in a certain fashion by Bismarck's wars of unification, the question was posed again in the twentieth century when an aggressive Germany tried twice to conquer Europe. Agreed on crushing Hitler and denazifying Germany during the Second World War, the wartime Allies then found themselves incapable of working together and imposing a general peace treaty on defeated Germany (pages 964–966). Instead, Germany was divided into two antagonistic states by 1949, and the German question continued to fester as national unity disappeared.

The Federal Republic of Germany—commonly known as West Germany—was the larger of the two, with 45 million inhabitants as opposed to 18 million in East Germany. Formed out of the American, British, and French zones of occupation and based on freely expressed popular sovereignty, the Federal Republic claimed that the Communist dictatorship installed by the Russians lacked free elections and hence all legal basis. While concentrating on completing its metamorphosis from defeated enemy to invaluable ally within NATO and the Common Market, West Germany also sought with some success to undermine the East German Communist regime. Between 1949 and 1954, it welcomed with open arms 2.3 million East German refugees seeking political freedom and economic opportunity, and it refused to have diplomatic relations with any state (except the Soviet Union) that recognized East Germany as a legal government. East Germany, first looted by the Soviets and then constantly losing its best workers to West Germany, limped along while the Federal Republic boomed. But the building of the Berlin Wall in 1961 (page 982) changed all that. It sealed the refugees' last escape route through West Berlin and allowed East Germany to stabilize and eventually become the world's most prosperous Communist country.

As the popular socialist major of West Berlin, Willy Brandt understood the significance of the Berlin Wall and the lack of an energetic U.S. response to

Willy Brandt in Poland, 1970 Chancellor Brandt's gesture at the Warsaw memorial to the Jewish victims of Nazi terrorism was criticized by some West Germans but praised by many more. This picture reached an enormous audience, appearing in hundreds of newspapers in both the East and the West. *(Süddeutscher Verlag)*

its construction. He saw the painful limitations of West Germany's official hard line when the Allies had, in fact, accepted the postwar status quo. Thus Brandt became convinced that a revitalized West Germany needed a new foreign policy, just as the German Social Democratic party he headed had abandoned doctrinaire Marxian socialism to become a broad-based opposition party after the Second World War. After a long battle and two bitter electoral defeats in the 1960s, Brandt became foreign minister in a coalition government in 1966 and won the chancellorship in 1969.

Brandt's victory marked the Federal Republic's political coming of age. First, it brought the Social Democrats to national power for the first time since the 1920s and showed that genuine two-party political democracy had taken firm hold. Second, it was a graphic indication of West Germany's new-found liberalism and political tolerance, for the gravel-voiced Brandt was a very unconventional German. Illegitimate son of a poor, unwed shop-girl, and a fire-breathing Socialist in his youth, Brandt had fled to Norway in the 1930s and had fought against Nazi Germany in the Second World War. Yet the electorate judged the man himself, turning a deaf ear to smears and innuendoes about treason and low birth. Third, Brandt showed that West Germany, postwar Europe's economic giant and political dwarf, was now both prepared and willing to launch major initiatives in European affairs.

The essence of Brandt's policy was to seek genuine peace and reconciliation with the communist East, as Adenauer had already done with France and the West. He negotiated treaties with the Soviet Union, Poland, and Czechoslovakia, which accepted existing state boundaries in return for a mutual renunciation of force or the threat of force. Thus West Germany abandoned the fiction that the "provisional" loss of eastern territory to Poland and the Soviet Union (see Map 30.3), agreed to by the Big Four at the Potsdam Conference in 1945, might some day be altered in Germany's favor in the final peace treaty that would never come. In addition, Brandt shrewdly made German ratification of these bilateral treaties conditional on a new agreement between the wartime Big Four, an agreement that solemnly guaranteed the freedom of West Berlin, that perennial source of bitter cold war conflict. Finally, using the imaginative formula of "two German states within one German nation," Brandt's government broke decisively with the past and entered into direct relations with East Germany, aiming for modest practical improvements rather than unattainable reunification.

Since all his initiatives required both American and Russian consent, Brandt constantly reiterated that none of these changes affected the respective military alliances of NATO and the Warsaw Pact. Yet, by boldly establishing "normal relations" with the communist East, West Germany seemed not only to turn another page on its ever-more-distant Nazi past, but on many bitter cold war conflicts as well. Thus West Germany's eastern peace settlement contributed to a general reduction in East-West tensions, which included a limited agreement on nuclear arms control between the United States and the Soviet Union in 1972. And with the German question apparently resolved, West Germany had freed itself to assume without reservations a leading role in Europe. In the future, it would often join with its Common Market partners in an attempt to insulate East-West relations within Europe from the enduring Soviet-American power struggle that characterized the rest of the world.

Political Crisis in the United States

The late 1960s and early 1970s also marked the end of the postwar era in the United States. The natural leader of the Atlantic alliance fell into a long and self-destructive political crisis, which weakened the nation at home and abroad and echoed throughout the 1970s.

The crisis in the United States had numerous manifestations, ranging from apparently uncontrollable annual summer riots to brutal political assassinations, which struck down Martin Luther King and both President John F. Kennedy and his younger brother Robert. But it first reached vast proportions in connection with President Johnson's leadership during the undeclared Vietnam War. Thus President Johnson, who wanted to go down in history as a master reformer and healer of old wounds (pages 983–984), left new ones as his most enduring legacy.

American involvement in Vietnam had its origins in the cold war and the ideology of containment (page 966). From the late 1940s on, most Americans and their leaders viewed the world in terms of a constant struggle to stop the spread of communism, although they were not prepared to try to roll back communism where it already existed. As Europe began to revive and China established a Communist government in 1949, efforts to contain communism shifted to Asia. The bloody Korean War (1950–1953) ended in stalemate, but the United States did succeed in preventing a Communist government in South Korea. After the defeat of the French in Indochina in 1954, the Eisenhower administration refused to sign the Geneva accords that temporarily divided the country into two zones pending national unification by means of free elections. President Eisenhower then proceeded to acquiesce in the refusal of the anti-communist South Vietnamese government to accept the verdict of elections and provided it with military aid. President Kennedy greatly increased the number of American "military advisers," to 16,000, and had the existing South Vietnamese leader deposed in 1963 when he refused to follow American directives.

After successfully portraying his opponent, Barry Goldwater, as a trigger-happy extremist in a nuclear age and resoundingly winning the 1964 election on a peace platform, President Johnson proceeded to expand the American role in the Vietnam conflict. As Johnson explained to his ambassador in Saigon, "I am not going to lose Vietnam. I am not going to be the President who saw Southeast Asia go the way China went."[4] American strategy was to "escalate" the war sufficiently to break the will of the North Vietnamese and their southern allies, without resorting to "overkill" that might risk war with the entire communist bloc. Thus the South received massive military aid, American forces in South Vietnam gradually grew to a half-million men, and the United States bombed North Vietnam with ever-greater intensity. But there was no invasion of the North, nor were essential seaborne military supplies from the Soviet Union ever disrupted. In the end, the strategy of limited war backfired. It was the Americans themselves who grew weary, and the American leadership that cracked.

The undeclared war in Vietnam, fought nightly on American television, eventually divided the nation. Initial support was strong. The politicians, the media, and the population as a whole saw the war as part of a legitimate defense against communist totalitarianism in all poor countries. But in 1966 and 1967, influential opinion leaders like the *New York Times* and the *Washington Post* turned hostile, and the television networks soon followed. A growing number of critics denounced the war as an immoral and unsuccessful intrusion into a complex and distant civil war. There were major protests, often led by college students. Criticism reached a crescendo after the Vietcong "Tet Offensive" in January 1968. This, the Communists' first major attack with conventional weapons on major cities, failed militarily: the Vietcong suffered heavy losses and the attack did not spark a mass uprising. But U.S. critics of the Vietnam War interpreted the bloody battle as a decisive American defeat, clear proof that a Vietcong victory was inevitable. And although public opinion polls never showed more than 20 percent of the people supporting American withdrawal before that became the announced policy after the November 1968 elections, America's leaders now lost all heart. After an ambiguous defeat in the New Hampshire primary, President Johnson tacitly admitted defeat: he called for negotiations with North Vietnam and announced that he would not stand for re-election.

Elected by a razor-slim margin in 1968, President Richard Nixon sought to gradually disengage America from Vietnam and the accompanying national crisis. He restated the long-standing American objective of containment in Vietnam, of aiding the "South Vietnamese people to determine their own political future without outside interference."[5] Using American military power more effectively, while simultaneously pursuing peace talks with the North Vietnamese, Nixon cut American forces in Vietnam from 550,000 to 24,000 in four years. The cost of the war dropped from $25 billion a year under Johnson to $3 billion under Nixon. Moreover, President Nixon launched a daring flank attack in diplomacy. He journeyed to China in 1971 and reached a spectacular if limited reconciliation with Communist China, which took advantage of China's growing fears of the Soviet Union and undermined North Vietnam's position. In January 1973, fortified by the overwhelming endorsement of the people in his 1972 electoral triumph, President Nixon and Secretary of State Henry Kissinger finally reached a peace agreement with North Vietnam. The agreement allowed remaining American forces to complete their withdrawal, while the United States reserved the right to resume bombing if the accords were broken. South Vietnamese forces seemed to hold their own, and the storm of crisis seemed past.

Instead, as the Arab oil embargo unhinged the international economy, the United States reaped the Watergate whirlwind. Like some other recent American presidents, Nixon authorized spying activities that went beyond the law. But in an atmosphere in which a huge series of secret government documents —later known as the "Pentagon Papers"—could be stolen and then given to the country's most influential newspaper for publication as part of its anti–Vietnam War campaign, Nixon went further than his predecessors. He authorized special units to use various illegal means to stop the leaking of government secrets to the press. One such group broke into the Democratic party headquarters in Washington's Watergate complex in June 1972 and was promptly arrested. Eventually, the media and the machinery of Congressional investigation turned the breakin and later efforts to hush up the bungled job into a great moral issue. In 1974 a beleaguered Nixon was forced to resign in disgrace, as the political crisis in the United States reached its culmination.

The consequences of renewed political crisis during the Watergate affair were profound. First, it resulted in a major shift of power away from the presidency toward Congress, especially in foreign affairs.

Nixon in China, 1972 Shown here toasting U.S.–China friendship with Chinese Premier Chou En-lai in Peking in February 1972, President Nixon took advantage of Chinese fears of the Soviet Union to establish good relations with Asia's Communist giant. Arriving after twenty-five years of mutual hostility, reconciliation with China was Nixon's finest achievement. *(UPI/Bettmann Newsphotos)*

Therefore, as American aid to South Vietnam diminished in 1973 and as an emboldened North Vietnam launched a general invasion against South Vietnamese armies in early 1974, first President Nixon and then President Gerald Ford stood by because Congress refused to permit any American response. After more than thirty-five years of battle, the Vietnamese Communists unified their country in 1975 as a totalitarian state—a second consequence of the U.S. crisis. Third, the belated fall of South Vietnam in the wake of Watergate shook America's postwar pride and confidence. Generally interpreted as a disastrous American military defeat, the Vietnam aftermath left the United States divided and uncertain about its proper role in world affairs. The long-dominant belief that the interests of the United States required an unending global struggle against the spread of communism was seriously damaged. In the 1970s, however, no alternative concept received general support, unless it was a narrow preoccupation with the multiplying problems of the troubled international economy.

The Helsinki Agreement, 1975 President Ford signs the historic accord guaranteeing European borders and calling for improvements in human rights. On the far left is Helmut Schmidt of West Germany, flanked by a jovial Erich Honecker savoring the fullest possible diplomatic recognition of his East German Communist state. *(UPI/Bettmann Newsphotos)*

Recent Developments

The complex political crisis in the United States during the Vietnam War and West Germany's reconciliation with eastern Europe under Willy Brandt were clearly major turning points in recent history. The power and prestige of the United States had suffered a serious decline, while West Germany had opened the door to major diplomatic agreements regarding Europe. Or so it seemed to many at the time. Yet the ultimate significance of these turning points remains uncertain, as may be seen by examining the often contradictory course of recent developments.

Brandt's Eastern initiatives and Nixon's phased withdrawal from Vietnam were part of many-sided Western efforts to reduce East-West tensions in the early 1970s. This policy of *détente,* or progressive relaxation of cold war tensions, reached its apogee with the Conference on Security and Cooperation in Europe, a thirty-five nation summit that opened negotiations in Helsinki, Finland, in 1973 and reached a final agreement in 1975. Including all European nations (except isolationist Albania), the United States, and Canada, the Final Act of the Helsinki Conference had certain elements of a general European peace treaty, like those signed at Vienna in 1815 and at Versailles in 1919. It formally agreed that Europe's existing political frontiers, including those separating the two Germanies, could not be changed by force and provided for increased East-West economic and cultural relations as well. Thus the Atlantic alliance solemnly accepted the territorial status quo in eastern Europe, as well as the Soviet Union's gains from World War Two. In return for this major concession, the Soviet Union and its allies agreed to numerous provisions guaranteeing the human rights and political freedoms of their peoples. The Final Act was a compromise embodying Western concerns for human rights and Soviet preoccupations with military security and control of eastern Europe. Optimists saw a bright new day breaking in international relations.

These hopes gradually faded in the later 1970s. The Soviet Union and its allies would ignore the human rights provisions of the Helsinki agreement (see above). Moreover, East-West political competition remained very much alive outside Europe. Many Americans became convinced that the Soviet Union was taking advantage of détente, steadily building up its military might and pushing for political gains in Africa, Asia, and Latin America. Having been expelled from Egypt by Anwar Sadat after the 1973 war with Israel, the Soviets sought and won toeholds in South Yemen, Somalia, and later Ethiopia. Having supported guerrilla wars against the Portuguese in Angola and Mozambique, the Soviet Union was rewarded with Marxian regimes in both countries. The spectacular 1975 airlift of 20,000 Cubans to Angola to help the new Marxian government consolidate its power rattled Americans' nerves and increased their suspicions.

But it was in Afghanistan that Soviet action seemed most contrary to the spirit of détente. The Soviet Union had long been interested in its Islamic neighbor, and in April 1978, a pro-Soviet coup established a Marxist regime there. This new government soon made itself unpopular, and rebellion spread through the countryside. To preserve Communist rule, the Soviet Union in December 1979 suddenly airlifted crack troops to Kabul, the capital, and occupied Afghanistan with 100,000 men. Alarmed by the scale and precision of the Soviet invasion, many Americans feared that the oil-rich states of the Persian Gulf would be next and searched for an appropriate response.

President Carter tried to lead the Atlantic alliance beyond verbal condemnation. He ordered a halt to extra sales of American grain—one of the few commodities the Soviet Union really needed from the United States—to the Soviet Union. But among its European allies only Great Britain supported the American policy of economic sanctions. France, and especially West Germany, argued that the Soviets' deplorable action in Afghanistan should not be turned into an East-West confrontation and tried to salvage as much as possible of détente within Europe. President Carter, they implied, had overreacted. The Afghanistan crisis again revealed serious differences within the Atlantic alliance, differences that had been surfacing periodically ever since General De Gaulle's independent course in the 1960s.

The alliance showed the same lack of concerted action when an independent trade union rose in Poland (see page 1037), most notably when western Europe again refused to follow the United States in imposing economic sanctions against Poland and the Soviet Union after the declaration of martial law in Poland in December 1981. Some observers concluded that the alliance had lost the will to think and act decisively in relations with the Soviet bloc. They saw inaction as part of a larger problem of growing disunity within the Western democracies, where debate and dissent were so pervasive that consistent and courageous action was virtually impossible and decline almost inevitable. Others noted that occasional dramatic differences within the alliance reflected the fact that the Common Market and the United States had drifted apart and become economic rivals.

Yet, despite its very real difficulties, the Atlantic alliance, formed in the late 1940s to check Soviet expansion in Europe, endured and remained true to its original purpose in the 1980s. The U.S. military buildup launched by Jimmy Carter in his last years in office was accelerated by President Ronald Reagan, who was swept into office in 1980 by the wave of patriotism following an agonizing hostage crisis in Iran. The new American leadership was convinced that the military balance had tipped in favor of the Soviet Union. Increasing defense spending rapidly, the Reagan administration concentrated especially on nuclear arms and an expanded navy as keys to a resurgence of American power in the post-Vietnam era. Somewhat reluctantly, and in the face of large protest demonstrations, European governments agreed that

American Hostages in Iran Blindfolded and hands tied, American employees at the U.S. embassy in Teheran are threatened and humiliated by their militant Iranian captors on the first day of their ordeal. In their anguish over the hostages, Americans tended to blame President Carter for weakness, though all the hostages eventually did return to the United States. *(UPI/Bettmann Newsphotos)*

NATO's forces had to be strengthened. They also reluctantly agreed to install medium-range American cruise missiles with nuclear warheads on their soil, in response to the vast arsenal of medium-range "European" missiles that the Soviet Union had targeted to destroy all important targets in western Europe without even calling on Soviet bombers or missile-launching submarines. Thus western Europeans accepted the need to maintain some kind of rough nuclear and general military balance in Europe to guarantee their freedom and genuine independence (see Map 32.2). Increasingly unable to act as a unit in local conflicts in Africa, Asia, the Middle East, or Central America because of different perceptions and interests, the Atlantic alliance, reinforced by a rich network of common cultural and political values, remained a powerful force defending the heartland of Western civilization.

THE SOVIET BLOC

The fluctuations in Western response to the Soviet bloc were tied in part to puzzling ambiguities within the Soviet system itself. Ever since Lenin, and certainly since Stalin, the Soviet Union has combined political dictatorship with egalitarian ideology, for example; and there has been a strong tendency in the West to see the Soviet Union in terms of black or white, of archvillain or great hero.

Map 32.2 The Use of Nuclear Power in the 1980s One major consequence of the growing use of nuclear power to generate electricity is that many countries have developed the expertise necessary to make nuclear weapons should they so choose.

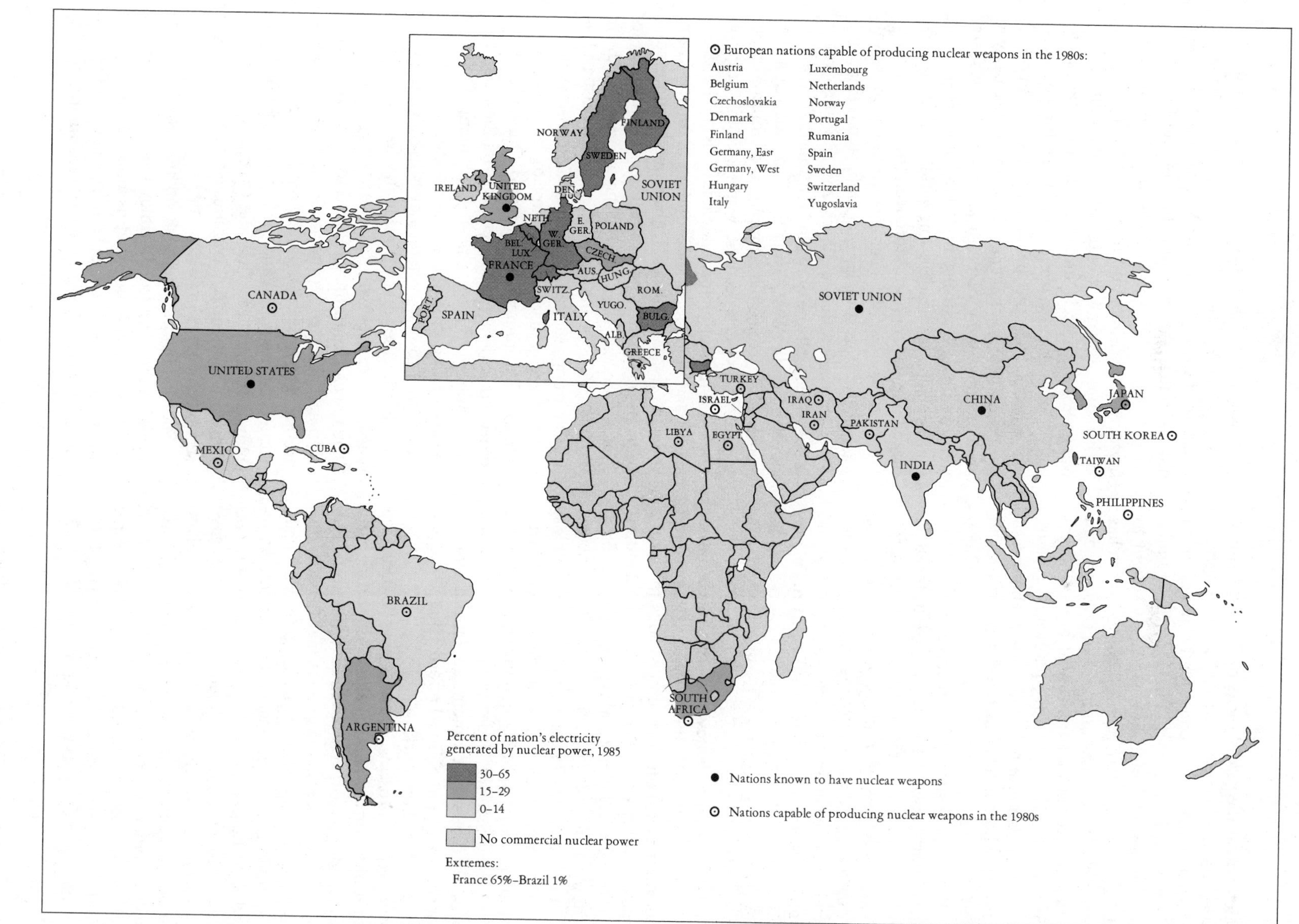
⊙ European nations capable of producing nuclear weapons in the 1980s:
Austria
Belgium
Czechoslovakia
Denmark
Finland
Germany, East
Germany, West
Hungary
Italy
Luxembourg
Netherlands
Norway
Portugal
Rumania
Spain
Sweden
Switzerland
Yugoslavia
NORWAY
SWEDEN
FINLAND
IRELAND
UNITED KINGDOM
DEN.
SOVIET UNION
NETH.
BEL.
LUX.
W. GER.
E. GER.
POLAND
CZECH.
FRANCE
AUS.
HUNG.
ROM.
SWITZ.
YUGO.
BULG.
PORT.
SPAIN
ITALY
ALB.
GREECE
CANADA
UNITED STATES
MEXICO
CUBA
BRAZIL
ARGENTINA
SOVIET UNION
TURKEY
ISRAEL
IRAQ
IRAN
LIBYA
EGYPT
PAKISTAN
CHINA
INDIA
JAPAN
SOUTH KOREA
TAIWAN
PHILIPPINES
SOUTH AFRICA
Percent of nation's electricity generated by nuclear power, 1985
30–65
15–29
0–14
No commercial nuclear power
Extremes:
France 65%–Brazil 1%
● Nations known to have nuclear weapons
⊙ Nations capable of producing nuclear weapons in the 1980s

In fact, and at the risk of oversimplification, these extremes may be regarded as equally inappropriate. The Soviet Union has consistently remained a somber gray in its behavior. First, the Communist party in the Soviet Union has steadfastly sought to maintain its monopoly of political power, which has not been difficult because communism is wrapped in Russian nationalism and traditional authoritarianism. Second, there has been an equally strong desire to preserve the Communist system throughout eastern Europe, where it has much less support than in the Soviet Union and is therefore subject to liberation efforts, which have been unsuccessful thus far. Third, military power has held the system together, providing a firm basis for continuous but cautious efforts to expand the Soviet sphere of influence. These enduring realities dominate the recent past, as may be seen by looking at the invasion of Czechoslovakia, the Brezhnev era, and the fate of Solidarity in Poland.

The Czechoslovak Experiment

In the wake of Khrushchev's reforms in the Soviet Union (pages 980–981), the 1960s brought modest liberalization and more consumer goods to eastern Europe, as well as somewhat greater national autonomy, especially in Poland and Rumania. Czechoslovakia moved more slowly than its Communist neighbors, but in January 1968, it began making up for lost time. The reform elements in the Czechoslovak Communist party gained a majority and voted out the long-time Stalinist leader in favor of Alexander Dubček. The new government launched a series of major economic and political reforms that fascinated observers around the world.

Educated in Moscow, Dubček was a dedicated Communist. But he and his allies within the party were also idealists, who believed that they could reconcile genuine socialism with personal freedom and internal party democracy. Thus local decision making by trade unions, managers, and consumers replaced rigid bureaucratic planning. Censorship was relaxed, and mindless ideological conformity gave way to exciting free expression. People responded enthusiastically, and the reform program proved enormously popular. Czechoslovakia had been eastern Europe's only advanced industrial state before the Second World War, and Dubček was reviving traditions that were still deeply cherished.

Although Dubček remembered the lesson of the Hungarian revolution (page 981) and constantly proclaimed his loyalty to the Warsaw Pact of Communist states, the determination of the Czech reformers to build "socialism with a human face" frightened hard-line Communists. In March 1968, Polish students took to the streets shouting, "We want a Polish Dubček" and "Long Live Czechoslovakia!" Czechoslovakia was obviously setting a dangerous example for the peoples of eastern Europe, tempting them to challenge the Communist party's absolute monopoly of political power. These fears were particularly strong in Poland and East Germany, where the leaders knew full well that they lacked popular support. Moreover, the Soviet Union attached great military significance to Czechoslovakia because of its strategic geographical position, and Moscow feared that a liberalized Czechoslovakia would eventually be drawn to neutralism, or even to the democratic West. Thus the East bloc countries launched a concerted campaign of intimidation against the Czech leaders, warning ominously of "counter-revolutionary tendencies" in public statements and demanding a restoration of Soviet orthodoxy in private meetings. Dubček made minor concessions on defense, but his regime was unwilling to knuckle under. The Soviet response was brutal. In August 1968, 500,000 Russian and allied eastern European troops suddenly occupied Czechoslovakia.

The Czechs made no attempt to resist militarily. The Soviets immediately arrested Dubček and the other top leaders, but to their chagrin, they found no collaborators to form a new government. Thus, instead of being shot, the arrested Czech leaders were flown to Moscow, where they surrendered to demands after they and their country had been threatened by Brezhnev with the most severe punishments. The Czech Communists agreed to reimpose censorship and accepted an indefinite stationing of Soviet troops on their soil. Gradually but inexorably, the reform program was abandoned and its supporters removed from office. Thus the Czechoslovak experiment in humanizing communism and making it serve the needs of ordinary citizens failed.

Shortly after the Czechoslovak invasion, Brezhnev declared the so-called Brezhnev Doctrine, according to which Soviet Russia and its allies had the right to intervene in any socialist country whenever they saw the need. The Chinese drew the reasonable conclu-

The End of Reform In August 1968 Soviet tanks rumbled into Prague to extinguish Czechoslovakian efforts to build a humane socialism. Here people watch the massive invasion from the sidewalks, knowing full well the suicidal danger of armed resistance. *(PP/Magnum)*

sion that they might be next, which encouraged them to seek the reconciliation with the United States that helped Richard Nixon obtain a Vietnam agreement with Hanoi. Predictably, the occupation of Czechoslovakia raised a storm of protest. Many Communist parties in western Europe were harshly critical, partly out of conviction and partly to limit their electoral losses. But the occupation did not seriously alter ongoing Western efforts—mostly notably, those of West Germany's Willy Brandt—to secure better relations with the East-bloc countries. The reason was simple. The West considered Czechoslovakia to be part of Russia's sphere of influence, for better or worse. Thus Stalin's empire remained solidly in place, and it seemed that change in eastern Europe could only continue to follow developments in the Soviet Union for years to come.

The Soviet Union

The 1968 invasion of Czechoslovakia was probably the crucial event of the Brezhnev era, which really lasted beyond the aging leader's death in 1982, until the emergence in 1985 of Mikhail Gorbachev (see page 1036). The invasion demonstrated unmistakably the intense conservatism of Russia's ruling elite and its determination to maintain the status quo in the Soviet bloc. It showed that Russia's Communist leaders were less inclined to accept fundamental reforms than were their Western counterparts. Thus the failure of both the Czechoslovak experiment and the student revolution in France proved that similar hopes of reconciling socialism with freedom were illusive on both sides of the iron curtain in the late 1960s. But whereas the aftermath of 1968's romantic upheaval in France brought a number of social and political reforms, notably for women and in higher education, the aftermath of 1968 in Czechoslovakia witnessed only a long step backward to the Stalinist regime.

Intervention in Czechoslovakia also brought further re-Stalinization of Soviet Russia, though with collective rather than personal dictatorship and without uncontrolled terror. This compromise seemed to suit the leaders and most of the people. Whether Westerners liked it or not, Soviet Russia appeared quite stable in the 1970s and early 1980s.

A gradually rising standard of living for ordinary people contributed greatly to stability. By 1974 two-thirds of the nation's families had television sets, almost 60 percent had sewing and washing machines, and about half had some kind of refrigerator. The economic crisis of the 1970s markedly slowed the rate of improvement, and long lines and innumerable shortages persisted. But long-suffering Soviet consumers compared the present with the recent past and not with conditions abroad. The enduring differences between the life of the elite and the life of ordinary people also reinforced the system. Ambitious individuals still had tremendous incentive to do as the state wished, in order to gain access to special, well-stocked stores, attend special schools, and travel abroad.

Another source of stability was that ordinary Russians remained more intensely nationalistic than almost any other people in the world. The party leaders successfully identified themselves with this patriotism, stressing their role in saving the motherland during the Second World War and protecting it now from foreign foes, including eastern European "counter-revolutionaries." By playing on nationalist feelings, de-Stalinization was very easily reversed. Many ordinary Russians considered an attack on Stalin to be an attack on the great sacrifices they had willingly made for their nation. Similarly, ordinary Russians took enormous pride in their country's military power, and young men accepted an inescapable three-year hitch in the army without question. The cult of Lenin, which replaced the cult of Stalin, also had nationalistic overtones, which neutralized the general cynicism about Communist ideology.

The weight of history also contributed to the preservation of the status quo. For centuries, the tsars were uncompromising absolutists, who taught their subjects that undivided and hence unquestioned authority was essential for the good of the state. Moreover, the politically dominant Great Russians constitute only half of the total Soviet population. As their action in Czechoslovakia showed, the Great Russian leaders feared that greater freedom and open political competition might result in demands for autonomy and even independence, not only by eastern European nationalities, but by non-Russian nationalities within the Soviet Union itself. Thus Western-style liberalism and democracy appeared as alien and divisive political philosophies that would undermine Russia's power and achievements.

The strength of the government was expressed in the re-Stalinization of culture and art. Free expression and open protest disappeared. In 1968, when a small group of dissenters appeared in Red Square to protest the invasion of Czechoslovakia, they were arrested before they could unfurl their banners. This proved to be the high point of dissent, for in the 1970s Brezhnev and company made certain that public dissent did not infect Soviet intellectuals. The slightest acts of open nonconformity and protest were severely punished, but with sophisticated, cunning methods.

Most frequently, dissidents were blacklisted and thus rendered unable to find a decent job, since the government was the only employer. This fate was enough to keep most in line. More determined but unrenowned protesters were quietly imprisoned in jails or mental institutions. Celebrated nonconformists such as Solzhenitsyn were permanently expelled from the country. Once again, Jews were persecuted as a "foreign" element, though some were eventually permitted to emigrate to Israel.

As the distinguished Russian dissident historian Roy Medvedev summed it up:

The technology of repression has become more refined in recent years. Before, repression always went much farther than necessary. Stalin killed millions of people when arresting 1000 would have enabled him to control the people. Our leaders . . . found out eventually that you don't have to put people in prison or in a psychiatric hospital to silence them. There are other ways.[6]

Political Developments Within the Atlantic Alliance and Soviet Eastern Europe, 1961–1985

Aug 1961	Construction of the Berlin Wall
Nov 1963	Assassination of U.S. President John F. Kennedy
Aug 1964	Tonkin Gulf Resolution: escalation of American involvement in Vietnam
Nov 1964	Re-election of U.S. President Lyndon B. Johnson
Jan 1968	Tet Offensive of Vietcong in Vietnam
Aug 1968	Soviet invasion of Czechoslovakia: Dubček forced to abandon liberal reform program
Nov 1968	Election of U.S. President Richard M. Nixon
1969–1973	Chancellor Willy Brandt negotiates reconciliation between West Germany and Communist eastern Europe
Dec 1970	Strikes in Poland in protest against large price rises; fall of government of Wladyslaw Gomulka
Feb 1972	Nixon visits Premier Chou En-lai in Peking; re-establishes good relations with Communist China
May 1972	Salt I Treaty between the United States and the Soviet Union
Jan 1973	Paris Accords between the United States and North Vietnam
Oct 1973	Fourth Arab-Israeli War; OPEC quadruples price of oil
Aug 1974	Nixon resigns from presidency over the Watergate scandal; Gerald R. Ford takes over as U.S. president
April 1975	Fall of Saigon to the Communists; reunification of North and South Vietnam
July 1975	Helsinki Agreement: Atlantic alliance accepts eastern European status quo in return for Soviet human-rights guarantees
Nov 1976	Election of U.S. President Jimmy Carter
1978–1979	Islamic revolution in Iran: oil production collapses, OPEC doubles the price of oil
March 1979	Camp David Accords between Israel and Egypt
May 1979	Election of British Prime Minister Margaret Thatcher
June 1979	Salt II Treaty between the United States and the Soviet Union
Nov 1979–Jan 1981	Iranian hostage crisis
Dec 1979	Soviet invasion of Afghanistan
Aug 1980	Occupation of the Lenin Shipyards in Gdansk: Polish government accedes to Solidarity's demands
Nov 1980	Election of U.S. President Ronald Reagan
May 1981	Election of French President François Mitterrand
Dec 1981	General Jaruzelski proclaims martial law in Poland; Solidarity leaders arrested
1982	Death of Soviet First Secretary Leonid Brezhnev
1983	Installation of American cruise and Pershing missiles in western Europe
March 1985	Mikhail Gorbachev becomes First Secretary of the Soviet Communist Party
Nov 1985	Reagan-Gorbachev summit in Geneva

Superpower Summit, 1985 At their Geneva meeting U.S. President Reagan and Soviet leader Gorbachev vigorously debated arms control and the many issues that separated their governments. Smiling frequently for the press and locked in an intense campaign for public support, especially in western Europe, they agreed only to meet again. *(Wide World Photos)*

Thus the worst aspects of Stalin's totalitarianism had been eliminated, but rule by a self-perpetuating Communist elite in the Soviet Union appeared as solid as ever throughout the 1970s.

That elite seemed equally secure in the 1980s, as far as any challenge from below was concerned. The long-established system of administrative controls continued to stretch downward from the central ministries and state committees to provincial cities, and from there to factories, neighborhoods, and villages. At each level of this massive state bureaucracy, the overlapping hierarchy of the Communist party, with its 17.5 million members, continued to watch over all decisions and manipulate every aspect of national life. Organized opposition was simply impossible, and the average Soviet citizen left politics to the bosses.

Yet the massive state and party bureaucracy was a mixed blessing. It discouraged economic efficiency and personal initiative as well as political dissent and intellectual innovation. It safeguarded the elite, but it also promoted apathy in the masses. Therefore, when the ailing Brezhnev finally died in 1982, his successor, the long-time chief of the secret police, Yuri Andropov, tried to invigorate the system. Andropov introduced modest reforms to improve economic performance and campaigned against worker absenteeism and high-level corruption. Relatively little came of these efforts, for both Andropov and his successor died in office in little more than a year. But Andropov's efforts combined with the dreary procession of state funerals in Red Square to set the stage for the emergence in March 1985 of Mikhail Gorbachev, the most vigorous Soviet leader in a generation.

The fifty-four-year-old Gorbachev was smart, charming, and tough. As long-time Soviet foreign minister Andrei Gromyko reportedly said, "This man has a nice smile, but he has got iron teeth."[7] In his first year in office, Gorbachev attacked corruption and incompetence in the upper reaches of the bureaucracy. Gorbachev launched a strong campaign against alcoholism and drunkenness, which were also deadly scourges of Soviet society. He seemed determined to use tough measures to make both the elite and the masses "shape up," so that the economy would perform better while the Communist party as a whole maintained firm control.

The new Soviet leader also seemed tough and determined in international affairs. He and his colleagues made clear that they would not permit any major deviation from the Communist model in eastern Europe, like the one that had only recently occurred in Poland (see discussion below). Gorbachev repeatedly attacked President Reagan's plan to build a space shield against nuclear missiles, popularly known as "Star Wars," and tried to exploit existing differences between the United States and its European allies on defense matters. The outcome of all these initiatives was uncertain in early 1986, but Mikhail Gorbachev seemed firmly in command and a leader to be reckoned with.

The Solidarity Revolution

While Soviet leaders seemed quite secure in the last years of the Brezhnev era, their satellite empire witnessed a spectacular resurgence of popular protest. Polish workers joined together en masse to fight peacefully for freedom and self-determination, while the world watched in amazement.

Poland was an unruly satellite from the beginning. Stalin said that introducing communism to Poland was like putting a saddle on a cow. Efforts to saddle the cow—really a spirited stallion—led to widespread riots in1956 (see page 981). As a result, the Polish Communists dropped efforts to impose Soviet-style collectivization on the peasants and to break the Roman Catholic church. Most agricultural land remained in private hands as the Catholic church thrived. Long a symbol of Poland's powerful patriotism, the Catholic church succeeded in holding the allegiance of rural people as they poured into the new industrial centers. With an independent agriculture and a vigorous church, the Communists failed to monopolize society.

They also failed to manage the economy effectively. The 1960s saw little economic improvement. When the government suddenly announced large price increases right before Christmas in 1970, Poland's working class rose again in angry protest. Factories were occupied and strikers were shot, but Wladyslaw Gomulka fell from power. Edward Gierek, the new Communist leader, then wagered that massive inflows of Western capital and technology, especially from a now-friendly West Germany, could produce a Polish "economic miracle" that would win popular support for the regime. Instead, bureaucratic incompetence coupled with worldwide recession put the economy into a nose dive by the mid-1970s. Workers, intellectuals, and the church became increasingly restive. Then the real "Polish miracle" occurred: Cardinal Karol Wojtyla, archbishop of Krakow, was elected pope in 1978. In June 1979, he returned for an astonishing pilgrimage across his native land. Preaching love of Christ and country and the "inalienable rights of man," Pope John Paul II electrified the Polish nation. The economic crisis became a spiritual crisis as well.

In August 1980, as scattered strikes to protest higher meat prices spread, the 16,000 workers at the gigantic Lenin Shipyards in Gdansk (formerly known as Danzig), laid down their tools and occupied the showpiece plant. As other workers along the Baltic coast joined "in solidarity," the strikers advanced truly revolutionary demands: the right to form free trade unions, the right to strike, freedom of speech, release of political prisoners, and economic reforms. After eighteen days of shipyard occupation, as families brought food to the gates and priests said mass daily amid huge overhead cranes, the government gave in and accepted the workers' demands in the Gdansk Agreement. In a state where the Communist party claimed to rule on behalf of the proletariat, a working-class revolt had won an unprecedented victory.

Led by a feisty Lenin Shipyards electrician and devout Catholic named Lech Walesa, the workers proceeded to organize their free and democratic trade union. They called it "Solidarity." Joined by intellectuals and supported by the Catholic church, Solidarity became the union of a nation. By March 1981, it had a membership of 9.5 million, of 12.5 million who were theoretically eligible. A full-time staff of 40,000 linked the union members and their sections together with modern communications technology and vital information. Solidarity created its own press service and published newspapers, as cultural and intellectual freedom blossomed in Poland. Solidarity's leaders had tremendous well-organized support, and the threat of calling a nationwide strike gave them real power in ongoing negotiations with the Communist bosses who replaced Gierek.

But if Solidarity had power, it did not try to take power. History, the Brezhnev Doctrine, and virulent

The Rise of Solidarity This photo shows the determination and mass action that allowed Polish workers to triumph in August 1980. Backed by a crowd of enthusiastic supporters, leader Lech Walesa announces the historic Gdansk Agreement to striking workers at the main gate of the Lenin Shipyards. *(Jean Gaumy/Magnum)*

attacks from Communist neighbors all guaranteed the intervention of the Red Army if Polish Communists "lost control." And since Poland's 35 million population had a long tradition of fierce patriotism and romantic revolt against both Russians and Germans, a terrible bloodbath would be the inevitable tragic consequence. Thus the Solidarity revolution was always a "self-limiting revolution," aiming at defending the cultural and trade union freedoms won in the Gdansk Agreement, without directly challenging the Communist monopoly of political power.

Solidarity's combination of strength and moderation explains why it lasted so long before it was crushed. The Soviet Union, already condemned worldwide for its invasion of Afghanistan, decided to play a waiting game of threats and pressure. After a crisis in March 1981 that followed police beatings of Solidarity activists, Walesa settled for minor government concessions, and Solidarity again dropped plans for a massive general strike. It was a turning point. Criticism of Walesa's moderate leadership and calls for local self-government in unions and factories grew. Solidarity lost its cohesiveness. The worsening economic crisis also encouraged grassroots radicalism and frustration: a hunger-march banner proclaimed that "A hungry nation can eat its rulers."[8] With an eye on Western public opinion, the Polish Communist leadership shrewdly denounced Solidarity for promoting economic collapse and provoking Russian invasion. In December 1981, the Communist leader General Jaruzelski suddenly struck in the dead of subfreezing night, proclaiming martial law and cutting all communications, arresting Solidarity's leaders and "saving" the nation.

The rise and fall of Solidarity was a major historical development. Jaruzelski's "invasion by proxy" again showed the Soviet Union's determination to maintain communist orthodoxy in its Eastern empire, which clearly rested on fear and old-fashioned military might. But the Solidarity revolution also showed the enduring appeal of other old-fashioned values—cultural freedom, trade union rights, patriotic nationalism, and Catholic piety. And the fact that Poland lived enthusiastically by these values for sixteen months meant that General Jaruzelski proceeded cautiously with communist "normalization." Solidarity failed, but only in part.

THE FUTURE IN PERSPECTIVE

What about the future? For centuries, astrologers and scientists, experts and ordinary people, have been trying to answer this question. Although it may seem that the study of what has been has little to say about what will be, the study of history over a long period is actually very useful in this regard. It helps put the future in perspective.

In 1931 a distinguished Harvard professor of genetics examined the prospects for the human race in an article read by millions. Among his predictions was that "in the year 2500 the population of the world should be about 3,500 millions, or about twice the figures of today."[9] In fact, the population of the world reached 4 billion in the 1970s and, outside the highly developed countries of Europe and North America, is still growing rapidly. The six-century projection of the learned expert was proved dead wrong in less than fifty years (see Map 32.3).

History is full of such erroneous predictions, a few of which we have mentioned in this book. Yet lack of success has not diminished the age-old desire to look into the future. Self-proclaimed experts even pretend that they have created a new science of futurology. With great pomposity they often act as if their hunches and guesses about future human developments were inescapable realities. Yet the study of history teaches healthy skepticism regarding such predictions, however scientific they may appear. Past results suggest that most such predictions will simply not come true, or not in the anticipated way. Thus history provides some psychological protection from the fantastic visions of modern astrologers.

This protection is particularly valuable today, because a great many projections into the future are quite pessimistic, just as they were very optimistic in the 1950s and 1960s. Many people in the Western world seem convinced that conditions are going to get worse rather than better. They fear, for example, that trade wars will permanently cripple the world economy, that pollution will destroy the environment, and that the traditional family will disappear. Until very recently, many experts and politicians were predicting that the energy crisis—in the form of skyrocketing oil prices—meant disaster, in the form of lower standards of living at best and the collapse of civilization at worst. Now some of these same experts worry that the unexpected sharp decline in oil prices will bankrupt both Third World oil producers, such as Mexico, and the large American banks that have lent them so much money. It is heartening to know that most such predictions will almost certainly not prove true, just as the same knowledge of likely error is sobering in more optimistic ages.

One of the more frightening and pessimistic predictions currently in vogue is that the northern nations of Europe and North America will increasingly find themselves locked in a life-and-death struggle with the poor, overpopulated southern nations of Africa, Asia, and South America. This North-South conflict, it is predicted, will replace the cold war struggle of East and West with a much more dangerous international class and race conflict of rich versus poor, white versus colored. Such, it is said, is the bitter legacy of Western imperialism.

As Map 32.4 shows, there is indeed an enormous gap between the very wealthy nations of noncommunist western Europe and North America and the very poor nations of much of Africa and Asia. Yet closer examination does not reveal a growing split between two sharply defined economic camps. On the contrary, there are five or six distinct categories of nations in terms of income level. The communist

Map 32.3 World Population Density Population densities vary enormously. The highest densities are in western Europe and east Asia. The United States and the Soviet Union are both sparsely populated, with most people concentrated in a few large urban areas.

Map 32.4 Estimated GNP per Capita Income in the Early 1980s

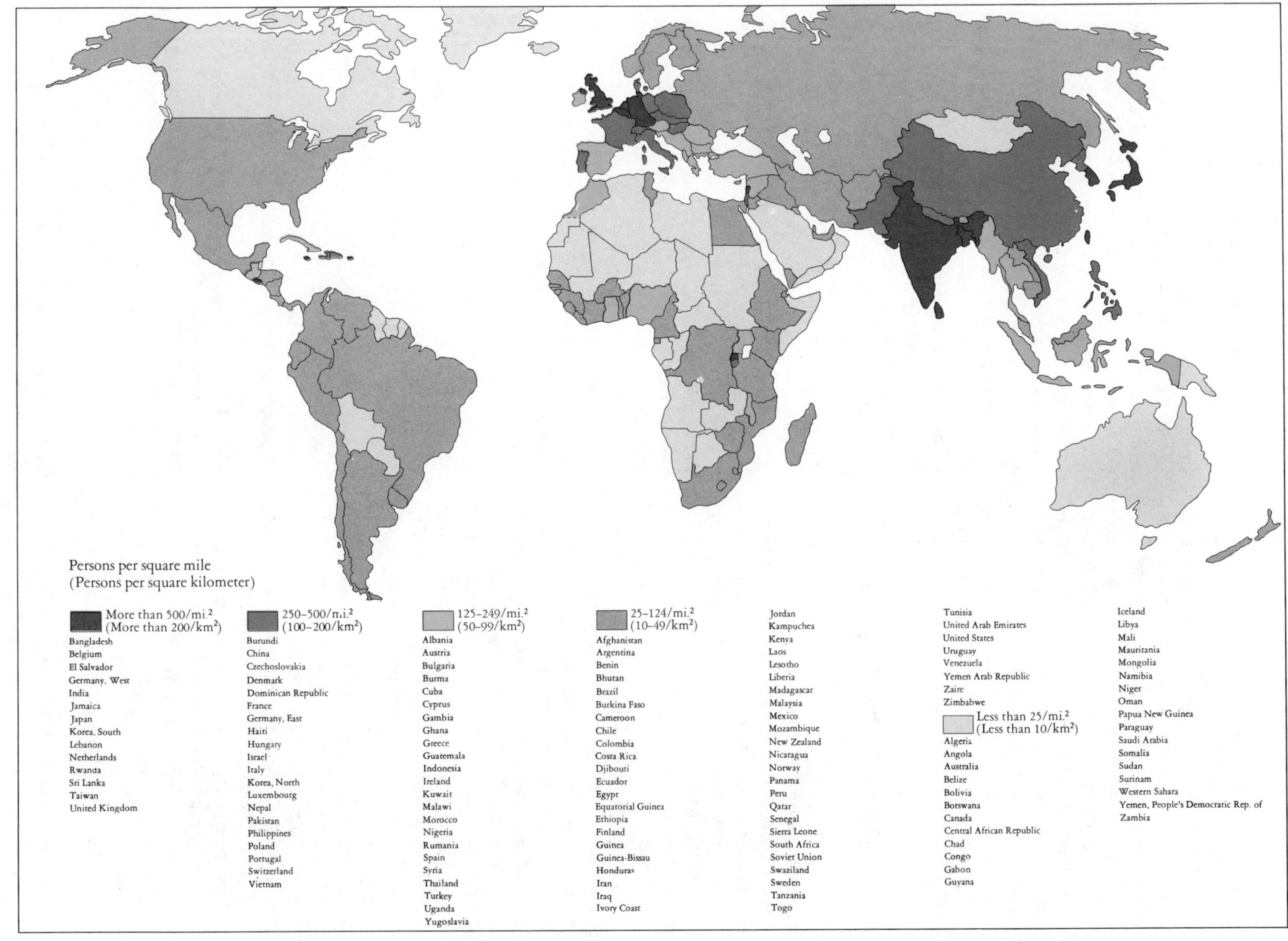

Persons per square mile
(Persons per square kilometer)
More than 500/mi.^{2} (More than 200/km^2)
Bangladesh
Belgium
El Salvador
Germany, West
India
Jamaica
Japan
Korea, South
Lebanon
Netherlands
Rwanda
Sri Lanka
Taiwan
United Kingdom
250–500/mi.^{2} (100–200/km^2)
Burundi
China
Czechoslovakia
Denmark
Dominican Republic
France
Germany, East
Haiti
Hungary
Israel
Italy
Korea, North
Luxembourg
Nepal
Pakistan
Philippines
Poland
Portugal
Switzerland
Vietnam
125–249/mi.^{2} (50–99/km^2)
Albania
Austria
Bulgaria
Burma
Cuba
Cyprus
Gambia
Ghana
Greece
Guatemala
Indonesia
Ireland
Kuwait
Malawi
Morocco
Nigeria
Rumania
Spain
Syria
Thailand
Turkey
Uganda
Yugoslavia
25–124/mi.^{2} (10–49/km^2)
Afghanistan
Argentina
Benin
Bhutan
Brazil
Burkina Faso
Cameroon
Chile
Colombia
Costa Rica
Djibouti
Ecuador
Egypt
Equatorial Guinea
Ethiopia
Finland
Guinea
Guinea-Bissau
Honduras
Iran
Iraq
Ivory Coast
Jordan
Kampuchea
Kenya
Laos
Lesotho
Liberia
Madagascar
Malaysia
Mexico
Mozambique
New Zealand
Nicaragua
Norway
Panama
Peru
Qatar
Senegal
Sierra Leone
South Africa
Soviet Union
Swaziland
Sweden
Tanzania
Togo
Tunisia
United Arab Emirates
United States
Uruguay
Venezuela
Yemen Arab Republic
Zaire
Zimbabwe
Less than 25/mi.^{2} (Less than 10/km^2)
Algeria
Angola
Australia
Belize
Bolivia
Botswana
Canada
Central African Republic
Chad
Congo
Gabon
Guyana
Iceland
Libya
Mali
Mauritania
Mongolia
Namibia
Niger
Oman
Papua New Guinea
Paraguay
Saudi Arabia
Somalia
Sudan
Surinam
Western Sahara
Yemen, People's Democratic Rep. of
Zambia

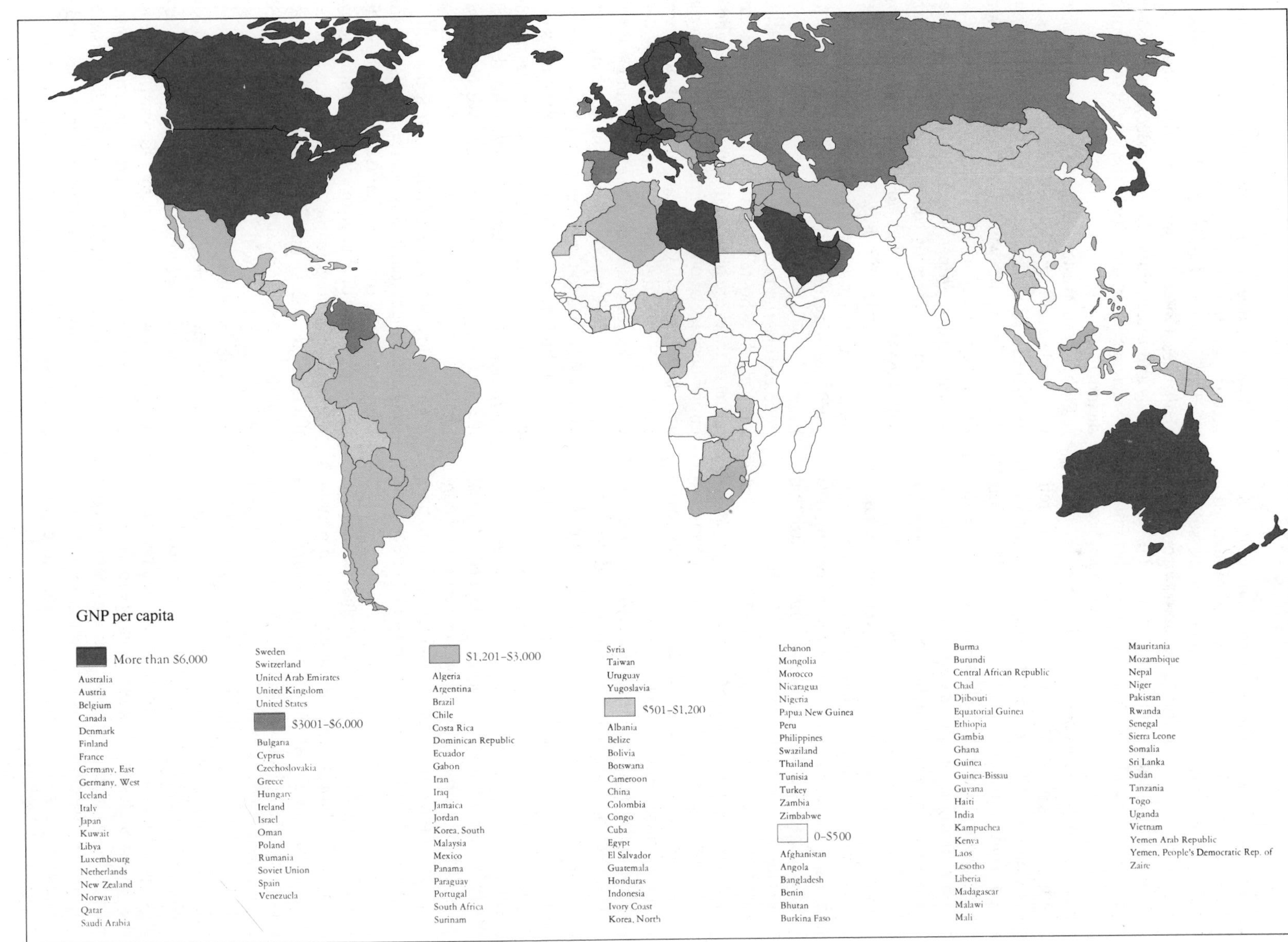
GNP per capita
More than $6,000
Australia
Austria
Belgium
Canada
Denmark
Finland
France
Germany, East
Germany, West
Iceland
Italy
Japan
Kuwait
Libya
Luxembourg
Netherlands
New Zealand
Norway
Qatar
Saudi Arabia
Sweden
Switzerland
United Arab Emirates
United Kingdom
United States
$3001–$6,000
Bulgaria
Cyprus
Czechoslovakia
Greece
Hungary
Ireland
Israel
Oman
Poland
Rumania
Soviet Union
Spain
Venezuela
$1,201–$3,000
Algeria
Argentina
Brazil
Chile
Costa Rica
Dominican Republic
Ecuador
Gabon
Iran
Iraq
Jamaica
Jordan
Korea, South
Malaysia
Mexico
Panama
Paraguay
Portugal
South Africa
Surinam
Syria
Taiwan
Uruguay
Yugoslavia
$501–$1,200
Albania
Belize
Bolivia
Botswana
Cameroon
China
Colombia
Congo
Cuba
Egypt
El Salvador
Guatemala
Honduras
Indonesia
Ivory Coast
Korea, North
Lebanon
Mongolia
Morocco
Nicaragua
Nigeria
Papua New Guinea
Peru
Philippines
Swaziland
Thailand
Tunisia
Turkey
Zambia
Zimbabwe
0–$500
Afghanistan
Angola
Bangladesh
Benin
Bhutan
Burkina Faso
Burma
Burundi
Central African Republic
Chad
Djibouti
Equatorial Guinea
Ethiopia
Gambia
Ghana
Guinea
Guinea-Bissau
Guyana
Haiti
India
Kampuchea
Kenya
Laos
Lesotho
Liberia
Madagascar
Malawi
Mali
Mauritania
Mozambique
Nepal
Niger
Pakistan
Rwanda
Senegal
Sierra Leone
Somalia
Sri Lanka
Sudan
Tanzania
Togo
Uganda
Vietnam
Yemen Arab Republic
Yemen, People's Democratic Rep. of
Zaire

countries of eastern Europe form something of a middle-income group, as do the major oil-exporting states, which, contrary to common belief, are still behind the wealthier countries of western Europe. Poverty in parts of Latin America is severe, but as the map shows, standards of living are substantially higher there than in much of Africa and Asia, both of which encompass considerable variation.

When one considers differences in culture, religion, politics, and historical development, the supposed split between "rich" and "poor" nations breaks down still further. Thus a global class war between rich and poor appears unlikely in the foreseeable future. A more reasonable expectation is continuing pressure to reduce international economic differences through taxation and welfare measures, as has already occurred domestically in the wealthy nations. Such pressure may well bring at least modest success, for the wealthy nations generally realize that an exclusively Western viewpoint on global issues is unrealistic and self-defeating. The true legacy of Western imperialism is one small world.

It is this that makes the nuclear arms race so ominous. Not only do the United States and the Soviet Union possess unbelievably destructive, ever-expanding nuclear arsenals, but Great Britain, France, China, and India all have "the bomb," and probably Israel and South Africa do as well. Other countries are equipped or desire to "go nuclear" (see Map 32.2). Thus some gloomy experts have predicted that twenty or thirty states will have nuclear weapons in the 1990s. In a world increasingly plagued by local wars and ferocious regional conflicts, they have concluded that nuclear war is almost inevitable and have speculated that the human race is an "endangered species."

Such predictions and the undeniable seriousness of the arms race appear to have jolted Western populations out of their customary fatalism regarding nuclear weapons, at least temporarily. Efforts to reduce or even halt the nuclear buildup in the Soviet Union and the NATO alliance have blossomed again. Moreover, the recent revival of the antinuclear movement has drawn broad popular support and enlisted creditable mainstream leaders, such as Catholic bishops in the United States and Protestant clergy in West Germany. An optimist can hope that comparable concern in non-Western areas may yet develop to help create the global political will necessary to control nuclear proliferation before it is too late.

Whatever does or does not happen, the study of history puts the future in perspective in other ways. We have seen that every age has its problems and challenges. Others before us have trod these paths of crisis and uncertainty. This knowledge helps save us from exaggerated self-pity in the face of our own predicaments.

Perhaps our Western heritage may even inspire us with pride and measured self-confidence. We stand, momentarily, at the end of the long procession of Western civilization winding through the ages. Sometimes the procession has wandered, or backtracked, or done terrible things. But it has also carried the efforts and sacrifices of generations of toiling, struggling ancestors. Through no effort of our own, we are the beneficiaries of those sacrifices and achievements. Now that it is our turn to carry the torch onward, we may remember these ties with our forebears.

To change the metaphor, we in the West are like a card player who has been dealt many good cards. Some of them are obvious, like our technical and scientific heritage or our commitments to human rights and the individual. Others are not so obvious, sometimes half-forgotten or even hidden up the sleeve. One thinks, for example, of the Christian Democrats, the moderate Catholic party, which emerged after World War Two to play such an important role in the western European renaissance. Or one thinks of the dismantling of colonial empires, which was a victory of Western ideals of liberty and nationhood as well as a defeat for Western imperialism. We hold a good hand.

Our study of history, of mighty struggles and fearsome challenges, of shining achievements and tragic failures, gives a sense of what is the essence of life itself: the process of change over time. Again and again we have seen how peoples and societies evolve, influenced by ideas, human passions, and material conditions. As sure as anything is sure, this process of change over time will continue, as the future becomes the present and then the past. And students of history are better prepared to make sense of this unfolding process because they have already observed it. They know how change goes forward, on the basis of existing historical forces, and their projections will probably be as good as those of the futurologists. Students of history are also prepared for the new and unexpected in human development, for they have already seen great breakthroughs and revolutions.

They have an understanding of how things really happen.

NOTES

1. Quoted by W. Laqueur, *Europe Since Hitler,* Penguin Books, Baltimore, 1972, p. 9.
2. *Wall Street Journal,* June 25, 1985, pp. 1, 20.
3. Quoted by Kessing's Research Report, *Germany and East Europe Since 1945: From the Potsdam Agreement to Chancellor Brandt's "Ostpolitik,"* Charles Scribner's Sons, New York, 1973, pp. 284–285.
4. Quoted by S. E. Morison et al., *A Concise History of the American Republic,* Oxford University Press, New York, 1977, p. 735.
5. Richard Nixon, *Public Papers, 1969,* U.S. Government Printing Office, Washington, D.C., 1971, p. 371.
6. Quoted by H. Smith, *The Russians,* Quadrangle/New York Times, New York, 1976, pp. 455–456.
7. Quoted in *Time,* January 6, 1986, p. 66.
8. T. G. Ash, *The Polish Revolution: Solidarity,* Charles Scribner's Sons, New York, 1983, p. 186.
9. E. M. East, in *Scientific Monthly,* April 1931; also in *Reader's Digest* 19 (May 1931): 151.

SUGGESTED READING

Many of the studies cited in the Suggested Reading for Chapters 30 and 31 are also of value for the years since 1968. Journalistic accounts in major newspapers and magazines are also invaluable tools for an understanding of recent developments. Among general works W. Laqueur, *Europe Since Hitler,* rev. ed. (1982), and W. Keylor, *The Twentieth Century: An International History* (1984), are particularly helpful with their extensive, up-to-date bibliographies. B. Jones, *The Making of Contemporary Europe* (1980), is a good brief account, while G. Parker, *The Logic of Unity* (1975), analyzes the forces working for and against European integration. D Swann, *The Economics of the Common Market,* 5th ed. (1984), carries developments into the 1980s. L. Barzini, *The Europeans* (1983), draws engaging group portraits of the different European peoples today and is strongly recommended. On West Germany since 1968, L. Whetten, *Germany's Ostpolitik* (1971), and W. Patterson and G. Smith, eds., *The West German Model: Perspectives on a Stable State* (1981), are good introductions. Willy Brandt eloquently states his case for reconciliation with the East in *A Peace Policy for Europe* (1969). The spiritual dimension of West German recovery is probed by G. Grass in his world-famous novel *The Tin Drum* (1963), as well as in the novels of H. Böll. W. Laqueur, *The Germans* (1985), is a highly recommended contemporary report by a famous historian doubling as a journalist.

Among the many books to come out of the Czechoslovak experience in 1968, three are particularly recommended: H. Schwartz, *Prague's 200 Days: The Struggle for Democracy in Czechoslovakia* (1969); I. Svitak, *The Czechoslovak Experiment, 1968–1969* (1971); and Z. Zeman, *Prague Spring* (1969). T. Ash, *The Polish Revolution: Solidarity* (1983), is the best book on the subject and is highly recommended. It may be compared with a less sympathetic account by N. Ascherson, *The Polish August: The Self-Limiting Revolution* (1982). A. Bramberg, ed., *Poland: Genesis of a Revolution* (1983), is a valuable collection of documents with extensive commentary, while R. Leslie, *The History of Poland Since 1863* (1981), provides long-term perspective. On the Soviet Union, in addition to works cited in Chapter 30, D. Shipler, *Russia: Broken Idols, Solemn Dreams* (1983), is a solid report by an American journalist, while A. Shevchenko, *Breaking with Moscow* (1985), is the altogether fascinating autobiography of a top Russian diplomat who defected to the United States. A. De Porte, *Europe Between the Superpowers: The Enduring Balance* (1979), and J. Hough and M. Fainsod, *How the Soviet Union Is Governed* (1979), are major scholarly studies.

Among innumerable works on recent economic developments, L. Thurow, *The Zero-Sum Society* (1981), is an interesting example of early 1980s pessimism in the United States, and it may be compared with the engaging and informative work by J. Eatwell, *Whatever Happened to Britain? The Economics of Decline* (1982). W. Rostow, *The World Economy: History and Prospect* (1977), is a massive scholarly tome by a perennial optimist, and P. Hawkins, *The Next Economy* (1983), contains intelligent insights that merit consideration by the ordinary citizen. Three major intellectual works, which are rather somber in their projections, are R. Heilbroner, *An Inquiry into the Human Prospect* (1974), and J. Revel, *The Totalitarian Temptation* (1977) and *How Democracies Perish* (1983).

CHAPTER OPENER CREDITS

NOTES ON THE ILLUSTRATIONS

CHAPTER OPENER CREDITS

Title page: Louvre/Cliché des Musées Nationaux
Chapter 21: Versailles/Cliché des Musées Nationaux
Chapter 22: Süddeutscher Verlag
Chapter 23: Historical Pictures Service, Chicago
Chapter 24: BBC Hulton/The Bettmann Archive
Chapter 25: Library of Congress
Chapter 26: Sir J. Benjamin Stone Collection, Birmingham Public Libraries
Chapter 27: Süddeutscher Verlag
Chapter 28: Historical Pictures Service, Chicago
Chapter 29: Archiv/Photo Researchers
Chapter 30: Leonard Freed/Magnum
Chapter 31: Henri Cartier-Bresson/Magnum
Chapter 32: Mark Antman/The Image Works

NOTES ON THE ILLUSTRATIONS

Page 666 Jacques-Louis David (French, 1748–1825), *The Tennis Court Oath.*

Page 673 John Trumbull (American, 1756–1843), *The Declaration of Independence.* Oil on canvas, 1786. 21⅛ by 31⅛ inches.

Page 674 E. C. Mills, *Signing of Treaty of Amity and Commerce and of Alliance between France and the United States.*

Page 675 This portrait of Louis XVI by Joseph-Siffrein Duplessis, French portrait painter (1725–1802), hangs in the Marie Antoinette Gallery at Versailles.

Page 679 This drawing by Persin de Prieur, "Premier assaut contre La Bastille," can be seen in the Musée Carnavalet, Paris.

Page 685 "Un Comité révolutionnaire sous la Terreur," after Alexandre Évariste Fragonard, French historical painter (1780–1850).

Page 689 Jacques-Louis David (French, 1748–1825), *Napoleon Crossing the Alps.* Oil on canvas.

Page 699 Fritz the giant steam hammer at the Krupp steelworks in Germany, photographed on 16 September 1861.

Page 702 James Hargreaves (d. 1778), English inventor, weaver, and mechanic, invented the spinning jenny about 1765.

Page 705 Engraving by Henry Beighton, 1717, of the atmospheric steam engine invented about 1705 by Thomas Newcomen, English blacksmith (1663–1729).

Page 707 The Northern locomotive *Fire Fly* on a narrow field bridge. Photo by Matthew Brady (American, 1823–1896), famous photographer of the Civil War.

Page 708 Honoré Daumier (1808–1879), *The Third-Class Carriage.* Oil on canvas. Daumier was both a caricaturist and a serious painter.

Page 712 The Cockerill works at Seraing, Belgium, at night. Lithograph by E. Toovey, Brussels, 1852.

Page 713 Royal visit to steelworks in Crewe, Cheshire: the tire-expanding machine, February 1866.

Page 718 The textile factory of Messrs Swainson, Birley and Co. near Manchester, extant until 1966: 7 stories high, 158 yards long, 18 yards wide, 660 windows, 32,500 panes of glass. The building was subsequently taken over by Horrock, Crewdson and renamed Fishwich Mills.

Page 719 From *Parliamentary Papers,* 1842, vol. XV.

Page 726 "Proclamation of the Roman Republic," 1848 lithograph by Bertarelli, Milan.

Page 731 Yohann Hochle, *Ball in the Winter Riding School,* 1815.

Page 733 *Count Clemens von Metternich* (1773–1859) by Sir Thomas Lawrence, English painter (1769–1830).

Page 740 Left to right: K. Marx, F. Engels (rear), with Marx's daughters: Jenny, Eleanor, and Laura, photographed in the 1860s.

Page 742 Eugene Delacroix (1798–1863), French painter and leader of the Romantic school.

Page 745 *Liszt am Klavier,* 1840, by Josef Danhauser, German painter (1805–1845).

Page 747 Eugene Delacroix (French, 1798–1863), *Les Massacres de Scio.* Louvre. This dramatic interpretation of a contemporary event scandalized Paris Salon visitors in 1824.

Page 749 From *Punch,* 1846. The humorous weekly *Punch*—founded in 1841 by the British journalist and sociologist Henry Mayhew (1812–1887) and others—is the most famous of its kind. Its cartoons and caricatures became a powerful vehicle of political and social comment.

Page 752 *The Legislative Belly,* lithograph by Honoré Daumier (1808–1879).

Page 760 Paul Gustav Doré (French illustrator and painter, 1833–1883), *Over London by Rail* from his *London,* published in 1872.

Page 764 "The Court for King Cholera," cartoon from *Punch,* XXIII (1852), 139.

Page 768 Cross-section of a Parisian house, about 1850, from Edmund Texier, *Tableauade Paris,* Paris, 1852, vol. I, p. 65.

Page 770 Opening of steam-propelled tramways by the locomotive *Harding* in Paris between the railroad stations of Montparnasse and Austerlitz. From *L'Illustration,* 19 August 1876.

Page 774 *Un Coin de Table,* 1904, by Paul-Émile Chabas, French painter (1869–1937). Oil on canvas.

Page 778 Market for servants, situated just outside the ancient boundary wall (the Kitai Yard) of Moscow and open every day of the year, Sundays being the busiest. From *The Illustrated London News,* 1 November 1850, p. 458. England had no fully illustrated newspaper until the first number of the weekly *Illustrated London News* appeared on 14 May 1842, with 16 printed pages and 32 woodcuts.

Page 791 Sir Frederick William Burton (Irish watercolorist, 1816–1900), portrait of George Eliot (Mary Anne Cross), 1865.

Page 794 From *Album of Photographic Views, 1890–1899, for the Construction of the Novoselitsa Branches of the Southwestern Railway in the Ukraine.*

Page 798 Demolition of part of the Latin Quarter in 1860. Engraving from a drawing by Félix Thorigny.

Page 810 Merchants of Nijni-Novgorod drinking tea. From *L'Illustration,* 29 August 1905.

Page 816 Assassination of 62 hostages in Haxo Road, Belville, France, by the Communards, 1872.

Page 826 Sir Benjamin Stone's photograph of a steamer on the Aswan Dam in 1907. Giant statues of Ramses II guard the ancient Egyptian rock temples he built at Abu Simbel. These were preserved at vast expense when the Aswan Dam was rebuilt in the 1960s and its rising water level threatened to flood them.

Page 836 Ellis Island pens, photographed in 1907.

Page 855 Min-Chiang-Chek, prisoner number 7 who was condemned to death for murdering missionaries at Kucheng. *The Graphic,* 23 November 1895.

Page 861 *The Congress at Berlin in 1878* by Anton von Werner, German painter of portraits and historical subjects (1843–1915).

Page 876 Panoramic view of Sackville Street and wharf area heavily shelled by British gunboat on Liffey River during the Easter Rising. *The Graphic,* 1916.

Page 894 Berlin family living in railway boxcar after World War I.

Page 900 Edmund Engelmann took this and other photographs secretly in May 1938 while Freud's apartment was under surveillance by the Gestapo. His chance for survival was about 50 percent. When leaving Vienna it was too dangerous for him to take the negatives, so he left them with an acquaintance. After the war this acquaintance had died, and Engelmann recovered these unique photographs only with great difficulty.

Page 904 Frank Lloyd Wright (American architect, 1869–1959), Falling Water, Bear Run, Pennsylvania—perhaps the greatest modern house in America, 1936. The largely self-taught Wright was an exponent of what he called "organic architecture": the idea that a building should blend in with its setting and be harmonious with nature.

Page 906 *Guernica,* 1937, by Pablo Picasso, Spanish painter and sculptor (1881–1973). The original oil on canvas, 11 feet, 5½ inches high by 25 feet, 5¾ inches wide, is in the Museo del Prado, Madrid.

Page 908 Mary Pickford (1893–1979) photographed by Hartsook in 1918. Rudolph Valentino (1895–1926) as he appeared in *Four Horsemen of the Apocalypse* (1921).

Page 920 Scene in San Francisco in 1934, photographed by Dorothea Lange.

Page 927 100,000 Nazi Storm Troopers gathered in the Luitpodarena in Nuremberg, Germany, to hear Adolf Hitler on Brown Shirt Day at the Nazi Party convention, 20 September 1936.

Page 929 French caricature by C. Leavdre, 1898.

Page 949 The cartoon "Stepping Stones to Glory" by Sir David Low (1891–1963) appeared in the London *Evening Standard* on 8 July 1936.

Page 956 East German troops supervising construction workers at the Berlin Wall, photographed from West Berlin.

Page 963 Rabaul Harbor, New Britain. U.S. Air Force North American B-25 passing over Japanese ship.

Page 971 The *Deutscher Verlag* building in Berlin after impassable street had been cleared of rubble, photographed on 6 July 1945.

Page 986 Muro Central in the Palacio Nacional, Mexico City, painted 1929–1935 by José Clemente Orozco (1883–1949), Mexican painter of the modernist school.

Page 990 Demonstrators link arms across Boulevard St. Michel on Left Bank during Paris riots of May 1968.

Page 995 First atomic bomb test at Bikini Atoll, in photograph released 26 July 1946.

Page 997 Astronaut Edwin E. Aldrin, Jr., leaving the lunar module. Apollo II was launched in Florida on 16 July 1969. Astronauts Neil A. Armstrong and Aldrin landed on the moon on 20 July while Michael Collins circled in the main spacecraft until rejoined by the others on 21 July. The astronauts returned to Earth on 24 July, when they were picked up in the Pacific Ocean.

Page 1006 Students in the Boulevard Saint Michel in Paris protesting the closing of the surburban Nanterre University, photographed on 3 May 1968.

Page 1014 Nuclear plant in the Loire Valley of France.

INDEX

Absolutism: falls in France, 682
Abstract expressionism, 905–906
Acton, Sir John, 743
Adams, John, 671
Adenauer, Konrad, 970
Afghanistan, Soviet invasion of, 1029
Africa: Western imperialism in, 841–845; response to imperialism, 849–850; end of imperialism in, 976–978
Agriculture: role in Industrial Revolution, 700; effect of Industrial Revolution on, 775; collectivization in Russia, 933, 980
Aiguillon, duke of, 680
Akhmatova, Anna, 979
Albania, 865
Alexander, king of Yugoslavia, 928
Alexander I, tsar of Russia, 693, 694, 730, 732
Alexander II, tsar of Russia, 805, 811, 838
Alexander III, tsar of Russia, 811, 861
Alexandra, tsarina of Russia, 878–879
Alexandria, 834
Algeciras Conference, 863
Algeria, 841, 844, 974, 978
Alliance for Progress, 988
Alliance of the Three Emperors, 861
All Quiet on the Western Front (Remarque), 868–869
Alsace, 860, 889
Alvarez, Luis, 999
America. *See* North America; United States
American Challenge, The (Servan-Schreiber), 997
American Revolution: origins of, 670–672; colonies win independence, 672–673; framing of Constitution, 673–674; impact on Europe, 674–675
Amiens, Treaty of, 691
Anaximander, 788
Andropov, Yuri, 1036
Anglican church. *See* Church of England
Anglo-French Entente, 863
Anglo-Russian Agreement, 863
Anglo-Saxons, 863
Angola, 842, 1029
Anti-Corn Law League, 750
Anti-Semitism: Dreyfus affair, 817; in 19th-century Austria, 821; in Russia, 838–839, 1034; Nazism, 914, 929, 940, 945, 953
Antiwar movement, 1026
Apollo Program, 997
Arabi, Ahmed, 834
Arab-Israeli War, 1018–1019
Arabs: during W.W. I, 871; and African nationalism, 976–977; war with Israel, 1018–1019
Architecture: modern, 903–905
Argentina, immigration in, 837, 838–839, 985
Aristocracy: in 1900, 722. *See also* Nobility

Arkwright, Richard, 701
Arrow Cross, 927
Art: romantic movement, 741–743, 744–746; rise of realism, 790–792; modernism, 903, 905–907; and artist, in communist Russia, 934, 979; in Nazi Germany, 944
Artists. *See* Art
Ashton, T.S., 724
Asia: and Western imperialism, 831–833, 845; emigration from, 840; responses to imperialism, 849–856; end of imperialism in, 975–977
Astaire, Fred, 909
Astronomy: modern, 996
Atlantic Alliance, 1023–1030
Atlantic Charter, 958
Atomic bomb, 963, 994–996
Atomic physics, 996
Auden, W.H., 902
Auerstadt, battle of, 693
Augustine, bishop of Hippo Regius. *See* St. Augustine
Austerlitz, battle of, 693
Australia, 828, 829, 831, 836, 837, 840, 963
Austria: issues Declaration of Pillnitz, 683; and First Coalition against Napoleon, 683, 684, 685, 687; in Second Coalition, defeated, 691; in Third Coalition, 693; as Napoleon's ally, 693, 694; and balance of power struggle, 730; forms Holy Alliance, 732; empire described, 733–734; 1848 Revolution, 754–756; unification of Italy, 799–803; and unification of Germany, 803–808; and Austro-Hungarian Empire, 820–821; system of alliances, power blocs before 1914, 860–864; in Balkan Wars, 864–866; in W.W. I, 871, 876; independent republic proclaimed, 886–887; 1919 peace treaty, 891; and Nazism, 940, 947, 950
Austro-Hungarian Empire, 820–821; in system of alliances, rival blocs before 1914, 860–864; in Balkan wars, 864–866; in W.W. I., 871, 876; surrenders to Allies, 886
Austro-Prussian War of 1866, 805–806
Authoritarianism, 926–929. *See also* Absolutism
Autobiography (Garibaldi), 801
Automobile, 706, 1003

Babies. *See* Infants
Bacon, Francis, 992
Bacterial revolution, 765–767
Balance of power, 730
Baldwin, Stanley, 909, 915–916
Balkans, 838, 860, 864–866
Balkan wars, 865–866
Balzac, Honoré de, 790
Banks, 700, 714, 916–918
Baring, Evelyn (Lord Cromer), 835
Barth, Karl, 902
Bastille, march on, 679–680
Bauhaus, 905
Baumgarten, Hermann, 807–808
Bay of Pigs, 987
Beethoven, Ludwig van, 744, 745–746
Belgium: industrialization of, 710, 714; in Africa, 842; Germany attacks, 866; in W.W. I, 867–868; atrocities in, 871; occupies Ruhr, 910–913; Nazis occupy, 951; post-W.W. II recovery, 972. *See also* Netherlands
Belgrade, bombardment of, 866
Bentham, Jeremy, 765
Berg, Alban, 907
Bergson, Henri, 896
Beria, Lavrenti, 980
Berlin, 756, 757, 842, 982
Berlin Wall, 982, 1023–1024
Bernal, John Desmond, 993
Bethmann-Hollweg, Theobald van, 866
Big Science, 996–998
Bill of Rights, American, 668, 673
Bill of Rights, English, 674
Birth control, 785, 1007, 1008
Birth of a Nation (film), 907
Birthrate: decline in, 785, 836, 1008, 1011
Bismarck, Otto von: in Revolution of 1848, 757; in unification of Germany, 804–808; as chancellor of German Empire, 813–814; calls imperialism conference, 842–844; and European system of alliances, 860–861
Black Hand, The, 866
Blacks: and civil rights movement, 983–984. *See also* Slavery
Blake, William, 716
Blanc, Louis, 739, 752, 753
Blitzkrieg, 950
Blum, Léon, 922
Boers, 842
Boer Wars, 842, 863
Bohemia, 733
Bolsheviks, 880–885, 934
Bonaparte, Louis Napoleon. *See* Napoleon III
Bonaparte, Napoleon. *See* Napoleon I
Borodino, battle of, 694
Bosnia, 860, 865–866
Boston Tea Party, 672
Bourbon dynasty, 694
Bourgeoisie: in Revolutionary France, 676; in Marxian socialism, 739–741
Boxer Rebellion, 856
Brandt, Willy, 1023–1025, 1028
Brassey, Thomas, 709
Brazil, 837, 839, 985–987
Brazza, Pierre de, 842
Breast-feeding. *See* Nursing of babies
Brest-Litovsk, Treaty of, 884, 930
Brezhnev, Leonid, 982
Brezhnev Doctrine, 1032
Briand, Aristide, 913
Bright, John, 750
Britain. *See* England; Great Britain
Britain, Battle of, 951
British Empire. *See* Great Britain
Brothers Karamazov, The (Dostoevsky), 786
Brunel, Isambard Kingdom, 709
Brüning, Heinrich, 942
Bulgaria: independence from Ottoman, 820; in Balkan wars, 865; in W.W. I, 871; in 1919 peace treaty, 891; forced into alliance with Germany, 951; Russia occupies, 965

Bullitt, William, 964
Burckhardt, Jacob, 799
Burke, Edmund, 682
Byron, George Gordon, 743, 746

Cabinet of Dr. Caligari, The (film), 908
Cairo, 834
Camus, Albert, 901
Canada: French, British control of, 828; immigration in, 836, 837
Canton, 832
Capital (Marx), 822
Capitalism: and Industrial Revolution, 701, 714–715; and foreign investment, 830–831; Roosevelt's efforts to reform, 918–920
Cardenas, Lazaro, 982
Cardinals. *See* Papacy
Carlsbad Decrees, 732
Carter, Jimmy, 1020, 1029
Casablanca Conference, 959
Castle, The (Kafka), 903
Castlereagh, Robert Stewart, 730, 732, 735, 747
Castro, Fidel, 982, 987–988
Catherine II (the Great), empress of Russia: organizes League of Armed Neutrality, 672–673
Catholic church. *See* Roman Catholic church
Cavaignac, Louis, 754, 796
Cavour, Camillo Benso di, 801, 802–803
Central Powers, 871, 876
CERN (European Council for Nuclear Research), 996, 999, 1021
Cézanne, Paul, 905
Chadwick, Edwin, 716, 765
Chamberlain, Neville, 950
Champagne, 868
Chaplin, Charlie, 907
Charles X, king of France, 750–751
Chartist movement, 720, 750
Chaumont, Treaty of, 694
Cheka, 885
Chemistry, 787–788
Chiang Kai-shek, 975
Child labor, 703, 717–718
Child rearing. *See* Children; Family
Children: child labor, 703, 717–718; rearing of in 1900, 784–787; in W.W. I, 874. *See also* Family; Infants
Chile, 985
China: "opening" of, 833; emigrants from, 840; Russia in, 845; and response to imperialism, 854–856, civil war in, 966, 967; Mao in power, 975–976; Nixon in, 1026
Chopin, Frédéric, 744
Christ. *See* Jesus Christ
Christian church. *See* Christianity; Roman Catholic church
Christianity: and working classes in 1900, 778–779; and Western imperialism, 847–848; in modern age, 896, 901–902
Church of England: members as Irish landlords, 722
Churchill, Winston: on battle of Omdurman, 844; in W.W. II, 951, 958–964; at Teheran conference, 964–966; at Yalta conference, 965–966; "iron curtain" speech, 966; out of office, 973
Cities: effect of Industrial Revolution on, 717; 19th-century life in, 762–792; industry's effect on growth, 762–765; conditions in 19th century, 763–765; public health movement in, 765; urban planning, 767–771; development of public transportation, 769–771; social structures in, 771–772; middle classes in, 772–775; working classes in, 775–780; family life in, 780–787. *See also* Urban life
Civil Rights Act of 1964, 983
Civil rights movement, 983–984
Classicism: romantic movement as revolt against, 741
Class structure: 1900 urban, 771–780; changing modern, 1000–1002
Class struggle, in Marxian socialism, 739–740
Clemenceau, Georges, 876, 889
Clergy. *See* Christianity; Roman Catholic Church
Clermont (ship), 829
Climate: influence on Greek life, ; of Italy, ; Northumbrian, ;
Clothing: increased use of cotton, 702; consciousness of, in 1900, 774; "ready-made," 777
Coal, 704, 707
Coal and Steel Community, European, 974
Cobden, Richard, 750, 845
Cockerill, John, 711–712
Cockerill, William, 711
Coercive Acts, 672
Cold war, 964–968, 972
Coleridge, Samuel Taylor, 743
Collectivization, in Russia, 932–933
Cologne, 769
Colonialism: collapse of in Asia, Africa, 975–977. *See also* Imperialism
Combination Acts, 720
Comecon, 1020
Commerce: 19th-century growth of international, 828–830. *See also* Trade
Committee of Public Safety, 684–687
Common Market, 972, 974, 978
Commons. *See* Parliament, English
Common Sense (Paine), 672
Commune, Parisian, 815–816
Communications, international, 829
Communism: Bolsheviks renamed Communists, 884; and Lenin win out in Russian civil war, 885; in Germany, 914; in France, 921–922; in Spanish civil war, 922; as type of totalitarianism, 928; and Stalin in Russia from 1928, 929–936; in Germany, 942; expansion into eastern European cold war, 964–968; wins out in Chinese civil war, 966
Communist Manifesto (Marx), 739, 821, 880
Computers, electronic, 994, 1021–1022
Comte, Auguste, 788
Concorde (airplane), 996, 998
Condition of the Working Class in England, The (Engels), 716
Conference on Security and Cooperation in Europe, 1028
Congo, Belgian imperialism in, 842
Congress of Berlin, 860, 864

Congress of Troppau, 732
Congress of Vienna, 728, 730–731, 799
Conrad, Joseph, 849
Conservatism: Metternich's, 732–734; and authoritarianism, 926–928
Conservative party, British, 915, 921, 970
Constable, John, 741, 744
Constitutional Charters, France, 750, 751
Constitutional Convention, 673–674
Constitution of the U.S., 673–674
Consumer societies, modern, 1003–1005
Contemporary society. *See* Modern life
Continental system, Napoleon's, 693–694
Contraception. *See* Birth control
Coral Sea, battle of, 962
Corn Laws, 748–750
Cort, Henry, 706
Cottage industry: "sweated industries," 777
Cotton goods, 702
Council of Europe, 972
Craftspersons, in 1900, 775–776
Craft unions. *See* Unions, labor
Crédit Mobilier, 714, 739
Crick, Francis, 1000
Crimean War, 801, 809
Critique of Political Economy (Marx), 822
Cromer, Lord (Evelyn Baring), 835
Crompton, Samuel, 701–702
Crown of St. Stephen, 754
Crystal Palace fair, 709
Cuba, 840; missile crisis, 982; revolution in, 987–988
Cubism, 906
Curie, Marie, 897
Czechoslovakia: republic proclaimed, 886; joins Little Entente, 910; Nazis occupy, 950; Russia occupies, 965, 967; treaty with West Germany, 1025; Soviet invasion of, 1032–1033J
Czechs, 733, 737, 754–756

Dadaism, 906
"Daffodils" (Wordsworth), 743
Danton, Georges Jacques, 684, 687
Dardanelles, 871
Darwin, Charles, 789–790
da Vinci, Leonardo, 906
Dawes, Charles G., 913
Dawes plan, 913
Debt, international, 1020–1021
Declaration of Independence, 668, 672, 680
Declaration of Pillnitz, 683
Declaration of the Rights of Man, 668, 680, 690
Decline of the West (Spengler), 903
De Gasperi, Alcide, 969
De Gaulle, Charles, 961, 969, 974, 978, 1006
Delacroix, Eugène, 744, 746
Delcassé, Theophile, 863
Democracy: 19th-century ideas on, 736
Democracy in America (de Tocqueville), 753
Denikin, Anton, 885
Denmark: war over Schleswig-Holstein, 758, 805; Nazis occupy, 951
Depression of 1929, 916–922
Détente, 1028–1029
Diaghilev, Sergei, 907
Díaz, Porfirio, 985
Dictatorships. *See* Absolutism; Totalitarianism
Diet: in 18th century, 678; effect of Industrial Revolution on, 717; Irish dependence on potatoes, 723–724; of middle class in 1900, 773–774; in W.W. I, 873, 874; in post W.W. II era, 1003
Directory (French), 688, 689
Discrimination, racial. *See* Racism
Disease: venereal, 785; in 19th-century cities, 762, 765; bacterial revolution controls, 765–767. *See also* Medicine
Disraeli, Benjamin, 819, 845
Divorce: rising rate of, 1012
DNA, 1000
Doctors. *See* Physicians
Doctor Zhivago (Pasternak), 981
Domestic servants. *See* Servants
Dostoevsky, Feodor, 786
Double Helix, The (Watson), 1000
Dowries, 780
Dreiser, Theodore, 791
Dreyfus, Alfred, 817
Drinking: among working class in 1900, 776, 777–778
Droz, Gustave, 784
Drugs: opium trade, 832
Drunkenness. *See* Drinking
Dubček, Alexander, 1032
Duma, 812–813, 878, 879
Dumas, Alexander, 744
Dutch. *See* Holland; Netherlands

Eastern Europe: West's struggle with Stalin over, 966–967, 968; satellite regimes under Soviet rule, 978–980; under Khrushchev, 981; in postwar era, 1005; under Brezhnev, 1032–1033, 1034
Eastern Orthodox church. *See* Greek Orthodox church; Russian Orthodox church
Easter Rebellion, 876
East India Company, 672, 701, 852
East Indies, 845
Eating. *See* Diet
Economic Consequences of the Peace (Keynes), 910
Economy: crisis of, as cause of French Revolution, 675–677; of French Republic, 686–687; and the Industrial Revolution, 700–703, 707, 709–715, 716–717; theories of, 735–736, 738–741; growth of international, 828–835; in W.W. I, 872; German reparations, 909–913; post-W.W. I, inflation in western Europe, 912–913; Great Depression, 916–922; post-W.W. II recovery in western Europe, 968–974; postwar U.S., 983; in Latin America, 984–987; recent problems in, 1016–1019
Edo (Tokyo) Bay, 833
Education: importance of, in 1900, 774; free, compulsory in France, 817; Britain establishes school system in India, 852; in Stalinist Russia, 936; postwar changes in, 1005

Egypt: Napoleon campaign in, 688; West in, 834–835; British in, 842, 845, 962; Nasser in power, 978
Einstein, Albert, 897–899, 994
Eisenhower, Dwight D., 963, 981, 983, 1025
Eisenstein, Sergei, 909, 979
El Alamein, battle of, 962
Elba, Napoleon's escape from, 731
Electricity, 787–788
Elimination of Poverty, The (Louis Napoleon), 796
Eliot, George (Mary Ann Evans), 791
Eliot, T.S., 902, 903
Emigration. *See* Migrations
Empires. *See* Imperialism
Enabling Act, 944
Energy: and Industrial Revolution, 703–704; requirements for, sources of, 703–704; steam as source of, 704–706; law of conservation of, 787; research on atomic, 974; energy crisis of 1970s, 1017–1019, 1022
Engels, Friedrich, 716, 740
England: Industrial Revolution in, 700–710; continent uses industrial methods of, 710–714; new capital/labor classes, 714–720; romantic movement in, 741–746. *See also* Great Britain
Enlightenment: influence on liberalism, 669; romantic movement as revolt against, 741J
Entertainment. *See* Recreation
Environment, 993
Equality, concept of, 668–669, 674, 735
Erhard, Ludwig, 970–971
Essay on the Principle of Population (Malthus), 736
Estates (orders) of French society, 677–678
Estates General of France, 677, 678
Estonia, 951
Ethiopia, 842, 947, 950
Europe: revolutionary era, 668–695; in Industrial Revolution, 700–724; ideologies and upheavals, from 1815 to 1850, 728–758; urban life in, 762–787; triumph of science and thought, 787–792; age of nationalism, 796–824; expansion and imperialism, 828–856; World War I, 860–877; Russian Revolution, 878–885; peace settlement, 885–891; age of anxiety from 1919 to 1939, 896–922; rise of totalitarianism, 926–947; World War II, 947–953; war ends, recovery, cold war, 958–988; life in postwar era, 922–1012; economy of 1970s, 1980s, 1016–1023; Atlantic alliance, 1023–1030
European Coal and Steel Community, 974
European Council for Nuclear Research, 996, 999, 1021
European Economic Community, 974
Evolution, theory of, 788–790
Existentialism, 900–901
Expansion. *See* Overseas expansion
Exploration. *See* Overseas expansion
Expressionism, 905–906

Factories: rise of, in Industrial Revolution, 701–703, 708; working conditions in, 702–703, 717–720; child labor in, 703, 717–718; early owners of, 714–715; crafts transferred to, 775–776
Factory Act of 1833, 719
Fairbanks, Douglas, Sr., 907
Family: as economic unit in early factories, 718–719; urban, in 1900, 776, 780–787; postwar changes in, 1007–1009. *See also* Marriage
Famine: in 18th, 19th-century Ireland, 720–724; in 20th-century Russia, 930, 933
Faraday, Michael, 788
Farming. *See* Agriculture
Fascism: in France, 921; in Spain, 922; as type of totalitarianism, 928; in Italy, 936–939; in Germany, 939–947
Faulkner, William, 902
Federalists, 674
Federal Republic of Germany. *See* West Germany
Ferdinand I, emperor of Austria, 732, 754, 756
Ferry, Jules, 817, 842, 844, 845
Films. *See* Motion pictures
Finance, 1016–1017
First Continental Congress, 672
First (Communist) International, 822
First World War. *See* World War I
Five-year plans (Russia), 929–930, 932–934, 936, 979
Flaubert, Gustave, 790
Florence, 799
Food. *See* Diet
Ford, Gerald, 1027
Foreign investment, 830–831
Formosa, Japan takes from China, 854
Fouché, Joseph, 690
Foulon, Joseph François, 679
Fourier, Charles, 739
Fourteen Points, 888
France: aid for American Revolution, 672; first phase of revolution, 675–680; National Assembly, 677–678, 680, 681, 682; limited monarchy, 680–682; war with Austria-Prussia, 683; monarchy falls, second phase of Revolution, 683–687; Thermidorean reaction and the Directory, 688; Napoleon's reign, 688–695; industrialization of, 710, 714; Bourbon monarchy restored, 728; Napoleon reappears, exiled again, 731; utopian socialism in, 738–739; romantic movement in, 744; supports Greek independence, 746; Revolution of 1830, 750–751; Revolution of 1848, Second Republic, 751–754, 797; Louis Napoleon in power, 754, 796–799; in Crimean War, 801; in war with Prussia, 808; Third Republic falls, Paris Commune crushed, 815–816; stability to 1914, 816–817; Dreyfus affair, 817; in Egypt, 834; in Africa, 842–845; reasons for imperialism, 845–848; defeated in 1871, 860; courts Russia, 861; courts Britain, 863; Germany plans to attack, 866; in World War I, 867–877, 886; at peace conference, 888–892; German reparations, 909–913; occupies Ruhr, 910–913; attracts artists, 914; Great Depression, 921–922; and Nazi Germany expansionism, 947; falls to Germany, 951; post-W.W. II conditions, 968–969; recovery in, 972, 974; in Algeria, 974, 978; in Indochina, 976; student revolts in, 1005–1006
Francis II, Holy Roman emperor, 693
Francis Ferdinand, archduke of Austria, 683, 865
Francis Joseph, emperor of Austria, 756, 820, 876
Franco, Francisco, 950

Franco–Prussian War of 1870–71, 808, 860
Frankfurt National Assembly, 757–758
Frederick VII, king of Denmark, 758
Frederick William III, king of Prussia, 693
Frederick William IV, king of Prussia, 756–757, 758, 803
French Revolution: causes of, 675–677; first phase, 677–682; Austro–Prussian War as result of, 683; monarchy falls, second phase of, 683–687; Reign of Terror, 687; Thermidorean reaction, the Directory, 687; rise of Napoleon, 688
Freud, Sigmund, 786–787, 821, 899–900
Freudian psychology, 786–787, 899–900
Fulton, Robert, 829
Fundamental Laws, 812–813
Future, perspective on, 1039–1043

Gambetta, Léon, 817
Gandhi, Mahatma, 975
Garibaldi, Giuseppe, 801–803
Gasoline, from coal, 994
Gauguin, Paul, 905
Gdansk Agreement, 1037–1038
General Motors strike, 920
Gentz, Friedrich von, 683
George III, king of England, 672
Géricault, Théodore, 741
German Confederation of the Rhine: formed, 693, 732; in Revolution of 1848, 756–758; and unification of Germany, 803–806; dissolved, 806
German Empire: formed, 808; from 1871 to 1914, 813–815; wins Franco–Prussian War, 860; system of alliances, rival blocs before 1914, 860–864; supports Austria–Hungary in Balkan wars, 866; plans to attack France, Russia, 866; invades Belgium, W.W. I begins, 866; in W.W. I, 867–877, 886
Germanic peoples, 863
German Workers' Party. *See* Nazism
Germany: Napoleon in, 693; industrialization of, 710, 712–713; German Confederation formed, 732; romanticism in, 741; and Revolution of 1848, 756–758; unification as German Empire, 803–808; as national state, 813–815; unions in, 823–824; trade with Britain, 829–830; emigration from, 837, 838; in Africa, 842–844; in Asia, 845; reasons for imperialism, 845–848; system of alliances, rival blocs before 1914, 860–864; supports Austria–Hungary in Balkan wars, 866; plans to attack France, Russia, 866; invades Belgium, W.W. I begins, 866; in W.W. I, 876–877; Brest–Litovsk treaty with Russia, 884; war ends, revolution in, 886–888; reparation issue, 889, 909–913; occupation of Ruhr, 910–913; Weimar Republic's government, 914; Great Depression, 916–918; Nazi, as totalitarian state, 928–929, 939–947; expansionism, 947–953; British, French declare war on, 951; in W.W. II, 951–953, 958–965; post–W.W. II conditions, 968–969; economic recovery in West Germany, 970–971, 972
Germinal (Zola), 791
Germ theory of disease, 766
Gestapo, 945
Giereck, Edward, 1037
Gioberti, Vincenzo, 799
Girondists, 684
Gish, Lillian, 907
Gladstone, William, 819
Goebbels, Joseph, 942, 944
Goethe, Johann W., 743
Gold standard, 811, 918
Goldwater, Barry, 1025
Gomulka, Wladyslaw, 981, 1037
Gorbachev, Mikhail, 1033, 1036–1037
Government. *See* State
Grand Empire, Napoleon's, 693–694
Grand National Consolidated Trades Union, 720
Great Britain: reorganizes empire, imposes more taxes on colonies, 670–672; colonies rebel, 672–673; recognizes colonies' independence, 673; Republican France declares war on, 684; defeats Napoleon at Trafalgar, 693; forms Fourth Coalition, defeats again, 758; Industrial Revolution in, 700–714; Continent uses industrial methods, 710–714; new capital/labor classes, 714–720; nonindustrialization, famine in Ireland, 720–724; balance of power struggle after Napoleon's defeat, 730; opposes Spain's return to Latin America, 732; supports Greek independence, 746; liberal reform in, 746–750; growth of 19th-century cities, 762; in Crimean War, 801; extends suffrage, social welfare measures, 817–818; Irish demand home rule, 819; growth in trade, foreign investment, 828–831; in China, 832; in Egypt, 834–835; emigration from, 837; in Africa, 842, 844; in Asia, 845; reasons for imperialism, 845–848; in India, 851–853; rivalry with Germany, 861–864; declares war on Germany, W.W. I begins, 866; in W.W. I, 866–867, 886; at peace conference, 888–892; movies, radio in, 909; and German reparations, 909–913; in 1920s, 914–916; Great Depression, 916–918; recovery, reform in, 921–922; and Nazi Germany's expansionism, 947–950; in W.W. II, 951, 958–964; in cold war, 964–968; post–W.W. II conditions, 968–971; refuses to join economic plan, 972; loses India, other colonies, 975–976. *See also* England
Great Day of His Wrath, The (Martin painting), 741–742
Great Depression, 916–922, 942
Great Powers, 730, 746
Great Train Robbery (film), 907
Greece: national liberation movement, 746; in Balkan wars, 865; Nazis conquer, 951
Greek Orthodox church: and Greek national aspirations, 746
Greene, Graham, 902
Grimm, Jacob and Wilhelm, 744
Gromyko, Andrei, 1036
Gropius, Walter, 905
Guadalcanal, 962
Guernica (Picasso), 906–907
Guizot, François, 751
Gypsies, 953

Habsburg Dynasty: description of empire, 733–734; and Austrian Revolution of 1848, 754–756. *See also* Austro–Hungarian Empire; Holy Roman Empire

Halévy, Elie, 928
Hancock, John, 672
Hardy, Thomas, 791
Hargreaves, James, 701
Harkort, Fritz, 712–713
Haussmann, Georges, 767
Health. *See* Medicine
Heart of Darkness (Conrad), 849
Hébert, Jacques, 687
Hebrews. *See* Jews
Hegel, Georg, 740
Heidegger, Martin, 901
Heisenberg, Werner, 899
Hellas. *See* Greece
Hellenism. *See* Greece
Helsinki Conference, 1028–1029
Herder, Johann, 737
Hernani (Hugo), 744
Herzegovina, 860, 865
Highways. *See* Roads
Himmler, Heinrich, 947, 953
Hindenburg, Paul von, 871, 873, 942, 944
Hindus, 852, 853
Hiroshima, 963
History: as seen by romantics, 742–743
Hitler, Adolph, 821, 901, 909; collapse of beer hall plot, imprisoned, 914, 940; in power, domestic policies, 939–947; international policies, W.W. I, 947–953, 958–964; suicide, 963
Hobsbawm, Eric, 728
Hobson, J.A., 848–849
Ho Chi Minh, 976
Hoffmann, Ernst, 746
Holland: in Japan, 832; in Africa, 842; in Asia, 845; Nazis occupy, 951; post–W.W.II recovery, 972. *See also* Netherlands
Holstein, 758
Holy Alliance, 732
Holy Roman Empire: abolished by Napoleon, 693
Hong Kong, 832
Hoover, Herbert, 918
Hospitals, 766–767
House of Commons. *See* Parliament, English
House of Lords. *See* Parliament, English
Hugo, Victor, 744
Human Comedy, The (Balzac), 790
Hunchback of Notre Dame, The (Hugo), 744
Hungary: Magyars dominate, 733; in Austrian Revolution of 1848, 754–756; as part of Austro-Hungarian Empire, 820–821; independent republic proclaimed, 886; 1919 peace treaty, 891; Little Entente formed against, 910; conservative authoritarianism in, 927; forced into alliance with Germany, 951; Russia occupies, 965; revolt in, 981. *See also* Austro-Hungarian Empire
Huxley, Aldous, 902

Illegitimacy: urban, in 1900, 780–781
Immigration. *See* Migrations
Immunology, 766–767
Imperialism, Western: in late 19th century, 828–856; "new," 840–849; in Africa, 841–845; in Asia, 845; causes of, 845–848; critics of, 848–849; responses to, 849–856; collapse of in Asia, Africa, 975–977
Impressionism, 905
Income: of handloom weavers, 702; effect of Industrial Revolution on, 709, 716; Ricardo's theory on, 736; 1900 urban, 771, 775
Income tax, in 1900, 772
India: British colony, 828; West in, 845; response to imperialism, 851–853; role in decolonization, division of, 975
Indian National Congress, 853
Indians, American: effect of Spanish expansion on, 831
Indochina, 845, 951, 976, 1025–1026
Industrial Revolution: in England, 700–710; origins of, 700–701; and first factories, 701–703; energy problems in, 703–704; Watt's steam engine, 705–706; coming of railroads, 706–709; and economic growth, 709; spread of, 710–714; Continent lags in industrialization, 710–711; agents of, 711–714; capital-labor relations, 714–720; factory owners, 714–715; workers, 715–717; working conditions, 717–720; growth of unions, 720; population pressures, 720–722; nonindustrialization, famine in Ireland, 722–724; effect on urban growth, 762–765; effect on urban structure, 771–780; in Russia, 810–812
Industry: cottage, 701; revolution in, 700–720; in 19th-century Russia, 810–812; under five-year plans, 933–934
Infants: changing patterns of care for, 784; caring for in 1900, 784–785. *See also* Children
Inflation: in Germany in 1920s, 912–913; in 1970s, 1019
Inquiry into the Nature and Causes of the Wealth of Nations (Adam Smith), 735
International Working Men's Association, 822
Investment, foreign, 830–831
Iran, 1020, 1029
Iraq, 891
Ireland: urban workers from, 719; nonindustrialization, famine in, 721–724; struggle over home rule, 819; emigrants from, 836–837; 1916 uprising, 876; Catholic south granted autonomy, 916
Iron: production stagnates, 704; and Industrial Revolution, 706
Iron Curtain, 966
Ismail, khedive of Egypt, 834
Isolationism, American, 891
Israel: creation of modern, 976; defeated in Egypt, 978; in war with Arabs, 1018–1019. *See also* Hebrews; Jews
Italy: Napoleon's victories in, 688, 693; unification of, 799–803; in Egypt, 834; emigration from, 837, 839–840; in Africa, 842; in Triple Alliance, 860; in W.W. I, 871; at peace conference, 889, 891; under Mussolini, 936–939; in W.W. II, 947, 949–950, 951, 962–963; post–W.W. II conditions, 969; recovery in, 972. *See also* Rome

Jacobins, 683, 684
Jacob's Room (Woolf), 902
Japan: industrializes, 710; and Russian war, 812; West's intrusion in, 832–833; emigrants from, 840; and response to imperialism, 853–854; becomes imperialistic, 854; in

W.W. I, 871; gains colonies from Germany in 1919, 889; joins Italy, German alliance, 950; attacks U.S., in W.W. II, 951, 958–964
Jaruzelski, General, 1038–1039
Jaspers, Carl, 901
Java, Dutch in, 845
Jefferson, Thomas, 668, 672, 680
Jena, battle of, 693
Jenner, Edward, 766
Jesus Christ. *See* Christianity
Jet aircraft, 994
Jews: dominate banking in France, 718; Dreyfus affair, 817; and anti-Semitism in 19th-century Austria, 821; as migrants, 838–839, 840; promised national homeland by Britain, 891; and Nazi's anti-Semitism, 914, 929, 939, 940, 945, 953; in Palestine after W.W. II, 976; in Russia, 979, 1034
Joffre, Joseph, 867
John Paul II, pope, 1037
Johnson, Lyndon, 983, 1025–1026
Johnson, Samuel, 741
Joyce, James, 902
Judeo-Christian tradition, 669
Junkers, 814

Kafka, Franz, 903
Kaganovich, Lazar, 982
Kandinsky, Wassily, 906
Kaunitz, Eleonora von, 732
Keats, John, 743
Kellogg, Frank B., 914
Kellogg-Briand Pact, 914
Kennedy, John F., 982, 983, 987, 997, 1025
Kerensky, Alexander, 879, 881
Keynes, John Maynard, 910, 918
Khadafy, Muammar, 1018
Khartoum, battle of, 844
Khrushchev, Nikita, 980–982
Kierkegaard, Søren, 902
King, Martin Luther, 983, 1025
Kingship. *See* Monarchy
Kinship ties, 719, 782
Kipling, Rudyard, 847, 849, 889
Kirov, Sergei, 934
Kissinger, Henry, 1026
Kitchener, Horatio H., 844, 852
Koch, Robert, 766
Koestler, Arthur, 934
Kollontai, Alexandra, 936
Königgrätz, battle of, 806
Korea, 812, 854, 967
Korean War, 970, 1025
Kornilov, Lavr, 881
Kossuth, Louis, 754
Kubitschek, president of Brazil, 987
Kulaks, 932–933
Kulturkampf, 813–814
Kun, Béla, 927
Kuomintang, 975

Labor: effect of Industrial Revolution on, 702–703, 714–720; child, 703, 717–718; in 1900, 775–780; division of by sex, 783; and socialism, 822–824; in W.W.I, 874; collective bargaining established, 920. *See also* Unions, labor
Labouchère, Henry, 849
Labour party, British, 824, 915, 921, 970, 975, 1002
Lafayette, marquis de, 672, 675, 680
Laissez-faire doctrine, 735
Lake Chad, 844
Lake Shore Apartments, Chicago, 905
Lamarck, Jean Baptiste, 788–789
Lamartine, Alphonse de, 744, 752, 796, 798
Language: role in modern philosophy, 901
Lateran Agreement of 1929, 939
Latin America: colonial, 732; economic nationalism in, 984–987; Cuban revolution, 1098–1099. *See also* South America
Latvia, 951
Law: Napoleon's civil code of 1800, 689
Lawrence of Arabia, 871
League of Armed Neutrality, 673
League of Nations, 886, 889, 891, 947
Learning. *See* Education
Le Corbusier, 904, 905
Ledru-Rollin, Alexandre, 752
Legislative Assembly (France), 683
Leisure. *See* Recreation
Lélia (Sand), 744
Lenin, Vladimir Ilyich, 879–885, 891, 909, 928, 929, 930
Leo XIII, pope, 817
Leonardo da Vinci. *See* da Vinci, Leonardo
Leopold II, king of Belgium, 842
Lewis, C.S., 902
Liberalism: central ideas of, 668, 733, 928; roots of, 669; attraction of, 669–670
Liberia, 842
Liberty, concept of, 668, 735
Liberty Leading the People (Delacroix painting), 744
Liebenfels, Lanz von, 940
Liebknecht, Karl, 888
Liège, industrialization, 711
Life expectancy, 1008, 1012, 1022
List, Friedrich, 713–714, 811, 838
Lister, Joseph, 766–767
Liszt, Franz, 745
Literature: romantic movement, 743–744; realism in, 790–792; 20th century, 902–903; Russian, 934, 981
Lithuania, 951
Little Entente, 910
Liverpool and Manchester Railway, 706–708
Lloyd George, David, 819, 863, 874, 888–890
Locarno treaties, 913
Locke, John, 669
Lodge, Henry Cabot, 891
Logical empiricism, 900–901
Lombardy, and unification of Italy, 799, 801
London: Crystal Palace exposition, 709; filth in, 763–764, 766; music halls, 778
London *Daily Mail*, 864, 909

Loos, Adolf, 904
Lords, House of. *See* Parliament, English
Lorraine, 860, 867, 889
Los Alamos laboratory, 994
Louis XV, king of France, 675
Louis XVI, king of France: dominated by nobility, 677–678; accepts constitutional monarchy, 682; guillotined, 684
Louis XVIII, king of France, 694–695, 730, 731, 750
Louis Napoleon. *See* Napoleon III
Louis Philippe, king of France, 751
Lovett, William, 776
Low Countries. *See* Netherlands
Loyalists, in American Revolution, 672
Luddites, 716
Ludendorff, Erich, 871, 873, 886, 940
Lueger, Karl, 821, 940
Lunéville, Treaty of, 691
Lusitania, 871
Luxemburg, Rosa, 888
Lyell, Charles, 788
Lyrical Ballads (Wordsworth/Coleridge), 743

MacArthur, Douglas, 962
MacDonald, Ramsay, 915, 921
Macedonia: Serbia takes from Ottoman Empire, 865
MacMahon, Marie Edmé, 817
Madame Bovary (Flaubert), 790
Magyars, 733, 820, 821
Malaya, 840
Malthus, Thomas, 736
Managers, as emerging social elite, 1001–1002
Manchu dynasty, 832, 854, 856
Manchuria, 812, 854
Manhattan Project, 994
Manufacturing. *See* Industrial Revolution; Industry
Mao Tse–tung, 975–976
Marcel, Gabriel, 902
Marconi, Guglielmo, 909
Marie Antoinette, queen of France, 681, 683
Maritain, Jacques, 902
Markets: effect of Industrial Revolution on, 707–708
Marne, first battle of, 867; second battle of, 886
Marriage: in cities of 1900, 780–781, 782–784; postwar changes in, 1007–1012. *See also* Family; Women
Marshall, George C., 966
Marshall Plan or economic aid to Europe, 966–967, 970
Martin, John, 741–742
Marx, Karl, 714, 716, 788, 796; life and views, 739–741; in London, 821–822; and Russian Revolution, 878; influence on Lenin, 880
Marxian socialism, 739–741, 821, 880, 897, 929. *See also* Communism
Massachusetts, beginnings of American Revolution in, 672
Mass transportation, 764, 769–771
Masturbation, 785–786
Masurian Lakes, 871
Matisse, Henry, 905
Matteotti, Giacomo, 938
Matter, and energy, 899
Mazzini, Giuseppe, 737, 799
Mechanics: Newton's, 787
Medicine: bacterial revolution, 765–767; Freudian psychology, 899–900
Medvedev, Roy, 1034
Meiji Restoration, 853
Mein Kampf (Hitler), 914, 940, 941, 942
Melba, Nellie, 909
Menarche, age of, 1008
Mendeleev, Dmitri, 787
Menopause, age of, 1008
Mental illness, 786–787, 899–900
Mercantilism: Adam Smith's criticism of, 735–736
Metternich, Klemens von, 747; and Napoleon, 694; and balance of power, 730–731; conservative policies of, 732–734; opposes Greek national war, 746; flees in 1848, 754
Mexico, 833, 985
Miasmatic theory of disease, 765–766
Michelet, Jules, 737
Mickey Mouse, 909
Microwave technology, 994
Middle class: new industrial, 716; rise of in France, 676–677; effect on representative government, 728; as political factor in England, 749–750; in 19th-century reform efforts, 750–751; in cities of 1900, 771, 772–775; changes in modern, 1000–1002
Middlemarch (Eliot), 791
Midway Island, battle of, 962
Mies van der Rohe, Ludwig, 905
Migrants, 837–840
Migrations: of Irish to America, 723, 724; of 19th-century Europeans, 835–840; of 19th-century Asians, 840
Milan: in Revolutions of 1848, 756
Mill, John Stuart, 817
Mines Act of 1842, 719
Mining: use of steam in, 704–705, 706; use of women, children in, 718, 719
Missionaries, 847–848
Mitterrand, François, 1021
Modern life: science and technology, 992–1000; emergence of a new society, 1000–1007; women and family in, 1007–1012; perspectives on future, 1039–1043
Modern society: movies and radio in, 907–909; changing class structure, 1000–1002; social security, welfare reforms, 1002; rising affluence, 1002–1005; discontent, student revolts, 1005–1007; postwar roles of women and marriage, 1007–1012; lifespans in, 1012, 1022
Modern thought: uncertainty in, 896–903; the new physics, 897– 899; Freudian psychology, 899–900; modern philosophies, 900–901; revival of Christianity, 901–902; modern literature, 0art, music, 902–907
Mohammed Ali, 834
Molotov, Vyacheslav, 980, 982
Moltke, Helmuth von, 866
Mona Lisa, 906
Monarchy: fall of in France, 675–688
Monet, Claude, 709
Monetary systems: international, 1016–1017
Monnet, Jean, 971, 972

Monroe Doctrine, 732
Montesquieu, Charles-Louis, Baron de, 669
Moon, manned spacecraft on, 997
Morality: 1900 middle-class code of, 775; working class code of, 776, 777
Morocco, 863
Mortality rates, 767, 836
Moscow, 694; uprising in, 812
Motherhood. *See* Family; Women
Motion pictures, 907–909
Mountain (French political group), 684
Movies. *See* Motion pictures
Mozambique, 842, 1029
Mr., Mrs., and Baby (Droz), 784
Munich, 940
Music: romanticism, 744–746; modern, 907
Music halls, 778
Muslims: at battle of Omdurman, 844; and British in India, 852–853
Mussolini, Benito, 909; in power, 936–939; opposes, then joins Hitler, attacks Ethiopia, 947, 950; deposed, 962–963
My Secret Life (anonymous), 781–782

Nagasaki, bombing of, 963
Nanking, Treaty of, 832
Naples: and unification of Italy, 799, 803
Napoleon I, emperor of France: rules France, 688–690; England defeats at Trafalgar, 693; becomes emperor, 693; European wars of, 693–695; defeated in Russia, abdicates, 694; defeated at Waterloo, 695, 731; reappears, exiled again, 731; in Egypt, 834
Napoleon III, emperor of France (Louis Napoleon): wins election of 1848, 754, 796; and rebuilding of Paris, 767, 797; reasons for election, 796–797; as president of Second Republic, 797; as emperor, 797–799; and Cavour, 801; and Bismarck, 805, 807
Napoleonic Ideas (Napoleon), 796
Nasser, Gamal Abdel, 978, 1018
National Assembly of France, 677–678, 680, 681, 682, 797, 798, 815–816
National Association for the Advancement of Colored People, 983
National Convention (France), 684, 687–688
Nationalism: and French Republic's success in war, 687, 737; concept of, 736–737; triumphs in Europe, 796–824; in France, 796–799; in Italy, 799–803; in Germany, 803–808; and the modernizing of Russia, 810–813; from 1871 to 1914, 813–821; as cause of W.W. I, 867; Nazism grows out of, 929; German, in Vienna, 940; Hitler's, 945; spreads to colonial territories, 975–977; economic, in Latin America, 984
National Labor Relations Act, 920
National People's party, China, 975
National Recovery Administration, 919
National Socialist German Workers' party. *See* Nazism
National System of Political Economy (List), 714
Nations. *See* Nationalism; State
NATO (North Atlantic Treaty Organization), 967, 974, 1030
Nature: romanticism's concern with, 741, 743; modern environmental movement, 993
Navarino, battle of, 746
Nazism: as type of totalitarianism, 928; and Germany, 939–947; and expansionism, 947–956; and racial imperialism, 951–953
Nelson, Horatio, 693
Netherlands: declares war on Britain, 672; and First Coalition against France, 683, 684, 685, 687; as part of Grand Empire, 693; united under Dutch monarchy, 730
Newcomen, Thomas, 705
New Deal, 918–920, 983
New Economic Policy, 930, 932
New Harmony, Indiana, 720
Newton, Isaac, 787
Nicholas I, tsar of Russia, 756
Nicholas II, tsar of Russia, 812, 866, 878–879
Nietzsche, Friedrich, 896, 901
Nigeria, missionaries in, 848
Nile River, 844
Nimitz, Chester, 962
1984 (Orwell), 903
Nivelle, Robert, 868, 876
Nixon, Richard, 1016, 1026, 1033
Nobel Peace prize, 913
Nobility: and French Revolution, 676–678
Normandy: in W.W. II, 963
North Africa, in World War II, 962
North America: revolution of British colonies, 670–675; railroads in settlement of, 828–829; immigration to, 835–836; discrimination against Asians, 840. *See also* Canada; United States
North Atlantic Treaty Organization (NATO), 967, 974
Northcliffe, Lord, 909
North German Confederation, 806, 807
Norway: women's suffrage in, 813; breaks with Sweden, 820; migration from, 840; Socialist party growth in, 921; Nazis occupy, 951; post-W.W. II recovery, 972
NRA (National Recovery Administration), 919
Nuremberg Laws, 945
Nursing of babies, 784
Nutrition: need to improve knowledge of, 1002. *See also* Diet

October Manifesto, 812
Oedipal complex, 787
OEEC (Organization of European Economic Cooperation), 970, 972
Oil, price of, 1016, 1017–1019, 1020
Omdurman, battle of, 844
On the Origin of Species by the Means of Natural Selection (Darwin), 789
One Day in the Life of Ivan Denisovich (Solzhenitsyn), 981
"Open Door" policy, 855
Opium trade, 832
Oppenheimer, J. Robert, 994
Organization of European Economic Cooperation (OEEC), 970, 972
Organization of Petroleum Exporting Countries (OPEC), 1018–1019, 1020

Orthodox Christianity. *See* Eastern Orthodox church; Greek Orthodox church
Orwell, George, 903
O'Sullivan, John Louis, 737
Ottoman Turks: driven from Greece, 746; in Egypt, 834–835; empire dying, 860, 861, 864; destroyed, 865, 871
Overseas expansion. *See* Imperialism
Owen, Robert, 720

Pacific, World War II in, 962
Paganini, Niccolò, 745
Paine, Thomas, 672, 682
Painting. *See* Art
Pakistan, creation of, 975
Palacký, Francis, 737, 756
Palestine: Arabs and Jews in, 976
Palmerston, Lord, 758
Panama Canal, 829
Panama Canal Zone, 847
Pankhurst, Emmeline, 813
Papacy: in Italian unification, 799; Pius IX declares infallibility, 814; in post–W.W. I Italy, 937; Vatican proclaimed independent state, 939
Papal States, 802
Papen, Franz von, 942, 944
Paris: uprising of poor in French Revolution, 679–680; rebuilding of, 767–769, 797; surrenders to Bismarck, 808; Paris Commune, 815–816; as artistic center, 914. *See also* France
Paris, Peace of (1814), 730
Paris, Peace of (1815), 731
Paris, Treaty of 1783, 673
Parlement of Paris, 677
Parliament, English: in American Revolution, 670, 671; and 19th–century reform movement, 747–750; Lords vs. Commons in 1901–1910, 819; rules India, 852
Passchendaele, 868
Pasternak, Boris, 981
Pasteur, Louis, 766, 787
Pasteurization, 766
Peace of Paris of 1814, 730
Peace of Paris of 1815, 731
Peace of Villafranca, 801
Pearl Harbor, attack on, 951, 958
Peasantry: in Russia, 884, 932–933; as third estate in France, 676, 678; after French revolution, 680; conditions among Irish, 721–724; collectivization of in Stalinist Russia, 932–933; collectivization in China, 975–976; recent decline of, 1002
Peel, Robert, 750
Peking, 832, 856
People, The (Michelet), 737
People's Budget, 819, 863
People's Charter, 750
Père Goriot (Balzac), 790
Pereire, Emile and Isaac, 714, 739
Périer, Casimir, 751
Perry, Matthew, 833, 853
Peru, 840
Pétain, Henri–Philippe, 876, 951
"Peterloo, Battle of," 749
Petrograd Soviet of Workers' and Soldiers' Deputies, 880
Philippines, 840, 845, 976
Philosophy: liberalism, 668, 733; conservatism, 732–734; radical theories, 735–741; of science, 788; determinism, 790; modern, 896–897; logical empiricism, existentialism, 900, 901
Physicians: women as, in Soviet Russia, 936. *See also* Medicine
Physics: development of thermodynamics, 787; modern advances in, 897–899, 994, 998
Picasso, Pablo, 906
Pickford, Mary, 907
Pillnitz, Declaration of, 683
Pilsudski, Joseph, 928
Pius VII, pope, 690
Pius IX, pope, 800, 814
Planck, Max, 897, 899, 902
Poincaré, Raymond, 910, 914
Poland: and nationalism, 812; gains territory in 1919, 891; signs pact with France, 910; conservative authoritarianism in, 928; Nazis, Russians occupy, 950, 951, 965; revolt in, 981; treaty with West Germany, 1023–1025; and Solidarity movement, 1029, 1037–1039
Popes. *See* Papacy
Popular Front, 921–922
Population: 19th–century growth, 720–722; growth in Ireland, 723; toll of Great Famine in Ireland, 724; Malthusian theory of, 736; growth in 19th–century cities, 762–763; 19th–century explosion as impetus for migration, 836–837
Port Arthur, 854
Portugal: conservative authoritarianism in, 928
Potsdam Conference, 966
Power. *See* Energy
Prague, "defenestration of," 756
Premarital sex, 780–781
Priestly, Joseph, 682
Professional class, rise of, 772–773
Prokofiev, Sergei, 979
Proletariat, in Marxian socialism, 739–740
Propaganda: during W.W. I, 871, 876; radio, movies used for, 909; Stalin's use of, 930, 934; Hitler's use of, 940, 942–944
Prostitution: urban, in 1900, 781–782
Protestantism: identification with French industrialism, 714; in modern age, 901
Protestant Reformation: Luther and, 901
Proudhon, Pierre Joseph, 739
Proust, Marcel, 902
Prussia: issues Declaration of Pillnitz, 683; and First Coalition, 683, 684, 685, 687; at war with Napoleon, 693, 694; gains territory from France, 730; and balance of power struggle, 730–731; forms Holy Alliance, 732; and 1848 Revolution, 756–758; and unification of Germany, 803–808; rivalry with Britain, 863
Psychology, Freudian, 786–787, 899–900
Public health: 19th–century advances in, 735

Public transportation, 764, 769–771
Purges, Stalin's, 934, 979–980
Pushkin, Alexander, 744
"Putting-out" system, 680–681, 701, 777

Quadruple Alliance, 694, 728, 730, 731
Quakers, 714
Quest of the Historical Jesus, The (Schweitzer), 901
Quo Vadis (film), 907

Racism: and Asian migrants, 840; and imperialism, 847, 849; of British in India, 853; Nazism grows out of, 929; and Nazism, 940, 952–953
Radar, invention of, 993–994
Radiation Laboratory, University of California at Berkeley, 999
Radical political concepts: liberalism, 735–736; nationalism, 736–738; utopian socialism, 738–739; Marxian socialism, 739–741
Radio, 909
Raft of the Medusa, The (Géricault painting), 741
Railroads: invention, spread of, 706–709; in Russia, 810–811; facilitate trade, 828–829; investment in, 831
Rasputin, 878–879
Rathenau, Walter, 872
Reagan, Ronald, 1021, 1029
Realism, in literature, 790–792
Recreation: of middle classes in 1900, 773–774; of working classes, 777–778; movies and radio, 907–909; in postwar era, 1003–1005
"Red Shirts," 802
Reflections on the Revolution in France (Burke), 682
Reform Bill of 1832, 749
Refrigerated transportation, 829
Reichstag, 813, 942, 944
Reign of Terror, in French Revolution, 687
Relativity, Einstein's theory of, 897–899
Religion: and science, 789–790; popular in 18th century, 682; and working class in 1900, 778–780; in modern age, 901; in Soviet Russia, 935
Remarque, Erich, 868–869
Remembrance of Things Past (Proust), 902
Reparations, World War I, 909–913
Representative government, 668–670, 736
Republicanism, of 19th-century liberals, 736
Resistance movement, World War II, 901, 959–961
Revisionism, 824
Revolutionary era: ideas of liberty, equality, 668–670; American Revolution, 670–675; French Revolution, 675–688; Industrial Revolution, 700–720; "dual" revolution, 728; revolution in France, 1830, 750–751; 1848 revolutions in Europe, 751–758
Rhineland, 757, 814, 912, 948
Ricardo, David, 736, 740
Riefenstahl, Leni, 909
Rite of Spring, The (Stravinsky), 907
Roads: Assyrian, 706
Robespierre, Maximilien, 682, 683, 684–687
Rogers, Ginger, 909
Roman Catholic church: in conflict with Republican France, 682; signs concordat of 1801, 690; Bismarck attacks, 813–814; France severs ties with, 817; and modern thinkers, 902; in Mussolini's Italy, 937, 939. *See also* Papacy
Romantic love, 780, 784
Romantic movement, 741–746
Rome: part of Italy in 1870, 799, 801. *See also* Papacy
Rome, Treaty of, 974
Rome–Berlin Axis, 950
Rommel, Erwin, 962
Roosevelt, Franklin D., 909; and New Deal, 918–920; in W.W. II, 958–964; at Teheran Conference, 964–966; at Yalta Conference, dies, 966
"Rotten boroughs," 749
Rousseau, Jean Jacques, 741, 743
Roux, Jacques, 684
Ruhr, occupation of, 910–913
Rumania: breaks with Ottoman Empire, 820, 865; joins Little Entente, 910; forced into alliance with Germany, 951; Russia occupies, 965
Russia: in Napoleonic wars, 693, 694; industrializes, 704, 710; and balance of power struggle after Napoleon's defeat, 730; forms Holy Alliance, 732; supports Greek independence, 746; modernization of, 808–813; further industrialization of, 810–812; Revolution of 1905, 812–813; steam power in, 829; immigration in, 837; Jewish emigration from, 838–839; in Asia, 845; and war with Japan, 854; in Bismarck's system of alliances, rival blocs before 1914, 860–864; support sought by Serbs, 865; in Balkan wars, 865–866; in W.W. I, 869–871, 877; revolution in, 878–885; imperial Russia falls, 878–879; provisional government, 879–880; Lenin and the Bolshevik revolution, 880–881; Trotsky seizes power, 883; dictatorship and civil war, 884–885; Lenin, Bolsheviks win, 885; quits W.W. I, 884; Stalinist, as totalitarian state, 929–936; in pact with Hitler, 950; occupies Poland, 951; Hitler invades, 951; in W.W. II, 951, 953, 958–964; in cold war, 964–968; in post–W.W. II period, 978–980; Stalin dies, Khrushchev in power, 980–982; recent economic problems, 1020; treat with West Germany, 1025; and Helsinki agreement, 1029; occupies Afghanistan, 1029; Soviet bloc, 1030–1039; occupies Czechoslovakia, 1032–1033
Russian Orthodox church, 878. *See also* Eastern Orthodox church
Russian Revolution of 1917, 878–885; imperial Russia falls, 878–879; provisional government, 879–880; Lenin and the Bolshevik revolution, 880–881; Trotsky seizes power, 883–884; dictatorship and civil war, 884–885; Lenin, Bolsheviks win, 885
Rutherford, Ernest, 899, 993, 996

Sadat, Anwar, 1018, 1029
Sailing ships. *See* Ships
St. Augustine: tradition revived, 901
St. Peter's Fields, Manchester, 749
Saint-Simon, Henri de: *Mémoires* quoted, 788; ideas of, 739
Salazar, Antonio de Oliveira, 928

Samurai, 853
Sand, George, 744
Sanitation: in 19th century, 763–765; public health movement, 765
Sans-culottes, 684, 685, 686, 687, 688
Sarajevo, 866
Sardinia, 799–803
Sartre, Jean Paul, 901
Sassoon, Siegfried, 868
Savery, Thomas, 705
Savoy Villa at Poissy, 905
Scandinavia: response to Great Depression, 921. *See also* Denmark; Norway; Sweden
Schleswig-Holstein, 758, 805
Schlieffen, Alfred von, 866
Schönberg, Arnold, 907
Schools. *See* Education
Schuman, Robert (statesman), 969, 972
Schumann, Robert (composer), 745
Schweitzer, Albert, 901
Science: bacterial revolution, 765–767; Freudian psychology, 786–787; triumphs in modern thought, 787–788; growth of social sciences, 788–790; the new physics, 897–899; postwar developments in, 992–1000; and military needs, 992, 993–996; and environmental problems, 992; rise of "Big," 996–998; life of scientists, 998–1000; funding for, 1021–1022
Scientific instruments: cost of, 996
Scientists, modern, 998–1000
Scotland: identification with English industrialization, 714. *See also* Great Britain
Scott, Sir Walter, 722, 743
Second Continental Congress, 672
Second Empire, French, 797
Second International, 822
Second World War. *See* World War II
Sennett, Mack, 907
Separation of powers in government, 673–674
September Massacres, 683
Serbia: breaks from Ottoman Empire, 820; in Balkan wars, 865– 866; in W.W. I, 871; unites with Slavs to form Yugoslavia, 887
Serfdom: abolished by Napoleon, 693–694; abolished in Russia, 809
Servan-Schreiber, Jean Jacques, 997
Servants: as indicator of wealth, 772, 773–774; domestic, in 19th century, 776–777J
Seven Years' War, 672
Sexuality: premarital, in 1900, 780–781; and marriage manuals, 784; and Freud's theories, 900; in Stalinist Russia, 936. *See also* Prostitution
Shipping, 829
Ships: steam, 829; refrigerated, 829; submarines in W.W.I, 979
Shogun, 853
Shostakovich, Dimitri, 979
Sicily: and unification of Italy, 799, 802
Siéyès, Abbé, 678, 689
Silva, Anna da, 801
Sino-Japanese War (1894–95), 855
Sister Carrie (Dreiser), 791
Six Acts, 749
Slaves and slavery: Asians in, 840; West agrees to work to stop, 842
Slavs, 887; in Austrian Empire, 733
Smith, Adam, 735–736
Smolensk, Napoleon in, 694
Social class: in 19th century, 771–780
Social Darwinism, 789, 847
Social Function of Science, The (Bernal), 993
Socialism: French Revolution and development of, 686; utopian, 738–739; Marxian, 739–741; in French Second Republic, 753–754; Bismarck opposes in Germany, 814; vs. nationalism, 821–824; in W.W. I, 872, 877; and provisional Russian government, 879; and 1918 revolution in Germany, 887–888; in Scandinavia, 921; in France, 921–922; Stalin's communism as perversion of, 929; and Mussolini's Italy, 937
Social science, 788–790
Social security system: Bismarck initiates, 814; in U.S., 920, 983; reforms, improvements in, 1002–1005
Solidarity (Polish union), 1029, 1037–1039
Solzhenitsyn, Alexander, 981, 1034
Somme, battle of the, 868, 873
Sophia, archduchess of Austria, 756
Sorel, Georges, 896–897
Sound and the Fury, The (Faulkner), 902
South America: Britain opposes return of to Spain, 732; immigration in, 837, 839, 840. *See also* Latin America
South German Confederation, 732
Soviet Union. *See* Russia
Space research, 996–997
Spain: declares war on Britain, 672; Republican France declares war on, 684; rebels against Napoleon, 694; grants constitution, 732; in Africa, 841; civil war in, 922, 950
Spanish-American War, 847
Spanish Civil War, 922, 950
Spencer, Herbert, 790
Spengler, Oswald, 903
Spinning of yarn, 701
Sports, in 1900, 778
SS (Nazi group), 945, 953
"Stagflation," 1019
Stalin, Joseph: and totalitarian Russia, 929–936; signs pact with Hitler, 950; Hitler invades Russia, 951; in W.W. II, 958–964; at Teheran Conference, 964–966; at Yalta Conference, 966; at Potsdam Conference, 966; in postwar era, 978–980; attacked by Khrushchev, 980
Stalingrad, Nazi defeat at, 961–962
"Stalin's Heirs" (Yevtushenko), 981–982
Stamp Act, 670–671
Standard of living: in Industrial Revolution, 717; in 19th century, 771–780, 822; in Russia, 935, 981, 1034; postwar era, 1002–1003
Stanley, H. M., 842
Starry Night, The (van Gogh painting), 905
State: triumph of modern national, 796–824; modern authoritarian, totalitarian, 926–929
Statistics, use of, 788

Steam engine, 705–706
Steam power, 705–706, 829
Stein, Gertrude, 914
Stephenson, George, 707
Stern, Karl, 902
Stolypin, Peter, 813
Storm and Stress group *(Sturm und Drang)*, 741
Storm troopers (Nazi), 944–945
Strasser, Gregor, 942
Stravinsky, Igor, 907
"Stream of consciousness," 902
Streetcars, 769–770
Stresemann, Gustav, 913, 914
Strutt, Jedediah, 718
Student revolts, 1005–1007
Sturm und Drang, 741
Submarine warfare, 871
Sudan, 845, 849
Sudetenland, 950
Suez Canal, 829, 834, 845, 962
Suffrage, 720; 19th-century liberal ideas on, 736; and 19th-century reform in England, 747, 750; in early 19th-century France, 750, 751–752; under Napoleon, 797, 799; growth of universal, 813; extended in England, 817; after W.W. I, 874
Sullivan, Louis H., 904
Sun Yat-sen, 856, 975
Surgeons. *See* Physicians
Surrealism, 906
Swaddling of infants, 785
Sweden: Third Coalition against France, 693; industrializes, 710; Norway breaks from, 820; emigration from, 840; socialist party growth, 921
Switzerland, 880
Syria, 891
System of Positive Philosophy (Comte), 788

Taft-Hartley Act, 983
Tai Ping rebellion, 855
Taiwan, 975
Talleyrand, Charles de, 730, 731
Tannenberg, battle of, 871
Tariffs: and industrialization, 713–714; and England's Corn Law, 750; and German Zollverein, 803; raised by Russia, 811; raised by Germany, other countries follow, 814; raised by U.S., Europe, 828; reduced through Common Market, 974
Tawfiq, khedive of Egypt, 834
Taxation: of American colonies, 670–672; in France before revolution, 675–676; income, 772
Technological developments: and Industrial Revolution, 700–710, 711–714; scientific research, 787–788; in Communist Russia, 933–934; postwar, 992–1000; and military needs, 992, 993–995; and environment, 993; life of technologists, 998–1000
Teheran Conference, 964–965
Teke tribe, 842
Telescope, 996
Ten Hours Act, 750
Terrorism, 934
Tess of the D'Urbervilles (Hardy), 791
Textile industry: as English cottage industry, 701; revolution in, 701–703; exports, 828
Thatcher, Margaret, 1021
Theology. *See* Religion
"Thermidorian reaction," 687–688
Thermodynamics, 787
Thiers, Adolphe, 816
Thought. *See* Modern thought; Philosophy
Three Emperors' League, 860–861
Tilsit, treaties of, 693
Tirpitz, Admiral, 863
Tito, Marshal, 980
Tocqueville, Alexis de, 753
Tolstoy, Leo, 791
Tory party, 747–749
Totalitarianism: of Germany in W.W. I, 874; in Orwell's *1984*, 903; in modern state, 926–929; in Stalinist Russia, 929–936; in Mussolini's Italy, 936–939; in Nazi Germany, 939–947; in China, 975
Tourism, 1003–1005
Towns: effect of Industrial Revolution, 709. *See also* Cities
Toynbee, Arnold, 902, 968
Tractus Logico-Philosophicus (Wittgenstein), 900
Trade: 19th-century international growth in, 828–830. *See also* Commerce
Trade unions. *See* Unions, labor
Trafalgar, battle of, 693
Transportation: railroads, 706–709, 810–811; public, 764, 769–771; advances in, 828–829, 996
Treaty of Amiens, 691
Treaty of Brest-Litovsk, 884, 885
Treaty of Chaumont, 694
Treaty of Lunéville, 691
Treaty of Nanking, 832
Treaty of Paris of 1783, 673
Treaty of Rome, 974
Treaty of Tilsit, 693
Treaty of Versailles, 888–892, 909–910
Treitschke, Heinrich von, 847
Trial, The (Kafka), 903
Triple Alliance, 860, 861, 871
Triumph of the Will, The (Riefenstahl), 909
Troppau, Congress of, 732
Trotsky, Leon, 883–884, 885, 930–932
Truman, Harry, 966, 983
Truman Doctrine, 966
Turkey: in Balkan wars, 866; and 1919 peace treaty, 891. *See also* Ottoman Turks
Turner, J. M. W., 709, 744
Tuscany, 799
Two Sicilies, 732
Tzu Hsi, 855

Ukraine, 812, 951
Ulster, Protestantism in, 722, 819
Ulysses (Joyce), 902
Underwear, increased use of, 702

Unemployment, 916, 918, 919, 920, 942, 1020, 1022
Unions, labor: beginnings in Great Britain, 720; and Russian revolution of 1905, 812; growth of moderate social movement, 822–824; in W.W. I, 872, 874; growth in U.S., 920; lose power under communism, 933; and Taft-Hartley Act, 903; Polish Solidarity Union, 1029, 1037–1039
United Nations, 965–966, 976
United Provinces of the Netherlands. *See* Holland; Netherlands
United States: British colonies revolt, 670–675; origins of revolution, 670–673; colonies win independence, 673–675; framing the Constitution, 673–674; proclaims Monroe Doctrine, 732; religion in 1900, 779–780; steam transport in, 829; in Japan, 832–833; 19th-century immigration to, 835–840; Asian immigrants in, 840; in Asia, 845; reasons for imperialism, 845–848; relations with Britain improve, 863; in W.W. I, 811, 886; at peace conference, 888–892; rejects Versailles treaty, 891–892; movies, radio in, 907–909; isolationism in, 910; German reparations, 913; Great Depression, 916–917; New Deal, 918–920; in W.W. II, 951, 958–964; in cold war, 964–968; Marshall plan and European recovery, 966, 970; aids French in Indochina, 976; postwar posterity, 983; civil rights movement, 983–984; postwar era in, 992–1012; political crisis in, 1025–1027; Vietnam war, 1025–1026J
Universities: student revolts in, 1005–1007
Urban life: in 19th century, 762–792. *See also* Cities
Urban planning, 767–769
Ure, Andrew, 716
Utopian socialism, 738–739

Valentino, Rudolph, 907
Valéry, Paul, 897
van Gogh, Vincent, 905
Vargas, Getulio, 985–987
Vatican. *See* Papacy
Venetia, 799, 801
Venice, 803; becomes part of Italy, 806
Verdun, battle of, 873
Versailles: revolutionists march on, 681; Treaty of, 888–892, 909–910
Vichy government, 951
Victor Emmanuel, Sardinia, 799, 803
Victor Emmanuel III, king of Italy, 937
Victoria, queen of England, 878
Vienna: Congress of, 728, 730–731; in revolution of 1848, 756; 19th-century rebuilding of, 769; and anti-Semitism, 821; Hitler in, 940
Vietnam, 854, 976
Vietnam war, 1007, 1025–1027
Vigny, Alfred de, 744
Villafranca, peace of, 801
Voting rights. *See* Suffrage
Voting Rights Act of 1965, 983

Walesa, Lech, 1037–1038
War and Peace (Tolstoy), 791
Warfare: first total effort under French Republic, 687; W.W. I "total war" concept, 872–874; air war of W.W. II, 951; mass, atomic bombings used in, 963–964; and modern technology, 993–995
Washington, George, 672
Waste Land, The (Eliot), 903
Watergate, 1026
Waterloo, battle of, 695, 731
Watson, James, 1000
Watt, James, 705–706
Waugh, Evelyn, 902
Wealth of Nations (Smith), 735–736
Weavers, wages of, 702
Weimar Republic, 910, 914, 940
Welfare, 1002, 1021
Welfare state, 984, 1002
Western Europe: postwar recovery of, 968–978; life in postwar era, 1005
West Germany, 969–971, 972, 1021, 1023–1025, 1028. *See also* GermanyJ
Wet nursing. *See* Nursing
Whaling industry, and opening of Japan, 832–833
What Is Property? (Proudhon), 739
What Is the Third Estate? (Siéyès), 678, 689
Whig party, 749
White-collar class, 772–773
"White man's burden," 847
White Russians, 884–885
Wilkinson, John, 706
William I, king of Prussia: reforms army, 803; and Bismarck, 804, 807; proclaimed emperor, 808; assassination attempt, 814
William II, emperor of Germany: forces Bismarck to resign, 814–815, 861; supports Austria-Hungary in Balkans, 866
Wilson, Woodrow, 871, 872, 888, 889, 891
Windischgrätz, Alfred, 756
Witte, Sergei, 811–812
Wittgenstein, Ludwig, 900–901
Women: march on Versailles, 680–681; middle class, in 1900, 773; as domestics, 776–777; in cities of 1900, 780–787; and suffrage, 813; in W.W. I, 874; in Stalinist Russia, 936; in Mussolini's Italy, 939; under Nazism, 945; in postwar era, 1003, 1007–1012
Woolf, Virginia, 902
Wordsworth, William, 716, 743, 744
Working class: development of, 708; early factory workers, 715–720; in cities of 1900, 771–772, 775–780; stabilization of, 1002. *See also* Labor; Peasantry
Works Progress Administration (WPA), 920
World War I, 860–877, 885–891; Bismarck's alliances, rival blocs before, 860–864; outbreak of, 864–866; origins of, 866–867; first battle of the Marne, 867; Russia in, 869–871; neutral countries, U.S. enter, 871; on the homefront, 872–877; social impact of, 874–875; Russia makes peace, 884; end of, 886; Treaty of Versailles, 888–891; U.S. rejects treaty, 891–892
World War II: early years of Nazi expansion, 947; appeasement by France, England, 947–949; Italy, Japan join Germany, 950; Hitler, Stalin sign pact, 950; Britain, France declare

war, France falls, Hitler rules most of Europe, 950–951; Hitler invades Russia, 951; Japan attacks Pearl Harbor, U.S. in war, 951; Hitler's "final solution," 953; the U.S.–British alliance, 958–961; battles of, 961–964; Germany surrenders, U.S. drops atomic bomb on Japan, war ends, 963–964
Wozzeck (Berg), 907
WPA (Works Progress Administration), 920
Wright, Frank Lloyd, 904
Writers. *See* Literature

Yalta conference, 966, 979
Yevtushenko, Yevgeny, 981–982
Yokohama, 853
Young Plan, 913
Ypsilanti, Alexander, 746
Yugoslavia: formed, 887; joins Little Entente, 910; conservative authoritarianism in, 928; Nazis conquer, 951; Russia occupies, 965; Tito breaks with Stalin, 980

Zemstvo, 809–810
Zhdanov, Andrei, 979
Zola, Emile, 790–791, 817
Zollverein, 714, 803
Zoning laws, 769
Zulus, 842